erception

the Microstructure of
E. Rumelhart, James L.

the Microstructure of
ical Models, by James L.
PDP Research Group

the Mind-Brain,

edited by

Computational Models of Cognition

Editors

Jerome A. Feldman
Patrick J. Hayes
David E. Rumelhart

Neurophilosophy

Toward a Unified Science of the Mind-Brain

Patricia Smith Churchland

A Bradford Book
The MIT Press
Cambridge, Massachusetts
London, England

This book was set in Palatino by Achorn Graphic Services and printed and bound by Halliday Lithograph in the United States of America.

Library of Congress Cataloging-in-Publication Data

Churchland, Patricia Smith.
  Neurophilosophy: toward a unified science of the mind-brain.
  (Computational models of cognition and perception)
  "A Bradford book."
  Bibliography: p.
  Includes index.
  1. Neuropsychology—Philosophy. 2. Mind-brain
identity theory. 3. Neurology—Philosophy. I. Title. II. Series.
  [DNLM: 1. Neurology. 2. Neuropsychology.
WL 100 C562n]
QP360.C49 1986   152   85-23706
ISBN 0-262-03116-7

Contents

Preface

In the mid-seventies I discovered that my patience with most main-stream philosophy had run out. What had instead begun to seem promising was the new wave in philosophical method, which ceased to pander to "ordinary language" and which began in earnest to reverse the antiscientific bias typical of "linguistic analysis." Even here I had a major misgiving, however, because the sciences embraced by the new wave as relevant to understanding the nature of the mind did not include neuroscience. Indeed, the best of what there was had espoused a novel and sophisticated form of dualism—theory dualism—that dismissed neuroscience as largely irrelevant to theories in psychology and philosophy. Since I was a materialist and hence believed that the mind is the brain, it seemed obvious that a wider understanding of neuroscience could not fail to be useful if I wanted to know how we see, how we think and reason and decide. I therefore decided to find out in detail whether what was already known in neuroscience was of any use in understanding cognitive functions. Beginning with a cautious paddling at the available edges of neuroscience, I quickly found myself venturing further and further from shore, and finally setting full sail.

In the midst of the unencumbered delights of discovering what was known about nervous systems and how neurobiologists got that knowledge, questions of a distinctly philosophical nature continued to make demanding background noises: Is it possible that we could have one grand, unified theory of the mind-brain? What would such a theory look like? Is a reductionist strategy reasonable or not? As a philosopher, I had found myself driven to the neurosciences, but having immersed myself in the neurosciences, I found I could not leave the philosophy alone either. For those far-reaching, wide-embracing questions asked about neuroscientific research I well recognized to be philosophical questions—moreover, questions where philosophers of science and historians of science have had useful things to say. It is now evident that where one discipline ends and the other begins no longer matters, for it is in the nature of the case that the boundaries are ill defined. This book is thus the result of what I came to regard as *neurophilosophical inquiries*.

Given the range of topics I needed to know about, I was throughout the project necessarily dependent on the willingness of neuroscientists to explain their research, to tell me what they thought was important and why, and to give advice on who else to talk to and what to read. My worst fear—that as a philosopher I would be considered an utter waste of time—was virtually never realized. Invariably neuroscientists were exceedingly generous, often going beyond explanations asked, allowing me to observe or participate in experiments, explaining details of techniques, and drawing back the curtain on the wider vision that motivated their research.

From time to time I found considerable disagreement among neuroscientists on fundamental issues, and at first I tacitly assumed that there must be someone who *really* knew what was what and who could settle for me what is the Truth. In the end I knew that I had to make up my own mind, and do it the way any neuroscientist would: find out as much as I reasonably could about the issue and go with what seemed most reasonable. A vague decision procedure, to be sure, but the only one I know of.

Without the generosity and patience of many people, not only neuroscientists, but also philosophers, psychologists, and computer scientists, this book would still be a shapeless intention. To Larry Jordan I am especially indebted for giving me a basis in neurophysiology and in laboratory techniques and for convincing me that it is essential to think about how organisms move. I also owe an enormous debt to Rodolfo Llinás, whose unique blend of experimental understanding and drive for theory gave me a sense of what a large, unifying framework for neurobiology and psychology might look like and how known data would figure in that framework. For similar reasons, I am grateful to Francis Crick, whose general understanding of the entire field of vision and sense of how theoretical problems in neurobiology might be solved directed me in getting a grip on the functional questions. More than anyone else, Llinás and Crick have made neuroscience seem like the most exciting thing in the world and consequently rekindled—and, I suspect, realigned—my philosophical preoccupations.

Among philosophers, my first and greatest debt is to Paul M. Churchland, who has been a partner in the venture from the very beginning. It was he especially who convinced me of the importance of bringing science and the philosophy of science to bear on questions in the philosophy of mind, and this has made all the difference in thinking about consciousness, cognition, and subjective experience, and about the general framework needed for a unified science of the mind-brain. Consistently naturalistic in his approach to philosophical questions, and robustly skeptical of folk psychology, he pointed me in the direction of the neurosciences. Dan Dennett made a difference in countless ways, one of which was convincing me to write the book in the first place. In addition, by taking a blue pencil to the manuscript in several of its incarnations, he helped me avoid many mistakes. Best of all, perhaps, he set an example of how philosophy ought to be done. Stephen Stich also gave me unstinting encouragement and advice, and his ruthless clarity helped keep mushiness from creeping in. To Jerry Feldman I owe a debt of thanks for a careful reading of the manuscript and for much useful criticism and advice. Cliff Hooker discussed large parts of the manuscript with me as well, and his general conception of the development of philosophy since the turn of the century provided an organizing focus.

Many other people gave me ideas, advice, and invaluable conversation or read some substantial section of the manuscript and suggested revisions. I should mention especially the following: Ted Bullock, Jeff Foss, Don Griffin, Alastair Hannay, Stevan Harnad, Ken Heilman, Don Herzog, Geoffrey Hinton, Marcel Kinsbourne, Marta Kutas, Michael Gazzaniga, Ron Giere, Lisa Lloyd, Vernon Mountcastle, David Olton, Andras Pellionisz, Susan Schefchyk, Martin Sereno, Terry Sejnowski, Allison Shalinsky, Aaron Smith, Michael Stack, Larry Weiskrantz, Chris Wood, David Zipser, and Steve Zucker. I want also to thank Harry and Betty Stanton of MIT Press/Bradford Books for their genteel encouragement and for making the production end of publication almost fun. Gustav Szabo designed the cover, and I am grateful to him for working out exactly the right theme. Finally, thanks to Darlene Stack for the ready supply of buck-you-uppo and for entertaining us through many a Manitoba blizzard.

For financial support, my greatest debt is to the Social Sciences and Humanities Research Council of Canada, without whose generous funding in providing release time from teaching this project would have been impossible (grants 410–81–0182, 451–83–3049). I am also grateful to the University of California at San Diego for support in the final stages of preparation of the manuscript (grants RJ111–G, RK91–G). In addition, I should like to thank the Institute for Advanced Study in Princeton for giving me a peaceful and productive year in 1982–1983, during which large portions of the book moved into position. I owe a special debt to the University of Manitoba for having the courage to support me in a host of important ways on a project that was not, by most lights, conventional.

PSC
La Jolla 1985

Neurophilosophy

One ought to know that on the one hand pleasure, joy, laughter, and games, and on the other, grief, sorrow, discontent, and dissatisfaction arise only from the brain. It is especially by it that we think, comprehend, see, and hear, that we distinguish the ugly from the beautiful, the bad from the good, the agreeable from the disagreeable. . . .
Hippocrates

Philosophy is like the mother who gave birth to and endowed all the other sciences. Therefore, one should not scorn her in her nakedness and poverty, but should hope, rather, that part of her Don Quixote ideal will live on in her children so that they do not sink into philistinism.
Albert Einstein, 1932

General Introduction

Squirming out from the primordial ooze, our evolutionary ancestors harbored within themselves a perfectly astounding invention—the excitable cell. Such is a cell that can pass a tiny electrical effect down its extent and that, in concert with clumps and configurations of similarly excitable cells, can be appropriately excited so that the organism may move, thereby feeding, fleeing, fighting, or reproducing. From the very beginning, mobile creatures whose excitable cells were capable of conveying information about conditions outside the body had a survival advantage over those whose movements were independent of whatever was going on outside. Obviously, the organism that flees in the absence of predators and feeds willy-nilly is doomed to be prey for those more lucky organisms fitted out with cells coordinating *representations of the world·* with *movement in the world.* With increased complexity of behavioral repertoire comes increased capacity for representing the environment.

Our own brains are massive mounds of excitable cells, which somehow contrive collectively to contain a rich representation of the outside world, as well as to enable the muscles to accomplish such feats as catching a ball, playing the violin, and talking, in addition of course to the fundamental feeding, fleeing, fighting, and reproducing. Additionally, the human brain, like the brains of other species, contains information about itself and about other brains, though to be sure, we do not standardly apprehend the information under that description.

Lurching out from the comfortable cave that is our commonsense conception of things, human brains have come to represent the sun, not as a god driven about in a golden chariot but as a nuclear fire; and the earth, not as a sheet with fat-cheeked cherubs blowing from the four corners but as a ball hurtling about the sun; and the heart, not as a cauldron for concocting animal spirits but as a pump for blood. We want also to understand our brains, and thus the brain investigates the brain, emburdened no doubt with a pack of misconceptions not unlike those impeding the investigation of the sun or the heart, but empowered for all that to disemburden itself and to bootstrap its way to insight and understanding.

It is within this context that certain intriguing problems arise—problems concerning how to study the brain, how to conceive of what it is up to, and how our commonsense conceptions of ourselves might fit or fail to fit with what we discover. Some of these have traditionally been recognized as philosophical problems. For example: Are mental states identical to brain states? Are mental states reducible to brain states? What sort of business is reduction? What are emergent properties and are there any? What, if anything, is special about the subjective point of view? Are conscious experiences physiologically understandable? What are representations and how can a brain represent the world outside itself?

Such philosophical questions are synoptic in character, in the sense that they are very general and very broad. But they are not of an entirely different nature from synoptic problems traditionally characterized as empirical: How is color vision produced? How does the brain learn and how does it store information? What are representations and how does a brain represent the world outside itself? Is the human brain more complicated than it is smart?

The questions, whether asked by philosophers or by neuroscientists, are all part of the same general investigation, with some questions finding a natural home in both philosophy and neuroscience. In any case it is the same curiosity that bids them forth, and it is perhaps best to see them all simply as questions about the brain and the mind—or the mind-brain—rather than as questions *for* philosophy or *for* neuroscience or *for* psychology. Administrative distinctions have a purpose so far as providing office space and salaries is concerned, but they should not dictate methods or constitute impedimenta to easy exchange. This is not to deny that there are divisions of labor—indeed, within neuroscience itself there are divisions of labor—but it is to argue that such divisions neither imply nor justify radical differences in methodology.

Philosophical problems were once thought to admit of a priori solutions, where such solutions were to be dredged somehow out of a "pure reason," perhaps by a contemplation unfettered and uncontaminated by the grubbiness of empirical facts. Though a convenience to those of the armchair persuasion, the dogma resulted in a rather anti-intellectual and scoffing attitude toward science in general, and when the philosophy was philosophy of mind, toward neuroscience in particular. But with the publication in the 1960s of Quine's *Word and Object* and Sellars's *Science, Perception and Reality*, it came to be seen that philosophy at its best and properly conceived is continuous with the empirical sciences, and that while problems and solutions can be more or less synoptic, this is a difference in degree, not a difference in kind. Although theories may be more or less distant from observations, they are interesting only insofar as they can touch, finally, upon observations. Sometimes the route to observations may, as in theoretical physics, be a long one through much theory, but a route there must finally be.

What used to pass for a priori arguments about the impossibility of science discovering this or that (such as the impossibility of discovering that space is non-Euclidean or that mental states are brain states) were sometimes merely arguments based on what could or could not be imagined by some individual philosopher. Since what can or cannot be imagined about the empirical world is not independent of what is already understood and believed about the empirical world, failures of imaginability were all too often owed to ignorance or to inflexible imaginations.

The sustaining conviction of this book is that top-down strategies (as characteristic of philosophy, cognitive psychology, and artificial intelligence research) and bottom-up strategies (as characteristic of the neurosciences) for solving the mysteries of mind-brain function should not be pursued in icy isolation from one another. What is envisaged instead is a rich interanimation between the two, which can be expected to provoke a fruitful co-evolution of theories, models, and methods, where each informs, corrects, and inspires the other.

For neuroscientists, a sense of how to get a grip on the big questions and of the appropriate overarching framework with which to pursue hands-on research is essential—essential, that is, if neuroscientists are not to lose themselves, sinking blissfully into the sweet, teeming minutiae, or inching with manful dedication down a dead-end warren. For philosophers, an understanding of what progress has been made in neuroscience is essential to sustain and constrain theories about such things as how representations relate to the world, whether representations are propositional in nature, how organisms learn, whether mental states are emergent with respect to brain states, whether conscious states are a single type of state, and so on. It is essential, that is, if philosophers are not to remain boxed within the narrow canyons of the commonsense conception of the world or to content themselves with heroically plumping up the pillows of decrepit dogma.

The guiding aim of the book is to paint in broad strokes the outlines of a very general framework suited to the development of a unified theory of the mind-brain. Additionally, it aims to bestir a yen for the enrichment and excitement to be had by an interanimation of philosophy, psychology, and neuroscience, or more generally, of top-down and bottom-up research.

In a way, nothing is more obvious than that philosophers of mind could profit from knowing at least something of what there is to know about how the brain works. After all, one might say, how could the empirical facts about the nervous system fail to be relevant to studies in the philosophy of mind. But there are interesting rejoinders to this. For example, it may be argued, as dualists do argue, that the mind is a separate and distinct entity from the brain, so that information about the brain will not tell us much about the mind (chapter 8). Or it may be argued that even if materialism is true, the properties characteristic of mental states are emergent with respect to brain states (chapter 8), or perhaps that neuroscientific findings are too fine grained to be pertinent to large-scale questions, or that neuroscience is methodologically confined to *structural* theories whereas what philosophers and psychologists (top-downish ones anyway) seek are *functional* characterizations of mental processes (chapter 9). These are some reasons for looking askance at neuroscience. I think each of them is wrong, though none is obviously or trivially wrong. Part of what I shall try to show is how these arguments fail.

At the same time, however, it has also seemed obvious that neuroscientists could profit from the philosophical research that has gone into answering the following questions: What sort of business is *reduction*? What conditions should be satisfied in order that *identifications* of phenomena can be made? How are we to understand in a general way what *representing* is? How are we to assess the prospects for a *unified account* of mind-brain function? How might language relate to the world? Many philosophers suspect that neuroscientists have been less than willing to see the importance to their own research of addressing the larger, synoptic questions and of examining the integrity of their governing paradigm, but have preferred to get on with writing "safe" grant proposals and undertaking unadventurous research.

It is also complained that when neuroscientists do address the larger questions, they tend to turn to outdated and discredited positivist ideas about what science is and about the nature of theories, meaning, and explanation. How widespread the faults are I cannot begin to estimate, but certainly there is some substance to the philosophers' complaints. Undoubtedly our understanding of science has come a long way since the heyday of logical empiricism, and it is important that some of the ground-breaking work of the past two decades in the history and philosophy of science be made accessible.

Accordingly, an abiding concern in writing this book is to present philosophical research and insights in a coherent and readable fashion, trying to balance between providing sufficient detail to make points thoroughly and being clear enough and clean enough so that neuroscientists do not give up on it as painfully abstruse, or "philosophical" in the bad sense of the word—that is, perverse, dark, and anyhow pointless. Philosophical detail is apt to dissolve into mere crinkum-crankum, and it is my intention to risk snubbing the niceties in order to preserve an uncluttered pattern of the main arguments.

In the most straightforward sense, what is wanted is a unified theory of how the mind-brain works. We want a theory of how the mind-brain represents whatever it represents, and of the nature of the computational processes underlying behavior. The collective effort to devise such a theory will be constrained by empirical facts at all levels, including neurophysiological, ethological, and psychological facts. In addition, it will be colored by pretheoretic hunches concerning what a theory could look like and what are the basic principles of mind-brain operation. More fundamentally perhaps, it will also be affected by opinions concerning whether such an enterprise is even reasonable at all.

The idea that ultimately there should be a unified theory of the brain—a theory that encompasses all levels of description—has of course been around for a long time. But the idea has typically seemed both surpassingly vague and pathetically remote. In truth, it really has been less a palpable conception than a misty ideal toward which science, in the very long haul, might progress. Consequently, philosophy has tended to ignore developments in the neurosciences and pretty much to go its own way. Likewise, research in the neurosciences has proceeded without much heed to what philosophers had to say about the nature of knowledge or of mental states. Quite simply, neither found the other useful, and the two disciplines have had largely independent histories. Contact was made only seldom, and then it usually consisted in desultory sparring on the "mind-body problem."

But things are changing. Developments in neuroscience and in philosophy, as well as developments in psychology and computer science, have brought the disciplines to the stage where there are common problems, and there is a gathering sense of the benefits for research in cross-talk. For one thing, neuroscience has progressed to the point where we can begin to theorize productively about basic principles of whole brain function and hence to address the questions concerning how the brain represents, learns, and produces behavior. Second, many philosophers have moved away from the view that philosophy is an a priori discipline in which philosophers can discover the a priori principles that neuroscientific theories had better honor on peril of being found wrong. Consequently, there has been a reevaluation of the significance of neuroscientific and psychological findings for philosophical research. Third, psychology has begun to deepen our understanding of certain mental processes, such as memory and visual perception, in a way that permits us to see to what extent orthodox conceptions are misconceptions, and how neural mechanisms might implement the functions. Fourth, work in computer science and computer modeling of networks has helped to generate concepts of information processing, representation, and computation that take us well beyond the earlier ideas and provide at least a general sense of how to address the question of subintrospective mind-brain processes.

We have entered a time when the idea of a unified theory of how the brain works is no longer impossibly remote. Trying to figure out a theory to explain how neural assemblies function, and thus to find a theoretical interface between high-level functions and lower-level neuronal functions, is indeed something one can do without straying into the murky domain of crackpot "science." My early conviction was simply that neuroscience must contribute essentially to the theoretical enterprise because we cannot expect to understand the brain-behavior relationship unless we understand what neurons do and how they are interconnected. Studying the neurosciences has deepened that conviction and has resulted as well in a reorientation of my philosophical pursuits. Theorizing about the brain and the behavior it produces will require both an understanding of fine-grained facts about nervous systems and large-scale framework conceptions. The more informed our brains are by science at all levels of analysis, the better will be our brains' theoretical evolution. Thus, the co-evolution of macrotheory and microtheory—broadly, of neuroscience and psychology—is a major methodological theme throughout. The strategy shaping the book, therefore, has been to introduce philosophy and neuroscience, each to the other.

Ideally, I should have liked to begin by presenting *theoretically relevant* neuroscience. The problem in pursuing that ideal is that in the very early stages of theory development, judgments about what is and is not theoretically relevant are necessarily naive. That is, there must exist a robust, commanding, and widely adopted theory against which to assess the theoretical importance of data, and no large-scale theory of brain function has yet succeeded in achieving such a status within neuroscience. This does not mean that there are no theories, only that there is no Governing Paradigm in the Kuhnian sense. Accordingly, my way of dealing with the problem is to begin in Part I by presenting some rudimentary neurophysiology, some rudimentary neuroanatomy, a glimpse into neurology and into neuropsychology, and a précis of a few methods used to study nervous systems.

I am painfully aware of how voluminously much I have left out of my introduction to neuroscience, but my hope is twofold: that I have presented enough so that philosophers may now approach textbooks and review papers without being intimidated, and that I have said enough so that the newly emerging theoretical frameworks presented in chapter 10 can be understood. I present these frameworks as examples of what a large-scale theory of brain function might look like, but at the same time I acknowledge that none has yet, and none might ever, achieve the status of Governing Paradigm.

Philosophers who are expecting to find in the introduction to neuroscience a point-by-point guide of just what facts in neuroscience are relevant to just which traditional philosophical problems will be disappointed. I have made some occasional efforts in that direction, but in the main my eye is on the overarching question of the nature of a unified, integrating theory of how, at all its levels of description, the brain works. If philosophers are to address that question, it cannot be in ignorance of what science already knows about nervous systems. Moreover, if the theoretical framework discussed in chapter 10 is even close to being right, then at least some traditional philosophical questions about the mind will, like old soldiers, just fade away, and new, very different problems will take their place.

In Part II I attempt to introduce neuroscientists to philosophy, and in the main, this means an introduction to philosophy of mind as informed by philosophy of science. When philosophers consider the question of a unified theory of the mind-brain, they focus on a number of problems. For example, what would a theory have to be like in order to account for what we think we know about the nature of mental states? To some philosophers, and to some neuroscientists in a philosophical mood, it has seemed that a unified theory of the mind-brain is an unattainable goal, perhaps even a preposterous goal. Some of the reasons derive from the enormous conceptual differences between explanations at the psychological level of description and explanations at the level of the single cell. Other reasons originate in deep-seated theories about the nature of representations and computations. Still others are based on a misunderstanding of the nature of intertheoretic reduction.

Many issues at this level of abstraction are still highly contentious, and the "conventional wisdom" is a bit like a collection of small lily pads distributed in a rather large pond. But philosophers have made distinctive progress on certain key issues, such as whether there is a nonphysical mind, and these results can be succinctly rendered. Part of the task in the introduction to philosophy of mind is to clarify the problems sufficiently so that all sorts of common confusions are kept at bay. The other part is to orient neuroscientists to one perspective on how these abstract problems may be confronted. This perspective is in no sense a complete answer to anything, but it is a view informed by philosophers· who make sense to me and neuroscientists who make sense to me. This perspective has two prominent features: one argues for the ultimate correctability of even our most deep-seated convictions about the nature of our mental life, and the other delineates a theory of intertheoretic reduction for science generally. The two converge in defense of an approach to finding a unified theory of the mind-brain that envisages the co-evolution of theories at all levels of description.

Thus, the framework for discussion of neuroscientifically relevant philosophy is the overarching question of the nature and possibility of devising a unified theory to explain how the mind-brain works. In dealing with the possibility of intertheoretic reduction, I have found it most useful to organize the discussion with the primary focus not on neuroscience but on theories elsewhere in science. This is essentially because neuroscience is a relatively young science, and by distancing ourselves from it somewhat, and by surveying dispassionately sciences with long histories, mature theories, and a rich theoretical evolution, it is to be hoped that analogies and disanalogies can be discerned that will be instructive in confronting the issues at hand. Intertheoretic reduction is a feature of the historical evolution of theories, and it therefore needs to be understood by reference to actual instances.

As before, I am acutely aware of the sketchiness of the picture, and undoubtedly other philosophers would go about the business in a different manner. But my hope is again twofold: that I have said enough to give a coherent picture that both makes philosophical sense and meshes appropriately with ongoing science; and that I have said enough so that neuroscientists can approach the relevant philosophical literature without being flummoxed.

Parts I and II are in many respects independent of each other, reflecting the essentially independent histories of philosophy and neuroscience. But the two sorts of enterprise converge as we collectively set about trying to devise, not merely dream of, theories of how the mind-brain works, and Part III represents one converging stream. In Part III, I discuss the status and significance of theory in neuroscience, and I present three interrelated examples of nascent theories. This Part exhibits an instance of a large-scale theoretical framework purportedly suitable for explaining molar effects in terms of neuronal behavior, and at the same time it provides an illustration of the convergence of philosophical and neuroscientific research. A paramount reason why these neurobiologically based theories of brain functions will be of interest to philosophers is that they may contain the foundations of a new paradigm for characterizing representations and computations. To the extent that they do so, they constitute a counterexample to those who argue for a uniquely psychological theory of representations and computation.

A characterization of the nature of *representations* is fundamental to answering how it is that we can see or intercept a target or solve problems, whether we consider these accomplishments in psychological terms or in neurobiological terms. The same is true of the *processes* operating on representations—the computations. Questions concerning representations and computations have long been at the heart of philosophical theories about the way the mind works, and it is clear that they are now central to neurobiological theorizing about the way the brain works. My selection of theoretical examples in Part III is motivated by the very traditional philosophical preoccupation with what it is to represent something and by the judgment that neuroscience has a great deal to teach us about how brains represent.

Certainly I do not suppose that the particular theoretical investigations that I have chosen to discuss are the only points where an interanimation of neuroscience and philosophy is possible. They happened to be ones that appealed to my imagination. Indeed, I think the possibilities are legion. I end the book where I do largely for a grindingly practical reason: it is long enough.

So far the ropes thrown across the divide are those from philosophy and from neuroscience, and it will be wondered where ethology and the assorted psychological sciences are thought to fit in the envisaged scheme of things. The fast answer is that they have an absolutely essential role in the enterprise of getting a unified theory of how the mind-brain works. Detailed understanding of the behavioral parameters is essential if we are to know what, exactly, is to be explained by reference to neural mechanisms. Additionally, theories of cognitive and subcognitive processes tendered by psychology, for example, can be expected to co-evolve with neurobiological theories, and these theories are likely to be party to any intertheoretic reduction that eventuates.

My emphasis has not been on ethology and the psychological sciences, however, and this for several reasons. First, the standard objections to the possibility of a unified theory of the mind-brain are typically philosophical, inasmuch as they draw on very general and very abstract considerations. If I am to defend the reasonableness of searching for a unified theory, I must answer these objections. Second, the theme of representations and their nature has been worked most thoroughly in a philosophical context, though where the psychological sciences offer relevant principles and pertinent data, I try to draw these in. Even so, the research in psychology and ethology is insufficiently discussed, and this because a third and familiar practical reason began to assert itself: the book is already long enough.

It is difficult to resist the excitement that now typifies so much research in the neurosciences and the related psychological sciences. The excitement is generated in part because neuroscience is *science*, and in pushing back the bounds of darkness it is discovering surprising new things and teaching us how some aspect of the universe works. But it is also because the discoveries have immediately to do with a very special realm of the universe, *ourselves*—with that miraculous mound of excitable cells lodged in our skulls that makes us what we are. In a straightforward sense, we are discovering what we are and how to make sense of ourselves. This is as much a part of *anyone's* philosophical aspirations, be they ancient or modern, untutored or scholarly, as any quest there is.

PART I

Some Elementary Neuroscience

Chapter 1

The Science of Nervous Systems: A Historical Sketch

As long as our brain is a mystery, the universe—the reflection of the structure of the brain—will also be a mystery.
Santiago Ramón y Cajal, ca. 1898

1.1 Introduction

If you root yourself to the ground, you can afford to be stupid. But if you move, you must have mechanisms for moving, and mechanisms to ensure that the movement is not utterly arbitrary and independent of what is going on outside. Consider a simple protochordate, the sea squirt. The newborn must swim about and feed itself until it finds a suitable niche, at which time it backs in and attaches itself permanently. Once attached, the sea squirt's mechanisms for movement become excess baggage, and it wisely supplements its diet by feasting on its smartest parts.

Animals are movers, and some of them display astonishing agility. How is it possible for an owl to dive, almost silently, out of the night sky and to entrap a scurrying mouse in its talons? Both organisms are on the move, yet the owl's timing is precise, and it neither crashes into the ground nor comes up empty-handed. How is it possible simply to walk, and to walk at varying speeds and over sundry obstacles? Look at a nervous system that is not performing normally because it has been altered by drugs, or by disease, or by trauma to the inner ear, for example, and we get a glimpse of the awesome complexity that underlies the smooth coordination we standardly take for granted. What is going on inside a canary when it learns the motor skill for song production, or inside wolves when they know how to organize themselves to bring down a deer? How is it that we see, hear, and figure things out?

Neurons are excitable cells, and neurons on the sensory periphery are activated by such things as photons or vibration, while neurons on the motor periphery cause the contraction of muscles. In between are neurons that orchestrate the sequence of muscle cell contractions permitting the organism to move so as to deal appropriately with the world outside its nervous system, by fleeing, feeding, and so forth. Neurons are the basic elements of nervous systems; they are evolution's solution to the problem of adaptive movement. But how do they work, and what is excitation? How do they produce effects as different as awareness of light and awareness of touch? How are they orchestrated so that the organism can make its way in the world?

In trying to understand the functional principles governing the human nervous system, we must remind ourselves that our brain has evolved from earlier kinds of brains—that our kind of brain was not built from scratch especially for us, but has capacities and limitations that are due to its historical origins. The pressure for nervous systems to evolve has derived not from the intrinsic beauty of rationality or from some indwelling goodness attaching to cognition, but primarily from the need for animals successfully to predict events in their environment, including of course events originating in other organisms (Dawkins and Krebs 1978, Llinás (in press)). The fundamental nature of cognition is rooted in the tricks by which assorted representational schemas give organisms a competitive advantage in predicting. Representational structures themselves must be organized to enable informed motor performance and will bear the stamp of their raison d'être.

Keeping in mind the biological evolution of the physical nervous system is therefore important in the theoretical undertaking, but relevant also is the cultural evolution of the *science* of nervous systems. Brains are exceedingly complex and delicate, and they give up their secrets with exasperating reluctance. Understanding something of how the knowledge was won, how conflicting theories were resolved, how technological advances made a difference, and so forth, anchors modern neuroscience and renders it more accessible. The historical perspective enables us both to articulate the fundamental assumptions inherent in current understanding that are owed to historical origins and to test those assumptions for adequacy. It helps us to see how even our most secure convictions can turn out to be misconceptions and how we can be taken by surprise. A sense of how we have come to be where we are is essential if we are to know where to go from here.

What follows is a very brief glimpse into some high points in the history of neurophysiology. By necessity, the historical sketch is very selective, and in the main I have followed the particular thread that has led to an understanding of what the basic structural elements of nervous systems are and a little about their modus operandi. Deferred until later is that part of the history concerned with the neurophysiological implementation of psychological functions.

1.2 Historical Sketch

By Galen's time (200 B.C.) a good deal of the naked-eye anatomy of the nervous system had been discovered. Galen was a Greek anatomist and physician, and he knew that movement depended on the muscles and that the whitish cords in the muscles were somehow critical. These cords are nerves, and the nerves are really cables containing strands of axon bundles. Galen's hypothesis was that the nerves transported one of the pneumata—psychic pneuma—to the muscles and that the muscle then puffed up as the pneuma permeated it, thereby producing movement. In Galen's conception the psychic pneuma was breath or air, though as he thought of it, breath was not merely physical stuff as we now believe it to be, but was infused with vital spirit. Galen's account was a beginning, though it uneasily bedded together the mechanistic and the vitalistic, and it was to persist as orthodoxy until nineteenth-century biologists and anatomists finally knew enough to replace it.

Descartes (1596–1650), though sometimes misunderstood on the matter, had a conception of bodily movement more consistently materialist than Galen. Captivated by the uncanny versatility of clockwork mechanisms and elaborate water fountain systems, Descartes believed the body to be a machine, albeit an exquisitely complicated machine. He agreed that muscles moved in virtue of the infusion of animal spirits, but he considered the latter to be

> nothing but material bodies and their one peculiarity is that they are bodies of extreme minuteness and that they move very quickly like . . . particles of the flame. . . . (1649; in Haldane and Ross 1911:336)

Clearly, there was nothing very spiritual about his "animal spirits." He was especially eager to get a mechanistic account of the reflexes, for he saw such actions as instances in which

> members may be moved by . . . objects of the senses and by . . . animal spirits without the aid of the soul. (1649; in Haldane and Ross 1911:339)

Cognizant of the involuntary nature of reflex action, he demonstrated this with the eye blink, observing that

> . . . it is not by the intervention of the soul that they close, . . . but it is because the machine of our body is so formed that the move-

ment of this hand towards our eyes excites another movement in our brain, which conducts the animal spirits into the muscles which cause the eyelids to close. (1649; in Haldane and Ross 1911:338)

The conception is evidently and ardently mechanistic. Elsewhere he described the reflex causal chain in the following way, illustrating his hypothesis with the drawing shown in figure 1.1. Suppose the skin of the foot is touched by a burning ember. This displaces the skin, which pulls a tiny thread stretching from the foot to brain. This in turn pulls open a pore in the brain, permitting the animal spirits to flow down, inflating the muscles and causing movement. What *was* beyond a mechanistic account, in his view, was voluntary action on the part of humans, for this, he thought, required a rational, immaterial soul and the free exercise of will. This was the legendary ghost rendering majestic the machine of the body.

Descartes was also struck by what is indeed a striking thing: that organisms perceive what they do and move as they do in virtue of something remote from their muscles and sense organs, namely, the brain. The nerves are essentially message cables to and from the brain. As Descartes remarked:

It is however easily proved that the soul feels those things that affect the body not in so far as it is in each member of the body, but only in so far as it is in the brain, where the nerves by their movements convey to it the diverse actions of the external objects which touch the parts of the body. (1644; in Haldane and Ross 1911:293)

The eerie case of phantom limbs teaches us, in Descartes's opinion, that "[the] pain in the hand is not felt by the mind inasmuch as it is in the hand, but as it is in the brain" (1644; in Haldane and Ross 1911:294). (It often happens that after a limb has been amputated, the patient says it feels as though the limb is still there, that it has a distinct position and orientation, and that it has sensations, typically painful ones. Sometimes the phantom limb disappears; sometimes it persists indefinitely.)

Others ventured to extend the mechanistic conception to cover not only involuntary behavior and "all those actions which are common to us and the brutes," but to voluntary behavior of rational humans as well. La Mettrie, most notably, put the case in a general way in his book, *L'Homme machine* (1748), and claimed there was no fundamental difference between humans and animals. "Irritation" of the nerves, he believed, would account for all behavior, both intelligent and

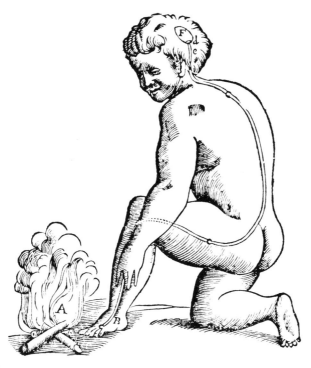

Figure 1.1
Descartes's explanation of the mechanism subserving reflex movement. ". . . the particles of this fire have force enough to displace the area of skin they touch; and thus
pulling the little thread *cc*, which you see to be attached there, they simultaneously
open the entrance to the pore *de* where this thread terminates [in the brain]. . . . [Next,]
. . . the animal spirits in its cavities begin immediately to make their way into the
nerves, and so into the muscles that give rise to movements. . . ." (From Descartes
1664; in Hall 1972:34.)

reflex. But unfortunately for La Mettrie, the times were far from ready for such stormy and heretical ideas, and he paid the harsh price of the iconoclast. He was hounded and reviled by the clergy, banished from France, and finally exiled even from liberal Holland. Eventually he was invited to the court of Frederick the Great of Prussia, where Voltaire was also in residence.

In his mechanistic conception of animal spirits and bodily function Descartes was undoubtedly a maverick, just barely remaining respectable through his constant caveats that he was probably wrong and that he submitted entirely to the authority of the Catholic church. Orthodoxy continued to pronounce animal spirits and vital forces as immaterial and ghostly and to see nervous activity as requiring vital forces.

Nevertheless, the idea that nerves were conduits for animal spirits gradually lost ground and was put to a particularly telling test by the great Dutch biologist, Jan Swammerdam (1637–1680). In one experiment he removed a frog's leg muscle together with parts of the nerves attached to it, finding, as others had before him, that the muscle would contract if the nerve were merely pinched or irritated. He reasoned that if mere mechanical deformation of the nerve was sufficient to produce muscle contraction, then "pneuma" from the brain could not be necessary, and ordinary physical properties could as well be the causal agents.

In a second and equally telling experiment Swammerdam tested the claim that muscles move in virtue of an infusion of pneuma that puffs them up (figure 1.2). Using an elegantly simple method, he found that the volume of muscle did not increase during contraction by nerve stimulation as the pneuma theory predicted. He simply placed the muscle in an enclosed chamber from which projected a tube containing water, and he noted whether there was any displacement of the water drop when the muscle contracted. There was none. From this he inferred that the muscle changed shape, but that ". . . no matter of sensible or comprehensible bulk flows through the nerves into the muscles" (*Biblia naturae*, published posthumously 1738). Others performed cruder versions of this test on living subjects by immersing an arm in water, contracting the muscle, and then measuring the water displacement. Of course these experiments did not convince everyone that the animal spirit hypothesis should be abandoned, but they did stimulate research on the physical properties of nerves and muscles.

A major advance in understanding was made by François Magendie in 1822. By experimenting on animals, he found that the nerve roots on the dorsal part of the spinal cord carry sensory information

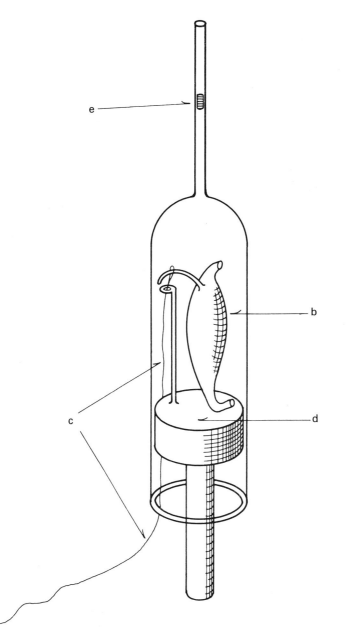

Figure 1.2
Swammerdam's experiment designed to test whether muscle volume increases during contraction. At *e* in the thin tube is a drop of water, which will be caused to rise if the muscle *b* increases in volume when stimulated mechanically (*c*) to contract. (Redrawn from Swammerdam 1737–8.)

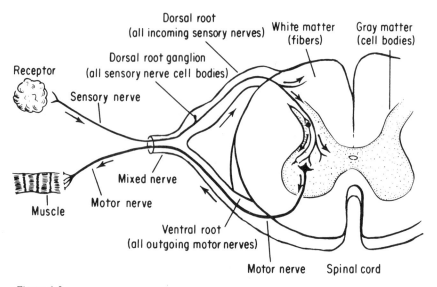

Figure 1.3
Organization of peripheral nerves viewed in a cross section of spinal cord at right angles to the cord. Afferent fibers transmit information in to the spinal cord via the dorsal root, and efferent fibers carry motor information out of the spinal cord and on to the muscles via the ventral root. (From Thompson (1975). *Introduction to Physiological Psychology.* New York: Harper and Row.)

from the periphery to the cord, while the ventral roots carried motor messages to the muscles (figure 1.3). This discovery of the separation of function of the nerves was exceedingly important in establishing the principle that different functions are executed by different parts of the nervous system. (As it happened, this was an instance of rediscovery, since unbeknownst to the scientific community, Herophilus and Erasistratus had recognized this division of labor some two thousand years before Magendie's experiments.) The general rule that dorsal roots carry sensory information inward and ventral roots carry motor information outward became known as the Bell-Magendie law, though it appears that Charles Bell (see below) in fact had not correctly identified the function of the dorsal roots.

Charles Bell (1774–1842) pioneered experimental research into the cause of differences in sensory qualities. By poking himself smartly on the tongue with a sharp needle, he noticed that for some areas he could elicit a sensation of pain, but for others he could elicit no pain whatever, but only a slightly metallic taste. Despite the identity of the stimulus, the effect was markedly different, and this moved Bell to believe that the difference was due to the nerves or to the brain and not to the nature of the stimulus. He also noticed that perceptions of light can be produced by pressing on the side of the eyeball.

At the time the prevailing view held that the quality of the sensation was essentially determined by the nature of the stimulus, though some organs such as the retina were thought to be more sensitive than the skin, and so could pick up delicate vibrations such as light, whereas the skin did not. Magendie as well as Bell now saw that this view must be false, and Magendie demonstrated it rather dramatically in the course of treating patients with cataracts. In his clinical practice he had to insert a sharp needle into the eye, and he observed that although penetration of the cornea was initially very painful, when the probing needle touched the retina it did not cause excruciating pain as the old theory predicted, and indeed caused no pain whatsoever. Instead, it produced sensations of light.

Johannes Müller (1801–1858) extended Magendie's investigation. According to his results, which became known as "the law of specific nerve energies," each nerve has its own peculiar "energy" or quality, in that it is part of a system capable of yielding one determinate kind of sensation only. Müller thoroughly canvassed the sense organs to see if he could produce the characteristic sensation and only that sensation by a variety of means. He found that sensations of touch, for example, could be elicited by mechanical influences, chemical influences, heat, electricity, and "stimulus of the blood" (as in congestion and inflammation). Müller's own statement of his conclusions reveals a change in the understanding of how and what the brain represents:

> Therefore, sensation is not the conduction of a quality or state of external bodies to consciousness, but a conduction of a quality or a state of our nerves to consciousness, excited by an external cause. (1835; in Clarke and O'Malley 1968:206)

This an echo of Descartes's earlier ruminations, and it marks a special point in the development of our understanding of how nervous systems represent the world outside. For it became evident that the brain in some sense has to reconstruct the world from the effects on nerves, and hence that the nature of the world is not sheerly "given" to us. It is in some measure a product of our brains.

Müller is standardly honored in biological histories as "the father of modern physiology." He was extraordinarily prolific, allegedly producing a paper every seven weeks from the age of nineteen until his death. He probed a wide range of areas, including histology, embryology, the physiology of motion, foetal life, nerves, and vision, and the anatomy of vertebrates and invertebrates. He was professor of anatomy and physiology in Berlin, and an impressive number of famous researchers got their start under his wise and inspiring tutelage. However, he still adhered to the immaterial conception of animal spirits, which he believed to course through the nerves at speeds too high to be measurable. One of his most illustrious students, Hermann von Helmholtz, challenged the vitalistic assumption in an imaginative and grand-scale fashion, and then went on to astound the world by actually measuring the velocity of impulse conduction in a nerve.

Helmholtz (1821–1894) was an uncompromising materialist in his conception of the causes of nervous effects. Educated in physics, Helmholtz was intrigued and provoked by the law of conservation of energy and by its general implications for biology. He reasoned that if the law was correct, and energy could be transformed but neither created nor destroyed, then there appeared to be no room for a vital force that exerted itself and went into abeyance ex nihilo. He therefore undertook to see whether the law might after all be applicable to living organisms, and thus he began to explore the relation between metabolic body processes and the heat generated by the muscles.

He started by showing that during muscular activity, changes take place in the muscles that could be accounted for simply as the oxidation of nutrients consumed by the organism. He then showed that ordinary chemical reactions were capable of producing all the physical activity and heat generated by the organism, and that so far as the question of energy was concerned, the body could be viewed as a mechanical device for transforming energy from one form to another. Special forces and spirits need not enter into it. Of course, this was not a decisive blow against vitalism, since Helmholtz had shown only that it was possible to explain the energy output of the organism in terms of energy input, not how in fact to explain it. Nevertheless, the approach he took and his meticulous care did have the effect of altering attitudes toward a mechanistic methodology, and his use of physics and quantitative analyses was widely admired and adopted.

Helmholtz then tested Müller's claim that nerve impulses traveled at immeasurable speeds. His methods were elegantly simple and quantitative. He measured the velocity of nerve conduction by stimulating the nerve at different points and noting how long it took for the muscle to contract. He found, to great amazement, that it was slower even than the speed of sound. In his preparation he calculated conduction velocity at a mere thirty meters per second (figure 1.4).

The results were wrenching in their consequences, for it was generally assumed that nervous effects were instantaneous—that one felt

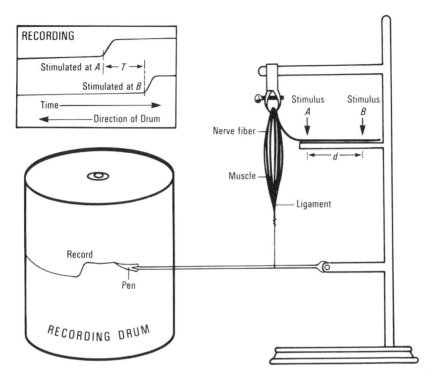

Figure 1.4
Schematic version of the apparatus Helmholtz used to measure the velocity of a nerve impulse. A nerve-muscle preparation is set up so that, when the muscle contracts, it pulls a pen upward. This leaves a mark on a recording drum. Helmholtz showed that when the nerve is stimulated at point B, the muscle will twitch later than if the stimulus is applied at point A. By measuring the actual time difference, T, he was able to calculate the impulse velocity. This velocity is obtained by dividing d (the distance between A and B) by T (the extra time it takes for the muscle to twitch if the nerve is stimulated at B rather than at A). (Reproduced from *Psychology* by Henry Gleitman, by permission of W. W. Norton and Co., Inc. Copyright © 1981 by W. W. Norton and Co., Inc.)

the touch the instant one was touched, or that one's hand went out the instant one decided to reach. The idea that the whole business takes time was rather shocking. Helmholtz's father described his own thoughts regarding his son's findings:

> As regards your work, the results at first appeared to me surprising, since I regard the idea and its bodily expression not as successive but as instantaneous, a single living act that only becomes bodily and mental on reflection, and I could as little reconcile myself to your view as I could admit a star that had disappeared

in Abraham's time should still be visible. (Letter to Hermann von Helmholtz in Koenigsberger 1906:67)

Another student of Müller's, Emil du Bois-Reymond (1818–1896), was the first to demonstrate (1843) that the nervous effect was in fact an electrical phenomenon and that a wave of electrical activity passes down a nerve. It had been well known that nerves could be excited by "galvanism," but establishing that electricity was the essential feature of normal nerve function was of great significance and established the basis for further physiological investigation. Certainly by this time the idea that a fluid, immaterial or otherwise, is transported in nerves to cause nervous effects had ceased to be interesting.

The pressing question now concerned the constituents of nerves and how such constituents were able to produce electrical effects. Slowly it began to emerge that the basic elements are neurons—cells with central bodies from which long filaments extend—but this hypothesis was hard won and was crucially dependent on a variety of technological discoveries. A number of difficulties obstructed the way of research here. For one thing, the chromatic aberrations of the early microscopes meant that artifacts constantly bedeviled observations, and it was not until the development of the achromatic compound microscope that it became possible to make reliable observations of nervous tissue.

Even so, other artifactual problems plagued research, since nervous tissue degenerates unless properly fixated and the differences between fresh and old preparations are so profound that old preparations are useless. It had to be painfully discovered that water-mounted slides were to be avoided because the change in osmotic pressure changed the cell dramatically. Moreover, as we now know, nervous tissue is packed cheek to jowl with cells, some of which are not neurons at all, but adjunct glial cells. Ingenious stains were eventually found that would highlight select numbers of neurons so they could be picked out visually from the dense thicket (figures 1.5, 1.6). Though invaluable, staining was to a troublesome extent an art, and the resulting preparations did not just emblazon their truths for anyone to read. The observations of the preparations had to be interpreted, and not infrequently there were disputes about what they truly showed. Finally, it had to be slowly and arduously discovered that unlike, say, red blood cells, which can be captured in their entirety in the image of the microscope, neurons have long processes extending well beyond the cell body or "soma."

Histologists, for example Purkyně (1837), saw cell bodies through the microscope, and on other slides they also saw the long, skinny

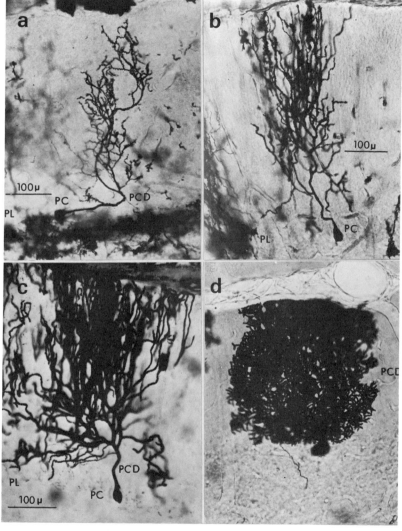

Figure 1.5
Neurons (Purkinje cells) in the cerebellar cortex of (a) the frog, (b) the alligator, (c) the pigeon, and (d) the cat. Stained by the Golgi method. (From Llinás and Hillman (1969). In *Neurobiology of cerebellar evolution and development*, ed. R. Llinás. Chicago: The American Medical Association.)

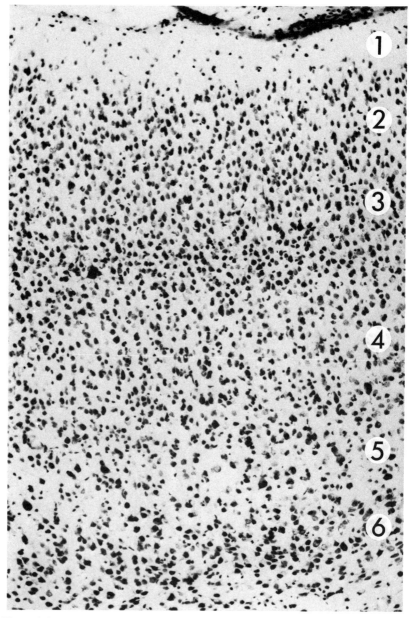

Figure 1.6
Photomicrograph of neurons in a cross section of the visual cortex of the mink. The stain used is cresyl violet (Nissl stain), which stains the cell bodies of all neurons. The cortex shown here is about 1.2 mm thick, and its six distinct layers can also be seen. (Courtesy S. McConnell and S. LeVay.)

"fibers" that we now call axons, but it was not until Remak ventured the opinion in 1838 that axons might be extensions of cell bodies that anyone suspected that neurons were radically different in shape from blood cells. As staining and fixation techniques improved, this fact finally became indisputable (Hannover 1840). Using a carmine stain and new fixation techniques, Deiters (1865) saw for the first time a luxuriant arborization of very thin and delicate dendrites extending from the cell body, and on the basis of observed structural differences he drew a distinction between "protoplasmic processes" (axons) and "nervous processes" (dendrites).

These assorted discoveries prompted the question, What are the connections between neurons? Connections of some kind there must certainly be, since reflex action clearly required a connection between ingoing sensory effects and outgoing motor effects, and, following Magendie, it was known that the sensory nerves were a distinct cable from the motor nerves.

Camillo Golgi (1843–1926) took the view that neurons must fuse or "anastomose" and that in order for the nervous system to do what it does, it must be one continuous nerve net or "reticulum" (1883). This became known as the "reticularist theory." A particularly important factor in observations was Golgi's development of a new staining technique using silver. To understand the fundamental principles of nervous system organization, it was necessary to know what the basic structure was, and hence researchers urgently needed a stain that would allow a single cell to be observed in its entirety. The staining technique discovered by Golgi had several remarkable properties. It selectively stained only a few cells in the tissue examined (1–10%), and to those selected it did what was wanted: it impregnated the soma, dendrites, and axons. This meant that for the first time researchers could observe the fundamental nervous units. The Golgi technique made it possible to investigate the nervous system in a powerful new way, and Golgi, by its means and through meticulous observations, addressed the question of the structural relations between neurons. He concluded, rightly, that dendrites do not anastomose as he thought axons did. He also conjectured, wrongly however, that dendrites likely served a nutritive rather than a nervous function. His reason for this opinion was that he thought his stained preparations showed dendrites terminating on blood vessels.

That neurons are independent units and do not fuse to form a continuous whole was known as the "neuron theory." To a modern ear this seems a rather odd label, since reticularists and neuronists alike believed there were neurons, but differed on whether it was in the nature of neurons to fuse cytoplasmically or to be separate units.

However, the word "neuron" was adopted by Waldeyer in his 1891 review of the controversy, and he used it to mean "independent cell."[1] Until Waldeyer's review, a variety of other expressions were used to denote what we now call neurons, and indeed the nomenclature was chaotic. This was of course a reflection of the fact that the nature of the anatomy of nervous tissue was just beginning to be understood.

The axon anastomoses hypothesized by the reticularists proved exasperatingly elusive, though considering how tiny is the gap between an axon terminal and the abutting cell body or dendrite, it is not surprising that some (for example, Held (1897)) thought they had observed terminals fusing with somas. Golgi staining is a subtle and rather tricky technique, even now. For one thing, considerable skill is required to know when the staining is still incomplete, inasmuch as the stain has not yet made its way to the far-flung ends of the neuronal processes, and when the staining is past completion, inasmuch as the stain begins to impregnate neighboring glial cells. Moreover, not a little inference and conjecture goes into drawings made from Golgi preparations, and sometimes things just do not go very well, especially for the novice.[2] Not surprisingly, therefore, the disagreement between the reticularists and the neuronists was not neatly solvable simply by looking through the microscope at Golgi-stained preparations. And the controversy was not without heat, for it concerned a fundamental property of nervous systems, the outcome mattered enormously, and for a long while the evidence was equivocal. However, by the turn of the century the reticularist hypothesis seemed to have lost considerable ground, and the camp was composed mainly of diehards.

Experiments with neuronal growth and degeneration proved to be singularly revealing of the independence of neurons, one from the other. Wilhelm His (1888) showed in a series of experiments that foetal neurons definitely start out as independent entities and then proceed to extend their axonal and dendritic processes. There seemed no evidence that they subsequently fused. In the mirror image of His's tests, Forel (1887) found that when a cell body is damaged, only the axon attached to it degenerates, and conversely, that when an axon is damaged, only its cell body shows the typical degenerative signs.

Moreover, it was known (Kühne 1862) that at the neuromuscular junction axons can be found in special pitted areas of the muscle fibers, but they do not actually penetrate the muscle membrane. This was important because it meant that axons could transmit their effects to the muscles, making them contract, without making direct contact with the muscle cell itself. Finally, as a result of Santiago Ramón y Cajal's (1852–1934) anatomical studies, making brilliant use of the Golgi method of staining, it appeared that axons had terminal bulbs that came very close to the membranes of other cells but did not actually fuse with them. In Ramón y Cajal's words:

> This is not to deny indirect anastomosis . . . but to affirm simply that never having seen them, we dismiss them from our opinion. (1888; in Clarke and O'Malley 1968:112)

Apparently, part of what stiffened Golgi's unbendable conviction was his expectation that unless neurons formed a continuous net, the manner of their communication would be unexplainable and that, in consequence, the old, vitalistic theories would be disinterred and revived to account for neuronal interaction. As Golgi saw it, the coordinated nature of sensory-guided movement implied that the nerves were part of a *system*, and this counted against individual action of nerve cells. As he remarked in his speech accepting the 1906 Nobel Prize for medicine,

> I cannot abandon the idea of a unitarian action of the nervous system without being uneasy that by so doing I shall become reconciled to the old beliefs. (1908; in Clarke and O'Malley 1968:96)

Ramón y Cajal, who by 1888 was foremost among the neuronists, was equally mechanistic (he likened vitalists to the villagers who believed Prince Borghese's automobile to be propelled by a horse inside). Ramón y Cajal was not insensitive to Golgi's worries about neuronal communication, but he thought it reasonable to conjecture that electrical induction might well account for all interneuronal communication. As it turns out, this conjecture was wrong, though some neurons apparently do communicate in that fashion. But in the neurons Ramón y Cajal studied, interneuronal communication is a highly complex bit of *biochemical* business, with complex molecules acting as messengers from one neuron to the next (section 2.3). Golgi's hunch that neuronal interaction would be staggeringly difficult to figure out should neurons be distinct units is, alas, the discouraging truth, though the gloomy expectation that mystical forces and substances would be invoked has not been borne out, at least not so far as the communication between cells is concerned.

Despite their different theories on the nature of neuronal connections and despite the purple cast the controversy had sometimes taken, Ramón y Cajal and Golgi were jointly awarded the Nobel Prize for physiology and medicine in 1906. Though convinced that neurons were independent entities, Ramón y Cajal acknowledges that the case was not yet closed, for with light microscopy one could not be certain of having followed fibers to their very end. Moreover, he agreed with Golgi that the reticularist view would, if true, make life easier, but he concluded that the reticularist hypothesis was unsupported by the evidence. As he put it:

> From the analytic point of view it would be very convenient and economical if all the nerve centers formed a continuous network intermediate between motor nerves and sensitive and sensory nerves. Unfortunately, nature seems to ignore our intellectual need for convenience and unity, and is very often pleased with complexity and diversity. (1908; in Clarke and O'Malley 1968:128)

Also in 1906, C. S. Sherrington (1857–1952) published his landmark book, *The Integrative Action of the Nervous System*, in which he used the expression "synapse" as a name for the communication structures of neurons in virtue of which one neuron can transmit a signal across a gap to another neuron. Sherrington's claim that the nervous system contained synapses was based not on direct observation of synaptic junctions but on inferences drawn in consequence of careful studies of simple reflexes in dogs.

His reasoning was straightforward and convincing. He knew the length of one reflex arc in the animal (two feet) and he knew the velocity of nerve conduction (200 feet per second), which meant that if conduction along nerve fibers were the only mode of signal transmission, the response latency should be about 10 milliseconds. In fact, Sherrington discovered it to be much longer—about 100 milliseconds. Accordingly, he inferred that conduction along nerve fibers was not the only mode of signal transmission and that the signal must be transmitted across a gap between sensory neurons and motor neurons by a slower process. These special areas where neurons communicate came to be known as "synapses."

Observation of synaptic junctions finally became possible by means of the electron microscope in the 1950s. Using stains, and patiently piecing together micrographs from serial sections a few microns thick, researchers could observe the cell membranes and trace their perimeters. It became evident that there were specialized structures from which the signals were sent and where they were received. These showed up in the electron microscope photographs as darkened (electron-dense) smudges on the membrane, with congregations of little round vesicles milling about the smudges on the sending side. The synaptic gap between neurons was measured as about 200 angstroms (figure 1.7).

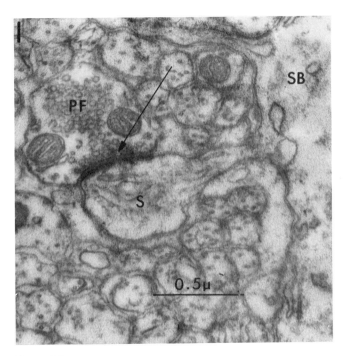

Figure 1.7
Electron micrograph showing the area of synaptic contact between two cells in the cerebellar cortex of the cat. The presynaptic cell is a parallel fiber (PF), and the postsynaptic cell is a branchlet on a dendrite of a Purkinje cell, designated (S). The arrow designates the synapse. The pre- and postsynaptic membranes are separated by a 200 angstrom cleft. Note the presence of electron-dense fuzz subjacent to the membranes and within the cleft, and the cluster of synaptic vesicles in the presynaptic cell. (From Llinás and Hillman (1969). In *Neurobiology of cerebellar evolution and development*, ed. R. Llinás. Chicago: The American Medical Association.)

When the reticularist theory was all but consigned to oblivion, the electron microscope revealed a synaptic junction that did not fit the standard mold; the gap was much smaller (only about 20 angstroms), and there were no vesicles. Recently it has become clear that these junctions are the sort that would have gladdened the heart of Golgi, for (as figure 1.8 shows) at these junctions there are tiny protein culverts connecting one neuron to the next (Furshpan and Potter 1959, Llinás, Baker, and Sotelo 1974). Nevertheless, this represents no triumph for the reticularist theory, since the existence of *any* discontinuities in neural circuits constitutes an embarrassment to this view, and in every nervous system so far studied the overwhelming preponderance of neurons are indeed units, unfused and distinct, though in constant and subtle communication with one another.

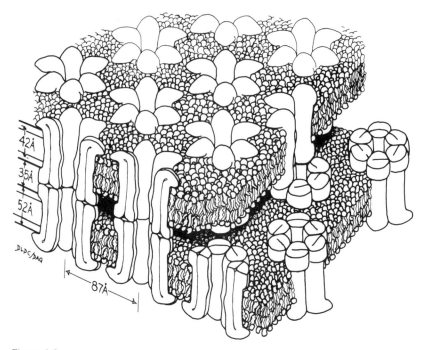

Figure 1.8
Schematic representation of an electrical synapse. The gap between the two cells is bridged at the point where opposing channels abut. The channels, composed of protein units, span the membrane and permit the exchange of small ions such as Na^+ and K^+ (From Makowski et al. 1977.)

In order to begin to understand how nervous systems work, it was essential to discover their basic functional units and how those units operate. In this enterprise, certainly, structural discoveries and functional discoveries were mutually dependent. Some hundred years elapsed between Helmholtz's measurement of the speed of signal conduction in nerves and the first observations of the microstructure of neurons through the electron microscope. During that period it was found that neurons are highly specialized cells, with a unique morphology and specialized cellular structures to subserve communication. Study of the nature of that communication became intense and was greatly aided by the squid, which has a motor neuron with a long axon unusually large in diameter. This giant axon of the obliging squid was our first entry into the complexities of how neurons communicate and respond to the signals of other neurons. As a result of research in those hundred years, what we might call the "neuron paradigm" came to be established, in the sense that the basic framework for research on neurons was widely espoused.

In this historical sketch I have touched on only some developments in early neuroscience and have gradually narrowed my focus to single out research on the neuron. Nonetheless, it should be emphasized that at the same time intensive efforts were being made to understand how large-scale functions might be implemented in the brain. Hypotheses were generated concerning how functions were either localized or distributed in the brain and how nervous tissue was organized. From neurologists studying the behavioral effects of lesions in the brain (lesions resulting from strokes or gunshot wounds, for example), from electrophysiologists stimulating and recording from diverse spots in the nervous system, and from anatomists investigating the routes traversed by bundles of axons and the styles of circuitry distinctive of certain parts of the brain, organizational features of the nervous system began to be investigated. These investigations, though extremely important, did not yield the correlative "neuronal ensemble paradigm," which might be expected to specify the fundamentals of what counted as a neuronal *ensemble* and how it functioned. In contrast to the general consensus reached by the 1950s concerning the fundamentals of the structure and function of individual neurons, many conflicts and puzzles concerning large-scale functions and their implementation have remained unresolved. These developments in the history of neuroscience will be briefly discussed in Chapter 4.

In those hundred years stretching from the research of Helmholtz to the introduction of the electron microscope into the laboratory, the elements for the blossoming of the science of nervous systems were formed. And indeed, blossom it did—spectacularly, prolifically, and sometimes in profoundly puzzling ways. To continue to trace, even sketchily, the emergence of knowledge through a historical sweep is impossible here, and perforce the better course will be to continue by presenting a synopsis of currently accepted theories on the nature of neuronal functioning and neuronal organization.

Selected Readings

Brazier, Mary A. B. (1984). *A history of neurophysiology in the 17th and 18th centuries.* New York: Raven.

Clarke, Edwin, and C. D. O'Malley (1968). *The human brain and spinal cord: A historical study illustrated by writings from antiquity to the twentieth century.* Berkeley and Los Angeles: University of California Press.

Neuburger, Max (1897). *Die historische Entwicklung der experimentellen Gehirn- und Rückenmarksphysiologie vor Flourens.* Stuttgart: Ferdinand Enke Verlag. (English translation by Edwin Clarke (1981). *The historical development of experimental brain and spinal cord physiology before Flourens.* Baltimore: The Johns Hopkins University Press.)

Rose, Clifford F., and W. F. Bynum (1982). *Historical aspects of the neurosciences.* New York: Raven.

Chapter 2
Modern Theory of Neurons

I doubt if we can even guess what Natural Selection has achieved, without some help from the way function has been embodied in actual structures. The reason is simple. Natural Selection is more ingenious than we are.
F. H. C. Crick, 1985

2.1   Introduction

If we are to understand how the mind-brain works, it is essential that we understand as much as possible about the fundamental elements of nervous systems, namely, neurons. Limits on the number of neurons, on the number of connections between neurons, and, perhaps most importantly, on the time course of neuronal events will highly constrain models of perception, memory, learning, and sensorimotor control. For example, it is worth dwelling on the constraints imposed by this temporal fact: events in the world of silicon chips happen in the *nanosecond* (10^{-9}) range, whereas events in the neuronal world happen in the *millisecond* (10^{-3}) range. Brain events are ponderously slow compared to silicon events, yet in a race to complete a perceptual recognition task, the brain leaves the computer far back in the dust. The brain routinely accomplishes perceptual recognition tasks in something on the order of 100–200 milliseconds, whereas tasks of much lesser complexity will take a huge conventional computer days. This immediately implies that however the brain accomplishes perceptual recognition, it cannot be by millions of steps arranged in sequence. There is simply not enough time. (This will be discussed in more detail in chapter 10. See also Feldman 1985.)

It is also worth dwelling on the fact that neurons are plastic, that their informationally relevant parts grow and shrink, that they are dynamic. Nor is their plasticity a nuisance or an ignorable nicety; it appears to be essential to their functioning as information-processing units. Again, as we search for models and theories to understand the nature of cognitive abilities, this fact will constrain our theorizing.

Moreover, considerations of plasticity in conjunction with limits on the number of neurons and the number of connections may be theoretically significant in the following way. Models of learning and memory that invest all the processing complexity in *connections*, and next to none in the neuron itself, may well find that the model must postulate many more units than the nervous system has. The number of neurons and their finite if large number of connections also restrict the range of possible models (Feldman and Ballard 1982).

Finally, it is useful to know that neurons and their modus operandi are essentially the same in all nervous systems—our neurons and the neurons of slugs, worms, and spiders share a fundamental similarity. There are differences between vertebrates and invertebrates, but these differences pale beside the preponderant similarities. Even our neurochemistry is fundamentally similar to that of the humblest organism slithering about on the ocean floor.

What matters here is not that this humbling thought pricks our eminently prickable vanity, but that it reminds us that we, in all our cognitive glory, *evolved*, and that our capacities, marvelous as they are, cannot be a bolt from the blue. Which means that models for human cognition are inadequate if they imply a thoroughgoing discontinuity with animal cognition. It is also a reminder that if we want to understand the nature of the information processing that underlies such functions as thinking and sensorimotor control, our theories must be constrained by how neurons are in fact orchestrated, and we cannot understand *that* without knowing a good deal about neurons themselves, about their connections to other neurons, and about how they form these connections. It is therefore a methodological constraint of the greatest importance (figure 2.1).

Nervous systems are information-processing machines, and in order to understand how they enable an organism to learn and remember, to see and problem solve, to care for the young and recognize danger, it is essential to understand the machine itself, both at the level of the basic elements that make up the machine and at the level of organization of elements. In this chapter the focus will be on neurons—on their structure and their manner of functioning.

2.2   *The Cellular Components of Nervous Systems*

The human brain weighs about three pounds and has a volume of about three pints. It contains some 10^{12} neurons, or perhaps as many as 10^{14}; the count is only an estimate. When the body is resting, the nervous system consumes about 20 percent of the body's oxygen supply, which is the lion's share, considering that the brain accounts

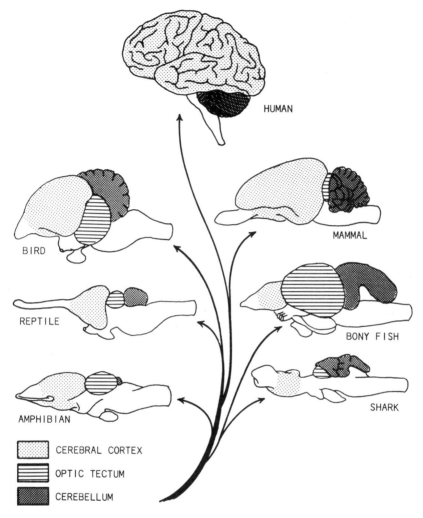

Figure 2.1
Lateral view of several vertebrate brains showing relative development of major brain divisions. Brains not drawn to scale. (Modified from Northcutt (1977). In *McGraw-Hill Encyclopedia of Science and Technology*. New York: McGraw-Hill.)

for only about 2 percent of the body's mass and that skeletal muscles, the kidneys, the heart, the liver, and so on, also demand oxygen. The central nervous system (CNS) consists of the brain and spinal cord; the peripheral nervous system (PNS) consists of all the nervous structures external to the brain and spinal cord, such as the fibers innervating the muscles and the sensory receptors in the skin. The retina is considered part of the CNS (figure 2.2).

Neurons
Neurons are the basic nervous elements and are differentiated into a cell body, or *soma*, and *processes*[1] (projections) extending out from the soma. The soma is the vital center of the cell, containing the nucleus and RNA, and it has structures that manufacture protein, much of which is shipped down the axon by a complex system of axonal transport. Processes are usually distinguished as *axons* or *dendrites*, but not all neurons have both. Axons are the principal output apparatus, and dendrites principally receive and integrate signals. Some sensory neurons in the skin have only an axon, and some neurons in the olfactory lobe have only dendrites. A single axon generally protrudes from the soma, and commonly it will branch extensively toward its end. In contrast, a dense arborization of dendrites often extends from the soma (figure 2.3). (See also figure 1.5.) In many types of neurons the dendrites are covered with stubby branchlets called *spines* that serve as the dominant points of contact with other neurons.

Neurons vary in size, but even the largest is exceedingly small. In the human nervous system, dendrites may be about 0.5 microns in diameter, and the soma of a motor neuron is about 20–70 microns wide. The largest axons are about 20 microns across, but they are long—some as long as the spinal cord. There is considerable variation between different types of neurons, with some showing fairly obvious specializations suited to their function. The squid was discovered to have motor neurons with relatively large axons (roughly one millimeter in diameter). Given its size, the giant axon of the squid could be impaled quite easily by recording and stimulating electrodes, allowing the electrochemical properties of axons to be investigated (Hodgkin and Huxley 1952). (These properties will be discussed in section 2.3.)

At birth, the primate nervous system has virtually all the neurons it will ever have. The only known exception is the olfactory system, in which neurons are continuously induced. Growth of axons and dendrites, as well as of the spines on dendrites, is prolific, especially in the first few years of life. In the midst of this luxuriant growth, how-

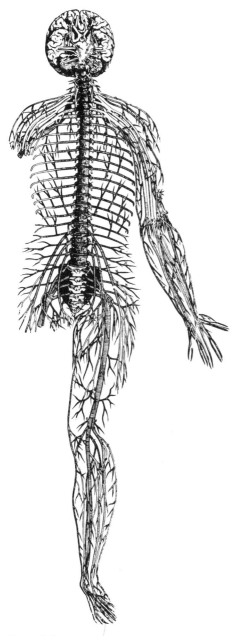

Figure 2.2
Drawing by Vesalius (1543) showing the brain, the spinal column, and the peripheral nerves, whose innervation of the trunk and limbs delineates the human form. (From Saunders and O'Malley 1950.)

ever, there is also massive selective death of neurons in early infancy, and between 15 and 85 percent of the original neuron pool is doomed. This appears to be a programmed death, and it is a crucial part of normal infant brain development, but exactly why it happens and precisely what are the principles of culling are not fully understood. (See also chapter 3.) There is additionally what one might call ordinary "grim reaper death," which fells about a thousand neurons per day in the adult brain after forty—a rather appalling statistic given the lack of replacements. Still, dendritic growth continues and surviving neurons apparently take up the slack. That the brain manages well enough even so is indicative of its plasticity.

Synapses are the points of communication between neurons, where processes make quasi-permanent junctions with the soma or processes of another neuron, and they appear to be highly specialized (figure 1.7, 1.8). It is usually presumed that signal transmission occurs only at synaptic junctions, but this is not known for sure. It may be that weak influences are transmitted at spots where the membranes lack specialized synaptic apparatus but are in close proximity. Commonly an axon will synapse on a dendrite or on the somas of other neurons, but it may synapse on other axons, and in some cases dendrites synapse on other dendrites and on somas. The number of synapses on each neuron varies widely, but it is large— approximately 5,000 on a mammalian motor neuron, and approximately 90,000 on a single Purkinje cell in the human cerebellar cortex (figure 2.4). Altogether, there are estimated to be about 10^{15} connections in the human nervous system, give or take an order of magnitude.

Functionally, neurons are classed as sensory neurons, motor neurons, or interneurons. Sensory neurons transduce physical signals, such as light or mechanical deformation, into electrical signals that they pass on. Motor neurons terminate on muscles to produce contractions. Interneurons are a mixed bag of everything else in between sensory neurons and motor neurons. Neurons come in a wide variety of types, and the types differ greatly in such properties as size, axonal length, and characteristic pattern of dendritic arborization (figure 2.4). In lower animals there is much less evidence of specialization, and in invertebrates the division of processes into axons and dendrites is not seen, dendrites being a later achievement than axons.

Neuroglia
Nervous tissue consists not only of neurons but also of special ancillary cells called *neuroglia*. These cells were first described and recog-

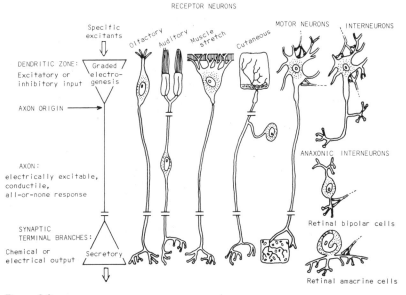

Figure 2.3
Basic functional and structural features of neurons, as shown in a variety of afferent (incoming) neurons, efferent (outgoing) neurons, and interneurons. The diagram illustrates the idea that impulse origin rather than cell-body position is the most reasonable focal point for the analysis of neuron structure in functional terms, at least for those neurons with an axon process. (Modified from Bodian 1967.)

nized as distinct from neurons in 1856 by Rudolf Virchow, who coined the term "neuroglia" because "glia" means glue, and he thought of them as a kind of glue in which nerve cells are planted. Their assorted properties, to the extent that they are known, turn out to be remarkable, though stickiness is not among them. One type of glial cell, the Schwann cell, wraps itself around and around the axonal process of a peripheral cell to provide an insulating sheath that permits faster conduction of the nervous impulse. The oligodendrocytes perform the same service for CNS axons. The sheath so formed is called *myelin*. Ensheathing is intensively cultivated during infancy and tapers off as the child approaches puberty; nevertheless, some myelinization in the cerebral cortex continues until about age forty (figures 2.5, 2.6).

   True myelin is peculiar to vertebrates, though even in vertebrates not all neurons are myelinated. Phylogenetically older neurons, such as the thin C-fibers that innervate the skin and carry information about pain (and probably many other things as well) are not myelinated. The association between neurons and glial cells varies greatly,

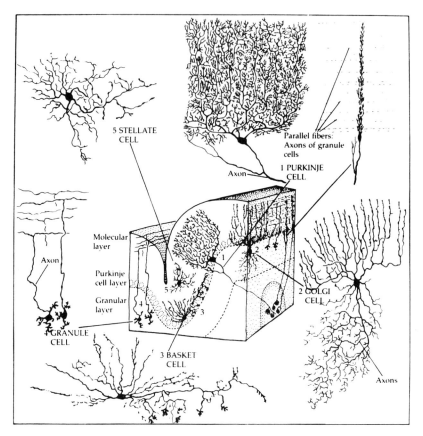

Figure 2.4
Types of neurons. The human cerebellum has over 10^{10} cells but only five neuronal types. Each type has its characteristic shape, branching pattern, connectivity pattern, and position. See figures 2.1 and 3.1 for the position of the cerebellum in relation to other brain divisions. (From Kuffler, Nicholls, and Martin (1984). *From Neuron to Brain.* 2nd ed. Sunderland, Mass.: Sinauer.)

and in some cases axons merely fit into a groove of a neighboring glial cell. Some neuroglia function as fences (astrocytes) and as filters (ependymal cells) in isolating neurons from blood but not from their special nutrient bath. Yet others, the microglia, function as phago-cytes or scavengers, cleaning up dead neurons and assorted detritus. The operation of neurons is so dazzling that glial cells tend not to get their share of the limelight. Nevertheless, outnumbering neurons by about ten to one, they are crucial to the proper functioning of the nervous system, though research is only beginning to reveal just how many tasks they are relied upon to perform. Certainly degeneration

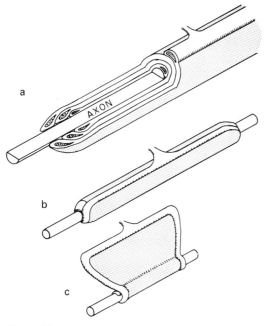

Figure 2.5
Diagram of a myelinated axon. (a) Part of the myelin is cut away to show the inner layers. (b) A glial cell that forms the myelin sheath is shown completely rolled up around a segment of axon. (c) Diagram of an axon segment and an unrolled glial cell. (Modified from Hirano and Dembitzer 1967.)

of the glia, for example of the Schwann cells and oligodendrocytes that make up the myelin sheaths, is devastating to proper sensorimotor control. Multiple sclerosis is one such demyelinating disease.

Where there are tracts of axons encased in myelin, the tissue appears lighter in color than where there are clumps of somas and their bushes of dendrites, which have a distinctly grayish (or pinkish) hue. It is the presence of myelin that makes the difference between white and gray matter, for only axons are myelinated. In a section of nervous tissue, this color difference is easily visible with the naked eye (figure 2.7).[2]

Receptors
Receptors hold a special fascination, perhaps because it is the range of stimuli to which receptors are sensitive that limits the kinds of things we sense in the world. Receptors are the interface between world and brain, and our conception of what the universe is like and what we

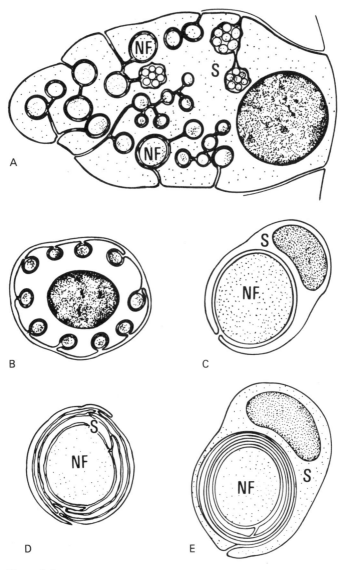

Figure 2.6
Schematic diagram of various forms of ensheathment known to occur in relation to neuron fibers. (A) Large glial cells ensheath axons singly or in groups (as in the leech). (B) Small undifferentiated nerve fibers may be enclosed in individual troughs of glial cell membrane (as in vertebrate peripheral nervous system). (C) Large nerve fibers may be surrounded by a single glial cell (as in insect peripheral nervous system). (D) Large nerve fibers may be surrounded by multiple layers of glial cell (as in insects). (E) Systematic spiralization and compaction lead to the myelin characteristic of the vertebrate peripheral nerve. (Modified from Bunge 1968.)

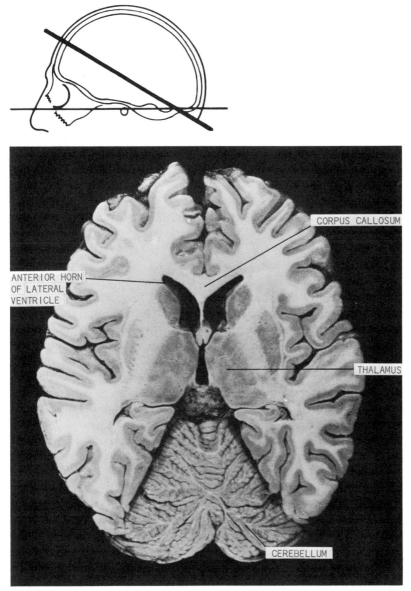

Figure 2.7
A section of the human brain at 20 degrees from the specified plane. The cerebral cortex
shows as the gray rind on the outer surface, following the folds of tissue. The cerebellar
cortex is also visible, as a rind following the very deep folds of the cerebellar white
matter. The corpus callosum consists of myelinated nerve fibers, and so appears white.
The thalamus contains a large consolidation of cell bodies and appears gray. (From
Matsui and Hirano (1978). *An Atlas of the Human Brain for Computerized Tomography.*
Copyright © Igaku-Shoin, Tokyo/New York.)

take to be the truth about the universe is inescapably connected to the response characteristics of cells at the periphery. This is what struck Magendie, and later Müller, in their experiments on the specificity of receptors in responding to distinct kinds of physical stimuli. It is probably also the source of the deep currents in Kant's plea for constraints in epistemology—constraints that would acknowledge that our access to the world is always *mediated* access, access via the nervous system. The human nervous system, after all, is a physical thing, with physical limits and physical modes of operation. Kant argued that we can know the world only as it appears to us—as it is presented to us—not as it is in itself. (See chapter 6.) When I open my eyes and look about me, it is as though I see the world as anything sees it, as it really is, in its nakedness and in its entirety. But what I see is a function not only of how the world is but also of how my visual receptors respond to one narrow parameter of the world's properties (electromagnetic radiation in the 0.4–0.75 micrometer range) and of how my brain is formed to manipulate those responses.

Nervous systems have evolved specialized receptors for detecting a wide range of physical parameters. The classical distinction into "five senses" is notoriously inept, since there are receptors not only for taste, smell, sound, sight, and touch but for a miscellany of other things as well. There are proprioceptors for detecting changes in position of the head, kinesthetic receptors in the muscles and the tendons to detect stretch, receptors for visceral distension and for lung stretch, and receptors in the carotid arteries to detect levels of oxygen in the arterial blood. Besides being incomplete, the classical taxonomy is imperspicuous. For example, the category "touch" rakes together diverse perceptions, including light touch, erotic sensations, light and deep pressure, vibration, a variety of temperature sensations, and a wide assortment of painful sensations.

Snug within the confines of our own perceptual world, it is jolting to realize that other animals are richly receptive where we are stony blind. Bees can detect ultraviolet light; snakes have pits for electromagnetic waves in the infrared range; flies have gyroscopic strain gauges; aquatic vertebrates can detect water displacement by means of lateral-line organs; pigeons have ferromagnets for orienting with respect to the earth's magnetic field, sharks can pick up and use low-frequency (0.1–20 Hz) electric fields; electric fish are sensitive to high frequency (50–5,000 Hz) current. A human submerging into the ocean depths finds an engulfing silence, but for an electric fish the watery world is rich in electromagnetic events, and it uses electrolocation and electrocommunication to great advantage (Bullock, Orkand,

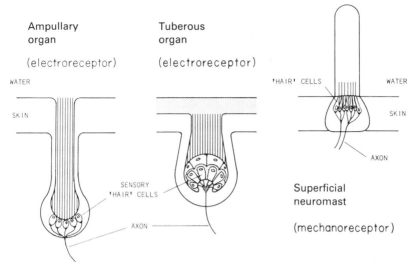

Figure 2.8
Diagram of two different electroreceptors and a mechanoreceptor found in the lateral line organs of fish. (Modified from Dijkgraaf 1967 and Szabo 1974.)

and Grinnell 1977). The world as perceived by humans is not the world as perceived by any organism. Rather, it is that narrow dimension of the world evolution has permitted our specialized receptors to detect (figure 2.8).

Even in very simple organisms, specialized receptors are found. The jellyfish, too far down the evolutionary ladder to have the benefit of organs for digestion and reproduction, nonetheless has complex eyes and statocysts (organs for detecting gravity, acceleration, and vibration). The jellyfish moves, and its first need is for receptors to inform its movement, since its survival depends on its moving in directed fashion. It does an organism no good to have a fancy digestive organ unless its movements ensure that things—and the right things—get put into it. It makes sense that the evolution of complex receptors to steer useful movement would be an early evolutionary development, and there is a correlation between the complexity of behavioral repertoire and specialization of central nervous tissue, on the one hand, and specialization of receptors and development of complex sense organs, on the other (Bullock, Orkand, and Grinnell 1977).

2.3   *How Do Neurons Work?*

Basic Electrical Effects

The distinctive thing about neurons is that they are instruments of communication; they receive, integrate, and send signals. Exactly how neurons do this is a complex story whose many subtleties are only beginning to be understood. Initially, the basic story will suffice, and the central elements in the basic story are fourfold: (1) *ions* in the extracellular and intracellular fluid, (2) a *voltage difference* across the cell membrane, (3) *single ion channels* distributed about the membrane that are specialized to control cross-membrane passage of distinct ion types, and (4) *voltage-sensitive changes* in single ion channels that transiently open the gates in the channels to permit ions to cross the cell membrane.

The cell membrane is a remarkable sort of sheet, dividing cytoplasm on the inside of the cell from the extracellular fluid on the outside. The membrane is nonuniformly dotted with tiny pores, specialized to control passage only of certain items. Both the intracellular and the extracellular fluids contain ions, which are molecules or atoms that have gained or lost electrons and consequently are negatively or positively charged. The plot of the basic electrochemical story depends on two general classes of ions: large negatively charged organic ions concentrated inside the cell, and inorganic ions with systematically changeable concentration profiles inside and outside the cell.

The large organic ions inside the cell cannot pass through the membrane, and their net charge is negative. Consequently, this affects the distribution of ions to which the membrane *is* permeable, since positively charged ions will tend to congregate inside the cell to balance the negative charge. The inorganic ions that figure in the story are potassium (K^+), sodium (Na^+), calcium (Ca^{++}), and chloride (Cl^-).

The high internal concentration of fixed negative charges is offset by just about the right number of cations. These are mainly K^+, because the membrane is much more permeable to K^+ than to either Na^+ or Ca^{++}, and because a sodium-potassium pump in the membrane draws in K^+ and dumps out Na^+. When the cell is at rest (that is, unless the membrane is stimulated), the Na^+ and Ca^{++} channels block the passage of Na^+ and Ca^{++}. Thus, K^+ concentrates inside the cell, and Na^+ and Ca^{++} concentrate outside (figures 2.9, 2.10). When the cell is stimulated, for example by an electric current or by a particular chemical, there is a change in membrane permeability to Na^+ and Ca^{++}. The principal instruments of this change reside in the structure of the single channel.

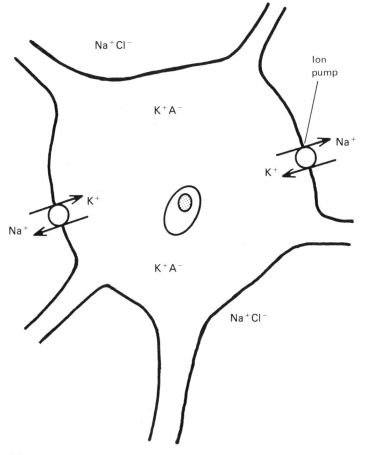

Figure 2.9
Schematic diagram of a neuron soma, showing the internal concentration of inorganic ions A^- and K^+, and the external concentration of NA^+ and Cl^-. The sodium-potassium pump in the membrane ejects Na^+ and hauls in K^+. (From Shepherd (1983). *Neurobiology*. New York: Oxford University Press.)

What accounts for the voltage drop across the membrane? Essentially, the organic anions together with the fact that among cations, only K^+ can cross the membrane to the cell's interior. Because the K^+ moves inward from areas of low K^+ concentration to areas of high K^+ concentration, it is said to move up its *concentration gradient*, and it does so because of the anion attraction inside. It therefore moves down its *electrical gradient*. At some point equilibrium between the two forces is achieved, in the sense that there is no net movement of K^+ across the membrane, and the electrical force required to keep K^+

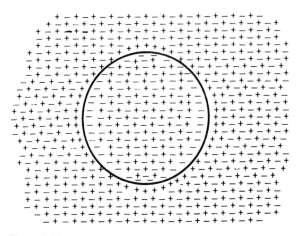

Figure 2.10
Schematic cross section of a neuron process showing the concentration of negative charges along the inside of the membrane and positive charges along the outside. (Reprinted with permission of the publisher from Koester (1981). Ch. 3 of *Principles of Neural Science*, ed. E. R. Kandel and J. H. Schwartz, pp. 27–35. Copyright © 1981 by Elsevier Science Publishing Co., Inc.)

at its concentration gradient can be calculated. This calculation yields the electrical *potential* for K^+ across the membrane. For example, in some neurons the equilibrium potential for K^+ (no *net* movement of K^+) is -70 millivolts (mv). The electromotive force is the force tending to equalize the charges, and the *electric potential* is a measure in volts of the electromotive force. In the neuron, accordingly, the organic anions exert an electromotive force of about -70 mv to pull K^+ up its concentration gradient. The actual recorded voltage across the membrane of the cell at rest is its *resting potential,* and this will be fairly close to the calculated potential for K^+.

Although -70 mv might seem to be an inconsequential voltage, in the cellular circumstances it is actually enormously powerful. This can be understood by observing that since a cross section of the membrane is only 50 angstroms thick, then its voltage equivalent across a one centimeter membrane thickness is 140,000 volts. An electric field of this magnitude is evidently capable of exerting a strong effect on macromolecules with a dipole moment, and it appears that single channels have as constituents precisely such macromolecules (Neher and Stevens 1979).

In sum, the consequence of the differential permeability of the membrane to the ions is that when the cell is at rest, there is a voltage across the membrane such that the inside of the cell membrane is negatively charged with respect to the outside (its resting potential).

Intracellular recording by microelectrode

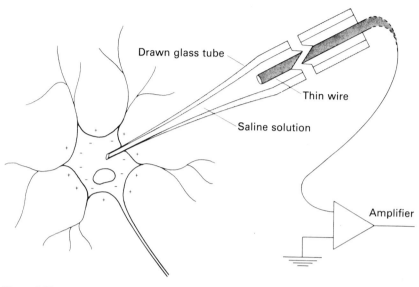

Figure 2.11
Idealized experiment for measuring the potential difference across the cell membrane. The electrode is a fine glass capillary with a tip no more than 0.1 micrometer in diameter filled with a saline solution.

By convention, the voltage is given as that of the inside relative to that of the outside, and since at rest the inside is negative relative to the outside, the voltage is expressed as a negative number of millivolts (e.g., -70 mv or -55 mv) (figure 2.11). The membrane is thus polarized, and the communicative functions of neurons depend on coordinated changes in the polarization of the membrane. The next step in the discussion will therefore concern how neurons exploit changes in potential so as to transmit information—from the outside world, to one another, and to the muscles and glands. The principal factor in the cell that is now believed to account for excitability, and hence for signaling, is the voltage-dependent conformational change in the molecular structure of single channels that permits a brief influx either of Na^+ or of Ca^{++}, depending on the channel type (Kuffler, Nicholls, and Martin 1984).

Synaptic Potentials
The dendrites and the soma of a neuron are bedizened with a profusion of synaptic connections (figure 2.12), and thousands of signals may be received at various places in the dendritic bush or on the cell

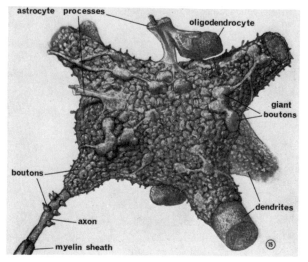

Figure 2.12
Synaptic end bulbs (boutons) on the surface of a motor neuron. (From Poritsky 1969.)

body during the space of a millisecond. The incoming signal is caused by a chemical acting on specialized membrane sites and it results in a change in the membrane's resting potential. The change in resting potential induced by an incoming signal at the synapse is the *synaptic potential*.

The postsynaptic response at any given site on the membrane may be a *decrease* in the membrane potential, for example from −70 mv to −60 mv. Such a membrane *depolarization* is brought about chiefly by changes in the permeability of the membrane that permit a brief influx of Na$^+$ or Ca^{++}. Alternatively, depending on the synaptic events, the postsynaptic response may be an *increase* in the membrane potential, for example, from −70 mv to −80 mv. This type of effect on membrane potential is referred to as *hyperpolarization* and can be achieved by the influx of Cl$^-$, the efflux of K$^+$, or both (figure 2.13).

The synaptic potential is transient, and the permeability profile of the membrane at its resting potential is quickly restored. The size of the synaptic potential is directly related to the number of single channels opened in response to the stimulating event and hence to the density of single channels in the vicinity of the stimulus; the greater the number of Na$^+$ channels, the higher the probability that a Na$^+$ channel will be opened after the depolarizing stimulus (Kuffler, Nicholls, and Martin 1984). At a given location a large stimulus will

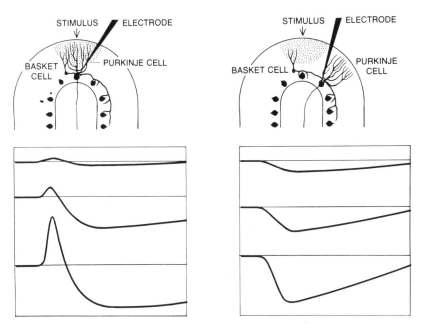

Figure 2.13
The soma of a Purkinje cell in the vicinity of stimulation is briefly depolarized (upward deflection), the degree of depolarization being a function of the stimulus intensity. A Purkinje cell outside that preferred area receives inhibitory input from the activated axon of a basket cell and is transiently hyperpolarized (downward deflection). (Courtesy R. Llinás.)

cause a potential with a greater amplitude than a small stimulus only if there is a greater number of single channels that it can affect.

The net movement of ions across the membrane constitutes a current, and this current spreads along the membrane from the focal site, decrementing with distance. The spread of current is affected by a number of factors, including the resistance of the cytoplasm, the resistance of the membrane, and the diameter of the dendrite. Since many synaptic potentials may be generated in close proximity within a narrow time slice, there arises the question of the nature of the interaction of synaptic potentials.

Suppose a dendrite's membrane is depolarized at some particular spot. As the current spreads, it will interact with current generated at that same place at a slightly earlier time, or with current generated elsewhere and elsewhen. For example, if it is adjacent to an area where the membrane is hyperpolarized, then the two effects will tend to cancel one another, or if it is adjacent to a depolarization, the effects will summate. Potentials therefore interact as currents sum to create a larger depolarization; or, if the effects were hyperpolarizing, to prevent depolarization; or, if the effects are opposite, to interfere and cancel. Because the amplitude of synaptic potentials is determined by channel density, stimulus size, and summation, they are called *graded potentials*. In this respect they contrast, as we shall shortly see, with *action potentials*.

It is presumed that by means of this complex interfusion and integration of synaptic potentials in the soma and dendrites, information is processed, though complete understanding of what is going on still eludes us. (But see chapter 10 for discussion of a theory that addresses this matter.) Nevertheless, it is easy to see that the relative position of stimuli on the dendrites, the width of the fiber, the density of ionic channels, the availability of energy, and so on, will play a role in the overall character of the integration of signals. If, as it seems, dendritic growth and synaptogenesis are connected to learning, we will want to know what the rather bewildering interfusion of potentials comes to in informational terms.

If, after the integration of depolarizing and hyperpolarizing potentials, there is sufficient current to depolarize the membrane of the axon hillock by a certain critical amount known as the "firing level" (about 10 mv), then the cell produces a large and dramatic output. (The axon hillock is the region of the neuron where the axon emanates from the soma.) Under these conditions, the axon will relay a depolarizing signal—an *impulse*—from the hillock to its terminal bulbs, using a mechanism described below that typifies axons. Depolarizing synaptic potentials are called *excitatory* postsynaptic potentials (EPSPs) because they contribute to the generation of an impulse in axons by bringing the membrane potential closer to the firing level. Because hyperpolarizing potentials tend to diminish the probability of the generation of an impulse, they are called *inhibitory* postsynaptic potentials (IPSPs) (figure 2.14).

Action Potentials
Axons are long, thin projections, sometimes a few millimeters, sometimes a meter or more in length. If a message is to be sent from one end to the other, it is necessary to ensure that the signal does not peter out en route and that the same message reaches the end as was put in at the beginning. This capacity for long-distance transmission is achieved by an increase in the density of Na^+ channels all along the axon membrane. What makes these channels special is that they are voltage-sensitive, and with depolarization they cease briefly to gate Na^+, thereby permitting Na^+ to rush into the cell down its electrical

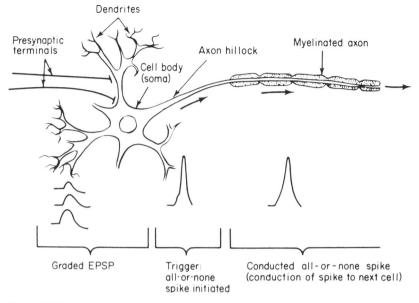

Figure 2.14
Summary diagram showing location on a motor neuron of the events responsible for impulse initiation. Dendrites and cell bodies respond with graded *excitatory synaptic potentials* (EPSPs) or *inhibitory synaptic potentials* (IPSPs); the action potential is triggered in the axon hillock and travels undiminished down the axon. IPSPs are not shown. (From Thompson (1967). *Foundations of Physiological Psychology.* New York: Harper and Row.)

and concentration gradients (figure 2.15). In the studied cases each channel has a mean channel current of about 1–2 picoamps and is open for a mean time of 0.7 msec (Sigworth and Neher 1980). When channel density is sufficiently great, therefore, the total current crossing a patch of membrane in a millisecond can be substantial, and because the channels are voltage-sensitive, this in itself can cause a special, self-amplifying effect.

Suppose incoming signals depolarize the membrane of the axon hillock by about 10 mv, as Na^+ ions move inside the cell. This inward Na^+ current results in a transient change in additional Na^+ channels in the axon membrane, thereby allowing even more Na^+ to enter the cell, depolarizing the membrane further, which then induces changes in yet more Na^+ channels to allow further Na^+ influx. Thus, a self-generating, explosive effect is produced. If the initial depolarizing current is large enough that the net influx of Na^+ is greater than the efflux of K^+ ions, the positive feedback results in a sudden large influx of Na^+. In absolute terms the number of ions crossing the

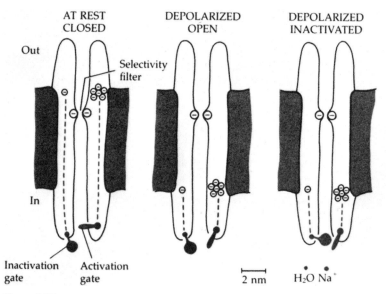

Figure 2.15
Voltage-sensitive sodium channel, drawn schematically to scale according to biochemical, electron microscopic, and electrophysiological information. Ionic selectivity is provided by a constriction lined with negative charges near the outer surface of the membrane. The activation gate near the inner surface opens in association with translocation of negative charges across the membrane from out to in. The inactivation gate blocks the inner mouth of the channel and prevents closing of the activation gate. Water molecule and hydrated sodium ion are drawn to scale for comparison. (Modified from Kuffler, Nicholls, and Martin (1984). *From Neuron to Brain.* 2nd ed. Sunderland, Mass.: Sinauer.)

membrane is actually quite small, but it is sufficient to change the membrane polarity dramatically from something on the order of -70 mv to something on the order of $+55$ mv (Kuffler, Nicholls, and Martin 1984).

Since the mean channel open time is only 0.7 msec, the summed increase in permeability to Na^+ of any given membrane patch is a very brief affair. As the membrane potential reverses from, say, -70 mv to $+55$ mv, Na^+ conductance is suddenly inactivated, and K^+ begins to move out of the cell, which initiates the restoration of the resting potential. Given a 10 mv depolarization, there is therefore a temporal *sequence* of voltage-sensitive changes in the membrane permeability: an abrupt increase in Na^+ permeability, followed by an abrupt inactivation of Na^+ permeability and an increase in outward K^+ current (figure 2.16). This precisely timed sequence of membrane events is a neuron *impulse,* and a membrane's capacity to generate

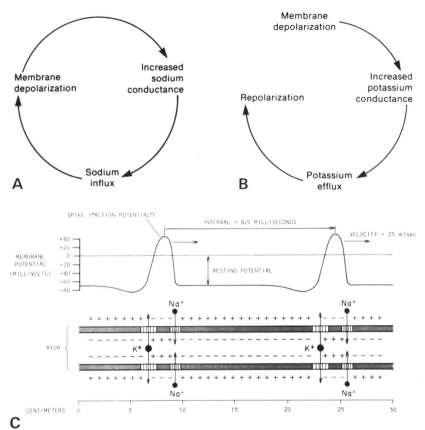

Figure 2.16
(A) Positive feedback effect resulting from above threshold depolarization of the membrane. (B) Restoration of the membrane's resting potential. (C) Propagation of a nerve impulse along the axon. The large change in potential is initiated by a small influx of sodium ions, which opens voltage-sensitive sodium channels, changing the potential further. The membrane's resting potential is restored as the sodium channels are inactivated, and potassium channels open to permit an outflow of potassium ions. This sequence of events begins at the axon hillock and continues down the length of the axon.

impulses is what is meant by excitability. (This gives only a simplified version of the sequence of membrane events. See Llinás 1984a.)

The impulse is also called an *action potential*, where the modifier "action" indicates that the large change in membrane polarization vastly exceeds the triggering depolarization contributed by the stimulus. If we put a recording electrode inside the axon and attach the recording electrode to an oscilloscope, the visual pattern produced by the impulse will appear on the screen as a spike; hence, impulses are also referred to as "spikes" (figure 2.16).

During the brief interval when the membrane is permeable to Na^+, the potential across the membrane at the relevant segment changes enormously as a consequence of the inward Na^+ current. This current will spread along the membrane, which will cause depolarization in the adjacent areas of the membrane, and Na^+ channels located there will, in their turn, undergo a conformational change to allow Na^+ current, thereby engaging the regenerative process to permit an influx of Na^+ ions in that region, and so on down the length of the membrane (figure 2.16). Therefore, the drama in the axon does not end with the production of a localized spike, for when an action potential is produced at the hillock, the spreading current depolarizes the neighboring membrane downstream, which in turn generates an action potential and consequently depolarizes *its* downstream neighborhood membrane, and so on.

In this fashion, a wave of depolarization and repolarization travels from the trigger zone in the axon hillock down the length of the axon. (It *could* travel the reverse direction, and can be made to do so in the laboratory, but in the untampered neuron it does not.) The signal does not alter in its journey down the axon, because the amplitude of the spike does not diminish as it travels. As long as there is one spike, this ensures that the adjacent membrane will be depolarized above its threshold, which means it will spike, and so on to the fiber end. During its spiking phase the axon cannot spike again; this is called its refractory period (figure 2.16). One might think of this by analogy with a slingshot that cannot fire again immediately but requires an interval for the sling to be repositioned and to regain a store of energy. The single channels have to be reconfigured, Na^+ has to be pumped out, and the neuron membrane has to regain its balance of electric potentials.

In view of the importance of time constraints imposed by the nervous system on modeling, it should be mentioned that the time course for a spike is some 0.2–5.0 msec, depending on the neuron, and this means that there is an upper limit on the spiking frequency of any given neuron. In humans some neurons can spike 500 times per second. For purposes of rough calculation, let us say that a spike takes about 1 msec. Now if a perceptual recognition task takes about 100 msec, then there can be *at most* 100 information-processing steps between input and output. Models that require ten thousand or a million steps are going to be out by several orders of magnitude.

The basic account of the electrophysiology of neurons was worked out by Hodgkin and Huxley in 1952, but not until recently has the structural basis for these properties been understood. In what amounts to a revolution in understanding the nature of neurons (see Junge 1981, Kuffler, Nicholls, and Martin 1984), researchers have begun to reduce electrophysiologically defined properties such as spiking and synaptic potentials to the basic molecular biochemistry of cell membranes. More precisely, it appears that the framework is emerging for a reduction of the action potential, the synaptic potential, the refractory period, and so forth, as defined in terms of electrophysiological theory, to the "kinetics" of single-channel currents and single-channel macromolecule organization, as described by molecular biology. This is evidently a development of great significance, since it begins to forge reductive connections between neurophysiology and biochemistry. If we can also determine the neurophysiological basis for behavior (see below), then we shall actually begin to see the outlines of a general, unified framework for comprehending the nature of nervous system function (Llinás 1984a).

It should also be acknowledged that despite the discussion's generalized reference to "the neuron," in fact different types of neuron vary tremendously along a number of dimensions and there is no typical neuron. The observed differences presumably reflect such factors as differences in membrane properties, channel density, and channel properties and can be assumed to have an explainable functional significance. Moreover, as Llinás (1984a) has emphasized, there are not merely the Na^+, Ca^{++}, and K^+ conductances already discussed. In the soma, for example, one might find a Ca^{++}-dependent K^+ conductance and a "fast transient" K^+ conductance, as well as a voltage-dependent K^+ conductance. The number of voltage-dependent ionic conductances present in a particular neuron may be greater than ten.

The conventional wisdom until recently held that dendrites do not spike, but as a result of work originated by Llinás in the mid-1970s (Llinás and Hess 1976) it was discovered that Purkinje cells in the cerebellum do have spiking dendrites (figure 2.17). Since then, dendritic spiking has been discovered in a wide range of CNS neurons, including neurons in the hippocampus and the spinal cord. (For a discussion, see Llinás 1984a.) On the other side of the coin, there are neurons with short axons, for example amacrine cells in the retina, that do not spike at all. Thus, the criterion that identifies a neuronal process on the basis of whether or not it spikes has collapsed; there are both nonspiking axons and spiking dendrites.

The amplitude of the spike is largely invariant and does not increase or decrease with the size of the stimulus. Variation in signal can be produced by altering the *frequency* of spikes in a train or by

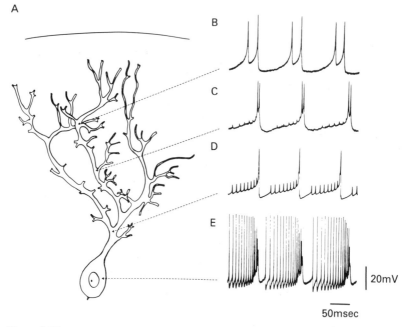

Figure 2.17
Sodium and calcium action potentials in (A) a Purkinje cell. (B) Depolarization of the
dendrite produced long-duration calcium action potentials, and (E) depolarization of
the soma produced high-frequency sodium action potentials, interrupted periodically
by a calcium action potential that was followed by a transient hyperpolarization. (C)
and (D) represent the effects of the passive spread of depolarization from the soma.
(From Llinás and Sugimori 1980.)

producing special *patterns* in a train of impulses through the combined use of hyperpolarizing and depolarizing currents. Frequently
neurons show a low rate of spontaneous spiking (spiking without
externally induced depolarization, perhaps by inward leakage of Na^+
or Ca^{++}), and this base rate of firing is increased by depolarizing
currents and decreased by hyperpolarizing currents (figures 2.18,
2.19).

Why the brain uses so much energy will now be evident. Neurons
must continuously maintain the ionic gradients essential to receiving
and sending information. If a neuron routinely handles a thousand
depolarizing signals in the space of a second or so, and if it spikes
several hundred times a second, its energy consumption will have to
be lavish. Evolution stumbled upon one energy-saving device in myelin. The strategy here is that if glial cells ensheath the axon to form
an insulating cover, then depolarizing current from one action poten-

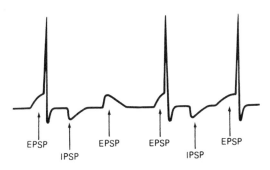

EPSP   EPSP   EPSP   EPSP
        IPSP   IPSP

Figure 2.18
Interactions of excitatory and inhibitory synaptic potentials (EPSPs and IPSPs) in an otherwise silent cell. Each of the synaptic potentials illustrated here is usually produced by the synchronous action of many presynaptic neurons. (Reprinted with permission of the publisher from Kandel (1981a). Ch. 7 of *Principles of Neural Science,* ed. E. R. Kandel and J. H. Schwartz, pp. 63–80. Copyright © 1981 by Elsevier Science Publishing Co., Inc.)

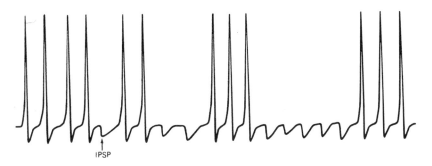

IPSP

Figure 2.19
Sculpting role of inhibition, shown here to produce changes in the firing pattern of a spontaneously active neuron. (Reprinted with permission of the publisher from Kandel (1981a). Ch. 7 of *Principles of Neural Science,* ed. E. R. Kandel and J. H. Schwartz, pp. 63–80. Copyright © 1981 by Elsevier Science Publishing Co., Inc.)

tial will travel further down the axon and so the energy-intensive action potential need occur only at wider intervals. This is called *saltatory conduction,* because the spikes, as it were, jump down the axon in long strides (figure 2.14).

Rolled-up Schwann cells are strung along peripheral fibers like sausages on a string, and the action potentials occur only at the exposed membrane between the Schwann cells, the "nodes of Ranvier." A large, well-myelinated axon in a human motor neuron can conduct an impulse up to 130 meters per second, whereas an unmyelinated fiber is much slower, sending impulses at only about 0.5 meters per second. These are factors concerning propagation of a signal within a neuron, but there is the additional matter of sending a signal from one neuron to another.

Neuronal Integration
There are two fundamental types of connection between neurons: electrical synapses and chemical synapses. Electrical synapses are of two types: (1) those generating *field potentials,* in which sending and receiving neurons are so closely positioned that current flow in one induces field changes in its neighbor, and (2) *gap junctions,* which consist of supremely thin protein tubes connecting the axon of one neuron to the dendrite or axon of another (figure 1.8). The tubes are so narrow as to permit the transfer of only very small ions such as Na^+ or K^+, and it is via the transfer of these ions that signals are transmitted from one neuron to the next.

Electrical synapses were for some time believed to be unique to primitive nervous systems, and though demonstrating their existence in the mammalian CNS is extremely difficult, research in the past ten years has shown electrical coupling in cells in the hippocampus and cells in the inferior olive that project to the cerebellum (Llinás, Baker, and Sotelo 1974). The intriguing question now is whether electrically coupled cells have a special functional significance in nervous systems.

The leading hypothesis focuses on the major difference between chemically coupled cells and electrically coupled cells, namely that the absence of synaptic delay (see below) in electrically coupled cells means that they can fire synchronously. Such synchronicity, along with positive feedback, appears to have an important role in generating rhythmic patterns typical of various CNS structures (Bower and Llinás 1983, MacVicar and Dudek 1980). In the case of the cells in the inferior olive, the electrical coupling may serve to establish synchronous firing of bands of Purkinje cells in the cerebellum. Since Purkinje cells are known to be crucial in subserving sensorimotor coordination, this general line of research has suggested that the synchronizing of rhythmic patterns in sets of neurons may embody a fundamental principle of neuronal organization underlying sensorimotor coordination (Llinás 1984b, 1984c).

Chemical synapses (figures 1.7, 2.20) have been most intensively studied in the giant synapse of the squid, and at the synaptic terminal it is Ca^{++} ions and Ca^{++} channels that play the crucial role (Llinás 1982). When a depolarizing wave reaches an end bulb of an axon, it opens voltage-sensitive Ca^{++} channels. Ca^{++} rushes into the cell and causes little vesicles containing neurotransmitter substance to fuse with the outer membrane at specialized zones (Heuser and Reese

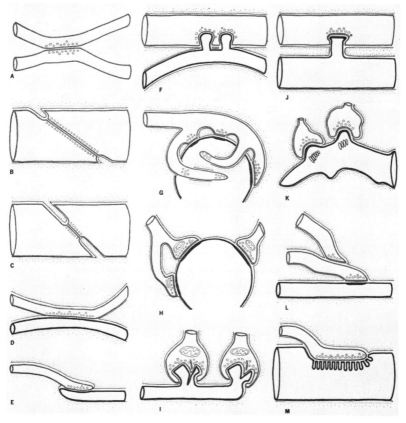

Figure 2.20
Types of synapses revealed by electron microscopy. (A) Axon-axon synapse in jellyfish. (B) Earthworm septal synapse with electrical transmission in either direction. (C) Crustacean synapse similar to (B). (D) Axon-axon synapse-in-passing, typical of invertebrates. (E) Axon terminal ending on a dendrite in invertebrate. (F) Crustacean giant-fiber-to-motor-neuron synapse, with postsynaptic motor fiber invaginated into the giant fiber. (G) Axon arborization-to-soma synapse typical of vertebrate brain cells. (H) Terminal buttons of axon arborizations typical of certain neurons in vertebrates. (I) Ribbon synapses between rod cell endings and dendrites of ganglion cells of vertebrate retina, with presynaptic specialization. (J) Synapse between giant fibers of squid stellate ganglion, postsynaptic invaginated into presynaptic. (K) Spine synapse (axon-dendrite) from cerebral cortical dendrite of vertebrates with postsynaptic specialization. (L) Serial synapse, permitting presynaptic inhibition. (M) Specialized neuromuscular endings found in vertebrate skeletal muscle, with postsynaptic grooves. (From Bullock and Horridge (1965). *Structure and Function in the Nervous Systems of Invertebrates.* W. H. Freeman and Co. Copyright © 1965.)

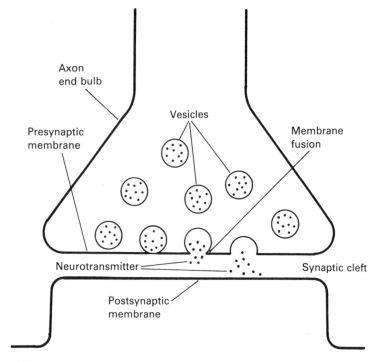

Figure 2.21
Schematic diagram showing release of neurotransmitter (synaptic vesicle exocytosis) as vesicle membrane fuses with end bulb membrane. (After Heuser and Reese 1979.)

1979). As the vesicle membrane fuses with the cell membrane, the neurotransmitter substance is released into the extracellular space that separates the axon from the adjacent neuronal process. Some of the neurotransmitter diffuses across the synaptic cleft and binds itself to specialized sites on the receiving cell—the postsynaptic membrane (figures 2.21, 2.22).

The time between the arrival of the signal at the synaptic terminal and the onset of the generation of a postsynaptic potential is known as the *synaptic delay*. It comprises three component delays: the time it takes (1) for Ca^{++} channels to open, (2) for the vesicles to fuse and release neurotransmitter, and (3) for the transmitter to diffuse across the synaptic cleft. The actual time of the synaptic delay is about one millisecond, which is remarkably short considering the complex molecular scenario (Llinás 1982).

Depending on which transmitter is released and on the character of the receptor sites, the neurotransmitter may produce a depolarization (an EPSP) or a hyperpolarization (an IPSP). The process of interfusion

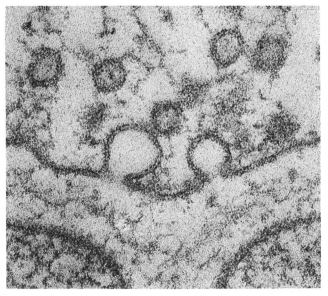

Figure 2.22
Electron micrograph showing how the synaptic vesicles fuse with the cell membrane as the neurotransmitter is discharged. (Micrograph produced by Dr. John E. Heuser of Washington University School of Medicine, St. Louis, Mo.)

and integration of current then begins in the receiving cell, as described earlier. In the studied cases unused transmitter is typically broken down and the components are retrieved by the presynaptic membrane for use next time, or sometimes they are retrieved by local glial cells. The transmitter that is bound to receptor sites must be quickly removed by enzymatic activity, if it is not to have a prolonged effect.

If the functional value of electrical coupling of cells is the synchronicity it permits, what is the distinct functional value to a nervous system of chemical synaptic coupling? Part of the answer is that it enables *amplification* of the signal. A current passed by electrical coupling from a small axon to a large soma is in danger of being ineffective. But if instead the signal in the axon causes at the end bulb the release of a flood of neurotransmitter molecules that depolarize the postsynaptic membrane across a substantial area, then the signal received will be nontrivial. In this fashion, a Ca^{++} current in the end bulb of one neuron can cause a substantial depolarization of another cell's membrane. Depending on the system's needs, therefore, the neurons may be coupled either electrically or chemically.

As outlined above, Ca^{++} is essential for synaptic transmission, and in some cells dendritic spiking is dependent on Ca^{++}. Moreover, it turns out that Ca^{++} is also important in the spiking of embryonic neurons, and in the dynamics of the growth cone at the tip of embryonic neurons. These assorted roles of Ca^{++} are suggestive of a deeper connection, and the joint functions of Ca^{++} at the synapse and in the growth cone have prompted Llinás (1979, 1982) to hypothesize that synaptic terminals are modified growth cones. This is a unifying conception of considerable power, and a succinct version of the reasoning runs as follows: in development, Ca^{++} may regulate the addition of new membrane at the growth cone by promoting the fusion of vesicle membrane and cell membrane, similar to the process seen in synaptic transmission. In the mature neuron the growth is subdued, and new membrane introduced into the cell membrane at synaptic signaling is recycled rather than left in place (Llinás and Sugimori 1979).

Transmission at chemical synapses is susceptible to an assortment of types of influence, and the nervous system takes advantage of all of them under special conditions (Cooper, Bloom, and Roth 1982, Snyder 1980). It can be affected by changes in the amount of transmitter released from the presynaptic membrane, changes in the amount of transmitter retrieved and the efficiency of retrieval, changes in the synthesis of transmitter within the sending cell, the number of receptor sites available, and changes in the responding chemicals inside the receptor cell.

In what is perhaps the simplest form of memory, a neuron increases its concentration of intracellular Ca^{++} as a result of a high rate of impulses (tetanus) reaching the presynaptic terminal. This means that more transmitter is released, with consequent alteration in the response pattern of the postsynaptic membrane. This alteration shows itself in a steady increase in the amplitude of the EPSPs (figure 2.23). This phenomenon is called post-tetanic potentiation, and the modification may last for minutes, or even an hour in some cells. As to the number of receptor sites, the advent of the electron microscope has made it possible to count them, and it is important to note that with age and stimulation the number of synapses increases. In particular, it has been found that with high-frequency stimulation additional synapses will flower in short order, suggesting a further mechanism for memory (Lee et al. 1980). It should also be remarked that some chemicals may function not as specific neurotransmitters but as neuromodulators, affecting the sensitivity of the postsynaptic neuron without actually inducing postsynaptic potentials.

In one of the most celebrated discoveries concerning how synaptic events subserve plasticity in behavior, Kandel and his colleagues

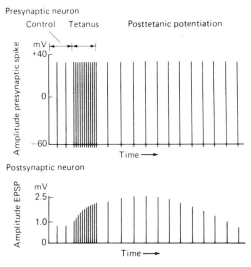

Figure 2.23
Post-tetanic potential: simultaneous recordings from a presynaptic neuron and its postsynaptic target cell. (In order to show events that occur over a long time, the sweep speed of this experiment has been compressed so that each presynaptic and postsynaptic potential appears as a simple line.) During the control period the presynaptic neuron is stimulated at a rate of 1/sec and produces a PSP of about 1 mv. The presynaptic neuron is then stimulated for several seconds at a higher rate of 5/sec. During this tetanus the PSP increases in size. After several seconds of tetanus, the presynaptic neuron is returned to its control rate of firing of 1/sec; however, the PSP it produces continues to be facilitated for many minutes and in some cells for several hours. (Reprinted with permission of the publisher from Kandel (1981b). Ch. 8 of *Principles of Neural Science*, ed. E. R. Kandel and J. H. Schwartz, pp. 81–90. Copyright © 1981 by Elsevier Science Publishing Co., Inc.)

(Kandel 1979, Hawkins and Kandel 1984) have shown that changes in Ca^{++} current (and hence changes in the amount of neurotransmitter released) are central in producing habituation and sensitization in the sea hare *Aplysia Californica* (This example will be discussed in more detail in the next subsection.)

The vulnerability of chemical synapses to modification by assorted chemicals has been exploited by organisms that have evolved the capacity to produce neurotoxins to be used as weapons. The snake venom alpha-bungarotoxin, like curare (the arrow poison used by Amazon Indians), works by binding to special receptor sites on muscles and resisting breakdown. This prevents the neurotransmitter acetylcholine from binding to produce depolarizing current to contract muscles. The muscles, therefore, are paralyzed. Botulinus toxin (a common cause of food poisoning) also produces paralysis, but achieves this by preventing the release of acetylcholine from the pre-synaptic membrane. In this case receptor sites are available, but there is no acetylcholine to bind to them, so once again paralysis is the result. Other neurotoxins, such as black widow spider venom, increase the discharge from the presynaptic membrane, causing the muscle cells to be excessively stimulated, resulting in rigidity and tremor.

Although the human nervous system has not evolved venom pouches or poison sacs, we have learned how to synthesize certain neurochemicals in the laboratory and how to use them to intervene directly in the neurotransmitting affairs of neurons. Neuropharmacology is the study of chemicals that affect neurons, and in recent times it has become an area of intense research as scientists try to discover effective treatment for diseases of the nervous system. Perhaps because of its immediacy to clinical concerns, neuropharmacology has become a glamor discipline within the wider domain of neuroscience. Three discoveries in particular have propelled it into public attention.

First was the discovery in the 1950s that certain drugs dramatically curtailed psychotic symptoms in many patients, enabling them, if not to lead completely normal lives, at least to live outside the asylum walls. In the short run these drugs calm violent and wildly excitable patients, and in the long run they abolish hallucinations and ameliorate disorders of thought. Since schizophrenia is a devastating and widespread mental disease, finding even a consistently palliative drug has had profound social significance. Such findings naturally engendered the hope that knowledge of how the drugs worked would lead to knowledge of the disease and its etiology, and thereby to knowledge of prevention.

Second were discoveries, also in the 1950s, that led to the treatment of Parkinson's disease, also known as the shaking palsy. Parkinson's disease is characterized by muscular rigidity, tremor, and akinesia (a diminished ability to make voluntary movements). It was found in autopsies that the brains of patients with Parkinson's disease had abnormally low levels of the neurotransmitter dopamine and that one motor area rich in dopamine-producing neurons (the substantia nigra) had degenerated. This suggested that dopamine deficiency was the root cause of the disease and that the motor dysfunctions could be alleviated by giving the patients the drug L-dopa (which converts to dopamine in the brain). The idea was tried, with considerable though not unalloyed success, and L-dopa is now the drug of choice for reducing the effects of Parkinson's disease. This too was an important discovery, for Parkinson's disease afflicts large numbers of people in their declining years. (For a short paper on recent developments in the treatment of Parkinson's disease, see Larsen and Calne 1982.)

Third was the revelation in the late 1970s that the nervous system manufactures and uses its own opiate-like substances—the *endogenous opiates*, as they came to be known (Hughes et al. 1975). It was found that there are at least five, three of which were classed as "endorphins" and two as "enkephalins." Though this discovery suggested a practical application in the relief of pain and of mood disorders, it also raised many questions. What are the opiates doing in the brain in the first place? Will we find endogenous tranquilizers and endogenous antidepressants?[3] Are certain diseases of the mind caused by imbalances in these chemicals? Can I be addicted to my own chemicals?

Investigation of the neurochemicals that have some role in the synaptic transmission of signals is accordingly important not only for determining what is going on at the cellular level. It is important also because it shows us that chemical events at the cellular level can have enormous effects on the brain's affairs as characterized at the psychological level of description. This is significant for those who oppose the idea of a unified science of the mind-brain, either because they believe the mind to be a distinct substance, because they believe mental properties to be emergent, or because they believe psychological theory to be irreducible to neurobiological theory. (See chapters 7–9.) Not that neuropharmacology can now yield anything like a decisive demonstration of the falsity of these views, but it can undermine certain favored theses about how very different and separate are brain states and mental states. By inches it helps to erode the metaphysical conviction that one's *self* is an affair apart from that mound of biological stuff hidden under the skull. It can help to shift the burden of proof to those who deny that there can be a science of the mind. Therefore, after a few simple illustrations of neurons as they participate in *networks*, I shall dwell a bit further on neuropharmacological considerations.

Some Simple Wiring Diagrams
To understand what the brain does, it is necessary to understand the connections between neurons at the sensory periphery and neurons at the motor periphery—that is, to understand how the neurons form a circuit to constitute an information-processing system. Because the intervening network is typically exceedingly complex, studying examples in which the neuronal connections between sensory input and behavioral output are very simple has been an important step in

seeing how input-output effects are achieved and in developing models of the intervening information processing. There are about twenty cases in invertebrate research in which the circuitry underlying a specific behavior pattern is known in great detail. These include swimming in the leech and the crayfish, walking in the locust, and a substantial number of behavior patterns in *Aplysia* such as inking, egg-laying, gill withdrawal, habituation, and sensitization (Bullock 1984).

To amplify the earlier mention of the cellular basis of simple habituation and sensitization, I shall illustrate the revolutionary discoveries in the neurobiology of behavior with the neuronal circuits in *Aplysia* (figure 2.24) that mediate gill withdrawal following stimulation of the siphon, habituation to a gentle stimulus, and sensitization after a painful stimulus to the head. Habituation is the decrement of a response to a repeated, benign stimulation. Sensitization consists in a heightened response to a benign stimulus following receipt of a painful stimulus.

In *Aplysia* the circuit leading from the siphon's sensory periphery to the motor periphery of the gill is very simple, as can be seen in the schematic wiring diagram in figure 2.25. It shows one of the 24 sensory neurons innervating the siphon in direct synaptic contact with the motor neurons innervating the gill. (Only one of the six gill motor neurons is shown.) The connection between the sensory neuron in the siphon and the motor in the gill muscle is *monosynaptic*, because only one synapse mediates input and output. There is also a second pathway formed by a branch of the sensory axon, which is disynaptic because it routes through the facilitating interneuron located between the sensory and motor neurons.

In the habituation experiments the animal's siphon is repeatedly stimulated with a gentle squirt of sea water, and after a few trials the gill withdrawal response decrements. Briefly, what Kandel and his colleagues found was that at the terminal bulbs of the sensory neuron the inward Ca^{++} current decreased during the habituation trials, which resulted in a decreased neurotransmitter release at the synaptic junction, with the result that the motor neuron was less depolarized and hence caused smaller contractions in the gill muscle.

In sensitization roughly the opposite happens; there is an increase in Ca^{++} current and hence an increase in the volume of neurotransmitter released into the synaptic cleft. However, this effect requires the mediation of the facilitatory interneuron, whose axon terminates on the end bulb of the sensory neuron (presynaptic facilitation) (figure 2.25). When the tail is given a noxious stimulus, the facilitatory interneuron releases serotonin, which then initiates a four-step

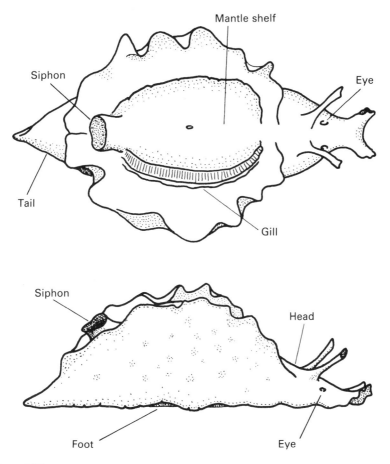

Figure 2.24
Top view and side view of the sea hare, *Aplysia Californica*. When the mantle shelf is stimulated, the gill contracts.

sequence of chemical events: (1) an elevation in the level of cyclic AMP (adenosine monophosphate) in the sensory neuron's end bulb, which causes (2) an elevation in an enzyme (cyclic AMP-dependent protein kinase), which causes (3) a decrease in the number of open K^+ channels, which causes (4) an increase in the number of open Ca^{++} channels.

Like sensitization, classical conditioning requires the facilitating interneuron. Conditioning is, however, more complex, because the close timing of the conditioned stimulus (CS) and the unconditioned stimulus (UCS) is essential in the system's selecting the particular

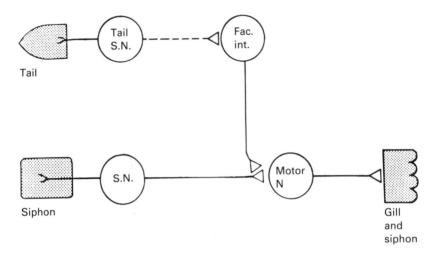

Figure 2.25
Partial neuronal circuit for the *Aplysia* gill and siphon withdrawal reflex and its modification. Mechanosensory neurons (S.N.) from the siphon make direct excitatory synaptic connections onto gill and siphon motor neurons. Tail sensory neurons excite facilitator interneurons, which produce presynaptic facilitation of the siphon sensory neurons. (From Hawkins and Kandel (1984). In *Neurobiology of Learning and Memory*, ed. G. Lynch, J. L. McGaugh, and N. M. Weinberger. New York: Guilford.)

stimulus to which it is sensitized. It appears that the temporal contiguity of CS and UCS causes an enhancement of Ca^{++} current in the sensory neurons on later occasions, though exactly how this happens is not yet understood.

Each of these forms of plasticity—habituation, sensitization, classical conditioning—appears to employ a relatively small set of specified cellular events, and Hawkins and Kandel (1984) have suggested that there might exist a general cellular "alphabet," in the sense that each of the various types of behavioral plasticity employs a distinct combination of the fundamental cellular event-types (figure 2.26). Possibly, they argue, other forms of plasticity such as associative learning, extinction, and stimulus generalization might have reductive explanations in terms of precise sequences of cellular events. They present for experimental evaluation models of kinds of plasticity based on that hypothesis.

To further illustrate how groups of neurons might be connected to yield a complex effect, consider the circuit in figure 2.27, which is a model for contrast enhancement. In every studied organism it has been found that sensory neurons typically send collaterals (axon branches) to interneurons that have an inhibitory effect on the neigh-

A

Habituation

B

Sensitization

C

Classical conditioning

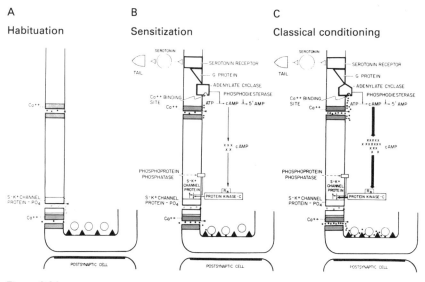

Figure 2.26
Cellular mechanisms of habituation, sensitization, and classical conditioning of the
Aplysia gill and siphon withdrawal reflex. (A) Habituation: Repeated stimulation of a
siphon sensory neuron (the presynaptic cell in the figure) produces prolonged inactivation of Ca^{++} channels in that neuron (represented by the closed gates), leading to a
decrease in Ca^{++} influx during each action potential and decreased transmitter release.
(B) Sensitization: Stimulation of the tail produces prolonged inactivation of K^{+} channels in the siphon sensory neuron through a sequence of steps involving cAMP (cyclic
adenosine monophosphate) and protein phosphorylation. Closing these channels produces broadening of subsequent action potentials, which in turn produces an increase
in Ca^{++} influx and increased transmitter release. (C) Classical conditioning: Tail stimulation produces amplified facilitation of transmitter release from the siphon sensory
neuron if the tail stimulation is preceded by action potentials in the sensory neuron.
This effect may be due to "priming" of the adenyl cyclase by Ca^{++} that enters the
sensory neuron during the action potentials, so that the cyclase produces more cAMP
when it is activated by tail stimulation. (From Hawkins and Kandel (1984). In *Neurobiology of Learning and Memory*, ed. G. Lynch, J. L. McGaugh, and N. M. Weinberger. New
York: Guilford.)

boring sensory neurons. This is called lateral inhibition, and it appears to be a common arrangement in nervous tissue, being found in
the retina, the skin, the olfactory epithelium, and the gustatory
epithelium. The effect of a lateral inhibition circuit is to enhance the
contrast between highly stimulated neurons and their nonstimulated
neighbors, since the stimulated cells fire at a high rate and the inhibited cells fire at a rate lower than their base rate. Some such arrangement in the retina is believed to figure in the perceptual effect
known as "Mach bands." The effect is easily seen in figure 2.28. The

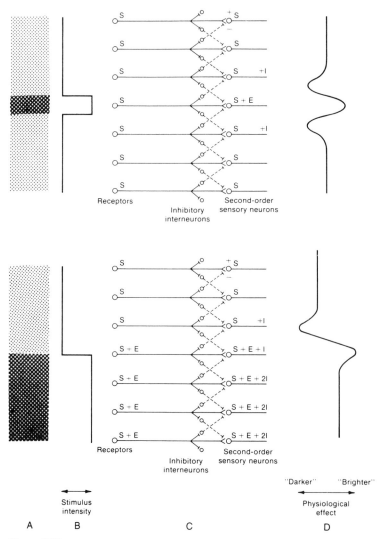

Figure 2.27
Lateral inhibition. (A) A pattern of uniformly gray areas with sharp edges, representing
a visual field seen by an eye. (B) The stimulus plotted as intensity (horizontal) against
spatial extent (vertical), emphasizing the uniformity of the physical intensity within
each area. (C) A network of receptors and second-order neurons with reciprocal inhibitory connections via interneurons (broken lines). Spontaneous activity in the receptors
(S) is augmented by excitation (E) due to light. The network causes the second-order
neurons to show S activity augmented by E and/or reduced by inhibition (I) in single or
double (2I) dose. (D) The output, equivalent to our sensation, plotted as darker or
lighter than the background due to S. This sort of arrangement probably explains the
Mach bands illusion seen in figure 2.28. (From Bullock, Orkand, and Grinnell (1977).
Introduction to Nervous Systems. W. H. Freeman and Co. Copyright © 1977.)

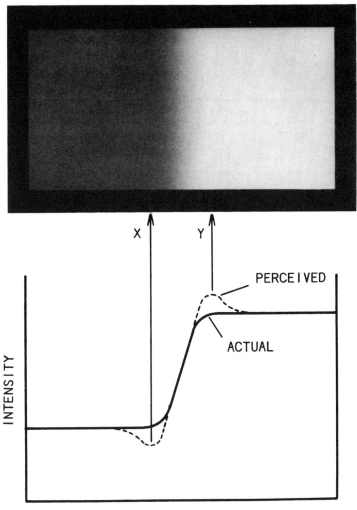

Figure 2.28
Although there is a smooth reduction in light intensity from right to left in the photograph, there appears to be a bright band at Y and a dark band at X. These are Mach band patterns. (Modified from Cornsweet (1970). *Visual Perception*. New York: Academic Press.)

Mach bands visible in the boundary area between a light region and a dark region appear as a sharper change in light intensity than actually obtains.

How contrast enhancement works in the hypothetical circuit can be observed in figure 2.27. All cells have a base firing rate, cells stimulated by the light have an increased firing rate, and each inhibitory neuron decreases the firing rate of its postsynaptic cell by some specified amount. Consider the cell that is on the boundary of the increase in stimulus intensity. Excited by the stimulus, it will fire at a higher than base rate, and it will therefore excite an inhibitory interneuron that synapses on the cells that are its immediate neighbors. One of its neighboring cells, unaffected by the light stimulus, will have its base rate decreased by the inhibitory interneuron, while the neighbor on the other side, despite being excited by the light stimulus, will fire less vigorously than the boundary cell because it receives inhibitory stimuli from excited neighbors on both sides. Since the cells at the boundary of the area receiving the stimulus are inhibited only by neighbors on one side, they have the highest firing rate. Although this is a highly simplified and schematic representation of how a network of neurons might interact to yield contrast enhancement, it illustrates how complex effects can be derived from appropriately connected simple units.

These examples of simple circuits are meant to provide only an introductory illustration of how neurons can be wired up to constitute an information-processing and a learning network. Nevertheless, they should help to make clear why neurobiologists have insisted it is necessary to understand the architectural and physiological properties of nervous systems. The reason is that such properties provide essential clues both to how networks can generate complex representations of the external world and of the internal nervous-system world and to the nature of the computations performed by large, interconnected arrays of neurons. In chapter 3 I will say more about some architectural properties of nervous systems believed to be especially significant in constructing a theory of the nature of neural network function. In chapter 10 I will discuss some theoretical developments arising out of, or at least directly inspired by, neuroanatomy and neurophysiology.

Concluding Remarks
Although the membranes of all body cells are polarized and have the ability to depolarize and repolarize, neurons are special both because their single channel configurations permit them to exploit this capacity in a *coordinated and systematic* fashion and because they are joined

together in a network. The result is that neurons can represent features of the world and can coordinate the occurrence of such features with muscular movement.

The fundamental principle is deadly simple, but at the same time almost endlessly versatile. Increased complexity will essentially be a matter of adding components of the same basic type; the neurons in a flatworm and the neurons in a human brain work on the same *fundamental* principles. From which it does not follow, however, that the capacities of the human brain are essentially just those of a densely packed conglomeration of flatworm ganglia. The marvelous thing about electrical circuits is that adding components is not merely a matter of enlarging the system, but sometimes means changing the system's capacities in novel and remarkable ways. In particular, the evolutionary step that interposes neurons between sensory neurons and motor neurons is revolutionary: it permits the building-in of a basic world-representation, and it can provide for increasingly fancy up-dating of that world-representation through learning. As the interneuron pool proliferates under evolutionary pressure for more competitive sensorimotor coordination, the innate world-representation improves and the dimensions of plasticity ramify.

2.4 Neurotransmitters and Other Neurochemicals

On a simple view of things it might have been predicted that the nervous system would need to produce just two chemicals to serve as neurotransmitters—one for excitation and one for inhibition. Even adjusted upward for Nature's tendency to scrounge, the prediction is not even close. There are at least forty known neurally active substances sloshing around in the nervous system, and it is a near certainty that more will be coaxed into revealing themselves. What are all these substances doing in the brain? Has Nature been wantonly extravagant in producing such variety, or does the variety reflect diversity in function?

These questions become especially fascinating in light of the synthesis of certain drugs that mimic, enhance, or obstruct the action of some of these substances and that moreover can have quite consistent and distinct psychological effects. Some may produce hallucinations, others reduce hallucinations; some alter moods to produce euphoria, others produce despair, anxiety, and hopelessness; some heighten arousal, others tranquilize; some are amnestic, others facilitate memory; some alleviate pain, others produce excessive drinking, eating, or unseemly sexual behavior. These drugs produce changes in the brain, mainly, it is believed, at synaptic junctions, and they provide a means for interfering in the nervous system that may help us understand what various parts of the brain do.

The assorted endogenous neurochemicals are not distributed randomly in the brain. First to be considered is Dale's law, which says that any given neuron synthesizes and releases only one type of transmitter, though it may have receptor sites fitted for any number of diverse transmitters. The law seems to hold generally for adult neurons, but, interestingly enough, it is known to be violated by developing neurons in the very young. In any event, the accepted classification specifies neurons as *dopaminergic* if they typically release the transmitter dopamine, *cholinergic* if they typically release acetylcholine, and so on for the set of neurotransmitters.

Several techniques have been devised to locate neurons with a characteristic transmitter. For example, by treating a neurochemical so that it will fluoresce, researchers have been able to show areas of the brain where it is concentrated and thereby to identify the location of neurons releasing it. Dopamine has been found to concentrate in neurons in an area of the brain called the substantia nigra and in the midbrain tegmentum (figure 2.29). Some of these neurons project to the forebrain where, given behavioral evidence, they are thought to play some role in mood regulation. But dopamine is not found *exclusively* in these areas, and minute amounts are found hither and yon, including in the spinal cord.

It was hoped that particular neurochemicals might be found exclusively in certain tracts and areas whose function was more or less well defined, but these hopes have been disappointed. For example, it would perhaps have been easier if the enkephalins were found solely in tracts that carry pain information or mediate the pain response, but this has not turned out to be the case. Though enkephalin is concentrated in certain ﹫pots, these spots are not what one would expect if it were primarily a neurochemical for the nociceptive system. For example, it is found in the primary photoreceptors of the spiny lobster. It is also noteworthy that endorphins are found in a wide range of organisms, including leeches, spiders, lobsters, rats, and monkeys.

Additionally, it is evident now that there is no sharp division between the chemicals found in the brain and the hormones found elsewhere in the body. Consequently, the once sharp distinction between secretion of peptides by glands in the endocrine system and secretion of peptides at the synaptic terminal is fast losing its edge. All the peripheral peptide hormones—for example, the gut peptide cholecystokinin and the sex hormone estradiol—have been found in the brain, and peptides originally believed unique to the brain—for

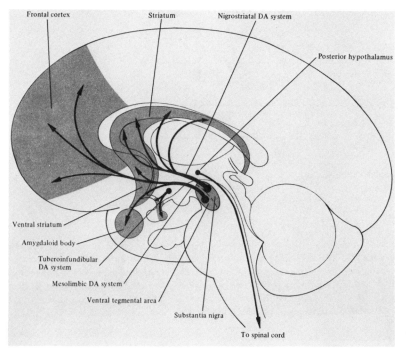

Figure 2.29
The nigrostriatal dopamine system originates in the substantia nigra and terminates in the main dorsal part of the striatum. Damage to this system results in Parkinsonian symptoms. The ventral tegmental area gives rise to the mesolimbic dopamine system, which terminates in the ventral striatum, amygdaloid body, frontal lobe, and some other basal forebrain areas. The tuberoinfundibular system innervates the intermediate lobes of the pituitary and the nearby median eminence, and dopamine neurons in the posterior hypothalamus project to the spinal cord. (From Heimer (1983). *The Human Brain and Spinal Cord.* Copyright © 1983 by Springer-Verlag.)

example, β-endorphin—are found outside the nervous system (Rehfeld 1980).

Moreover, the assumption that each transmitting substance has a one-trick profile, producing either just excitatory or just inhibitory effects on the postsynaptic neuron, is false. At least one neurotransmitter—serotonin—has been shown in *Aplysia* to cause either excitation or one of two styles of inhibition on the postsynaptic neurons, depending on the receptor structures. That this versatility is a general feature of transmitting substances is suspected but not yet proven (Paupardin-Tritsch and Gerschenfeld 1975).

Although each of the forty or so substances has been found to have some neural effect, especially at synaptic junctions, so far only eleven are demonstrated to function as transmitters. To count as a transmit-

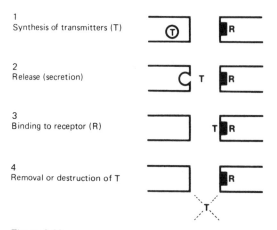

Figure 2.30
Four biochemical steps in synaptic transmission: (1) synthesis of the neurotransmitter substance (T), (2) release of transmitter into the synaptic cleft, (3) binding of the transmitter to the postsynaptic receptor (R), and (4) removal or destruction of the transmitter substance. (Reprinted with permission of the publisher from Schwartz (1981). Ch. 10 of *Principles of Neural Science*, ed. E. R. Kandel and J. H. Schwartz, pp. 106–120. Copyright © 1981 by Elsevier Science Publishing Co., Inc.)

ter, a substance must satisfy four conditions: (1) it must be synthesized in the presynaptic neurons, (2) it must be released from the presynaptic terminal, (3) it must be shown to cause EPSPs or IPSPs, and (4) there must be mechanisms for its removal from the scene of action (figure 2.30).

Demonstrating that a neurochemical passes muster on each of the four counts is exceedingly difficult, and to date only eleven have passed all four, though many others have been shown to pass some, and answers are awaited for many tests. The list of canonical transmitters includes acetylcholine (an excitatory substance released by motor neurons at the neuromuscular junctions, and by other neurons in the CNS as well), dopamine (so far found to be inhibitory), norepinephrine (also called noradrenalin), serotonin, and GABA (γ-aminobutyric acid, another inhibitory transmitter) (tables 2.1, 2.2).

Not all inhibitory transmitters have precisely the same causal profile, however. Norepinephrine appears to have a longer and slower course of action than, for example, serotonin (Taylor and Stone 1981). Some neurochemicals are thought to have a modulatory role in regulating the effects of a transmitter on the receiving cells, and there is evidence that some neurotransmitters act on voltage-sensitive channels as well as at the standard receptor sites, thus affecting the response properties of neurons in a range of subtle ways

Table 2.1
Canonical transmitter substances

Acetylcholine	γ-Aminobutyric acid (GABA)
Dopamine	Glycine
Norepinephrine	Glutamate
Epinephrine	Aspartate
Serotonin	Taurine
Histamine	

Source: Feldman and Quenzer (1984). *Fundamentals of Neuropsychopharmacology.*

Table 2.2
Neuroactive peptides

Gut-brain peptides
    vasoactive intestinal polypeptide (VIP)
    cholecystokinin octapeptide (CCK-8)
    substance P
    neurotensin
    methionine enkephalin
    leucine enkephalin
    insulin
    glucagon
Hypothalamic-releasing hormones
    thyrotropin-releasing hormone (TRH)
    luteinizing hormone-releasing hormone (LHRH)
    somatostatin (growth hormone release-inhibiting factor, SRIF)
Pituitary Peptides
    adrenocorticotropin (ACTH)
    β-endorphin
    α-Melanocyte-stimulating hormone (α-MSH)
Others
    angiotensin II
    bradykinin
    vasopressin
    oxytocin
    carnosine
    bombesin

Source: Snyder (1980). Brain peptides as neurotransmitters. *Science* 209:976–983.

(Nicoll 1982). The subtlety and complexity of interneuronal communication far outstrips the "excite-inhibit" repertoire, and we are only beginning to understand what the assorted chemicals do (Taylor and Stone 1981, Dismukes 1980).

Fine-grained detail has accumulated concerning such things as the molecular structure, location, synthesis, blocking agents, and enhancing agents of the various neurochemicals, but there is still nothing remotely resembling a comprehensive *theory* of what they do or of how the known psychological effects result from tinkering with them. We may know that cocaine acts by blocking the uptake of norepinephrine, leaving norepinephrine lying about in the synaptic cleft to continue its work unabated, but how that produces euphoria is a smooth-walled mystery.

The absence of theory here is not surprising. For one thing, until much more is known about the details of brain business and about how noradrenergic neurons fit into the grander scheme of things, merely focusing on the one change we happen to know cocaine produces cannot be expected to tell us much. Second, until we have higher-level concepts to describe what configurations of neurons are doing, we have no means of bridging the gap between molecular descriptions and molar descriptions. The mystery will not be solved merely by finding out about the molecular details of the slew of neurochemicals, but neither will it be solved without much of that detail. (See Miczek, Thompson, and Shuster 1982, Mayer 1975, Cooper, Bloom, and Roth 1982.)

Neuroleptics
Largely because of their clinical significance, the antipsychotic drugs (called *neuroleptics:* "that which takes the neuron") have been the focus of concentrated study. In the treatment of schizophrenia the phenothiazines, of which chlorpromazine is the most renowned, are extensively used, and it is estimated that some fifty million patients have been treated with them. For roughly a decade they were used without any clear idea of how they affected the CNS and were therefore prescribed mainly on the strength of their behavioral effects, much as antianxiety pills such as Librium and Valium are still used (Kolata 1979a).

Research now indicates that the phenothiazines block the dopamine receptor sites, and the evidence has come from the cellular as well as the behavioral level. In vitro studies show that chlorpromazine does bind to dopamine receptor sites, though it has as well been linked to an increase in norepinephrine turnover. A problematic side effect of chlorpromazine therapy that also points to dopamine involvement is that patients on extended chlorpromazine treatment may eventually develop motor symptoms similar to those of patients suffering from Parkinson's disease. From another direction it has been found that amphetamine, which stimulates dopamine receptors, will induce "amphetamine psychosis" and in otherwise mild schizophrenics will induce acute psychotic symptoms. (See Feldman and Quenzer 1984.)

The possibility has been considered that the phenothiazines work not by zeroing in on the psychotic effects per se but rather by sedating or tranquilizing the brain. Though this possibility is not yet ruled out, some evidence against it was found in a comparison of the effects of sedatives such as barbiturates and of neuroleptics, which shows them to be quite distinct. Though neuroleptics are not widely regarded as a *cure* for schizophrenia, in virtue of their specific effects in treating a hitherto intractable disease they have engendered optimism for the discovery of a cure and even for the means to prevent the disease altogether.

Once the connection to dopamine was made, the hypothesis that naturally formed itself was this: if neuroleptics antagonize dopamine, then perhaps schizophrenia has its origin in the malfunction of dopaminergic neurons, such that there is an excessive amount of dopamine in the CNS. Schizophrenia, it might be said, is "hyperdopaminia." So far, efforts to prove this have been less than decisive, and the heady expectation of the early days that a simple solution was all but in hand has quietly given over to a tempered belief that an answer, probably not all that simple, will eventually be untangled as part of a more comprehensive theory of neurobiology.

Whether a dopamine flood is the root cause of schizophrenia is not yet established, and even assuming dopaminergic neurons are the culprits, there is an assortment of ways in which they might be malfunctioning. They might be too active and thus release too much dopamine, but alternatively the mechanisms for synthesis might be abnormally hearty, or the mechanisms for breakdown might be abnormally sluggish, or, in a different vein, the postsynaptic neurons might be overly sensitive to dopamine or might have cultivated too many receptor sites—all of which are consistent with chlorpromazine's demonstrated capacity to reduce symptoms. Though chlorpromazine alteration of dopaminergic transmission does of course make dopaminergic neurons prime suspects, the trouble is that such facts are entirely consistent with the possibility that some biochemical impropriety (e.g., an enzymatic muck-up) further upstream is the underlying cause (or, more difficult yet, one of several underlying causal factors). Additionally, it is likely that psychological factors of a complex nature also play a role in altering the balance of the chemical soup, even as such alterations in the soup in turn affect the psychological states. Hence, an adequate account of schizophrenia, clinical depression, sociopathy, and so forth, would need to integrate biological and psychological descriptions (Kety 1978).

Still, the hopeful thing is that the array of possibilities is after all an array of empirical and testable possibilities. And the evidence is snowballing that schizophrenia is a somatogenically based disease, like, for example, Parkinson's disease or diabetes, rather than a disease that originates in strictly psychological elements such as guilt, shame, repression, and the like. A first source of evidence for this derives from comparison of the effectiveness of phenothiazine therapy with other therapeutic techniques such as psychotherapy. For very seriously afflicted patients, drug therapy is generally considered more effective in reducing symptoms than psychotherapy, more effective than placebos, and more effective than psychotherapy and placebos combined (Davis and Garver 1978). For milder afflictions, the case is far less clear.

Second, examination of the brains of schizophrenics in autopsies or by using three-dimensional scanning techniques (described in chapter 5) shows that there are some systematic differences between such brains and those of normal subjects. For example, the ventricles of chronic schizophrenics are typically larger, and the level of activity in the forebrain is substantially reduced. There are also distinct differences between normal subjects and chronic schizophrenics in the distribution of cerebral blood flow, in the gross electrical activity of the brain as measured by the electroencephalograph, and in glucose uptake patterns as measured by positron emission tomography (Ingvar 1982, Buchsbaum et al. 1982, Buchsbaum et al. 1984). (See chapter 5 for an explanation of these techniques.) Exactly what these findings mean is far from clear, but they do add another piece to the puzzle.

Third, there is strong evidence of familial susceptibility to schizophrenia. In one study it was found that if one monozygotic twin is schizophrenic, then there is about a 45 percent chance the second one will be so as well. The risk drops to about 13 percent if the twins are fraternal. The incidence of schizophrenia in the general population is roughly 1 percent. Additional studies on adopted children in Denmark also indicates an inherited susceptibility to the disease (Kety et al. 1975). Another study compared children born to schizophrenic parents but reared by normal parents with the opposite situation (children born to normal parents but reared by affected parents) and a control group (children born to normal parents and adopted by normal parents) (Wender, Rosenthal, and Kety 1974). The results pointed to a genetic effect: roughly 18 percent of the first group became schizophrenic, whereas the incidence of schizophrenia in the second group and the control group was the same, about 10 percent. (For a collection of papers on schizophrenia as a somatogenic disease, see Henn and Nasrallah 1982.)

As a result of the work on familial histories and schizophrenia, the hypothesis that there is a genetic susceptibility to schizophrenia seems correct, though there is still considerable controversy concerning the adequacy of experimental controls and the interpretation of the data. No one has claimed that the genetic factor is all there is to it, for even assuming there is a gene implicated in the causal history of schizophrenia, environmental factors, whatever they are found to be, are certainly relevant. Otherwise the chance of a second monozygotic twin having schizophrenia if the first does would be 1 rather than .45. In this respect schizophrenia could be like phenylketonuria (PKU), a recessive disorder caused by a deficiency of an enzyme, which results in high levels of phenylalanine in the brain. It is a serious disease for those on a diet rich in protein, which contains phenylalanine, but it does not show up on a meat-restricted diet (Rosenberg 1980). Certain environmental conditions may trigger schizophrenic symptoms, whereas in an environment free of those factors a carrier of the gene may be largely free of the disease. For example, being raised by parents who are schizophrenic appears to be one relevant environmental condition.

Matters could be, and probably are, horrendously complicated. What is now classified as a single disorder—schizophrenia—may in fact be a number of causally unrelated types of disease (Crow et al. 1982), and even if some type of schizophrenia has a genetic basis, the modes of transmission and epigenetic factors have yet to be determined. It is worth bearing in mind that some genetically based diseases such as Sanfilippo's syndrome have essentially one clinical presentation but are producible by the presence of either of two distinct genes, and for all we know now this may be the case for schizophrenia. (For review papers, see Buchsbaum and Haier 1978 and Crowe 1982.)

This discussion of attempts to understand schizophrenia as a neurochemical disease has touched on only a sprinkling of current developments, and then only superficially. And schizophrenia is not the only mental disorder to be so studied; depressive disorders, the dementias, dyslexia, and sleep disorders are examples where genetic and neurochemical studies are bearing fruit. (For example, see Whitehouse et al. 1982.) Nor are *mental* disorders the only ones in this category; diseases involving the motor system (for example, Parkinson's disease, Huntington's chorea, and myasthenia gravis) are also instances where research in neurochemistry has been pursued with considerable success (Spokes 1981). For wider and more thorough discussions, the reader may consult works recommended in the reference section.

The discovery that it is possible to change the brain directly and alleviate the catastrophic effects of brain disease has far-reaching social importance. Brain disorders are widespread, and demographic distribution being what it is, the number of older citizens steadily increases—with the result that the number of patients with strokes, Parkinson's disease, Alzheimer's disease, and so forth, will also be on the upswing. The social and personal costs of brain disorders are enormous, and the possibility that we might really understand and manipulate some of the causally relevant conditions seems an increasingly real possibility. In this context it is useful to mention that a new technique for treating Parkinson's disease is being developed, a technique that presents an important moral issue, especially since it may conceivably be applied more generally to other disorders.

The issue is this. As a result of research in neural implants, it was found that foetal neurons extracted from a specified area of a rat's brain and injected into the same area of another rat's brain established themselves there as functioning elements in the nervous system. Thus, neurons extracted from the substantia nigra of a foetal rat and injected into the brain of a rat with lesions in the substantia nigra continued to live and began to produce dopamine, the neurotransmitter in deficit since the destruction of the substantia nigra. The dopamine deficiency suffered by the brain-lesioned rat was accordingly made good to some degree, and the motor deficits were diminished though not abolished. Because the brain is isolated from the immune system by the "blood-brain barrier" (the neurons are not directly nourished by the bloodstream but are "fed" by the intervening neuroglial cells), brain grafts are less susceptible to rejection by the immune system as a foreign invader. Although this immunological privilege, as it is called, has been demonstrated in the rat, it is not yet known whether primate brains enjoy the same property and will accept foreign neurons (Barker and Billingham 1977).

Now under study is the possibility that humans with Parkinson's disease might be treated by injecting foetal neurons into the brain. This would be far better than treatment with L-dopa, because the brain's need for dopamine is continuous but the drug can only be taken at discrete intervals, and because in the long term Parkinson's patients on this drug tend to develop psychiatric symptoms, some of the motor deficits reappear, and the drug seems to have declining efficacy. A replacement of the atrophied neurons by healthy neurons would be a vast improvement. A similar case can now be made for treating diabetes with foetal cells from the pancreas, and it is possible that replacing neurons in the hippocampus may help patients with Alzheimer's disease. Foetal neurons implanted into the hippocampus even show a tendency to establish projections to the appropriate regions of the host brain, and more remarkably, they appear to establish functional synapses, though this is still under investigation (Bjorklund and Stenevi 1977 and 1984, Freed 1983).

The most effective implant cells are foetal cells, and if it should turn out that cell transplants in humans must use cells from human foetuses rather than from animal foetuses, the moral issue comes into focus. So far no human foetal cells have been used in neural implants, and the experiments with implants in the brain of humans with Parkinson's disease have all used cells from the patient's own adrenal medulla (Bjorklund and Stenevi 1984). These experiments have resulted in little if any restoration of capacity, but the belief is that human foetal cells would be more effective. One question to be raised here is this: is it acceptable to use neural tissue obtained from aborted human foetuses? Assuming for this discussion the moral propriety of abortion, should the cells be used to alleviate the ravages of cruel diseases such as Alzheimer's?

The issue may be sidestepped to some degree if some clever neurobiologist discovers how to produce the desired cells in tissue cultures. Even then, however, those who believe that the human soul is infused in the morula at the moment of conception may find the tissue culturing immoral on grounds that foetal neurons in tissue culture are "ensouled." Naturally neuroscientists are wary of undertaking any research that might provoke an imbroglio, however misguided its motivation. Thus, there is the further sociological and political issue concerning how to educate the public such that a rational, nonsuperstitious judgment can be made. (See also the discussion concerning materialism and dualism in chapters 7 and 8.) In any event, there is a real need for experimental studies on the efficacy of implantation of human foetal neurons in treatment of such disorders as Parkinson's and Alzheimer's disease.

Although these questions are intriguing, I shall take them no further in this book. My intent here is merely to flag the questions, partly for their intrinsic interest, and partly because the issue of the use of human foetuses will likely come to legislation in the near future. It is an issue of profound practical significance, and one on which cooperation between neuroscientists and philosophers will be essential. I do not believe there are any a priori answers, and the more empirical information available in considering the question, the more informed will be the conclusions drawn.

Advances in our understanding of the biological factors in diseases such as schizophrenia also raise questions leading in a quite different direction. The developments in understanding madness that have shifted from the demonic possession theory popular from the sixteenth to eighteenth centuries, to the psychoanalytic theory advocated by Freud and widely practiced in the twentieth century, and now to biochemical theories, do not merely represent a change in clinical approach but penetrate to our everyday conception of ourselves.

Assuming that diseases such as schizophrenia do have a basis we can describe in biochemical terms, this invites the idea that we might enhance our knowledge generally, of the sane as well as the insane, should we acquire knowledge of the biochemical aspects of emotions, moods, and desires and of cognitive development and organization. If the desires, fears, inclinations, and dispositions of the insane are in some measure a function of the neurochemicals in the brain, then so are those of the sane. This line of thought leads to broad questions concerning the nature of the integration of psychological theory and neuroscientific theory, and the possibility of reduction. Because these questions require a substantial philosophical and neuroscientific setting, they will be deferred until chapters 8 through 10.

Sex and Neurochemicals
One dimension of the psychology of an organism where its neurochemistry is manifestly relevant is reproduction and the congeries of behavior patterns related to it. Gender identity is crucially connected to the presence of certain steroids, the gonadal hormones. Until rather recently it was widely supposed that the role of gonadal hormones did not include intervention in the business of the CNS, but it is now known that they are found in regionally specific parts of the brain and that sexual differentiation of the brain takes place at their behest (McEwen et al. 1974, Pfaff and McEwen 1983).

From the point of view of natural selection, sex is a good thing, since it provides the medium for mixing genetic material and hence for maximizing variation. Sexual reproduction requires dimorphism (two forms), and in many animals, including of course all mammals, there is a dimorphism of behavior as well as of reproductive organs and various other bodily features. Dimorphism in behavior is a method of ensuring that individuals recognize each other as appropriate mating partners and recognize that the timing is appropriate. It also ensures that coupling gets the reproductive parts where they should be for successful reproduction. Parental nurturing behavior is also advantageous, and consequently many brains may have built-in dispositions for nest building, feeding the young, foiling predators, and so on.

In normal adult animals (rats and horses are well-known examples) priming by gonadal hormones—androgen for males and estrogen for females—activates reproductive behavior. In the developing organism the presence of gonadal hormones has a quite different effect, hidden from casual view. At this early stage the hormones function to set the brain's development on a course that establishes its gender. The brain of the developing organism thus becomes male or female, and subsequent influx of hormone in the adult organism will not be able to reverse the changes wrought in the brain.

An organism with an XY chromosome pair is a genetic male,[4] and at some point in his early development testosterone will be manufactured by his emerging testes and released in his body. Some will affect maturation of the gonads, and some will reach his CNS where, during a certain critical period in which particular neurons are maximally sensitive to testosterone, it will induce organizational changes in the brain that "masculinize" it. The critical period varies from species to species. In most animals studied it is confined to foetal stages, and in humans it is believed to encompass the third and fourth months of gestation. Rats, ever obliging to the experimenter, have a critical period that extends a few days beyond birth.

Until the influx of testosterone the brain is bipotential—that is, capable of becoming characteristically male or female. This means that brain sex is not simply a matter of genetic sex, and indeed the two can be dissociated such that a genetic male can have a female brain, and a genetic female can have a male brain. So-called experiments of nature are one indicator of this sort of dissociation. Freemartins are cows (genetic females) with a male twin. They are invariably infertile, and in the pasture behave more like bulls than like cows. Even before ultrastructural studies of brains revealed what differences there could be between male and female neuronal organization, the freemartin phenomenon suggested that there was a masculinization of the female's brain as a result of the foetal environment she shared with her male twin. In the human case a pathological condition called *androgen insensitivity* results in a genetic male who is phenotypically female both in external genitalia and in sexual orientation (Ehrhardt and Baker 1974).

In the laboratory male rats deprived of testosterone during their critical period never show male reproductive behavior (mounting, intromission), though they do show female reproductive behavior, measured by frequency of lordosis (female presenting posture—raised rump, concave back). It is important to note that for such animals, priming with testosterone after the critical period fails to elicit mounting. Females exposed to testosterone during the critical period are masculinized; their adult behavior is characteristically male and their lordosis quotient is low and not much enhanced by priming with estrogen. The androgenization of the developing brain appears to be irreversible and enduring.

Taking such standard behavior patterns as mounting and intromission as an index of characteristic male reproductive behavior and lordosis as an index of female reproductive behavior, it is evident that genetic sex determines brain sex only via the intermediary auspices of gonadal hormones. Such indexes are admittedly rather restricted and other behavior profiles such as display patterns, offspring-care behavior, song, nest building, etc., can, where appropriate, be taken into account.

Establishing behavioral indexes for characteristically male or characteristically female behavior is notoriously difficult, and in the pioneering stages researchers have tended to adopt fairly conventional and crude descriptions. How to extend animal studies to the human case, how to refine and reconfigure the indexes of what is masculine and what is feminine, and how to extend studies to include nonreproductive behavior as well are questions for further research. However, the point of emphasis here is that, using narrowly defined indexes of the masculine and feminine in behavior, it is clear that such adult behavior is crucially affected by early exposure of the brain to testosterone and that this exposure determines whether exposure as an adult to gonadal hormones will be effective in producing characteristic reproductive behavior. There also seems to be a distinct feminizing of the brain, so that a female brain is not one that merely missed out on androgenization (Goy and McEwen 1977, Feder 1984).

What exactly does testosterone do in the brain, and what does brain androgenization mean in terms of neuronal structure and organization? To begin with, rat studies show selected areas in the brain where testosterone concentrates, and these areas include the hypothalamus, the pre-optic area, the amygdala, the midbrain, and the spinal cord. Within these regions are specialized neurons that contain protein receptors fitted for estradiol. Testosterone molecules enter such cells, convert to estradiol, and link up with the receptors. The protein-hormone pair migrate to the cell nucleus and enter it, where they interact with the genes to affect the program for protein synthesis (figures 2.31, 2.32).

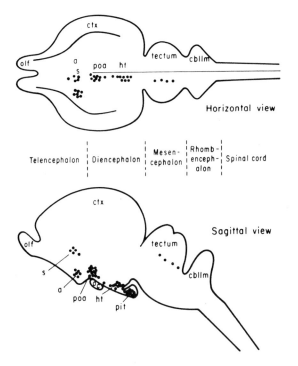

Figure 2.31
Abstract representation of a "generalized vertebrate brain," showing locations of estradiol- and testosterone-concentrating neurons common to all vertebrates so far studied. The top drawing is a horizontal view, and the bottom a sagittal view. Black dots represent groups of steroid-concentrating cells. Abbreviations: *a*, amygdala; *cbllm*, cerebellum; *ctx*, cortex; *ht*, nuclei in hypothalamus; *oc*, optic chiasm; *olf*, olfactory bulb; *pit*, pituitary; *poa*, pre-optic area; *s*, septum. (From Morrell and Pfaff 1981.)

Paradoxically, it is estradiol, a female hormone, to which testosterone converts and which articulates the androgenization of the brain. Why then, does the estradiol routinely produced by developing females not itself androgenize the brain? The answer is that in the foetus the liver produces a protective protein—alphafetoprotein—that binds estrogen in the blood and prevents it from entering the cerebrospinal fluid and so from reaching the brain. Testosterone is not so bound and accordingly is free to find its way unencumbered to the brain. This answer suggests the following test: administer estradiol directly to the brain of infant female rats to see whether it produces the characteristic androgenization seen in males. The outcome is that it does indeed androgenize the brain of the genetic female (McEwen 1976, McEwen et al. 1974).

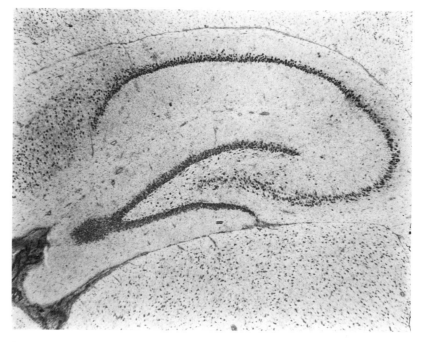

Figure 2.32
Steroid-hormone receptors in rat hippocampus, located by administering a radioactively tagged steroid. (Courtesy John Gerlach and Bruce McEwen.)

Precisely how the hormone-protein pair influence the genetic program for protein synthesis has not yet been uncovered, but it is suspected that there is a connection to neurotransmitter production. Heritage and Stumpf (1980) have found a proximity of hormone-sequestering cells and neurons that release transmitters such as dopamine and norepinephrine, and the project now is to divine the significance of that connection.

The possibility that arborization and connectivity patterns are altered is under exploration. Toran-Allerand (1978) found that hormone-sensitive neurons in vitro respond to application of estradiol by teeming growth of dendrites and axons. Raisman and Field (1973) found distinct patterns of synaptic connections in the pre-optic area of male rat brains. If genetic male rats were deprived of testosterone during their critical period, the synaptic connections of that area resembled the characteristic female pattern. The evidence points most convincingly in these cases to distinctions in circuitry and connectivity as a result of sexual differentiation induced by testosterone.

Morphological differences between male and female rat brains are

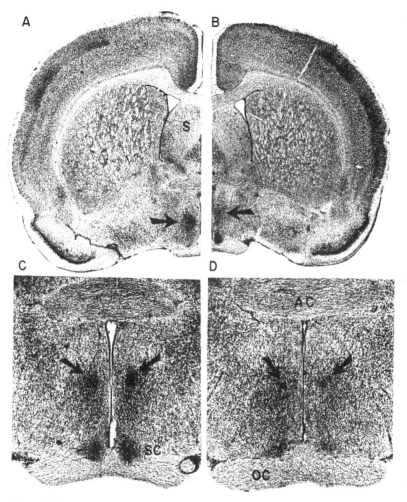

Figure 2.33
Visible differences in male (A and C) and female (B and D) rat brains. Tissue is stained with thionin, which stains acidic structures in cell bodies. Arrows point to medial preoptic nucleus (in the hypothalamus), which appears to be more densely packed and well defined in the male. (From R. A. Gorski 1979b.)

visible with the naked eye. Gorski et al. (1978) found an area near the hypothalamus that, when stained, shows a large, well-formed nucleus of cells in the male and a much smaller, diffuse pattern in the female (figure 2.33). Legions of outstanding questions present themselves here, not the least of which is how differentiation in neuronal morphology explains the dimorphism in behavior. Gradually answers are being pieced together, and the search for connections

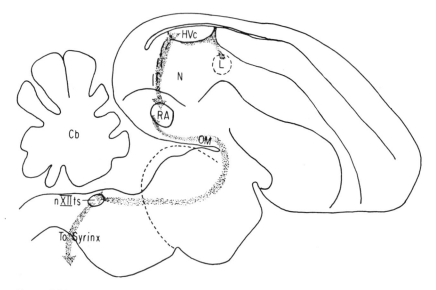

Figure 2.34
Drawing of a sagittal section of the brain of an adult male canary. HVc and RA are the two forebrain nuclei involved in song control. L, the auditory projection of the caudal neostriatum (N), sends fibers that end in a field apposed to ventral HVc, presumably enabling the learning of a song repertoire by reference to auditory information. nXII is the caudal half of the hypoglossal nucleus, formed by the motor neurons that innervate the muscles of the trachea and syrinx. Cb is the cerebellum. (From Nottebohm 1981.)

between steroid-sensitive neurons and reproductive behavior is beginning to yield impressive results. For example, male mating vocalizations in a range of different bird species are mediated by specialized nuclei whose neurons are steroid binding. Nottebohm has found in canary brains a pair of forebrain nuclei[5] that are large in males and small in females, and whose size can be manipulated by manipulating the availability of testosterone (figure 2.34) (Nottebohm 1981, De-Voogd and Nottebohm 1981). In canaries only the male is a songster, and Nottebohm has shown that well-developed nuclei are essential in the canary's learning and producing his song. Castrated males have diminished song-control nuclei and cease to sing; females ovarectomized and given testosterone grow song-control nuclei and learn to sing, albeit not with the customary virtuosity of intact males. Similar connections have been found in zebra finches by Konishi and Gurney (1982), in the oyster toadfish by Fine et al. (1982), and in frogs by Kelley (1980).

And what of our brains—do they too show sexual differentiation? By now it is evident that it is not so much a question of *whether* there is sexual dimorphism in the brains of humans but of how much, what kind, whether there are any differences in cognitive capacities, and in what dimensions of behavior it shows up. Evolution is not likely to have been able to disengage the deeply embedded binding specificity of gonadal hormones in the brain from the rest of the program for brain development and maturation of gonads. Sex is nothing if not basic, and although small-scale modification of surface features of the reproductive package is not improbable (for example, receptivity of the female outside the estrus period—humans, pygmy chimpanzees, rhesus monkeys, macaque monkeys), modification of deep principles that are fundamental to a wide range of structural elements is wholly improbable. Moreover, what we know from pathological studies in human endocrinology confirms rather than falsifies the hypothesis that humans share with other animals a sexual differentiation of the brain.

Already mentioned was the condition known as androgen insensitivity, where the organism cannot use the testosterone it generates. Though there are no discernible effects on genetic females, genetic males with this condition are both phenotypically female and female in sexual preference. On the other hand, human females subjected to androgen in utero as a result of a genetically determined defect in the functioning of the adrenal gland have genitalia masculinized in varying degrees, though their internal reproductive organs are female. These females show varying degrees of masculinized behavior, as measured in terms of playmates preferred, initiation of rough-and-tumble fighting, and intense energy expenditure. These tendencies persist despite surgical correction of genitalia, hormone replacement therapy, and being raised as females, although most are heterosexual (Ehrhardt and Baker 1974).

Pioneer studies in lateralization of function also point to some behavioral differences between male and female children in the degree of hemispheric specialization, which has led to the speculation that male brains are more thoroughly lateralized than female brains (Witelson 1976, Waber 1976). In a study on rhesus monkeys in which an area of the prefrontal cortex was lesioned, Goldman and her colleagues (1974) found sex-dependent effects on a variety of tests requiring spatial discrimination. Male monkeys, both adults and infants, were impaired on the tests, whereas only female *adults* were impaired. Young females were unaffected. The results were taken to imply a dimorphism in the development of prefrontal cortex subserving the cognitive processes involved. This performance difference was abolished in females prenatally exposed to androgen. An anatomical difference in the caudal (rear) portion of the corpus callosum of humans has been found; in females it tends to be larger and more bulbous than in males (de Lacoste-Utamsing and Holloway 1982). What this implies for psychological functions is not known.

Probably human male brains are androgenized in varying degrees and female brains are feminized in varying degrees, but how this shows itself in cognitive capacities, emotional responses, social interaction, and so on, is very much an open and empirically approachable question. It would not be surprising if the differences were found to have only a rough and approximate fit to current North American attitudes concerning what is masculine in behavior and what is feminine. Certainly the sheer existence of differentiation in neural morphology should not encourage a rejuvenation of the superstitions revered in some one culture or other. Folk tales specifying manliness as typified by sporting competitiveness and saloon camaraderie, and femininity as typified by lace and lullabies in the nursery, should not be mistaken for empirically tried and true theory.

Ethological studies are of tremendous importance to the enterprise, and it should not be assumed that available data confirm the prevailing conceits of folk sociology. Even among primates there is stunning diversity in sexually dimorphic behavior and in social structure. In some species, for example the hamadryas baboon, care of the offspring is a female task (Kummer 1968); in others, such as the marmoset, tending the young is, apart from suckling, a shared affair (Jolly 1972); in still others (the Barbary macaque) all males of the troop casually share in helping tend the infants. Some primates are largely solitary (orangutans), some have monogamous pair-bonding (marmosets), some have harems (hamadryas baboons), some are promiscuous (Anubis baboons), and in some species the females make a regular circuit of the appropriate males (Barbary macaques).

Competitiveness seen in females may be a function of species, social structure, the sex of an intruder, the availability of food and suitable males, and so on, but entirely absent it demonstrably is not. Sexual dimorphism tends to be accentuated in polygynous species, but it is too early to tell what, if anything, this implies about humans (Hrdy 1981, Krebs and Davies 1978).

The difficult thing about studying sexual dimorphism in humans is objectivity, for there is a fatal tendency to search selectively for facts to confirm a coddled hypothesis. Coddled science is bad science, and so it will be here. The degree to which culture and education overlie such hard-wired dispositions as exist is also an empirical question, not to be settled by culturally selective anthropology or species-selective ethology. Assuming that not all social behavior is hard wired, then the educational and cultural overlay we choose is a function of what we value, and this, finally, is a moral matter. All things considered, I believe we should welcome research on sexual differentiation in neuronal morphology, though the swill that can be expected from the popular press will doubtless smother some enthusiasm. Still, it is better to know than not to know.

Selected Readings

Akil, Huda, S. J. Watson, E. Young, M. E. Lewis, H. Khachaturian, and J. M. Walker (1984). Endogenous opioids: Biology and function. *Annual Review of Neuroscience* 7:223–255.

Bjorklund, Anders, and Ulf Stenevi (1984). Intracerebral neural implants: Neuronal replacement and reconstruction of damaged circuitries. *Annual Review of Neuroscience* 7:279–308.

Bullock, T. H., R. Orkand, and A. Grinnell (1977). *Introduction to nervous systems.* San Francisco: W. H. Freeman.

Cooper, J. R., F. E. Bloom, and R. H. Roth (1982). *The biochemical basis of neuropharmacology.* 2nd ed. New York: Oxford University Press.

DeVoogd, T. J., and F. Nottebohm (1981). Sex differences in dendritic morphology of a song control nucleus in the canary: A quantitative Golgi study. *Journal of Comparative Neurology* 196:309–316.

Feder, H. H. (1984). Hormones and sexual behavior. *Annual Review of Psychology* 35:165–200.

Hawkins, Robert D., and Eric R. Kandel (1984). Steps toward a cell-biological alphabet for elementary forms of learning. In *Neurobiology of learning and memory*, ed. G. Lynch, J. L. McGaugh, and N. M. Weinberger, 385–404. New York: Guilford.

Henn, Fritz A., and Henry A. Nasrallah, eds. (1982). *Schizophrenia as a brain disease.* New York: Oxford University Press.

Iverson, Leslie L. (1979). The chemistry of the brain. *Scientific American* 241/3:134–149.

Iverson, Leslie L., and Martin M. Rosser (1984). Human learning and memory dysfunction: Neurochemical changes in senile dementia. In *Neurobiology of learning and memory*, ed. G. Lynch, J. L. McGaugh, and N. M. Weinberger, 363–367. New York: Guilford.

Kandel, Eric, and James H. Schwartz, eds. (1981). *Principles of neural science.* New York, Amsterdam, Oxford: Elsevier/North-Holland.

Shepherd, Gordon M. (1983). *Neurobiology.* New York: Oxford University Press.

Chapter 3

Functional Neuroanatomy

Understanding the mind may not be as intricate as our vanity hoped or our intellect feared.
Rodolfo Llinás, 1986

3.1 Introduction

If we are to understand how the brain works, we must understand not only the nature of the basic units, the neurons, but also how populations of neurons are configured, such that their orchestrated activity permits the organism to make its way in the world. An impression common outside of neuroscience is that in their organization, nervous systems resemble nothing so much as an endless, untended bramblescape—foreboding, hopelessly tangled, and defiantly intractable. Accordingly, on the bramblescape theory of brain design, figuring out how the brain works is a faintly ludicrous business, since there are too many neurons, too many branches, too many thorns.

The bramblescape theory is terminally naive. Although nervous systems are indeed complex, neuroanatomists have discovered that they are no hodgepodge, but instead are highly orderly and exhibit great regularity in their structural design. As new techniques are devised, and as earlier techniques are pushed into further reaches, new dimensions of structural regimentation reveal themselves. If, as it now seems, more genetic material is devoted to structuring the brain than to structuring any other organ in the body (Bantle and Hahn 1976), then a key element in constructing a theory of what the brain is doing and how it does it must be the physical organization of the brain itself. In a sense, in the nervous system you are who you talk to; therefore, understanding which neurons talk to which is of the essence.

The relation between physiology and anatomy is one of mutual abetting, for as more physiology is brought within scientific ken, more structural data will emerge, which in turn spawns new functional exploration, and so on. Moreover, the distinction between structure and function is not, at bottom, a fundamental division in kinds. Roughly, a concept is functional (physiological) if it specifies the job description; it is structural (anatomical) if it specifies what units in the machine perform the job. The distinction is a relative one, however, inasmuch as concepts can be employed both at one level of description to specify a function executed by structural units and at a higher level of organization to give a structural specification for the higher-level functional concepts. And at a lower level of analysis, the hitherto structural units are characterized functionally relative to the units that execute their lower-level function. As Christensen et al. (1980) put it, ". . . one neuroscientist's mechanism is another's phenomenology" (p. 342). This relativity certainly does not mean that the distinction between structure and function is useless, but only that it cannot be expected to shoulder too much metaphysical weight. (For further discussion, see chapter 10.)

I shall touch on five dimensions of neuronal organization in this chapter: pathways, laminae, topographical maps, columns, and nervous system development. In each case I shall provide only a few examples to illustrate the organizational feature; for a more complete introduction to the organization of nervous systems, see the selected readings at the end of the chapter. There are other dimensions of order, such as lateral inhibition and center-surround organization, which I shall not discuss here. To orient the reader, I will first introduce the principal anatomical divisions in the human brain, relying on the figures to provide supplementary detail.

3.2 Principal Anatomical Divisions

Based largely on features grossly observable in dissection, the traditional anatomical division of the brain distinguishes five main structures (figure 3.1): (1) the telencephalon, which consists of the cerebral hemispheres, (2) the diencephalon, which consists of the thalamus and the hypothalamus, (3) the mesencephalon or midbrain, (4) the metencephalon, which is the cerebellum and the pons, and (5) the medulla oblongata, sometimes called the "myelencephalon." These classifications are still used, though as progress is made in understanding how nervous systems work, how they evolved, and how they develop, different classifications, functionally more revealing, can be expected to emerge.

In humans, the cerebral hemispheres are very large (see figure 2.1) and markedly wrinkled, as the expanding cortical sheet has folded to stay within the confines of a skull small enough for the human female

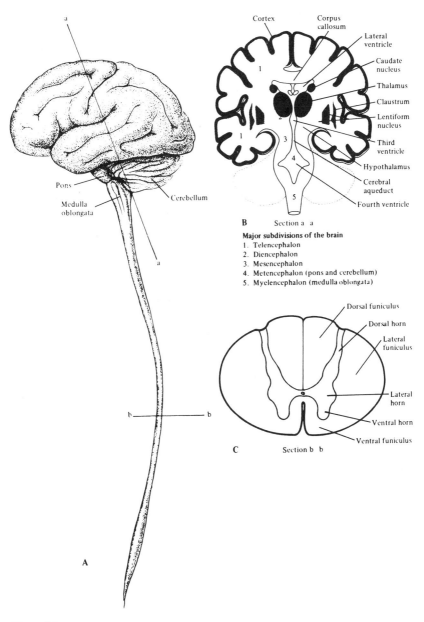

Cortex

Corpus
callosum

Lateral
ventricle

Caudate
nucleus

Thalamus

Claustrum

Lentiform
nucleus

Third
ventricle

Hypothalamus

Cerebral
aqueduct

Fourth ventricle

Pons

Medulla
oblongata

Cerebellum

B   Section a a

Major subdivisions of the brain
1. Telencephalon
2. Diencephalon
3. Mesencephalon
4. Metencephalon (pons and cerebellum)
5. Myelencephalon (medulla oblongata)

Dorsal funiculus

Dorsal horn

Lateral
funiculus

Lateral
horn

Ventral horn

Ventral funiculus

C   Section b b

A

Figure 3.1
The central nervous system consists of (A) the brain and spinal cord. Gray and white matter are distributed as shown in cross sections through (B) the brain and (C) the spinal cord. (From Heimer (1983). *The Human Brain and Spinal Cord.* Copyright © 1983 by Springer-Verlag.)

to deliver at birth. A fissure is called a *sulcus*, and the ridge between sulci is a *gyrus*. The surface of the hemispheres is the *cerebral cortex*, about 2 millimeters deep (figure 3.2), below which are white-matter *tracts* (bundles of nerve fibers), the most renowned of which is perhaps the corpus callosum, which connects the two hemispheres. What differentiates white matter from gray matter is this: the gray matter consists mainly of cell bodies and dendrites and looks gray when fixed in formaldehyde, whereas the white matter consists mainly of axons covered with myelin, which has a whitish appearance.

Major sulci and gyri in the cerebral hemispheres constitute a basis for further anatomical divisions into *lobes* (figure 3.3). A more fine-grained division was proposed by Brodmann (1909), who mapped the brain into fifty distinct regions on the basis of cytoarchitectural criteria (figure 3.4). (See section 3.4 for the explanation of his method.) The Brodmann numbers are still commonly used in identifying cortical regions, though in those regions such as 17 and 18 where physiologists have found functionally important differences within a specific Brodmann area, new numbering systems have become necessary. (See section 3.5.)

Subcortical gray structures important to note for later purposes include the hippocampus and the amygdala, which are located within the temporal lobe and are phylogenetically ancient (figure 3.5). These structures, especially the hippocampus, are currently under intense investigation for their role in memory. (See chapters 4 and 5.) There are other large gray subcortical structures, such as the basal ganglia, which figure importantly in motor control.

The thalamus, considered part of the diencephalon, is also a subcortical gray structure. Shaped like an egg and bearing complementary right and left halves, the thalamus is sometimes regarded as a kind of brain within the brain. It is a major integrating center, and all sensory tracts except the olfactory tract converge here before sensory signals are processed and passed on to the relevant cortical area. The *lateral geniculate nuclei (LGN)* are prominent thalamic structures, one nucleus situated on each side of the thalamus, toward the rear. (By "nucleus" is typically meant a well-differentiated clump of cell bodies and dendrites; in effect, the internal clumpy analogue of the outer rind-like cortex.) The LGN are recipients of massive projections from the retina and in turn project massively to specific areas of the cerebral cortex.

The midbrain (mesencephalon) contains a variety of structures that function as integration and relay centers for incoming and outgoing signals, and it is the connecting point for several cranial nerves con-

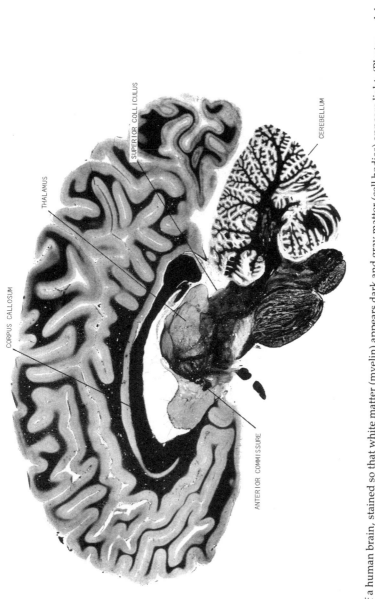

CORPUS CALLOSUM

THALAMUS

SUPERIOR COLLICULUS

CEREBELLUM

ANTERIOR COMMISSURE

Figure 3.2
Sagittal section of a human brain, stained so that white matter (myelin) appears dark and gray matter (cell bodies) appears light. (Photograph by Van Hoesen and Reimann from the Yakovlev Collection, appearing in Heimer (1983). *The Human Brain and Spinal Cord.* Copyright © 1983 by Springer-Verlag.)

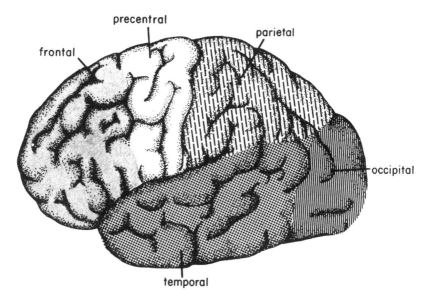

Figure 3.3
Major subdivisions of the brain in relation to prominent sulci and gyri. (From Thompson (1975). *Introduction to Physiological Psychology*. New York: Harper and Row.)

trolling movement of the eyeballs. On the dorsal side, seen by lifting up the cerebrum, are two pairs of lumps—the *superior colliculus* (see figure 3.2), which is important for visual reflexes, and the *inferior colliculus*, which integrates incoming auditory signals. The *reticular formation*, a diffuse feltwork of neurons implicated in arousal and in the cycles of sleeping, dreaming, and waking, is prominent in the midbrain, but extends from the thalamus to the medulla. Also found in the midbrain are nuclei for the oculomotor nerve; nuclei for the trigeminal nerve, which carries afferent information from the teeth, face, and sinuses; nuclei subserving motor control that are inhibited during dreaming ostensibly to prevent dream-correlated movement; and the substantia nigra, whose atrophy is linked to Parkinson's disease.

The cerebellum and the pons are the principal anatomical structures of the metencephalon. The cerebellum, deeply fissured in humans and other primates (see figure 3.2), mediates motor coordination and has a highly regular, and therefore inviting, pattern of cellular organization and connectivity. It will be discussed further in illustrating hypotheses in theoretical neurobiology in chapter 10. The medulla contains nuclei controlling vital functions such as heartbeat and respiration, and it is the controlling point for more cranial

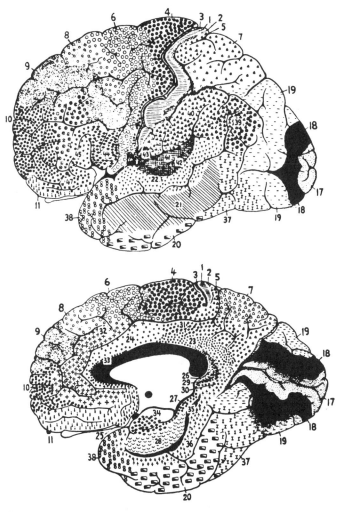

Figure 3.4
Brodmann's (1909) areas of the cerebral cortex, based on cytoarchitectural criteria.

nerves, including the facial, cochlear, and vestibular nerves. The medulla shades off into the spinal cord, which extends down the spinal column. The spinal cord contains descending tracts, most of which figure in motor control, and ascending tracts, which carry sensory signals. It also contains the wiring to execute various reflexes independently of input from the brain, such as the relatively simple knee-jerk reflex and, at least in cats, the much more complex business of smoothly rhythmic locomotion.

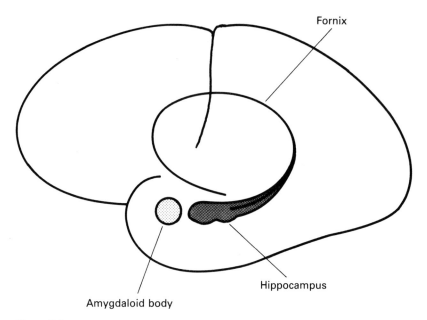

Figure 3.5
Schematic diagram showing the relative positions deep within the brain of the hippocampus, the amygdaloid body, and the fornix, as they would be seen if the brain were transparent. (From Heimer (1983). *The Human Brain and Spinal Cord*. Copyright © 1983 by Springer-Verlag.)

Deep within these brain structures are the *ventricles*, cavities filled with cerebrospinal fluid (CSF) (figures 2.7 and 3.6). The CSF is cooked up by specialized structures in the ventricles called the choroid plexus, and a trickle of CSF emerges from ventricle openings near the cerebellum to bathe the brain within the protective sheath of dura. Blockage of the cerebral aqueduct during prenatal development causes an excessive accumulation of CSF in the ventricles, which expands them abnormally and results in the condition known as hydrocephalus.

3.3   Pathways and Tracts

If a feather touches your hand, sensory neurons detect the event and you feel a typical sensation at the touched spot. Where does the signal from the peripheral neurons go such that you end up having the feeling and knowing the location of the contact? If you fixate an object while turning your head, your eyes move so as to compensate

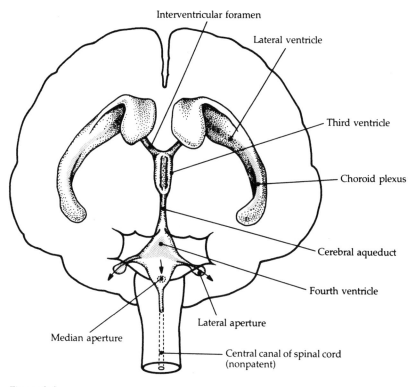

Figure 3.6
The brain's ventricles. Frontal view of the brain, as if it were transparent, showing the cavernous areas that are filled with cerebrospinal fluid (CSF). Three tiny apertures, a median and two lateral apertures, permit the escape of CSF into the narrow space between the brain and its membrane overcoats. (From Angevine and Cotman (1981). *Principles of Neuroanatomy*. New York: Oxford University Press.)

for the movement of your head. What is the circuitry that sustains the tracking?

To answer such questions, neuroanatomists have charted the pathways of neurons from the periphery, in the spinal cord, and in the brain itself. Early research relied heavily on two techniques: (1) the injection of special dyes that were taken up by neurons, and (2) damaging a neuron, giving it time to degenerate down its length, and then tracing the line of degeneration. Sometimes neurons postsynaptic to the damaged neuron also show atrophying responses to the damage, and this permits tracing the pathway further.

Recently it was found that radioactively labeled amino acids are taken up by neurons, incorporated into proteins, and then shipped by axonal transport down the length of the axon. Sometimes the labeled material moves across the synaptic junction and is further taken up by the postsynaptic neuron and shipped to its axon terminus. An enzyme, horseradish peroxidase, has the singular advantage of moving in the other direction. Placed at the axon terminal, it will be taken up and transported by the retrograde system *up* the axon to the cell body, and will fill the entire neuron in all its ramifications. Using both techniques, a double labeling of pathways can be performed that permits great precision in determining the projection profile of a group of neurons. These techniques have been invaluable in charting the pathway organization in nervous systems. Physiological techniques, which involve electrical stimulation at one site and recording from other sites, are equally crucial and are used in conjunction with the anatomical methods (Heimer and Robards 1981).

Results using assorted methods have converged, and consequently a great deal has been uncovered concerning the routes traversed by sensory and motor signals in the CNS, though the picture is less complete for humans than for other animals, and even in the most studied preparations there remain many gaps in detail. To illustrate some of what has been established, consider the pathways in the auditory system (figure 3.7), showing substantial but incomplete cross-over of auditory nerve fibers in the brain stem and four synaptic junctions between the auditory nerve and the cortex. The somatosensory system has two quite distinct routes (figure 3.8). The lemniscal system subserves the perception of a variety of sensations, including movement of hairs, fine touch, deep pressure, and limb position. This system has a well-defined pathway up the spinal cord, synapsing in a specific area of the thalamus and then projecting to a well-defined area of the cortex.

The second major route is the spinothalamic system, thought to signal mainly painful stimuli and temperature. This pathway occupies a quite different space in the spinal cord, terminates in its own location of the thalamus, and then projects to the cortex.

The vestibulo-ocular reflex (VOR) enables an organism to track an object smoothly even while the head is moving in any of its possible parameters. The crucial part of the circuit for this reflex originates in the vestibular apparatus in the inner ear, where receptor neurons detect acceleration of fluid in their semicircular canal and project to the vestibular nuclei in the brain stem and then to the oculomotor nerves that direct the extraocular muscles to move the eyeball (figure 3.9). Therefore, there are only three synapses between the receptor neurons in the vestibular apparatus and the ocular muscles control-

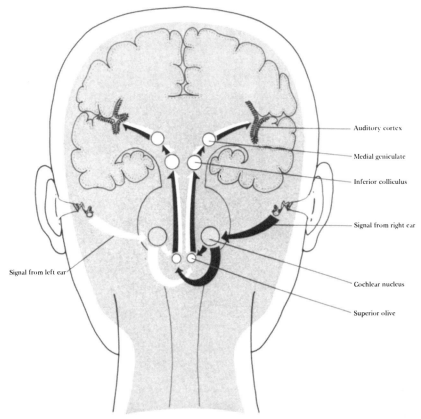

Figure 3.7
Pathways to auditory cortex from the ear. Back view of the brain with coronal section. (From Lindsay and Norman (1977). *Human Information Processing*. 2nd ed. New York: Academic Press.)

ling eyeball movement. This, together with the fact that the ocular muscles are not used to apply force to external loads (as our arm muscles are when we heft a hammer, for example) has made the VOR a system whose functional properties are especially amenable to study. One functional theory to explain how it works will be discussed in chapter 10. (It should be mentioned, however, that the VOR is not entirely controlled by signals in those circuits, since there are influences from other sources, for example from the cerebellum.)

The visual system has two main pathways: (1) from the retina to the superior colliculus, to the cortex, and (2) from the retina to the LGN, to the cortex. It is the latter pathway that is essential for experienced visual perception in humans, and it has been argued that the signals

A. SPINOTHALAMIC PATHWAY

B. LEMNISCAL PATHWAY

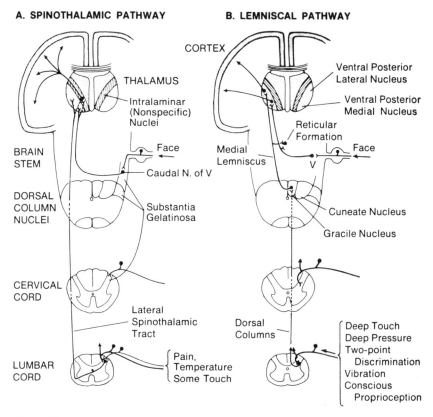

Figure 3.8
Ascending pathways of the somatosensory system. (From Shepherd (1983). *Neurobiology*. New York: Oxford University Press.)

from the collicular route are the basis for the perceptual judgments of blindsight patients (see chapter 5). The optic nerve carrying fibers from each eyeball divides at the optic chiasm, with half the fibers crossing over and half proceeding on the same side. As a result, all the fibers representing the left visual field (originating on the right hemiretina) in each eye go to the right hemisphere, and all the fibers representing the right visual field (originating on the left hemiretina) go to the left hemisphere (figure 3.10). The first synaptic relay is in the LGN, where fibers layer themselves according to the retina of origin. In primates the fibers from the right eye occupy laminae 5, 3, and 2, and fibers from the left eye occupy laminae 6, 4, and 1. (Laminae are discussed in the next section.) After leaving the LGN, fibers proceed in orderly fashion to specified layers in specified areas of the cortex. A large number go to area 17, otherwise known as the *primary visual*

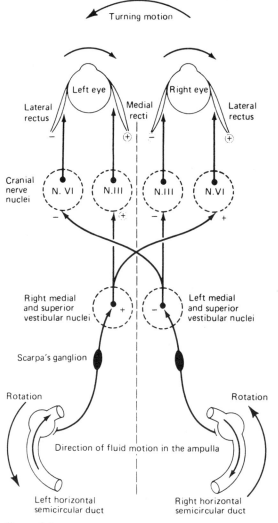

Figure 3.9
Schematic circuit diagram for the initial phase of the vestibulo-ocular reflex arc. In-
crease (+) or decrease (−) in rate of firing along a particular pathway is indicated.
(Reprinted by permission of the publisher from J. P. Kelly (1981b). Ch. 35 of *Principles of
Neural Science*, ed. E. R. Kandel and J. H. Schwartz, pp. 406–418. Copyright © 1981 by
Elsevier Science Publishing Co., Inc.)

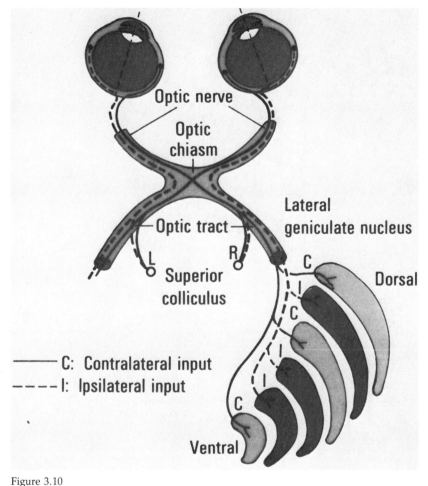

Figure 3.10
Projection of the retinas upon the superior colliculus and the lateral geniculate nucleus.
(Modified from J. P. Kelly 1981a.)

cortex or the *striate cortex* and there are massive reciprocal connections
going from the cortex back to the LGN.

On the classical conception, visual processing is hierarchical, and
information moves up through a series of levels from the LGN, to the
primary visual cortex, to the "association cortex," and onward, becoming more abstract, cross-modal, and interpreted at each level.
Most simply, the idea is that successive levels involve feature extrac-
tion of an increasingly abstract type—ascending, for example, from
cells that respond to brightness contrast, to cells that respond to light

boundaries in specific orientations in specific parts of the visual field, to cells that respond to light boundaries in divergent parts of the visual field, to cells that respond to changes in boundaries (corners and edges) (Hubel and Wiesel 1965, 1977). Higher yet are cells responding preferentially to a hand, or to a conspecific face, independently of stimulus size and position (Gross, Rocha-Miranda, and Bender 1972, Desimone et al. 1984). Finally, the logic leads us to conjecture, perhaps there are cells whose conditions of response are even more abstract and complex, such as a cell that would respond uniquely to the presence of Grandmother—hence the celebrated "grandmother cell" hypothesis (Barlow 1972).

The classical conception, however, is now widely regarded as requiring substantial revision. (Merzenich and Kaas 1980, Stone and Dreher 1982, Stone 1983). The most important factor here is that structural and functional differences have been discovered among the ganglion cells leaving the retina, and these differences are systematically preserved in later aspects of the projection system. This in turn has led to the hypothesis that what was believed to be a straightforward *sequential* organization is really (or is additionally) a diversely *parallel* organization, with at least three distinct streams (figure 3.11). Retinal ganglion cells divide into three types, referred to simply as X, Y, and W fibers. Each type has distinct receptive field properties, response properties, conduction velocities, and originating locations on the retina; each also has a distinctive projection pattern to the LGN (and for W and Y cells, to the superior colliculus) and finally to the striate cortex.

Part of what encouraged the classical conception was the finding by Hubel and Wiesel (1977) that many cells in area 17 are tuned to respond to highly specific events. For example, cells in a certain column are maximally responsive when a vertical bar of light is presented to the animal; cells in an adjacent column are maximally responsive to a bar of light a few degrees off the vertical; and so forth. Other cells in the striate cortex are maximally responsive to changes in boundaries. Additionally, Hubel and Wiesel had figured out how the response properties of what they called "complex cells" *could be* a function of convergent input from sets of simple cells, and how the response properties of "hypercomplex cells" *could be* the function of convergent input from complex cells. The feature-extraction hypothesis seemed compelling and elegant, and it quickly became the standard textbook account. One crucial test of the hypothesis is this: destruction of area 17 should entail destruction of the first cortical feature-extraction mechanism, with the result that pattern recognition should not be possible in animals with lesions to this area.

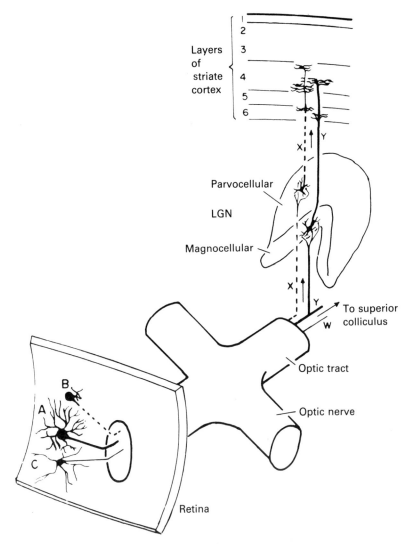

Figure 3.11
Schematic representation of the parallel organization of the pathways from retina to
cortex in the monkey. Three of the major morphological classes of retinal ganglion cells
are represented; the A and B cells are assumed to be the counterparts of the physiologically distinguished Y- and X-like cells, and the C cells to be the counterparts of one of
the subgroups of W-like ganglion cells. The X and Y cells project to the lateral geniculate nucleus (LGN), the W- and Y-like cells to the superior colliculus (not shown).
Within the LGN, X cells terminate in the upper (parvocellular) laminae, Y cells in the
lower (magnocellular) laminae. Their activities are separately relayed to striate cortex
(area 17), where they terminate in different laminae and activate different groups of
cortical cells. (From Stone and Dreher 1982.)

Surprisingly, experiments by Sprague, Berlucchi, and their colleagues have consistently failed to bear out the prediction. Lesions to areas 17–18 result in diminution of visual acuity, but they do not destroy the capacity to discriminate patterns or even to learn new pattern discriminations (Sprague et al. 1977, Berlucchi and Sprague 1981). On the other hand, destruction of extrastriate areas does impair pattern discrimination. These experiments clearly imply that extrastriate cortical areas make some independent contribution to pattern recognition, and together with the neuroanatomical and neurophysiological discoveries, they argue for a parallel-processing model for vision. What *functional* principles might be implemented by such a parallel architecture remain obscure, but some possibilities are considered in chapter 10.

Also problematic for the classical hierarchical conception are recent discoveries showing that the cortex has not merely one or two areas whose cells are arranged in a topographic map representing the retina, but that it abounds in topographic maps. Topographic mapping is the dimension of orderliness featured in the next subsection, and the significance of multiple maps will be raised there.

It should finally be noted that another classification for pathways uses neurochemical criteria, identifying a pathway according to the characteristic neurochemical found in the axons of the group. For example, the locus coeruleus is a small nucleus in the brainstem, the axons projecting from which release norepinephrine (figure 3.12). Axons from this structure are interesting because they project throughout the brain, including all over the cerebral cortex, the spinal cord, and the cerebellum. This unusually wide spread of projections has led to the functional conjecture that the locus coeruleus system serves a regulatory role, perhaps in regulating attentional and arousal states in the brain as a whole. Axons bearing dopamine, axons bearing serotonin, and so forth, are slowly being identified, and the neuron groups in question are consequently sometimes referred to as "the dopamine system" "the serotonin system," and so forth. (See also figure 2.29.) The extent to which the neurochemical classification of pathways converges with other classifications is still undetermined.

Though I have provided merely a glimpse in this section into what is known about tracts and pathways, I trust it will nonetheless be enough to fortify my claim that understanding structure is essential for figuring out theories of function. (See selected readings at the chapter end.)

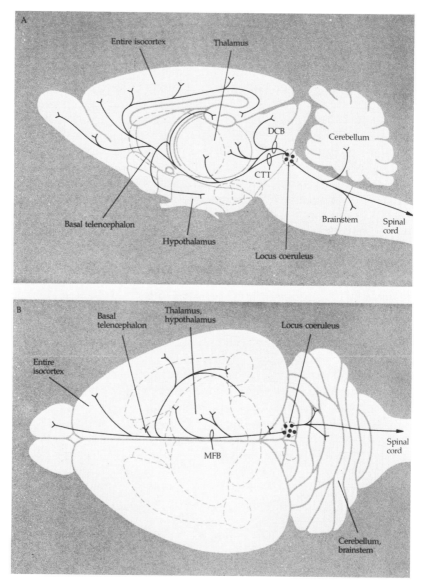

Figure 3.12
Locus coeruleus norepinephrine system. (From Angevine and Cotman (1981). *Principles of Neuroanatomy*. New York: Oxford University Press.)

3.4   The Laminar Structure of the Cortex

It has long been known that the cortex of the cerebral hemispheres is not just a uniform slab of neural tissue but is stratified into six layers or *laminae*. The original basis for the claim was anatomical and depended on observations of the segregation of cell types and of cell processes to distinct levels (figure 3.13). (See also figure 1.6.) Staining techniques make it possible to observe the stratification, and it can be seen, for example, that the topmost layer contains few cell bodies, that layer V contains many large pyramidal cells, that layer IV contains no pyramidal cells, and so forth.

Nor is the laminar profile constant across diverse areas of the cortex. For example, in a comparison of the motor cortex and the sensory cortex some interesting differences emerge. In the motor cortex layer V is thick and is richly populated by large pyramidal cells, whereas layer IV is relatively thin and is sparsely populated by incoming fibers terminating on cells at that level. The somatosensory cortex has the reverse pattern. It was on the basis of such cytoarchitectural features that Brodmann segmented the cerebral cortex into fifty so-called Brodmann areas. (See again figure 3.4.)

What is the functional significance of laminar organization? The answer has been elusive, but new data reinforce the conviction that functional significance it must indeed have, if we could but light upon it. For example, it has been found that one specific cell type, the pyramidal cells, are the dominant efferent cells, and that pyramidal cells at distinct levels methodically project to specific areas (figure 3.14). For example, pyramidal cells from layer III make callosal connections, whereas those connecting to the spinal cord and superior colliculus come only from layer V. Afferent fibers also have a methodical termination pattern: fibers from the thalamus terminate largely in the middle layers, callosal fibers and incoming ipsilateral cortical fibers terminate in the same layer from which they originated (Jones 1981). Each class of cells originating in the retina projects to a specific lamina of the LGN, whose cells in turn terminate in specific laminae in areas 17 and 18 (figure 3.11). The topmost layer is scanty in cell bodies and contains more horizontal dendritic connections. It is the last to develop in neurogenesis, and it is phylogenetically more recent.

Structures other than the cerebral cortex also exhibit a laminar organization. The superior colliculus, the cerebellum, the thalamus, the olfactory lobe, and the hippocampus all follow the stratification principle. In addition to its horizontal stratification, the cortex also has a highly structured *vertical* organization in virtue of which narrow cy-

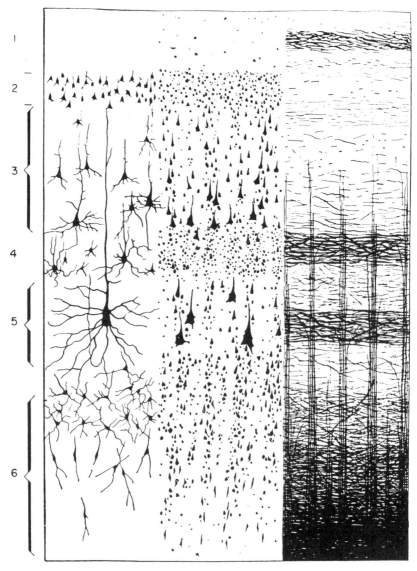

Figure 3.13
A general schema of the laminar nature of the cerebral cortex, based on data derived from three different staining techniques. Left, Golgi method; center, Nissl method; right, Weigert myelin stain. (From Ranson and Clark (1959). *The Anatomy of the Nervous System.* 10th ed. Philadelphia: Saunders.)

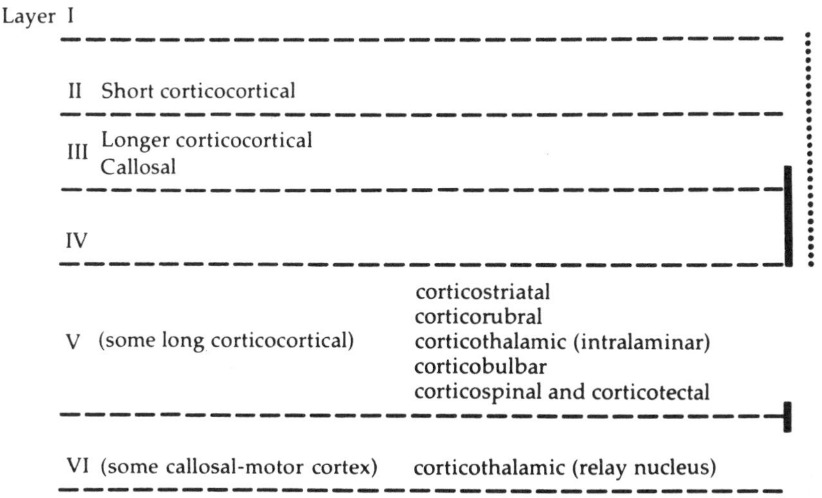

Layer I

II   Short corticocortical

III   Longer corticocortical
      Callosal

IV

V   (some long corticocortical)   corticostriatal
                                     corticorubral
                                     corticothalamic (intralaminar)
                                     corticobulbar
                                     corticospinal and corticotectal

VI   (some callosal-motor cortex)   corticothalamic (relay nucleus)

Figure 3.14
Laminar distribution of somata of cortical efferent (pyramidal) cells in monkeys. Vertical lines to right indicate zones of termination in sensory cortex of thalamic (solid lines)
and corticocortical (interrupted line) afferents. In areas outside the primary sensory
areas, thalamic fibers do not terminate in layer IV. (From Jones (1981). In *The Organization of the Cerebral Cortex*, ed. F. O. Schmitt et al. Cambridge, Mass.: MIT Press.)

lindrical aggregations of cells form rich interconnections. This columnar organization superimposed on the laminar organization will be
discussed below.

Such systematicity strongly indicates that the laminar structure is
the brain's solution to a fundamental functional problem, or that
some sort of economy in information processing is achieved by such
precise stratification (Van Essen and Maunsell 1983). Exactly what the
problem-solution pair is, however, has not been obvious. In this discussion the question of theory may be usefully delayed until further
dimensions of order have been discussed, since the various dimensions of order may well be a *package* solution to certain functional
problems, rather than independent solutions to independent problems. (See also chapter 10.)

3.5   Topographic Maps in Nervous Systems

One of the most promising and puzzling discoveries about the organization of nervous systems is that many structures abide by a
principle of topographic mapping, whereby neighborhood relations
of cells at one periphery are preserved in the arrangement of cells at
other locations in the projection system. If we think of the neurons at

the sensory periphery as forming a receptor sheet, then deformed versions of that sheet are represented in a large number of CNS regions. Whatever the functional principle served, it must be served successfully, since wide areas of the cerebral cortex as well as other structures abound in such maps, and new research is turning up more all the time.

In order to constrain the theorizing about what the functional principle is, it will be necessary to provide a fuller portrait of topographic maps in nervous systems. The standard methods for determining a topographic arrangement exploit neuroanatomical facts and crucially involve electrophysiological techniques. For sensory systems the basic strategy is to stimulate at the periphery and record from cells in the area under study. For motor systems the strategy is to stimulate centrally and record effects further downstream. The most thoroughly studied animals are the cat and various species of monkey, and there are interesting differences between species. Much less is known about this dimension of order in the human cortex since clinical justification rarely exists for the relevant experiments. Nevertheless, available data indicate that topographic mapping is a very general principle of organization also applicable to the human brain. (See especially chapter 5 and Penfield and Roberts 1959.)

Retinotopic Maps
As we have seen, retinal ganglion cells terminating in the LGN are neatly arranged in six laminae. It has also been found that the cells in each lamina are arranged in a topographic representation of the retina. In other words, adjacent cells have adjacent receptive fields, and more specifically, the spatial relations on the retina are preserved in the spatial organization of the neurons. (The receptive field of a cell is the area in the visual field that evokes a maximal response in the cell in question.) Additionally, all of the six maps in the LGN are in visuotopic register, so that a perpendicular through the LGN touches the same part of each retinal field. This arrangement is believed to subserve the stereoscopic functions executed in cortical visual areas of primates (Allman 1977).

The superior colliculus is also a laminar structure, and a number of its principal layers sustain a map of the relevant periphery. The topmost level is retinotopic, and the bottommost layer appears to be a motor map. When a given location on the motor map is stimulated, the eyes move so as to foveate the location that is the receptive field for the cell in the retinotopic map perpendicular to the stimulated motor cell. This enables the eyes to foveate quickly on targets discerned in peripheral vision, a sort of visual grasp reflex. This suggests that the motor map is a representation of the motor space of the extraocular muscles. (See chapter 10.)

Different classes of cells in the LGN project to specific laminae in the striate cortex, and on the classical conception of how visual information is processed to yield perception, only the striate cortex was thought to have a definable retinotopic map. Other visually responsive areas were thought to be less specific and more interpreted, and were sometimes referred to as "psychological cortex," in contrast to striate cortex, which was believed to be processing at a more basic level in the hierarchy. Unpredictably, it turns out that there are multiple retinotopic maps in the cortex. In the owl monkey, which has been intensively studied by Allman and his colleagues at the California Institute of Technology, sixteen distinct visual areas (monomodal areas) have been found in the cortex of *each* hemisphere. About ten of these have been found to be markedly topographic, displaying a highly ordered and complete representation of the retina, and the remaining seven show topography in varying degrees (figure 3.15). Even "psychological cortex," it appears, has a retinotopic organization. Research on these matters is by no means complete, and as research continues, even more visuotopic areas may be discovered.

Important also in addressing the functional significance of topographic organization are the characteristic ways in which distinct retinotopic maps are distorted. For example, some areas have greater representation for central parts of the visual field than others, and in some the field is split and wrapped around another map (figure 3.15). It is not yet settled how best to interpret the systematic distortion, but Allman (1977) argues that the wraparound design of V-II, together with expanded representation of the center of the visual field in V-I and V-II, may have emerged as the capacity for stereoscopic vision evolved. In a similar vein, Merzenich and Kaas make these observations:

> The split in representation allows a second-order representation (such as V-II or DL) to wrap around a first-order transformation (such as the adjoining V-I or MT) with minimal distortion and matched or congruent borders. This arrangement also permits short interconnections between paired representations. (1980:26)

Also functionally relevant are the massive reciprocal connections between the thalamus and the various cortical areas responsive to visual stimuli, between the superior colliculus and those cortical areas, and finally between one cortical area and another. These connections, moreover, are highly regimented. For example, intracortical projections typically arise from layer II, projections to the opposite

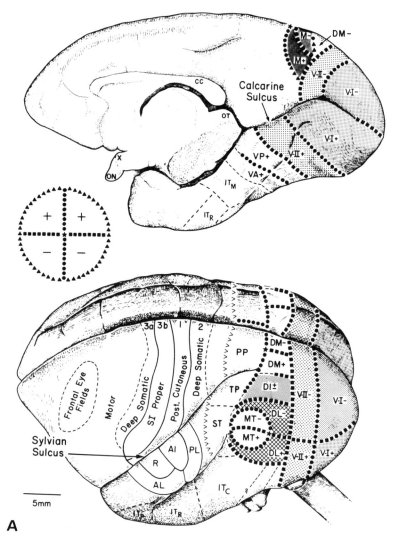

Figure 3.15
(A) Sixteen retinotopic maps have been discovered on the cortex of the owl monkey.
Above is the ventromedial view; below is a dorsolateral view. On the left is a perimeter
chart of the visual field. The symbols on this chart are superimposed on the surface of
the visual cortex. (+) indicates upper quadrant representation; (−), lower quadrants.

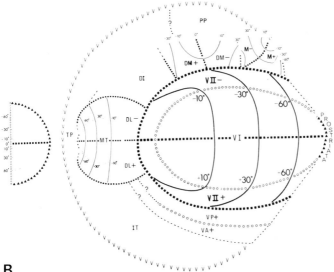

B

Figure 3.15 (continued)

(B) Schematic unfolding of the visual cortex of the left hemisphere of the owl monkey. The unfolded visual cortex is approximately a hemispherical surface, which is viewed from above in this diagram.

Abbreviations: AI, first auditory area; AL, anterolateral auditory area; CC, corpus callosum; DI, dorsointermediate visual area; DL, dorsolateral visual area; DM, dorsomedial visual area; IT, inferotemporal visual cortex (c, caudal; m, medial; r, rostral; p, polar); M, medial visual area; MT, middle temporal visual area; ON, optic nerve; OT, optic tectum; PL, posterolateral auditory area; PP, posterior parietal visual cortex; R, rostral auditory area; ST, superior temporal visual area; TP, temporoparietal visual cortex; VA, ventral anterior visual area; V-I, first visual area; V-II, second visual area; VP, ventral posterior visual area; X, optic chiasm. (From Allman 1982. Reconstructing the evolution of the brain in primates. In *Primate Brain Evolution*, ed. E. Armstrong and D. Falk. New York: Plenum. Based on Allman and Kaas 1971.)

hemisphere arise from lower parts of layer III, and so forth. (See again figure 3.14.)

An additional organizational feature of the visual system is that as cells from the LGN project to specified layers of the striate cortex, they do so in chunks alternately from one eye and then from the other, producing "ocular dominance bands" of neurons in the cortex (Hubel, Wiesel, and LeVay 1977) (figure 3.16). A similar sort of banding of terminating fibers has now been found in the prefrontal cortex, where fibers terminating in the principal sulcus and originating in the homologous area of the contralateral hemisphere form bands, with

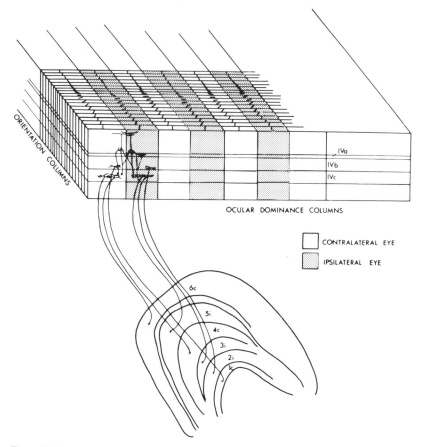

Figure 3.16
Schematic diagram of the postulated columnar organization of the primary visual cortex in the macaque. Cells in a given orientation column (slab) respond preferentially to stimuli in a specific orientation. Neurons in different laminae in the lateral geniculate project to layer IV of the cortex, and interneurons distribute the effects vertically and (to some degree) horizontally. At right angles to the orientation slabs are ocular dominance columns, formed in virtue of the sorting of afferents, either from the right eye or from the left eye. Neurons in a given column are more likely to be driven by stimuli to one eye, either the right or the left. (From Hubel and Wiesel 1972.)

fibers from elsewhere interpolated between them (Goldman-Rakic 1981). In the case of the striate cortex the ocular dominance bands are believed to figure essentially in stereoptic vision. In experiments on cats and monkeys it has been found that if one eyelid is sutured shut during a critical period in infancy, the bands representing that eye are strikingly reduced in width. If the sutures are removed from that lid and the other lid is sutured, then after a period of time the "deprived" cortical bands expand to a more normal width.

The discovery of multiple retinotopic maps on the cortex of primates is of enormous importance, and continued research may reveal yet other maps, less obvious even than those already found. Still, the question of their functional utility remains tantalizing. Why does the brain have these maps? What does it do with them? As Francis Crick has noted (in conversation), we must guard lest our own logic for map use mislead us here. After all, there is no one *in* the brain to look at the maps. It is not as though the maps are read and followed by anyone, so whatever their logic, it is *their* logic.

Cochleotopic Maps
The cochlea, a structure of the ear, is a coiled tube containing specialized membranes, fluids, and organs. In virtue of the structures in the middle ear, certain deformations in the air are transformed into wave patterns in the cochlear fluid, which in turn are transduced into electrical signals in specialized receptor cells (figure 3.17). These signals are transmitted up the auditory pathway to the cerebral cortex, and the final consequence of these activities is that we hear sounds. (For a basic introduction to the auditory system, see Lindsay and Norman 1977; for a more detailed account, see Uttal 1973.)

The cochlea is so constructed that high frequency tones stimulate receptor cells at the base of the cochlea, and progressively lower tones stimulate cells up the length of the cochlea, with the lowest-frequency tones stimulating cells at the cochlear apex. The neighborhood relations in the frequency spectrum are preserved in the axonal layout in the auditory nerve, so that a neuron with a characteristic frequency of, say, 1500 Hz will lie between neurons with characteristic frequencies of 1600 Hz and 1400 Hz.[1] This preservation of neighborhood relations is called a *cochleotopic* or *tonotopic* map, and the orderly mapping of neurons with sound frequencies is preserved at each synaptic station on the way to the cortex: the cochlear nuclei, the superior olivary nuclei, the inferior colliculi, the medial geniculate nuclei of the thalamus, and finally, diverse areas of auditory cortex (figure 3.7). Because each of these integrative nuclei contains divisions that congregate neurons containing distinctive source-specific information,

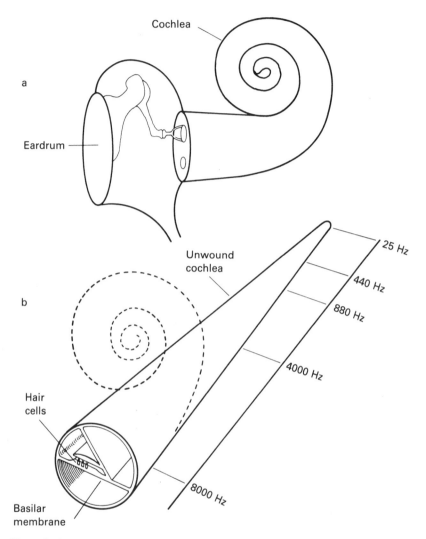

Figure 3.17
(a) Position of the cochlea relative to the eardrum, showing the mechanical delivery of acoustic energy to the base of the cochlea. This particular arrangement serves to match impedances so that vibrations are efficiently transferred from the gaseous medium of the atmosphere to the higher-density liquid medium within the cochlea. (b) The "un-rolled" cochlea. Points along the internal membrane are mechanically resonant to specific frequencies. Membrane motion at a resonant point stimulates the local hair cells. Acoustic frequency is thus spatially coded in the nervous system. (Based on Von Békésy 1960.)

this is not a simple serial processing system, but a system complemented with extensive parallel processing.

There are at least six distinct cochleotopic maps on the temporal cortex of the macaque monkey, and four on that of the owl monkey, each with its own properties and its own source of thalamic neurons (Merzenich and Brugge 1973) (figure 3.18). How many cochleotopic maps are on the human temporal cortex is not yet known, but on the basis of other primate studies it would be surprising if there were fewer than six on each hemisphere. (In at least some animals there is also a degree of auditory mapping in the superior colliculus.) Nor is it yet known whether each representational region has a distinct function or exactly what such functions might be. There is also extensive bilateral representation of sounds from the inferior colliculus on up, so that sounds detected by cells in the right ear, for example, are represented in both right and left hemispheres. These intercalated representations are believed to be the basis for the several binaural "comparators" that integrate information from both ears to enable localization of sound sources (Merzenich and Kaas 1980).

Somatotopic Maps
Sensory receptors in the hand enable us to feel light touch, pressure, vibration, temperature, and pain, and also to know the position of the hand and the joints. Distinct receptor neurons are sensitive to each of these features, and neurons higher in the projection system preserve the modality uniqueness.

Each peripheral neuron has a receptive field such that the neuron will maximally respond when a particular part of the skin, for example, is stimulated with its preferred stimulus—say, light touch. Size of receptive field varies, and some neurons, such as those in the lemniscal system with receptive fields in the skin of the fingers, have much smaller receptive fields than those for the skin of the back. Greater perceptual acuity is achieved with a large group of neurons, each of which has a small receptive field, than with a few neurons, each of which has a large receptive field.

Neurons carrying information from the sensory periphery terminate at selected areas of the thalamus, where they are arranged in a somatotopic representation of the body. These thalamic areas in turn project to selected areas of the cortex, all in very orderly fashion and with substantial reciprocal projections from the cortex. In the cortex neurons are again mapped in such a way as to preserve neighborhood relations of body parts, though there are some interesting discontinuities. Accordingly, neurons responsive to stimuli on the index finger are between neurons responsive to stimuli on the thumb and

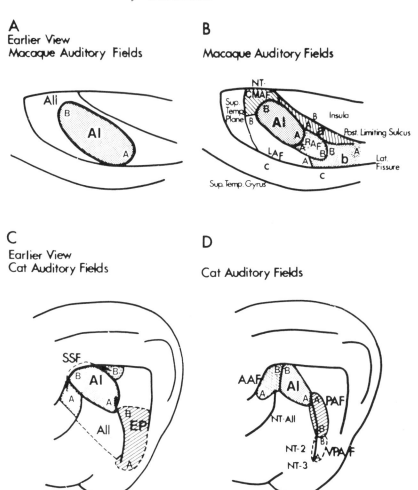

Figure 3.18
Traditional (A and C) and current (B and D) views of the organization of auditory cortex in monkeys and carnivores. In all figures the representations of the cochlear apex (A) and base (B) are indicated in those fields where cochleotopic organization has been described. In the traditional view, only primary (AI) and secondary (AII) auditory fields were described. Later, AI was redefined and five additional auditory fields with distinct architectonic and electrophysiological characteristics were described. Abbreviations: LAF, lateral auditory field; AAF, anterior auditory field; PAF, posterior auditory field; VPAF, ventroposterior field; RAF, rostrolateral field; NT, nontopographic; NT-CMAF, caudomedial auditory field. Fields A and B are shown on a view of the surface of the superior temporal plane and dorsolateral surface of the superior temporal gyrus. (From Merzenich and Kaas 1980.)

those for the middle finger, but distant from those for the big toe or the scalp. This organization yields somatotopic maps on the cortex of the sensory surface, the muscles, and the joints. In general, the lemniscal system exhibits precise mappings of the body onto neurons of the somatosensory cortex. The spinothalamic system projects to different areas, and here mapping is thought to be coarser and less precise. Neurons in this system tend to have larger receptive fields, and individual neurons may be receptive to an assortment of types of stimuli.

Early research indicated one major somatosensory map, designated as SI, and a smaller area, SII, but recent research has revealed many more complete somatotopic maps in the area behind the central sulcus (figure 3.19). Six have already been found in each hemisphere of the owl and macaque monkeys, and the search is not yet complete. Distinct somatotopically arranged areas of cortex appear to be specialized for distinct submodalities, such as joint position, cutaneous stimulation, or "deep somatic" (muscle) parameters. The maps are not simple duplications of one another, and there are important differences between somatotopically mapped regions. The differences range along such parameters as origin of terminating fibers, destiny of projecting fibers, receptive field, and response properties of the neurons. As with retinotopic and cochleotopic maps, it is suspected that the human cortex will be at least as richly endowed with somatotopic maps as are the already investigated species. And for somatosensory processing, as for visual processing, the classical sequential model seems to be ceding ground to a parallel model (Kaas et al. 1981).

One principle governing map distortion is based on the population of neurons representing a particular body area. In the case of certain maps some body areas such as the hands and lips are more represented than others, since those areas have a higher density of receptive neurons, which in turn have smaller receptive fields. It has been found that the amount of cortex activated by a stimulus in a given receptive field is roughly constant, whatever the peripheral area (Sur, Merzenich, and Kaas 1980). This means that when a body part is innervated by many neurons, each of which has a small receptive field, that body part will appear magnified on the cortical map relative to an area in which there are fewer neurons, each of which has a large receptive field. Accordingly, a cortical map may show a much larger area for the fingers than for the trunk.

Other distortions are not so readily explicable. For example, in the owl monkey there are substantial differences between area 3b and

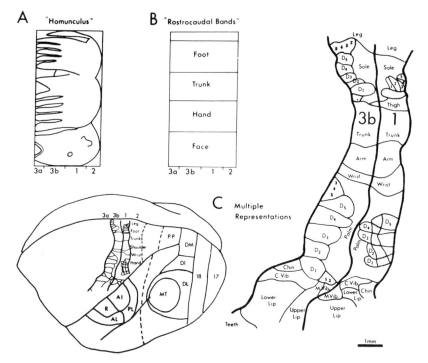

Figure 3.19
Three conceptions of the organization of postcentral parietal somatosensory cortex (SI)
of monkeys, and some details of the two cutaneous representations in owl monkeys.
(A) The traditional concept has been that a single body representation occupies four
architectonic fields. (B) A modification of the traditional concept is that major body
parts are represented across all architectonic fields in bands. (C) Data indicate that the
SI region contains multiple representations. Some of the features of the two cutaneous
representations in areas 3b and 1 are shown on a dorsolateral view of the brain on the
lower left and in more detail on the right. Somatotopic maps are shown in relation to
retinotopic and auditory maps. Portions of cortex activated by given body parts are
outlined. The digits of the hand are numbered. Closer view is given on the right.
Abbreviations: C. vib, chin vibrissae; M. vib, mandibular vibrissae. (From Kaas et al.
1981.)

area 1 in the mapping of the hand, inasmuch as the map in area 3b
has a much more extensive representation of the glabrous surface
than does the map in area 1, and the representation of the back of the
hand is split. The reason for this and what it means for the processing
of somatosensory information is still obscure. But it is hard to stifle
the hunch that topographic relations contain the key to communication between neuronal ensembles.

Maps in the Motor System

Like its sensory cohorts, the motor cortex (area 4) is organized topographically, such that adjacent regions of cortex are connected to adjacent groups of muscles, and this topographic ordering is preserved in the motor aspects of the spinal cord. In the motor cortex the fingers and the tongue have a greater representation on cortical regions than the leg, owing to their higher density of innervation by motor neurons. Area 6, immediately in front of the motor strip, also has a topographic layout, though it is smaller. As mentioned earlier, the superior colliculus too is organized in laminar fashion, and one layer appears to contain a topographic representation of the activity of extraocular muscles controlling eyeball movement. As with cortical mapping of the sensory epithelia, research on motor organization is intensive, and it would not be surprising if less obvious and more abstract motor maps were revealed in areas hitherto suspected to be devoid of them (Asanuma and Rosen 1972, Schiller and Stryker 1972, Robinson 1972).

3.6   Vertical Columns

The cortex, as we have just seen, displays order in the horizontal plane. In work begun by Lorente de Nó in the 1930s, it has been discovered that the cortex also displays a dimension of order in the *vertical* plane. More specifically, it appears that cells aggregate in column-like bundles about 0.5 to 1.0 mm in width. The columns are defined in terms of input-output relationships and intrinsic local circuitry (figure 3.20) (Szentágothai 1975, 1979, Mountcastle 1979, Goldman-Rakic 1981).

The functional role of these columns is by no means fully understood, but it is evident that one basis for the aggregation of neurons into columns is a common termination point for axons originating in focal zones elsewhere—for example, in the thalamus, the homologous area in the contralateral hemisphere, or other cortical areas. As Jones (1981) puts it, these bundles are "punctate zones of terminations." In the case of fibers originating in the thalamus, the modality and spatial properties specific to the thalamic fibers terminating in a focal zone are to some degree imposed on the neurons occupying other lamina in that zone. More simply, this means that a given set of thalamic fibers carrying information about, say, pressure on the left knee will terminate largely in a circumscribed area of the somatosensory cortex, and neurons within the respective narrow vertical column will have related response properties and receptive fields.

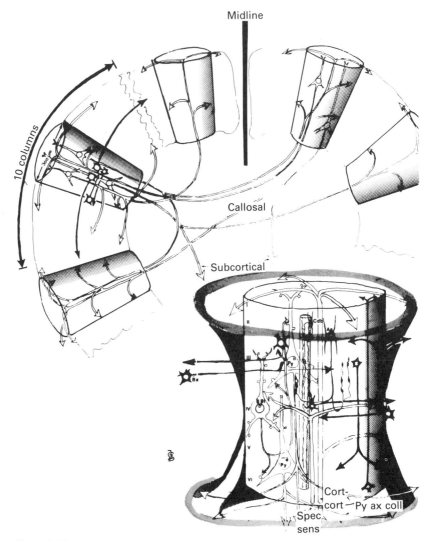

Figure 3.20
Schematic diagram showing the organizational principle of similarly interconnected
columns, each about 150–300 micrometers in diameter and containing about 5,000 cells.
One of the cylindrical columns is shown in more detail (lower right) with a few representative excitatory pyramidal cells (in outline) and a few horizontally-acting longer-
range inhibitory interneurons (in full black). The pattern of intracolumnar arborization
and the stratification of excitation and inhibition give the column a widening at the
surface and base and a corsetting in the middle region. (Courtesy J. Szentágothai.)

In single-cell studies of the somatosensory cortex Mountcastle (1957) found that vertical electrode penetrations encountered cells with a common receptive field, a common profile for adaptation to external stimuli, and a common submodality to which they were responsive. Oblique penetrations encountered units belonging to distinct submodalities, having distinct receptive fields and distinct adaptation profiles. Mountcastle concluded that in its movement on the horizontal axis the obliquely penetrating electrode crossed vertical boundaries of functional modules in the brain. More particularly, the results revealed columnar organization ordered along two dimensions: columns for body surface ranged along one axis (X), and columns for specific submodalities ranged along the orthogonal axis (Y) (figure 3.21).

In analogous research on the striate (primary visual) cortex, Hubel and Wiesel (1968) also found evidence for a columnar organization. As noted earlier, they reported that certain columns of cells are selectively tuned to respond to specific complex stimuli. These columns run roughly orthogonal to the ocular-dominance bands, exhibiting again the two-dimensional ordering of properties. Asanuma (1975) has reported columnar modules in the motor cortex, and others (e.g., Sousa-Pinta 1973, Merzenich and Brugge 1973) have found a columnar organization in cochleotopically mapped areas of the cortex. Once again, a two-dimensional order is revealed: columns arranged along the X axis respond according to frequency, yielding isofrequency bands. Roughly orthogonal to these bands are columns arranged on the Y axis that deal with the binaural aspect of hearing, either by summating responses from the two ears or by inhibiting the ipsilateral response (figure 3.22). This is a splendidly sensible organization for the localization of sounds, since binaural disparity can be employed to determine location only when waves have the same frequency. The intersection of isofrequency columns and binaural processing columns would facilitate such localization (Suga 1977). (For a general discussion of columnar organization, see Mountcastle 1979.)

To this point in the discussion of the hypothesis that the planar laminae of the cortex are crossed by vertical columns, the emphasis has been on the focal terminations of fibers. However, additional physiological features lend credence to the hypothesis that those column-like aggregations must be of fundamental significance for information processing in the cortex. Specifically, there are both *excitatory vertical connections* within the column-like aggregation supplied by one type of interneuron (small and spiny), and *inhibitory connections* made to

Columnar and laminar
organization of cerebral cortex

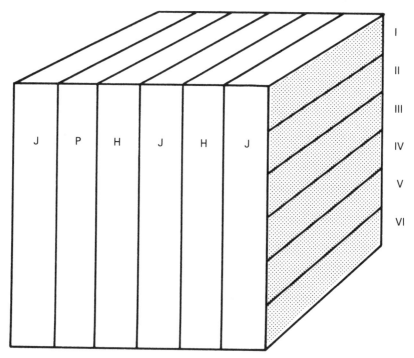

Figure 3.21
Columnar organization of the somatosensory cortex demonstrated physiologically.
Each column is specific for a submodality. The examples shown here are for joint (J),
pressure (P), and hair (H) stimulation. (Reprinted with permission of the publisher
from Kandel (1981c). Ch. 17 of *Principles of Neural Science,* ed. E. R. Kandel and J. H.
Schwartz, pp. 184–198. Copyright © 1981 by Elsevier Science Publishing Co., Inc.
Based on Mountcastle 1957.)

neurons at the perimeter of the column and to cells in neighboring
columns (figure 3.23).

The excitatory interneuron mediates between the input and the
output of the aggregation. It makes synaptic contact with the incoming thalamic fibers, and it sends axon branches vertically along the
columnar aggregation to synapse on the output pyramidal cells at
various laminar levels. Given this circuitry, it is reasonable to postulate that columns are input-output modules. As for the inhibitory

A. Cochlear Rep. in two Cat
   Auditory Fields (AAF and AI)

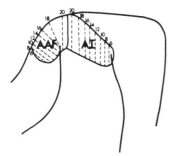

B. Binaural Bands within AI

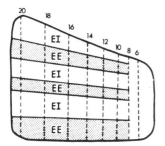

Figure 3.22
(A) Cochleotopic representation within two auditory fields (AAF and AI) in the cat. Numbers represent locations along the cochlear sensory epithelium measured from the cochlear apex. (B) Highly schematized drawing of the internal organization of AI. This field is marked by a series of alternating functional binaural bands, orthogonal to the isofrequency contours of the fields. Within a given binaural band, all neurons are either excited by the stimulation of both ears (EE bands), or excited by the stimulation of the contralateral ear and inhibited by the stimulation of the ipsilateral ear (EI bands). The lowest frequency part of AI (at the right) has not been studied in sufficient detail to determine its internal binaural organization. (From Merzenich and Kaas 1980.)

interneurons, given what is known about the modality specificity and receptive field specificity of afferent and efferent cells in the columnar aggregate, it appears that between them, the Golgi type II and the basket cells function to reduce noise and to focus the signal.[2]

Moreover, evidence is accumulating that the *output* of columns is also compartmentalized. In studies on the prefrontal cortex Goldman-Rakic (1981) has shown that there is a parcellation of fibers departing from one cortical column and terminating in another cortical column, and that the prefrontal cortex, like the somatosensory and visual cortex, displays a columnar organization. She and her colleagues

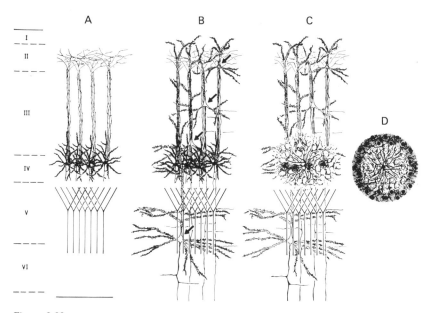

Figure 3.23
Semischematic figure showing postulated input-output columns based upon bundling of thalamocortical fibers. Focal nature of such input is maintained throughout thickness of cortex by small spiny cells with vertical axons (A) that receive thalamocortical synapses. Vertical axons, by synapsing on pyramidal cells in all layers (B), ensure that the input column is also an output column. Focal nature of inputs is thought to be maintained and "focused" by putatively inhibitory Golgi II cells, also receiving thalamic synapses (C) and serving to inhibit (D) small spiny cells less strongly excited at perimeter of thalamic input zone (black stipple). Bar represents approximately 500 micrometers. (From Jones (1981). In *The Organization of the Cerebral Cortex*, ed. F. O. Schmitt et al. Cambridge, Mass.: MIT Press.)

have also found that distinct projection pathways from the prefrontal cortex to the hippocampus form distinct columnar terminations in the hippocampus. (Also see Goldman-Rakic 1984.)

It is also possible that the columnar aggregates are themselves organized in some fashion into larger units, which Mountcastle (1979) calls *macrocolumns*. The boundary conditions of these units are fixed in terms of the static and dynamic properties of the neurons; for example, in the visual cortex such properties would include ocularity and the place in the visual field that excites the neurons. Investigating the extrinsic connections of the larger unit and of the modules that compose the larger unit has provided an underpinning for the observation that large-scale functions are not discretely localized in the brain, but are distributed. The data show that distinct modules within the macrocolumn enjoy their own peculiar extrinsic connections to modules outside the macrocolumn. As Mountcastle says:

> Thus the total set of modules of a large entity is fractionated into subsets, each linked by a particular pattern of connections to similarly segregated subsets in other large entities. The linked sets of modules of the several entities are defined as a distributed system. (1979:37)

This connectivity arrangement implies that a microcolumn can belong both to a given macrocolumn and to a number of distributed systems. This in turn would explain why local lesions typically do not destroy a particular functional capacity, but rather tend to degrade it to a degree roughly proportional to the size of the lesion and to the general importance of the structure in subserving the capacity (Mountcastle 1979).

Much remains to be discovered concerning just which columnar aggregates talk to which other columnar aggregates, and such information will undoubtedly be central both in understanding the brain as a massively parallel information-processing system and in understanding what is going on in the brain at a number of levels of organization. It is, for example, a matter of considerable significance that roughly 80 percent of an aggregate's connections—incoming and outgoing—are with other *cortical* neurons. Why cortical neurons have so much to say to one another and what the nature of the messages is will undoubtedly become apparent as the intricacy of the computational architecture comes to be understood in greater detail.

It will be apparent that if one starts by thinking of the cortex as a sheet, it is essential to update this conception to accommodate the data concerning pathways, laminae, maps, and columns. With increasing degrees of accuracy we can think of the cortex as a *stack* of sheets, then as a stack of *sheets with methodical vertical connections,* then as a stack of sheets, *some of which are topographically mapped,* with methodical vertical connections, and finally, as *containing cells with highly specific origins and projections.* Seeing so much architectural purpose, one is virtually driven to conclude that the secret of the brain's computational and representational capacities cannot be understood independently of understanding its functional architecture.

3.7   Neural Development

The brain of an adult organism is remarkably orderly in its organization, but perhaps what is most astonishing about such organization is that no master intelligence guides its construction—it grows natu-

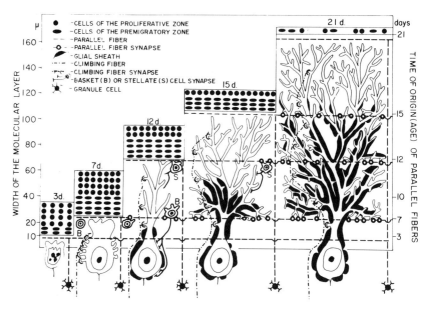

Figure 3.24
Diagrammatic illustration of some major events in the maturation of a Purkinje cell and of the molecular layer. If the parallel fibers are traced through the columns from left to right, it is seen that the fiber formed on day 7 has no synapses on that day, but that it has synapses with basket cells on day 12 and an increasing number of synapses with Purkinje cells from day 15 onward. Likewise, the parallel fiber formed on day 12 has no synapses at that time, but has synapses with a stellate cell on day 15. The displacement and growth of a climbing fiber is indicated on the left side of the Purkinje cell. (From Altman 1972.)

rally, starting from a few cells induced from epithelial cells early in the biography of the developing embryo. Studies in developmental neurobiology have begun to reveal how strictly patterned is the genesis of the nervous system, and how very puzzling are the principles that govern its development (figure 3.24).

Consider, for example, a motor neuron in the spinal cord of an adult monkey. First, its causal ancestor in the embryo was a precursor cell (neuroblast), from which it must have differentiated in a mitotic division. This differentiation results in its having the distinctive properties of a motor neuron, not those of a mechanoreceptor or a Purkinje cell or some other type of neuron. Second, it must migrate from the point of origin to the right place in the spinal cord. Then it must grow its connections; the dendrites must sprout and make contact with the right neurons to form the right circuits, and the axon must find its way out of the spinal cord via the proper route (the ventral horn, not the dorsal horn). It must go to the muscles—more particularly, if it is a dorsolateral axon it must innervate the limb muscles, and if it is a ventromedial axon it must innervate the axial muscles. There is evidence that the various neuronal pools in the spinal cord preferentially "seek" specified muscle fibers to innervate, a remarkable and almost uncanny route-finding accomplishment (Rakic 1975).

An equally extraordinary story can be told for all other neurons. For example, a retinal ganglion cell must have ganglion cell shape and response properties, migrate from the site of origin to the most superficial layer of the retina, establish dendritic connections with the right cells in the retina, find its way down the rather long route to the LGN, either crossing or not crossing, depending on whether it is a nasal or a temporal fiber, find the suitable layer in the LGN to terminate in and do so in such a way as to preserve retinotopic mapping, and make appropriate connections with the neurons that project elsewhere. Sometimes errors are made, but errant neurons are typically eliminated as development proceeds. It is not known how errors are recognized, or why the errant neuron fails to survive.

The electrophysiological properties of spiking neurons also undergo a distinctive evolution. In their early stages the spiking of these cells is based on calcium current. At later stages spiking may have both a calcium and a sodium component, but eventually the sodium component dominates and the calcium component declines. This physiological sequence has not yet been fully explained, but it appears to be an important feature of neurogenesis and may be especially significant for learning. (See especially Llinás and Sugimori 1979, Llinás 1984a, 1984c.)

Exuberant proliferation of cells followed by selective cell death seems to be a standard mode of operation in neuronal development. Depending on the neuronal structure, between 15 percent and 85 percent of the original neuronal pool may be eliminated in selective cell death. In one case (the chick) a whole tract, projecting from the visual cortex to the spinal cord, grows and then dies. The principle of selection is not yet understood, but functional participation is believed to be important. It may be that functionally busy neurons receive more nourishment than the functionally more idle and hence become more robust, a variation on the "them that works, eats" rule (Cowan 1979, Truman 1984).

In addition to the culling of entire cells, there is in certain populations a massive retraction of cell processes (axons and dendrites) in young neurons following a luxurious flourishing. For example, in the adult organism each muscle cell is usually innervated by a single motor neuron axon. However, at an earlier period in neurogenesis many axons will have emerged to make contact with the given muscle cell, and in subsequent development all but one retract, presumably through some sort of competition. Once matters have settled down, process proliferation in some cell types appears to resume.

Intervention in the normal course of neurogenesis has yielded valuable insights into the causal agents. A particularly illuminating technique pioneered by R. W. Sperry has been to transplant an extra (supernumerary) limb or to rotate an eye after cutting the optic nerve and to study the nature of the subsequent innervation as well as the behavior of the organism. Sperry found, for example, that if an extra leg bud is grafted onto a chick embryo alongside the normal leg, it will be innervated by motor neurons. Specifically, it will be innervated by the motor neurons normally innervating the trunk (Sperry 1963). In studies on the frog in which the optic nerve had been sectioned and the eye rotated 180 degrees, he also found that retinal ganglion axons will regenerate, but they follow the route of the original axons back to the optic tectum. The behavioral consequence is that the frog snaps 180 degrees *away* from where the eye detects a fly.

This systematicity suggests some principled way in which neurons determine where they are to terminate and with whom they are to make contact. Sperry has hypothesized that a "chemical affinity" exists between the growing neurons and the tissue of destination. Some evidence supports this view, indicating that in forming connections, neurons are aided by protein "labels" acquired on their membranes in the differentiation process, in virtue of which they can match with complementary neurons and be recognized (Cowan 1979). The development of a nervous system is plainly a matter of great subtlety and complexity, and much more remains to be discovered about the chemical factors that affect neurogenesis and about other mechanisms that may be involved. (For a discussion on the developmental profile of the neocortex, see Rakic 1981.)

We have seen that the width of ocular dominance bands can be influenced by suturing one eye shut and thereby depriving the relevant cortical area of activity. This implies that there is some stimulus-dependent plasticity in the organization of the cortex and that within the genetically delimited parameters there is scope for environmental effects. How much of the organizational profile depends on the genetic program, as well as the manner of dependence, is under study, and one important discovery bearing on these questions has been made by Martha Constantine-Paton and her colleagues (1981).

The background is this: in the frog the optic tectum is the dominant visual processing structure, and such cortex as the frog brain has plays no crucial role in vision. (In humans the superior colliculus is the anatomical homologue to the frog's optic tectum.) Unlike mammalian retinal projections, in which retinal fibers are sorted according to visual hemifield, the retinal projection of the frog exhibits sorting only according to retinas; virtually all fibers from the right eye project to the left optic tectum, and virtually all fibers from the left eye project to the right optic tectum. There is therefore no interdigitation of ocular dominance bands in the frog tectum. Constantine-Paton's question was this: what happens to tectal organization if a third eye is transplanted into the frog brain early in neurogenesis? The experiment consisted in transplanting a developing eye (eye primordium) from one tadpole into another tadpole, placing it, for example, midway between the two normal eyes (figure 3.25). Once the tadpole had become a mature frog, radioactively labeled amino acids could be injected into the eye, allowing the fiber pathways to be traced. Moreover, by recording from selected areas in the optic tectum while the retina was stimulated with light, it was possible to test the electrophysiological properties of the projections.

The first finding was that the retinal fibers from the supernumerary eye make their way to one or the other tectum just as retinal fibers normally do. They may all go to the left or all go to the right. The second finding was that the fibers from the supernumerary eye and the fibers from the normal eye *compete* for tectal space, with the result that bands of tectal cells, sorted according to eye of origin, are formed and interdigitate in a manner strikingly reminiscent of the ocular dominance bands seen in mammalian visual cortex. An overall retinotopic map is superimposed on the band-pattern, though the map is somewhat ajumble because the two eyes, owing to how they are positioned on the head, have visual fields that are not sufficiently isomorphic. The supernumerary eye, though functional, actually impedes performance on fly-snapping tasks, evidently because the retinotopic map in the tectum is not a faithful representation of any one visual field and because the motor connections are not suited to this unusual arrangement (Constantine-Paton and Law 1982).

To explain the formation of bands and maps, Constantine-Paton has argued that two mechanisms are at work. First, there is a general chemical affinity between retinal axons and tectal tissue, in virtue of which fibers grow to the tectum rather than somewhere else, and more specifically, they grow to specified areas within the tectum, rather than just indifferently to any tectal area. Once fibers are in the right general area, a second mechanism is responsible for further organizational refinement of tectal cells.

As a result of this additional mechanism, cells are maintained as neighbors as a function of conformity in responsivity; crudely, cells that respond together, live together. The basic idea is simple: synaptic

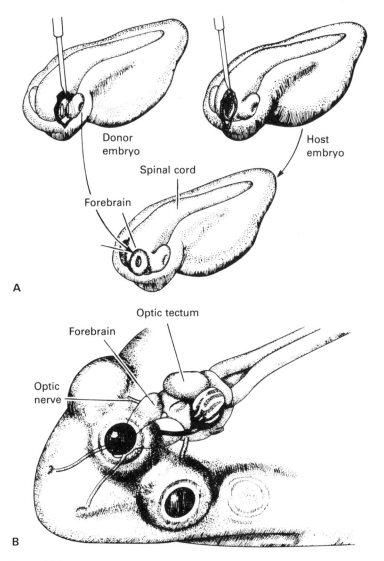

Figure 3.25
(A) Surgical procedure that produces a three-eyed frog requires that an eye primordium be taken from one frog embryo and introduced into a second embryo after tissue has been removed to make room for it. At the time of transplantation each embryo is some three millimeters long and each eye primordium is an outpouching from the developing forebrain. (B) Mature three-eyed frog has two normal eyes positioned correctly on its head and a third eye either in front of a normal eye or on top of the head. In about three-fourths of all cases the third eye competes with a normal eye to establish axon terminals in one tectum. (From Constantine-Paton and Law (1982). The development of maps and stripes in the brain. Copyright © 1982 by Scientific American, Inc. All rights reserved.)

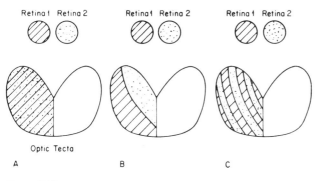

Figure 3.26
Schematic explanation of banding when retinal ganglion cells from two eyes (retina 1 and retina 2) innervate one tectal lobe. (A) Complete overlap of the terminals from the two eyes. Expected if only retinal ganglion cell-to-tectal cell affinities are involved in generating the retinotectal map. (B) One of several ways the two retinal projections could divide the tectal plate. Expected if ganglion-cell axons merely obtained some aligning cue from the tectal plate and sorted so as to reestablish the nearest-neighbor relationships of the retinal ganglion-cell bodies. (C) Interdigitating termination bands. Expected if ganglion cell terminals from each retina are sorted so as to maximize contact with particular regions of the tectum *and* maintain the nearest-neighbor relationships of their retinal-cell bodies. (From Constantine-Paton (1981). In *The Organization of the Cerebral Cortex*, ed. F. O. Schmitt et al. Cambridge, Mass.: MIT Press.)

communication between one incoming retinal fiber and a tectal cell is increased when the signal from that retinal fiber is correlated with signals from other retinal fibers, and that correlation is most likely when the fibers originate in the same area of the retina. The tectal cells in some way reinforce synaptic connections when conditions of strong correlation of signals are satisfied. Thus, neighborhood relations are preserved, nonneighborhood connections atrophy, and the neurons gradually render the map more precise and form themselves into interdigitating eye-dominance bands (figure 3.26). Working out the details of the suggestion and putting them to experimental test is, of course, anything but simple.

An outstanding implication of this research is that one dimension of cortical organization in mammals, namely the ocular dominance bands, may well be a function, not of genetic specification, but of broader principles governing neuronal competition for space. Evidently frog DNA does not code for the formation of ocular dominance bands, yet form they will, when fibers are forced to compete for tectal space.

The means whereby a nervous system succeeds in developing from a few precursor cells in the embryo to a fully differentiated, specialized, wired-up neuronal machine is beginning to be understood. This knowledge is likely to play a crucial role in theories of how brains learn, how they represent the world, and what sort of business learning really is—what constraints there are, and what degrees of freedom. Understanding how neuronal order arises out of such modest beginnings is bound to help us understand the fundamental principles of brain function. (For a short and excellent introduction to neuronal development, see Cowan 1979; for a collection of papers, see Patterson and Purves 1982.)

3.8   A Brief Remark Concerning Invertebrates

Although the discussion in this chapter has focused exclusively on vertebrate nervous systems, invertebrates deserve special (if lamentably brief) notice because their nervous systems have been particularly valuable in the search for an explanation of functional properties in terms of structural properties. One reason is that the nervous systems in animals such as the leech, *Hirudo*, and the sea hare, *Aplysia*, are simpler and have many fewer neurons. *Hirudo*'s entire population is a mere 14,000 neurons (*Aplysia* has about 20,000), but even so it has a nontrivial behavioral repertoire. There is, however, a further respect in which invertebrates are amenable to research: they display a remarkably high degree of structural invariance at the micro level from one individual to another. For example, the leech has twenty-one ganglia in addition to the head and tail brains, and in each ganglion (cluster of somas) the neuronal pool is rigorously stereotyped, in the sense that its neurons are quite precisely determined in shape, size, axonal branching, location, biochemistry, pattern of connectivity, electrophysiological properties, and function (figure 3.27).

A neuron responsive to pressure, for example, is found in segmental ganglia in every individual *Hirudo* in exactly the same location relative to other neurons, having precisely the same morphology,

Central nervous system

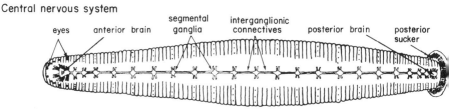

Figure 3.27
Diagram of the leech showing the head brain, tail brain, and intervening segmental ganglia. (Adapted from Weisblat and Kristan 1985.)

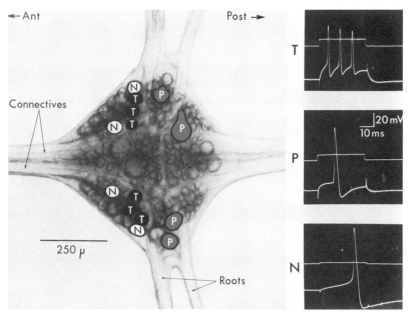

Figure 3.28
Segmental ganglion seen from its ventral aspect, and action potentials of identified cells. Cells labeled include the T, P, and N mechanosensory cells, which respond to touch, pressure, and noxious mechanical stimulation of the skin. (*Right*) The intracellular recordings of T, P, and N action potentials were elicited by passing depolarizing current through the microelectrode. The T cells fire repeatedly during a maintained depolarization; N cells fire spontaneously and have a large undershoot. (From Nicholls and Baylor 1968.)

essentially the same spike profile, and so forth (figure 3.28). Such neurons, duplicated across individuals, are referred to as "identified neurons," and their presence, along with the relatively small number of neurons in the total nervous system population, has made it possible to determine the entire physiological basis of behavior patterns such as swimming in *Hirudo* (Stent and Kristan 1981) and habituation and sensitization in *Aplysia* (Kandel 1979). In *Hirudo* about 20 to 30 percent of the roughly 200 neurons in each segmental hemiganglion have been "identified."

3.9   Conclusions

Anyone with theoretical proclivities will find in all this order not only constraints that any theory of brain function must honor but also the very fire to ignite the theoretical imagination. The neuroanatomical information is sufficiently rich at this stage that the greening of theory that articulates the principles of brain function seems inevitable. At a minimum, those whose skepticism concerning brain research was based on a bramblescape conception should be willing to see that the detailed orderliness belies their presumption of impenetrable tangle.

The volume of research classed under the broad rubric of functional neuroanatomy is enormous, and it is not possible to summarize even the research devoted to a single aspect.[3] Moreover, the order we know about is in part a function of the techniques we have for making it show up, and there may be further realms of order waiting for the curtain to be pulled aside, had we but the appropriate techniques. The order we know about is in part also a function of available theoretical frameworks that characterize brain function and can guide and motivate experimental investigations. A dimension of order may be found only after a theory, robustly successful on a number of counts, deduces that it ought to be there. With so much known about the neuroanatomy and neurophysiology of nervous systems, what is now needed are theories of brain function that will begin to pull the data together, to pose new questions, and to compete for epistemological space. This further matter of theory in neuroscience will be explored in chapter 10.

Selected Readings

Barr, Murray L. (1974). *The human nervous system: An anatomical viewpoint.* 2nd ed. New York: Harper and Row.

Cowan, W. Maxwell (1979). The development of the brain. *Scientific American* 241/ 3:112–133.

Heimer, Lennart (1983). *The human brain and spinal cord: Functional neuroanatomy and dissection guide.* New York: Springer-Verlag.

Heimer, Lennart, and Martine J. Robards, eds. (1981). *Neuroanatomical tract-tracing methods.* New York: Plenum.

Magistretti, Pierre J., John H. Morrison, and Floyd E. Bloom, eds. (1984). Nervous system development and repair. *Discussions in Neurosciences* 1/2 (special issue).

Merzenich, M. M., and J. H. Kaas (1980). Principles of organization of sensory-perceptual systems in mammals. *Progress in Psychobiology and Physiological Psychology* 9:1–42.

Schmitt, F. O., F. G. Worden, G. Adelman, and S. G. Dennis, eds. (1981). *The organization of the cerebral cortex.* Cambridge, Mass.: MIT Press.

Spitzer, Nicholas C., ed. (1982). *Neuronal development.* New York: Plenum.

Chapter 4

Higher Functions: Early Work

I cannot conceive what even the very highest nervous centres can possibly be, except developments out of lower nervous centres, which no one doubts to represent impressions and movements.
J. Hughlings Jackson, 1875

4.1 Introduction

No claim about how the nervous system works can properly be assessed or understood without understanding the methods used to obtain the data. This holds whether the claim is that dopamine is a neurotransmitter or that the left hemisphere is specialized for speech. Otherwise, one simply takes the claims on faith, or on the authority of "established" science. In earlier sections my discussion of methods was regrettably perfunctory, a decision dictated by considerations of simplicity and space and permitted by dint of substantial consensus regarding what is established at the level of basic neuroscience. However, in a discussion of the so-called higher functions, the necessity of referring to methods overwhelms the restraints of other scruples. At this stage in the neuropsychological study of higher functions, much is still contentious, and precious little concerning the brain's role in higher functions can really be said to be established. Nor is there yet available anything like a fleshed-out theory of the kinematics and dynamics of the higher functions themselves. Hence the authority on whose granite shoulders we yearn to be boosted is not yet available.

As things stand, there are many suppliant hypotheses, but few that pass through the gates; different methods often yield conflicting and confusing results; there are deep problems concerning how to interpret results; the taxonomy of higher functions is itself ill defined and theoretically impoverished; in a few cases the conclusions researchers wish to draw disastrously outstrip their meager, shivering data; and finally, the popular picture of higher functions and the brain is often drawn from the popular accounts of hemispheric specialization, where these are rife with guesses disguised as confirmed hypotheses and flimsy suppositions masquerading as solid truths of neuropsychology.

None of which should in the least discredit neuropsychology in its attempts to get a grip on higher functions. For here the problems are appallingly difficult, many methods are in their infancy, and any field can be plundered by popularizers who hoist an hypothesis out of its carefully surrounding guard of hedges, qualification, caveats, and scare-quotes. Nor does it mean that neuropsychological research can safely be ignored, since masses of provocative data have been uncovered that are important pieces of the puzzle, and in any case, neuropsychological questions will not be answered by sitting on our hands and looking the other way.

In the main, research on higher functions in the brain has focused both on questions concerning what parts of the brain carry out or otherwise figure in certain jobs and on determining what kinds of jobs the brain does. Crudely, the most prominent research ideology underwriting neuropsychology is that psychological theory (specifying a taxonomy of functions and a theory of their interconnections) should cooperate with neural mapping hypotheses to fix the areas that participate in particular functions, so that these results can then be used by neurophysiologists to figure out *how* the brain does what it does.

Though that research ideology has much to recommend it, neuropsychology on the hoof is much less straightforward. The central reason is this: even determining what the general categories of higher functions are is a deeply empirical-theoretical task, and it is becoming increasingly evident that in a literal sense we do not yet understand *what* "higher" capacities the brain has, or whether conventional categories come even close to carving Nature at her proverbial joints. Certainly we do not know a priori what the brain really does, nor just what cognitive and subcognitive capacities it really has. We have to find that out in the way we have to find out anything else about the nature of the empirical world. These themes will be developed more fully in the philosophical framework of Part II, but in order to provide an initial perspective on why neuropsychology is methodologically so difficult, it will be useful to touch on them now.

In seeking neuroanatomical substrates for psychological functions, earlier neuropsychologists often gave pride of place to traits of character such as cleverness or diligence, and postulated neural centers of cleverness or diligence—places wherein the diligent or clever operations were carried out. More recent trends favor categories specifying different capacities, such as "speech production" and "declarative memory," and still others suggest a general distinction between "analytic" capacities and "holistic" or "synthetic" capacities. But what is the psychological *theory* that provides the categorial framework and guides the seach for neural substrates?

The answer is that at this time psychological theory is in *statu nascendi*. What is needed, but what does not yet exist, is a fleshed-out and robust theory of what the fundamental cognitive capacities are, of the subcognitive capacities providing the lower-level basis for cognitive capacities, of the nature of processes that intervene between input and output, and of the nature of the representations used at various levels of organization. The starting point for theorizing was of course folk psychology, just as the starting point for modern physics was folk physics (see chapters 6 and 7). Thus, according to our folk psychological conception, we have a memory, we are conscious, some memories fade with time, rehearsing helps us remember, one recollection sometimes triggers related recollections, and so forth. Equipped just with the folk psychological notion of memory, we might well expect that there is a single, unified kind of process or mechanism in the brain that subserves remembering.

As psychologists and neuroscientists know well, folk psychology does not take us very far; moreover, the boundaries of its basic categories may have to be substantially redrawn. The investigation of memory by psychologists has revealed a wide range of behavioral data that has led to attempts to extend and redraw the basic folk psychological conception. For example, it has been claimed that there is a short-term memory, which stores information for short periods, and a long-term memory, which stores it more permanently. So far, however, these postulated capacities are understood essentially in behavioral terms, not in terms of the well-defined internal processes, cognitive and subcognitive, that must underlie them.

Even for these ostensibly straightforward postulations, researchers disagree on whether there are really two distinct capacities, because the characteristics of the postulated memory stores vary as a function of the materials to be recalled, the type of task set in the experiment, the strategies, and the subjects (Craik 1984). They also disagree on whether there is a third element such as the rehearsal buffer (Atkinson and Shiffrin 1968) between the other two, how the various structures are related, and what the subcognitive processes are in virtue of which people remember and forget. Moreover, remembering is not self-evidently a *single* kind of process: free recall gives results different from cued recall, which in turn gives results different from recognition tests (Craik and Lockhart 1972; Squire and Cohen 1984). In addition, it has been argued on the basis of careful animal studies that working memory is dissociable from reference memory (Olton, Becker, and Handelmann 1979) and that spatial-map memory is dissociable from nonspatial memory (O'Keefe and Nadel 1978).

Some data discovered by neuropsychologists are so remarkable, and so contrary to customary assumptions, that they suggest that some basic assumptions about memory may be in need of radical revision. Consider, for example, patients who are so profoundly amnesic that they cannot remember the doctor they have seen day in and day out, or what they had for breakfast, or anything of a close relative's visit earlier in the day. Yet these patients can learn some quite complex things, such as how to do mirror reading or how to solve the Tower of Hanoi puzzle shown in figure 4.1 (though they do not remember *that* they have encountered the puzzle before or *that* they have learned to solve it) (Milner, Corkin, and Teuber 1968, Squire and Cohen 1984). Moreover, their memory for events that occurred before the brain damage (retrograde memory) is quite normal. Pertinent to the matter of a categorial framework for psychological functions is the fact that there is as yet no principled description specifying what general class of thing these amnesic patients can still learn and what they cannot, and why they remember certain things and not others. So far, no theoretically grounded description has been winnowed out to specify the nature of the two capacities, if such indeed there be.

At first, it might be thought that if distinct capacities really exist, they might be distinguished as follows: one involves *knowing how*, and hence concerns the acquisition of motor skills, and the other involves *knowing that*, and hence is a matter of the acquisition of cognitive information. That will not do, however, because learning to solve the Tower of Hanoi puzzle is not merely acquiring a motor skill, such as learning to ride a unicycle (*if* that itself is a purely motor skill). It also requires something that we might, in our innocence, call intelligence.

Insofar as the learning in these cases has a cognitive dimension, one cannot just explain it on the basis of a cognitive-noncognitive division. Indeed, these cases raise fundamental and disquieting questions concerning what it is for a process to be a cognitive process at all, what processes underlie skill acquisition, and what it is for behavior to be intelligent. (Also see chapter 10.) What makes the amnesic studies so intriguing is that it is far from obvious what unifies the assorted things that profound amnesics can still learn. From examining the class of things so far discovered that amnesics can remember, it is not obvious how to predict what else they can remember and

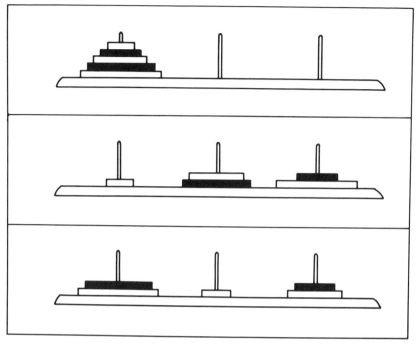

Figure 4.1
The Tower of Hanoi puzzle used to test cognitive skill learning in amnesic patients. To solve the puzzle, subjects must move the five blocks shown in the top panel to the rightmost peg. The rules are that only one block can be moved at a time, and a large block can never be placed on a smaller block. The optimal solution requires 31 moves. The middle panel shows an arrangement of blocks that leads directly to the optimal solution, and the bottom panel shows an arrangement that does not lead directly to solution because it is not on the optimal solution path. (From Squire and Cohen (1984). In *Neurobiology of Learning and Memory*, ed. G. Lynch, J. L. McGaugh, and N. M. Weinberger. New York: Guilford.)

what they will not be able to learn. Which entails that we do not yet know what the capacities are (Warrington 1979).[1]

Learning and memory are at the dead center of cognition, if anything is, and as their categories are revised and redrawn, the theoretical landscape of higher functions is undergoing tremendous transformations. The general category of learning has already fragmented into a variety of kinds of process, and indeed the term "learning" is now often replaced by the broader and less theoretically burdened expression "plasticity."

Among kinds of nervous system plasticity already believed to be distinct phenomena are habituation, sensitization, classical conditioning, operant conditioning, imprinting, habit formation, post-tetanic potentiation, imitation, song learning (in birds), one-shot learning to avoid nausea-producing foods, and cognitive mapping, in addition to which are the apparently high-level phenomena distinguished in terms of what is learned, such as learning language, learning who is a conspecific, learning to read, learning social skills, learning mathematical skills, learning to learn more efficiently, learning to lower blood pressure, and heaven knows what else. Whether these involve common or distinct mechanisms, and how many distinct processes there really are, remains to be discovered. Whether anything like an *empirically justified* distinction between the cognitive and the noncognitive will survive, or if it does, whether it will confirm even a rough approximation of our current hunches, also remains to be discovered.

The theoretical problem that emerges from a study of the work on memory, learning, and other higher functions, such as consciousness, is this: if the psychological (functional) taxonomy is ill defined, then the search for neural substrates for those functions will be correspondingly ill defined. There are, certainly, remarkable data, found at all levels in psychology and neuroscience, but precisely how to interpret the data in terms of a theory of neurobiological capacities, representations, and processes is yet to be discovered.

Standing back from the details of individual experiments, what we want to know is how humans and other animals learn, what makes them smart, how they plan and problem solve, how they recollect and forget, how their brains differ when their personalities differ, how they can be self-aware, what consciousness is. The treacherous difficulty here is that we cannot be sure when we are asking the right questions. We do not know whether such categories as "emotion," "declarative memory," "procedural memory," "learning," and "consciousness" pick out a unified, single, *natural* kind, or whether these categories herd together quite motley collections of disparate phenomena—whether searching for the neural substrate for "memory" is like looking for the "principle" that unites jewels, such as amethysts, diamonds, amber, and pearls.

Jewels do not form a *natural kind*, in the sense that there are natural laws about their properties and behavior. They are *accidental kinds*, unified not by their nature but by social convention. It may be that commonsense theory (folk psychology) is so misconceived, and its taxonomy so askew, that even the formulation of our questions thwarts our inquiry. (This will be further considered in chapters 7 through 10.)

The difficulties here are such as to make one fear that we cannot get a theory until we have one—that acquisition of theory, like acquisition of wealth or breeding stock, is limited to those who already have it. And indeed, getting started is notoriously difficult, for unless there is a solid and substantial theory of psychological functions and how they interlace, one has only the clumsiest of hunches as to what to look for. But such a dilemma is of course the way of it in science generally, and any successful science got to where it did by heroic and stubborn bootstrapping. Viewed from atop a long-secured theoretical keep, the climb may seem deceptively simple. For example, modern chemical theory seems so evident, straightforward, and right, that it is well to remember that in its stormy formation some of the deepest convictions and the most safe and obvious assumptions of available alchemical theory and common sense had to be overturned; that in its nascent stages, it was commonly considered preposterous and objectionable where it was at loggerheads with the "self-evident"; that it doggedly pulled itself up by its own bootstraps.

I do not, therefore, regard the current "pretheoretical" situation in cognitive neurobiology as cause for despair with the field. On the contrary, it is perhaps the prospect of emerging theory that gives cognitive neurobiology and psychology an especial excitement. This is the frontier, after all, and it is to be expected that there will be rough edges, false starts, and considerable theoretical derring-do. Nor do I view it as psychology's job to hew out the theory in advance of neuroscientific discovery. Rather, psychology and neuroscience will need to cooperate and co-evolve, if a successful theoretical framework is to emerge.

The rationale for emphasizing the importance of techniques and methods will now be clearer. So long as the categorial framework is itself being invented and revised, it does not provide us with secure background assumptions, and in consequence we need to know how data are obtained in order to try to understand what they might mean, and whether they might mean that the categories must be reconfigured.

These reflections raise further questions about the evolution of a theory of higher functions and about the relations between neuroscience and psychology, and it raises very general questions about the status and significance of folk psychology. Such questions will be the focus of chapters 6 through 10. One further introductory observation, however, should be made.

As neuroscience develops, specialized disciplines within the field acquire special names. The term "neurology" once covered any study of nervous systems, but with the splitting off of psychiatry in the 1930s it is now used mainly to mean "clinical neurology," which is the study of abnormalities in human nervous systems. Neurologists are usually medical doctors and work in hospitals. "Neuropsychology" is a term of more recent vintage, having been first used in a serious publication by D. O. Hebb in 1949. It is typically applied to studies of the relation between the human brain and behavior, and it has a wider focus than "clinical neurology." Neuropsychologists are usually Ph.D.s and are often found in university psychology and physiology departments. "Physiological psychology" is a term occasionally used to cover the same ground, although it sometimes includes animal studies of brain and behavior and is perhaps a less fashionable term.

A neurobiologist typically works on the brain-behavior relationship in nonhuman species, but there are those called "neurobiologists" whose work is indistinguishable from that of others who are called "neurophysiologists," and undoubtedly there are still others who call themselves "neurobiologists" to distinguish themselves from people who are in psychology departments. And some of the latter are called "psychobiologists" but like to distinguish themselves from others who are neuropsychologists or just plain psychologists. I try to use the term "cognitive neurobiologist" very widely, to cover those whose research is concerned with matters cognitive, *broadly* conceived, and is constrained and informed by neuroscientific results. Patently, the divisions are less than precise, and it may be that as neuroscience in general evolves, a more orderly set of distinctions will emerge.

Finally, in keeping with my governing strategy, this section will in no sense be a survey. The selected readings section at the end of the chapter lists neuropsychology texts that already fulfill that need. Rather, I shall choose what has caught my attention, either for what it suggests concerning the prospects for a unified theory of the mind-brain or for how it indicates the importance of a co-evolutionary strategy for neuroscience and psychology at all levels of investigation. Moreover, the literature in this area is vast—there seem to be papers as far as the eye can see and in every direction. As a result, I shall sin by omission, sometimes knowingly and regretfully, sometimes in ignorance. My hope is that by providing a summary discussion of particular methods and selected results, I might enable the reader to inspect the literature more fruitfully and with greater circumspection.

4.2   Cerebral Specialization and Naturally Occurring Lesions

There are ancient reports of observations of striking behavioral deficits, such as paralysis or weakness on one side of the body, or sudden onset of disturbances in speech. A stroke is the result either of a blockage of a blood vessel that cuts off the blood supply to a particular area of the brain or of a rupture of a blood vessel causing interruption of the blood supply downstream. If there is no blood supply, there is no oxygen, and if there is no oxygen, neuronal death swiftly follows. Strokes are common in advanced age, and the nature of the behavioral deficit following a stroke has been found to be linked to the area of the brain damaged by oxygen deprivation. Study of stroke victims has become an important source of information concerning specialization of function, and it was also one of the earliest sources. Nevertheless, behavioral deficits do not wear their causes on their sleeves, and for early physicians the study of deficits was confounded in many ways.

For one thing, behavioral deficits can be caused not only by strokes but also by tumors, traumas, infectious diseases, degenerating nervous diseases (e.g., Parkinson's disease and multiple sclerosis), psychiatric diseases (e.g., schizophrenia), and neurogenetic disorders (e.g., Huntington's chorea). Hence, it would have been exceedingly difficult for early physicians to find much pattern in the medley of symptoms their patients presented. Moreover, comparison of cases was limited from one geographical region to the next, and testing could be neither thorough nor standardized. Until rather recently, then, neurological diagnoses were largely intuitions in the dark. For example, paralysis resulting from a stroke is not self-evidently distinguishable from paralysis resulting from a tumor, from excess eating of a certain chick-pea (lathyrism), from hysterical paralysis, or from a demyelinating disease. Moreover, neurologically based disorders such as strokes and tumors often involve personality changes, sometimes subtle, sometimes not so subtle. Even itemizing the roster of possible causes, let alone isolating the particular cause of a particular patient's malady, is knowledge hard won.

Disturbances in speech resulting from strokes are rather common, owing to the manner in which the cerebral blood vessels branch (figures 4.2, 4.3). The middle cerebral artery feeds a wide area of the frontal cortex, and interruption of blood flow in the left middle cerebral artery is often followed by loss of speech or *aphasia*. So far as is known, the first person to make the connection between frontal cortex and speech production was Franz Joseph Gall (1758–1828). History remembers Gall largely for his phrenology or "cranioscopy," as he called it, and his reputation as a crackpot has overshadowed his deserved reputation as a fine anatomist and a pioneering localizationist.

Using better dissection techniques than others, Gall made postmortem inspection of as many brains as he could get his hands on, where

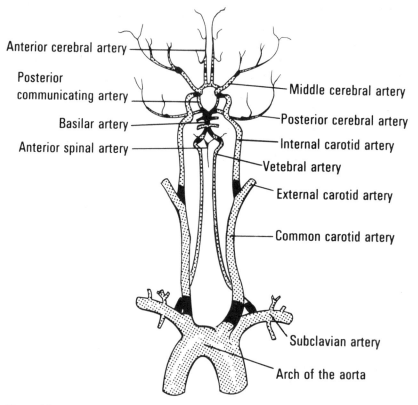

Anterior cerebral artery

Posterior
communicating artery

Basilar artery

Anterior spinal artery

Middle cerebral artery

Posterior cerebral artery

Internal carotid artery

Vetebral artery

External carotid artery

Common carotid artery

Subclavian artery

Arch of the aorta

Figure 4.2
The blood vessels of the brain. The darkened areas show the common sites of arterio-
sclerosis and obstruction in the cerebral vessels. (From McDowell (1979). In *Textbook
of Medicine*, ed. P. B. Beeson, W. McDermott, and J. B. Wyngaarden. Philadelphia:
Saunders.)

he had documented the patient's capacities, dispositions, and traits
before death. He became convinced that the brain was not an undifferentiated mass subserving a soul with distinct faculties, and that it
must itself be divided into distinct "organs," damage to which resulted in impaired behavior. He put the matter of brain localization
thus:

> . . . but it would be also quite inconceivable that a single organ
> absolutely homogenous throughout could present phenomena
> so different and give rise to manifestation of moral qualities and
> intellectual faculties so various and dissimilar. (1812; in Clarke
> and O'Malley 1968:477)

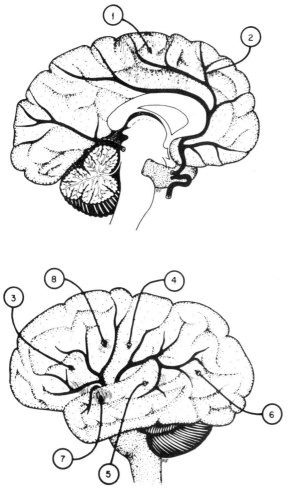

Figure 4.3
Lesions affecting language and speech processes. (1) Area involves frontoparietal region and the corpus callosum with only transient loss of speech as a result of inclusion
in the supplementary motor area. (2) Supplementary motor area of either hemisphere.
Stimulation produces arrest of ongoing speech and initiation of repetitive nonvoluntary
vocalization. Lesions result in abnormalities in initiation, continuation, and inhibition
of speech. (3) Broca's area. Lesions typically produce agrammatism, poor articulation,
and abnormal writing. (4) Lesions result in apraxia of lips and tongue and lead to
disintegration of speech as a whole. (5) Lesions cause disintegration of phonetic hearing. (6) Lesions lead to disintegration of rational speech and to disturbance of the
understanding of logical, grammatical constructions. (7) Lesions produce word
deafness and severe motor aphasia. (8) Area where electrical stimulation results in
perseveration of speech. (From Gazzaniga (1975). In *Handbook of Psychobiology*, ed. M. S.
Gazzaniga and C. Blakemore. New York: Academic Press.)

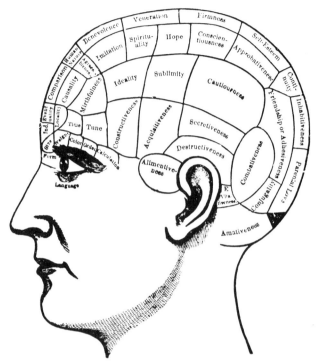

Figure 4.4
Phrenological location of faculties according to the scheme of Spurzheim. (Reproduced in Clarke and O'Malley 1968.)

The phrenology came in with Gall's belief that superlative developments of a capacity or trait required superlative development of the relevant brain center, which in turn would be reflected in the shape of the skull as the enlarged neural mass grew against the cranial cap—hence, the infamous bumps on the head. He thought that sexual appetite, for example, was a function of the cerebellum, and hence a consuming appetite could be detected by feeling a telltale lump on the lower rear of the head (figure 4.4).

The bumps were both the glory and the undoing of Gall, and he and his followers, notoriously Spurzheim, were often the deserving objects of derision, in part because their overweening zeal in fishing for correlations between character traits and cranial bumps overcame any dispassionate interest in testing their claims. Pierre Flourens (1784–1867) was perhaps their most devastating critic, and as a result of his lesion studies on chickens and pigeons, he disputed not only the bumps theory but also the more general principles of the localization of function, arguing instead that intellectual functions were widely spread on the cerebrum (Flourens 1824). Thus, at this stage in the history of neurology there was a polarization of hypotheses: localizationist at one end and holistic at the other.

Despite fearsome criticism of it, the general principle of brain specialization still stood as phrenology crumbled, and that principle became increasingly respectable—though alas for Gall, the more so the greater the distance from his name. Bouillaud (1796–1875) and Auburtin (1825–1893) pursued the idea of a connection between the frontal lobes and speech, and in postmortem examination Bouillaud confirmed Gall's observation. Auburtin had a patient who had attempted suicide and succeeded only in shooting off a flap of his skull cap, revealing the intact brain beneath. Auburtin reported his remarkable findings on this man to the Société d'Anthopologie de Paris in 1861:

> During the interrogation [of the patient] the blade of a large spatula was placed on the anterior lobes; by means of light pressure speech was suddenly stopped; a word that had been commenced was cut in two. The faculty of speech reappeared as soon as the compression ceased . . . . . compression applied with moderation and discretion did not affect the general functions of the brain; limited to the anterior lobes it suspended only the faculty of speech. (1861; in Clarke and O'Malley 1968:492–493)

As it happened, Paul Broca (1824–1880) heard Auburtin's report, and subsequently the two of them examined a patient with speech loss who, for unrelated reasons, was not expected to live. Postmortem examination of that patient did reveal that the second and third frontal convolutions on the left side were destroyed (see figure 4.5) (Broca 1861). The autopsy was critically regarded, however, because the brain was never cut, and surface examination revealed massive damage to wide areas of the brain, not merely to the frontal convolutions. Undeterred, Broca cautiously examined twenty-two further cases and, some two years after the test with Auburtin, ventured the claim that typically only the *left*, not the right, frontal convolutions were implicated in speech loss, and moreover that essentially only the productive capacity of speech was lost, not the capacity for comprehension (Broca 1863).

The data did seem to imply a high degree of specificity of the cortical area Broca explored, though many questions remained, and still remain, concerning how to interpret such specificity and what it entails about the task specificity of local brain structures. The area in question came to be referred to as "Broca's area," and the type of

Broca's area   **Wernicke's area**

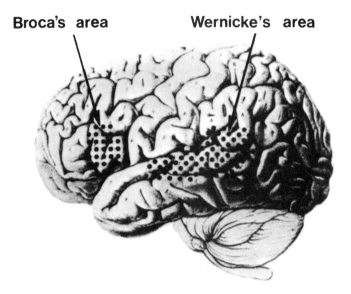

Figure 4.5
The position of Broca's and Wernicke's areas. (From Blakemore (1977) *Mechanics of the Mind.* Cambridge: Cambridge University Press.)

language disorder typified by production deficits is generally referred to as "Broca's aphasia." Whether the disorder bearing his name is caused by lesions to exactly the area bearing his name is not established (see Mohr 1973, Zangwill 1975), though it is often assumed to be. One problem is that naturally occurring lesions are rarely if ever confined just to Broca's area but involve wider cortical regions, and surgical excision of Broca's area has not always resulted in permanent aphasia.

In 1874 Carl Wernicke published a monograph in which he claimed that there was a second major center for language and that it was located on the first and second temporal convolutions (figure 4.5). He had observed that some patients show a language deficit not in expression, but in comprehension. Unlike patients with Broca's aphasia, these patients often talk volubly, but what they say is incoherent and nonsensical, a kind of word salad. They cannot carry out simple commands, they cannot identify objects seen or felt, and they seem strangely unaware that they have any deficits.

Wernicke referred to this syndrome as "sensory aphasia," and "Wernicke's aphasia" came to be the label for a wide range of comprehension deficits. Wernicke argued that the area he identified was the center for language understanding and that since it was connected to Broca's area by a fiber bundle, an interruption of that tract would result in a third distinctive language disorder, which he called "conduction aphasia." Such patients can understand speech and are aware of their deficit, which is that they produce fluent nonsense. Although his critics, especially Marie and Head, were doubtful that symptoms came so neatly packaged or that the lesions responsible for the symptoms were so discretely localized, Wernicke was convinced that there were discrete areas that governed reading and writing, the lesioning of which produced the observed deficits, alexia and agraphia.[2]

But what exactly had the localizationists found, and what exactly did their findings mean? There certainly were some difficulties with the data because Nature does not tailor her lesions to suit inquiring neurologists, the extent and area of lesions varies greatly from one individual to another,[3] and when there is a speech disturbance, it is seldom if ever the only behavioral deficit. Broca himself remarked worriedly upon the variability from case to case. Until a few years ago the location of the lesion was impossible to detect while the patient was alive, and by postmortem time there were often additional lesions (Smith 1984).

Moreover, there were problems of interpretation. Evidently Gall had thought of the "organ" for speech on the model of organs such as the heart and liver—that is, as a discrete, largely independent, island-like entity. Certainly that model of cortical specialization, as applied to the entire spectrum of psychological functions, ran afoul of the evidence that the whole brain is involved in varying degrees in intelligent functions and in memory. Against the localization theory, Goltz found in 1892 that decorticated animals could walk about and respond, that subcortical structures were involved in memory and the voluntary movements, and that there was often substantial, if partial, recovery of function after stroke and trauma. (Regarding residual functions following decortication, see also Kolb and Whishaw 1984.)

In an important conceptual breakthrough, the British neurologist Hughlings Jackson attempted to reconcile the conflicting data. As he observed in 1864, there are local symptoms, and local symptoms imply some degree of localization of lesions; hence, he argued that some acceptable but fuzzy way of construing "local" was necessary. For example, lesions to the primary visual cortex typically result in blindness, not in deafness, paralysis, or aphasia. Jackson's special concern was epilepsy, and in his astute observation of many epileptic patients he noted that the symptoms could be confined to a particular body area. For example, one patient had spasms confined to one side of her body, and her seizures always began with a tingling in her fingers that proceeded to spread up her arms and down her legs. At the same time, Jackson well knew that surgical removal of a chunk of cortex might yield no discernible effects.

Hughlings Jackson was profoundly influenced by Herbert Spencer's evolutionary conception of nervous system function,[4] and he came to view the brain as an integrated set of systems organized in a hierarchy, with sensorimotor representation featured at every level but with increasing complexity and sophistication. Accordingly, his way of reconciling the discrepancies between the "discrete organs" hypothesis and the "holistic" hypothesis was first to replace the exact margins espoused by organ theory with imprecise boundaries and then to argue for multiple representation in various places at various levels of the hierarchies. This implied a division of labor in the nervous system, but a division made many times over, a division that was fuzzy, overlapping, partially redundant, and increasingly specialized; and moreover, a division of labor that had the potential for reorganization in the event of damage. On Jackson's hypothesis, with the destruction of high-level structures the more complicated versions of behavior would also be impaired, but so long as the lower-level structures were intact, simpler "low-level" versions would remain.

This rich if inchoate framework for understanding brain function caught the imagination of many neurologists and remained until the present a powerful conception within which to guide research and interpret results. It was consistent both with there being some nontrivial degree of specialization by nervous tissue and with the sparing and the restoration of function. Its emphasis on evolutionary considerations and its departure from strict localizationist tenets gave it enduring influence.

There are many spellbinding cases in the annals of neurology, but the strange case of Phineas Gage holds special fascination, and it helped foster the idea that the frontal lobes had some special role in personality traits. Gage was the foreman of a railway gang laying track in Vermont, and in 1848, while he was tamping a charge of dynamite at the bottom of a hole, a spark ignited the dynamite, sending the tamping rod up the hole and through the left frontal area of Gage's head. A few minutes later Gage was conscious and speaking, and after convalescing from an ensuing infection, he put on his boots and went to town, apparently completely recovered. However, in the words of his friends, "He was no longer Gage." His personality had changed dramatically.

Once reliable, affable, and considerate, Gage was now irascible, short-tempered, impulsive, profane, and wont recklessly to indulge his "animal propensities" (Harlow 1868). Unable to resume his old job, he earned his bread as a circus exhibit. The striking change in personality and the correlated destruction of frontal lobe tissue naturally prompted widespread curiosity about the nature of the link, and about what it was that the frontal lobes, more highly convoluted and developed in man than in other primates, could be doing in the general scheme of brain function.

Some information about frontal lobe function came from animal ablation studies, in which selected bits of neural tissue were surgically removed and the effects documented. The research of Leonardo Bianchi (1848–1927) was exceptionally good, and in describing the effects of frontal lobe ablation in monkeys, he observed,

> [It] does not so much interfere with the perceptions taken singly, as it does disaggregate the personality, and incapacitate for serialising and synthesizing groups of representations. (1895; in Clarke and O'Malley 1968:544–545)

He also noticed a loss of "psychic tone," by which he meant that the surgically altered animals lacked initiative and inquisitiveness and seemed indifferent to their surroundings. However, it was not until the 1960s that further intensive and systematic studies were made of the effects of frontal lobe lesions in animals. There was of course no body of data from induced lesions in frontal lobes of humans—none, that is, until the 1940s, when the surgeons Walter Freeman and J. W. Watts popularized frontal lobotomies for psychiatric patients and the behavioral effects of this "cure" were assessed. (See Kolb and Whishaw 1980; Valenstein 1973.) Although it was generally assumed that the frontal cortex was the seat of intelligence, Hebb showed in 1939 that epileptic patients who had undergone frontal lobe surgery showed no diminution in IQ, and later studies on lobotomy patients confirmed this result (Hebb and Penfield 1940). As testing procedures improved, it became evident that frontal lobe patients have deficits in planning and in sequencing motor behavior, and they tend to show stereotyped and inflexible behavior patterns. (For a short review paper, see Milner and Petrides 1984.)

Useful as they are, studies of naturally lesioned brains have severe limitations. As Kolb and Whishaw observe (1980:92), lesions may result in at least three quite different effects on behavior: (1) loss of function, (2) release of function, and (3) disorganization of function. Thus, in addition to the problems already mentioned was the perplexing question of how to interpret a link between a lesion and a behavioral deficit, a question that persists even when the lesion is conveniently circumscribed and the deficit well defined. Can it be simply and straightforwardly inferred, "If A is the lesioned area and the patient can no longer do Y, then A is the center for Y"? For many reasons, the answer must be no.

For one thing, the area A might be *necessary* for the function Y, without being both necessary *and* sufficient as the description "center" implies. Moreover, lesions in area A might result in interference with other brain areas that are critical for Y, without A itself being either necessary or sufficient for Y. It is known that acute lesions may disturb functions elsewhere in the brain (Heilman and Valenstein 1979), and a behavioral deficit may be the result of such secondary, nonspecific causes (also called "diaschisis"). Finally, there might be no "center" for Y at all. (For a general discussion of the problems in interpreting lesion data, see Kolb and Whishaw 1980; Smith 1984.)

An illustration of this last situation can be found in a famous report by Déjerine in 1892. He had a patient who awoke one morning and discovered that he could no longer read, though he could speak and understand. He could even write, but he failed utterly to read what he had written. In addition, he had lost vision in his right visual field. This syndrome is now referred to as alexia without agraphia, or pure word blindness. If we may infer a center for every function that can be selectively impaired, then it could be concluded that Déjerine's patient had a lesion in his "reading center." (Déjerine himself did not draw this conclusion, but rather thought alexia to be a version of aphasia.)

That conclusion is doubtful for several reasons. First, anthropological considerations indicate that reading is a cultural achievement that emerged long after humans had evolved. Second, since reading requires visual and linguistic capacities, and since postmortem examinations of patients with pure alexia typically show lesions both in the visual cortex and in the corpus callosum, it may be more reasonable to suggest (Geschwind 1965; Sperry and Gazzaniga 1967) that the deficit in Déjerine's patient may be the result of a disconnection between the relevant "linguistic" and "visual" areas of the brain. (For more on alexia without agraphia, see Vignolo 1983.)

Notice too that breezy use of the aforementioned simple inferential scheme will yield a bizarre catalogue of centers—including, for example, a center for inhibiting religious fanaticism, since lesions in certain areas of the temporal lobe sometimes result in a patient's acquiring a besotted religious zeal. Add to this centers for being able to make gestures on command, for prevention of halting speech, for inhibition of cursing and swearing, and so on, and the willy-nilly nature of Gall's phrenological catalogue comes back to haunt us.

The interpretation of lesion results is further complicated because function is frequently at least partially restored after a time, but the degree of restoration varies considerably from patient to patient, and it is often impossible to predict. This does not mean that hypotheses concerning localization of function are hopeless, but it does mean that they have to be framed within a context where all interpretive complications are taken into account.

Andrew Kertesz has suggested five principles to guide the interpretation of lesion data. He says the function of an area may be related to the lesion if

1. The same functional deficit always follows the lesion.
2. The same deficit is not produced by other, independent lesions.
3. The deficit is measured according to standardized and meaningful methods.
4. The lesion location is determined objectively and accurately.
5. Biological variables such as time from onset, age, etiology and so forth are controlled. (1983a:18)

The simple inferential scheme "If A is the lesioned area and the patient can no longer do Y, then A is the center for Y" is widely recognized to be fallacious, and in the neurological literature descriptions of the form "A is the center for Y" have largely been abandoned in favor of "A has elements underlying the function Y" or "A is involved with Y," once there is evidence from control lesions that the deficit is not the result of diaschisis. Claims so couched are obviously made with greater caution, not only regarding what the link is between areas of the brain and certain functions, but also regarding what the real categories of brain function are. Hence, part of what neurologists have labored to understand is the nature of the functional organization that underlies the behavior of intact brains. (For a discussion of the history of lateralization hypotheses in the nineteenth century, see Harrington 1985.)

4.3 Mapping the Brain by Electrical Stimulation

Once the electrical properties of the nerves were discovered, the possibility presented itself of using electricity to stimulate directly isolated and specific parts of the nervous system to see if this produced isolated and specific effects. The first well-designed and significant studies on the nervous system using electrical stimulation were undertaken by two German physiologists, Eduard Hitzig (1838–1907) and Gustav Theodor Fritsch (1838–1927), and the method has been of enormous and enduring importance.

Since the brain itself does not contain pain receptors, one of the beauties of the method is that experiments can be undertaken without the confounding effects of a general anesthetic. Initially, Hitzig and Fritsch merely stuck electrodes on the back of the head and noted that when current was applied, the eyes moved. Conjecturing that "the cerebrum . . . is endowed with electric excitability . . . ," they decided to go under the skull and investigate the brain more directly. Using dogs as their experimental animal, they surgically removed segments of the skull. They then placed electrodes on the exposed cortex and stimulated the tissue using very weak currents.

In a report published in 1870 they claimed they had obtained contractions of specific muscle groups from stimulation of specific areas of the cortex, that the relevant area for a given muscle group was small, that it was constant from dog to dog, and that contraction of muscle groups on the body's *left* side was produced by stimulation of the relevant cortical area on the *right* hemisphere. To consolidate their results, they produced a crude map of the motor cortex, showing which muscle groups correlated with which areas of the cortical convolution immediately in front of the central sulcus, an area designated as motor cortex.

Because other cortical areas can also induce movement when electrically stimulated, Hitzig and Fritsch used their stimulation results in conjunction with ablation studies, finding that destruction in these other areas did not affect motor output, but that destruction of selected locations on the precentral convolution did result in weakness and sometimes temporary paralysis of the limbs, and in clumsy and crude movement of the limbs. The interleaving of the two methods was critical in determining areas of specialization, for the stimulation studies seemed to corroborate Jackson's hypothesis of multiple and hierarchical sensorimotor representation; wide areas of the brain might contain motor representations, but only certain narrower areas were specialized for fine or complex movements. The areas designated "motor" were so designated not only because specific motor effects were produced by circumscribed electrical stimulation but also because extirpation of those areas resulted in motor deficits.

David Ferrier (1843–1928) refined the techniques of Hitzig and Fritsch and repeated their results in primates, again combining stimulation and ablation studies to home in on the specific areas specialized in movement of particular muscle groups. He more clearly delineated the motor cortex, which he called a "motor center," and he took his data as evidence supporting localizationist theory (Ferrier 1876).

The first electrical stimulation study on a human subject was performed in 1874 in Cincinnati by an American physician, Roberts Bartholow, on his housemaid, Mary Rafferty, who apparently had a cancer of the skull that had eroded the skin and bone, leaving parts of her brain exposed. Bartholow inserted electrodes into her brain and was able to induce focal convulsions and sensations. For example, he induced contractions of the upper and lower extremities on the right side after stimulation of the left cerebrum. His account of this experiment makes chilling reading, as Mary is described as complaining of a very strong and unpleasant feeling (Bartholow 1874) in her right arm and leg. Bartholow was roundly condemned for using techniques on a patient that were not motivated by clinical and therapeutic considerations, and consequently he languished as a medical outcast. Nevertheless, the work did show that a human brain could be electrically stimulated to produce effects related to those found in animal experiments.

Ferrier believed that his work with primates suggested that in humans too the motor cortex was crucial for voluntary movement and that documentation on natural lesions and on epilepsy fit together with his animal studies (Ferrier 1890). It was an inferential leap with attendant uncertainties, but the evidence was decidedly intriguing. Because researchers were understandably reluctant to use humans as subjects for electrical stimulation experiments unless there was a clear clinical justification, the possibility of using this mapping technique on humans to understand more of higher functions remained largely in abeyance until Wilder Penfield saw in it an invaluable clinical tool, and one that might thereby have theoretical spin-off. Of this, more in section 5.4.

Finer and more detailed examination of the motor and sensory cortex in animals was conducted by C. S. Sherrington (1875–1952) and A. S. F. Grünbaum (1869–1921),[5] who not only improved upon the mapping of the cortex but also delineated the difficulties and limitations of electrical stimulation as a method, some of which remain with us still (figure 4.6). They noticed that if an area of the cortex is stimulated at a particular time, this alters the response characteristic at that point *and* elsewhere in neighboring cortex, sometimes facilitating responses, sometimes resulting in reversal (from extension to flexion of a joint), sometimes producing a different movement altogether. The borders of areas as determined by electrical stimulation may vary as a function of what is stimulated when. As Grünbaum and Sherrington ruefully point out in discussing the motor field:

> Thus if the anterior border is delimited by stimulating a series of cortical points in succession from behind forward, the anterior limit of the field is found farther anterior than if determined by

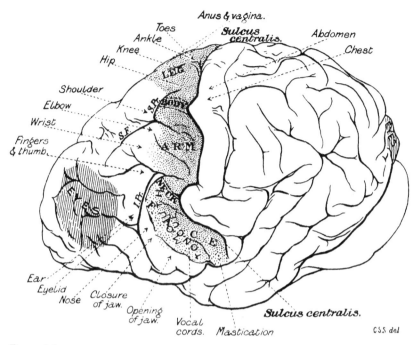

Figure 4.6
The mapping of the motor areas of a chimpanzee brain by Grünbaum and Sherrington (1902). (Reproduced as figure 128 in Clarke and O'Malley 1968.)

stimulating a series of points starting well in front of the limit and followed from before backward. (Leyton and Sherrington 1917; in Clarke and O'Malley 1968:523)

That is, the results are different when working back to front than when working front to back. The time course of events induced in the cortex could therefore not be ignored in trying to determine location. The motor cortex, Grünbaum and Sherrington argued, is labile, and "functional instability" of the motor cortex seemed to be a fact of cortical organization—a fact, moreover, that undermined localization hypotheses that postulated exact, fixed, and time-independent boundaries. (See section 5.4 and Mateer 1983 for a discussion of recent developments in electrical stimulation techniques.)

Selected Readings

Adams, R. D., and M. Victor (1981). *Principles of neurology.* 2nd ed. New York: McGraw-Hill.
Galaburda, Albert M., and Marek-Marsel Mesulam (1983). Neuroanatomical aspects of

cerebral localization. In *Localization in neuropsychology*, ed. A. Kertesz, 21–61. New York: Academic Press.

Harrington, Anne (1985). Nineteenth-century ideas on hemisphere differences and "duality of mind." *Behavioral and Brain Sciences* 8/4:617–659.

Hecaen, Henri, and Martin L. Albert, eds. (1978). *Human neuropsychology*. New York: Wiley.

Heilman, Kenneth M., and Edward Valenstein, eds. (1979). *Clinical neuropsychology*. New York: Oxford University Press.

Kolb, Bryan, and Ian Q. Whishaw (1980). *Fundamentals of human neuropsychology*. San Francisco: W. H. Freeman.

Mateer, Catherine A. (1983). Localization of language and visuospatial functions by electrical stimulation. In *Localization in neuropsychology*, ed. A. Kertesz, 153–183. New York: Academic Press.

Valenstein, Elliot S. (1973). *Brain control*. New York: Wiley.

Chapter 5
Higher Functions: Neuropsychology and Neurology

Apart from the technical and methodological difficulties, perhaps the most serious obstacle in the way of real advance in the study of those aspects of cortical activity that are commonly (if obscurely) referred to as "higher functions," is the absence, in most of neuroscience, of a sure theoretical framework.
W. Maxwell Cowan 1981

5.1 Introduction

Results from lesion studies and from electrical stimulation studies made it evident that the organization of the brain conformed neither to the strict localization model nor to the holistic model, which took *degree* of activity as opposed to *area* of activity as the important variable. The strict localization hypotheses were undermined by a number of findings, both clinical and experimental. For example, in experiments with monkeys Glees and Cole (1950) determined through stimulation studies an area of the motor cortex specific to movement of the thumb, then surgically removed the area and allowed the monkey time to recover from paralysis. During this period the monkey recovered motor function of the thumb. When Glees and Cole reexamined the cortical area, they found that cells bordering the lesion, whose stimulation hitherto did not move the thumb on stimulation, now moved the thumb. These too were lesioned out, and the monkeys again recovered the capacity to move the thumb. These studies, like Lashley's (1933, 1937), did not show there was no cortical specialization for function, but only that strict localization of function was doubtful.

On the other hand, quite specific effects resulting from brain lesions have been observed both in clinical studies and in the laboratory. For example, monkeys with hippocampal lesions show deficits in spatial learning (Olton, Becker, and Handelmann 1979), and humans with bilateral lesions to the hippocampus, amygdala, and temporal lobe show profound anterograde amnesia (Scoville and Milner 1957).

To illustrate the specificity of particular cortical areas, consider color agnosia, studied intensively in the patient W.K. by Kinsbourne and Warrington (1964). W.K. suffered a highly circumscribed lesion to the left posterior cortex, in an area on the borderline between visually responsive areas and areas subserving language. Tested once his condition stabilized, he was found to display a largely isolated deficit in color representation. He was unable either to identify correctly the color of objects or to pick out objects in response to a color named. Nor could he correctly identify the color of the sky, trees, or a stop light. The exceptions here, remarkably, were "white," "gray," and "black." For example, he might say that a stop light is blue or purple, and his responses were no better than chance. On the other hand, he was unproblematically able to match and sort colors, such as pieces of wool, to say whether two samples were the same or different in color, and to say of a picture with a green sky that the sky was the wrong color, though his performance in *naming* the color of sky was at chance. His nonverbal representation for colors seemed, therefore, intact, whereas his verbal representation for colors appeared to be disconnected from the nonverbal. He remained largely unaware of the deficit, presumably because, as Kinsbourne and Warrington observed, "like a sensory aphasic who cannot detect the errors in his own speech, the patient has no means of discovering his mistakes, and he therefore continues unhesitatingly in his wrong use of the names of the colors" (p. 299).

As another example, consider Mrs. B., a patient also studied by Kinsbourne and Warrington (1963a). As demonstrated at autopsy, she had a small, highly circumscribed lesion in the border area between the inferior temporal lobe and the occipital lobe. Her clinical pattern showed a highly selective deficit: she had difficulty in perceiving the *whole* of what was shown, though she could, one by one, perceive the parts. For example, if shown for a brief period a set of geometrical forms, she could identify one, usually the left, well enough, but her simultaneous perception of the whole scene was very limited. Given enough time, she could identify other forms in the picture. Shown a word, she could identify individual letters, but she could not read the whole word. By reading each letter aloud, however, she could then reconstruct the word and by that laborious means identify it. The impairment could not be attributed to a defect in vision or to general intellectual deterioration, but appeared to be specific to simultaneous form perception.

Like Déjerine's (1892) patient (chapter 4), Mrs. B. was able to write from dictation, but she could neither copy written sentences nor read what she had written. Kinsbourne and Warrington suggest that if other patients reportedly suffering from pure alexia were tested for nonverbal form perception as well as for reading, they might be found to be like Mrs. B. in having this more general deficit involving simultaneous form perception. The deeper account of the nature of the capacity in question remains, obviously, to be determined. But this clinical example, and many others like it, imply a specificity in function for circumscribed brain regions that undercuts thoroughly holistic hypotheses.

That the brain has some degree of specialization is evident from clinical studies as well as from stimulation studies, but by 1950 at least, it was very clear that the task-*specificity* of distinct areas was not to be understood on the model of the task-*dedication* of distinct segments of an assembly line or distinct parts of body, such as lungs, heart, and kidney. The tug-of-war between localizationists and antilocalizationists has largely given over to questions about how the brain could be organized such that there can be (partial) recovery of function after certain kinds of lesions, but no recovery after other kinds, and about what "specialization" means in terms of the organization of nervous tissue. This is hard enough to answer with respect to the primary visual cortex, the somatosensory cortex, the motor strip, and so forth, but it is far more difficult with regard to the inbetween areas referred to as "association cortex." Cowan (1981) gives a concise summation of the problems:

> It is not only that we lack a straightforward means of activating most of the associational areas; for many of these areas we hardly know what types of questions to pose. (p. xviii)

Contributing pieces to the puzzle of cerebral organization and higher functions are studies at many levels, including neuroembryology and neuroanatomy, as well as clinical and behavioral studies. In this chapter I shall focus on the latter type of research.

One of the most remarkable and fascinating domains of study at this level has involved the search for differences in functional specialization of the two cerebral hemispheres. This research was greatly stimulated by the neurological finding that severe epilepsy could be treated by surgical section of the commissures connecting the hemispheres. Patients who have undergone this treatment are an invaluable source of information about brain organization, and the subtle disunity detected in their cognitive lives also motivated philosophical questions about the unity of consciousness, the unity of the self, control, and the nature of the distinction between voluntary and involuntary behavior. Sections 5.2 and 5.3 will therefore focus on the lateralization research, section 5.4 will discuss techniques for determining intrahemispheric specialization of function, and section 5.5 will briefly summarize some neurological data that may help to unseat assorted philosophical prejudices about higher functions and what we know of them.

5.2 Hemispheric Lateralization of Functions: Split-Brain Studies

The Technique
The most prominent connection between the cerebral hemispheres is a thick communicating sheet of neurons called the *great cerebral commissure* or the *corpus callosum*. There are additional connecting commissures, including the anterior, the posterior, the habenular, and the hippocampal commissures, and since the brain is not divided at all in the midbrain and brain stem, there are presumably communicating routes via these structures as well (figure 5.1). (See also figures 2.7, 3.2.)

The clinical situation was apprehended as follows. Certain patients suffered severe epilepsy that was not significantly controlled by drugs, the severity and frequency of their seizures making anything resembling normal living impossible. To neurologists studying epilepsy, it appeared that seizures spread from the epileptic focus to undamaged areas, and hence the idea arose that the seizures might be diminished if the electrical storm could be prevented from spreading from the epileptic hemisphere to the normal hemisphere. By cutting the corpus callosum, such spread might be curtailed. The surgical procedure was first attempted by William van Wagenen and R. Yorke Herren in the 1940s, but without significant clinical success—but also, surprisingly, without significant impairment to the patient. Apparently Van Wagenen did not usually section the anterior commissure, and he may not always have entirely sectioned the corpus callosum.

Puzzling over what this large mass of fibers did in the brain, researchers began to study in animals the effects of callosal section, and in the 1950s Ronald Myers and Roger Sperry discovered that with the proper method, they could teach one hemisphere of a cat's brain to perform a certain task, while the other hemisphere remained ignorant of it. In their procedure they cut not only the commissures but also the optic chiasm (figure 5.2), which meant that all information from the right eye went to the left hemisphere, and vice versa. So merely by patching one eye, they could exclusively condition one hemisphere to respond to a visual stimulus. This was a remarkable result,

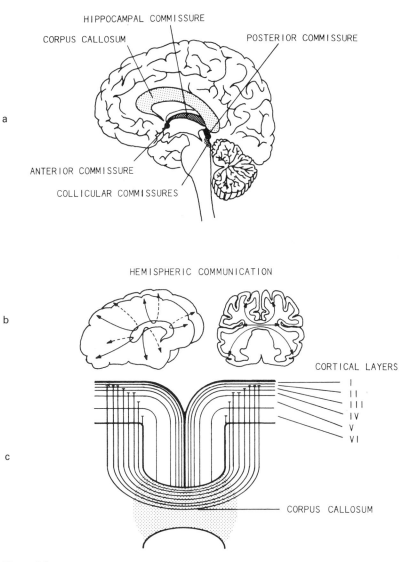

Figure 5.1
(a) Position of major interhemispheric connections in the human brain as seen in sagittal section. (b) Interhemispheric fibers largely connect homologous areas in the two half-brains. (c) In addition, they terminate mostly in the cortical laminae from which they arose in the opposite hemisphere. (From Gazzaniga and LeDoux (1978). *The Integrated Mind*. New York: Plenum.)

for it seemed to imply that the unity of the cerebral pair was a matter of whether or not they received the same information, not of some higher-order unifying principle, and it raised puzzling questions about why evolution apparently lavished on the nervous system *two* cognitive processing systems.

Improving upon Van Wagenen's earlier procedures, Joseph Bogen and Peter Vogel in the 1960s again tried commissurotomy for intractable epilepsy, and this time undoubted clinical success was achieved. Some two dozen patients underwent commissurotomy, in which the entire length of the corpus callosum was sectioned, as well as the anterior commissure (Bogen, Fisher, and Vogel 1965). This set of patients was subsequently intensively and ingeniously studied by Roger Sperry and his group at the California Institute of Technology. Contrary to the earlier studies on Van Wagenen's patients, these studies showed that the commissurotomy produced definite and striking effects, and moreover that the effects were not unrelated to the results earlier obtained with cats. In the 1970s Donald Wilson of the Dartmouth Medical School began to use the technique, but with some differences (Wilson et al. 1977). In his method the surgery was done in two stages, and the anterior commissure was spared. This series became known as the *Eastern series*, in contrast to the first group, which is often referred to as the *California series* or the *Bogen series*.

The Disconnection Effect
This work clearly established that, under suitable conditions, one could show a definite disconnection between the cognitive activities of the two hemispheres—that each hemisphere had, so to speak, a life or unity or integrity of its own. Since the procedures under which the disconnection effect can be made to show up are well known, a highly condensed description will suffice here (figure 5.2) (Gazzaniga and LeDoux 1978, Levy-Agresti and Sperry 1968, Sperry 1974).

In one experimental setup, visual information is sent exclusively to one hemisphere and then a question is posed to see whether the information is available to the other hemisphere. For example, the subject fixates on the midpoint, and a tachistoscope is used to flash a signal to one visual hemifield for a designated period, roughly 200 milliseconds (figure 5.3). (Unlike Myers and Sperry's cats, these patients have an intact optic chiasma, which means that ordinarily visual information goes to both hemispheres. By confining the signal to one visual *hemifield*, the experimenter can ensure that the signal goes to only one hemisphere.)

If the word "spoon" is flashed to the right hemisphere and the

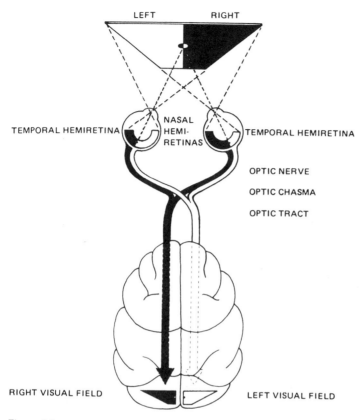

Figure 5.2
Information in the right visual field goes to the left hemisphere, and information in the left visual field to the right hemisphere. Information presented to each *eye* is projected equally to both hemispheres. In order to ensure that information is presented to only one hemisphere, the subject must fixate the midline and the visual stimulus is briefly flashed. (From Gazzaniga and LeDoux (1978). *The Integrated Mind*. New York: Plenum.)

subject is asked to report what he saw, he answers "nothing," but if he is asked to use his left hand to feel under a cloth for the object seen, the left hand picks out a spoon. Evidently, the right hemisphere knows that it saw a spoon and hence the left hand acts on that information; the left hemisphere knows nothing and hence, being the linguistically fluent hemisphere, says it knows nothing.

In another study (Levy, Trevarthen, and Sperry 1972), subjects were asked to fixate the midpoint, and then a composite (chimeric) figure was flashed. Generally the subject's verbal reports corresponded to the picture flashed to the left hemisphere, and when the subject was asked to point to the person seen, the hand (either right

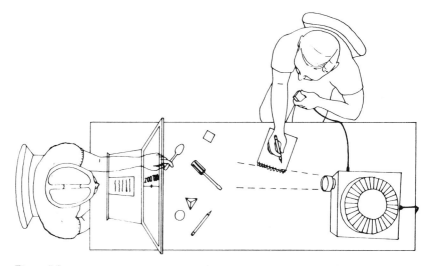

Figure 5.3
The basic testing arrangement used for the examination of lateralized visual and
stereognostic functions. Here the subject picks out by feeling with his left hand the
object that was visually presented to his right hemisphere. (From Gazzaniga and
LeDoux (1978). *The Integrated Mind*. New York: Plenum.)

or left) would point to the picture corresponding to the one flashed to
the right hemisphere (figure 5.4). Noteworthy also in these studies is
the phenomenon of *completion*, whereby an incomplete figure is apprehended as complete. Although only half a face or figure was presented to each hemisphere, what was seen by each hemisphere was
not an incomplete figure but a whole, completed figure. Why and
how the figure is filled in is not understood.

Having established a disconnection effect, researchers saw also the
opportunity to tease out evidence for differential specialization of the
hemispheres. But before turning to those matters, I want to consider
briefly the disconnection effect and its implications for tacit assumptions about unity of self and unity of control.

One is accustomed to thinking of oneself as a single, unified, coherent *self*. The possibility that underlying that customary conception is
something diverse and divisible, something whose coherence may be
tied to coherence of input and output or to anatomical connectedness,
rather than to an "intrinsic coherence of selfness," is the possibility
ushered in by the split-brain studies. At first blush it is a startling
possibility.

In the aftermull of reading studies of split-brain subjects one is
inevitably provoked to wonder about their inner life and to ask,

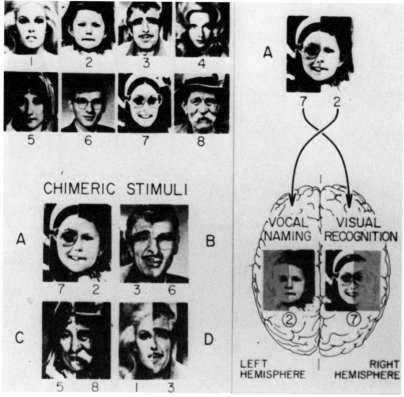

CHIMERIC STIMULI

Figure 5.4
The test for the simultaneous perception of faces by the two hemispheres. On the right: diagram of projection of a chimeric stimulus presented to the split-brain subject. Verbally, the split-brain subject reports seeing 2, but the left hand points to 7 as the seen face. In either case, what is seen is reported to be a whole face. (From Levy, Trevarthen, and Sperry 1972.)

"What would happen to *me* if my brain were bisected?" Evidently it would be different from having a kidney removed, but the difference it would make to oneself is far from obvious. Disconnection can be demonstrated in commissurotomized subjects. So much is clear. But hard on the heels of the observation comes the inescapable inclination to infer that they have two of something where the rest of us have only one. But two of *what*? Two minds perhaps, or two souls, or two selves, or two persons, two centers of consciousness, two centers of cognition, two centers of control, two wills, or what? How do these categories relate to each other? For example, if there is more than one center of cognition, does this mean there is more than one center of control, or more than one center of consciousness? Or more than one mind? How do we know *which* of these things intact brains have one of and split-brain subjects have more than one of? What is becoming evident is that we do not have an adequate theoretical framework within which we can answer these questions, and that the disconnection effects should be taken as an occasion for finding out more about the brain such that we can begin to understand the results, rather than for forcing the results to fit with our prescientific assumptions. (The question of the revision of our folk psychological preconceptions will be discussed at length in chapters 8 and 9.)

Dualists will have a special problem with interpretation—namely, how to reconcile the results with their conception of the mind or soul as a nonphysical substance in causal interaction with the nervous system. Of course, it is possible that a dualist might see in the results reason to abandon dualism, but if he is bound irrevocably to the Cartesian conception, he needs to find an interpretation of the results that is consistent with the assumption that the mind is a nonphysical substance. (A discussion of the merits of materialism and dualism can be found in chapter 8.)

To be more explicit about the dualist's dilemma, consider that, on a dualist conception, the self (or mind or what have you) *has an intrinsic unity*—that is, a unity owed to the nature of mental substances rather than dependent upon the anatomical or physiological organization of the underlying brain. Indeed, for those dualists who believe that the self survives brain death, this is a crucial consideration. The brain may rot entirely, but the soul, argues the dualist, is immortal.

Accordingly, to deny the relevance of anatomical disconnection to unity of self, dualists have argued with some ingenuity either that everyone normally has *two* minds (Puccetti 1981) or that no one— even the split-brain patients—has more than one (Eccles 1977). On either alternative, commissurotomy allegedly makes no difference whatever to the unity of self (or selves). There is, however, a price to pay in each case.

The first view entails believing that each skull houses two persons/ two minds, and that even oneself is not, so to speak, *one*self. The second view has to downplay the abilities and complexities of one hemisphere (the right) and to identify the specialties of the other hemisphere with the expression of consciousness so as to deny that one of them (again the right) is fancy enough to have consciousness and selfhood.

The trouble is, however, that several split-brain patients have linguistic capacities not only in the left hemisphere but also show increasingly impressive capacities for comprehension and expression in the right hemisphere (see the next subsection). These cases look like straightforward counterexamples to the hypothesis, and to insist that in these cases only the left hemisphere is conscious begins to look like dogmatism. Since the motivation for each of the dualist alternatives is not simply to make sense of the phenomenon but to make science conform to antecedent convictions about the nonphysical nature of the mind, neither position is prepared to concede the possibility that our commonsense framework is theoretically too impoverished to sustain an adequate interpretation of the disconnection effect.

The dualist's attempts to force an adequate interpretation out of commonsense conceptions are nonetheless instructive in showing how very inadequate that framework really is and, pari passu, how inadequate dualism itself is. The disconnection phenomenon does resist assimilation within the commonsense, orthodox conception of ourselves, and it begins to be evident that we do not have the theoretical resources available to give sure-footed interpretations. Nonetheless, what *not* to do here is more easily specified than what to do, inasmuch as some interpretations stumble rather obviously and some inferences are clearly maladroit. For example, ample evidence has accumulated that even in the normal case there is a great deal of complex, clever, *cognitive* processing that is not available to awareness, such as the processing that underlies the production and comprehension of grammatical sentences. It is very smart processing that is also inaccessible to introspection. Accordingly, it cannot be inferred that

"if there are two cognitive modules, then there are two centers of consciousness."

Again, since there is ample prima facie evidence for some degree of consciousness in nonverbal children, deaf-mutes, aphasics, and many animals (Patricia S. Churchland 1983), it cannot, in the absence of much argument, be assumed that

"if x has no linguistic productions, then x is not conscious."

But what conditions must be satisfied for an organism to be conscious, or for an organism to have more than one center of consciousness? Does the fact that dolphins sleep one hemisphere at a time mean that they have more than our complement of centers of control/consciousness/cognition? Unity of self apparently does not require complete connectedness of information, since humans characteristically fail on occasion to notice patent contradictions in their beliefs and even in their desires (Stich 1978, Nisbett and Ross 1980), so how much connectedness and integration is required for unity of self? Are the split-brain subjects so very different from those humans with split personalities? What is the basis for postulating distinct centers or modules? These are empirical questions for which we need empirical, as opposed to a priori, answers. (For a further discussion of revisions to the concept of consciousness, see chapter 9.)

Until much more is known about the mind-brain, these questions will have to wait for an answer, tantalizing though they may be. As things stand, the notions of a center of consciousness, or a center of control, let alone "mind," "self," "person," and "soul," are theoretically so ill defined that we are at a loss to know how to count such things. In the absence of a psychological and neuroscientific theory concerning cognition, consciousness, attention, and so on, counting centers of consciousness and the like is essentially a guess-and-by-golly affair.

Until we know *what* we are counting, we cannot begin to count—and we cannot even say with much confidence that we have *one* of whatever it is that split-brain subjects seem to have two of. It is like trying to count blood types before there was a theory about the constituents of blood and how they differed from organism to organism, or like trying before Cantor to decide whether there was more than one infinite set; without a sound set theory, it was like clawing at the air. To the amusement of future historians, current debates on the number of selves in split-brain subjects may be seen as akin to nineteenth-century debates in biology over whether each organism or organism-part had its own vital spirit, and over what happens to the vital spirit of a bisected worm whose parts squirm off in separate directions to begin lives of their own. What I find especially important in the split-brain results is the suggestion that our familiar conceptions, such as "center of consciousness" and "self," do not have the empirical integrity they are often assumed to have. (For more discussion on these questions, see Patricia S. Churchland 1983, Dennett 1978b, 1979, Griffin 1984, and the commentaries on Puccetti 1981.)

Clues to Lateralization

If the two hemispheres have different capacities, some evidence for those differences ought to show up in the behavior of split-brain subjects when the hemispheres are separately stimulated. Hence, such subjects present a unique opportunity to investigate whether there are differences and what their nature is. To those of us looking in from the outside, the early results of studies investigating this possibility appeared to show that the left hemisphere (LH) had linguistic capacities that the right hemisphere (RH) lacked, and that the RH had certain nonverbal skills in which it was superior to the LH, for example, facial recognition and manipulospatial skills.

Some descendant hypotheses that bear a family resemblance to these ancestral hypotheses do seem to be true, but as research progressed, matters revealed themselves to be considerably more complicated, and newer methods have not always led to a convergence of theory. Besides these two hypotheses, other claims for differential specialization, initially walking in long strides, have become enmired in controversy concerning methods, statistical analysis, population samples, interpretation, and so forth. In this category are hypotheses to the effect that the RH is specialized for musical capacities and for certain emotional responses.

As well, there are some hypotheses which are just plain wild and woolly; for example, that the RH is imaginative and creative while the LH is analytical, stodgy, and plodding, that the dichotomies of mental life limned in Eastern religions such as yin and yang have their neural home in the left and right hemispheres, respectively, and that one hemisphere (usually thought to be the left) is more under the thumb of the superego than the other. Airport bookstalls display books specifying therapeutic exercises to bring up the "tone" of a "neglected" hemisphere, and there are those moved 'to champion right hemisphere rights. But let us start where matters are clearest and the consensus on results is substantial, namely with the hypothesis that linguistic skills are lateralized to the LH.

The performance of split-brain subjects in the specially devised tests indicated one clear asymmetry in the linguistic performance of the two hemispheres. Specifically, the LH could give verbal answers to questions, whereas the RH could not (Gazzaniga, Bogen, and Sperry 1962, Levy-Agresti and Sperry 1968). This much seemed to corroborate other neurological findings of correlations between LH lesions and linguistic deficits. But a more finely specified characterization of the capacities was needed to determine whether the RH lacked simply motor control for speech, or the wider capacity for expression, or the capacity for understanding language and for manipulating linguistic representations, or the capacity to think in language, or some more deeply characterized capacity that resulted in lack of productive capacity, and so forth. Wanted are the answers to questions such as these: When one thinks in words to oneself is this a process going on in the LH and not the RH? Does the RH normally contribute in some way to the processing underlying language? If the RH does not use language as a representational medium, what does it use? What is the evolutionary basis for a division of labor, and are there performance asymmetries in other animals?

In none of the tests on the California series of patients were spoken or written answers produced by the RH; hence, it was concluded that the RH lacked expressive capacity for language. The problem therefore was to determine the nature and extent of comprehension by the RH. Subjects from this series appeared to have severely limited but significant linguistic comprehension in the RH; the RH could match simple, concrete nouns with pictures, but performance dropped on complex nouns and on verbs. When words were spoken aloud, the left hand could retrieve the matching object. Although it was argued that the RH must understand language to the extent of understanding the task demand, this was tendentious since visual demonstrations were always and repeatedly given along with verbal explanations.

The LH could produce a smile when flashed the word "smile," but the RH never did. Nevertheless, the verbal command to make a fist with the left hand or raise the left arm could be obeyed. Moreover, the RH was unable to match pictures according to rhyming names, to distinguish singular from plural or past from present, and to determine from the syntax, subject and object. One theory was that such limited capacity for understanding as the RH did have was different in kind from that of the LH, and that for the RH linguistic symbols were qualitatively on a par with any other visual or acoustic stimulus (Levy 1982).

To deny the RH *any* linguistic facility was too strong, since the left hand could point to and retrieve objects matching words and vice versa, and when the RH was asked, "What do monkeys eat a lot of?", the left hand responded by searching in the cloth bag of plastic fruit and pulling out the banana. In any case it remained a possibility that the testing methods might favor the LH and give misleading results, and that the RH might have a greater capacity than hitherto detected by the tachistoscopic method. Zaidel (1975) set out to examine the possibility that if words were presented for a longer period, comprehension performance of the RH might improve. He therefore devised a special contact lens—the Z lens—that was designed to block out light to half the retina and hence to restrict information to one hemifield and thence to one hemisphere. In this way he could control visual stimuli to one hemisphere while permitting a longer scan than the tachistoscopic method (figure 5.5).

Based on a series of tests with the Z lens, Zaidel reported significant linguistic comprehension in the RH of split-brain subjects in the California series. Given time to scan, the RH demonstrated rather complex comprehension, performing roughly like a normal-ten-year old and proving able to assemble letters into words and recognize a wide range of words, including verbs (that is, it could match verbs and pictures of actions). Oddly, the RH still did nothing

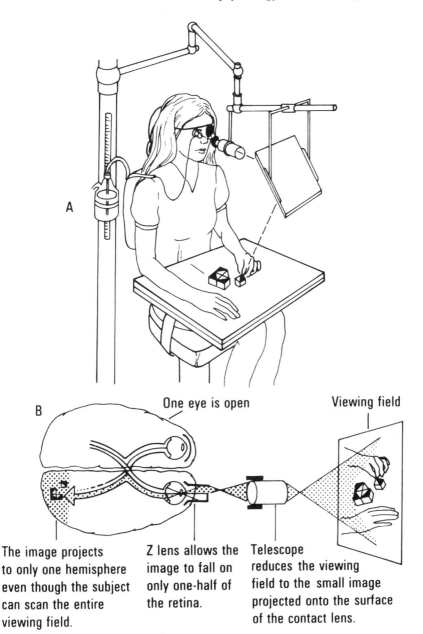

The image projects to only one hemisphere even though the subject can scan the entire viewing field.

Z lens allows the image to fall on only one-half of the retina.

Telescope reduces the viewing field to the small image projected onto the surface of the contact lens.

Figure 5.5
The Z lens. The lens set-up keeps the patient's field of view lateralized to one hemisphere. One eye is patched, and the image is projected to only one-half of the retina of the other eye. (From Springer and Deutsch (1981). *Left Brain, Right Brain.* W. H. Freeman and Co. Copyright © 1981. Adapted from Zaidel 1978.)

when the request "Smile" was visually presented. Syntactic performance was still inferior, as measured by the Token Test in which subjects are asked to execute such commands as "Pick up either the blue circle or the red triangle" and "Put the green circle on the blue triangle."

This work greatly complicated the theory that language—motor control of speech, comprehension, *the works*—was lateralized to the left hemisphere. Some researchers came to favor the theory that aspects of linguistic skill are lateralized in varying degrees and that comprehension is more bilateral than had been thought previously, though the left hemisphere is preeminent for motor control. Exclusive control it probably does not have, since it is known from neurological cases that aphasic patients with LH lesions can sometimes utter oaths, sing well-known songs, or repeat well-rehearsed phrases, as in the case of the proctologist who was severely aphasic but who would on occasion flawlessly deliver his ritual diatribe against the use of Preparation H. Allegedly, the "automatic" nature of such utterances implies that they are more like reflexive responses than like intentional speech, but matters are too ill defined here for that claim to mean a great deal.

Zaidel's results indicated an even greater linguistic capacity of the RH than the first studies had demonstrated, and one resolution of the disparity was to claim that the earlier performance profile of the RH may have been an artifact of the experimental procedure. On the other hand, Zaidel's work is by no means beyond controversy. Skepticism over whether the Z lens can be counted on to restrict light absolutely to one hemifield has inevitably and reasonably been voiced. Moreover, Zaidel's results are based essentially on just two of the split-brain patients, L.B. and N.G., and in Gazzaniga's earlier testing of six subjects in the California series, including L.B. and N.G., the four others apparently failed to show any evidence of RH language functions (Gazzaniga 1983). Generalizing from the sample consisting of L.B. and N.G. may well be misleading, therefore, the more so since studies of the Eastern series of patients revealed that only three of twenty-eight patients had any linguistic comprehension in the RH (Gazzaniga 1983). The question of the extent and nature of the RH's capacity to comprehend language became increasingly complex, and the disagreement began to heat up.

Other complexities began to crowd into the picture. The reliability of tests in which questions were presented out loud to the subject came under scrutiny. There seems to be some scope for ipsilateral (same side) mediation of hand movements in addition to the more standard contralateral (other side) control. When a command is given out loud, it is received by both hemispheres and the LH may some-times initiate left hand movements. Accordingly, some of the early tests showing good linguistic comprehension by the RH may have been queered by an insufficiently careful method of stimulus presentation.

To avoid this sort of contamination, Kimura's (1967) technique us-ing auditory stimuli seems preferable. The anatomical situation is as follows: in the auditory system there is a major projection from each ear to the contralateral hemisphere, but there is also a smaller ipsilat-eral projection. (See figure 3.7.) Ordinarily, a message piped into one ear goes to both hemispheres. However, Kimura argued that when there are competing messages from each ear, only the message in the contralateral pathway gets through and the message in the smaller ipsilateral pathway is blocked. In order to deliver an auditory mes-sage selectively to one hemisphere, it is necessary to pipe a different message to each ear. Accordingly, in the testing arrangement the subject wears headphones and a distinct message is *simultaneously* presented to each ear. Kimura's technique for testing asymmetries by presenting competing messages to the ears is called "dichotic listening."

Although the theory has been generally accepted and the dichotic listening method has been widely used in studying lateralization in normal subjects as well as split-brain subjects, disquieting evidence that the ipsilateral message does sometimes get through has begun to emerge. Gordon (1980) found in his study of the California series of split-brain subjects that the commands presented dichotically to the left ear did sometimes reach the LH—often enough to raise a caution about results obtained using the method.

As the capacities of the RH were explored in greater detail, it was found that if the LH of split-brain subjects was occupied in an ex-traneous task, the RH would respond to a dichotically presented command such as "Point to the ceiling" with the appropriate action (Gordon 1980). In one rather dramatic example where different com-mands were sent to the two hemispheres, the left arm did the bidding of the RH and pointed to the ceiling while the right arm at the behest of the LH scratched the table. It might be reasoned that the lack of response by the RH in earlier tests to the request "Smile" was due not to failure of comprehension on the part of the RH but to other factors, such as dominance of the LH for control of brain stem mechanisms involved in motor ouput.

Clinical studies of patients with right hemisphere lesions give only ambiguous support to the hypothesis that normally the RH has no role in language, inasmuch as some studies report deficits whereas others can find no significant differences in language performance between RH lesioned patients and controls. For example, some neurologists (Critchley 1962, Gainotti et al. 1983, Gardner et al. 1983) have claimed that with sufficiently subtle tests, striking linguistic deficits can be seen in RH lesioned patients. Such patients apparently show diminished spontaneity in conversation, hesitation and blocking in finding the right word, and difficulty in giving definitions and paraphrases; moreover, they have difficulty seeing the point of a joke or are obtuse with metaphor and double entendre, and they have trouble summarizing a fable or telling a brief story. (See also Myers and Linebaugh 1981.) On the other hand, a well-controlled study by Brookshire and Nicholas (1984) found that RH lesioned patients were as well able to extract the main points of a paragraph as were controls.

The linguistic deficits allegedly presented by RH patients are certainly not just like those presented by LH patients, and until the clinical picture is better defined, it might be safest to postpone concluding that language is strictly a left hemisphere operation. Just what sort of role the RH plays is unclear, nor is it well understood just what the cognitive and subcognitive functions subserving linguistic performance are such that we should test for deficits in those functions. Such linguistic theory as we do have seems to wither before the monumental task of characterizing the deeper capacities of both the RH and the LH in virtue of which humans display their wide range of linguistic and cognitive accomplishments. (See especially Gardner et al. 1983.)

Although a rarity, left hemispherectomies in adults have been performed for the treatment of tumors. In the first report of such a case, Zollinger (1935) observed that the patient recovered some speech and was able to carry out verbal commands. More recently, Burklund and Smith (1977) report two cases of left hemispherectomy on right-handers in which the patient showed a consistent and gradual increase in verbal capacities until the neoplasm invaded the right hemisphere and the patients died. Both patients showed quite similar and definite recovery of language functions. For example, a month after surgery one patient was able to answer "yes" and "no" appropriately and asked the nurse, "You got a match?" Five months after surgery he made no errors in counting or in reciting the days of the week, and only two errors in completing eight sentences. His spontaneous speech was limited, but his residual verbal capacities were striking.

Clearly, in these patients the RH was not mute, let alone alinguistic, and although neither survived the surgery longer than two years, the pattern of recovery invites the speculation that performance might have continued to improve. Since these data do not comport very well with neurological data on LH lesions, an explanation is needed. Smith (1966, 1972) has offered the intriguing suggestion that when the hemispheres are intact, there is a complex cooperative relation between the RH and the LH, with the LH exerting dominance and control and inhibiting RH language. These inhibitory effects continue so long as there is LH tissue but are diminished or extinguished with left hemispherectomy and with commissurotomy, whereupon the RH is permitted some participation in linguistic business. Initially Smith's hypothesis received derisory rejection from orthodox opinion, but it is now being taken seriously as a testable hypothesis (Sperry 1982).

The well-worn maxim that the inevitable sequel to lesions in Broca's area is complete loss of speech is called into question by the clinical observations of Mohr (1973) and Zangwill (1975), who saw unusual verbal capacity in several adult patients following surgical excision of tissue including Broca's area. These patients were all right-handers. Roughly a month after surgery they were speaking well and answering questions; for example, when asked, "What is a dwarf?", one patient said, "A child is a normal human being in the process of growing up and a dwarf could be a fully matured human being" (Zangwill 1975). On the basis of other data, it seems doubtful that these subjects had bilateral linguistic representation prior to the growth of the tumors, and it seems unlikely that in each case the surgeons were just mistaken about what neural areas were removed. These cases are certainly problematic for the hypothesis that lesions to Broca's area result in Broca's aphasia, but since the language functions are likely managed by other areas in the LH, they do not constitute evidence for RH linguistic capacity.

Textbook accounts of split-brain research naturally strive to present a clean package, uncluttered with details of exceptions and variations, and clear of data tables, descriptions of methods, and individual histories. So between the farm-gate and the shop window, as it were, a lot of the messiness endemic to the actual research is cured out.

For example, there is in fact substantial individual variation in capacities of split-brain subjects, acknowledged for example by Gazzaniga in his twenty-year retrospective (1983) and by Sperry in his Nobel lecture (1982), but it goes largely unmentioned in general descriptions. Because they are searching for the generalization, the researchers themselves tend to play down the individual variation in capacities, but variation there certainly is. Left out of textbook accounts is the fact that most split-brain patients give virtually no responses at all to stimuli presented to the RH, not even to simple perceptual matching tests. Others are capable of some rudimentary linguistic comprehension, and still others display assorted shades of proficiency. In addition, the sample size is small, and all split-brain subjects have a neurological pathology—namely, epilepsy.

Moreover, there is just enough evidence to give life to the suggestion that the greater the linguistic competence of the RH, the greater is its skill in the other things it is allegedly good at, such as manipulospatial tasks (Gazzaniga and Smylie 1984). Those who show no capacity for language even on simple matching tests apparently do not show RH superiority on constructive and spatial tasks. No response is not very interesting, and consequently the subjects with nonresponsive RHs are not the ones who are studied intensively. Are they atypical? It is not yet clear who *is* typical.

Two patients from the Eastern series have been found to have striking and sophisticated RH capacities not only for linguistic comprehension but also for expression (Gazzaniga and LeDoux 1978, Gazzaniga 1983). They are unusual in this regard, and it is believed that neurological damage to the LH in childhood resulted in a bilateral representation of language and that they are therefore not typical. Nevertheless, there are two respects in which the results from the studies of the split-brain subjects P.S. and V.P. merit particular reflection. The first concerns how the LH explains and renders coherent the behavior initiated by the RH, and the second concerns the cognitive capacities of the RH when it is linguistically competent.

How does the LH of a split-brain patient think about the behavior intended not by it, but by the intentions of the RH to which it had no access, either before or after the event? The answer is deeply interesting, for the LH does not appear to go through a conscious process of seeing the behavior as uncaused by it, wondering how on earth it happened, and then deliberately fabricating a story to explain it. On the contrary, it smoothly incorporates the behavior into its scheme of things, providing a coherent and plausible explanation without conscious puzzlement or mendacity. Consider the following examples.

A picture of a snowy scene is flashed to the RH and a picture of a chicken's claw is flashed to the LH. An array of pictures is then placed before the subject, who is to select with each hand a picture that best matches the flashed picture (figure 5.6). In this setup P.S.'s left hand selected a shovel to go with the snowy scene, and his right hand selected a chicken's head to match the claw. When asked to explain the choices, the verbally more fluent hemisphere responded thus: "That's easy, the chicken claw goes with the chicken and you need a shovel to clean out the chicken shed." The response of the LH thus

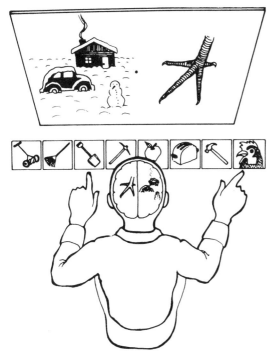

Figure 5.6
The method used in presenting two different cognitive tasks simultaneously, one to each hemisphere. The left hemisphere was required to select the match for what it saw (the chicken claw), while the right was to select the match for what it saw (the snowy scene). After each hemisphere responded, the subject was asked to explain the behavior. (From Gazzaniga and LeDoux (1978). *The Integrated Mind*. New York: Plenum.)

makes sense of the left hand action using the resources available to the LH, and the response is unstrained and coherent.

P.S. understood the surgery, and he understood that his hemispheres were disconnected and could act independently of each other—or perhaps I should say that his LH and possibly his RH understood these things. But notice that in the case in question the LH does not respond by saying that what the left hand does is not its responsibility, or that the RH controls the left hand, or, most significantly, that it does not know why the left hand reached for the shovel. The LH responds as though the motivating factors for the left hand's action were its own.

What is striking, therefore, is that given its understanding, the LH of P.S. does not explain the actions of the left hand as something the RH did. Even when just reminded of the RH's ability, the LH persists in explaining the action as though the action were something it intended all along to do. In case after case the LH integrates the actions initiated by the RH into its own scheme of things. (For more examples and discussions, see Gazzaniga 1985.)

This confabulation appears to be natural, untroubled, and appropriate, and there is no evidence whatsoever that the subject is consciously making things up. Other commissurotomized subjects show that same apparently irresistible tendency to quench ostensible paradoxes by confabulation. (See Gazzaniga 1983 and 1985.) It is as though the theoretical framework the brain uses to make sense of its world will not tolerate or will not accommodate certain kinds of aberrant data or aberrant thoughts. The data that parts of one's body act without one's intentions may be consistently rejected by healthy brains in favor of some more plausible hypothesis. Or thoughts concerning disunity may never earn a working place in a brain's representational system of the world because they are inconsistent with its basic principles for organizing its world, or if they do, the effects on the representational framework may be a disastrous disintegration.

Making sense of the world is probably as basic a function as just about anything else the brain does, and the nature of the representational system and the principles of its organization can be investigated empirically (Gardner et al. 1983). Moreover, from an entirely different area of research, evidence accumulates that *normally*, explanation of choices, moods, judgments, and so forth, are less introspection-driven than they are theory-driven (Nisbett and Ross 1980). What seems exciting and promising is that the results from this research on split-brain patients, the results from social psychology, and the philosophical theory underwriting revisionary materialism (chapters 8 and 9) are converging. (See also Patricia Churchland 1983.)

The first point leads to the second, which is that the real value of the split-brain research may lie less in what it reveals concerning anatomical organization—which hemisphere is dominant for which capacities—than in the light it sheds on the *cognitive organization* of the brain. After all, it could be said that neurological studies (stroke patients, Wada tests (see section 5.3), and so forth) had already revealed roughly as much as the split-brain studies about lateralization. With split-brain patients it is possible to investigate such things as what difference linguistic capacity makes to the cognitive skills of an RH (the evidence so far suggests that it doesn't help; see Gazzaniga and Smylie 1984), whether there is competition between the hemispheres for processing resources (there seems to be; see Holtzman and Gazzaniga 1982), whether there is paracallosal transfer of information and what its character is (there is, and it seems to be very abstract), what the deeper capacities of the hemispheres are, and what the nature of attention, memory, and so forth really is.

At this point, I should like to conclude with a crisp summary of results from split-brain research, but the complications are such that I am deterred from so doing. So far as lateralization is concerned, the most securely battened-down conclusion to emerge from the split-brain studies and related neurological studies is this: the LH is preeminent in the motor control of speech and generally far outstrips the RH in comprehension; the RH generally outperforms the LH in manipulospatial tasks. Is the LH lateralized for language? It depends on what "lateralized" means. (See also Allen 1983.) If it is defined to mean merely that the LH in many brains performs better on verbal tasks than the RH, then indeed language is lateralized to the LH. If it means that the RH has no significant linguistic *capacities* or that the RH contributes nothing to normal linguistic processing, or that the neural tissue in the LH is specialized for linguistic capacities but the neural tissue of the RH is not, then the claim is still *sub judice*. There is an abundance of provocative data and of ingenious tricks for investigating the brain, but exactly what it all means in terms of definable capacities remains deeply puzzling.

5.3 Hemispheric Lateralization: Neuropsychological Techniques

5.3.1 The Wada Test (Amytal Aphasia Test)
As a means of establishing before surgery where motor control for speech was lateralized, J. Wada devised the method of injecting the barbiturate sodium amytal into either the left or the right carotid artery; the left carotid supplies blood to the left hemisphere, the right carotid to the right hemisphere (figures 4.2, 4.3). The effect of the drug is to suppress neural activity; hence, by administering it selectively to one hemisphere at a time, it is possible to anesthetize one hemisphere while the other remains active. (See Wada 1949, Wada and Rasmussen 1960.)

Briefly, in the Wada test a needle is inserted into one carotid artery and the patient is required to raise both arms and to perform a verbal task such as counting backward by threes from one hundred. As the drug is released into the artery, the arm contralateral to the inactivated hemisphere droops and falls, and cessation of speech is taken as reliable evidence for dominance of motor control in the inactivated hemisphere. For example, suppose the patient is right-handed and the amytal is injected into the left carotid. As activity in the LH is suppressed, the right arm will drop and speech will probably cease.

The patient may then be asked to hum a melody, make pitch discriminations, or something of the kind, as the capacities of the RH are investigated.

Findings at the Montreal Neurological Institute, where the test was developed, show that some 90 percent of right-handers and 70 percent of left-handers have speech lateralized to the LH. The remaining group is a mixed bag, with some showing speech lateralized to the RH, and some left-handers showing bilateral motor control for speech (Rasmussen and Milner 1977). Before generalizing the results to the population at large, it should be recalled that all these tests were done on neurological patients, most of whom were epileptic.

With this much description of the Wada test, it might be imagined that sodium amytal is the perfect means for exploring the capacities of the two hemispheres, for at first glance it looks like reversible hemispherectomy. The appearance is misleading, however, for a variety of reasons. Although the test has been an invaluable clinical tool and has yielded precious theoretical data, it is severely limited.

Because there are risks with the drug and with the procedures, the test is kept as short as possible—just long enough to get the piece of information that makes it worth the patient's risk to undergo the test. Anything else is a bonus. The whole business usually lasts no longer than two to six minutes, which means that detailed testing of the subtleties of RH comprehension of language is just not possible. Coarse-grained questions such as "Which hemisphere is dominant for motor control of speech?" can be answered, but more fine-grained questions requiring lengthy tests cannot.

Unacquainted with the hazards of the procedure, I once asked if it would be possible for me to undergo a left-sided Wada test. My objective was simple enough; I wanted to see what it was like to have an inactive LH and to find out whether, with only the RH active, there is still awareness, experience, thinking, and so on. I reasoned that even if my RH was mute, once the amytal had worn off, the RH should be able to transfer memories to the LH and the LH could then report. And of course I expected that "yes-no" questions concerning my conscious states could be put to me during the procedure—for example, "Are you aware in the usual way of what is going on?"

As a number of neurologists have explained, the plan was ill conceived. First, the procedure carries risks one would not normally take simply for the sake of science. Sometimes a piece of plaque is dislodged from the arterial wall and plugs a blood vessel. Second, I was told I would not get what I was after in any case, because patients typically have only confused and scanty recollections of the events during the test, regardless of which hemisphere is suppressed. As

Bryan Kolb described it, they tend to give confabulated answers to questions, and they appear unable to recollect even such striking things as the paralysis to one arm. Even their descriptions of mood and feelings during the test are at variance with behavior observed by the researchers.

For example, a person who was weepy and frightened during the test may recall feeling happy. The explanation for lack of recall is not evident, though my assumption that a left-sided test would make *no* difference to the RH was apparently naive. For some patients the explanation may be that there was some "leakage" of amytal to the other hemisphere. About half the patients show some crossover on angiography (a method of tracing the vascular system by injecting it with radio-opaque dye), and it may be that minute amounts "leak" into the other hemisphere even in the remaining cases.

Accordingly, taking the Wada test may be roughly analogous to being abruptly made very drunk, with comparable confusion and lack of recall. Moreover, it may be that even if the LH has some access to the information acquired by the RH during the test, the information is so discordant with the principles of unity that the brain (or the individual hemisphere) uses to make sense of its world that the LH cannot integrate such implications of disunity any more than the LH of split-brain patients can, and hence it simply denies the discordant datum and confabulates.

As an index of the complexity in this domain, one other set of results using the Wada test is important. Kinsbourne (1971) reported on three severely aphasic right-handers who had some measure of residual speech. For example, one could utter single words and name objects, the second could read aloud, and the third could repeat words spoken to him. In the Wada tests given these patients it was apparent that motor control for residual speech was now an RH function. That is, a right-sided amytal injection arrested speech and phonation entirely, but not so a left-sided injection.

Studies of Normal Brains
In order to counterbalance hypotheses formed in clinical studies, neuropsychologists tried to devise ways of investigating functional asymmetries in the brains of neurologically normal subjects. The problem of finding a suitable technique was formidable, since what was needed was a way of lateralizing the presentation of a stimulus to one hemisphere despite the fact that an intact corpus callosum could be expected to thwart that aim in routine transfer of information from one hemisphere to the other. However, it was found that in lateralized tachistoscopic presentations (in which the subject fixates on the

midpoint and a stimulus is flashed for less than 200 msec in one or the other hemifield), normal subjects showed performance asymmetries. In particular, words flashed to the right visual hemifield were more likely to be identified than words flashed to the left hemifield.

It was reasoned that the hemisphere that received the stimulus directly had an advantage over the hemisphere that received it via the corpus callosum and that, when the stimulus was linguistic, the advantage of the left hemisphere would precipitate out as a performance asymmetry. Why the hemisphere receiving the stimulus directly should have an advantage—assuming it really does—is still unexplained, but since the performance asymmetry is apparently a robust phenomenon, the tachistoscopic technique gained currency and is now widely presumed to reveal asymmetries in brain function.

With the applicability of the technique justified on the basis of performance asymmetries, further performance asymmetries are assumed to reflect asymmetries in hemispheric function. Words are flashed to test for asymmetries in linguistic capacities, while pictures of faces and arrangements of dots and shapes have been used to test for asymmetries in nonlinguistic performance. On the whole, the latter have been less reliable in producing asymmetries than the former.

The dichotic listening configuration has also been widely used with normal subjects (Kimura 1967). The theory is that items simultaneously presented to the ears go exclusively to the contralateral hemisphere (the smaller ipsilateral channel being suppressed; but see section 5.2) and that the hemisphere that receives the information directly somehow has an advantage over the one whose reception is indirect.

The rationale here is as before. Verbal stimuli presented to the left ear are less likely to be identified than those presented to the right; hence, the stimuli can be presumed to have lateralized effects, almost as though they were strictly lateralized to one hemisphere. For example, if words are simultaneously presented to both ears, most right-handed subjects will identify more of those presented to the right ear than of those presented to the left. This is known as a right ear advantage (REA). A left ear advantage (LEA) may be obtained for melodies. Since there are performance asymmetries, direct information must be favored, and if the hemisphere has an expertise for the directly received information, performance asymmetries will result. Thus the theory behind the technique.

Lateralized tachistoscopic presentations and dichotic listening tests are the major means of studying lateralization of function in normal brains, though other techniques have been used. For example, dichaptic tests have been developed in which objects with different shapes are placed in the hands of the subject, who later tries to identify them visually (Witelson 1976). A left hand advantage is obtained. How good are these techniques, and what have they revealed about the brain?

Even the best techniques are bedeviled by serious problems, some of which will be outlined here. As Springer and Deutsch (1981) point out, the Wada test indicates that in some 95 percent of right-handers speech production is lateralized to the left, yet only about 80 percent of the right-handers show a right ear advantage, and only about 70 percent show a right visual field advantage. Nor does a given individual who shows an REA correctly identify *all* words presented to his right ear and *none* to his left; on the contrary, he may correctly identify 75 percent of the words presented to his right ear and 50 percent of those presented to his left (Berlin 1977). The advantage is statistical, not absolute. When the left-ear words are identified, this is not interpreted as evidence for RH comprehension but is explained instead in terms of transfer of information across the corpus callosum.

This flexibility in interpretation is not without a price, however, for it seems to jeopardize the justification for the method. Moreover, the measures from the tachistoscopic tests and the dichotic listening tests are not highly correlated, though they purportedly measure the same capacity. A significant percentage of right-handers show an LEA instead of an REA, and some are more successful in identifying words in the left visual field than in the right. Nor are the results for a single individual stable, for a subject may show an REA one week and an LEA the next, though the brain is generally assumed not to have a correspondingly unstable organization.

Particular dangers attend those hypotheses concerning cerebral organization that are based entirely on behavioral studies of neurologically intact subjects and without corroborating evidence from neurological cases. For example, in 1976 Levy and Reid published a paper claiming that in the left-handed population, handwriting posture predicted which hemisphere was dominant for language. More specifically, they observed that some left-handed subjects used an inverted handwriting posture (in which the hand is in a hooked position) and some used a straight posture. According to the hypothesis, for those with the straight posture language was lateralized to the RH, and for those with inverted posture language was lateralized to the LH. Behavioral studies on left-handed neurologically intact subjects that used other indices of lateralization were found to comport with the hypothesis: for example, "hookers" tended to have REAs, and "pushers" tended to have LEAs. The correlation between assorted studies was impressive (but see McKeever 1979), and a robust and reliable regularity seemed to have been discovered. The results caused considerable stir, and researchers doing behavioral studies sorted their populations accordingly.

It all came unstuck, however, when the hypothesis was tested more directly on neurological patients. In amytal tesing of four left-handed patients, Volpe, Sidtis, and Gazzaniga (1981) found that all three patients who had a straight posture had speech lateralized to the LH, and the fourth patient, who had an inverted posture, had speech lateralized to the RH—both findings contrary to Levy and Reid's prediction. Since the results in the Wada test are in each case opposite to what the hypothesis predicted, the hypothesis has been falsified, notwithstanding the reliable correlation of behavioral indices using neurologically intact subjects. Indeed, those very correlations must, for all their reliability and robustness, be the object of some searching methodological questions. What are the reliable correlations an index of?

Finally, there arises the inexorable and vexing question of what the results mean. Do they show that a capacity is lateralized? Or merely that one hemisphere is dominant for that capacity? And what exactly does "dominant" mean here? Or do they show that one hemisphere is more efficient than the other in the performance of a certain task? What precisely are the capacities in question? Does the size of the REA reflect the degree of lateralization, or the inefficiency of commissural transfer, or what? (See Berlin 1977.) Might the performance asymmetries sometimes reflect idiosyncratic differences in attentional bias (Kinsbourne 1974, 1982), in listening and viewing strategy (Springer 1977), or in assorted other variables yet to be factored out? How much farther ahead are we if all we have learned from these studies on normal brains are such things as that on certain kinds of tests 70 percent of the right-handed subjects correctly identify 60 percent of the words flashed to the left hemisphere and 40 percent of those flashed to the right? (See also Marshall 1981.)

The volume of literature reporting behavioral asymmetries with assorted stimuli staggers the imagination, and it has probably doubled since these words were written. It is impossible to escape wondering whether there has been a random-data-gathering binge, motivated less by concern to test theory than by the certainty of getting results, and made tempting by the ready accessibility of testable undergraduates and by the relatively simple nature of the testing arrangements. On the one hand the beauty of the dichotic listening model and lateralized tachistoscopic presentation is that they can be used on neurologically intact subjects. Testing is not nearly as difficult as, say, doing lesion studies in animals, and the equipment is minimal. As techniques go in neuroscience, they are easy.

On the other hand, it has allowed researchers to simply go asymmetry hunting, and notice that just about any asymmetry is reportable. If you are bent on finding an asymmetry, just keep redesigning the stimulus classes until you get one, for the possibilities here are quite literally endless. Moreover, as the volume of literature grows, asymmetries become even more reportable as they fit or fail to fit with other reports already in the literature. Trying to determine what is and what is not significant in the literature surpasses the herculean, and it may be that, as Stevan Harnad once said to me, the best thing to do is wait ten years until all the chaff has blown off, and we can see what is really solid and of lasting value.

In attempts to characterize the deeper capacities underlying the observed performance asymmetries, it has been argued (Levy-Agresti and Sperry 1968, Bradshaw and Nettleton 1981) that the hemispheres use distinct processing strategies or styles and that they use different codes and different modes of operation. Specifically, it has been claimed that the LH is an analytic processor, operating in a sequential manner, and specializes in handling temporal sequencing, whereas the RH processes in a synthetic, Gestalt, and holistic fashion, using parallel rather than sequential processing, and specializes in spatial information. For short, the LH is an analytic-temporal processor, and the RH a synthetic-spatial processor.

Though the drive for a deeper characterization of capacities is laudable, this hypothesis almost certainly gets us no closer to the truth. For one thing, there is no theory about what analytic processing is, and certainly no one has the slightest idea what "holistic" or "global" processing might be. Assuming that the LH is specialized for language skills and the RH for facial recognition, it in no way follows either that the underlying neural mechanisms in the LH are language-like or that those in the RH are like the processes we are introspectively aware of when we recognize a face. Recognizing a face seems, to introspection, to be an all-of-a-bunch affair, but from the point of view of the brain it is hardly likely to be so, considering that the process must begin at the retina with the excitation of individual cells. (See also Allen 1983.) Second, dividing space and time across the hemispheres looks contrived, since many perceptual problems and motor problems, for example, certainly involve both parameters (Morgan 1981, McKeever 1981).

There are also nagging methodological problems with the hypothesis. What kinds of tests show that a holistic processor is at work? Or an analytic processor? The hypothesis is far too vague to inform here, and the worry is that any given performance asymmetry can be taken as showing either holistic processing or analytic processing, depending on how one chooses to describe the operations underlying it. (See especially Marshall 1981.) The dangers of reasoning from a performance asymmetry, to a designation of the hemisphere responsible, to styles of processing, and thus in a circle are entirely too real.

Furthermore, it is surely implausible to suppose that the brain deals with space and time separately; from what we do know of its operations, there is a spatiotemporal integration. (See chapter 10; also Pellionisz and Llinás 1982.) At this stage, the hypothesis is really a metaphor in search of a reality to give it substance, and it may be more misleading than helpful. Evolutionary studies and comparative neuroanatomy are likely to be crucial in coming to understand the nature of the deeper capacities and of the underlying neural processes, and how there comes to be a division of labor. Performance asymmetries in humans, intriguing though they may be, are probably the outcome of too many complex operations to be very enlightening for the deeper questions. (For a recent review of the literature and a discussion of conceptual issues in lateralization studies, see Allen 1983.)

Summary
Although the descriptions of methods in this section have been kept to cursory outlines, the overarching intent was to act on the principle that what the data mean cannot be answered without knowing how the data were obtained. It is important to emphasize the intricacies and pitfalls of methods in this research because the data and the interpretations based on the data are only as good as the methods. It matters tremendously if, for example, certain performance asymmetries turn out to be artifacts of the testing procedures rather than consequences of differential capacities of neural regions. Capacities of neural regions cannot be tested directly but must be inferred from behavior together with certain crucial assumptions about other capacities of other neural regions and about where information goes to and comes from. Should these assumptions be less than certain, the inference is that much more shaky. And of course the vast majority of such assumptions are still themselves in need of confirmation.

What gives a method unimpeachable credentials is a confirmed theory of brain function that backs it up, but of course at this stage what we need methods for is to *get* a theory of brain function. Thus, progress is made slowly, in bits and pieces, and with continual readjustment, revision, and modification even of the seemingly secure and well-established bits. Though I have focused exclusively on linguistic capacities in this section, similar difficulties and problems attend hypotheses concerning nonlinguistic capacities, such as manipulospatial capacities. Worse and more numerous difficulties beset hypotheses concerning lateralization of emotions and musical and mathematical capacities. (For good discussions, see Springer and Deutsch 1981, Kolb and Whishaw 1980, Allen 1983, Bryden 1982.)

5.4   Techniques for Intrahemispheric Localization of Functions

Electrical Stimulation Mapping

The value of direct electrical stimulation of the brain in plotting functional areas had been evident since the early work of Hitzig and Fritsch (section 4.3), and during the 1940s it was found that it could be used as a means of charting the cortex for speech areas in patients about to undergo surgical excision of epileptogenic foci. Using the technique, surgeons were able to determine before excision what cortical areas were involved with speech and hence what areas to spare. The results of this technique, which was developed by Wilder Penfield and his colleagues at the Montreal Neurological Institute, turned out to have considerable theoretical as well as practical importance (Penfield and Roberts 1959).

The procedure involved turning down a flap of skull and placing electrodes directly on the cortical surface. The patient remained comfortable and awake, with just local analgesia for the craniotomy. Using weak current, Penfield stimulated selected areas of the brain while the patient engaged in specified verbal tasks, and observers recorded effects. Usually patients were shown pictures and asked to name objects, to count, to read, and to write. When interference occurred—such as arrest of speech, hesitation, inability to find the right word, or misnaming—the site of stimulation was marked as within the cortical speech area. Speech itself was never induced by electrical stimulation, though occasionally vowel sounds ("oh," "ah") were elicited. The technique was also used in mapping sensory and motor areas of the cortex.

The results of the research challenged prevailing hypotheses about what cortical areas were specialized for speech functions. Arrest of speech and misnaming occurred not only where they were expected, namely in Broca's area, but also in the posterior zones and in Wernicke's area, which on current theory was supposed to be dedicated to language comprehension. There was also a pronounced interference effect in the superior or supplementary motor area. (See figure

3.4, Brodmann area 6.) Moreover, the zones marked as susceptible to interference were much more extensive than expected, and the boundaries of the cortical speech area varied from person to person. On the basis of this method, the claim that Broca's area was responsible for speech and Wernicke's area was responsible for comprehension looked far too simple.

More recently, the technique has been refined by George Ojemann and his colleagues (Ojemann 1983, Mateer 1983), who test for more than just interference with speech itself, looking for interference with language-related behavior such as mimicry of orofacial movements, short-term memory, and phoneme identification. A number of striking and highly discrete effects have revealed themselves.

For example, at one particular location stimulation consistently interferes with naming but with no other function, and yet at a site merely 0.5 centimeters away there is no interference with naming at all. At some locations only orofacial mimicry is disrupted by stimulation, at others only short-term memory, at others some combination of functions, and so on. In one patient who was bilingual in Greek and English, the discreteness of location of language functions was especially dramatic, inasmuch as at one site only naming in English was disrupted, and at a nearby site only naming in Greek was disrupted (figure 5.7).

The locations at which stimulation disrupts a specified function seem to be stable in a given individual during the test period, and there is some preliminary evidence that there is considerable stability across a stretch of time (on the order of months), as well as some subtle changes. Locations vary across individuals, so that sites where naming is disrupted will not be at exactly the same place for each person. Ojemann has suggested that the cortical sites participating in particular language functions may be organized in columnar fashion, much as the somatosensory cortex and the visual cortex are (chapter 3). This work has taken localization hypotheses in an updated and appealing direction.

Ojemann and his colleagues have also studied interference effects when specific areas of the thalamus are stimulated and have found errors in naming, perseveration in misnaming, and subtle effects on short-term memory. Clearly, subcortical mechanisms cannot be ignored in trying to understand the business of language. Other subcortical areas have also been found to be implicated in language (Naeser et al. 1982), and the idea that the cortical structures will tell the whole story is fast losing ground.

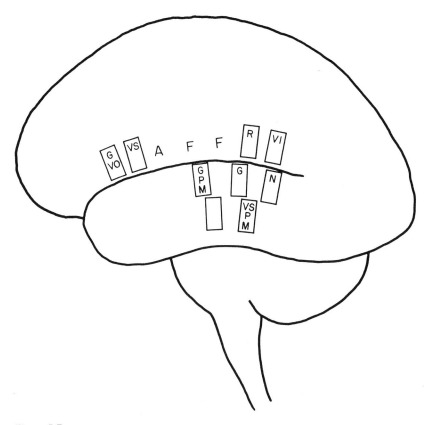

Figure 5.7
Stimulation mapping of six language-related functions at nine sites on the cortex of a 30-year-old female, bilingual in English and Greek. Each site stimulated is represented by a rectangle, and symbols within the rectangle represent significant errors evoked at that site. Abbreviations: N, naming in English; G, naming in Greek; R, reading; VI, short-term verbal memory, with stimulation during input to memory; VS, memory with stimulation during presumed time of storage; VO, memory with stimulation at time of retrieval; P, phoneme identification; M, mimicry of sequences of orofacial movements; A, site of speech arrest; F, site of evoked facial movement and sensation. (From Ojemann 1983.)

Noninvasive Techniques
In the yarns of science fiction, a Dr. Strangefish has cunningly crafted a device which, when placed near the head of our hero, will miraculously read off his every fear, plan, and secret thought. Although nothing as roundly magical as that has been invented, in the last decade several new devices have made it possible to "see" brains and brain activity without opening the skull. In their reality-bound way, some of these devices are every inch a miracle, and their practical and

theoretical significance has been enormous. They have made it possible to find tumors before surgery, to locate lesions, to determine whether zones of the brain are differentially active under differing conditions, to determine abnormalities in specified zones, and so on. Unlike the fanciful machine of Dr. Strangefish, they do not permit brain-reading of thoughts and plans, but they can reveal useful things, such as areas of heightened or depressed activity, which, together with information from other fields in neuroscience, can inform localization hypotheses and clinical diagnoses.

The Electroencephalograph (EEG)   The *electroencephalograph* is a simple device first used by Hans Berger in 1929 that records the effects of putting electrodes on the scalp (figure 5.8). It was found that if the ouput of recording electrodes was amplified and converted into lines on a piece of chart paper, certain characteristic wave patterns were reliably obtained in a range of distinct brain conditions (figure 5.9). Highly distinctive patterns are obtained during epileptic seizures and are now diagnostic.

The EEG has been important as a clinical tool in diagnosing such things as deafness in infants and in establishing a criterion of brain death (Kelly 1981). It has also been invaluable in investigating what the brain is up to during sleep—indeed, it has permitted revolutionary discoveries about the nature of the sleeping brain. Using the EEG

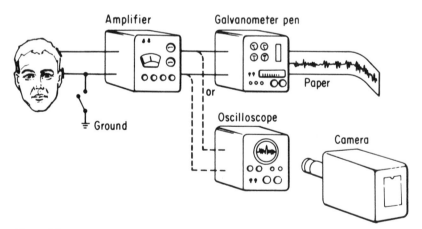

Figure 5.8
Diagram of EEG recording system. The scalp electrode records the voltage changes generated by brain activity, and the electrode on the ear provides the ground. The signals received from the brain are amplified and displayed on a polygraph or on an oscilloscope. (From Thompson (1967). *Foundations of Physiological Psychology*. New York: Harper and Row.)

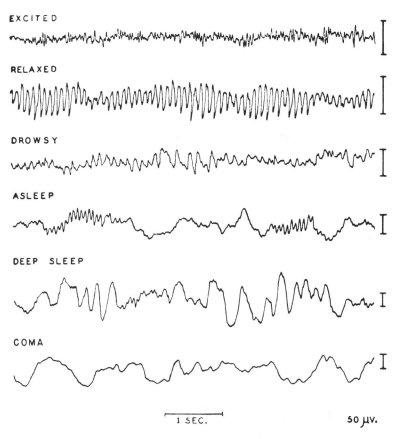

EXCITED

RELAXED

DROWSY

ASLEEP

DEEP SLEEP

COMA

1 SEC.   50 μV.

Figure 5.9
Characteristic EEG traces during variations in states of consciousness. (From Penfield
and Jasper (1954). *Epilepsy and the Functional Anatomy of the Human Brain*. Copyright ©
1954 by Little, Brown and Co.)

to monitor sleep, researchers have found that during sleep the brain
activity displays a typical sequence of waveform types, with characteristic durations and regular patterns (figure 5.10). On the basis of
superficial criteria, sleep appears to be essentially just one kind of
state, and it has often been assumed to be a passive affair, resulting
more from sensory cool-down than neuronal activity. Hence, it was
surprising to find that from the point of view of neuronal activity the
brain's sleep state is not a single, uniform type of state but encompasses at least four different sorts of state, as measured by differences
in pattern produced on the EEG, and that sleep is in some manner
actively brought about by neuronal mechanisms.

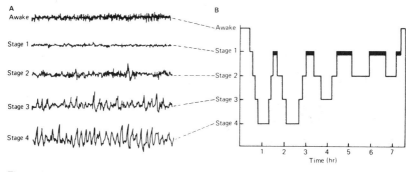

Figure 5.10

(A) EEG recordings during different stages of wakefulness and sleep. Each trace shown represents 30 seconds. The top recording of low voltage fast activity is that of an awake brain. The next four represent successively deeper stages of non-REM slow-wave sleep. Stage 1 REM sleep can be distinguished from stage 1 non-REM sleep only by additional data concerning eye movements and eye muscle contractions. (B) A typical night's pattern of sleep staging in a young adult. The time spent in REM sleep is represented by a dark bar. The first REM period is usually short, about 5 to 10 minutes, but REM periods tend to lengthen in successive cycles. The amount of stage 2 non-REM sleep increases until it occupies all of the non-REM period. (Reprinted by permission of the publisher from D. D. Kelly (1981). Ch. 40 of *Principles of Neural Science*, ed. E. R. Kandel and J. H. Schwartz, pp. 472–485. Copyright © 1981 by Elsevier Science Publishing Co., Inc.)

One stage is characterized both by a distinct waveform and by a set of behavioral indexes, which include increase in heart rate and blood pressure, cessation of gastrointestinal movements, a decrease in muscle tone, and (most distinctively) activity in the extraocular muscles, which is easily seen as *rapid eye movement* (REM). There is also activity in the middle ear muscles. Aserinsky and Kleitman (1953) found that visual dreaming typically occurs during REM sleep, and though dreaming was once suspected to be confined largely to the REM period, it is now evident that some sort of dream-like "mentation," perhaps of a less visual nature and more closely akin to waking thought, takes place during other stages as well (Foulkes 1966). What does seem clear, however, is that a higher percentage of dream recall can be obtained immediately after arousal from REM sleep than after arousal from other stages. The remaining three stages, identified principally by characteristic patterns of waveforms but also indexed by arousability of the sleeper, are classified as *non–rapid eye movement* (NREM) *sleep*. The temporal profile for a sleeper's night shows a pattern of stages that is fairly standard both in sequencing and in duration of stages (figure 5.10). It is of interest that the REM periods increase in length with each cycle. Of course, the waveforms do not reveal anything about the *content* of a dream; nevertheless, there is some evidence that the emotional and visual vivacity of dreams is greater in the later periods.

REM sleep periods appear to alternate in a set fashion with NREM periods, with the REM duration starting at about 5 to 10 minutes after sleep onset and increasing with each cycle. Periods of stage 4 sleep cease about midway in the sleep cycle, and the stage 2 durations increase. In addition to the systematicity observable within an individual's sleeping periods, there are also patterns distinctive of developmental stages. For example, infants show the highest percentage of sleeping time spent in REM sleep (50 percent at birth, 30 to 35 percent at age 2, and 25 percent about age 10). There is a distinct decline in percentage of REM sleep in adolescence followed by an increase in middle age and another sharp decline after age 60. Percentage of stage 4 sleep declines continuously from infancy, and typically this stage is entirely absent in old age. Analogous stages of sleep have been recorded in nonhuman primates and in small rodents and birds, stage 4 NREM as well as REM being observable.

Apparently the brain will maintain something like a quota of REM sleep in the long run. For example, it has been found (Clemes and Dement 1967) that when normal subjects are deprived of REM sleep, a REM rebound occurs on subsequent nights. That is, the REM stages are both more frequent and longer in duration, and the longer the deprivation, the larger the rebound. REM sleep deprivation does seem to be correlated with irritability and increased sexual behavior, but so far there has been no solid demonstration that anything like cognitive disintegration occurs as a result of REM sleep deprivation.

Because of the frequency with which psychiatric patients complain of sleep disorders, one line of research undertakes to explore the possibility that certain psychiatric disorders may be correlated with abnormalities in the sleep cycle and its characteristic stages. In particular, it has been suggested that abnormal onset of the first REM period typifies patients with chronic depression (Kupfer and Foster 1972, 1975). There is also evidence that symptoms in depressives (endogenous but not reactive depressives) may be relieved to some degree by giving a jolt to the sleep-awake cycle, for example by depriving the patient of REM periods (Pflug and Tolle 1971, Vogel et al. 1975).

What the brain is up to during REM sleep or during other NREM stages is not understood, nor is it settled whether dreaming (REMing and other mentation) has a functional role in the brain's economy or whether it is an incidental by-product of no use in itself. On the useful side, Roffwarg, Muzio, and Dement (1966) argue that dreaming stimulates the CNS, thereby promoting maturation. Crick and Mitchison (1983) suggest that dreaming has an important housekeeping function, inasmuch as it involves putting noise in the system and culling out by a forgetting procedure those cognitive patterns that are activated by mere noise rather than by a genuine information-bearing signal. Although this is consistent with the data, so are many other hypotheses, such as Jouvet's (see below), and it is still too early to tell whether it is on the right track.[1] In any case, given the regularity of REM occurrence and the rebound effect of REM-deprived subjects, it does seem plausible that when the brain goes into the REM stage, some point is served, and the brain is not merely idling, doodling, or "knitting up the ravell'd sleeve of care." On the strength of traditional conceptions, one is inclined think of sleep as loafing, but from the point of view of the economy of the brain, it is likely no such thing.

Of importance here too is the fact that organisms are vulnerable to predators when asleep, and during REM sleep there is a mechanism in the brain stem that turns on to inhibit movement that might otherwise be triggered by dream states (Jouvet 1967). Cats in whom the mechanism has been lesioned show well-integrated movement during REM periods, exhibiting the usual range of stereotypical behavior including flight, exploration, rage, and grooming.

Jouvet's hypothesis concerning the function of dreaming says that at least in lower animals the brain rehearses important motor-coordination patterns during dreaming, in preparation for real encounters in the waking state. The rehearsal is made safe by the brain-stem inhibition of the output motor mechanisms. In contrast to the Crick-Mitchison forgetting function for dreaming, Jouvet's hypothesis envisages that much of the dream pattern is genetically programmed and that consolidation and streamlining of motor control are the object.

The work on sleep and dreaming in the last thirty years has been revolutionary in its impact on our conception of the nature of sleep. Once assumed to be an essentially passive and largely homogeneous affair, sleep has been shown to have an organization and dynamic that negates the old conception. Moreover, the research raises questions about whether there are different kinds of conscious states, and different ways or different levels of being aware that we have yet to understand. Moreover, if cognitive reorganization or consolidation does take place during various sleep stages, this raises further questions about the nature and function of consciousness (waking consciousness at least) in cognitive activity generally. Roughly a third of one's life is devoted to sleep, and it may well be that important cognitive work of some variety is carried out by the brain while sensory input and motor output are curtailed. Philosophically speaking, the research on sleep and dreaming is of interest both because it is an instance of the fragmentation and redesign of a folk concept (sleeping) as a result of psychological and neuroscientific research and because it bears upon traditional questions concerning what it is to be conscious. (See also chapters 7 and 9.)

The discussion of the EEG has so far proceeded without raising the question of the neural basis (the electrogenesis) of the recorded waveforms, and this should be raised now. The answer, in brief, is that the neural basis is not understood. It might be hoped that a given squiggle on the recording represents the summation of action potentials of a functionally significant neuronal ensemble, but so far there are no solid data to confirm the hope. As Bullock, Orkand, and Grinnell (1977) note, in addition to effects from action potentials there may well be effects from slowly changing potentials due to an assortment of cellular and extracellular activities.

Moreover, neurons may be grouped so that some field effects are canceled, some are amplified, some interfere, and so forth. One of the more thorough critics of certain uses of the technique, C. C. Wood, comments (in unpublished work),

> Whether or not activity in a particular group of neurons is evident in macropotential recordings depends upon the geometry of the active cells and cell aggregates, the pattern of synaptic activation, the degree of temporal and spatial synchronization, the spatial relationships between recording electrodes and the active tissue, and the amount and form of simultaneous activity in other groups of neurons.

To get even close to determining the electrogenesis of macropotentials recorded at the scalp one would need, at the very least, to record field potentials from neural tissue itself. Moreover, one would need simultaneous, intracellular recordings from large numbers of adjacent cells, and here the technology peters out. Notice too that whether the recorded activity is owed, principally or in part, to a *functionally significant neuronal ensemble* has certainly not been demonstrated. As will be evident from the foregoing discussion of sleep and dreaming, this does not entail that EEG data can be dismissed as useless, and certainly their clinical use does not depend on having settled the question of electrogenesis for a given macropotential. But for assessing the theoretical significance of the recordings it is important to know that what the EEG recordings signify in terms of the anatomical and physiological substrate is not understood. This issue will become especially important for evoked-potential research (see below).

Event-Related Potentials (ERPs)   Event-related potentials (ERPs; also known as "evoked potentials") are obtained by taking a series of EEG epochs (for example, 60 or 100 or 500) and averaging them together, ostensibly to filter out the noise and retain the signal. For example, the same stimulus, such as a shock at a specified voltage applied to a fingertip, is presented on many trials to a number of subjects, the wave patterns are recorded by the EEG, and finally these recordings are averaged by the computer (figure 5.11). The ERP waves are standardly displayed as an average across a number of trials.

The theoretical interest in ERPs derives from the possibility that specific waveforms can be correlated with specific types of cognitive and subcognitive processes taking place in the mind-brain, and that on the basis of confirmed correlations the nature of the processes can then be investigated (Kutas and Hillyard 1984). Given this possibility, the defining strategy of cognitive psychophysiology is to investigate cognitive processes through ERP effects.

Conventionally, the ERP recording is divided into the early components (patterns that occur up to 40 msec after the onset of the stimulus) and later components (those that occur after the 40 msec mark). Components are labeled according to time of peak latency (e.g., 100 msec) and by whether they are positive in polarity (typically represented as downgoing on the recording) or negative (typically upgoing). Thus, a P300 is a positive, downgoing, wave occurring 300 msec after stimulus presentation, and an N100 is a negative wave occurring 100 msec after stimulus presentation.

Some ERP results are both striking and robust. For example, there is a distinct wave that begins to appear about 31 msec after an electrical stimulus has been applied to the finger, and the size of the wave varies as a function of the size of the voltage (figure 5.12). If the stimulus is sufficiently large to be consciously experienced, then an N100 is recorded. It has also been found that where the subject receives the stimulus on both hands, but *attends* to only one hand, there is a clear difference in late components (P100, P470).

This difference between early and late components in sensitivity to attention is robust. The early components are stimulus bound; they occur whether or not the subject is attending and are not significantly modulated even if he is anesthetized. They are therefore called *exogenous components*, in contrast to the later components such as the P300,

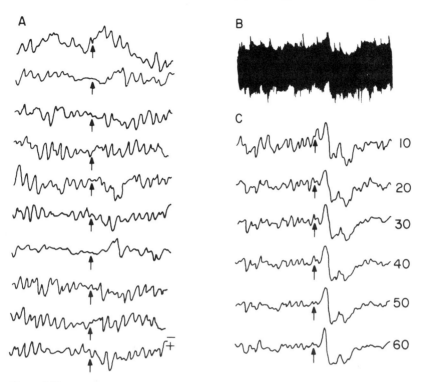

Figure 5.11
An illustration of the signal-averaging procedure as applied to electroencephalographic data. (A) Single trials. Epochs of raw EEG recorded from vertex of a subject. The time of stimulus-onset is indicated by the arrow. Note the absence of any obvious pattern of response to the stimulus in the raw record. (B) Sixty such records are superimposed. The superimposition marginally enhances the configuration of the evoked response but the details are difficult to discern. (C) Sequence of successive averages of the same data, cumulatively adding 10 trials to each epoch. Note the increasing clarity of the records. (From Donchin (1975). In *International Symposium on Signal Analysis and Pattern Recognition in Biomedical Engineering*, ed. G. F. Inbar. New York: Wiley.)

which are in general highly susceptible to internal conditions and hence are called *endogenous components* (Sutton et al. 1967).

A large P300 can be reliably produced in the so-called oddball paradigm. In this condition a subject is asked to sit before a television screen and is sequentially presented with objects from two antecedently defined categories, where objects from one category occur with high probability, say 80 percent of the time, and objects from the other category occur only 20 percent of the time. For example, the objects may be red (80 percent) and blue (20 percent). The subject is

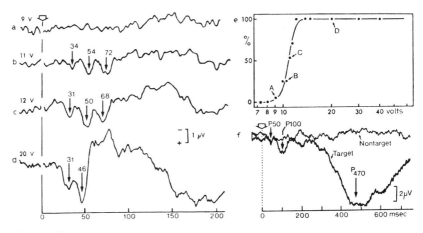

Figure 5.12
Conscious sensation and somatosensory evoked potentials (SEP) for faint stimuli. (a)–
(d) SEPs to an electric pulse (0.1 msec duration) to the third finger of the left hand in a
normal adult. The SEP is recorded from the contralateral parietal scalp focus. Three
hundred (300) trials are averaged. The voltage of the stimuli delivered at the time of the
vertical line (hollow arrow) is 9 V (a), 11 V (b), 12 V (c), and 20 V (d). Time in msec along
the abscissa. Voltage calibration of 1 μm. The black arrows identify the early positive
SEP components that disclose a latency shift for faint stimuli (b,c). No SEP can be
identified for the 9 V stimuli (a). (e) Detection by the subject in the same experiment
with a plot of the number of trials detected in each run (ordinate, percent) as a function
of the voltage of the finger stimuli (abscissa, volts). The letters identify the corresponding SEP records in (a)–(d). (f) SEP to near-threshold electric stimuli to the index
finger of one hand in a selective attention paradigm involving random series of stimuli
delivered to 4 different fingers at a fast rate (mean random frequency 150/min). The two
superimposed traces compare SEPs to identical stimuli that were designated either as
targets to be mentally counted (thicker line) or in other runs as nontargets to be ignored
while the subject identified stimuli to the opposite hand (thinner line). The early P50
SEP component is not modified, but large P100 and P470 components occur for the
targets. (From J. E. Desmedt, J. Debecker, and D. Robertson 1979. In *Cognitive Components in Cerebral Event-Related Potentials and Selective Attention*, ed. J. E. Desmedt. Basel:
Karger.)

required to count objects from one category. It has been found that
large-amplitude P300 waves reliably occur on those occasions when
subjects are presented with the less probable stimulus, and the rarer
the stimulus, the larger the P300 amplitude (Duncan-Johnson and
Donchin 1977). The oddball paradigm has many versions, and the
categories can be quite abstract—for example, male vs. female names,
politicians vs. entertainers, and so forth (Kutas, McCarthy, and Donchin 1977). The omission of an expected stimulus will also yield a
P300 component (Picton et al. 1974). It has been found in addition
that semantically strange sentences, such as "The boy ate eggs and

cement," will reliably yield a large-amplitude N400 component (Kutas and Hillyard 1980).

What does the P300 component, for example, signify, and how are we to interpret the data? What can it tell us concerning information processing in the mind-brain? The dominant strategy here is to try to correlate the presence of the P300 (or other waveforms) with particular psychological states or processes. By refining the set of conditions under which the P300 can be elicited, and by examining the sequelae as well, ERP researchers hope to find hypotheses concerning the underlying processes (Donchin et al. 1983). On this basis it has been hypothesized that the P300 represents the making of a decision, or the updating of a world-model, or surprise, and so forth.

One danger here, however, is that the conditions under which a waveform is elicited may be such a mixed bag that it is not plausible to suppose that the wave represents a *unitary* function of any kind. It could happen that a large set of information-processing functions is executed during the period when the EEG shows a given waveform, and even that membership in the set varies from occasion to occasion. For example, because of its sensitivity to a widely diverse range of conditions, one waveform, called the contingent negative variation, is now suspected by a number of researchers to have no corresponding unitary function, despite being reliably elicited under assorted conditions. Indeed, for none of the endogenous components has it been established what, if any, is the unitary information-processing function manifested in the waveform. This is true even of the P300, which has been intensively and imaginatively explored.

For those who are skeptical about the integrity and value of ERP research the difficulties over interpretation are at the heart of the matter. The problem, succinctly, is that it is simply not understood what the waveforms mean, either in terms of their electrogenesis or in terms of higher-level functional processes, which they are presumed to manifest.

It was already observed in the discussion of EEG recordings that we do not know how to explain the macropotentials in terms of underlying micropotentials. Since ERPs are averages of EEG recordings, ERP research inherits the EEG interpretation problem. If anything, the problem is greater for ERP research inasmuch as sequential features of a recording one second long are alleged to manifest specific psychological or neurophysiological processes. For all one can tell from the ERP, some features of the recording may be entirely independent of information-processing transactions. Nor has it been ruled out that the very averaging techniques designed to make significant features show up actually mask important differences in psychological or neuronal processes that obtain from occasion to occasion. A major concern, therefore, is that if we do not understand the anatomical and physiological substrate for the ERP, the assumption that the averaging technique extracts signal out of noise may be mere wishful thinking. (For an excellent and detailed discussion of the problems connected with inferring information about the nervous system from ERP measurements, see Wood and Allison 1981.)

The nature of the neuronal substrate is rather better understood in the case of the early components, where the evidence shows them to be linked to signal transmission from the periphery, and animal studies and lesion studies have yielded converging results. But for the endogenous components, such as the P300, no one has a well-supported theory concerning what the neuronal substrate is. It cannot even be assumed that the effects are owed primarily to cortical activity, since thalamic activity, for example, could also affect the recording. Direct recording from the cortical surface could at least narrow down the alternatives here, but it still will not reveal the source of the effect.

Assuming that the methodological justification of evoked-potential research is that it helps bridge the gap between neuroscience at the micro level and psychology at the macro level, then it must address the matter of the neuronal substrate for its data. Unless it does so, the possibility remains very much alive that a given peak or trough really does not mean anything in terms of a distinct step in the processing of information executed by a discrete neuronal ensemble.

If there are difficulties in hitching endogenous ERPs to the neuronal substrate, there are also difficulties in hitching them to information-processing functions at the macro level. Already mentioned is the problem of resolving the conditions for eliciting a waveform so that the waveform can be plausibly correlated with a specific cognitive or subcognitive process. An additional and serious difficulty concerns the individuation of the waveforms themselves. That is, how does one tell when the recording shows a P300 or a P500? It appears to me that the individuation of components—whether there is just one, and if so, which one it is—is by no means settled on the basis of the physical features of the recordings, and not infrequently involves a generous dollop of interpretation.

The temporal definition for a given waveform is not very fine, and the timing turns out to be a somewhat flexible criterion for individuation. For example, Donchin et al. (1983) argue that the P300 can occur anywhere between about 250 and 900 msec and can even occur after the motor response. The claim is that the onset of the P300 is later when the discrimination task is more difficult or complex. However, there is disagreement here, and what one researcher calls a P300, another researcher in another laboratory will insist is really a P450, a different wave altogether that manifests a different psychological process. How much deviation from the 300 msec mark matters? If a waveform at 900 msec is considered to be an instance of the same type as the one occurring at 300 msec, what are the criteria for determining this? Why should we be convinced the same process is manifest? Indeed, components may overlap, and this further complicates the business of determining whether a given peak should be identified as one component and whether it is the same as the one produced in a different run.

Factors other than temporal profile figure in the individuation decision, including, obviously, the shape of the trace. But some researchers wish also to use the conditions for production and the location on the scalp where the electrodes were placed. In fact, shape of trace is not decisive either, since, as researchers are quick to point out, not every squiggle marks a relevant difference, and moreover the wave can have varying amplitudes. Which squiggles do count? Well, that cannot be answered precisely either, and conditions of production and timing will bear upon that. But if the conditions of production vary, and so does the timing, how then do we tell which squiggle counts?

The problem is, none of these criteria can stand on its own, and none has a soundness independent of the others. But without a secure grounding of at least one criterion, either in the underlying physiology or in the higher-level psychology, the risk of circularity in reasoning is nontrivial. There is disagreement among laboratories about whether a recording shows a P300 or a P-something else, which is not resolved by temporal considerations, shape, or conditions of production, and unless these basic individuation issues can be settled to some degree, the program to correlate waveforms with stages in information processing must be similarly unsettled.

On the other hand, if the timing *is* deemed decisive, and a wave *must* peak at 300 msec to count as a P300, then all hell breaks loose, because no correlations between waves so specified and unitary psychological processes have a prayer of being established. So there has to be some flexibility. Yet once it is allowed that the time resolution of these waves need not be at all precise, the individuation problem becomes acute.

The circularity permitted by the mutually dependent criteria shows itself most clearly when trying to establish what psychological processes a wave, such as the P300, is to be correlated with. It is often possible to square putatively disconfirming data by saying that there really was a P300, but it happened at 800 msec, or it had a low amplitude, or the conditions of production were not standard, or there were overlapping components, and so on; alternatively, one might say there really was no P300 because the conditions of production were nonstandard, or the shape was not right, or the time was not right, and so forth. I do not say these disputes typify ERP research, but they are sometimes in evidence, and it is difficult to see how such disagreements can be resolved in principled fashion in the absence of independent criteria for individuation.

Despite its methodological tribulations, ERP research has an impressive following, largely, as its proponents rightly point out, because it is the only noninvasive way of collecting data on the brain activity of normal, awake, behaving humans. To be sure, a technique satisfying those specifications is highly desirable, and consequently there have been systematic attempts to refine experimental procedures and to construct more revealing mathematical analyses of the data. Moreover, ERP data can be useful in conjunction with results using other techniques in psychology and neuroscience, even though some of the methodological issues are unsolved. Perhaps the best example of this is the research of Hillyard and his colleagues concerning directed attention.

The basic ERP fact that Hillyard exploits is that the early components appear to be insensitive to directed attention, whereas later components are sensitive. The N100 appears to be the first component whose variation reflects what the subject is attending to, and it is modality indifferent. Hillyard's insight is that data concerning the N100—for example, what stimulus parameters it is sensitive to, whether specific combinations of properties have the same N100 profile—might be brought to bear in adjudicating the debate between early selection and late selection theories in cognitive psychology. For this aim, it can be left open what unitary function, if any, the N100 manifests.

Roughly, those favoring early selection (e.g., Broadbent 1970, Treisman 1969) argue that there is some early selection of stimuli based on simple physical properties and that only selected stimuli receive full analysis in subsequent processing. On these models the early *stimulus* selection is later followed by a *response* selection. By contrast, in late-selection theories (e.g., Norman 1969) the stimuli are thought to be fully analyzed before any selection occurs. Since the available behavioral data do not decisively cut against either theory, Hillyard and his colleagues have tried to design experiments that will provide ERP data indicating whether or not early selection occurs.

The idea in one experiment (Hansen and Hillyard 1983) is to measure how much difference it makes to the N100 whether a two-property stimulus has the right combination of properties to make it a candidate for a target stimulus. Let the stimulus be sound pips, and the properties be pitch and location. Subjects are to attend, for example, to high-pitched sounds emitted from the left; of sounds in this class, the target sounds will be those with long duration. Put crudely, the question is: if a sound has the "wrong" location, does that affect whether or not the other property, pitch, is processed? Hansen and Hillyard's analysis of the N100 indicates that it does affect whether or not there is N100 sensitivity to pitch in such a case, suggesting that the properties are not independently and fully analyzed, as the late-selection theory advocates, but that only selected stimuli are fully processed. (See also Hillyard et al. 1984; for a review of ERP research and cognitive theories, see Kutas and Hillyard 1984.)

5.5   Imaging Techniques

Computerized Axial Tomography (CT Scanners)
The principle of computerized axial tomography (CT scanning) is to rotate around the head an X-ray source that is coupled to a synchronously moving X-ray detector on the other side, and then to use a computer to reconstruct in visual form the variations in X-ray opacity of the brain. This gives a cross-sectional X-ray picture of the brain at one level or cut (hence "tomography"). For other "cuts" the procedure can be repeated at a different level. Normal brain scans are then compared to the scan under study to determine whether there are abnormalities.

This system was the pioneer of the computer-aided visual displays of the brain, and although it has been a valuable innovation, it has considerable limitations even as a diagnostic instrument. If an abnormality such as a tumor is to show up, it must have absorption properties different from those of normal tissue, and this is not always the case. Abnormalities may not show up on a CT scan until they are in the serious stages; small tumors may be missed, and demyelinating diseases such as multiple sclerosis are missed more often than they are detected. Additionally, there is always some risk in exposing the body to ionizing radiation, and frequent exposure is to be avoided. On the other hand, CT scanners are simple to use and are much cheaper than PET scanners (see below).

Cerebral Blood Flow (rCBF) Studies
This technique exploits the assumption that blood flow in a cerebral region is coupled to the metabolic needs of neurons in that region,

which in turn are coupled to the degree of activity of those neurons. Hence, if zones are differentially active according to function performed, this should be reflected in differences in the volume of blood supplying those zones during the relevant period of time. The trick is to find a way to make such regional differences in blood flow show up. The problem is solved by tagging the blood with a radioactive tracer (usually xenon 133). This is harmless to the brain and washes out quickly, but the electromagnetic radiation emitted by the tracer can be detected by a source outside the brain. Localized variations in blood flow can then be detected as greater concentrations of xenon 133. A computer then converts the data into visual form, coding concentrations by colors, and a portrait emerges of localized differences in cerebral blood flow. In order to establish a baseline, it was first necessary to establish the resting pattern in normal brains, and then deviations from the resting state could be observed when the subject was engaged in a specified task.

Magnificent images of brains going about their business have been produced by the rCBF technique. When a subject speaks, there is a typical "lighting up" both of LH areas in the temporal lobe and frontal lobe and of the larynx-mouth areas of motor and somatosensory cortex. Interestingly, roughly homologous areas in the RH also light up, though less intensely. A different pattern is seen when the subject reads silently, reads aloud, makes a voluntary movement, and so forth (see Lassen, Ingvar, and Skinhoj 1978). Of great clinical and theoretical interest are the characteristic differences in rCBF distribution between normals and schizophrenics, and between normals and patients with organic dementia (figures 5.13, 5.14).

The spatial resolution using this technique is one centimeter, and the temporal resolution is about two minutes, so variations taking place outside those limits will go undetected.

Positron-Emission Tomography (PET Scanners)
Although rCBF techniques yield revealing profiles of the active brain, it would be even better if it were possible to see what the brain is doing at a variety of distinct levels, from the top on down, and to have a portrait of the brain as a whole. One idea was to use the tomographic stratagem and to get even closer than rCBF studies to the metabolic processes by tagging glucose, the sole energy source for neurons, with such substances as radioactive fluorine (fluorine 18), which can insinuate itself into a glucose molecule and hence follow the metabolic pathway into the cell. As the atom of fluorine 18 decays, it emits positrons, which in turn interact with electrons, with the result that gamma rays are released and can be detected by a sensor

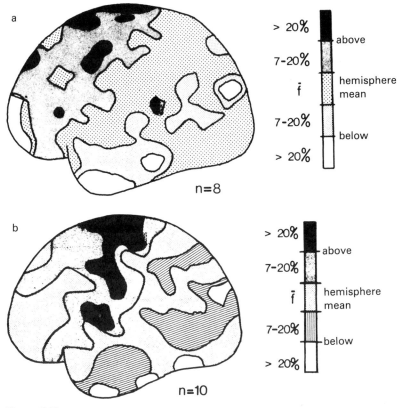

Figure 5.13
Cerebral blood flow (rCBF) distribution by the intra-arterial xenon 133 method in a group of normals (a) and patients with organic dementia (b) (mostly Alzheimer cases). Note the differences between the normal group and the dementia patients in rCBF distribution in the hyperfrontal and parieto-occipito-temporal regions. Relative flows are plotted in accordance with scales to the right. (From Ingvar 1982.)

outside the body. The greater the metabolic activity of a neural area, the more positron-labeled glucose is required, and the more gamma rays are emitted. A computer can reconstruct a color-coded image of the brain's metabolic activities on the basis of the measured distribution of gamma rays at a variety of distinct cuts from the top on down.

Twelve distinct cuts are created simultaneously, and regional variations in metabolic activity are plainly revealed, deep within the brain as well as on the cortical surface. The spatial resolution is usually about one centimeter, but in principle it could be made much finer by increasing the number of projections of the emission detector. Clinically the machine is very useful, and it is more accurate than the CT

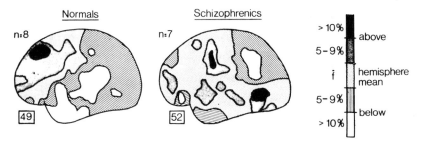

Figure 5.14
Distribution of cerebral blood flow at rest in eight normals and in seven highly psychotic chronic schizophrenics. Note that both groups showed about the same mean hemisphere flow rates (49 and 52 ml/10 g/0.1 min, respectively). However, the distribution of the flow is different. The schizophrenics show lower flow in frontal regions and higher flow in postcentral regions. (From Ingvar 1982.)

scanner in diagnosing Alzheimer's disease, tumors, epilepsy, and strokes. Cost of the machine is the main obstacle to getting better resolution. (See Ter-Pogossian, Raichle, and Sobel 1980; Sokoloff 1981.)

The use of PET scanning to help identify what regions of the brain are specialized for what particular functions is likely to become increasingly important. For example, Mishkin, Ungerleider, and Macko (1983) have used the technique to compare cortical activity in a blinded monkey and a seeing monkey. Specific areas in the blinded monkey showed reduced glucose utilization, and the presumption is that these areas are involved in the processing of visual information. To test the presumption independently, these data are compared to results from other methods, such as electrical stimulation, recording, lesion studies, injection of dyes, and so forth. A convergence of results would tend to confirm the anatomical hypothesis.[2]

The PET scanner is a kind of window on the brain's business, and by its means we can view differences in brain activity as a function of whether the person is doing mental arithmetic, recalling a conversation, analyzing musical chords using visual imagery, or analyzing musical chords *without* using visual imagery. In studies on normal subjects, Phelps and Mazziotta (1985) found distinctive patterns of glucose uptake correlated with such psychological states, demonstrating that differences in content of psychological state and in preferred cognitive strategy can be reflected in PET scan displays (figure 5.15). How finely PET-detected profiles correlate with subtle variations in mental state is not yet determined, and as resolution and technique improve, the hope is that we will find highly specific neural correlates that allow major breakthroughs in functional neuro-

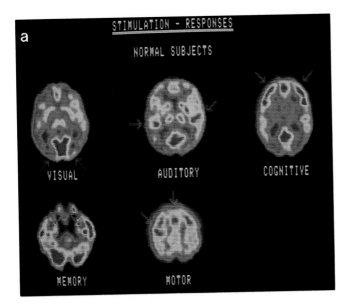

Figure 5.15

Functional neuroanatomy demonstrated in PET studies of normal subjects. (Tracer is 2-deoxy-2-[¹⁸F]fluoro-D-glucose (FDG).) Color scale is in units of micromolecules per minute per 100 grams, ranging from 2 (dark purple) to 45 (red). Hence, areas of high activation will appear red, and areas of lower activation will appear at the bluer end. (a) Visual stimulus consisting of full-field alternating checkerboard stimuli activated (27.6 ± 6.5 percent versus control) the full extent of the primary (medial) visual cortex (arrows). Auditory stimuli resulted in responses (17 to 25 percent increases compared to the control) that were symmetric in magnitude but asymmetric in distribution for the transverse temporal cortex (arrows). Image of cognitive task represents responses where a specific task was involved rather than passive perception of stimuli; arrows indicate activation of frontal cortex. Memory tasks (remembering information from a verbal auditory stimulus) caused bilateral activations of the mesial temporal cortex (hippocampus, parahippocampus). Motor task of a sequential finger movement of the right hand caused cortical metabolic activation of the left motor strip (lower arrow) and supplementary motor cortex (vertical arrow). (b) Auditory stimuli produced metabolic responses that varied with the content and in some cases with the strategy used by the subject to perform the task. In resting states (ears plugged, eyes open) left-right cerebral symmetry in glucose utilization is seen. In right-handed individuals verbal auditory stimuli predominantly activated and caused metabolic asymmetries (left > right = 5 to 16 percent) of the left hemisphere, whereas nonverbal stimuli (music) predominantly activated the right hemisphere (16 to 27 percent). Simultaneous stimulation with language and music caused bilateral activations of both hemispheres. (From Mazziotta et al. 1982.) (c) In subjects who listened to sequences of musical notes and were asked to determine whether notes in one sequence differed from those in another, the pattern of glucose utilization correlated with the strategy used by the subject. Persons using visual imagery strategies had predominantly left hemisphere asymmetries, and those who did not use this strategy had maximal activations in the right hemisphere. The timbre test required subjects to compare complex chords for similarities and differences, and consistently produced increases (22 percent versus control) in glucose utilization in the right hemisphere (arrow). (From Phelps and Mazziotta 1985. Courtesy of the American Association for the Advancement of Science.)

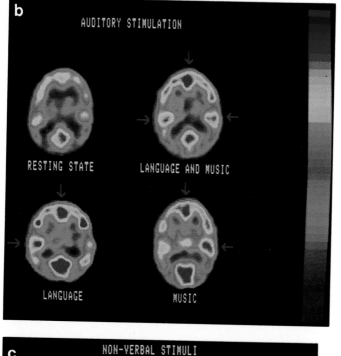

b

AUDITORY STIMULATION

RESTING STATE   LANGUAGE AND MUSIC

LANGUAGE   MUSIC

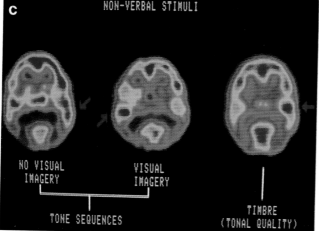

c

NON-VERBAL STIMULI

NO VISUAL IMAGERY   VISUAL IMAGERY

TONE SEQUENCES

TIMBRE (TONAL QUALITY)

anatomy. The limits of the technique have certainly not been reached. The major drawback to the PET scan technique is expense. It requires a powerful computer, a cyclotron to manufacture the needed isotopes, and technicians to run the machines.

Nuclear Magnetic Resonance (NMR) Imaging
Nuclear magnetic resonance (NMR) imaging produces far better images than the CT scanner, and without the use of radioactive substances and ionizing radiation. The secret of NMR imaging depends on a curious property of the nuclei of atoms: if the nucleus contains an uneven number of particles, then it has a spin and hence behaves like a magnet. Hydrogen and phosphorus, of which the body has large amounts, are atoms with such nuclei. When a substance containing such nuclei is placed in a magnetic field, the axis of spin of the nuclei is altered, and the magnets/nuclei orient themselves in conformity with the lines of force. Once regimented, they can be made to point in a new direction and then allowed to flip back. This manipulation provides information, for as the nuclei flip back, they release energy, and this emission can be monitored and used to reconstruct an image of where the hydrogen, for example, is concentrated and distributed.

The idea is to exploit the fact that substances such as hydrogen and phosphorus have nuclei that can be manipulated, can be manipulated selectively, and are unevenly distributed in the body. Hydrogen is of course found in water and in lipids, and there are subtle differences in the distribution of hydrogen in soft tissue that show up in NMR images. Hence, differences between normal brains and brains with tumors or other lesions are discernible. This sort of image provides anatomical information, but metabolic portraits—of special interest to the theoretician—may be obtainable as well. Phosphorus is a part of adenosine triphosphate, or ATP, which is the energy-storing molecule providing energy for all metabolic processes, including those in neurons. ATP is concentrated in regions of greatest metabolic activity, so greater concentrations of phosphorus can provide clues concerning what parts of the nervous system are subserving particular functions.

The technology for NMR imaging is still in its infancy, and NMR enthusiasts predict that it will replace CT scanning for diagnostic purposes and that as refinements are made it will be of increasing value to neurophysiology and neuropsychology. (For a good introduction, see R. Edelman 1984.)

5.6   *A Sample from Neurological Studies*

A primary source of insights concerning the organization of the nervous system and how it subserves behavior is clinical neurology; so it was long before the advent of such devices as PET scanners and autoradiography, and it remains so even now. For philosophers, who may tend to assume that the brain is pretty much dedicated to knowledge, abstract thought, and in general to the "higher functions," a singularly surprising thing to learn in neurology rounds is how often distinct neurological disorders include motor impairments of some description. Even in cases where cognitive deficits are particularly prominent, there are typically accompanying motor deficits. This, together with evolutionary considerations and neurophysiological data concerning how much of the brain is, in one way or another, implicated in motor control, should invite us to question any assumption that takes the brain to be chiefly a device for knowledge acquisition and only incidentally a device for sensorimotor control (see also chapter 10).

A theoretical value derived from studying neurological cases, therefore, is their potential for dislodging conventional assumptions. Such a study also helps generate an understanding of the organization of the nervous system and of the fact that underlying the smoothness of normal behavior is an extraordinarily intricate neuronal machine.

A number of years ago I began going regularly to neurology rounds at the Health Sciences Centre in Winnipeg, and these Thursday mornings became the focus of extended perplexity and wonder. My first patient I still recall with eidetic vividness. He was a professor emeritus from the medical college who had suffered a stroke deep in the brain, probably affecting the limbic structures, one consequence of which was that he would frequently and unaccountably cry. His face would suddenly sadden, the tears would wash down his cheeks, and his body would shake with sobs. Before he was presented, the neurologist explained that the crying behavior was not accompanied by the usual emotions or triggered by the usual events. The patient did not feel sad, did not feel like crying, and was not putting on an act, however convincing his behavior. And it was totally convincing, for it seemed to me almost impossible that someone could cry so heartrendingly, and yet not feel griefstricken.

The patient was questioned during the crying behavior as well as after, and he consistently explained, through his tears, that the behavior and the feelings were totally dissociated, and he would point to his head in a gesture of knowing exasperation. His behavior was as much a mystery to him as to the rest of us. In a commonsense way, I had assumed there could never be a dissociation between feelings of sadness and sadness behavior unless the subject was attempting to deceive, which this patient plainly was not. Indeed, I had known philosophers who said such dissociation could not happen. Yet here it was, and my commonsense assumption was taking a drubbing.

I began to ransack the neurological literature for answers, but my perplexity abated not at all, and each Thursday brought a fresh assault on the commonsense framework within which we standardly comprehend the behavior of normal brains—the framework within which we think about awareness, reasoning, unity of self, connectedness of cognitive capacities, connectedness of concepts and beliefs, and so forth. So long as the brain functions normally, the inadequacies of the commonsense framework can be hidden from view, but with a damaged brain the inadequacies of theory are unmasked.

Again and again one is dumbstruck by the problem of how to make sense of what one observes in the neurology ward. Such data seem to me crucially relevant in coming to understand how deficient folk psychology really is and how little we know of the deeper capacities underlying the known cognitive capacities of the brain. Received philosophical doctrine on the nature of rationality or the unity of self, for example, comes to seem made of very flimsy stuff. Neurology remains, therefore, endlessly engrossing. (For more discussion on folk psychology and its inadequacies, see chapters 8 and 9.)

The following is a small sample of cases intended to show something of what makes this domain of study important, theoretically as well as practically, to philosophers and neuroscientists. Aside from mirror reversal, none is very rare, and any neurologist in any large hospital will have seen them all, and more than once. Because the descriptions are highly simplified, it should be borne in mind that there is considerable variation among patients in the behavioral manifestation associated with a particular type of deficit. Syndrome descriptions constitute merely condensation points for clouds of behavioral abnormalities.

Facial Agnosia
Sometimes an RH lesion results in the patient's inability to recognize faces, including those of his family, those of famous people, and even his own face in a photograph. The patient may have normal vision, and can recognize and identify objects easily. This frequently seems to be an isolated disturbance, and the patient often compensates for the deficit by using other cues to identify people. For example, he

may identify his wife by her glasses or a hat—though if these are put on someone else, he will pick out that individual as his wife.

Recently it has been discovered that patients who are unable to recognize faces nonetheless show a large electrodermal skin conductance when shown faces familiar to them before the dysfunction, and they do not show a similar response to unfamiliar faces (Tranel and Damasio 1985). In one case the patient also showed the skin response to faces newly encountered. The data suggest that the physiological basis for facial recognition is intact in these patients, even though they have no conscious access to the information.

In part what these cases show is that recognition of individual conspecifics is not just an aspect of the general cognitive business subserving recognition of teacups, dogs, trees, and so forth. Something special is required, and thus important questions are raised about what that is and about the evolutionary significance of special mechanisms for recognition of conspecific individuals. Since the ability to identify others as individuals is found in many other species, including some insects (e.g., crickets), the questions raised here connect to questions regarding the brain's representational scheme of social relations and how it evolved.

Visual Agnosia

Patients otherwise unimpaired visually may be unable to identify by vision common objects, though they can name them if allowed to touch, hear, or smell them. They can faithfully copy a line drawing but remain unable to say what the object is. (See figure 5.16.) Sometimes this syndrome is found with color agnosia (inability to identify colors) and facial agnosia, and sometimes with alexia, and the lesions are usually in the areas of the visual cortex lying outside areas 17 and 18. Data from these cases are useful in determining the character and structure of sensory modules, in hypothesizing what precedes and follows certain elementary processes, and so forth. (For such a use, see Marr 1982.)

Blindsight

Anatomical studies of the visual system indicate that the striate cortex (primary visual cortex) receives a massive projection of neurons from the lateral geniculate nucleus, and earlier this area was widely regarded as the first major processing region for visual information. Lesioning the striate cortex was thought to result in complete blindness, and there was substantial evidence for this view. Nonetheless, it was found (Weiskrantz and Cowey 1967) that monkeys whose striate cortex had been excised showed a surprising residual visual

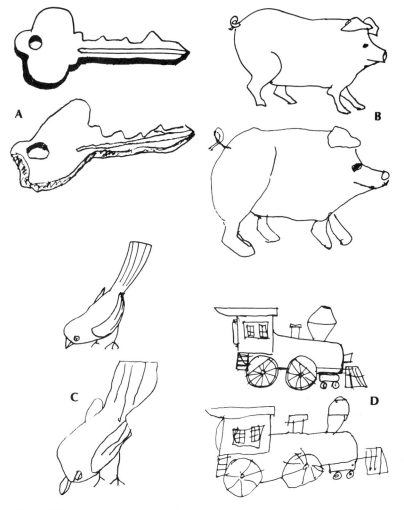

Figure 5.16
Copies of line drawings by a patient with visual agnosia. Before drawing, the patient could not identify any items, and after making copies, his attempts to identify what he had drawn were as follows: (A) "I still don't know." (B) "Could be a dog or any other animal." (C) "Could be a beach stump." (D) "A wagon or a car of some kind. The larger vehicle is being pulled by the smaller one." (From Rubens and Benson 1971.)

capacity. They could maneuver around large obstacles and could discriminate two-dimensional patterns, even when the entire striate cortex was removed. Other work on split-brain subjects had suggested that in addition to the major geniculostriate visual pathway, there must be a second pathway (Trevarthen 1970). Thus, to explain the residual capacity after striate lesions, it was hypothesized that the route through the superior colliculus provided the information on which the brain relied to make visual discriminations (figures 3.10, 3.11).

Naturally, the monkey studies raised the question of whether a comparable residual capacity could be found in humans with striate damage. In 1974 Weiskrantz et al. published their findings concerning a patient D.B. who, for medical reasons, had undergone surgical removal of the major portion of the striate cortex on the right hemisphere. As a result of the surgery, he was blind in the left visual field of both eyes (called a "homonymous hemianopia").[3] That is, on the run of standard clinical tests, and by his own description, D.B. was blind in his left visual field.

When tested for residual visual capacity, D.B. protested that he could see nothing, and he was therefore asked merely to guess his answers. In these tests he was indeed able to make discriminations with respect to coarse features of his environment, and he could do so with impressive accuracy. So long as the presentations were not too small, or the duration of the presentation not shorter than about 650 msec, he could correctly discriminate horizontal from vertical bars of light and X's from O's. He could also point with great accuracy to where *in his blind visual field* a point of light had been shining (accuracy of 29/30, 30/30 etc.). It was incontestable that his "guessing" was no mere guessing and that he was making use of visual information to form a judgment, despite the fact that he did not have consciously available visual information.

This first study of a human subject has been followed by others that tend to confirm the early findings, and testing procedures and controls have been refined to eliminate the possibility that the spared visual field has access to the visual stimuli presented to the blind visual field. Perenin and Jeannerod (1978) tested six subjects who had undergone complete decortication of one hemisphere, and in their residual visual capacities they were similar to D.B. Like him, they were strikingly accurate in pointing to visual targets in their blind visual fields and in distinguishing equiluminant patterns, such as triangles and circles. By contrast, two subjects whose blindness was owed to *pregeniculate* (chiasmatic) lesions were unable to perform above the chance level on the discrimination tests. This is a significant contrast because such lesions interrupt information from the retina to *anywhere,* and thus both the major geniculostriate pathway and the hypothesized second pathway would be deprived.

It should be mentioned that the second pathway hypothesis is still contentious, and some researchers believe that the blindsight phenomenon can be accounted for either by scattered light falling onto unimpaired parts of the visual field or by segments of the striate cortex that are spared. (See Campion, Latto, and Smith 1983 and the commentaries that follow.)

The blindsight cases are interesting for a number of reasons, one of which is that subjects are apparently providing a visual report on features of the environment but are not doing so on the basis of visual experiences. That is, the subjects appear to have no visual awareness of where the point of light is located, yet they can locate it. Sometimes the subjects acknowledge that they have a "feeling," such as a prickling or a feeling of "gunfire at a distance" (Richards 1973), but these experiences are not visual experiences. What is remarkable is that subjects who deny visual awareness can yet be consistently correct in pointing and in determining whether there is a circle or a square in their blind visual field.

It has sometimes seemed safe to assume that behavior at this level of sophistication *implies* awareness on the part of the subject, and that if a subject can systematically report the light's location, he must have visual experiences on which to base his judgment. These data certainly call that assumption into question, though it could be rescued by abandoning a further common assumption about awareness— namely, that if one is aware, then one knows one is aware. In other words, given the data, we cannot assume both that (1) if someone can observationally report on some current feature of the world, then he has experienced it and that (2) someone experiences something if and only if he is aware that he experienced it.

Whichever assumption gives way, it is evident that we need to revise our conception of what sort of state awareness is, though considering data just from the blindsight studies, we may not be clear about which assumption to revise, or indeed whether they both need revision. Other data will of course be relevant. For example, quite apart from clinical cases, signal detection theory makes it amply clear that whether or not someone experiences something is by no means the cut and dried affair one might have hoped it to be (Swets, Tanner, and Birdsall 1964). From the point of view of philosophy, it is important to see that this is an instance where empirical discoveries put pressure on us to make conceptual revisions (Patricia S. Churchland 1980a, 1983; see also chapters 7 and 8). The next case is an additional instance of this.

Blindness Denial

Also called Anton's syndrome, blindness denial is sometimes the sequel of a sudden onset of cortical blindness. The clinical picture is that such patients cannot see, but they somehow fail to recognize the deficit and persist in the belief that they can see. When asked whether there are visual defects, these patients will say that vision is quite normal, although they may complain that the lights are kept rather dim. When they bump into furniture, blindness denial patients typically confabulate, claiming that there is too much stuff around, that they are clumsy, and so forth. If asked to report visually, they again confabulate and willingly claim to see two fingers (the doctor holds up four), to see that the doctor's tie is brown (he has no tie), to see two nurses (there is one), and so forth. The confabulation is appropriate to the situation, and there is no evidence that the patients are deliberately making things up or that they are merely trying to keep a stiff upper lip.

Denial does not occur if the lesion is in the optic tract or even in the projection from the thalamus to the cortex, but only when the cortex is lesioned. It is anything but clear what is going on in these cases, and at most one can redescribe the symptoms in terms of capacities the patient has lost. Thus, as Kinsbourne (1980) describes it, the cerebral lesion has damaged the "analyzer" whose output indicates absence of visual input, and hence the patient is not aware of the absence of visual input. Unlike blind patients who admit their blindness, denial patients never acquire new and compensatory skills in maneuvering, and they tend to persist in stumbling around.

A related syndrome is found in patients with RH parietal lesions and left-sided paralysis. They frequently deny the paralysis and insist they can move quite normally; like blindness denial patients, they then confabulate wildly (but comfortably) to explain their behavior. They are puzzled and irritated by the suggestion that their limbs are paralyzed.

Though tempting, the suggestion that denial can be explained in terms of general confusion and intellectual deterioration or in terms of a determination to put up a good front is not in fact plausible. As Bisiach et al. report (in unpublished work), denial fractionates along function-specific lines. For example, a patient may deny blindness but be quite aware of dysphasia or hemiplegia. Moreover, the "confusion" is typically specific to denial, and the patient may be quite realistic and lucid on matters outside the problematic domain.

Notice that if the damage is only spinal but not cortical, patients typically *are* aware of their disability and do not deny it. Also part of this puzzling pattern are patients with jargon aphasia and lesions in the parietal and temporal regions. In contrast to patients with Broca's aphasia, these patients tend to be unaware of their deficits. Though otherwise unimpaired intellectually, they may fail completely to notice that their speech is unintelligible and their communicative efforts unsuccessful. It is widely believed that the denial syndrome is correlated with lesions in the limbic structures and does not occur when lesions are confined to the cortex. The premorbid personality of the patient may also be a factor, though this does not imply that the syndrome is psychiatric. (See especially Weinstein and Kahn 1955; Kinsbourne and Warrington 1963b.)

These cases are arresting because they challenge the general assumptions that if one cannot see or cannot move an arm, then one is aware—and aware without reservations—that one cannot see or cannot move the arm, and that if one is making unintelligible conversation, then one is aware, instantly, that one is not making sense. Such assumptions now appear problematic, and thus the blindness denial and other denial syndromes have implications that suggest revisions to the commonsense conception of what it is to be aware. Taken together with other cases that bear upon awareness, such as disconnection, hemineglect (see below), and blindsight, this case makes us stand back from the commonsense conceptions concerning consciousness and suggests that there is much to be learned about the conditions and dimensions of consciousness by studying the brain. (I discuss this further in chapters 8 and in Patricia S. Churchland 1983.)

Given the behavioral data, the usual clinical characterization of patients suffering from blindness denial is this: they are blind, but they are not aware that they are blind. However, it has been suggested to me by several philosophers that this case must be misdescribed, because, it is said, the following is a necessary feature of the concept of consciousness: so long as one is conscious, and so long as one can make judgments at all, *then* if one is not having visual experiences, one will be aware that one is not having visual experiences, and vice versa. In a word, you cannot fail to know whether you are blind. I do of course concede that the case *may* be misdescribed, inasmuch as we do not understand the empirical situation well enough to be certain what the correct description is. However, I cannot agree that we can know a priori that it *must* be misdescribed. On my view, what is claimed to be a necessary feature of the concept of consciousness is an empirical assumption that the phenomenon of blindness denial calls into question. And only the empirical facts will determine whether the assumption stands or falls.

Hemineglect
Also called hemi-inattention, hemineglect is a syndrome most commonly associated with right parietal lesions and accompanying lesions in the limbic structures or the reticular formation. Depending on severity, patients will ignore and seem unaware of events in the hemispace contralateral to the site of the lesion. They may dress and clean only the right side of body, eat only food on the right side of the plate, read only the right side of a page, and draw only the right side of a figure. Even when the page is placed entirely in the right hemispace, such patients still tend to read only the right side of the page. (See figure 5.17.) Asked to point directly in front of their bodies, hemineglect patients tend to point to the middle of their right hemispace.

These patients do not have a strictly visual defect in the left visual field, however, and occasionally they react to stimuli in the left hemispace. Generally they simply neglect this space, as though it were not there. Sometimes they deny ownership of the left arm or leg, asking whose it is or why it is in bed with them. In less severe cases ownership may be grudgingly admitted, but the limb is treated as an object. Sometimes a pain in the left limb will be reported as felt in the right.

Critchley reports a patient who addressed his left arm thus: "You bloody bastard! It's a lost soul, this bloody thing. It keeps following me around. It gets in my way when I read. I find my hand up by my face, waving about" (1979:118). It is also of interest that hemineglect patients may be unable to conjure images of left-sided space. Bisiach and Luzzatti (1978) found that patients asked to visualize a well-known square in Milan could provide details about right hemispace as they imagined themselves facing it, but not the left. The memories were there, however, for when asked to imagine approaching the square from the other dirction, these patients could now accurately describe the missing side, now on their right.

Studying deaf patients who have suffered RH lesions, Klima, Bellugi, and their colleagues at the Salk Institute have made a number of remarkable and rather paradoxical discoveries (Bellugi, Poizner, and Klima (forthcoming)). Their patients were all fluent in American Sign Language, and it has been found that though signing essentially involves visuospatial skills, signing deaf patients show the same corre-

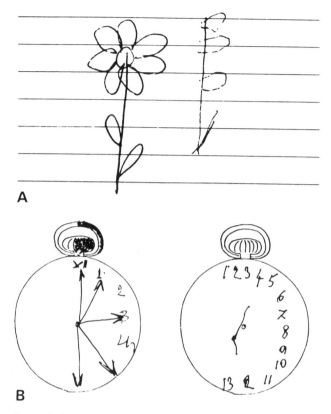

Figure 5.17
(A) Examiner's drawing of a daisy on left; patient with hemineglect drew daisy on right. (From Heilman et al. (1983). In *Localization in neuropsychology*, ed. A Kertesz. New York: Academic Press.) (B) Drawings of patients with hemineglect when asked to fill in the clock faces. (From Bisiach et al. 1981.)

lation of deficits and lesion sites as do speaking patients. That is, they present aphasic symptoms with LH lesions and visuospatial deficits with RH lesions. But what happens to the signing and comprehension capacities of left hemineglect patients? Are such patients able to use their left hemispace for communicative purposes?

The answer is complex and surprising. As a preliminary, it is important to know that space has a crucial role in signing—at the *lexical* level, to differentiate signs, at the *morphological* level, to make inflections, and at the *syntactic* level. In the last case, for example, nouns may be introduced into the discourse and associated with an arbitrary reference point in the horizontal plane, and later pronoun reference will be made by signing to these points. Relations between objects specified by the verb ("He chased her") will be specified in terms of the spatial relation and the direction of movement between the established points (Klima and Bellugi 1979).

Consider now one of the hemineglect signing subjects tested by Bellugi, Poizner, and Klima. When asked to describe her room, she squashed together all the furniture in her right hemifield. When asked the sign for "square" she omitted the left side. However, and this is the surprising result, she continued to use her *left* hemifield quite normally for syntactic purposes in signing. And her comprehension of signs, by signers making use of both hemifields, was normal. It appears that when space is used for syntactic representation, the subject is in some sense aware of space and the appropriate spatial relations between points, but when space is represented directly, as in describing a room, the representation of space is truncated.

One leading theory (Heilman 1979) is that hemineglect is a defect of orienting mechanisms; another is that it is a defect in arousal mechanisms (Kinsbourne 1977), although the research carried out by Bisiach and Luzzatti and by Bellugi, Poizner, and Klima suggests that representations of space may be crucially involved. In any event, since the nature and function of attention is so poorly understood, the theories constitute only a beginning. In concert with related phenomena, hemineglect raises important questions about brain mechanisms for attention, awareness, and consciousness and about the body scheme or body-in-space representation that the brain must have. And they emphasize once more the point that phenomenological access and the subjective point of view are by no means the final word but rather the merest beginning in our attempt to understand the nature of awareness, consciousness, and attention.

Calculating Oddities
The ability of ordinary humans to count, to perform arithmetic calculations, to solve complicated equations, and the like, is remarkable. Occasionally there is an exceptional development of calculating capacities, whereby an individual can perform complicated arithmetical calculations in his head and with great speed. Sometimes calculating prodigies also show autistic symptoms or may be demented (idiots savants), and their abilities may be highly confined (Sacks 1985).

Critchley (1979) describes several severely retarded individuals who had superlative calculating abilities. A famous example was Fleury, described as a "destructive imbecile," who produced the cube root of 465,484,375 (= 775) in thirteen seconds and had a prodigious memory for dates, but was unable to grasp even the rudiments of geometry. Some such prodigies remember all the stock market quotations from the newspaper for months running but are otherwise severely retarded. It is amazing enough when a calculating prodigy is also a mathematical genius, as for example in the case of Srinivasa Ramanujan,[4] but when general intellectual capacities are impaired and calculating stands alone, one is especially baffled about what this implies concerning arithmetic capacities. How are they standardly integrated with other intellectual capacities? How did they evolve? Why do they develop so superlatively in some retarded brains? Does such development perhaps take place at the expense of other faculties?

Stroke patients sometimes are unable to calculate at all, having lost all sense of the number series, of which of two numbers is greater, of how to count, of how to identify numerals, and so on. In other cases, a patient may be able to multiply but not add. When this is accompanied by aphasia, alexia, or defects of short-term memory, the anarithmia may be secondary, but sometimes it appears to be a relatively isolated deficit.

The inability to handle arithmetic notions can also be congenital and is not always accompanied by other intellectual deficits. In one especially remarkable case that came to my attention, the man was exceptionally intelligent but had from childhood lacked the ability to grasp numerical values and to perform even the simplest arithmetic operations. He could identify numbers between one and ten, but he did so without any real sense of what they meant, essentially as one could learn to identify nonsense symbols.

The inability was a source of great embarrassment to the man, who had, through ingenious compensatory strategies, managed to make himself very wealthy. All too aware of his inabilities, he hired accountants to perform the calculations he required, and because he saw the dangers in trusting one accountant, he had the figuring done by several competing firms. In order to deal with problems such as measuring amounts, he had his wife mark with colored lines the level to which containers were to be filled with, for example, fertilizer or seed. With extraordinary cunning he managed to cope successfully without numbers, partly of course by exploiting the calculating capacities he knew others possessed. His intellectual economy was the inverse of that of the idiots savants inasmuch as he appeared to lack only an "arithmetic module." That could indeed be a misdescription, for there may be subtle connected deficits that are not detectable by the casual observer or in the usual tests (McCloskey, Caramazza, and Basili (forthcoming)).

There are legions of cases that challenge our understanding of what the brain does and how it is organized. How can we explain the discovery that some hydrocephalic patients in whom the ventricles have expanded to occupy over 90 percent of the cranial cavity nonetheless have IQs in the normal and above-normal range and can complete a university degree (Berker 1985)?[5] What is it that changes in the brain when, as a result of a stroke, the patient's visual experiences are a mirror image of normal experiences, so that he can only read books held up to a mirror, writes the mirror image of his signature, runs around the baseball diamond from home plate to third, to second, to first, and home again, and attempts to drive on the left-hand side of the road? What does such a case tell us about the nature of spatial representation? How does it connect with the brain's representation of one's body-in-space? (See Heilman et al. 1980.)

Neurological studies were one of the earliest sources of wonder regarding the brain, and they continue to be absorbing. With the advent of new imaging techniques, it is possible to make headway in correlating lesions with performance deficits, and that is of course immensely valuable. For example, if we can correlate Alzheimer's disease (senile dementia) with degeneration in certain areas, and if we discover the degeneration is linked to a neurotransmitter deficiency (Perry and Perry 1982), then we can set about to interrupt and perhaps reverse the ravages that characterize that disease. Moreover, as I remarked at the outset, neurological studies are also vitally important for their capacity to unsettle and unseat our intuitions, our assumptions, and our commonplace verities about the nature of what the mind does. Unseated intuitions leave room for new theory, and that electrifies the curiosity and stokes up the theory-making machinery.

5.7   Conclusions

None of the methods discussed in this chapter yields a sure-fire means for telling us how and where certain higher functions are carried out in the brain. None of the experimental procedures is perfect and free of flaws. Nevertheless, each in its own way is useful, and what is to be hoped is that data from distinct experimental procedures will slowly converge upon a common hypothesis. Accordingly, human studies need to be conjoined with animal studies, clinical studies with studies of normals, lesion data with results from electrophysiological investigations (stimulation and recording), and both of these with anatomical information, behavioral data (ERPs, PET scans, tachistoscopic and reaction time studies, etc.), neuroembryological data, and so forth. Whitman Richards (1983:461) sums it up thus:

> If so many psychophysical experiments are flawed, why bother? One reason that motivates many of us to study behavior with imperfect designs is that our imperfections will usually differ from one set of experiments to another, thus allowing a convergence to the understanding of underlying mechanisms.

Selected Readings

Bryden, M. P. (1982). *Laterality: Functional asymmetry in the intact brain.* New York: Academic Press.

Feindel, W., R. S. J. Frackowiak, D. Gadian, P. L. Magistretti, and M. R. Zalutsky, eds. (1985). Brain metabolism and imaging. *Discussions in Neurosciences* 2/2 (special issue).

Galambos, Robert, and Steven A. Hillyard, eds. (1981). *Electrophysiological approaches to human cognitive processing.* (Based on a work session of the Neurosciences Research Program, 1981.) *Neurosciences Research Program Bulletin* 20:141–265.

Gazzaniga, Michael S., and Joseph E. LeDoux (1978). *The integrated mind.* New York: Plenum.

Hecaen, Henri, and Martin L. Albert, eds. (1978). *Human neuropsychology.* New York: Wiley.

Kertesz, Andrew, ed. (1983). *Localization in neuropsychology.* New York: Academic Press.

Kolb, Bryan, and Ian Q. Whishaw (1980). *Fundamentals of human neuropsychology.* San Francisco: W. H. Freeman.

Mendelson, Wallace B., J. Christian Gillin, and Richard Jed Wyatt (1977). *Human sleep and its disorders.* New York: Plenum.

Perecman, Ellen, ed. (1983). *Cognitive processing in the right hemisphere.* New York: Academic Press.

Squire, Larry R., and Nelson Butters, eds. (1984). *Neuropsychology of memory.* New York: Guilford.

Thompson, Richard F. (1975). *Introduction to physiological psychology.* New York: Harper and Row.

PART II

Recent Developments in the Philosophy of Science

Chapter 6

Introduction and Historical Sketch

There is no first philosophy.
W. V. O. Quine, 1969

6.1 Introduction

Within the domain of neuroscience, questions at one level of generality inevitably provoke questions at both higher and lower levels of generality. Wondering how the retina works, for example, leads down one path to inquiries about the microstructure of rods and cones, and thus to biochemistry, and eventually to physics. It also leads in the opposite direction, to inquiries about such things as the organization of neurons in the visual cortex and what functions are there carried out. Following that ball of yarn as it unwinds before us, questions of greater generality take form. How does the brain visually recognize shapes and colors, how does it recognize crows and water? How do we see? Conviction concerning how to go about answering these questions shades off as the questions become more broad, more general, or more abstract. As the ball of yarn rolls on, our curiosity begins to limn the shape of large and ominously general questions looming out of the fog. Can we develop a science of animal behavior, human behavior included? What will be the role of neuroscience in such a science? How can neuroscience and psychology be integrated?

The shape and character of a research program can be molded by the perspective one has on questions at levels up and down from where one's day to day efforts are directed. Neuroscientists, therefore, like scientists in all fields, are compelled on occasion to follow the ball of yarn past the gates of their paradigm, and thus to contemplate the coherence and consilience of their research within a broader framework. They are compelled, that is, to be philosophical.

The dawn of natural philosophy, which is to say, of science, was marked by a fascination with the disparities between appearance and reality; disparities between what seemed, given one's beliefs and some observations, to be true, but what, given other beliefs and observations, seemed to be false. Early philosophers were moved to suspect that how things appear may be the outcome of a deeper reality, hidden from view, and radically different from the appearance apprehended in observation. Their reflections on the nature of substance, change, motion, fire, and so forth, gave rise to bold theories about the deeper reality and about why it was not immediately perceived. Thus, for example, in a swashbuckling slice through the blooming, buzzing, confusing complexity the world presents, the ancient Greek philosopher Democritus (460–370 B.C.) claimed that the reality underlying appearances consisted of nothing but atoms and the void. The atoms, he hypothesized, hooked together in assorted ways, and differences in the appearance of substances were owed to differences in the shapes and collective organization of the fundamental atoms. Humans, like everything else in the universe, were at bottom just organized assemblies of atoms, although the organization was neither understood nor assumed to be simple. Minds, therefore, were conceived as being fundamentally material, and their remarkable capacities were a function of the remarkable organization of matter.

The force and vivacity of these ancient ruminations can be recaptured by recollections of appearance/reality discrepancies in one's childhood. Recall watching the moon scudding by the clouds on a windy night, and having that seemingly unassailable observation corrected with the claim that it is the clouds that are doing the scudding. How do you know? Line up the position of the moon with the top of the poplar tree, watch for three minutes, and see what has moved. A new observation conflicts with the old.

Recall the surprise at being told that the earth is a huge sphere and that it moves around the sun. How do you know? The answer here is longer, requiring gravitational theory and Newton's mechanics, and of these in turn one can ask, How do you know? In the third century B.C. Aristarchus offered a heliocentric view; the Sun was at the center, and the planets, including the Earth, moved about the sun in circles. The rationale for this theory derived from calculations Aristarchus had made of the distance of the Moon and Sun from the Earth, and on that basis he roughly gauged the relative sizes. Since the Sun was so vastly larger than the Earth, he thought its daily passage across the sky must be mere appearance, and that in reality it was the Earth that moved rather than the Sun.

Although his calculations were acceptable, Aristarchus could not explain how the Earth moved, since nothing was pushing it along, and prevailing Aristotelian theory required continuous application of a force to explain continuous movement. Nor could he explain why there was no observed stellar parallax unless the stars were infinitely far away, and that additional hypothesis seemed ad hoc and ludicrous. At the time, these were good objections to his theory, and the failure of his conjecture to fit with the only extant theory meant it failed to win widespread acceptance. Aristarchus's conjecture was right, as it turned out, but without the surrounding theory of mechanics no one could see how it might be right. Observations alone do not decide the worthiness of theory, and the interpretation of the observation requires surrounding confirmed theory.

If we cannot take appearances for granted, then it becomes perplexing how to get at the truth about the way the world really is. What can we take for granted as *given*, as *certain*, and what methods can we use to generate more knowledge? These are questions that have driven epistemology (theory of knowledge), and as we have come to acquire more knowledge about the universe and how it works, we have come to understand more about the business of knowledge acquisition.

Suppose the object of inquiry is not the nature of motion or of the Earth, but the nature of the mind. Is it possible that the reality of the mind's nature, of its structures and processes, is also different from the appearance? If the answer is yes, it means that neuroscience and experimental psychology may yield descriptions of inner states and processes that are deeper and different—perhaps radically different—from how we intuitively think of mental states and processes in ourselves.

And what about epistemology itself? Can we settle questions of the nature of knowledge in living organisms without an empirically based theory of how brains acquire knowledge? Or is it rather that theories concerning the nature of knowledge and knowledge acquisition are themselves constrained by empirical theory in neuroscience and experimental psychology? According to one viewpoint issuing from joint work in philosophy of science and philosophy of mind in contemporary North America, the answer to the last question is yes. To see why this is a plausible answer, a historical backdrop for the contemporary work is essential.

The history of philosophy is a complex and richly ornamented tapestry; I shall be following but one thread, and that is the thread leading to theories that make sense to me. As before, I must emphasize that what follows is in no sense a scholarly survey, nor is it a survey of the thoughts even of the philosophers I do discuss.[1] The rationale for including a brief look at the history of philosophy is simple. My ultimate objective is to make clear some recent developments in the philosophy of science. To do so, I must first say something about epistemology, and that in turn requires some remarks on the origins of contemporary epistemology. Hence the backward glance into the history of philosophy. My approach here is frankly idiosyncratic and opportunistic; I use what I need to make clear the current situation in science and philosophy.

6.2   Early Epistemology

Plato (429–347 B.C.)
Plato thought Reality was not to be found in the physical world (the world of sensibilia) at all but rather in the nonphysical world of intelligibilia, a world that housed mathematical entities and other nonphysical objects of thought. Only by turning away from the sensible world and by contemplating the nonphysical objects of intellection could real understanding be achieved. Mathematics was offered as the model of Knowledge and how it was to be won. Interaction with the physical world might yield opinion or mere belief, but it could never yield Knowledge of Reality. Pure contemplation was the proper occupation of the rational soul, itself a nonphysical substance capable of existence independent of the physical body. Since the theory postulates two distinct kinds of substances, mind-stuff and material-stuff, it is known as *substance dualism.*

Looked at in one way, Plato's theory is a desperate one. Faced with the difficulty of specifying how to distinguish reliable observations from illusory ones, good empirical theory from bad empirical theory, he turned his back on the muck and tangle that is the world and dismissed it *all* as mere appearance and not worth the trouble. Exercise of reason alone was Plato's avenue to knowledge. Although his position was an extreme one, certain of its themes have survived with surprising vitality. In particular, the idea that the mind has as its objects of knowledge and contemplation nonphysical intelligibilia has reappeared in countless guises as an argument for the special nature of the mental, for dualism of various types, for the mind's special access to itself, and for the impossibility of reducing psychology to neuroscience. (See chapters 7 and 8.)

Plato is the archetypal antinaturalist and contrasts vividly with contemporary naturalists who argue that the mind is the brain and that empirical science is indispensable to discovering the nature of the mind-brain, including the nature of the "Pure Reason" that Plato thought would lead us to truth. The greatest erosion to Plato's views was caused by the success of empirical science itself, and this erosion began on a grand scale during the Renaissance.

Descartes (1596–1650)

With the resurgence of scientific progress after the Dark Ages, there was a revitalization of attempts to determine how true empirical understanding might be acquired and how it could be distinguished from apparent knowledge. René Descartes had a keen and inquisitive empirical eye and developed empirical theories to explain such diverse phenomena as the movements of the planets and reflex behavior in living organisms. (See section 1.2.) He also wanted to establish a method that would distinguish what was genuine knowledge from bogus belief, and his strategy was to establish first what could be taken for granted as certain.

It seemed to him that the founding certitude was that he had thoughts, feelings, doubts, and so on. Whether the thoughts corresponded to an external reality was not established, but that they were a testament, indubitable and certain, to *inner* reality, Descartes took as established. The soul and its contents were self-evident to the soul, and thus the soul knew itself through self-examination—that is, through introspection. Descartes believed that "I think, therefore I am" (Cogito ergo sum) could constitute the foundation of the edifice of knowledge.

The distinction between reality and appearance could not apply to the soul's knowledge of itself; in matters concerning the mind and its contents, what seemed real to the mind was real. Having established a foundation, Descartes needed to specify the means for building. The rational soul came equipped with the means, he averred, because it conformed to an innately configured structure of ideas and principles, and it could distinguish the self-evident from the non-self-evident. It was, after all, a *rational* soul with a scheme of innate representations, and principles of logic were the principles of its dynamics.

Like Plato, Descartes was a substance dualist, and he took the soul to be a nonphysical substance in causal interaction with the body primarily through the auspices of the pineal gland. (See also chapter 1.) Ontology concerns what exists, and in Descartes's ontological theory both physical stuff and a distinctive mental stuff were believed to exist. His postulation of a distinctly mental substance was motivated at least in part by his reflections on the complexity of reasoning and of thinking in general. The rule-following aspect of reasoning, our ability to think about indefinitely many things as well as about abstract matters such as mathematics, our capacity to deliberate before action and to defer gratification, all suggested to Descartes that there was something entirely unique about the mind. So remarkable are these capacities, he opined, that they cannot be capacities of a merely physical substance. (For a further discussion of dualism, see chapter 8.)

Descartes is sometimes viewed as the father of modern philosophy, largely because of his attempts to find and characterize the systematicity both in science (natural philosophy, as it was then called) and in the individual's own internal scheme of understanding. He can be seen as developing an early cognitive theory, which addressed the nature of representations and the nature of the relations enjoyed by representations. The idea that our knowledge is a structure whose foundation is the contents of consciousness, and whose upper regions are in place insofar as they are justified, is an idea that has dominated epistemology until very recently. Together with the view that the contents of consciousness are apprehended largely without error by introspection, these ideas make up the core of a very powerful tradition in philosophy and the sciences. As for the Cartesian assumption that the mind has innate ideas that permit a priori knowledge concerning the nature of the world, it was ground underfoot by the empiricists.

Classical Empiricism

The nature of knowledge, the principles governing the accumulation of knowledge, its limitations, and its logic were the topics of inquiry for the empiricists. History remembers especially John Locke, George Berkeley, and David Hume in the eighteenth century and John Stuart Mill and Auguste Comte in the nineteenth. To be sure, they did not speak with one voice, but, highly simplified, the central theses of the empiricist theory of knowledge are as follows.

There are two kinds of things we can know about: (1) the nature of the empirical world (matters of fact) and (2) relations between ideas (matters of logic and mathematics). Propositions about the first domain are empirical propositions, and propositions about the second domain are "analytic" propositions.

Corresponding to this division is a division among kinds of truth: necessary truth and contingent truth. True analytic propositions are *necessarily* true, and their negations are necessarily false and imply a contradiction. For example, "The interior angles of a triangle sum to 180°" is a necessary truth of geometry, and the denial of that sentence is necessarily false. Similarly, "A bachelor is an unmarried man" is a necessary truth of language (that is, it is true by definition), not a factual truth about the way the world is. By contrast, a true empirical proposition is only *contingently* true. It is true in virtue of how the world is, as a matter of contingent fact. Its truth is not a matter of definitions. The world might have been different, and the proposition could have been false. For example, Pierre Trudeau is in fact bald, but there is nothing inherently contradictory about the statement "Trudeau is not bald."

In a bold stroke, the empiricists then claimed that there is a type of reasoning appropriate to each basic domain of thing to be known: observation and "experimental reasoning" for matters of fact, and "abstract (a priori) reasoning" for matters of mathematics and for analytic matters generally. In contrast to Descartes and the rationalists, they claimed that a priori reasoning cannot reveal truths about the nature of the world—about space, time, substance, existence, causation, the nature of the mind, and so forth. These matters, they argued, are matters of fact and hence are matters for empirical research.

It was the battle cry of empiricism that only observations and experimental reasoning can lead to factual knowledge. For mathematical, geometrical, and logical knowledge, however, a priori reasoning is appropriate, and confirmation by experimentation is irrelevant.[2] There are no other avenues to knowledge, and encroachment on the empirical domain by a priori reasoning leads, in the empiricist view, not to genuine knowledge but to the mere illusion of knowledge. Hume put the point most memorably:

> When we run over our libraries, persuaded of these principles, what havoc must we make? If we take in our hand any volume of divinity or school metaphysics, for instance, let us ask, *Does it contain any abstract reasoning concerning quantity and number?* No. *Does it contain any experimental reasoning concerning matter of fact and existence?* No. Commit it then to the flames, for it can contain nothing but sophistry and illusion. (Hume 1748; in Selby-Bigge 1894:165)

It is evident that a primary motivation in empiricist thought was the desire to characterize a method whereby respectable, worthy discoveries in science could be distinguished from mere speculation and idle theorizing, and from "authoritative" deliverances of sages and theologians. The empiricists envisioned the gradual construction of a sound and solid edifice of empirical knowledge whose foundations enjoyed the certainty of observations and whose upper structures were secured by induction on those below. The only statements permitted entry to the edifice of knowledge were those justified either by *direct observation* or *by inference* from other statements already justified. Observational statements were narrowly characterized to mean only statements that described what *strictly speaking* was observed and did not go beyond what could be sheerly observed. Thus, the statement "There is a lemon on the desk" would not, on this construal, count as observational, since something is not a lemon unless it grew on a lemon tree, tastes sour when put in the mouth, has juice inside (which, moreover, stings when put on an open wound), and will eventually rot. But none of these properties can I literally, truly *see* with my eyes as I sit here.

Strictly speaking, what I observe, the empiricists would claim, is an oblong, yellow patch in my visual field, and on the basis of past experience I *infer* that there is a lemon in front of me. What we immediately experience, they said, are not objects of the external world, but phenomenal properties such as patches of yellow, pains, tastes, smells, and so on. These are the raw data of the senses—*the Given*—which are the outcome of sensory interaction with the world. Hence, these sheerly given data came to be called *sense-data*.

But now a very troublesome question arises: What is the relation between sense-data and the external world? Do the internal representations resemble the objects in the world? A view commonly attributed to Locke says that there are important dimensions of resemblance, and that it is in virtue of the resemblance between representation and reality that we know the nature of reality. This sort of view is now called *naive realism*. Some empiricists, for example Berkeley, saw straightaway that there were acute problems with naive realism. In particular, if sense-data were the only access to reality, then claims of resemblance could never be justified and were nothing better than speculation. That is, if there is no unmediated access to reality, how do we justify claims about the nature of reality? Berkeley found it more plausible to think of our entire conception of objects in an external reality to be a sort of organizational imposition on sense-data supplied by the mind. On this view, so-called external reality is really nothing other than sets of actual and possible sense-data. This view is known as *idealism*.

Idealism has typically seemed an option of last resort, and a more obvious recourse is to suppose that external reality causes the sense-data, and that differences in sense-data features correspond to differences in the reality perceived. In short, we ought to be able to reason from effects to their causes. Hume systematically scrutinized this alternative, and the results were devastating. First, if sense-data can never be directly compared with reality, how do we ever know how faithful or unfaithful they are? If all the mind has observational access to are *effects* of the external world on sense organs, then, asked Hume, how can we arrive at true understanding concerning the nature of the *causes* of those effects? If it is not possible for us to approach reality save through the medium of our experiences, then justification of our beliefs about the external world may be impossible. Deductive justification is inappropriate, but inductive justification cannot get started without observation of the causes, and yet observation is always the *effect* of the causes we need to observe. Second, Hume asked what became the tormenting question for empiricism: How is "experimental reasoning" about causes and effects itself justified? In terms of deduction? That is impossible since the conclusions of inductive arguments are not deductively derivable from their premises. In terms of experimental reasoning? That, Hume pointed out, is arguing in a circle.

On one reading, Hume is an unqualified naturalist. He thought that much of our representation/knowledge system is neither governed nor organized by principles of logic, and that if we want to understand the cognitive domain, we must look to other—nonlogical—principles that will explain the *causal* factors involved. For example, he thought that we are *caused* to suppose that our sense-data faithfully represent reality; it is simply one aspect—an empirically explorable aspect—of the way the human mind works. This is interesting because it implies a criticism concerning the adequacy of a science of the mind that assumes that cognition is fundamentally logical (and language-like) in nature. To understand how the mind represents, and how representations are transformed and reconfigured, it will be necessary to investigate scientifically the causal principles that in fact govern the mind's operation. (A modern version of such criticism of the mind-as-logic-machine idea will be considered in chapters 9 and 10.)

Some of the importance of Hume's contribution to the empiricist theory of knowledge derives from his careful and ruthless working out of the implications of empiricist principles and from his discovery of profound and intractable problems that arise within the empiricist framework. In coping with these problems, later thinkers were eventually forced to abandon much of that framework, including the idea that science must have an absolute foundation of certainties given in sensory experience, that induction is the only principle available for empirical justification, that there is an absolute distinction between truths of language and truths of fact, and that the mind can know its nature through introspection. Important in the progress towards these revisions was Immanuel Kant.

Kant (1724–1804)

If the problem is to show how the mind may contain a faithful copy of Reality, as something knowable without mediation by the mind (or, as we would say, the brain), then Kant, agreeing with Hume, said the problem is unsolvable. All knowledge is mediated by the mind and its sundry faculties, which impose a structure and an organization on the input. Observations themselves are not "raw" but are apprehended through the lens of the mind's categories, and this includes our observations of our own inner goings-on. In more modern terms we might say that all observation is conceptualized, or highly processed, or theory-mediated, where the brain in its evolved and acquired wisdom supplies the theory (chapter 7).

Although Kant seems to have thought the categories used by the mind were in some sense a priori, and though he did not identify the mind with the brain, what is especially interesting in the present context is his insight that the mind's knowledge of *itself* is mediated. For if it is, then despite Descartes the mind is not transparent to itself. That is, introspective awareness may not yield truths about the way the mind works.

As Kant saw it, our knowledge of inner objects and processes is no more immediate than our knowledge of outer objects and processes. This means that there is nothing epistemologically unique or sacrosanct about introspectively based beliefs; they are not on an entirely different footing from beliefs about the outer world, and they have neither more nor less need for justification. Inner representations are not somehow privileged representations; the inner world is no more evident than the outer world. Inner truth is no more "given" than outer truth. Kant was nevertheless convinced that to the degree that the workings of the mind were knowable at all, it was philosophical reflection that would yield the central features of that knowledge.

Later philosophers inspired by Kant, notably the neo-Kantians, took a more naturalistic approach than Kant himself, claiming that psychological investigation was appropriate to learning the mind's operations and that such study would yield, not a priori truths about the mind's operations, but empirical principles characterizing its functions. This school of thought did not become popular among philosophers, however, partly because logicians in the nineteenth century (especially, for example, Frege) found abhorrent the idea that the laws of logic might be in some sense dependent on the empirical nature of the mind. The crux of the antipsychologizing thesis went like this: Rationality is essentially conformity with the laws of logic, but the validity of those laws cannot be equated with mere empirical truth of how the mind in fact operates. Such laws are universally and absolutely true, regardless of how some person's mind works, and regardless of how often someone's mental operations violate that law. The laws must be a priori truths. This doctrine of a special status for logic and hence for the logical operations of the mind was a powerful influence on British-American philosophy of mind. Evidently, if one has a cognitive theory that characterizes the mental representations as sentence-like and the operations on sentences as conforming to the laws of logic, then one will tend to assume that much of the investigation of the mind and its processes is a priori.

The Kantian theme that introspective knowledge is not epistemologically privileged began to provoke a revolutionary trend when it occurred to later philosophers (such as Feyerabend) that it implies the possibility that the entire framework of concepts for understanding our inner life might be reconfigured. If our beliefs about ourselves are mediated by concepts, then the question can always be raised whether those concepts are adequate to their task and whether our beliefs about our inner world can be improved by science in much the same way that our beliefs about the outer world are improved by science. This was not a view that Kant himself adopted, but it was nevertheless a view that his work inspired.

Peirce (1839–1914)
Many threads lead from the complexity and richness in Kant's thoughts, and one such thread was idealism, which espoused the notion that the world is nought but the mind's construction and that the only reality is mental reality. A different thread, which interests me more, is connected to the pragmatists in America, and Charles Sanders Peirce was the visionary pioneer of pragmatism. Peirce thought the idea of Unknowable Reality was metaphysical tomfoolery; he took instead the view that the only reality is the reality science discovers and that the *truth* about nature is what science *at the limit of inquiry* will say about nature. In the idealized long run, the completed science is a true description of reality; there is no other Truth and no other Reality. Accordingly, he was what we now call a *scientific realist*, and for him the completability of science was an idealized conception—it is that toward which we are progressing, though we may not in fact ever reach that end.

Peirce argued that the distinction between appearance and reality is an evolving one, becoming progressively more accurate as science evolves. In his view, the distinction can be drawn only within science, not from a metaphysical point outside all science. Moreover, he believed that if we want to understand knowledge and its acquisition, we must treat the knower and the knowing community as something to be investigated by scientific means, and that in such investigations we must avail ourselves of whatever in science is relevant—

physiology, psychology, history of science, and sociology as well as philosophy. In this regard Peirce, to an even greater degree than Hume and the neo-Kantians, was a naturalist.

Additionally, Peirce had a sensitive and subtle understanding of the dynamics and methodology of science. He distinguished among *crude induction, quantitative induction,* and *qualitative induction.* Crude induction is typified by the coarse generalizations made in everyday business—for example, "All gophers burrow underground." Quantitative induction is what we now call probability theory and statistical reasoning. Qualitative induction consists in framing conjectural hypotheses and then testing them to see if the facts falsify them. The hypotheses that survive the rigors of empirical testing are, by analogy with biological evolution, the ones most fit, and given the wider scientific enterprise within which they compete for approval, they are also the ones most likely to be true. We publicize and preserve the hypotheses that survive their trials by fire; the rest are forgotten and perish. In this fashion a body of integrated, coherent science evolves and asymptotically converges on truth.

One problem that troubled Peirce relentlessly is particularly interesting here, because it is akin to certain problems that have plagued artificial intelligence (AI) research: the indexing problem and (distantly related to it) the frame problem (chapter 9). Peirce's problem is this: when a scientist is trying to find an explanation for a phenomenon, there are *indefinitely* many hypotheses to be tried. Yet as a matter of psychological fact, his reasoning does not canvass the entire range but is always restricted to a handful of relevant or plausible possibilities. How does the mind-brain "fish" for relevant hypotheses? How is it equipped such that the billions of irrelevant ideas do not even come into awareness, there to be rejected?

It may be remarkable enough that when given a specific array, the mind-brain can select the hypotheses that are relevant, but how does it go about the different business of just lighting on relevant hypotheses without antecedently setting out all possibilities? Peirce felt driven to speculate that somehow there is a mechanism that has a sort of "tropism for truth," though he ruefully recognized what an unsatisfying and puzzling idea that is.

With William James (1842–1910), another pragmatist, the revered presumption that science, and knowledge generally, required foundational certainties began to seem questionable. If, agreeing with Kant, our sensory experience is interpreted experience, then the "certainties" of sensory evidence are only as good as the infused interpretation. Moreover, innateness of categories and concepts cannot guarantee truth—categories might be innate but false of the world—

and therefore interpretations are only as good as the empirical evidence supporting them. However it is that science makes progress, and James had views about that, it is not because it rests on a bedrock of certainties of sense or certainties of reason. These rather revolutionary thoughts of the pragmatists were perhaps ahead of their time. In any case, to British and Continental philosophers they seemed brash and Yankee, and their ideas did not take hold in philosophy until the later work of Kuhn, Quine, Feyerabend, Hanson, and other philosophers of science. In the meantime there were other important developments: the new logic, new theories of meaning, and the attempts by the logical empiricists to understand what made science *science*.

Frege (1848–1925) and Russell (1872–1971)
Gottlob Frege essentially invented modern mathematical logic. As this logic was to have profound effects on how philosophers rejuvenated the empiricist program of depicting the justificatory structure of science, it also had a profound effect on epistemology in general. As we shall see, some of those effects consisted in lending support to the antinaturalist theme and hence in discouraging the naturalist approach to epistemology and to the nature of the mind.

Frege, and somewhat later Bertrand Russell and his collaborator, A. N. Whitehead, devised a new theory of logic that was incomparably more powerful and illuminating than the old syllogistic logic of Aristotle. It provided the means for symbolizing sentences and logically important structures within sentences, as well as for characterizing the important relations between sentences. It provided a rigorous—mathematical—characterization of how a sentence can be proved from other sentences, and it permitted the construction of logical systems of axioms, rules, and theorems. Tarski (1944) later provided a mathematical characterization of the truth of sentences in a logical system. Without going into details, suffice it to say that the symbolic structures and the configuration of the relations between structures formed a *grand system*, where the structures, the relations, and the means for getting around in the system were all crystal clear.

Logic had, rather suddenly, been propelled from a primitive to a modern state. Certain hoary problems simply vanished under analysis using the new logic, and others were transformed from deep mysteries to manageable problems. Russell and Whitehead used their logic to do something truly spectacular—namely, to show how the whole of mathematics could be reduced to just logic and set theory. Although there were some residual problems with the reduction that eventually took on ominous proportions, the demonstration that one domain of knowledge and truth might be reduced to another, ostensibly more basic domain was profoundly important. It changed how people thought about mathematics, about logic, and about language. It began to seem possible that mathematical reasoning and scientific reasoning *in general* could be described in terms of sentences and the logical relations holding between them. And it gave new life to empiricism (logical empiricism) by holding out the vision that *the whole of science—and even the whole of one's cognitive system—might be systematized by logic in the way that the whole of mathematics was systematized.*

The early empiricists, such as Hume, conceived of the contents of the mind—the representations—as ideas, and to explain cognition they needed to postulate various mechanisms, one of which was the association of ideas. This conception was beset with many difficulties, not the least of which was that "ideas" were ill defined, and association appeared to have at best a limited role and was in any event not well understood. As mathematical logic flowered, some philosophers began to apply insights of logic to the philosophy of mind. They began to think that representations might usefully be modeled on sentences, and the relations between them could be characterized in terms of logic.

Oversimplifying, one could then think of the mind as essentially a kind of logic machine that operates on sentences. Further developments in logic, including remarkable developments in confirmation theory, inductive logic, decision theory, and theory of computability, seemed to underscore the fruitfulness of the approach (Hempel 1945; Boolos and Jeffrey 1974). Moreover, the well-defined nature of the logical concepts and the rigor of the system suggested that a system of logic might be implemented in a machine. Ideas from computability theory (Church 1936, Turing 1937a,b), together with ideas from linguistics (Chomsky 1965) and psychology (Neisser 1966), eventually converged to engender the now-familiar and virtually doctrinal computer metaphor for the mind's representations and computations (Fodor 1975). This gets somewhat ahead of the story, however, and to see the origins of the computer metaphor and why it achieved such wide acceptance, it is necessary to look briefly at the new, twentieth-century version of empiricism.

6.3 Logical Empiricism

A number of elements of the Zeitgeist make logical empiricism an understandable development. First, scientists and philosophers interested in science lost patience with continental and British idealism.[3] To many it seemed utterly sterile, confused, and full of metaphysical mushiness. A second factor was the fragmentation of the classical synthesis in physics of mechanics, electrodynamics, and thermodynamics—the synthesis that seemed to have left physics in an almost completed state. The special theory of relativity and the quantum theory were powerful new theories that replaced the old, and there was renewed excitement about the possibilities for physics. The revolution in biology wrought by Darwin made it seem possible to have a genuine science of biology, and work in physiology by Helmholtz, Pavlov, and others generated enormous excitement. It seemed possible that science might explain vision, learning, and so on, and that in general, it might explain how humans worked. Reflection about the nature of science and scientific progress, methodology and justification, and the nature of laws and explanations was an inevitable consequence. Third, the logic of Frege and Russell suggested the possibility of making a logical *system* out of science: one could show the logical relations between theories and evidence, between laws and instances, between foundations and superstructures.

Logical empiricism owed much of its original vitality to logical positivism, which was a movement established by scientists and philosophers of science in Vienna after the turn of the century. Logical positivism as a cohesive movement began in earnest with the regular convening of the Ernst Mach society in 1928, a group that eventually became known as the Vienna Circle. The society formally dissolved in 1938, and logical positivism as a movement came to an end. Logical empiricism, as a skein of theories about science and knowledge generally, was its heir, and its influence both within philosophy and in the sciences was enormous. By roughly 1970 logical empiricism had grown weak and toothless, and its newer progeny had taken over. Though its central principles were much changed, what endured was enthusiasm for science and scientifically justified theory, and the correlative suspicion of superstition, religion, and metaphysical maundering.

The Theses of Logical Empiricism
A seminal insight of the logical empiricists was that it might be possible to describe the systematicity in the set of scientific beliefs by means of modern formal logic. By widening the concept of "science" to include all knowledge, the logical empiricists developed a theory about the structure and system of *knowledge in general*. The deliverances of the senses were observations and yielded observation sentences; the sheerly sensory features of observations were referred to as "sense-data." It was argued that observation sentences provide the foundational certitude for science and knowledge generally, and

some (Russell (1924) and Carnap (1928) in his early work) believed that only sense-data sentences could be the real foundations. Others, such as Neurath (1932) and Carnap (1950) in his later work, took as the foundation physicalistic sentences that quantitatively described space-time points in the language of physics.

Sense-data sentences were thought to be incorrigible—that is, sentences about which the experiencer could not be mistaken, sentences where the experiencer's judgment could not be false. There were some disagreements about just how to construe sense-data sentences, but Carnap's early specification of them as *eigenpsychische*— minimal descriptions of private experience (e.g., "red here now," "pain here now")—was widely adopted. What are normally called observation sentences (e.g., "The bucket is full of water") were not considered to be as sound and sure as sense-data sentences, and on the contrary were thought to require justification by the allegedly firmer sense-data sentences. Logical truths and definitional truths were also incorrigible, not because of the nature of the Mind or Reality or some such, but because they express conventions of language. As Wittgenstein (1922) explained it, they are tautologies and empty of content. All the rest are factual statements ultimately dependent on sense-data sentences for their justification. If such factual statements bear the right logical relations to the foundations, they are justified, otherwise not.

A prevailing motivation of the logical empiricists was to characterize the fundamental difference between real science, which would provide truths about the nature of the universe, and unconstrained speculation, metaphysical posing, and assorted mush that was frequently dished out in fancy language as Philosophical Wisdom. Their targets were, among others, those idealists who talked about the unreality of space, time, and matter and who said a great deal about Spirit. The strategy was to describe a system of knowledge wherein every piece in the system had a proper justification. This broad aim of distinguishing science from its phony pretenders was shared by all the logical empiricists, whether they took as basic sense-data sentences or the physicalist sentences describing individual space-time points. Modern logic and analysis of language using modern logic provided the means for characterizing the justificatory credentials of genuine scientific propositions.

The account of *justification* was simple in its framework, and the details were to be filled in later. Unadorned, the idea was that a hypothesis was tested by deducing observation sentences from it, together with other initial conditions, and then determining experimentally whether the observations deduced were forthcoming under the specified conditions (Hempel 1965). Hypotheses that passed such tests were considered confirmed. This was called *hypothetico-deductive justification*, because it was *hypotheses* that were up for testing and because their observational consequences were *deduced* from the hypothesis together with statements describing the conditions of the test. Thus, the new logic was used in characterizing the relations between hypotheses and observation sentences.

The theory of *explanation* fit hand in glove with the theory of justification, and it too exploited the new logic. The general idea was that a phenomenon is explained when its occurrence is understood as part of a general pattern of such events in such circumstances. That is, a phenomenon is said to be explained when its occurrence can be *deduced* from a generalization describing the regular occurrence of events of that type in the specified conditions. To take a starkly simple example as the core case, we explain why a copper bar has expanded in the following way:

(1) Whenever copper is heated, it expands. (Nomological generalization or law)
(2) This bar is copper. (Initial condition)
(3) This bar was heated. (Initial condition)
(4) This bar expanded. (Explanandum)

The first sentence specifies a regularity found in nature; (2) and (3) specify the particular conditions that obtained. Notice that (4) logically follows from the earlier three, and given the set (1)–(3), the situation described in (4) is precisely what would be expected. Thus is the expansion of the copper bar explained. Less simple examples will involve a set of generalizations, and the list of initial conditions may be far longer. When we want to explain why in general copper expands when heated, then that statement becomes the explanandum and is deduced from a set of other nomologicals (laws) about metals, atomic structures, and heat.

However much the list of laws and initial conditions is embellished, however sophisticated the laws, and however delicate the initial conditions, the underlying form of explanation remains invariant. Naturally, it was recognized, working scientists will not always trouble themselves to set out the entire explanatory structure in their accounts and "obvious" clauses may be omitted, but in principle any explanation should fit into the general mold. To explain why the patient Smith is hyperreflexive, we may say, "His spinal cord was transected three months ago." But that suffices as an explanation only in virtue of the shared background knowledge that whenever the spinal cord is transected and some two months have passed, the spinal reflexes are hyperbolic. Otherwise, it would be no explanation at all. To go on to explain why the spinal reflexes are regularly enhanced in spinally transected organisms, we need to invoke a deeper network of generalizations about spinal reflexes and descending control, where "Whenever the spinal cord is transected, the spinal reflexes are hyperbolic" becomes the explanandum, itself deducible from the set of established generalizations. At some point in the explanatory chain the desired explanation will not be available, as we bump up against the walls of our ignorance. (See E. Nagel 1961, Hempel 1965.)

Since the generalizations describing lawful or law-like regularities are called *nomological* generalizations, and since the logical condition on getting an explanation of a phenomenon is that the sentence describing it be logically *deducible* from the nomological plus initial conditions, this was called the *deductive-nomological theory of explanation*. A vast improvement over relying on untrustworthy intuitions or clear and distinct ideas about when a phenomenon had been explained, the theory was an elegant achievement.

Fitting into the rest of the conception was a theory of meaning, and it was an essential feature of the wider program of distinguishing genuine science from pseudoscience. The view was that sense-data sentences have their meaning primitively, inasmuch as their meaning is tied to the raw sense-data themselves, whereas all other sentences have their meaning derivatively. Sentences that do not acquire their meaning in this way are strictly speaking meaningless, even though they may appear to have meaning. According to the *verification theory of meaning* (Carnap 1932; Schlick 1936), the meaning of a sentence is the method of its verification. Roughly, this means that for sense-data sentences the meaning is the sense-datum; for any other sentence the meaning is determined by the kinds of empirical consequences one could observe if it were true—that is, the kinds of effects one could observe if it were true. Put another way, according to this theory the meaning of a sentence is a function of its *empirical* content, either directly or derivatively.

Ultimately, this theory required that the meaning of theoretical expressions in physics and elsewhere (e.g., "electron," "force field") had somehow or other to be attached to sense-data, and even in the early days exactly how this could be accomplished was admitted to be a problem. The logical empiricists hoped it could be solved by tying the meaning of such terms to observable effects that could be produced in specified conditions. That is, given certain operations with research devices (Wilson cloud chambers, cyclotrons, etc.), certain observables (such as white tracks in a Wilson cloud chamber) will be forthcoming. The meaning of the expression is then equated with the operations that produce certain relevant observations. The hue and ry still heard in the halls of psychology and physiology departments concerning "operational definitions" has its origins in this attempt to reduce the meaning of theoretical expressions to bedrock observation sentences. To "operationalize" a term is to specify *as its meaning* the empirical conditions under which the phenomenon it describes will exhibit observable effects.

The theory of meaning also had as a corollary a criterion of meaningfulness that could sort terms and sentences into two distinct lots. Meaningful sentences were those that could, in one way or another, be verified by sensory evidence. Sentences that could not possibly be verified were considered meaningless on this criterion, even though they might appear to the unwary to have meaning. The logical empiricists' point was that if a sentence had no empirical consequences whatever, if its being true or false could make no possible difference to any experience one might have in the world, then the sentence was without content, though by virtue of its grammatical structure it might masquerade as meaningful. Sentences drawn from the idealists' literature were frequently held up as examples of what got tossed into the meaningless bin: "Nothing noths," "The Absolute is Absolute Being," etc. Their impatience here was fair enough, but they had a problem of their own: if they could not reduce the meaning of respectable *theoretical* expressions to basic observations, these expressions also ran the risk of being cast out as meaningless. It would be a classic case of throwing the baby out with the bathwater. Such a result would constitute a defeat for the theory of meaning. As we shall see in section 6.4, the logical empiricists did suffer a great defeat on this very issue.

Reduction was the focus of concentrated effort, because logical empiricists typically had the view that science should constitute a unified, coherent body of knowledge. Ultimately, they argued, less basic sciences such as chemistry should reduce to more basic sciences such as physics, and in the fullness of time an integrated account, including sciences of brain and behavior, ought to emerge. Within the framework of the logical empiricist program, philosophers of science tried to figure out a precise theory of what reduction is and what conditions must be satisfied to effect a reduction. The account enabled philosophers to characterize the relations between theories such as classical thermodynamics and statistical mechanics, and the relations between general disciplines such as chemistry and the more basic discipline of physics.

This account also prepared the ground for discussions concerning the conditions of and prospects for the unity of science (Oppenheim and Putnam 1958). The guiding conception (Nagel 1961) was that reduction is primarily a relation between theories and only derivatively a relation between phenomena. This insight was exceedingly important, because it counterbalanced the tendency to imagine reduction as a baffling *metaphysical* relation between things or properties, and, as we shall see, it made it possible to characterize reduction using the resources of mathematical logic.

Theories embody what is believed about a range of phenomena, and when reduction is achieved, two theories are discovered to be related in a special way. More specifically, the account claimed that when theories are reduced, the laws of the reduced theory are *logically deducible* from the more basic laws of the reducing theory plus special connecting statements called *bridge principles*. These principles would state, for example, that certain entities and properties described in the reduced theory are in fact identical to entities and properties in the reducing theory.

The favored example was the reduction of the laws of thermodynamics to the laws of statistical mechanics. In this case the bridge laws specify that in a gas the property of having a certain temperature is identical to the property of having a certain mean molecular kinetic energy. Given some simplifying assumptions, the Boyle-Charles law in classical thermodynamics is then deducible from the laws of statistical mechanics. If gaseous pressure is construed as the reactive effect of rebounding molecules, then '$P = \mu RT/V$' falls out swiftly. The reduction of the classical gas laws was touted as the paradigm of how reductions in science proceed, and the expectation was that all sciences would eventually be reduced to physics in a grand unity with bridge principles linking one tier to the next via identity statements.

In sum, logical empiricism presented a grand, coherent, and highly rigorous picture of science and, at the same time, of human knowledge. As we have seen, it included an account of the nature of explanation, of meaning, of justification, of reduction, of the foundations of knowledge and of how structures are built on the foundations, and finally, of how science is to be distinguished from pseudoscience. The accounts fitted together in such an impressive fashion as to give credence to the wider conception of the eventual unity of all science, and it was essentially logic that provided the unifying principle (Hooker 1975). Mathematical logic provided the wherewithal for much of the rigor, for the integration of the accounts, and for the definitiveness of crucial concepts. Clean and bold, logical empiricism had tremendous appeal.

6.4   *What Happened to Logical Empiricism?*

Any theory this elegant and this systematic deserved to be right. It was as though God had said, "Let there be order," and there was logical empiricism. But the order turned out to be superficial and contrived, and for all its singular virtues logical empiricism rather rapidly evolved into something very different. Since many contemporary objections to the idea of a science of the mind and to reductionism are based on a conception of science *as described by the logical empiricists*, it is important to know that the central conceptions of logical empiricism ceded their niche to a new breed of philosophy. Nevertheless, what this philosophy did inherit from logical empiricism was its respect for science and its conviction that theories must be testable against empirical evidence.

Virtually everything in logical empiricism was transformed: the theory of meaning, the criterion of meaningfulness, the theory of justification, the distinction between theory and observation, the claims of foundations, the theory of reduction, and even to some degree the theory of explanation. It was in the closer study of science itself, of its dynamics, methodology, and history, and also in the attempts to supply the details missing from the grand scheme, that the mistakes of logical empiricism began to show themselves. The story of how this came about is fascinating, but I shall limit discussion here to the barest outlines. (See Suppe 1977 and the papers in Morick 1972.)

Karl Popper is an unorthodox logical empiricist who resisted the idea that the body of scientific knowledge accumulates by the confirmation or verification of hypotheses. In a startlingly different picture of the dynamics of science (1935, 1963), he argued that hypotheses are worthy of acceptance only if they *resist falsification.* His point was devastating and simple: it is easy to find confirming instances of hypotheses—too easy for this to be the right methodology. Consider some simple hypothesis such as "All plants reproduce sexually." If all I need are confirmatory instances, I can start in the garden and discover that all 654 daisies reproduce sexually, all 953 violets reproduce sexually, and so on. In short order I shall have an impressive accumulation of positive instances. No botanist would be impressed, however, since I have not tried to find a disconfirming instance—I have not looked at cases that might be counterexamples. Before adopting a hypothesis, I should examine many different species of flowering plant, I should examine grasses and ferns, and in general I should try as hard as possible to falsify my hypothesis.

Consider another hypothesis, namely that Broca's area controls speech production. To establish the hypothesis, it is not enough to find a positive correlation between lesions in Broca's area and speech loss; one must find out whether there are patients with lesions in Broca's area and no speech loss, and whether there is speech loss with lesions elsewhere. Failure to falsify will then be significant, unlike the collection of verifying cases. Popper's claim was that if the scientist accepts hypotheses by finding confirming instances, he will end up believing a great many false hypotheses and following a great many dead ends. On the other hand, if he has a hypothesis that has withstood tough attempts at falsification, then he can accept that hypothesis—not as true, not as confirmed, but as the best hypothesis available so far. Because he had a wholly different picture of justification, Popper came to quite different views about the dynamics and structure of science, and of knowledge generally.

Furthermore, Popper disagreed with the assumption that what scientists should try to formulate are explanatory hypotheses with high probability. On the contrary, he said, hypotheses are interesting only if they are bold—that is, if they are improbable and thus likely to be falsified. For then, to withstand falsification by rigorous testing is a triumph, and such a hypothesis is significant. Safe (that is, probable) hypotheses are a dime a dozen, and the safest are logical truths. If what science is seeking is primarily a body of certain truths, it should stick to spinning out logical theorems. The trouble with such safety, however, is that it doesn't get us anywhere. Einstein's hypothesis that the geometry of space would be "warped" by large masses was, given the theory of the time, highly improbable. If Einstein was right, then during the solar eclipse a star would be seen in one position; if he was wrong, it would be seen in some other position. When the hypothesis withstood the falsifying test, this was profoundly significant.

Our understanding of the dynamics of the scientific enterprise was deepened dramatically by W. V. O. Quine (1953, 1960), who argued that interpreting the results of experimental procedures is a far more complex affair than it seems, and that contrary to the dream of logical empiricism the falsification of a hypothesis is not a straightforward affair, with logic our only counsel. Quine was inspired by the much earlier work of Pierre Duhem (1861–1916), who argued that hypotheses cannot be tested in isolation from the whole theoretical network in which they figure and hence that the idea of "crucial experiments" was far more messy than generally assumed. Quine was impressed by the force of Duhem's arguments and saw that they had radical implications for the logical empiricist theories of explanation, confirmation, and reduction. Duhem perceived that in practice, interpreting experimental results involves more than application of simple logical principles:

> Indeed, the demonstrative value of experimental method is far from being so rigorous or absolute: the conditions under which it functions are much more complicated than is supposed in what we have just said; the evaluation of results is much more delicate and subject to caution. (1914; tr. Philip Weiner 1953:185)

When we are in the business of testing a hypothesis or using a theory to deduce observable consequences, we tend to assume that failure of the predicted event implies that the hypothesis is false. Thus the textbook account of the structure of a crucial experiment: If hypothesis H and auxiliary assumptions A are true, then O will happen. When in the circumstance O fails to happen, H is disconfirmed.

Duhem saw that the failure of O to happen could quite as well be explained, not by H's falsity, but by the falsity of an auxiliary assumption. The experiment itself cannot tell us that it is H rather than one or more of the auxiliary assumptions in A that is false. All that logic can tell us is that somewhere in our assumptions there lurks a falsity; nothing in deductive logic tells us which assumption it is rational to believe is false. Moreover, in even the simplest experiments there is a wider network of laws and theory that is assumed to hold true; and, given the failure of O, it might be some part of the background network that is to blame. As Duhem put it, we "can never subject an isolated hypothesis to experimental test, but only a whole group of hypotheses . . ." (tr. Philip Weiner 1953:187). When the predicted event fails to occur, it is evident that *something* in the theoretical network must be changed, but nothing in the experiment tells us *what* should be changed.

Consider the following illustrations. Using Newton's laws and auxiliary assumptions concerning the orbits, velocities, and masses of the planets and the mass of the sun, astronomers predicted the orbit of the newly discovered planet Uranus. Schematically, they said, "If N and A_1 . . . A_n, then O." One of their auxiliary assumptions was simply that there were no other planetary bodies in the vicinity. In their observations the orbit of Uranus failed to correspond to O. Thus, O was false. The astronomers might then have concluded that Newton's laws were false, but in fact they sought to find the error instead in the auxiliary assumptions. Specifically, they modified the assumption that there were no other bodies. Instead, on the basis of what they did observe about the orbit of Uranus, they predicted there must be another planetary body close enough to Uranus to affect its orbit. Shortly thereafter, the planet Neptune was discovered through the telescope in just the place the astronomers predicted it would be found. In this case, then, one of the auxiliary assumptions in the original experiment was taken to be false.

But compare the next example. This time astronomers made a prediction about the orbit of Mercury (specifically, about the amount of its precession) based on Newton's laws and auxiliary assumptions concerning the size of the sun, and the size, velocities, and orbits of other planets. Schematically, they said, "If N and $A_1 \ldots A_n$ are true, then P," where P specified the orbit of Mercury and where one of the auxiliary assumptions again was that there were no other significant bodies in the vicinity. Again, the prediction was false, and P was not observed, but what was observed was instead a different orbit, P'.

Having succeeded so spectacularly on the earlier occasion by modifying an auxiliary assumption, astronomers again predicted an additional planetary body, which in anticipation they called Vulcan. But though they searched the heavens tirelessly, Vulcan was never found, and consequently some astronomers began to toy with the unthinkable possibility that not the auxiliary assumptions but Newton's laws were at fault. Nevertheless, they more or less shelved that dreaded possibility and vainly tried ever new ways of faulting the auxiliary assumptions, until the introduction of Einstein's general theory of relativity changed the picture. The new theory demanded new calculations, and it was found that the special theory of relativity plus the old auxiliary assumptions *did* have the observed orbit P' as a consequence. In the spirit of hypothetico-deduction, this was seen as an important test passed by the general theory of relativity. The Duhemian point here is that in neither case did the failure of the prediction tell us what was amiss, but only that somewhere in the network there was a flaw.

On the Quine-Duhem thesis, there is no such thing as a once-and-for-all crucial experiment in which a hypothesis is conclusively demonstrated to be false. A test for a hypothesis is crucial not absolutely, but *relative to background assumptions*. What we take to be the "bare facts" against which we test a hypothesis are statements held to be factual relative to background assumptions, and if those assumptions are called into question, their correlative "facts" are too. From the point of view of geocentrism, it is a "fact" that the earth does not move—an "observable fact." But if Copernicus was right, the facts themselves had to be reconceived.

Quine's point was this: there is no mechanical method or logic for determining exactly what to change in one's theory, and hence any hypothesis can in principle always be protected and the falsity "shifted" to other statements elsewhere in the theoretical network by making suitable and sometimes large-scale adjustments in the background theoretical network. *Any* sentence can be safeguarded from falsity and revision, so long as we are prepared to make appropriate adjustments to other parts of the theoretical network. Conversely, no sentence has special epistemic properties that protect it from revision (Quine 1960). Accordingly, it is possible for rational scientists such as Golgi and Ramón y Cajal to continue to disagree even after a great deal of data is accumulated. They differed not only on whether or not neurons formed a continuous net but also on the importance of the background assumption concerning a nutrient supply for the neurons. For Golgi that was of central importance, and hence he tended not to revise his background hypothesis that dendrites made contact with structures other than blood vessels. Ramón y Cajal, on the other hand, seemed ready to let the explanation of nutrient supply come later, so he was quite willing to interpret dendritic connections as neuronal connections.

Predictive failures in experimental situations are failures looking for a culprit. On the Quine-Duhem thesis, experiments test the theoretical network as a whole, and where the revisions should occur in the event of a predictive failure is not determined by formal logic alone.

But then come the difficult questions. How *should* we make rational revisions in our theoretical networks? How do we know where to assign blame? Evidently, in scientific practice a variety of considerations enter: if a hypothesis already explains a good deal and there is no other theory with which to replace it, scientists are reluctant to see it as the part to revise. If revising one deep feature in the theoretical network entails massive revision elsewhere, scientists are more likely to revise something else. Considerations of simplicity, unity of theory, success of existing theory, availability of a replacing theory, and so forth, make important contributions to a scientist's decision concerning what to alter given the predictive failure.

These are observations—and rather vague observations at that—about practice, but the normative questions about what *should* be scientific practice cannot be kept at bay. What are the correct principles for making decisions about data, and will following them lead to true theories? When should we be revolutionary in coping with data, and when conservative? If we are consistently revolutionary, we will never accumulate an "established" body of scientific knowledge; yet if we are consistently conservative, we will miss the munificence of scientific revolutions of the kind wrought by Galileo, Darwin, and Einstein. Sometimes it may even be reasonable to revise an observation judgment itself, or to reinterpret what was seen in the light of revision to theory elsewhere in the network. Thus, one may conclude that it cannot have been a blood vessel that one saw making contact with the dendrites, or that what one thought was a feature of the neuron was really an artifact of the staining procedure, and so on. As Quine remarks, in the extreme, the tail may come to wag the dog. Moreover, as any experimenter knows well, this is sometimes reasonable, in some sense of reasonable, since in the actual business of running experiments, in the hurly-burly of the laboratory, observation judgments are never quite as secure and unimpeachable as they are in philosophers' theories of observation.

In sum, given the Quine-Duhem thesis, the difficulty then confronting philosophers of science was how to characterize methodology in science—how to distinguish justified from unjustified revisions, how to provide principles for rational conduct in scientific inquiry. These were problems that clearly could not be solved within the framework of logical empiricism. One view is that the answers are to be found not by a priori pondering or by linguistic analysis but by empirical investigation wherever relevant. If, by means of psychology, history of science, and neuroscience, we can determine how the brain conducts its epistemic/cognitive business, then we can proceed to get a theory concerning how to maximize efficiency in that business and hence how to maximize rationality in scientific inquiry. That is, I think, the heart of Quine's view (1969). It is thoroughly naturalistic, and it is a view I find irresistible. (For further discussion, see chapters 9 and 10.)

Another important consequence of the Quine-Duhem thesis is this: in the face of a recalcitrant phenomenon—an event unexpected given our beliefs—the set of sentences we may consider revising includes not only what is conventionally called science but also our commonsense beliefs. Our knowledge is a richly interconnected whole, and it resists a principled epistemic division between scientific beliefs and nonscientific beliefs. As Einstein put it, "The whole of science is nothing more than a refinement of everyday thinking" (1949:55).

In a similar vein Quine has remarked that science is self-conscious common sense. Certainly common sense does get revised in the course of the accumulation of knowledge; we no longer believe that the Earth is flat, or that design in organisms betokens an Intelligent Designer, or that space is a vessel, or that heat is a fluid passing from hot objects to cold. What we call commonsense systems of beliefs about external macro objects, about colors, about heat, about motion, and so on, are best seen as just some hypotheses among others that the brain uses to theorize about the meager input it gets from its sensory periphery. Sometimes the theories humans collectively devise replace existing theories, presumably because they explain and predict in superior fashion. Primitive theories give way to sophisticated theories, and as the latter become the common coin of everyday life, they may then acquire the status of common sense. A remarkable thing about the human brain is that it can use those primitive theories to bootstrap its way to ever more comprehensive and powerful theories—to find the reality behind the appearances. (For a fuller discussion of this point, see chapters 7, 9, and 10.)

A consequence of Quine's view is that even our epistemological convictions about what it is to acquire knowledge and about the nature of explanation, justification, and confirmation—about the nature of the scientific enterprise itself—are subject to revision and to correction. As we come to understand how the brain works, we will come to learn about what it is for a brain to "theorize," to be "rational," and to "understand." We will discover general principles of brain operation that may change, and change radically, our existing epistemological conceptions.

It is in this sense that there is no *first* philosophy. There is no corpus of philosophical doctrine concerning science and epistemology such that we can be sure it is the Truth to which all science must conform. There is, as Quine remarks, no Archimedean point outside all science from which we can pronounce upon the acceptability of scientific theories. In abandoning the view that there is a First and Inviolable Philosophy, Quine (1960:3) urges us to adopt a metaphor coined by Neurath: "Science is like a boat, which we rebuild plank by plank while staying afloat in it. The philosopher and the scientist are in the same boat."

What Happened to the Verification Theory of Meaning?
According to the verification theory of meaning, the meaning of a nonobservation term was given by the set of empirical consequences of sentences containing the term. From the outset, there were problems with this view. Suppose that a certain empirical consequence depends on technology conceived but not yet invented. Is that part of the meaning? Suppose that a certain empirical consequence depends on physics not yet established—or not yet conceived. Or suppose that some boring little prediction is falsified. Does that change the meaning of the term? Suppose that sentences have empirical consequences that only occur to us tomorrow. Are they part of the meaning? And so forth. Moreover, it emerged that the meaning of the most respectable of theoretical terms was defined implicitly by the theory the terms figured in, not by the empirical consequences of the theory. Terms such as "force field," "energy," and "electromagnetic radiation" were prime examples where meaning was a function of the

embedding theory and where operational definitions were laughable. Although expressions such as "intelligence," "rationality," and "learning" do not yet have an embedding theory as rich and as rigorous as that enjoyed by the terms in physics, nevertheless it can be seen that to accept operational definitions as giving their meaning would be a mistake. As neurobiological and psychological theories that embed these expressions develop, their meaning will correspondingly become more precise. (See chapter 7.)

The damage inflicted to the verification theory of meaning by these criticisms was certainly severe, but the jugular was really opened by application of the Quine-Duhem thesis. Using that thesis, Quine made the point that empirical consequences are consequences of the whole theoretical network, never of individual sentences. In order to determine the empirical consequences of a hypothesis, we must specify the initial conditions—and the background theory that legitimates our use of them, as well as the wider background theory that provides the vocabulary in which the hypothesis is framed. Also to be factored in is the background theory that justifies the use of a particular measuring instrument, such as a voltmeter, or the use of an observing instrument, such as an electron microscope. If a single empirical hypothesis did have its *own* set of empirical consequences, then in the event of falsified prediction we would indeed know that it, rather than some other sentence, was false. But, as we saw earlier, whatever the result of the experiment, deductive logic itself does not decide for us which sentences to let go as false and which to retain as true. To paraphrase Quine, empirical statements do not have empirical consequences they can call their own. Whole theories have empirical consequences, and it is whole theories that are the basic units of meaning—not terms, not sentences, and not subparts of the network. To be acceptable as an account of nature, a theoretical network must, *as a whole,* touch an observational base, but not every acceptable sentence or term in the network must do so.

The meaning of theoretical terms is a function of the network of laws and theories in which they figure; thus, modification or correction of the laws will entail changes in the meaning of the terms involved. Moreover, Quine argued, even sentences we hitherto construed as definitions might be revised as we try to cope with falsified predictions and new empirical data. (For examples, see Paul M. Churchland 1979.) The empiricist doctrine of a fixed and unbridgeable rift between two kinds of truth (sentences true in virtue of their meaning and sentences true in virtue of the facts) and between two kinds of knowledge (knowledge of meaning and knowledge of facts) was consequently construed as empiricist dogma, and dogma we would do best to divest ourselves of (Quine 1953). Thus germinated the *network theory* of meaning. (See also chapters 8 and 9.)

What Happened to the Empirical Foundations?
From the standpoint of logical empiricism the nature and epistemological role of observation sentences were unproblematic. Observation sentences were known through experience, and they were the foundational "Given" of knowledge structures. To be known through observation seemed pretty straightforward, and to be justified solely on the basis of that observation seemed equally straightforward.

Theoretical sentences, on the other hand, were thought to be decidedly problematic, with respect both to meaning and to justification. However, the Quine-Duhem thesis raised the possibility that sometimes, in order to maximize coherence and explanatory power, revisions of sentences at the observation level may be necessary. Sometimes, perhaps, the foundational basis should be reconfigured if the advance in theory is sufficient to require it. Yet if the foundational sentences can be revised, they cannot serve as the enduring bedrock of science, on which theoretical superstructure is supposedly built.

Seeing the implications of the Quine-Duhem thesis, a number of philosophers began to examine what had seemed unproblematic, namely, observation sentences. Particularly influential was the work of Paul Feyerabend (1963a), N. R. Hanson (1967), and Mary Hesse (1970). Hesse pointed out that for knowledge structures to have a foundation of observation sentences that stand firm and inviolable while the theoretical sentences above them come and go, observation sentences must be independent of theoretical sentences. She therefore examined whether they were indeed independent, and hence whether there could be an independent observation language.

To begin with, it turned out that logical empiricism had no very clear definition of just what an observation sentence is. Sometimes it was defined as a sentence known through observation, but such a definition is blatantly circular. "Known directly through experience" is just as bad. "An observation predicate is one directly applicable to the empirical world" is fine except that it will not pick out predicates whose application is free from theory.

The point is, many theoretical predicates can be directly—noninferentially—applied to the world once the speaker's knowledge of the embedding theory is second nature to him. An experienced geologist can see that the term "glaciation" is applicable to a certain geological feature; an experienced neurologist can see, without going through intervening inferential steps, that a patient has Parkinson's disease; a seasoned farmer can see fire blight on pear trees; an astronomer can see red shifts; a physicist can see alpha particles in a bubble chamber; and so forth.

The other side of the coin is this: even if observation predicates are initially learned by direct association with properties in the world, their meaning is not independent of laws regarding such properties. This, argued Hesse, is a straightforward consequence of two things:

> (1) The direct association of predicates with types of empirical situations inevitably leaves a good deal of slack in what counts as an appropriate instance of the relevant type of situation. Situations are always complex and various; similarity is not a transitive relation; and the learning paradigms are often ill chosen.
>
> (2) The application of any predicate must therefore also be conditioned by some rough generalizations or laws, which relate the real occurrence of that feature to the occurrence of other features.

Suppose that a child hears the word "dog" in the vicinity of Rover and associates the word with something or other in that situation— possibly with all and only the dog himself, possibly with the-dog-in-this-room or with doggy-at-dinner, or with doggishness, or with the dog's tail or the dog's bark, or even with furry things. The word "dog" eventually comes to be more narrowly defined to fit standard usage not simply in virtue of the initial learning but in virtue of the additional information the child acquires about dogs through hearing the word in other contexts. Reclassification may take place for the child as a result of imparted generalizations about dogs. To take a crude example, if he hears "Dogs like table scraps," he will abandon a classification that applied "dog" to the wagging furry part of the animal.

Adults experience analogous events. A beginning neuroscientist's first observation through a microscope may produce puzzlement—it may be difficult to know what is artifact and what is part of the cell. ("*That's* endoplasmic reticulum??") Theory informs observation, and after a short while it becomes hard not to see, say, the end bulb. Notice that if I see something as an end bulb, then I imply that a whole range of additional properties will obtain: that it is at the end of an axon, that if tested it would be found to contain synaptic vesicles, that if we looked at it under an electron microscope we would see synapses, and so on. To apply the descriptive term "end bulb" to what is seen in the microscope is not a sheer, naked observation: it implies an indefinite number of generalizations applicable to the object. This cascade of indefinitely many implications is a general feature of the observational application of any descriptive term, whether it is "coyote," "red," or "synaptic vesicle."

The point is that because at some stage in language learning there must be learning by ostension (where the word is uttered and the object pointed to) and because the ostension can never rule out all interpretations but one, there is always room for reinterpretation and reclassification. Since sometimes that reclassification will result from pressure from generalizations, albeit folksy generalizations, the predicate cannot be considered immune from theory and hence is not independent of theory.

The second consideration also entails that reclassification can take place on the basis of newly acquired generalizations. Whales may initially be classed as fish, but new knowledge bids us reclassify them as mammals. Or the child learns about burning and knows that burning things are hot; and, among many other assorted things, he learns about rusting and touches rusty nails without getting burned. One day the nature of oxidation is explained, and he comes to classify burning and rusting together, even though fire is hot and rust is cold.

"Pain" may be first applied to a bashed finger and later extended to wider conditions: feet on a wintry day, the stomach after too many green apples, the skin after a burn, excessively loud sounds, an electric shock, headaches, loss of something loved. Are the sensations evoked on the different occasions exactly alike? Evidently not. (See also Churchland and Churchland 1981.) Reclassification at the behest of theory entails that the meaning of the terms cannot be independent of theory. And as Hesse emphasizes, since language learning involves application of a term in situations that are not identical to the situation in which it was learned, there are bound to be reclassifications. That is, observation terms are bound to be revised.

Despite agreement that the meaning of observation predicates is not independent of the laws in which those predicates figure, it may nevertheless seem that there is a residual core that is attached to the subjective experience or *quale*. "Warm," it may be argued, does have *some* of its meaning fixed by generalizations one believes, but some of its meaning is the subjective experience of warmth itself. All the rest could be swept away as false, and I would still know what "warm" means—namely, *that feeling*.

Seductive though the idea is, Paul M. Churchland (1979) has argued that it is less plausible than it seems. His view is that the spontaneous application of observation terms may exploit physiological and psychological stabilities—indeed, it is this stability that probably explains the attractiveness of the qualia doctrine. (See also chapter 8.)

But the network of laws is the primary and basic determiner of meaning. Here is his test case: Suppose a species of hominid evolved with eyes sensitive only to wavelengths in the infrared range. Hence, they detect temperature by means of the visual system. Consequently, they see warm things as whitish-grey, hot things as white, cool things as gray, cold things as black, and so on. In observations, where we use "hot" they use "crin." For example, they say that a boiling kettle is crin and an ice cube is not at all crin. Now, does "crin" mean "hot," or does it mean "white"?

If we translate on the assumption that "crin" means "hot," it turns out that the hominids espouse the same scientific laws concerning heat and temperature as we do, and they make most of the same perceptual discriminations we do. That is, ice cubes are cold and boiling kettles are hot. Suppose that for some reason we need to cooperate with them and hence that we need a good and efficient translation of their language. Then we will undoubtedly translate their "crin" as our "hot" and not as our "white." Why? Because we need the translation to communicate, and what we care about most is exchange of information—about, for example, whether something has the property that boils water, not whether someone's qualia are just like mine when he detects the property that boils water.

We might conceivably prefer the qualia-based translation, but if we do, then the beliefs we must then ascribe to the hominids, instead of being isomorphic with our beliefs, are very odd. On such a translation, they think that ice cubes are black, that white objects sizzle and turn gray when splashed with river water (we of course think that hot objects sizzle and turn cool), that gray objects turn white in the heat of the sun, and that white objects cause a painful burn; indeed, they turn out to believe all manner of rather bizarre things. When they shout the warning "It is crin, it is crin!" we take them to mean "It is white, it is white!"—and since we see no white objects of a threatening nature about, we are likely to get burned. To maximize translational efficiency, we will ignore as irrelevant the experiential differences between them and us. And so will they, since their translation of *our* beliefs, if guided by considerations of qualia, will ascribe systematically bizarre beliefs to us. When push comes to shove, laws are more important than qualia in determining meaning.

Empirical foundations of science and knowledge generally are not absolute and forever fixed; rather, they are foundations only relative to a particular encompassing network. What counts as the observable base will evolve and change as theory evolves and changes. Any observation sentence may, under pressure from evolving theory, be seen as false. When philosophers came to this realization, the traditional empiricist conception of the structure of knowledge had finally been recognized as a misconception.

As we have seen, logical empiricism underwent a truly substantial evolution, not at the hands of philosophers from an antiscientific school, but rather as a result of research by philosophers deeply interested in and committed to the scientific enterprise. The theories of confirmation, of justification, of meaning, of epistemological foundations, of the structure of science itself were all undermined, and logical empiricism, though still admired for its clarity and rigor, is now generally assumed to have collapsed. (The fate of the theory of reduction and the theory of explanation deserve their own space and will be considered separately in chapter 7.)

One legacy of the collapse is that some philosophers were moved to question the role of logic in unifying all aspects of the logical empiricists' picture. Perhaps, it has been conjectured, the beauty and systematicity of modern mathematical logic has led us astray, and the fundamental mistake is to suppose that we can understand knowledge on the model of sets of sentences standing in logical relations to one another, and mental processes on the model of logical transformations. Perhaps, after all, cognition cannot be understood as a fundamentally propositional-logical affair. But to know what sort of affair it is, perhaps we shall have to understand the brain itself (chapter 10). Perhaps philosophers and neuroscientists really are in the same boat.

6.5 Implications for a Theory of the Mind

That there is an absolute division between matters of meaning and matters of fact was a tenet of all variations on the empiricist theme, and its demise pulled the rug out from under those philosophers who practiced on the assumption that the solution to philosophical problems consisted in analyzing meanings. The facts, on this view, would have to follow where conceptual clarification first led. For the philosophy of mind in particular, the favored method was to "analyze" the "common" concepts used in talking about the mental in order to discover answers—either answers about the true nature of the mental and how it differs from the physical, or answers showing that the original problem was after all just a semantic misunderstanding. This was the dominant approach to questions in the philosophy of mind from about the 1940s to about the 1970s, though some never found it plausible (for example, J. J. C. Smart and Paul Feyerabend) and others even now remain faithful to the conceptual analysis style (for example, Anthony Kenny and Colin McGinn).

The method of analysis, to the extent that I understand it, proceeds by asking what is and is not conceivable or imaginable, by assaying whether something comports with the existing meaning of the words in question, and by amassing fine details on how "ordinary people" use the words or on "our concept" of the matter at hand. Empirical theories as well as philosophical theories about mental states and processes are sometimes criticized on the basis of whether or not they mesh with existing "ordinary usage"—as analyzed by the philosopher. For example, a standard criticism of the idea that mental states (e.g., pains, beliefs, perceptions) are in fact identical with brain states is the argument that brain states presumably occur at a certain time and a certain place in the brain, but we do not speak of mental states (e.g., a desire for tomato soup) as being at a specific spatial position, let alone at several inches behind the eyes.

Or it is pointed out that we speak of a pain as searing, and of a belief as true, but it is alleged that "It makes no sense to say that a brain state is searing, or true." It is urged that it is meaningless to say that the mental states are brain states because our concept of mental states is radically different from our concept of brain states. And so on. This style of argument, long typified by philosophy at Oxford, is on the wane even there, but it is still advanced quite seriously, and a forthright specimen of the genre can be found in a recent book on reduction and the mind by McGinn (1982). For example, he says,

> It is rather that mental concepts are intuitively such that no physical concepts *could* characterize the essential nature of the mental property denoted. In other words, it seems that mental concepts *already* contain the essence of mental phenomena and that physical concepts are necessarily unsuited to this role; . . . . (p. 19)

The method is suspect. First, whether a hypothesis makes sense to someone will not be independent of his background beliefs and assumptions. So what makes no sense to a dualist may make perfectly good sense to a physicalist. Nor are usage and intuition in general anywhere near as uniform and doctrinaire as the method must assume. Feyerabend was perhaps the most severe critic of the method, and bypassing the fashionable disputes, he went straight to the heart of its assumptions:

> The more people differ in their fundamental ideas, the more difficult will it be to uncover such regularities. Hence analysis of usage will work best in a closed society that is firmly held together by a powerful myth as was the philosophy in the Oxford of about 10 years ago. (1963a:192 (Morick))

Second, whether something is conceivable or imaginable is not independent of one's belief network and of one's capacity to imagine. It was easy for Galileo to conceive of the Earth as one planet among others moving about the Sun, but his detractors found it outrageous and inconceivable. Semmelweis could well imagine that tiny organisms invisible to the naked eye caused disease, but others found it laughable and inconceivable. Similarly, whether it is or is not part of the concept of mental states that no physical state *could* characterize the essential nature of the mental property denoted (McGinn, above) will depend on whether it is believed to be possible that mental states are brain states. For those who have a framework within which it *is* possible, *their* concepts of mental states and mental properties, and their intuitions, will run quite the opposite of McGinn's. Which means that the intuitions one has about certain concepts cannot decide anything about the actual empirical nature of what those concepts are believed to apply to. Feyerabend described the inadequacy of appealing to the common idiom as a source of truth in the following way:

> . . . in order to discuss the weaknesses of an all-pervasive system of thought such as is expressed by the "common idiom", it is not sufficient to compare it with "the facts". Many such facts are formulated in terms of the idiom and therefore already prejudiced in its favor. Also there are many facts which are inaccessible, *for empirical reasons,* to a person speaking a certain idiom, and which become accessible only if a different idiom is introduced. (1963b:145 (Borst))

A common philosophical tactic for criticizing neurobiological hypotheses concerning the identification of mental processes with brain processes used to be to brand these hypotheses as "incoherent" or to cite them, pityingly, as having tripped up on a "category error." Thus, the suggestion that the brain remembers or has knowledge or uses linguistic symbols is sometimes pilloried as a mere conceptual error that consists in taking categories appropriate to one domain and applying them to a different, inappropriate domain.[4] But one person's category error is another person's deep theory about the nature of the universe, and what is deemed appropriate or inappropriate in the application of categories depends tremendously on one's empirical beliefs and one's theoretical imagination (Rorty 1965).

The important thing for getting at the truth about brains is not whether in customary usage ordinary humans-in-the-street do say that persons remember but do not say that brains remember; rather, it is whether we ought to say that brains remember—whether, given the empirical facts, it is a reasonable hypothesis that brains remember. Customary usage is perhaps of anthropological interest, but it will not determine much about the nature of reality.

There is also a more general criticism of the method. Since in the normal course of scientific progress the meanings of words undergo change as a result of theory change, then when a hypothesis is advanced that would result in meaning change, this is not *of itself* an objection to the hypothesis. If we are to leave certain old doctrines behind as archaic, this inevitably entails leaving behind as archaic the old meanings. Hence, what to ancient ears may have sounded like an odd thing to say comes to seem entirely ordinary and correct. This is because the ancient ears are informed by ancient theory.

To make theoretical progress we precisely expect some degree of meaning change, and certainly if observation sentences are revised, then observational predicates undergo meaning change. Galileo's critics thought it was contradictory to say the Earth moved. Now if indeed it *was* part of the meaning of the word "Earth" that the Earth was stationary, then as people acquired evidence that the Earth moved, they thereby acquired reason to change the meaning. And, as remarked earlier, modifying beliefs and modifying meanings are not distinct and separable enterprises. The assumption that a new theory's adequacy is compromised if its terms fail to preserve synonymy with the terms of the old theory is perniciously conservative. For it implies that preservation of the status quo should override considerations of empirical adequacy. As Feyerabend pointed out,

> Arguments from synonymy judge a theory or point of view not by its capability to mimic the world but rather by its capability to mimic the descriptive terms of another point of view which for some reason is received favorably. (1963a:187 (Morick))

Feyerabend refused to acquiesce in the sacredness of the common idiom, in the empiricist theory of meaning, in the conventional wisdom concerning the absolute distinction between theory and observation, between fact and interpretation. Instead, he articulated a radically different, and less tidy, picture of science and common knowledge, and he was led to the view that perhaps the entire "common idiom" we use in talking about mental states and processes, and the mind in general, may be misconceived and empirically unsound. He concluded that the network of concepts we regularly use in understanding and explaining ourselves and others might need to be radically overhauled, including the observation language used to report our inner goings-on. Analyzing the common idiom, he explained, might tell us something about what we do believe, but "the question of the truth of the beliefs has not been touched" (1963b:144 (Borst)).

Like Kant, Feyerabend realized that our apprehension of our inner world is not more basic, privileged, or immediate than our apprehension of our outer world. Our understanding of our inner life is mediated by the concepts we use in apprehending mental states and processes. But unlike Kant, Feyerabend thought the whole fabric of mental concepts might be systematically improvable and revisable. (See also Rorty 1965; Paul M. Churchland 1979, 1981.) The nature and degree of doctrinal improvement is a matter for discovery in science, not for protective and proprietary linguistic analysis. Even if our observation sentences describing mental states and processes are, *relative to existing theory,* foundational, they form no part of an absolute foundation.

The destruction of the logical empiricist theory of empirical foundations and theory of meaning thus turned out to have profound implications for the philosophy of mind. It liberated philosophers both from the constraints of holding fixed the current meaning of certain words and from the limitations of what can (now) be imagined. It showed the sterility of limiting what can be discovered in science by what we currently mean. It permitted philosophers to see that empirical discoveries in psychology, neuroscience, artificial intelligence research, and so forth, could mold and shape and perhaps transmute the language of the mental.

Nonetheless, in an obvious sense and despite all the differences in detail, the naturalistic bent of the new developments in the philosophy of mind is akin not only to the pragmatism of Peirce and James but also to the spirit of empiricism in all its various incarnations. For the cardinal hunch is that to discover our nature we must see ourselves as organisms in Nature, to be understood by scientific methods and means. Hume's enthusiasm for a science of man has a decidedly contemporary ring:

> For to me it seems evident, that the essence of the mind being equally unknown to us with that of external bodies, it must be equally impossible to form any notion of its powers and qualities other than from careful and exact experiments, and the observation of those particular effects, which result from its different circumstances and situations. (1739, introduction)

Selected Readings

Ayer, A. J., ed. (1959). *Logical positivism.* New York: Free Press.
Butterfield, Herbert (1968). *The origins of modern science 1300–1800.* Toronto: Clarke, Irwin and Co.
Descartes, René (1649). *Les passions de l'âme.* English translation in E. S. Haldane and G. R. T. Ross (1911). *The philosophical works of Descartes.* 2 vols. Reprinted (1968). Cambridge: Cambridge University Press.
Feyerabend, Paul K. (1981). *Philosophical papers.* Vols. 1 and 2. Cambridge: Cambridge University Press.
Hume, David (1739). *A treatise of human nature.* Modern edition by L. A. Selby-Bigge (1888). Oxford: Clarendon Press.
James, William (1907). *Pragmatism: A new name for some old ways of thinking.* New York: Longmans, Green. (Reprinted in Frederick Burkhardt and Fredson Bowers, eds. (1975). *Pragmatism and the meaning of truth.* Cambridge, Mass.: Harvard University Press.)
Kant, Immanuel (1781). *Kritik der reinen Vernunft.* 2nd. ed. (1787). Translated and edited by N. Kemp Smith (1929). *Immanuel Kant's critique of pure reason.* Reprinted (1964). London: Macmillan.
Kuhn, Thomas S. (1962). *The structure of scientific revolutions.* 2nd ed. (1970). Chicago: University of Chicago Press.
Peirce, Charles Sanders (1931–1935). *The collected papers of Charles Sanders Peirce,* vols. 1–6, ed. Charles Hartshorne and Paul Weiss. Cambridge, Mass.: Harvard University Press.
Plato. *Plato: The Collected Dialogues.* (1961). Ed. Edith Hamilton and Huntington Cairns, eds. New York: Bollingen Foundation.
Popper, Karl R. (1963). *Conjectures and refutations: The growth of scientific knowledge.* New York: Basic Books. (2nd ed. (1965). New York: Harper and Row.)
Quine, W. V. O. (1953). *From a logical point of view.* Cambridge, Mass.: Harvard University Press.
Quine, W. V. O. (1969). Epistemology naturalized. In *Ontological relativity and other essays,* 69–90. New York: Columbia University Press.

Chapter 7
Reduction and the Mind-Body Problem

. . . [metaphysical systems] are the only means at our disposal for examining those parts of our knowledge which have already become observational and are therefore inaccessible to a criticism "on the basis of observation."
Paul K. Feyerabend, 1963

7.1 Introduction

In concluding the last chapter, I foreshadowed the implications for philosophy of mind of the major revisions in the platform features of logical empiricism. These changes permitted the development of a naturalistic conception that envisioned research on the mind-brain as an *empirical* investigation of the nature of mental states and processes, their causes, and their effects. Naturalism follows hard upon the heels of the understanding that there is no first philosophy. Inevitably the naturalistic approach leads us to inquire into the possibility of a unified theory of the mind-brain, wherein psychological states and processes are explained in terms of neuronal states and processes. A fundamental question concerning this possibility can be put as follows: Can mental states and processes be *reduced* to brain states and processes? Can one be a reductionist?

Not everyone expects mental states to reduce to brain states. On the contrary, it has been my observation that many philosophers and cognitive scientists, most of the artificial intelligentsia, not a few neuroscientists and biologists, and theologians generally, reject the possibility as unlikely—and not merely as unlikely, but as flatly preposterous. But what, precisely, are they denying, and what *is* reduction? The aim of this and the subsequent two chapters will be to understand and evaluate the objections to reductionist strategies. This is central to my program, for obviously, if reductionism is a hopeless cause, then it would be foolish to search for an explanation of mental states and processes in terms of brain states and processes.

Indeed, if reductionist strategies really are absurd, then it may well be wondered how neuroscience can be relevant to research in psychology, let alone to philosophical questions.

In chapter 8 I consider objections posed by dualists and by those who consider there to be an irreducible set of properties distinguishing mental states from any sort of physical state. In chapter 9 I consider antireductionist arguments formulated by contemporary philosophers who are part of the functionalist movement. Here I lay the groundwork for those chapters by offering an account of what reduction is, and what it is not.

7.2   Intertheoretic Reduction

The word "reduction" has a bewildering range of applications in the literature. "Reductionism" has come in some quarters to be used as a general term of insult and abuse. Sometimes it is used as a synonym for "behaviorism" (which is a case of the vague hounding the vague), or as a synonym for such diverse sins as "materialism," "bourgeois capitalism," "experimentalism," "vivisectionism," "communism," "militarism," "sociobiology," and "atheism." With such diversity, equivocation is inevitable, and often as not opposing sides in a debate on reductionism go right by each other because they have not agreed upon what they disagree about. How "reductionism" came to acquire such indiscriminate uses is beyond my ken, and perhaps it would be best to drop the word altogether and so avoid the inappropriate connotations. The dilemma is, however, that for the subject matter under consideration, "reduction," in the sense to be specified, *is* the right word. It is the word traditionally used in the relevant literature in science and in the philosophy of science, and there is no other word that begins to be appropriate. Therefore, I have decided to take my chances with "reduction" and to guard against misunderstanding by specifying the meaning I intend.

In the sense of "reduction" that is relevant here, reduction is first and foremost a relation between theories. Most simply, one theory, the *reduced* theory T_R, stands in a certain relation (specified below) to another more basic theory T_B. Statements that a phenomenon P_R reduces to another phenomenon P_B are derivative upon the more basic claim that the *theory* that characterizes the first reduces to the *theory* that characterizes the second.

Before I amplify and illustrate these points, a word about tactics. In order to clarify the nature of intertheoretic reduction and to begin to assess the prospects for reduction of psychological theories to neuroscience, it will be wisest not to focus on the very case at issue, namely neurobiological theories and psychological theories, but on cases at some remove from what is contentious. Otherwise, we not only lose clarity but also run the risk of begging all the important questions. The account of intertheoretic reduction should not be tailored to suit the specific case at issue but should be adequate to reduction in the sciences generally. Moreover, there do not yet exist fleshed-out neurobiological theories with reductive pretensions, let alone reductive success, and to introduce neuroscientific fiction in the analysis stage would only be confusing. By contrast, physics, chemistry, and genetics provide well-studied examples of theories that have reduced to other theories. Therefore, it will be most efficient to draw upon those examples in the history of science where two theories have eventually enjoyed an intertheoretic reduction and where the examples have been analyzed by historians and philosophers of science. Hence, examples from physics, chemistry, and biochemistry will figure prominently in illustrating the analysis of reduction. With an account of the intertheoretic relations and dynamics of reduction in hand, we can reopen the question of the ultimate reducibility of psychological theories to neurobiological theories.

To return to the issue, reduction is a relation between theories, and one phenomenon is said to reduce to another in virtue of the reduction of the relevant theories. For example, the claim that light has been reduced to electromagnetic radiation means (a) that the theory of optics has been reduced to the theory of electromagnetic radiation and (b) that the theory of optics is reduced in such a way that it is appropriate to identify light with electromagnetic radiation. Similarly, when we entertain the question of whether light is reducible to electromagnetic radiation, the fundamental question really is whether the theory of optics is reducible to the theory of electromagnetic radiation. Hence, when we raise the question of whether mental states are reducible to brain states, this question must be posed first in terms of whether some theory concerning the nature of mental states is reducible to a theory describing how neuronal ensembles work, and second in terms of whether it reduces in such a way that the mental states of T_R can be identified with the neuronal states of T_B. A good deal of muddle concerning reduction can be avoided with this initial clarification regarding reductive relations.

A consequence of intertheoretic reduction is explanatory unification, and in the sciences such unification is considered a good thing. If one theory can be explained by another and thus reduced to it, then our understanding of the phenomena described by the theory is greatly enhanced. For example, as a result of the reduction of the theory of optics to the theory of electromagnetism we came to understand why the laws of optics are as they are, and to this extent our understanding of how light behaves and what it is was enhanced.

Another important consequence of intertheoretic reduction is ontological simplification. Ontology pertains to what entities and properties exist, and in the event of intertheoretic reduction it may turn out that where we had thought there existed *two* different kinds of phenomena characterized by the laws of two different theories, there is in fact but *one* kind of phenomenon that is described by both theories.

For example, in the mid-nineteenth century it was widely supposed that light was one sort of phenomenon, and electromagnetic effects quite another. By the turn of the century the laws of optics had been reduced to the laws of electromagnetic theory, and we understood that light *is* electromagnetic radiation. We understood what light is for the very first time, in the sense that we understood why the laws of optics are as they are.

Ontological simplification may also be achieved, not by the reduction of one theory to another, but by the elimination of one theory by another. For example, the elimination of the caloric theory of heat by the kinetic theory of heat achieved ontological simplification, not by the identification of caloric with molecular kinetic energy, but by the claim that there is no such thing as caloric. Ontological simplification—simplification concerning what kinds of things we think exist—is thus a typical feature of reductions, and as these contrasting examples illustrate, the simplification may be achieved either through reduction and identification or through elimination. The general conditions under which the simplification takes one form rather than another will be discussed shortly.

Having said that reduction is a relation between theories, we must now characterize that relation. Under what conditions is one theory said to reduce to another? Recall that the crux of the answer provided by the logical empiricists was that for T_R to reduce to T_B it must be *logically derived* from T_B plus some extra stuff. This extra stuff included domain-specific boundary conditions, limiting assumptions, approximations, and so forth, but also crucial were the bridge principles. As prescribed by logical empiricism, it was the function of bridge principles to connect properties comprehended by the laws of T_R to properties comprehended by the laws of T_B. In the most straightforward case the bridge principles would *identify* the properties in the reduced theory with properties in the more basic theory.

The logical empiricist account is a huge improvement on the woolly intuitions that abound concerning reduction. By making theories the fundamental relata, much of the metaphysical bewilderment and dottiness concerning how entities or properties could be reduced simply vanished. Nevertheless, just as the logical empiricist accounts of empirical foundations and of meaning were revolutionized, so was the account of intertheoretic reduction. As historians and philosophers of science examined the dynamics of science, they found it necessary to disensnare themselves from a background myth abetting logical empiricism—namely, the myth that science is mainly a smoothly cumulative, orderly accretion of knowledge. Historians and philosophers of science began to see that science is a rather more turbulent affair and that sometimes one theory is completely displaced by another. Evidently, sometimes there are scientific revolutions in which the former assumptions about what is the correct theory, about what are the facts against which to test theories, and about what needs to be explained, are junked holus bolus. (See especially Kuhn 1962 and Feyerabend 1962.) Even the favored instances of apparently orderly accretions have turned out to be surprisingly disorderly on close inspection. Indeed, there is not one example from the history of science that exactly fits the logical empiricist pattern of reduction, and some outstanding cases do not fit at all, force and bowdlerize how you will (Hooker 1981).

The problem was that theories invariably had to be corrected and modified to get something suitable that could be deduced from the basic theory. With the modifications accomplished, it was not of course the old theory itself that was deduced, but at best a *corrected version* of the old theory. Theories range themselves on a spectrum of how much correction and revamping they require to get into deducible form. Some require relatively little correction in order to be reduced (as for example in the case of reducing the theory of optics to electromagnetic theory), but in other cases so much correction is needed that almost nothing save a few low-level, homey generalizations can be retained. Phlogiston theory of combustion and the demonic possession theory of nervous disorders are two such examples. In these cases the correction required was so thorough that it seemed more appropriate to think of the old theoretical ontology as displaced entirely by the new theoretical ontology. The spectrum accordingly has at one end reduced theories that have been largely retained after the reduction and at the other end theories that have been largely displaced, with sundry cases falling in between.

If the old theory has to be corrected before it can be logically derived from the new theory, then the logical empiricist conception of reduction needs modification. In particular, the expectation that the bridge principles are always necessary, and that their function is to correlate phenomena in the old theory with phenomena in the new, must be reconfigured. And this is a reconfiguring of enormous importance in thinking about reduction vis-à-vis psychology and neuroscience. Should the old theory be largely displaced, then bridge laws are typically dispensed with. We do not identify phlogiston with oxygen, nor do we identify the demons that were said to possess shaking palsy patients with dopamine deficiency. Presumably we could do so, inasmuch as there is no strictly formal (logical) reason not to, but there is no theoretical utility in these identifications. On the contrary, such identifications might perpetuate misunderstanding of what the new theories do. Instead, we say there is no such thing as phlogiston, and there are no such things as demons. In these cases, therefore, bridge principles play no role whatever.

In other cases where correlations are usefully forged, properties in the new theory are matched up with properties in the *corrected version* of the old theory. However, the reconfigured properties of the corrected version of the old theory are never more than approximations to the properties in the original theory. The rub is, therefore, that whenever the corrections to the old theory are anything more than relatively minor, it is always tendentious to claim that phenomena in the old theory are to be identified with phenomena in the reducing theory.

This dimension of scientific dynamics is important for our considerations because many standard objections to the possibility of a unified theory of the mind-brain depend on the assumption that the commonsense understanding of mental states—of consciousness, beliefs, desires, and so forth—is *correct*. Using this assumption, it is often argued that no identification between neuronal states and mental states is forthcoming. In a sense, this conviction too can be seen as a legacy of logical empiricism, which cited immediate experience as Given and hence as the certain foundation supporting the edifice of knowledge. In seeing that reductions typically involve revision and modification of the reduced theory, and that even outright elimination as well as reduction is a possibility, we should acknowledge the necessity of relaxing our conviction concerning the basic correctness of our understanding of the mental. To appreciate the kinds of possibilities inherent in the future evolution in neurobiological theory, we should consider how philosophers of science have improved upon the logical empiricist story.

If the logical empiricist account of reduction is procrustean and wrong, how then should the conditions for intertheoretic reduction be specified? Roughly, as follows: Within the new, reducing theory T_B, construct *an analogue* T_R^* of the laws, etc., of the theory that is to be reduced, T_R. The analogue T_R^* can then be logically deduced from the reducing theory T_B plus sentences specifying special conditions (e.g., frictionless surfaces, perfect elasticity). Generally, the analogue will be constructed with a view to mapping expressions of the old theory onto expressions of the new theory, laws of the old theory onto sentences (but not necessarily *laws*) of the new. Under these conditions the old theory reduces to the new. When reduction is successfully achieved, the new theory will explain the old theory, it will explain why the old theory worked as well as it did, and it will explain much where the old theory was buffaloed. (To see this account worked out in detail, see Paul M. Churchland 1979 and Hooker 1981. See also Patricia S. Churchland 1982.)

To digress briefly, I should mention that there are of course nonformal conditions on reduction as well. For example, it must be reasonable to believe that T_B is true—implying as well that T_B must have the right sort of fit with the rest of established science. Furthermore, T_B should apply to the same *domain* of phenomena as T_R. I hasten to point out, however, that the conditions for rationally preferring one theory to another have not, notoriously, been worked out (Kuhn 1962). Moreover, it is my view that they will not be well understood until we have a much more complete account of what the mind-brain is doing in virtue of which it constructs theories, and of what rationality of mind-brain processing really consists in. Clearly, therefore, although my account of intertheoretic reduction ideally should be supplemented by a theory of rationality, we shall nonetheless have to make do with an inchoate understanding of rationality, which is all we have, until neuroscience and psychology yield a more complete theory of mind-brain function.

How much of, or how closely, the old theory is mirrored in the analogue varies from case to case and is a function of how much correction the old theory requires. Most of the theory of optics could be preserved, only some of classical thermodynamics, and almost nothing of the caloric theory of heat and temperature. If a reduction is smooth, in the sense that most principles of T_R have close analogues in T_B, then the matching of cohort terms denoting properties can proceed and identities can be claimed. Informally, a similarity-fit means that property P_R of the reduced theory has much the same causal powers as the cohort property P_B of the basic theory.

Determining when the fit is close enough to claim identities between properties and entities of the old and those of the new is not a matter for formal criteria, and the decision is influenced by a variety of pragmatic and social considerations. The whim of the central investigators, the degree to which confusion will result from retention of the old terms, the desire to preserve or to break with past habits of thought, the related opportunities for publicizing the theory, cadging grants, and attracting disciples all enter into decisions concerning whether to claim identities and therewith retention or whether to make the more radical claim of displacement.[1] In fact, I do not think it matters very much that we establish criteria for determining when the reduced and the reducing theory resemble each other sufficiently to herald identities of properties (Patricia S. Churchland 1982).

The evolving unifications seen in science therefore encompass not only smooth reductions with cross-theoretic identifications but also rather "bumpy" reductions where cross-theoretic identifications are problematic and involve revision of the old theory's concepts, and outright elimination with no cross-theoretic identifications at all. Phlogiston, caloric fluid, the spirit of sal ammoniac, and demons are all examples in which the embedding theory was eliminated and no cross-theoretic identifications were made.

It is singularly important for the discussion of the reduction of mental states to brain states that intertheoretic unification does not require cross-theoretical identification of states and things, and that reduction may involve substantial correction of the reduced theory. For it is often assumed that a unified theory of the mind-brain requires a smooth reduction, such that types of mental states (as now conceived) are identified with types of brain states (as now conceived). However, to make such identifications a requirement is to hobble severely the theoretical development of neuroscience, for it implies that only a reduction on the retentive end of the spectrum will do, and that neither will any of the variously revisionary styles of reductive relations be acceptable nor will displacement be considered even possible.

So far as we can tell now, that may be analogous to the requirement that only a retentive reduction of alchemy will do, or only a retentive reduction of caloric theory. The requirement is excessively conservative insofar as it insists on the preservation of the reduced theory. At the same time, it is excessively bold, since it in effect predicts that of all the possible places on the reductive spectrum where it might fall, this reduction will in fact be at the retentive end.

Moreover, theories at distinct levels often co-evolve (Wimsatt 1976a), as each informs and corrects the other, and if a theory at one stage of its history cannot reduce a likely candidate at a higher level, it may grow and mature so that eventually it does succeed in the reductive goal. In the meantime the discoveries and problems of each theory may suggest modifications, developments, and experiments for the other, and thus the two evolve toward a reductive consummation. Transmission genetics and molecular genetics exemplify this sort of co-evolution. As things stand, molecular genetics has not completely reduced transmission genetics, but its development toward a richer theory that can effect the reduction is guided in part by results and hypotheses in transmission genetics, whose research is in turn inspired in part by questions arising from molecular genetics. In the course of their co-evolution it has become evident that the "genes" as characterized in early transmission genetics, likened unto beads on a string, do not exist, and consequently the generalizations of transmission genetics have had to accommodate the molecular discoveries. (See especially Philip Kitcher 1982; see also chapter 9.)

In chapter 9, where the co-evolution of theories will be discussed in more detail, we will see that early signs of such mutual influencing are now to be found in research on memory as neurobiologists, psychologists, and neurologists inform and correct one another. And in chapter 10 I shall present an example of the co-evolution, albeit in the early stages, of neurobiological and psychological hypotheses concerning the nature of attention. Both the reductive hypotheses from neurobiology and the behavioral observations from psychology are essential to the wider program of figuring out how the information storage and retrieval system(s) works and how each corrects and informs the other. It is of course conceivable that a richly developed psychology of memory will never be reduced by a richly developed neurobiology of memory, nor transmission genetics by molecular genetics, however the pairs co-evolve. On the other hand, it would be fallacious to argue and reckless to predict that since the reduction is not now available, it never will be.[2] (The genetics example is further discussed in chapter 9.)

It is often in this gradual co-evolutionary development of theories that the corrections and extensions to both theories are made, and from such theoretical interanimation may ultimately emerge a unified theoretical framework. At this final stage the reduced theory will have an explanation—of its properties, laws, entities, and so forth—in terms of the reducing theory. However, as Francis Crick has remarked (in conversation), by the time we get to the point of being able to sit down and crank out the derivation of one theory from another, most of the really exciting science is over—the inspired modeling, the wild and woolly imaginative flights, the wall-tumbling experiments, the fitting and revising and revolutionizing are pretty much behind us.

Admittedly, this is something of an exaggeration, inasmuch as scientific theories are ever incomplete, and there is always fun to be had. Nonetheless, this view is correct in emphasizing the importance of the co-evolutionary process in achieving a reductively integrated theory. The logical empiricists, in focusing exclusively on the final products of a long history of theoretical evolution, overlooked the dynamics of theoretical evolution. This is a serious oversight, since it is typically in a theory's evolution that the major reductive links are forged and the major revisions—categorial and ontological—are wrought.

Reductive achievements sometimes fall short of the complete reduction of one theory to another because the available mathematics is insufficient to the task. Thus, quantum mechanics has succeeded in explaining the macro properties of only the simplest of atoms, and whether more will be forthcoming depends on developments in mathematics. Some people tend to want to make a lot of this (for example, Popper (1977)), but it has seemed to me not to be a lesson of any great significance in contemplating a reductive strategy for psychology and neuroscience. In the case of quantum mechanics the mathematical limitations do not entail that the macro properties of the more complex atoms are emergent in some spooky sense, but only that for want of mathematical solutions, an approximation will have to suffice. In any case, whether the appropriate mathematics will be developed is very much an open question, and since the date of Popper's original remarks, more reductions have been accomplished by quantum mechanics. The important point is that the general outlines of the reductive story are in place. Finally, we have no reason at this stage for assuming that a reductive program in neuroscience will be stopped dead in its tracks because the enabling mathematics is unavailable.

Because I think it most unlikely that a theoretical unification of neuroscience and psychology will involve a *retentive* reduction of mental states *as currently understood* with neuronal states *as currently understood*, it may be useful to dwell briefly on several examples in which one theory largely displaces another. Classical mechanics (Newtonian mechanics) was succeeded by Einstein's special theory of relativity (STR). This theoretical development is generally recognized as an instance of reduction, and initially it may seem to be a case that falls at the retention end of the spectrum. After all, it might be pointed out, the two theories have a common subject matter: mass, motion, acceleration, and so on.

The appearance of retention, and thus the appearance of identifying phenomena in one theory with phenomena in the other, is deceptive, however, and the differences between the two theories are sufficiently radical to call STR a displacement rather than a retentive reduction of classical mechanics (CM). To illustrate, consider mass. As conceived within CM, $mass_{CM}$ is a property, intrinsic to an entity;

it does not vary from observer to observer as a function of his velocity relative to the object whose mass$_{CM}$ is at issue. Mass$_{STR}$ is entirely different. It is a relation between an entity and countless reference frames; and it will have a different value for each observer with a different velocity relative to the object whose mass$_{STR}$ is at issue.

If STR is correct, there is no such thing as mass$_{CM}$; conversely, if CM is correct, there is no such thing as mass$_{STR}$. Properties intrinsic to objects are not relations between objects; more different they cannot be. Which means therefore, that mass$_{CM}$ is not identifiable with mass$_{STR}$. Similar points can be made about momentum, energy, and so on (Feyerabend 1962).

Here, then, is an instance where an entire theoretical network of laws and concepts is reconfigured at the hands of the reducing theory. The laws of CM are not deducible from the laws of STR, and this for two reasons: (1) the laws of CM "hold" only under certain limiting conditions, and if we are to deduce anything resembling CM from STR we must add in the (false) assumption that these limiting conditions obtain, and (2) where the terms of CM express intrinsic properties, the corresponding terms of STR all express *relations*. Given this latter fact, CM is not deducible from STR at all. What can be logically deduced from STR (plus the false assumptions) is a set CM* of *analogues* of the laws of CM, analogues still expressed in the relativized vocabulary of STR. Insofar as this deduction explains the set of analogue laws CM* in terms of STR, it thereby explains classical mechanics.

STR, plus Limiting Assumptions
$\downarrow$ logically entails
CM*
    which is isomorphic with
CM

Speaking more strictly, the deduction explains why CM was as successful as it was, within the classical limits. And the deduction does show that STR has the resources to "take over" the explanatory and predictive jobs performed in the past by the original CM. That is why this case still counts as a successful intertheoretic reduction, despite the lack of a systematic set of intertheoretic identity statements.

A concern may yet linger: "What about mass itself—what about the phenomenon that exists in nature? Perhaps mass$_{CM}$ is not identical to mass$_{STR}$, but does mass itself reduce to mass$_{STR}$ or not?" In order to understand the question, we must know what the speaker means by "mass." Suppose he says, "Well, it is that property which things differentially have such that one thing is harder to push than another, such that some things weigh more than others, etc." Notice that in giving the answer, in effect he gives a theory of sorts—a dinky little theory perhaps, but his beliefs about what mass is are inevitably tied to generalizations of some sort. Because if he is to use the word, he must have classificatory schemata and some rule of application, be they homespun or not.

At this stage the earlier discussion of epistemological matters—of empirical foundations, theories, and observations—is particularly helpful. To suppose that there is a phenomenon, namely mass, that can be apprehended and understood independently of any theory is an illusion. Bare facts, neutral observation, theory-independent access to the world, and absolute foundations have gone to the wall with logical empiricism. (See chapter 6.) In the case under consideration the speaker's "mass" is characterized by the theory he provides, and hence his question boils down to this: does his dinky-theory (DT) that specifies $mass_{DT}$ reduce to STR in such a way that $mass_{DT}$ can be identified as the same thing as $mass_{STR}$? Now the question is answerable, and the answer is an unambiguous "no," since in his dinky-theory mass is a property, not a relation. Assuming that STR is correct, there is nothing in nature that corresponds to the speaker's conception of mass—nor, for that matter, to mass as conceived by CM. What is in nature, says STR, is relativistic mass—mass as described in STR.

What gets reduced are theories, and the stuff in the universe keeps doing whatever it is doing while we theorize and theories come and go. So the question "Does mass itself get reduced?" does not make any sense.

The second example also illustrates displacement, but this time it is a *folk theory* that is displaced by another. Such an example is especially pertinent to the mind-brain issue for the following reason: it is common for objections to the possibility of a theoretical unification of neuroscience and psychology to lean heavily on our current intuitions about our mental lives. The framework of concepts for such intuitions is frequently credited with being observationally true or self-evidently true. And this framework is often alleged to be irreducible to any theory in neuroscience. My strategy is to draw attention to the range of fates that can befall a conceptual framework, no matter that it is an intuitive, "observational" framework. If it is irreducible, that may be owed to its being so inadequate that it deserves displacement, or it may be that it will not be smoothly reduced, but instead revised, either in large or in small measure. As this example will show, even "observable" concepts may be reconfigured or eliminated, and occupying the station of "intuitive framework" or "folk theory" protects that framework neither from reduction of the revisionary type nor from outright elimination. (That our intuitive understanding of mental states and processes can be understood as a folk *theory* will be discussed in detail in section 7.3.)

Newtonian classical mechanics was itself the innovative challenger to a more primitive theory of motion derived from Aristotle. The central wisdom of Aristotle's theory of mechanics was this law: An object will continue in motion if and only if a force is continuously applied to keep it in motion. As Aristotle reasoned, if one stops pushing a boulder, it will stop moving; when sufficient force is applied, the boulder begins to move again, and it will continue to move so long as the force is applied. The motion of projectiles appeared to be a problem for the theory, since a rock hurled from a catapult, for example, continues in motion after release from the catapult and hence after release from the force applied by the catapult.

According to the theory, once the external force of the catapult is no longer applied, the object should drop straight down. Medieval physicists tried to solve the problem of projectile motion by postulating an internal force imparted to the object by the catapult. The rock continues to move after release from the catapult because it has been given an *impetus* that keeps it in motion. Why then does the object eventually fall? Because, the theory said, the internal force slowly dissipates, whereupon the object's weight causes it to fall. The theory recognized nothing fundamentally different between rectilinear motion and curvilinear motion—it was all just motion. Thus, a corollary to the theory was that objects could be given curved impetus, so that an object twirled around the end of a string allegedly continued in a circular path when released from the string.

This was the impetus theory of projectile motion, and it was to dominate physics until Galileo set the subject on the path that finally wound to Newton. The example is important for a number of reasons. First, it is crucial to understand that impetus theory was not smoothly reduced and largely retained by Newton's theory but was falsified and displaced by it. As a theory of mechanics, the impetus theory is misconceived and muddled from top to bottom. In contrast to the central wisdom of Aristotle, Newton's first law states that a body in uniform rectilinear motion will continue in uniform rectilinear motion unless acted on by a force; a force is required to *accelerate* a body but not to keep it in uniform motion. On Newton's theory there is no such thing as impetus *at all*; there is simply nothing in classical mechanics with which to identify impetus. "Momentum" may suggest itself, but momentum is not a *force*, whereas being a force was the whole point of impetus.

Additionally, the distinction fundamental to impetus theory—between being in motion and being at rest—is irrelevant to Newtonian dynamics, which instead draws a fundamental distinction between moving at constant velocity (either at rest or at unchanging speed) and moving at changing velocity (acclerating and decelerating). In addition, the failure to see the differences between motion in straight lines and motion deviating from straight lines was disastrous. The corollary concerning curved impetus was a muck-up and can easily be observed to be false—so easily, in fact, that the untroubled claims to have observed verifying instances look like first-rate cases of seeing what we believe.

The example is interesting for a second reason—namely, that something rather like impetus theory seems to be what many humans uninformed of classical mechanics tend to believe and act upon, even in the twentieth century. In a series of studies performed by McCloskey (1983), it was found that both in their behavior with regard to moving objects and in their verbal predictions and explanations, students were far more Aristotelian than Newtonian. In one test college subjects were asked to jog along and try to "bomb" a stationary target by dropping a golf ball on it. Typically, they thought the ball would fall straight down when released, and some even thought it would move backward. Therefore, they did not drop the ball until the hand holding it was directly over the target or even past it. In other experiments subjects tried to make a puck slide in a curved path by moving their arm in a curved path before releasing the puck. Additionally, they explained projectile motion in terms of a force imparted to objects that keeps them in motion but slowly dissipates, after which gravity takes over—an explanation reminiscent not of Newton but of the medieval physicists. Among students acquainted with classical mechanics there was a tendency to try to assimilate that theory to the impetus theory, for example by construing momentum as a cause of motion and in effect using "momentum" in much the same role in which the old theory used "impetus."

These experiments indicate that apart from the scientific community, most humans seem to employ a sort of *folk physics* or, as McCloskey calls it, *intuitive physics*. Although a person might not describe his set of beliefs concerning motion as a theory, given the role of such beliefs in explaining and predicting motion, it is nonetheless appropriate to credit the person with a folk theory. The set of beliefs is not likely the product of self-conscious theorizing, *but insofar as they are used to explain and predict motion of objects, they function for the person the way a consciously constructed theory functions.* Perhaps the folk theory is casually acquired as one learns one's native language, or perhaps there is some innate structure in the brain that fastens on this theory first. Whatever its origins, folk theory there does seem to be, and to someone uninformed of Newton's laws the folk theory seems to be self-evident and observably true—a bit of rock-solid commonsense. Moreover, like earlier impetus theorists, ordinary folk think they have observed what we know to be impossible trajectories for projectiles. (See McCloskey, Caramazza, and Green 1980, Clement 1982.)

To someone unacquainted with Newtonian theory the central wisdom of Aristotle's physics does seem intuitively dead obvious, and Newton's first law may well seem counterintuitive and outlandish. Only when it is experimentally shown how impetus theory and Newton's laws predict different effects—only when it is demonstrated how Newton's laws can explain why impetus theory worked as well as it did and how much more Newton's laws could explain—does the superiority of Newton's laws begin to dislodge the old dogma root and branch. Once the new theory becomes second nature, observations are made within its framework, not within the framework of the abandoned theory. Unless the old theory is deliberately dislodged and its falsity explicitly recognized, the inclination seems to be to force the new theory to knit itself, somehow or other, into the old theory.

This example illustrates several points that will be useful in the discussion of reducing mental states to brain states: first, that in reductive developments one theory can displace and falsify another; second, that sometimes what is displaced and falsified is a *folk theory* within which those who hold it make their observations; third, that despite the self-evidence of the folk theory, it can be demonstrated to be misconceived; and fourth, that as a newly acquired theory becomes familiar, it can be as routinely and casually used as the old folk theory. For example, a seasoned engineer uses Newtonian mechanics as effortlessly and "intuitively" as McCloskey's subjects use impetus theory. With routine use of a theory, one naturally makes economies in the sequence of inferential steps and comes to be able to predict the trajectory of a projectile without laborious deductions. One just knows, and knows without conscious effort at Newtonian reasoning, that a puck will not move in a curved path after release from a hand swung in a circle, and it will seem faintly bizarre that anyone should have thought otherwise.

A further pertinent observation is that even after a theory has been displaced by a competing theory, some people may continue to understand phenomena in terms of the displaced theory, quite as though it were not false. Unless explicitly taught to think of motion in a Newtonian framework, people seem disposed to employ the impetus theory. That they do so does not imply that the old theory has not really been falsified by the new theory; it merely means that some people do not know or care that it has been falsified. To construct a new theory and reduce the old is one thing; for the reducing theory to find its way into our hearts and minds is another.

A similar account can be given of folk thermodynamics, a hodgepodge theory of heat and temperature that was displaced by classical thermodynamics, which in turn was reduced, not very smoothly, by statistical mechanics. (See Paul M. Churchland 1979.) I suspect somewhat the same story can be told for folk theory of design in nature, which explained the organization exhibited in the working of the eye or the nature of reproduction, for example, in terms of an intelligent designer. That theory has been displaced by biology and the theory of evolution.

I do not suppose there is a neat sorting out of what is folk theory and what is a subsequent development that eventually found widespread acceptance in a particular culture. Alchemy might not be considered a folk chemistry, though many of its concepts and ideas became common coin, whereas animistic theories of weather and seasons, say, might be considered folk meteorology. I set no great store by getting a rigorous criterion to demarcate the folk theory from the folk-plus-one theory from protoscientific theory from genuinely scientific theory. Theories are, after all, natural phenomena; they evolve, and they cause changes in what people mean by certain expressions, in how they think, and in how they see the world. Some slip easily into the vernacular, others are isolated to small communities of the cognoscenti. Some are readily adopted by children but always seem foreign to their parents. Some, like heliocentrism and the theory of evolution, are disruptive of the wider metaphysics; others, like the germ theory of disease, are relatively inoffensive to the wider metaphysics; some are stopped in their tracks by war, barbarians, plagues, famine, or other acts of God.

To the extent that the new theory substantially displaces the old, there is a reconfiguring of *what needs to be explained*. Previous consensus on the explananda dissolves, and new explananda, conceived within the framework of the new theory, come to dominate research. For example, in Ptolemaic theory the Earth was the center of the universe around which revolved the celestial sphere, roughly as though the Earth were a small pea inside a gigantic revolving basketball. Indeed, it was thought that the sphere could be observed to turn daily around the inert Earth, an observation that seemed unproblematic and straightforward. Ptolemaic theorists therefore had to answer the question "What makes the celestial sphere turn?" and assorted hypotheses were advanced and discussed concerning the mechanism. However, since Newtonian theory dispensed altogether with the celestial sphere, the mechanism of its movement is no longer something that needs to be explained, and claims to have observed the sphere and its movement are misconceived and false.

Hence, Newtonian theory did not solve the problem of what makes the celestial sphere move by postulating an intricate set of gears, pulleys, and what have you. It rejected the explanandum as misconceived. There is no celestial sphere, so there is no problem about what makes it move. Moreover, one cannot observe it or its movements, though the apparent movement of the stars can be explained in Newtonian theory by reference to the Earth's motion. In addition, of course, the seemingly self-evident datum that the Earth is stationary is falsified by Newtonian theory. Thus can the observational data of one theory be revised by the victorious new theory.

Explananda of many earlier theories have suffered a kindred fate: Harvey did not try to explain how animal spirits are concocted in the heart; instead, he said that the heart is a pump for blood and tried to explain how it pumped. Modern biologists do not try to explain how vital spirit makes things alive; instead, they try to explain other things, such as how information is coded in DNA. (See Feyerabend 1963a.)

It is the contrast between competing theories that highlights flaws, foibles, and misconceptions in theories, and without that contrast it is often hard to avoid simply taking for granted the explananda, methods, and "self-evident data" of the prevailing paradigm. For this reason, Feyerabend exhorts us to encourage as many competing theories to bloom as possible, and to keep aflame the humbling thought that new theories may revise our old conceptions entirely, including our conceptions of what is obvious and what are the "facts" that need to be explained.

The relevance of this to the issue of an eventual unified theory of the mind-brain is this: what we take to be obvious or observational within the framework of intuitive psychology is not guaranteed correctness or survivability simply on the strength of that obviousness and observationality. As we have seen, even intuitive frameworks, and even observational concepts, can be reconfigured as science proceeds. Perhaps only by looking first at examples where the emotional stakes are lower can we begin to get enough distance to see that our "intuitive" conceptual framework for understanding ourselves, for introspecting, for observing, for explaining and predicting behavior may require revision or even elimination.

For the sake of completeness I should add that the theory of scientific explanation I adopt here is a modified form of the deductive-nomological (DN) model worked out by the logical empiricists (chapter 6; see also E. Nagel 1961). The important modifications are twofold. (1) Intertheoretic reduction is an instance of DN explanation, where what is explained is not a single event but a law or set of laws. Insofar as the account of intertheoretic reduction deviates from the logical empiricist conception, there are corresponding modifications in the theory of explanation. In particular, the theory must be modified to allow for explananda to be reconfigured rather than deduced as they stand. The model accommodates this change without strain. As noted earlier in the discussion of intertheoretic reduction, sometimes what is deduced is not the old law itself but a reconfigured version or analogue of the old law. Accordingly, it is not the old law that is explained, but its analogue. (2) Not all laws are universal generalizations; some are statistical generalizations. Thus, the basic model must be broadened to encompass explanations where the covering laws are probabilistic. This modification will not in fact play a significant role in the issues raised in this book, but to see how it works, interested readers should consult Salmon 1971. (A great many details concerning the deductive-nomological model of explanation that I must ignore here are cogently discussed in E. Nagel 1961 and Rescher 1970. For a more recent paper that answers many of the objections to this model, see Cupples 1977.)

Having declared my preference for the deductive-nomological theory of explanation, I emphatically add that I neither wish nor need to be doctrinaire about this. On the contrary, I adopt this theory only as a first approximation that enables us to discuss without folderol the important aspects of intertheoretic reduction. Accordingly, the framework for reduction and explanation is intended to accommodate explanations of the form described by Cummins (1983), in which a *capacity* at one level of organization is explained in terms of the coordinated functioning of capacities at a lower level of organization. The points that I find central are that reduction involves *explanation* and that typically reductions involve *corrections* of those levels of description that supply the explananda.

In any case I think the theory of explanation is bound to be provisional, since I expect that as theories of brain function mature, we will acquire a far deeper sense of what the brain is doing when it seeks explanations, what it counts as explanatory fit, what understanding comes to, and so on. And my conviction is that this deeper sense will take us beyond the paradigm in which explanations in general are characterized on the model of *logical* relation between *sentences*. (See chapters 9 and 10.) Rather, it may hypothesize very different sorts of relations between cognitive structures very different from sentences. Indeed, some of the shortcomings visible in the DN model cut so deep as to suggest the need for a very different paradigm (Van Fraassen 1980, Cummins 1983). In short, it may well be that as neuroscience matures, it will change profoundly our conception of cognitive activity and therewith our epistemology.

7.3   Mental States and Folk Psychology

What Theory Will Reduce to Neurobiological Theory?
The fundamental point of the foregoing section was that questions concerning the reduction of mental states to brain states front for the real question, which is whether one *theory* is reducible to another *theory*. The first piece of business, therefore, is to determine which theories are candidates for the relevant intertheoretic reduction. This crucial first step is often missed in discussion of reduction (see for example Sperry 1980, MacKay 1978, Eccles 1977), with the consequence that it is often hard to see what the issues are and what might count as evidence one way or another. In these circumstances the debates about reduction threaten to become an unavailing clash between precarious metaphors and amorphous intuitions.

What theory, then, is the candidate for reduction to neurobiological theory? It is the integrated body of generalizations describing the high-level states and processes and their causal interconnections that underlie behavior. Broadly speaking, this is the domain of scientific psychology, and especially in the last hundred years an enormous research effort has gone into discovering important generalizations about such functions as memory, learning, perception, development, language use, and so forth. Nevertheless, it is acknowledged on all sides that although some generalizations have been discovered, there does not yet exist an integrated body of generalizations—a comprehensive Theory—that delineates the psychological states and processes mediating perception, learning and memory, problem solving, cognitive mapping of an environment, and so forth. There is still an enormous amount we simply do not understand at the psychological level about the cognitive and sensorimotor capacities of organisms. There is therefore a great deal of research yet to be done, and it is evident that the candidate for reduction to neurobiological theory is some *future* theory. It is a yet-to-be-devised integrated account of the causal connections between psychological states and behavior.

Granting the unfinished status of scientific psychology, it is nevertheless clear that for many of the generalizations and discoveries that have been made by psychologists, the question of a future reduction to neurobiological generalizations is not tendentious. Consider, for example, the following generalizations:

1. Extinction of a learned response R is slower if on the learning trials the conditioned stimulus was correlated with the unconditioned stimulus with a probability less than 1.
2. An organism will not learn a response R to a conditioned stimulus K if K is presented simultaneously with or after the unconditioned stimulus L.
3. If two stimuli, such as two bars of light or two circles of light, are presented in a properly timed succession, the scene is perceived as *one* object moving in space.
4. Prelinguistic infants are able to give discriminative responses to every phoneme from every natural human language, but children who have learned a language are able to discriminate only those phonemes found in the language they have learned.
5. If a light-colored rectangle is placed flush against a dark-colored rectangle, one will see *at the border* a darkening of the lighter color (the Mach bands discussed in chapter 2).

The list could easily grow to encyclopedic length, but the point is that the possibility of a neurobiological reduction of these generalizations tends not to offend anyone. For the most part it is expected that brain-based explanations of why these generalizations and similar generalizations hold true will eventually be forthcoming. It is expected, for example, that learning curves of rats in T-mazes will have a neurobiological explanation, and research on the hippocampus and the cerebellum (interpositus nuclei) already lends support to this expectation (Olton, Becker, and Handelmann 1979, McCormick 1984).

Even so, some misgivings may linger about the possibility of reduction should it be assumed that a reductive strategy means an exclusively bottom-up strategy or that in the aftermath of the intertheoretic reduction the high-level theory will somehow wither away or be useless or in disgrace. These misgivings are really just bugbears, and they have no place in my framework for reduction.

Recall that on my account of intertheoretic reduction, one theory is reduced to another if it (or a corrected analogue of it) is *explained* by another. This does not entail that the reduced theory will somehow cease to be, or that the phenomena it describes cease to be. On the contrary, if the reduction is smooth, its reduction gives it—and its phenomena—a firmer place in the larger scheme of biological theory. If the reduction involves major correction, the corrected, reduced theory continues to play a role in prediction and explanation, and it too has a place in the larger scheme of things. Only if one theory is eliminated by another does it fall by the wayside.

Nor, it must be emphasized, does intertheoretic reduction imply an essentially "compositional" research strategy. By a "compositional strategy" is usually meant that one must first know all about the micro properties (the parts) before addressing the macro properties (the whole). True enough, higher-level capacities will be explained in terms of lower-level capacities or structures, but the order of *discovery* is not the same as the order of *explanation*. As a matter of discovery, coevolution of higher-level and lower-level theories is certain to be more productive than an isolated bottom-up strategy.

But if a reductive future for generalizations such as (1) through (5) of scientific psychology is not considered to be impossible or even contentious, then what is the issue? Is there a residual source of objections to intertheoretic reduction even after the story of the nature of intertheoretic reduction dispels some of the antireductionist bugbears? The answer is clearly yes. The residual problems are quite complex, and they condense around two substantial points. Simplified, the first can be stated thus: "Our ordinary understanding of our mental states provides the observational base against which the adequacy of any psychological theory must be tested, and this, it is argued on various grounds, is not reducible to neurobiology. The framework features of our commonsense understanding are unrevisable and inalienable." The reasons for this conclusion are very diverse, and the arguments supporting this general sense of the correctness of the commonsense framework will be the focus of chapter 8.

The second condensation point concerns representations and the nature of the computations over representations. Simplified, it runs as follows: "Theories of human cognition will be radically incomplete unless they can provide some characterization of *representations* and the *transitions between representations*. If cognition involves computation, then it involves operations on representations. So far the only line on such a characterization of representations depends on a conception of representation embodied in our ordinary understanding of mental states. But this is a conception that resists reduction, and generalizations concerning representations will not be reducible to neurobiological generalizations." Examples of generalizations that refer to representations can be found in social psychology, linguistics, perceptual psychology, and cognitive psychology. Consider as examples the following generalizations, drawn from Nisbett and Ross 1980:

6. People's inferences about what caused an event or an action are strongly influenced by the concreteness or the imaginability of available information.

7. When someone has an opinion on a emotionally significant matter, conflicting evidence is treated as if it were supporting, impressions formed on the basis of early evidence survive exposure to inconsistent evidence presented later, and beliefs survive the total discrediting of their evidence base.

Or consider a different sort of generalization from developmental linguistics:

8. There is a stage in language learning during which children "regularize" common irregular verbs, even though they have never heard instances of such regularizations. For example, they may say "camed" instead of "came," "gived" instead of "gave," "supposen't" instead of "isn't supposed to," and so forth.

The resistance to the goal of a unified theory, therefore, devolves not upon generalizations of such mien as (1) through (5) but upon generalizations that pertain to representations. If a significant part of human information processing involves operations on representations, and I agree that it must, then the quarrel is a singularly important one, for it concerns the future development of that domain of scientific psychology which addresses the cognitive capacities of humans and other organisms. Moreover, this antireductionist argument is relevant not only to the wider question of neuroscience-psychology unity of theory but also to the question of a unified theory at the *psychological* level. The reason is this: if generalizations (1) through (5) and their kind are reducible to neurobiological theory, but (6) through (8) and their kind are not, this forecasts a fragmentation of theory at the level of psychological states and processes.

It is important to try to find out whether or not the arguments against the unified conception are right, for the issue bears upon how we decide to do research. If we are persuaded that a unified theory is impossible and that some explanations of cognition, perception, and so forth, cannot ever be explained in terms of neurobiological theory, then this profoundly affects how we conceive of our long-term research goals, and that affects our more immediate research strategies. Which research intuitions to weed out and which to culture, which research visions to abandon and which to nurture, are affected in subtle and in substantial ways by how we come down on the question of intertheoretic reduction. If the antireductionist arguments are correct, then perhaps neurobiological research is largely irrelevant to research on cognition, perception, learning, and so forth. Because these two lines of resistance to intertheoretic reduction of psychology to neurobiology have methodological consequences, they deserve to be examined carefully. I am persuaded by neither line of resistance to the reductionist strategy, and in chapters 8 and 9 I shall try to explain why.

Virtually all arguments against reductionism, if they are not just confusions about what intertheoretic reduction is, depend on the designation of some aspect of our commonsense framework as correct and irreducible. Accordingly, the discussion of the soundness of these arguments must focus on that commonsense framework, its relation to scientific psychology, and its epistemological status. In this section I want to establish something that is of pivotal significance to later arguments—namely, the *correctability* of commonsense understanding of mental states and processes. In chapters 8 and 9 I shall extend that claim further by arguing that both the defining categories and the fundamental generalizations of our commonsense framework should be improved upon; that is, in all likelihood they ought to be revised. The theme of the co-evolution of scientific theories will be the background unification of all my arguments.

What Is Folk Psychology?
So far I have referred to our "commonsense framework for understanding mental states and processes" without being very precise about what is meant. For brevity's sake, I shall begin by replacing that long-winded description with a shorter label, namely "folk psychology." Now by folk psychology I mean that rough-hewn set of concepts, generalizations, and rules of thumb we all standardly use in explaining and predicting human behavior. Folk psychology is commonsense psychology—the psychological lore in virtue of which we explain behavior as the outcome of beliefs, desires, perceptions, expectations, goals, sensations, and so forth. It is a theory whose generalizations connect mental states to other mental states, to perceptions, and to actions. These homey generalizations are what provide the characterization of the mental states and processes referred to; they are what delimit the "facts" of mental life and define the explananda. Folk psychology is "intuitive psychology," and it shapes our conceptions of ourselves. As philosophers have analyzed it, the preeminent elements in folk psychological explanations of behavior include the concepts of *belief* and *desire*. Other elements will of course figure in, but these two are crucial and indispensable.

As an example of how the theory is put to work, we may start with a very simple case in which we need to explain why John flipped on the light switch:

> (1) "He wanted to see if his copy of *Middlemarch* was on his desk, he believed that the best way to find out was to turn on the light and look, he believed that in order to turn on the light he had to flip on the light switch, so he flipped on the light switch."

Ordinarily, it is not necessary to make so much explicit—indeed, it would be ludicrously pedantic to do so—and successful explanation can be highly elliptical. Depending on the situation, "He wanted to see if his copy of *Middlemarch* was on his desk" will frequently do, because all the rest can be left understood. The "fill" is not unnecessary; it is just so obvious that we can take it for granted. Two people who know each other very well may leave so much unspoken that it is hard for another to follow (see for example the dialogue in John Fowles's *Daniel Martin*). Sometimes, though, with small children or with someone unfamiliar with the culture, a greater degree of explicitness is required. Not even the explanation (1) is maximally explicit, however, for explanations require generalizations, and its generalizations are in the wings. Unspoken ("understood") generalizations do indeed serve in the background here, though they are sufficiently familiar and obvious that they are made explicit only on special occasions. One such generalization, albeit a low-level specimen, is this:

> (2) "Whenever a person wants to bring about a state *s, and* he believes that his doing *p* is a way to bring about *s, and* he believes that he can do *p, and* he can do *p*, then, barring conflicting desires or preferred strategies, he will do *p*."

Like the generalizations asserting a regularity between copper's being heated and its expanding, or between spinal injury and hyper-reflexivity, this generalization purports to describe a regularity in nature. Something rather like it seems to function in the routine reasoning about why persons behave as they do. Whether the generalization is accurate and whether it should be improved upon are not at issue here. The central point is that background generalizations, sometimes with a home-brewy lack of subtlety, figure in our day-to-day explanations of human behavior. Insofar as it enables us to make sense of and explain a certain range of phenomena, folk psychology resembles the folk physics discussed in section 7.2.

The network of generalizations of folk psychology appears to be extremely rich and complicated, and undoubtedly there are variations between the theoretical networks of diverse individuals. Henry James surely employed a more sophisticated psychological theory than Er-

nest Hemingway, though presumably they shared many general beliefs about why humans behave as they do. One way to begin to limn
the generalizations that figure in the commonsense theory of human
behavior is to press for expansions of action explanations in order to
force the implicit and "understood" background assumptions into
the open. This is similar to the method used to limn folk physics. For
example, many people thought that Richard Nixon knew about the
cover-up of the Watergate break-in. Why? Because, it will be said, he
was in the room when it was discussed. Why is that relevant?
Crudely, because if someone x has normal hearing, and someone else
y says "p" in a normal speaking voice in x's vicinity, and x knows the
language, then x hears that p. Similarly, we may conclude that a
person was lying because he must have seen the body (anyone with
normal vision, in broad daylight, standing two feet away would
have), that someone did believe that there was money in the safe
(why else did he break in and jimmy the lock), and so forth. Fodor
(1981) suggests other instances: "seeing that a is F is a normal cause of
believing that a is F; statements that p are normally caused by beliefs
that p; the belief that a thing is red is a normal cause of the inference
that the thing is colored..." (p. 25) (For more discussion on the background generalizations, see Paul M. Churchland 1970, 1979.)

Those who find these generalizations to have an excessively cracker-barrel flavor should recall that they are up for discussion precisely
so that antireductionist arguments citing the essential correctness of
folk psychology can be addressed. Admittedly, the generalizations do
have a cracker-barrel quality, but this is characteristic of folk theory
generally, and it does not in the least imply that they are simple-
minded. On the contrary, however folkish it is, folk psychology as a
framework of understanding is very complex. Moreover, folk psychology is where scientific psychology began, and if scientific psychology is to revise and improve upon folk psychology, it must know
what that framework consists of and whether and to what extent it
can be revised.

The insight that our psychological concepts are nodes in a background theory and that our explanations of human action proceed
within the framework of that theory is owed mainly to Sellars (1963)
and Feyerabend (1963b,c). It is an insight that has profoundly influenced research in the philosophy of mind. Together with the related work in epistemology and philosophy of science, the "theory"
theory of our commonsense beliefs about the mind has engendered
new understanding of the nature of mental concepts and rendered
tractable some baffling traditional questions, some of which pertain to
reduction.[3] Before discussing how these insights can help in confront-

ing the question of reduction and the mind-body problem, certain preliminary issues should be addressed.

The Origins of Folk Theory

One query to be raised about the Sellars-Feyerabend thesis is this: How do persons come by the folk theory? And where did it come from in the first place? Apparently, we do not learn folk psychology in the way we learn Newtonian theory or molecular genetics, nor do we typically make conscious or labored use of folk psychology generalizations.

Some of the theory may be acquired as we learn the language, and some of it may be acquired in a nonchalant and unreflective way as part of growing up among conspecifics. Some of it may indeed involve explicit instruction of old saws ("The bearer of bad news may be himself the object of dislike," "People don't like show-offs"), and some of it may involve imparting rather more recent information ("Pupil size of the person one is looking at affects beliefs about how friendly the person is"). The etiology of an individual's possession of a folk psychology is probably much like the etiology of his possession of a folk physics, and folk thermodynamics, and so forth. For all we can tell now, the mind-brain may have an innate disposition to favor and "grow" the rudiments of certain folk theories, including folk psychology and folk physics.

As to where the theory came from, certainly the image of a *homo habilis* Newton squatting at the cave mouth, pondering how to explain human behavior and finally sketching out the basics of folk psychology with jawbone and berry juice, is not very plausible. The ancestry of folk physics, folk thermodynamics, and folk theory of matter is similarly clouded in the mists of the far distant past, and a jawbone and berry juice theory is not plausible for any of them.

Sellars tells a kind of "just-so" story in which a primitive people begin to fashion a folk psychology by postulating inner states characterized on the model of overt speech. The folk discover it useful in certain conditions to say that someone is in a state analogous to the state he is in when he says out loud, "There is a rabbit." Thus, they come to attribute covert or inner speech states to each other, and thereby they come to attribute *thoughts* to each other. But this story was designed not so much to be anthropologically reasonable as to emphasize a logical point. Sellars's thesis was that beliefs and desires are *beliefs that p* and *desires that p*, and hence that the logic of such expressions is importantly related to the logic of overt utterances of "*p*."[4]

In order to characterize folk psychology, folk physics, and all the rest as theories, what is important is not that they originated in self-conscious construction, but that in their explanatory and predictive role *they function as theories*. In this respect, folk psychology and folk physics deserve to be called theories. Although it would be satisfying to know the origins of commonsense lore and to know how any individual comes to have the lore he has, our ignorance on these matters in no way impugns the claim that the lore should be considered a theory in the defined sense. For that claim concerns the epistemological status and function of the lore, not its origins.

Folk Theory and Rationality
Propositional attitudes are those mental states whose identity depends on a *proposition* specifying the content. If Jones has the belief that hawks eat mice, then the proposition "Hawks eat mice" specifies the content or "object" of his belief—in other words, it specifies what his belief *is*. Additionally, Jones might *be afraid* that hawks eat mice or *hope* that hawks eat mice, or *expect* or *wish* or *wonder whether* hawks eat mice, and in each case it is the proposition "Hawks eat mice" that defines the *content* of the propositional attitude. (Pains, tickles, and itches, by contrast, are not propositional attitudes.) We can chart the logical relations between propositional attitudes in virtue of the logical relations that obtain between the content sentences. Jones's belief that hawks eat mice and his belief that Leonard is a hawk entail his belief that Leonard eats mice. And so on.

Much dwelt upon is the observation that explanations of human behavior proceed by showing how the behavior was rational in the light of the subject's beliefs and desires, where it is the content of the beliefs and desires that make rational sense of the behavior. For example, Smith might say his reason for butchering the calves was that the cost of feed was increasing and that the price of beef cattle was declining. Smith's private deliberations must have gone something like this: "The cost of feed is increasing, the beef cattle market is declining, if I want to make a profit—and I do—my outlay must not exceed my income, therefore I should butcher the calves now." Replace "The cost of feed is increasing" with "I could never prove Fermat's last theorem," and the decision to butcher the calves is no longer reasonable in light of the contents of the mental states.

The point is, there is a "rational-in-the-light-of" relation between the contents of the mental states and the content of the decision, and some philosophers have wished to argue that this distinguishes *absolutely* explanations of intentional action from explanations in physics, biology, and other branches of science. According to this view, even if psychological explanations conform to the deductive-nomological pattern, it is not the deductive relation obtaining between the covering laws, initial conditions, and the explanandum that is important; rather, it is the internal, rational-in-the-light-of relations between the contents of mental states that do the explanatory work.

In particular, this special relation has been cited as grounds for rejecting the claim that explanations within folk psychology are causal explanations and that the generalizations of folk psychology are causal-explanatory. On the contrary, it has been argued, the generalizations are not causal, and the style of explanation in which they have a role is uniquely rational as opposed to causal. (See for example Dray 1963.) What produces human behavior, it is said, are reasons, not causes, and we understand behavior in virtue of finding a suitable *rationale*, not in virtue of finding *causal conditions.* And this has sometimes functioned as the basis for antireductionist arguments.

The observation that in explanations of human behavior a rationality relation connects statements about beliefs and desires with statements about behavior is entirely correct. What is mistaken is the inference that beliefs and desires therefore do not cause behavior. More generally, it is false that the existence of a rational relation between statements characterizing events precludes, or is somehow at loggerheads with, a causal connection between the events. This can be straightforwardly seen in a computer executing a deductive logic program, where the states the computer runs through are related by logic *and* by cause. Indeed, the program is precisely designed so that when certain causal relations obtain between machine states, then the appropriate logical relations also obtain between statements describing those states.

This existence of abstract or formal relations defined over contents or objects of "attitudes" is not, moreover, a feature unique to psychology. Ironically, it is in fact a point of deep similarity between psychological laws and laws elsewhere in science. There are laws containing numerical attitudes, between which arithmetical relations hold; laws containing vectorial attitudes, between which algebraic relations hold; and so forth. Once noticed, this parallel is striking, and it speaks for, rather than against, the similarity between folk psychology and other theories in the sciences. (See Paul M. Churchland 1970, 1979, 1981.) Consider the following:

Numerical Attitudes	*Propositional Attitudes*
x . . . has a mass$_{kg}$ of n	. . . believes that p
. . . has a charge$_{coul}$ of n	. . . desires that p
. . . has a temperature$_K$ of n	. . . perceives that p

. . . has energy$_i$ of n . . . hopes that p
   etc.   etc.

Not only is there a parallel with respect to attitudes identified via abstract objects (propositions and numbers); there is also a parallel in the laws that specify the abstract relations (logical and numerical) that obtain between distinct states. Recall the generalizations with which this section began and compare, for example, the following:

9. If a body x has a mass m, and if x suffers a net force of f, then x accelerates at f/m.
10. If a gas has a pressure P, and a volume V, and a quantity m, then barring very high pressure or density, it has a temperature of PV/mR, where R is the gas constant.

What I have wished to emphasize here is that there is nothing especially mentalistic, mystical, or noncausal about generalizations that exploit abstract relations between abstract objects. Generalizations in folk psychology do it, but so do generalizations in physics and chemistry. The existence of "rational-in-the-light-of" relations between objects of propositional attitudes fails to imply that psychological explanations are noncausal explanations. (See also chapter 9.)

Finally, it should be observed that propositions and the logical relations defined over them constitute an impressively powerful structure, and insofar as folk psychology exploits propositions as its domain of abstract objects, it inherits the power of that structure. That is, it inherits *as part of psychology* that systematicity which is inherent in the logical system of propositions. (See Fodor 1975.) It is this insight, made the more appealing by the discoveries of modern logic and by the construction of electronic devices conforming to logic, that has engendered a certain "logicist" conception of the mind. On this conception, the mind is fundamentally a sentential computing device, taking sentences as input from sensory transducers, performing logical operations on them, and issuing other sentences as output.

Folk Theory and Self-Knowledge
The hypothesis that we operate with a folk psychology in virtue of which we attribute psychological states to others and to ourselves may be resisted because the attribution to *ourselves* seems directly observational, without any mediating framework of categories and concepts. The attribution of beliefs and perceptions to others may be mediated by theory and inference, it may be argued, but surely one has direct and unmediated awareness of one's own mental states. No

theory is invoked, and none needed, to recognize what mental states one has. Or so it seems.

The impression of immediacy cannot, however, be taken at face value. To begin with, knowledge of the external world can seem quite as direct and immediate as knowledge of one's inner states. When I look out my window, it seems I immediately see a tree, and immediately see that it is larger than my computer, though I am unaware of deliberate classification or ponderous inferring—or even of lightning-fast inferring, for that matter. So far as data from introspection are concerned, I simply see a tree. Sometimes, to be sure, I have to undertake a bit of reasoning if I am puzzled about what I see, but correlatively, sometimes I undertake a bit of reasoning to determine what I really want or whether my current feeling of unease is embarrassment, anger, or frustration.

As far as the sheer impression of immediacy is concerned, outer perceptions seem as immediate as inner perceptions. But failure to introspect evidence of cognitive engagement of a conceptual framework does not imply that no conceptual framework is engaged. In the case of perception of the external world we certainly do not take introspection's impression of immediacy to be correct. Complex information processing, pattern recognition, and conceptualizing certainly underlie ostensibly simple and "direct" perceptual judgments. Consider for example a perceptual effect such as size constancy, in which the visual impression of a tree will be seen as larger than the visual impression of one's thumb, even though the latter occupies a larger area of the visual field. The perceptual judgment is as immediate as anything can be, inasmuch as there is no awareness of a period of calculation and reasoning. Nevertheless, the information processing enabling the judgment is likely to be subtle and complex.

Part of the trouble in addressing the "immediacy" objection is simply that it is hard to know what "immediate" is supposed to mean here. If it means "not mediated by subcognitive processes," the thesis is obviously mistaken. If it means "not mediated by cognitive processes," it is just as surely mistaken. If someone asks "Would you like to fly a hang-glider?", and Jones ponders a bit and says "Yes," then from what we already know in neurobiology and psychology, we can take it as read that a highly orchestrated sequence of complex mind-brain processes made it possible for Jones to tell us what he desires.

The intuition that recognition of mental states is somehow sheerly observational and free of cognitive interpretation must eventually confront the arguments considered earlier that undermined the logical empiricist conception of observation. The upshot of those arguments (see section 6.4) was that there is no independent observation language; that all observation terms are nodes in a conceptual framework and thus are interlaced with other observation terms and with theoretical terms; that all observation terms derive at least some of their meaning from the generalizations that embed them (Hesse 1970, Paul M. Churchland 1979). The observation predicates used in the recognition of inner states are no less interconnected with theory than the observation predicates used to describe the external world. Learning to apply mental predicates crucially involves learning appropriate generalizations that specify the conditions of correct application.

Just as learning the word "dog" involves learning generalizations about dogs, so learning words such as "is in pain" involves learning such things as that hunger, a bang on the thumb with a hammer, holding a snowball in bare hands for a long time, having one's hair pulled, eating too much candy, and sustaining a cut all cause pains; similarly for such expressions as "is anxious," "wants that p," "is frustrated," "likes a," and "believes that p." These generalizations are cut from fustian stuff, but the claim is not that they are *true* generalizations of folk psychology, but just that they *are* generalizations of folk psychology, and it is in virtue of such generalizations that the embedded categories are implicitly defined. Whether these generalizations are true, or grossly misconceived, or in need of major modification or minor fine tuning, are distinct questions.

Notice too that the conditions of application are really very diverse and that the felt sensations can be very different and yet still be called pain (Churchland and Churchland 1981). Certainly there is a learned component in the recognition of mental states, though presumably there is an innate mechanism for such learning. Awareness of inner states is a species of perception that is directed internally rather than externally, and the observational predicates employed in recognition of mental states enjoy no special status. Moreover, what may be a predicate applied by ponderous inference at one stage of life (e.g., the predicate "feeling intellectual satisfaction") may subsequently come to be routinely used and thus without studied application of the rules.

A traditional reason for supposing that introspective apprehension is unique derived from the epistemological enthusiasm for bedrock foundations to support the structure of knowledge, and it depended on the assumption that one could not err in recognition of one's own mental states. By contrast, error in perceiving the external world or in attributing mental states to others was considered commonplace. Now even supposing it were true that "inner sense" does not in fact err, notice that it does not follow that no theory (no categorial framework) is employed. The remarkable accuracy could be owed to a remarkably accurate application of a true theory in inner perception. But the traditional view wanted more, and hence it was argued that one *could not* be wrong—not merely that one mercifully, but contingently, escaped error. If we could not be wrong, that allegedly would be evidence for immediacy and directness.

The trouble is that we can be wrong and often are. Sometimes behavior is the outcome of desires we explicitly disavow or beliefs we explicitly deny. Even when the conditions are in no way pathological, we sometimes mistake the causes of our choices and judgments and misidentify the assorted influences on our behavior (Nisbett and Ross 1980, Gazzaniga and LeDoux 1978). A sensation of extreme cold can be mistaken for a sensation of heat, a dreamed pain can be seen to be unreal upon awakening, and in general expectation effects can induce errors in the perception of our mental states (Paul M. Churchland 1985).

Even though we may be understood to apprehend inner states such as beliefs and desires within the confines of a categorial framework, and even though it is agreed that we can err in the application of the categories of that framework, nevertheless it may be supposed that awareness itself is what is immediately apprehended, and hence apprehended without benefit of a categorial framework. Moreover, it may seem that in the phenomenon of awareness, those with enthusiasm for absolute foundations will have found what they seek. For it may seem that we cannot be mistaken that we are aware. This may be supposed to be the Cartesian corker that shows that some domain of our mental life is immediately and incorrigibly apprehended.

There has long been much ado about Descartes's argument and what it implies with regard to the self and self-knowledge. After seeing the possibility of doubting the truth of most of his beliefs about the world, Descartes found a case that he took to be immune to reasonable doubt. Paraphrasing, he said, "I cannot reasonably doubt that I think—that I am aware." Thus Descartes's memorable conclusion: "I think, therefore I am" (Cogito ergo sum). Now the issue in this section concerns whether one understands the mental states of oneself and others within a theoretical framework. For this issue, what is important is that the Cartesian argument fails to show that our inner goings-on are directly and immediately presented to us. It fails to show that no categorial framework or theory is employed in the application of predicates to one's own mental states.

Here's why. The first point is a reiteration of the earlier observation: awareness, whatever its neurobiological identity, is bound to be the outcome of much processing and brain activity. This is uncontentious.[5] Second, if cognitive categories figure in that processing, that is sufficient for my purposes. Given a suitably liberal reading of "cognitive," knowing that one is aware involves cognitive use of the concept of awareness. This is surely quite as uncontentious.[6] Third, it is compatible with the Cartesian argument that the relevant theoretical framework and the mechanisms for its application are such that whenever the brain goes into a state with the content "I am aware," it is always true that one is aware. But this will only be a matter of contingent fact about the way the brain works, not a necessary fact drawn from a priori philosophy.

Alternatively, for all we know now, it may happen that one's brain does sometimes go into a state with the content "I am aware" when it is false that one is aware, perhaps, for example, when the brain is in certain kinds of coma. Such might even be the stock response of the brain to sudden severe trauma. I certainly do not know that this never happens or never could happen. Intuitions consulted from the comfort of the armchair may be quite misleading concerning the nature of the empirical facts, here as elsewhere. From the armchair, it might have seemed to be safe to assume that if one is blind one cannot fail to be aware that one is blind or that if one makes accurate perceptual judgments about the world one must be perceptually aware. Yet, as we have seen (section 5.6) the assumptions seem to be false given the neurological data. The armchair hypotheses should present themselves as hypotheses open to evidence from the world, not as hidebound and unassailable truths of reason.

Here is a deeper reason for pausing: it is possible that the folk theory that gives "awareness" its meaning might turn out to be displaced by a superior theory. Accordingly, just as it turned out that there was no such thing as impetus, there may be no such thing as awareness. This is not as bizarre as it first sounds. Presumably there is *some* monitoring mechanism or other chugging away in the mind-brain in virtue of which our current employment of the concept "awareness" can get a foothold—just as there is something or other going on in the world in virtue of which the employment of the concept "impetus" got a foothold. But we may misapprehend it, folk psychology may be a thoroughly muddled theory of mental business, and a newer and better theory may yield a theoretically more satisfactory characterization of it. What is *it*? Well, whatever it is that we now, perhaps mistakenly, characterize as awareness, which some future theory may characterize in a quite different way.

In summary, introspective capacities do not appear to be incompatible with the "theory" theory of our commonsense understanding of mental life. On the contrary, one's apprehension of one's own mental states is a cognitive process that at some level exploits a conceptual framework. The nature of that process, the degrees of plasticity it may have, and the nature of the representations and their role in that process remain to be empirically discovered by cognitive neurobiology. Moreover, the notion of a conceptual or theoretical framework is still only roughly delimited and will itself need to be revised, extended, or perhaps eventually displaced, by cognitive neurobiology. I view the "theory" theory as a provisional conception that enables us to disentangle ourselves from a confining epistemology and a confining philosophy of mind. As neuroscience and scientific psychology collectively come to understand more about the nature of information processing, so we shall come to understand what theorizing is, and our inchoate conceptions will mature. Ultimately, to invoke again Neurath's metaphor, this plank in our boat will itself be changed. This is not a philosophical flaw in the "theory" theory; it is just a frank acknowledgment that we do not understand much at all about what it is for a brain to theorize.

Folk Psychology and a Nonphysical Mind
Finally, it may be argued against the "theory" theory of mental predicates that if mental states are states of a nonphysical mind, then our access to them must be direct rather than theory-mediated. The argument is simply a non sequitur. Even if the mind should be nonphysical, its access to its states and processes may be via a theory, and it may have lots of nonconscious mental reasoning and processing and lots of nonconscious beliefs and desires. Moreover, even the nonphysical mind may make mistakes and have false theories, one of which may be about its own states and how they interact. Nonphysicalness in and of itself implies nothing about immediacy, directness, and privileged access. The ontological question about what sort of substance the mind is must be distinguished from the epistemological question concerning how the mind knows itself.

7.4 Conclusions

Intertheoretic reduction is fundamentally a relation between theories, such that one theory T_1 is said to reduce to another theory T_2 if T_1 (or an analogue of it) is deducible from T_2. One phenomenon P_1 is said to reduce to another P_2 if the theory that characterizes P_1 reduces to a theory that characterizes P_2. Reductions in science are only rarely smooth reductions with uncomplicated cross-theoretical identifications. More typically, they are bumpy and thus involve varying degrees of revision to the reduced science. Sometimes the correction required is so massive that the candidate theory is better described as having been displaced outright.

Accordingly, neuroscientists should not at this stage of their inquiries feel compelled to envision the details of a future reduction of folk psychological generalizations, nor should they suppose themselves obliged to seek identifications between neurobiological states and psychological states *as characterized within folk psychology*. Identifications may be forthcoming, but then again they may not. Whether they are is an *empirical* matter, not an *a priori* matter. The crucial point is that identities are not required for reductions at a remove from the retentive end of the spectrum. So unless neuroscientists can tell in advance that they will not find any reason either to revise or to displace folk psychology, they are not honor bound to design their research to turn up such identities.

The objections to the reductionist program that envisions a unified theory of the mind-brain, in which psychological theory is ultimately explained by neurobiological theory, derive from two sources: (1) from a conviction that a subset of generalizations in scientific psychology are of such a nature as to resist reduction, and (2) from a conviction that folk psychology is both substantially correct and essentially irreducible to neurobiology. The generalizations in scientific psychology that are thought to be problematic are typically in the domains of cognitive psychology and social psychology and make reference to beliefs, inferences, or, in general, propositional representations. Insofar as these problematic generalizations rely on a theory of representations drawn from folk psychology, these two patterns of objection have a common element.

Although folk psychology has a profound familiarity and obviousness, and although the categories of folk psychology are observationally applied, it nevertheless remains true that folk psychology is a theoretical framework and hence a framework whose adequacy can be questioned and assessed. The adequacy of folk psychology is in no way secured by its seeming to be overwhelmingly obvious, by its being observationally applied, by its being applied introspectively, or even by its being innate, if such be the case. If we see that folk psychology has no right to epistemological privilege, and no immunity to revision and correction, then we can begin to see that its generalizations and categories can be corrected and improved upon. Indeed, an underlying theme in scientific psychology is that they can and are being modified and even superseded.

Once it is recognized that folk psychology is not immune to scientific improvement, this reveals the possibility that what will eventually reduce to neuroscience are generalizations of scientific psychology that have evolved a long way from the home "truths" of extant folk psychology. Moreover, as I shall argue in chapters 8 and 9, these generalizations will likely to be the product of a long co-evolution with neurobiology. What may eventually transpire, therefore, is a reduction of the evolved psychological theory, and this evolved theory may end up looking radically different from folk psychology—different even in its *categorial* profile. In other words, the psychological generalizations that are eventually considered ripe for reduction may be both richer and substantially revised relative to current generalizations in folk psychology. If that is the direction taken by the co-evolution of psychology and neuroscience, future historians of science will see folk psychology as having been largely displaced rather than smoothly reduced to neurobiology.

I have not argued that this will be the fate of folk psychology, but only that once we have seen that folk psychology has no more epistemological privilege than folk physics, that the categorial structure of folk psychology has no more sanctity and a priori consecration than that of folk physics, we can rid ourselves of a huge weight of argument that tempts us by appeal to the obviousness and the certain inviolability of folk psychology.

It must now be determined whether the two lines of argument against the reductionist program can show what is both irreducible and correct about folk psychology. It will not be sufficient for these arguments to defend just irreducibility, since irreducibility in a theory can be owed to its being so radically amiss that wholesale displacement is exactly what it deserves. Assuming that this chapter has established that folk psychology is assessable for its empirical adequacy and improvable by empirical research if found wanting, it will also not be enough for these arguments simply to point to a category's being observationally applied or seeming to be obvious. So much is entirely compatible with the inadequacy and falsity of a theory. Nor, of course, can the arguments quietly help themselves to assumptions about the correctness of the generalizations and categories. The focus of chapter 8 will be a set of arguments pertaining to the nature of our subjective experiences, and chapter 9 will examine and evaluate the arguments based on the theory of the nature of representations.

Selected Readings

Churchland, Paul M. (1979). *Scientific realism and the plasticity of mind*. Cambridge: Cambridge University Press.

Feyerabend, Paul K. (1981). *Philosophical papers*. Vols. 1 and 2. Cambridge: Cambridge University Press.

Hooker, C. A. (1981). Towards a general theory of reduction. Part I: Historical and scientific setting. Part II: Identity in reduction. Part III: Cross-categorial reduction. *Dialogue* 20:38–59, 201–236, 496–529.

Kuhn, Thomas S. (1962). *The structure of scientific revolutions*. 2nd ed. (1970). Chicago: University of Chicago Press.

Wimsatt, William (1976). Reductive explanation: a functional account. In *PSA 1974* (Proceedings of the Philosophy of Science Association), ed. R. S. Cohen, C. A. Hooker, A. C. Michalos, and J. W. van Evra, 671–710. Dordrecht, Holland: D. Reidel.

Chapter 8

Are Mental States Irreducible to Neurobiological States?

We are deceived at every level by our introspection.
F. H. C. Crick, 1979

8.1 Introduction

There are researchers in psychology, neuroscience, philosophy, and other fields who have concluded that no unified theory of how the mind-brain works will ever be devised and that at least some psychological phenomena are forever beyond the reductive reach of neuroscience. And some of these opinions survive the clarifying effect of the account of reduction presented in chapter 7. Study of brains is all very well, it may be allowed, but even in the long run it will not explain much of significance concerning how we learn, remember, speak, solve problems, and so on. Subjective experience, consciousness, reasoning, and even visual illusions are sometimes argued to be forever beyond the explanatory reach of neuroscience, regardless of unforeseen breakthroughs and surprising discoveries. No single reason rallies those who reject the possibility of a reduction, and there is little unity among the skeptics concerning why a reduction is impossible. Rather, there is a spectrum of arguments, some of which are deeply perplexing, others of which are less arguments than loving expressions of which intuitions one has vowed to shelter, come what may.

In this chapter and the next I want to examine those arguments that seem especially persuasive or challenging, in order to determine whether the skeptics are right. At the outset it is necessary to distinguish two very general patterns of argument. Arguments in the first class are advanced by those I refer to as "boggled skeptics," who say essentially that the brain is so horrendously complicated—there are too many neurons and too many connections—that the hope of understanding it is but a pipe dream. In all likelihood, the boggled skeptic laments, the human brain is more complicated than it is smart, and hence neuroscience cannot hope, even in the long run, to fathom the mysteries of how it works. Arguments in the second general class are advanced by those who find principled reasons for skepticism, deriving for example from the nature of subjective experience or from the fact that some mental states have meaning and significance. Those who advance arguments of this type I call "principled skeptics." (See also Patricia S. Churchland 1980a.)

The boggled skeptic may, of course, be right in his prediction. Notice though that what he advances *is* a prediction, and one that concerns the nature of the empirical world and whether, as a matter of empirical fact, our brains are smart enough to invent an adequate theory to explain certain empirical phenomena. Whether the boggled skeptic is correct is an empirical matter, and so far at least there is no empirical evidence to justify his gloomy prediction. So far as we can tell now, the human brain might be more smart than it is complicated.

That neuroscience is hard does not imply that it is impossible, and from the standpoint of ignorance it is rash to claim what *cannot* be known. Science and technology have frequently confounded prophecies concerning what could never be known or done. Problems unsolved by one researcher with one set of techniques and theories may be solved by another researcher with other techniques and theories. Does the boggled skeptic claim to know when an unsolved problem in neuroscience is also unsolvable for neuroscience? Improved technical means for investigating the brain have made possible in the last two decades research and results that would have dumbfounded earlier researchers. There is no predicting either what new techniques might show or what new theories might discover, and in this respect progress in neuroscience is as unpredictable as progress in any other science. If the practical implication of the boggled skeptic's reservation is that neuroscience might as well call it quits, then surely that would be an error. Even should there be impenetrable walls ahead, it is too soon to say that neuroscience has gone about as far as it can go. Beyond these few remarks, I will not directly discuss the case of the boggled skeptic, for the book as a whole constitutes an indirect invitation to him to reconsider his pessimistic forecast.

The arguments that I class together as defending *principled skepticism* are very diverse indeed, but they fall into roughly two—antagonistic—groups. The first orients itself around the view that there is a distinctive mental dimension that is not reducible to anything physical. Within this view there is a further division over whether this mental dimension actually harbors a separate mental *substance* such as the nonphysical mind or the soul ("substance dualism") or whether it is limited to nonphysical *properties* of the physical brain ("property dualism"). There are many variations on the basic theme, most of which are dismally muddled, but the dominant motivation concerns two aspects of mental life: subjective experience and the logical nature of thinking, reasoning, understanding, and so forth. Substance dualism and property dualism are perhaps the most familiar if not the most cogent of the antireductionist reservations, and the best of these arguments certainly jell the most common lay suspicion about reductionism. Dualism in its most plausible forms will be the focus of discussion in this chapter.

The second pattern of arguments defending a principled skepticism of reductionism has a slightly different basis. Here the orienting point is the hypothesis that the generalizations of psychology are *emergent* with respect to the generalizations of neuroscience and that mental states and processes constitute a domain of study *autonomous* with respect to neuroscience. At the same time, however, dualism is roundly rejected, and problems concerning consciousness and subjective experience tend to be put on the back burner. Despite its explicit rebuff to the dualists, this general position nevertheless shares with dualism a dominant motivation that fixes on the presumed logical nature of reasoning, understanding, problem solving, and so forth. Following the inspiration of the logical empiricists, proponents of this view model cognition on the sentential-logical structure of modern logic, such that representations are more or less sentence-like and computations are more or less logic-like. But cognition modeled as a *logical* business appears to be unexplainable in terms of the *causal* business in the underlying neuronal structure. Hence the claim for the emergence of generalizations and the autonomy of research. It is this second view that finds sympathy from most contemporary philosophers and psychologists who have antireductionist sentiments. The arguments in its support are broadly construed as *functionalist* in nature, and they will be discussed in detail in chapter 9.

8.2 Substance Dualism

One line of resistance to a program aimed at reducing psychological theory to neuroscience is taken by those who deny that the mind is identical with the brain and who conceive of the mind instead as a nonphysical substance. Their hypothesis is that mental states such as perceptions, thoughts, feelings, and sensations are states, not of the brain, but of a different substance altogether. This substance is characterized as independent of the body inasmuch as it allegedly survives the brain's disintegration, though it is considered to interact causally with the brain when the latter is intact.

On this hypothesis, no reduction of psychological theory to neuroscientific theory is forthcoming because the former is a theory about the states and processes of mind-substance, whereas the latter is a theory about the states and processes of a material substance, the brain. Each substance is thought to have its own laws and its own range of properties, hence research on the brain is not going to yield knowledge of the mind and its dynamics, nor, by parity of reasoning, will research on the mind tell us anything much about how the brain works.

What is the evidence for the hypothesis that minds are nonphysical substances in which mental states such as beliefs, desires, and sensations inhere? Descartes was particularly impressed by the human capacity for reasoning and for language, and though he was a keen mechanist, he simply could not imagine how a mechanical device could be designed so as to follow rules of reasoning and to use language creatively. What sort of mechanical devices were the paradigm that inspired Descartes's imagination? Clockwork machines and fountains. And though some were intricate indeed, by our standards even the most elaborate clockwork devices of the seventeenth century do not have a patch on modern symbol-manipulating machines that can perform such tasks as guiding the flight path of a cruise missile or regulating the activities of a spacecraft on Mars. The advent of the modern computer has stolen much of the thunder of Descartes's argument that reasoning betokens a nonphysical substance (Dennett 1978b, 1986). Nevertheless, as we shall see in chapter 9, the theme that reasoning, the *meaningfulness* of sentences in reasoning, and the *logical* relations between sentences used in reasoning eludes an explanation in physicalist terms is taken up by contemporary philosophers as the basis for antireductionist arguments. The outward form of the contemporary arguments is new and clever, but the motivating intuitions are discernibly Cartesian.

An intractable problem confronting substance dualism concerns the nature of the interaction between the two radically different kinds of substance. Soul-stuff allegedly has none of the properties of material-stuff and is not spatially extended, and the question therefore concerns how and where the two substances interact. This problem stymied Descartes, and his completely inadequate solution was to suggest that the "animal spirits" functioned to mediate between the two types of substance and that the subtle interaction took place in the pineal gland. But his animal spirits were composed of material stuff, albeit very fine material stuff, so the problem stood its ground.

Can the mind be affected by, say, electrical or magnetic fields? For Descartes, apparently not, for then it would have properties in common with matter, and its status as a radically different substance would be imperiled.

On the classical picture, essentially two types of items were exchanged at the station where mind and brain interacted, wherever it was, and these were sensations and volitions. The brain was thought to send sensations to the mind, which could then use them in perception. The mind, on the other hand, was thought to send volitions to the brain, which could then translate the volitions into motor effects. The higher functions of the mind, including reasoning, consciousness, moral feelings, and the emotions, were assumed to function independently of the brain, save for the extent to which perceptions might figure in these functions. Perceptions were excepted because they were to some extent dependent on sensations. This independence of the higher mental operations from the physical business of the brain was really the raison d'être of the substance dualist hypothesis, for it was these mental functions that seemed utterly inexplicable in material terms. Given a life of their own in the nonphysical mind, reasoning and consciousness and their kind should be amenable to nonmaterial explanations, and getting these seemed far easier than getting brain-based explanations. We shall see this theme concerning reasoning and consciousness reappear in assorted guises in virtually every antireductionist argument, including those most recently minted.

The hypothesized independence of reasoning and consciousness that makes substance dualism attractive is at the same time a chronic and aggravating problem that costs it credibility. The difficulty is straightforward: reasoning, consciousness, moral feelings, religious feelings, political convictions, aesthetic judgments, moods, even one's deep-seated personality traits—all can be affected if the brain is affected by drugs or by lesions, for example. The more we know about neurology and about neuropharmacology, the more evident it is that the functions in question are not remotely as independent as the classical hypothesis asserts. On the materialist hypothesis, the observed interdependence is precisely what would be expected, but it is distinctly embarrassing to the dualist hypothesis.

Recent hypotheses meant to explain the nature of the interaction between the nonphysical mind and the physical brain are not significant improvements upon Descartes's proposal. Although Eccles (1977, Eccles and Robinson 1984) has energetically addressed the problem, his theory of the interaction remains metaphorical. His explanatory flow diagram consists essentially of many arrows connecting the "mind" box to the box for the language areas of the human brain. The question that persists after study of the array of arrows is this: what is the manner of interaction, and how does the nonphysical mind bring about changes of state in the brain, and vice versa? The inescapable conclusion is that the arrow-array is after all as much an explanatory surd as the notion of Descartes's animal spirits finely but mysteriously "affecting" the nonmaterial substance in the confines of the pineal gland.

The unavailability of a solution to the manner of interaction between two radically different substances does not entail that substance dualism is false. For all we know now, further research may yet discover a solution. But with no leads at all and not even any serious plans for finding a solution, it does mean that the hypothesis has diminished appeal. This failure invites the conjecture that the problems the hypothesis was designed to solve might in fact be pseudoproblems, and in this respect they might be similar to the now-discarded problems of how the heart concocts vital spirits or how the tiny homunculi in sperm can themselves contain tinier homunculi containing even tinier sperm containing yet more tiny homunculi. The phenomena, as we now know for these cases, were radically misdescribed, and the corresponding problems, therefore, did not exist to be solved.

Additional difficulties further diminish the plausibility of substance dualism, and one such problem is drawn from evolutionary biology. Assuming that humans evolved from earlier mammalian species, that we and the chimpanzees share a common ancestor, and that we can trace our lineage back to single-celled organisms, then a question arises about where the soul-stuff came from. Do all organisms have it? If some organisms do not have such a substance, how did the others come to have it? Could it have evolved from physical stuff? If humans alone have minds, where did these substances come from? A theologically based answer is that nonphysical minds, unlike physical brains, are not an evolutionary product but were for the first time placed in contact with brains by divine intervention some 80,000 years (or in some calculations merely 6,000 years) ago. Since then, apparently, there has been continual intervention by a supernatural being to invest each human brain with its own nonphysical mind.

The price of espousing substance dualism begins to look too high, for among other things it entails arbitrary and unmotivated exceptions to the plausible and unified story of the development of intelligence provided by modern evolutionary biology. On the other side of the ledger, the compensatory explanatory payoff from the hypothesis seems meager. If chimpanzees or monkeys do not have minds, then presumably their learning, perception, feeling, and problem solving are explained in terms of brain function. But if theirs, then why not ours? In the absence of solid evidence for the separate existence of the mind, the appeal of substance dualism fades.

The hypothesis of substance dualism is also supposed to explain the unity of consciousness (the unity of the self), and it is alleged that such unity cannot be explained on a materialist hypothesis (Eccles 1977). The reasoning here is less than convincing, both because it is far from clear what the phenomenon is that the hypothesis is meant to explain and because it is far from clear how the hypothesis succeeds in explaining this ill-specified phenomenon.

Consider first the phenomenon. Certain questions immediately arise: How do nonconscious mental states comport with alleged unity of consciousness? How does all that nonconscious processing postulated in cognitive science fit into the picture? How do the split-brain results fit? Or the blindsight results? Or the cases of split personality? What about when the brain is in slow-wave sleep or in REM sleep? The questions are far too numerous for unity of consciousness to be a phenomenon in clear and unproblematic focus.

In a previous publication (1983) I argued that consciousness, as it is circumscribed in folk psychology, probably is not a natural kind, in much the way that impetus is not a natural kind. Nor, for example, do the categories "gems" or "dirt" delimit a natural kind. That is to say, *something* is going on all right, but it is doubtful that the generalizations and categories of folk psychology either do justice to that phenomenon or carve Nature at her joints. The evidence already indicates that consciousness is not a single type of brain process, and that if we think of consciousness as a kind of light that is either on or off, and that when on illuminates the contents of mental life, we are hopelessly mistaken. We already know that so-called subliminal experiences can affect "conscious" problem solving. We know that one can engage in a number of highly complex activities at once, even though not "paying attention" to them all. We know that brain activity as measured on the EEG during some REM sleep looks more like brain activity during fully awake periods than during other sleep periods. We know that some subjects who are in fact blind apparently fail to be aware that they are blind. We know that some patients with temporal lobe damage can learn complex cognitive skills and yet be completely unaware that they have done so—even while engaged in one of those very skills. And so on and on.[1] The brain undoubtedly has a number of mechanisms for monitoring brain processes, and the folk psychological categories of "awareness" and "consciousness" indifferently lump together an assortment of the mechanisms. As

322   The Philosophy of Science

neurobiology and neuropsychology probe the mechanisms and functions of the brain, a reconfiguring of categories can be predicted.

The second question to be asked of the substance dualist concerns how his hypothesis explains the phenomenon, whatever that phenomenon is. How is it that the nonphysical mind yields unity of consciousness? How does it unify experiences occurring at different times? If the answer is that the nonphysical mind unifies because the experiences are experiences of *one* substance, then that answer is also available to the materialist, who can say that the experiences are experiences of *one* brain. If the answer is that it is simply in the nature of the nonphysical mind to be unified and to provide unity, then the sense that an *explanation* has been provided loses its hold. It is like saying, "It just does." Moreover, the materialist is entitled to make the same futile move: it is simply in the nature of the brain to provide unity to experiences. This is a standoff, and neither hypothesis advances our understanding. Therefore, the dualist cannot claim that his case is supported by his being able, and the materialist's being unable, to explain the unity of consciousness.

A parallel discussion can be constructed concerning nonphysical minds and free will. Here the dualist credits his hypothesis with the ability to explain how humans have free will. In this instance too, it is far from clear what the phenomenon is or how dualism explains anything about it. A dualist hypothesis claiming that the nonphysical mind acts freely because it is the nature of the mind to do so leaves us without explanatory nuts and bolts. And as before, for every move the dualist makes here, the physicalist has a counterpart move. Again the result is a standoff, and the dualist can claim no advantage. (For the best recent discussion of the free will issue, see Dennett 1984b.)

The two primary foci for the dualist's conviction are the logical-meaningful dimension of cognition and the qualities of consciousness. The importance of these matters has struck dualist philosophers in different ways, with the consequence that some have gravitated to one focus and some to the other. One group has taken the nature of felt experience as *the* difficulty of paramount importance and hence has tended to side with materialists on the other question. That is, they expect that eventually the logical-meaningful dimension will ultimately have a causal neurobiological explanation. For these philosophers reasoning is not the stumbling block, partly because the idea that the logical-meaningful dimension of cognition is fundamentally noncausal is found objectionable. The second group has just the converse set of intuitions. Like reductionists, they think that ultimately consciousness and the qualities of felt experience will be explained in neurobiological terms. But for them, *the* difficulty of paramount importance lies in the logical-meaningful dimension of cognition. Here, they argue, are insurmountable problems for a reductionist strategy.[2] The reductionist has been useful to both camps by providing reductionist arguments for each to use against the other.

These dualist intuitions can be respectably sustained despite the hopeless problems of substance dualism in finding a coherent fit for the mind-substance in modern physics and biology. The general strategy in support of these intuitions has been to abandon the albatross idea of a distinct *substance* but to retain the idea of irreducibility. Thus, philosophers concerned with subjective experience have argued that subjective experience is an irreducible *property*, and philosophers concerned with the logical-meaningful dimension have argued for the irreducibility of cognitive *theory*. It is among these two, albeit inharmonious, groups that the most sophisticated antireductionist arguments are to be found, and characteristically they are not to be removed by a few casual rejoinders.

The next section will examine those arguments deriving from the nature of subjective experience, consciousness, and the like. Section 8.4 will then examine the second group of arguments, namely those that see the logical-meaningful aspect of mental life as noncausal and hence not amenable to neurobiological explanation.

8.3   Property Dualism and Subjective Experience

The nature of subjective experience has seemed to many people so striking and so extraordinary that it has been invoked repeatedly as the standing refutation of reductionism. The argument from subjective experience has been most powerful, not in the hands of the substance dualists, who have to contend with complications of their ghostly substance, but in the hands of the property dualists. Although there are nontrivial differences among the hypotheses advanced by assorted property dualists, the crux of the shared conviction is that even if the mind is the brain, the qualities of subjective experience are nevertheless emergent with respect to the brain and its properties. Subjective experience, goes the argument, has a character and a quality uniquely and irreducibly mental.

Since the notion of a property's being emergent makes an appearance in this argument, an explication of "emergence" is in order. In general, whether a property is emergent is a function of the reductive relation that holds—or rather, *fails* to hold—between two theories or conceptual frameworks. More specifically, a property P specified by its embedding theory T_1 is *emergent* with respect to the properties of an ostensibly reducing theory T_2 just in case

1. P has real instances,
2. P is co-occurrent with some property or complex feature recognized in T_2, but nevertheless
3. P cannot be reduced to any property postulated by or definable within T (Paul M. Churchland 1985)

As noted in the account of intertheoretic reduction outlined in chapter 7, the reducibility of one property to another depends on whether the theory that characterizes the property at issue reduces to the theory that characterizes the other. To put the matter informally, if a property of one theory has causal powers that are not equaled or comprehended by any property in the second, more basic theory, then the property is considered to be emergent with respect to the second theory. Accordingly, to claim that the qualitative features displayed in one's subjective experience are emergent with respect to the physical brain is to insist that the commonsense conceptual framework for apprehending and describing such psychological properties is not reducible to any future neuroscience.

Whether a property is emergent is therefore not a simple observational feature of the property, and so one cannot tell simply by inspecting a property whether or not it is emergent with respect to some other property, despite the conviction displayed by the occasional theorist lost in introspective reverie. (E. Nagel (1961) also points this out.) Nor of course do commonsense intuitions that two properties are substantially or even stunningly different entail anything about whether a future intertheoretic reduction might actually identify the two. Light may seem completely different from electromagnetic radiation, yet light turns out to *be* electromagnetic radiation. Having a high temperature seems supremely different from having a high mean molecular kinetic energy, yet it turns out that high temperture in a gas *is* high mean kinetic energy of the constituent molecules. Notice also that one does not provide *independent* evidence for the irreducibility of one property to another merely by claiming that the first is emergent relative to the second. That would be like saying of a property that it is irreducible because it is irreducible.

"Emergent property" is also used in the neuroscientific literature with a quite different sense roughly equivalent to "network property." Consider a set of cells in the retina that are wired so as to collectively constitute a movement detector, even though none of the individual cells is itself a movement detector. The functional property of being a movement detector may understandably be described as "emergent" relative to the individual neurons in the circuit. However, the functional property is certainly and obviously reducible to the neurophysiological properties of the network. Indeed, once we understand the network, we have the reductive story in hand. Although this is a useful sense of "emergence" (which Dennett calls "innocent emergence"), it is clearly not the sense intended by property dualists in their arguments against reductionism. Thus, when Sperry (1980) argues that mental states are emergent, he specifies that he means they are irreducible, not merely that they are network properties.

The claim that subjective experience is not reducible to brain states is to be understood within the wider framework of intertheoretic reduction, where it unpacks as the claim that psychology will not reduce to neuroscience; more specifically, that it will not reduce to neuroscience in such a way that subjective experiences can be identified with states of the brain. States of the brain are causally connected to subjective experience and give rise to the stream of events in awareness, the argument will agree, but the experience *itself*, with its unique qualities, cannot be identified with some process or aspect of neuronal activity. In contrast to the substance dualists, the property dualists do not believe there is a nonphysical substance in which experiences inhere. Rather, they claim that subjective experiences are produced by the brain and can in their turn affect the brain, but they are not themselves identifiable with any physical properties of the brain. On this view, we cannot say, for example, that feeling sad is a neuronal configuration in such and such a neuronal ensemble.

An analogy here may help. It has often been claimed that the *blueness* of (liquid) water is a property that is emergent relative to the microphysics of H_2O molecules, on the grounds that no amount of microphysical information could allow us to predict or to deduce that liquid aggregates of such molecules would have the peculiar qualitative character we call "blue." Blueness may systematically *co-occur* with aggregates of H_2O molecules, it is conceded, but it is a self-contained and irreducible property that appears *in addition to* the microphysical features of aggregated H_2O. It is, in a word, emergent.

Given the account of intertheoretic reduction outlined earlier, the fallacy of this reasoning is displayed with relative ease. For one thing, reduction does not require that reduced properties, as conceived within their older conceptual framework, be *deducible* or *predictable* from within the new reducing theory. Old frameworks are culturally idiosyncratic and highly various. It cannot be the obligation of new theories to predict how ignorant cultural epochs may happen to conceive of the complex phenomena in their explanatory domain. What they are obliged to do, if they are to achieve the reduction of earlier concepts, is nothing more and nothing less than to entail the existence of properties that systematically *mimic* the alleged causal powers of the properties to be reduced.

In the example at issue, the microphysics of H_2O molecules does indeed entail that liquid aggregates of them will *preferentially scatter incident electromagnetic radiation at a wavelength of about 0.46 μm.* It is this complex property that proves to have all of the causal powers of blueness (at least as it is manifested in liquid water). This microphysical property affects human observers in all the same ways as does blueness. It affects nonhuman instruments in all the same ways as does blueness (for example, it projects light through a prism into the same spectral position as does blueness). And so forth. Because of these systematic parallels, it is reasonable to *identify* the blueness of an object with its disposition to scatter (or reflect, or emit) electromagnetic waves preferentially at about 0.46 μm. That is the property that humans have been visually discriminating for millennia, though without appreciating its fine-grained nature. The blueness of water, therefore, is not an emergent property. On the contrary, it reduces rather smoothly, and as a coherent part of a systematic account in which the other colors are also reduced. (For simplicity's sake, I here ignore more recent accounts according to which color is a matter of the object's reflectances at, not one, but three critical wavelengths. Those new accounts are more complex, but the reductive lesson is the same.)

We must not be stampeded, therefore, either into accepting impossibly strong conditions on successful reduction or into forgetting the point of intertheoretic reduction, which is just to show that a new theoretical framework provides a parallel but markedly superior conception of an old and familiar domain. Neuroscience should not be required to meet standards of reduction more stringent than we impose elsewhere in science simply because the concepts it aspires to reduce are deeply entrenched in common sense.

Furthermore, it is true that at this stage in the history of science, subjective experience has not been successfully identified with and explained by states and processes in the brain. Insofar as it has not, then subjective experiences do not now enjoy a reduction to brain states. Nevertheless, this current state of science does not entail that no neuroscientific theory will ever reduce psychology. Analogously, in the eighteenth century it would have been true to say that temperature did not reduce, inasmuch as thermodynamics was still an autonomous science. This did not entail that it never would reduce to a more basic theory or that temperature is an emergent property. Indeed, by the late nineteenth century thermodynamics was the beneficiary of a triumphant reduction to statistical mechanics, at which time it was evident that temperature (of gases) is not emergent but is identical with mean molecular kinetic energy.

Now in saying that subjective experience is emergent, property dualists wish to claim not merely that the reduction of folk psychology to neuroscience eludes us here and now, but that it always will. In principle. Evidently this is much stronger than simply saying that psychology has not yet been reduced to neuroscience, which, after all, is a crashingly obvious thing to say. How does the property dualist propose to defend the opinion that neuroscience will never reduce psychology in such a way that subjective experience can be identified with states of the brain?

The main arguments derive from reflections on the special nature of subjective experiences. But the objections are not always either clear or well-defined, and in many cases one cannot tell what it is about subjective experiences that is to justify the prediction that neuroscience can never reduce psychology. Sometimes the arguments simply work fuzzy intuitions about what is and is not imaginable, or even about what is and is not desirable. Since it is impossible here to catalogue all the variations on this theme, let alone analyze them, instead I have selected for further discussion what I take to be the strongest and most coherent of the arguments. The arguments are extracted from Thomas Nagel's classic paper (1974) and Frank Jackson's more recent but destined-to-be classic paper (1982).[3] For the analysis and the criticism of these arguments, I have made extensive use of two works by Paul M. Churchland (1984, 1985).

Knowing from the Inside/Having a Point of View
For Nagel, there is something special about having an introspective capacity—a capacity to know one's thoughts, feelings, and sensations from the inside, as it were. One's experiences have a certain unmistakable phenomenological character, such as the felt quality of pain or the perceived character of red. One therefore has a subjective point of view. It is the *qualia* or qualitative character of experiences, sensations, feelings, and so forth, to which we have introspective access, and it is this that, in Nagel's view, is not reducible to neural states. These mental states resist reduction because introspective access to them has an essentially different character, yielding essentially different information, than does external access via neuroscience. The argument does exert a powerful attraction, but as stated it is still teasingly vague. In order to see exactly how it works, it is necessary to set out a more precise version.

(A)
(1) The qualia of my sensations are knowable to me by introspection.
(2) The properties of my brain states are *not* knowable to me by introspection.
Therefore:
(3) The qualia of my sensations ≠ the properties of my brain states.

A second argument, complementary to the first, seems also in play:

(B)
(1) The properties of my brain states are knowable by the various external senses.
(2) The qualia of my sensations are *not* knowable by the various external senses.
Therefore:
(3) The qualia of my sensations ≠ the properties of my brain states.

The general form of the argument seems to be this:

(1) a is F
(2) b is not F
Therefore:
(3) $a \neq b$

Leibniz's law says that $a = b$ if and only if a and b have every property in common. So if $a = b$, then if a is red, b is red, if a weighs ten pounds, then b weighs ten pounds, and so forth. If a is red and b is not, then $a \neq b$. Assuming their premises are true, arguments (A) and (B) appear to establish the nonidentity of brain states and mental states. But are their premises true?

Let us begin with argument (A). There is no quarrel with the first premise (the qualia of my sensations are known-to-me-by-introspection), especially since qualia are defined as those sensory qualities known by introspection, and in any case I have no wish to deny introspective awareness of sensations. In contrast, the second premise (the properties of my brain states are *not* known-to-me-by-introspection) looks decidedly troublesome. Its first problem is that it begs the very question at issue—that is, the question of whether or not mental states are identical to brain states. This is easy to see when we ask what the justification is for thinking that premise true.

The point is this: *if in fact* mental states are identical to brain states, then when I introspect a mental state, I do introspect the brain state with which it is identical. Needless to say, I may not *describe* my mental state as a brain state, but whether I do depends on what information I have about the brain, not upon whether the mental state really is identical to some brain state. The identity can be a fact about the world independently of my knowledge that it is a fact about the world. Similarly, when Jones swallows an aspirin, he thereby swallows acetylsalicylic acid, whether or not he thinks of himself thus; when Oedipus kissed Jocasta, he kissed his mother, whether or not he thought of himself thus. In short, identities may obtain even when we have not discovered that they do. The problem with the second premise is that the only justification for denying that introspective awareness of sensations *could be* introspective awareness of brain states derives from the assumption that mental states are not identical with brain states. And that is precisely what the argument is supposed to prove. Hence the charge of begging the question. (Although I have used (A) as an illustration, the same kind of criticism applies equally to (B).)

Other problems with these arguments are more subtle. One difficulty is best brought out by constructing an argument analogous to (A) or (B) with respect to the character of the properties under discussion and comparing the arguments for adequacy. Consider the following arguments:

(C)
(1) Smith believes Hitler to be a mass murderer.
(2) Smith does not believe Adolf Schicklgruber to be a mass murderer.
Therefore:
(3) Adolf Schicklgruber ≠ Adolf Hitler.

As it happens, however, Adolf Schicklgruber = Adolf Hitler, so the argument cannot be right.

Or consider another instance of the general argument form where the property taking the place of F is a complex property concerning what John believes or knows:

(D)
(1) Aspirin is *known by John to be a pain reliever.*
(2) Acetylsalicylic acid is *not* known by John to be a pain reliever.
Therefore:
(3) Aspirin ≠ acetylsalicylic acid.

And one final example more closely analogous to the arguments at issue:

(E)
(1) Temperature is *directly apprehendable by me as a feature of material objects*.
(2) Mean molecular kinetic energy is *not* directly apprehendable by me as a feature of material objects.
Therefore:
(3) Temperature $\neq$ mean molecular kinetic energy.

These arguments fail because being-recognized-as-a-something or being-believed-to-be-a-something is not a genuine feature of the object itself, but rather is a feature of the object *as apprehended under some description or other* or *as thought about in some manner*. Having a certain mass is a property of the object, but being-thought-by-Smith-to-have-a-certain-mass is not a genuine property of the object. Such queer properties are sometimes called "intentional properties" to reflect their thought-mediated dependency. Notice that in (B) the property is being-knowable-by-the-various-external-senses, and in (A) the property is being-known-by-me-by-introspection. Both are sterling examples of thought-dependent properties.

Now the arguments (C) through (E) are fallacious because they treat intentional properties as though they were genuine properties of the objects, and a mistake of this type is called the *intentional fallacy*. It is evident that the arguments designed to demonstrate the nonidentity of qualia and brain states are analogous to arguments (C) through (E). Consequently, they are equally fallacious, and the nonidentity of mental states and brain states cannot be considered established by arguments such as (A) and (B).[4]

The last difficulty with the arguments is better seen in a slightly different and more compelling version of the argument for the nonidentity of mental states and brain states, which I present and discuss below.

Knowing Our Sensations: Jackson's Argument

The strategy of this second argument once again involves showing that differences between knowing our states via introspection and knowing via nonintrospective means are of such a nature as to constitute grounds for denying the reducibility of psychology to neuroscience. In order to clarify those differences, Frank Jackson (1982) has constructed the following thought-experiment. Suppose that Mary is a neuroscientist who has lived her entire life in a room carefully controlled to display no colors, but only shades of white, gray, and black. Her information about the outside world is transmitted to her by means of a black-and-white television. Suppose further that one way or another she comes to know everything there is to know about the brain and how it works. That is, she comes to understand a completed neuroscience that, among other things, explains the nature of thinking, feeling, and perception, including the perception of colors. (This is all wildly unlikely, of course, but just suppose.)

Now for the argument: despite her knowing everything there is to know about the brain and about the visual system, there would still be something Mary would not know that her cohorts with a more regular childhood would, namely, the nature of the experience of seeing a red tomato. Granted, she knows all about the neural states at work when someone sees a red tomato—after all, she has the utopian neuroscience at hand. What she would not know is *what it is like to see red*—what it is like to have that specific experience. Conclusion: her utopian neuroscience leaves something out. This omission implies that there is something in psychology that is not captured by neuroscience, which in turn implies that psychology cannot be reduced to neuroscience.[5]

More formally and with some simplifications, the argument is this:

(F)
(1) Mary knows everything there is to know about brain states and their properties.
(2) It is not the case that Mary knows everything there is to know about sensations and their properties.
Therefore:
(3) Sensations and their properties $\neq$ brain states and their properties.

The argument is very interesting, and it gives an unusually clean line to the intuition that mental states are essentially private and have an irreducibly phenomenological character. Nonetheless I am not convinced, and I shall try to explain why.

First, I suspect that the intentional fallacy, which caused problems for arguments (A) and (B), likewise haunts the premises of argument (F). That aside, there are perhaps more revealing criticisms to be made. Paul M. Churchland (1985) and David Lewis (1983) have independently argued that "knows about" is used in different senses in the two premises. As they see it, one sense involves the manipulation of concepts, as when one knows about electromagnetic radiation and can use the concept "electromagnetic radiation" by having been tutored in the theory. The other sense involves a prelinguistic apprehension, as when one knows about electromagnetic radiation by having had one's retina stimulated in the light of day, though one cannot use the expression "electromagnetic radiation." The latter

sense may involve innate dispositions to make certain discriminations, for example. If the first premise uses "knows about" in the first
sense and the second uses it in the second sense, then the argument
founders on the fallacy of equivocation.

The important point is this: if there are two (at least) modes of
knowing about the world, then it is entirely possible that what one
knows about via one method is identical to what one knows about via
a different method. Pregnancy is something one can know about by
acquiring the relevant theory from a medical text or by being pregnant. What a childless obstetrician knows about is the very same
process as the process known by a pregnant but untutored woman.
They both know about pregnancy. By parity of reasoning, the object
of Mary's knowledge when she knows the neurophysiology of seeing
red might well be the very same state as the state known by her
tomato-picking cohort. Just as the obstetrician does not become pregnant by knowing all about pregnancy, so Mary does not have the
sensation of redness by knowing all about the neurophysiology of
perceiving and experiencing red. Clearly it is no argument in support
of nonidentity to say that Mary's knowledge fails to cause the sensation of redness. Whyever suppose that it should?

There is a further reservation about this argument. With the first
premise I take no issue, since we are asked to adopt it simply for the
sake of argument. The second premise, in contrast, is supposed to be
accepted because it is highly credible or perhaps dead obvious. Now
although it does have a first blush plausibility, it is the premise on
which the argument stands or falls, and closer scrutiny is required.

On a second look, its obviousness dissolves into contentiousness,
because the premise asks me to be confident about something that is
too far beyond the limits of what I know and understand. How can I
assess what Mary will know and understand if she knows *everything*
there is to know about the brain? Everything is a lot, and it means, in
all likelihood, that Mary has a radically different and deeper understanding of the brain than anything barely conceivable in our wildest
flights of fancy.

One might say well, if Mary knew everything about *existing* neuroscience, she would not know what it was like to experience red, and
knowing *absolutely* everything will just be more of the same. That is
an assumption to which the property dualist is not entitled to help
himself. For to know everything about the brain might well be qualitatively different, and it might be to possess a theory that would
permit exactly what the premise says it will not. First, utopian
neuroscience will probably look as much like existing neuroscience as
modern physics looks like Aristotelian physics. So it will not be just

more of the same. Second, all one need imagine is that Mary internalizes the theory in the way an engineer has internalized Newtonian physics, and she routinely makes introspective judgments about her own states using its concepts and principles. Like the engineer who does not have to make an effort but "sees" the world in a Newtonian manner, we may consider that Mary "sees" her internal world via the utopian neuroscience. Such a neuroscience might even tell her how to be very efficient at internalizing theories. It is, after all, the premise tells us, a *complete* neuroscience.

Intuitions and imaginability are, notoriously, a function of what we believe, and when we are very ignorant, our intuitions will be correspondingly naive. Gedanken-experiments are the stuff of theoretical science, but when their venue is so surpassing distant from established science that the pivotal intuition is not uncontroversially better than its opposite, then their utility in deciding issues is questionable.

Moreover, intuitions opposite to those funding premise (2) are not only readily available, they can even be fleshed out a bit. How can I be reasonably sure that Mary would not know what a red tomato looks like? Here is a test. Present her with her first red object, and see whether she can recognize it as a red object. Given that she is supposed to know absolutely *everything* there is to know about the nervous system, perhaps she could, by introspective use of her utopian neuroscience, tell that she has, say, a gamma state in her O patterns, which she knows from her utopian neuroscience is identical to having a red sensation. Thus, she might recognize redness on that basis.

The telling point is this: whether or not she can recognize redness is clearly an empirical question, and I do not see how in our ignorance we can confidently insist that she must fail. Short of begging the question, there is no a priori reason why this is impossible. For all I know, she might even be able to produce red in her imagination if she knows what brain states are relevant. One cannot be confident that such an exercise of the imagination must be empirically impossible. To insist that our make-believe Mary could not make introspective judgments using her neuroscience *because* mental qualia are not identical to brain states would, obviously, route the argument round in a circle.

How could an alchemist assess what he could and could not know if he knew everything about substances? How could a monk living in the Middle Ages assess what he could and could not know if he knew everything there was to know about biology? He might insist, for example, that even if you knew everything there was to know about biology, you still would not know the nature of the vital spirit. Well, we still do not have a complete biology, but even so we know more than this hypothetical monk thought we could. We know (a) that there is no such thing as vital spirit, and (b) that DNA is the "secret" of life—it is what all living things on the planet share.[6]

The central point of this reply to Jackson has been that he needs independent evidence for premise (2), since it is palpably not self-evident. It cannot be defended on a priori grounds, since its truth is an empirical question, and it cannot be defended on empirical grounds, since given the data so far, as good a case can be made for the negation of premise (2) as for premise (2) itself. I do not see, therefore, how it can be defended.

Concluding Remarks

There is a tendency to suppose that a dualist thesis, of either the substance or the property stripe, can be defended simply by noting and acknowledging that humans have an introspective capacity, that we are conscious, and that we are aware of our experiences. But it is a mistake to think that a reductionist need deny these observations. On the contrary, he might envision a reduction in which experiences, awareness, beliefs, perceptions, feelings, and so forth, as characterized in folk psychology, are identified with specific brain states. Such a reduction would fall on the retentive end of the inter-theoretic reduction spectrum, and hence it is a reduction that explicitly acknowledges the existence of mental states and consciousness, as now conceived. Nobody said light did not exist after the reduction of optics to electromagnetic theory; rather, they said light *is* electromagnetic radiation. And nobody said the laws of optics were useless or in disgrace. Notice that on this scenario, it would make perfectly good sense to talk about mental states causing brain states, since mental states turn out to *be* states of the brain (cf. Sperry 1980, Eccles 1977). Nor is a special notion of causation needed, as Sperry (1980) suggests.

Alternatively, a reductionist might envision a reduction in which a considerably evolved scientific psychology reduces to a considerably evolved neuroscience, such that our current conceptions of mental states and their nature are revised to some considerable extent. On this scenario, mental phenomena *as we now conceive of them* are not identified with brain states *as we now conceive of them*. This compares roughly with the bumpy reduction of Aristotelian physics to Newtonian physics, where "impetus" is not identified with anything in Newton's theory, because the phenomenon is reconceived. Even here, the reductionist in no way denies the existence of mental phenomena. Rather, he expects that we may now misconceive and misunderstand those phenomena and that a better, richer, and more comprehensive theory will be forthcoming. In the meantime he acknowledges the propriety of talking about mental phenomena in terms of whatever psychological theory is available, and he will enthusiastically support psychological research as a necessary part of an eventual reduction. (See chapter 9.) In the same way a molecular geneticist will enthusiastically support research in transmission genetics as a necessary part of an eventual reduction.

It is empirically possible that even a much-evolved and transformed psychology will fail to reduce to a much-evolved neuroscience. In that case mental phenomena, even newly conceived, will be emergent with respect to neural phenomena. Can we tell now that this will be the turn of the wheel? I think it is far too early to predict that psychology is forever beyond the reductive aspirations of neuroscience, and, as remarked earlier, one certainly cannot tell simply by observing the phenomena that no intertheoretic reduction is in the cards.

Nevertheless, there remains to be considered a set of powerful arguments that defend the hypothesis that psychology will not reduce to neuroscience. These arguments, still within the framework of property dualism, focus not on the phenomenological character of experience, not on the subjective point of view, but on the fact that mental states have a semantic dimension and that mental processes are, in some degree, logical. These arguments are the focus of the next section.

8.4   Intentionality and Intertheoretic Reduction

Conscious awareness is not the only aspect of our mental life that has seemed to defy explanation within neuroscience. The *representational* nature of thought has also appeared entirely beyond the capacity of a physical machine. A human can have thoughts not just about the here and now, but also about things dead and gone, about things that have never yet existed, and even about impossible things such as perpetual motion machines and methods for squaring the circle.

Furthermore, humans are in some degree rational, and our thoughts (or some subset of them) form a coherent, logically interconnected system. We may draw inferences, construct mathematical proofs, or find patterns in data, such as the rule for continuing the Eleusis series 1, 1, 2, 3, 5, 8, 13, . . . and the theory that explains the movements of the planets. We know when the evidence contradicts a hypothesis, and we can create hypotheses relevant to explaining an empirical phenomenon. We can figure out theories to explain the origin of the universe and the origin of species, and we can figure out how to make an airplane that will fly.

Physical devices, it has been argued, can be complex and intricate, but none have this rather astonishing capacity to represent and to reason. Nor, it may be pushed further, can physical devices ever have such a capacity, for it is a distinctly *mental* capacity. Representational thought is not the product of greater complexity of the physical device; it is the product of mentality. The distinctively human accomplishments cannot be explained merely by the hypothesis that human brains are exceedingly complex; they can be explained only by the hypothesis that we have internal states that are distinctively mental.

How, exactly, is this thesis defended? How can it be demonstrated that no physical machine can have representational states? In order to exhibit and to examine the arguments, it is necessary first to focus more finely on what, in a general way, it is for a state to be representational.

Traditionally, philosophers have said that thoughts have "aboutness," in the sense that they are about something external to the mental state itself. The belief that my computer sits on Einstein's old table is about my computer and its relation in space to a table that once was used by Einstein. Medieval philosophers were much intrigued by this "aboutness" dimension of thought, and in trying to understand the difference between thoughts and other states like pain, they described thoughts as "intending" something beyond themselves. (The thought that Einstein was imaginative is about Einstein, but a pain is just painful.) In consequence, the property of having "aboutness" came to be described as the property of *intentionality*. "Intentional" and "intentionality" as used by philosophers are therefore technical terms, not to be confused with the common use of "intentional" to mean "deliberate."

Intentionality proved to be more perplexing the more it was studied. When a belief is about something that exists, it is straightforward enough to say what in the world is the object of the belief. But when, for example, Smith believes that caloric is a fluid that makes things hot, or that Santa Claus will bring him toys, or that there is a proof for Goldbach's conjecture even though no one has ever found it, matters are less than straightforward. Some philosophers, such as Brentano and Meinong, tried to solve the problem by postulating a world of real but abstract objects to be the objects of thought. Other philosophers, such as Russell, thought the cure worse than the disease, or at least no better.

The paradigmatically intentional states are the propositional attitudes, such as x believes that p, x wants that p, x thinks that p, x intends to bring it about that p, and so forth. As discussed earlier, it is characteristic of propositional attitudes that they are identified by a sentence that specifies exactly what thought someone has. If Smith believes that there are polar bears in Churchill, then the sentence "There are polar bears in Churchill" identifies what belief Smith has. Put another way, the identifying sentence specifies the *content* of Smith's belief. Content sentences have meaning, and thus propositional attitudes may be characterized as having content or meaning. What meaning a particular state has, is specified by whether the state is a belief, a desire, a hope, etc., and by the relevant content sentence. More generally, representational states are states with meaning.

Given this clarification, the contemporary approach to intentionality has been to see questions concerning "aboutness" and the objects of thought as absorbed into the more general question concerning the contentfulness or meaningfulness of representational states. In those debates between physicalists and dualists where intentionality has been the issue, the division concerns whether or not it is possible for physical states to have content and whether or not physical states can be representational states. Having an adequate theory of linguistic meaning was thus a matter of the first importance, and questions concerning how thoughts have meaning and how elements of language have meaning attracted an immense research investment from philosophers. Matters are far from settled, but it appears that the *network theory of meaning* has emerged from the smoke as the most powerful and comprehensive theory (see below, this section). An important feature of this theory for our purposes is that, though compelling on independent grounds, it turns out to be compatible with physicalist theories of mental states and processes. Actually, it is compatible with both dualism and physicalism, but because it is compatible with physicalism it has been important in showing that the meaningfulness of mental states is not per se an obstacle to a physicalist theory of the mind-brain.

It has been a continuing theme in philosophical reflection that the human ability to reason and to have meaningful thoughts implies the existence of a unique capacity in us—a capacity so extraordinary that no sheerly physical mechanism could possibly account for it. Articulating these intuitions such that a clear and comprehensible argument results has taken a number of very different forms. One line, whose failures I have already spelled out in section 7.3, denies that rationally related states are causally related. The most recent arguments defend the emergence of cognitive psychological theory with respect to neurobiological theory on grounds of the special nature of meaningful and inference relations (see chapter 9). The focus in this section will be an influential argument owed to Karl Popper (1972, 1977) that appears to capture one dimension of the intuitions about meaning and logic in virtue of which it is thought that the capacity for thought is fundamentally nonphysical and emergent. Popper's argument closes in on the *semantic* dimension of propositional attitudes and on the *abstract* nature of their propositional objects.

Popper and the World of Intelligibilia
The crux of Popper's argument against reductionism depends on his idea that there exists a world of abstract, nonphysical objects with which we interact when we reason, discover a proof for a theorem, find consequences for a physical theory, use language, think about arithmetic or quantum mechanics or Gödel's incompleteness results. He calls this realm of abstract objects "World 3," and its denizens include arithmetic objects such as the integers, the irrational numbers, and the relations between them, mathematical objects, logical objects, and relations between them, scientific theories, the as-yet-undiscovered proof for Goldbach's conjecture, and the as-yet-undeduced consequences of theories in physics, neuroscience, and so forth. It also contains some "embodied" objects such as books and musical scores. Popper calls the physical world that conforms to physical laws "World 1," and he claims that mental events and processes belong to a distinct "World 2."

Popper argues that World 3 exists as an autonomous reality independent of ideas in minds, dispositions to verbal behavior, wiring in the brain, or any such. That is, World 3 is part of neither World 2 nor World 1. His reasoning here depends on the view that the laws of logic cannot simply amount to empirical generalizations about how persons reason, or even about how professional logicians reason. These laws of logic are norms or standards concerning what *ought to be*, and, by Popper's lights, the validity of these laws does not derive from the fact that logicians accept them. Rather, logicians accept these laws because they are valid, and their validity is an independent matter of World 3 relations among World 3 objects. Moreover, certain inferences are valid whether or not anyone has ever drawn those inferences or even entertained those propositions. This, as Popper sees it, can be explained only by postulating the real existence of logical systems and World 3 intelligibilia.[7]

How does this bear upon the issue of intertheoretic reduction? In the following way. Popper aims to show that World 2, the realm of mental states and processes, cannot be a subpart of World 1, and the argument boils down to this:

(1) World 3 can bring about changes in World 1, as for example when someone uses a theory to produce a steam engine that converts chemical to mechanical energy.

(2) However, World 3 cannot affect World 1 directly, but only through the intervention of World 2. That is, abstract objects cannot bring about changes in the physical world except as they are "grasped" and manipulated by thought processes. These processes in World 2 cannot be physical processes because only something nonphysical can interact with the nonphysical intelligibilia of World 3.

Therefore:

(3) World 2 cannot be part of World 1, which implies that mental states cannot be physical states.

Popper is confident that physicalism is incompatible with the existence of World 3 and that a reductionist's only defense is to deny that realm its reality. That will not be my strategy. Though I do find normative notions (rules, laws, etc.) deeply puzzling, and though I find my perplexity assuaged not at all by the postulation of a World 3, my objections to Popper's claims do not depend on arguing against his World 3. Rather, what seems to me in error is the claim in premise (2) that only something nonphysical can interact with the intelligibilia of World 3. One problem is that the claim simply begs the question at issue. For all Popper has argued, perhaps the right sort of physical thing—neural assemblies, maybe—*can* so interact. That theories cannot yield technology without the mediation of thought does not show that thought is *nonphysical* but only that thought is *necessary* for technology. A physicalist would state Popper's claim this way: theories cannot yield technology without the mediation of brains.

The claim is even more powerful because there are positive examples of purely physical systems whose workings we understand very well, which can prove theorems, solve equations, follow mathematical and logical laws, and in some instances learn from the past and readjust their rules accordingly—namely, computers. A computer is wired up and programmed such that by going through a sequence of physical states, it goes through a sequence of functional states, such as drawing a deductive inference from two premises. By "functional state" I mean a state that is characterized in terms of its causal relations with input states, output states, and other internal functional states. (See also chapter 9.) The machine's operations can be described and explained at the level of the circuitry or alternatively at a functional level in terms of what it is computing (Dennett 1978a). If, in performing logical inferences, computers interact with abstract objects of World 3, then Popper's second premise is undermined and the argument fails. If, in performing logical inferences, the computer is deemed to be innocent of interaction with World 3, then what fails is Popper's central assumption that inferences require interaction with the abstract objects of World 3.

Further, consider the possibility that going through a mental process, such as proving a theorem, is in the relevant respects like the computer's going through a functional process of proving that same theorem. That is, at some appropriately high level of description, the two processes are the same. It is this possibility that philosophers (Putnam 1967, Fodor 1975, Dennett 1978b) have developed into the philosophical theory known as *functionalism*. Functionalism, in its most general rendition, is just the thesis that the nature of our psychological states is a function of the high-level causal roles they play in the internal system of states that mediate between sensory input and behavioral output.

According to this thesis, mental states are *functional* states of the brain, and they stand in the same relation to the neural machine as functional states of a computer stand to the electronic machine. Mental states *could be* functional states of some nonphysical substance, but that they are functional states of the brain is the more likely possibility. The functional states of the computer are realized or implemented in its electrical circuits; similarly, mental states are realized or implemented in the neural stuff. The differences between functional descriptions and hardware descriptions turn out to be differences in what *level* of description is appropriate, not in whether what is described are physical states or nonphysical states. Descriptions of mental states are functional descriptions of physical states at a designated level. (See Dennett 1978a and 1981, Lycan 1981a and 1981b.)

To explain a given output of the computer, one describes the program it was executing, its input, and the functional stages that led to its output. At one appropriate level of description the computer may be said to be proving a theorem, in which it uses, say, the rule of double negation or the rule of modus ponens. A human theorem-prover may execute the same steps in proving the same theorem. Now we can think of folk psychology as a theory fragment partially describing the program(s) human brains execute. The programs that the brain executes and that we currently attempt to describe in folk psychological terms are evidently far more complicated than anything yet devised in computer science. And in the case of brains we do not yet have a neuroscientific theory in which to couch a machine-level description of what is going on, nor, of course, do we know that folk psychology is a basically correct description of the program. Nevertheless, the salient point is that computers offer a prime example of how it is possible to explain the rule-governed behavior of a purely physical machine without resorting to nonphysical hypotheses. (Functionalism will be more fully discussed in chapter 9.)

Moreover, in defense of his claim Popper seems to imply that it is more understandable how nonphysical states can interact with intelligibilia than how neural states might. In the absence of some theory concerning the nature of this interaction, this asymmetry of understanding is wishful thinking. Certainly saying that the mind "grasps" the denizens of the third realm is no theoretical advance whatever. How the postulated nonphysical states interact with neural states is, as shown earlier, in the same dire theoretical predicament.

Popper replies to the example of a computer executing logical operations by saying that computers are "designed by us—by human minds" and thus "both the computer and the laws of logic belong emphatically to what is here called World 3" (1977:76). But this does not meet the objection. Does the computer, which is a physical machine, interact with World 3 objects or not? If it does, then why not brains? Or does Popper perhaps mean that the functional states of computers really are not physical states after all? His reply misses entirely the point of the functionalist theory, which is that mental states are states described at a high level of functional organization and implemented in brains. If a frankly physical system such as a computer can follow rules and procedures, can conform to mathematical laws, and can deduce conclusions never before deduced by man or machine, then it is plain that one need not hypothesize nonphysical mechanisms merely on the strength of a system's capacity to follow rules and logical laws.

Still, it may be argued, our brains evolved, but computers are constructed, and therein lies the difference. But is this difference relevant to the question of whether our functional states are physical states? Suppose it turned out that our brains did not evolve but were in fact the design of some superintelligent beings from another galaxy who cleverly covered up all traces of their tinkering with the Earth's ecosystem. Or suppose, as some people do, that our mind-brains are designed by a god. How then should we describe our functional states? To be consistent, one who espouses Popper's theory should say either that our brains, like computers, are World 3 objects, in which case it is perfectly mysterious that we manage to interact with the physical world, or that our mental states are physical states. Neither answer fits Popper's scheme.

Finally, there is a rather simple reductio of Popper's argument. If he is right in arguing that because propositional attitudes stand in a relation to abstract entities, they are not physical states, then a perfectly parallel argument will show that the paradigmatically physical properties—mass, temperature, charge, etc.—are not physical properties. Recall the discussion in section 7.3 of numerical and vectorial attitudes, where examples of numerical attitudes included "...has a mass in kilograms of n," "...has a temperature in kelvins of n," "...has a charge in coulombs of n," and so on. Empirical laws exploiting the abstract relations defined over formal entities are found not only in psychology, where the states are propositional attitudes, but also in physics, where the states are numerical attitudes. Consider, for example, the law "For any x, m, and f, if a body x has a mass m, and x suffers a net force of f, then x accelerates at f/m." Now evidently numerical attitudes have truck with abstract (numerical) objects in World 3, and to parallel Popper's reasoning, they can interact with such objects only if the numerical attitudes are nonphysical. Hence, mass, temperature, charge, and paradigmatically physical magnitudes generally must also be nonphysical properties. Clearly, we are not going to buy *this* conclusion. But it is now highly problematic how we can refuse it, if we follow Popper to his conclusion concerning propositional attitudes.[8]

Intentionality: Intrinsic and Derived
Consider the following very simple argument:

> (1) If the intentionality of propositional attitudes is a physical property, then it should be possible to build a computer whose states have genuine intentionality.
> (2) But no computer model that simulates human propositional attitudes will have states with genuine intentionality.
> (3) Therefore: the intentionality of propositional attitudes is not a physical property.

Recall that for a state to have intentionality is basically for it to have meaning or content (or "aboutness") in the sense described above.[9]

The second premise bears the weight of the argument, and it requires a closer look. In its defense, it will be said that however sophisticated the behavioral output of the computer, and *however closely it may simulate the behavior of a person,* none of its linguistic outputs will really have meaning. To test this claim, suppose there has been built a robot with a behavioral repertoire much like my own, that it is fitted out with sensory receptors for seeing, hearing, smelling, and so forth, and motor effectors. This may require that its internal organization mimic my brain's organization even down to very low levels, but that is an empirical question to be decided by empirical research. Just assume that our internal systems are sufficiently similar that our behavioral repertoires resemble one another as closely as Popper's and mine do. Suppose also that the robot has a device for emitting sounds, and on a certain occasion after having its visual scanners trained on the morning news broadcast from Houston Space Center, it goes into an internal state identified by "The space shuttle was launched this morning," such that it then wheels into your office and emits the utterance "The space shuttle was launched this morning."

Appearances notwithstanding, continues the argument, the robot's utterance has meaning only because *we* give it meaning—that is, only because we interpret it as meaning what we mean when we say "The space shuttle was launched this morning." Without our interpretive grace, neither the robot's utterances nor its internal states have any meaning. If we are tempted to say that its internal state was the thought that the shuttle was launched this morning, then we must beware that its so-called thought state represents something about the shuttle only by our so interpreting. Its internal states are mere machine states, representing nothing and meaning nothing. In short, the meaning of its outputs and hence the intentionality of its states is *derived* from our meaning and the intentionality of our states. In contrast, *my* thought that the space shuttle was launched this morning has original and intrinsic meaning, rather than derived meaning. That is, the meaning of my internal state is not dependent on or a function of anyone's interpreting it to have a meaning, but is a matter of my meaning something by it. Thus the argument.

This argument has many puzzling aspects, the first of which pertains to what it must be assuming about how the states of biological persons have meaning and intentionality. To clarify this a bit, consider the meaning of my utterance "The space shuttle was launched this morning." What I mean by that, and whether you and I mean the same thing, depends in obvious and intricate ways on what else I believe. For example, if I should believe that a space shuttle is a banana and that to launch something is to put it in the blender, then what I mean is not what Walter Cronkite means when he says "The space shuttle was launched this morning." And what I believe is likewise different. To the extent that your background beliefs are very different from mine, the meaning of the words we use will be correspondingly different. To the extent that we share beliefs, our meanings will be shared. If my background theory of the heavens is Ptolemaic and yours is Copernican, then we shall mean something quite different by "planet." (Ptolemaic theory holds that planets are

344 The Philosophy of Science

stars not fixed on the celestial sphere; Copernican theory holds that planets are not stars but cold bodies revolving around the sun, and that Earth is a planet.)

What someone means by an utterance depends on the related beliefs that he has, and in turn the content of his beliefs is a function of what he means by certain expressions, in one big ball of wax (Quine 1960). The meaning of an expression for an individual is a function of the role that expression plays in his internal representational economy—that is, of how it is related to sensory input and behavioral output and of its inferential/computational role within the internal economy. Sparing the niceties, this is the *network theory of meaning*, otherwise known as the *holistic theory* or the *conceptual-role theory*. (See Paul M. Churchland 1979, Rosenberg 1974, Field 1977.) Translation is accordingly a matter of finding a mapping between alien representations and one's own such that the network of formal and material inferences holding among the alien representations closely mirrors the same network holding among our own. It is possible that representational economies may be so different that translations are not possible.

Meaning is therefore *relational* in the sense that what an expression means is a function of its inferential/computational role in the person's internal *system* of representations, his cognitive economy. This is not to say that an expression has meaning only if someone interprets or translates it as having a particular meaning. However, it does imply that isolated expressions do not somehow sheerly have meaning and that mentality cannot somehow magically endow an utterance with intrinsic meaning. What it does deny is that meaning is an intrinsic feature of mental states and that a state has the meaning it has regardless of the wider representational system. Moreover, it contrasts with a theory of meaning that says that the meaning of a word is the set of objects it is true of and that the meaning of a sentence is to be identified with the state of affairs that makes it true.[10]

With this brief background in theory of meaning, we can return to the central question raised at the outset: can the robot, whose behavior is very like my own, be said to have thoughts with meaning and more generally to have states that represent that *p*? Now in order to simulate my outer behavior as closely as the premise asserts, the robot will have to have an internal system of representations and computations of a richness roughly comparable to my own. Consequently, it will have elements whose roles have a pattern comparable to the roles played by elements in my internal economy. But if the elements in its internal economy are close analogues of my own, if their roles mirror those in my economy, then what else do they need to have meaning?

To refuse to assign meaning—meaning as genuine as it gets—to the robot's internal states would therefore be to apply a double standard, arbitrarily and to no useful purpose. To bridle here looks like dogmatism. What the robot means by an expression will, as with me, be a function of the role that expression plays in the internal representational economy of the robot. If I can find a mapping between its representational system and my own, then I shall have a translation of its utterances. So much is anyhow all one has to go on in ascribing intentionality to other humans. This is not to say that the robot's internal states have meaning only if I interpret them, for after all, the elements of its representational economy objectively bear the inferential/computational relations that they do to each other, regardless of whether I encounter the robot or not.

If the robot turns out to be a fake, inasmuch as its effects are really produced by a small boy hiding inside, then the intentionality *is* derived, for the robot has no system of representations of its own in virtue of which inferences are drawn and so forth. On the other hand, if it has a brain of electronic stuff, if its behavioral output is a product of its complex internal system of representations implemented in its brain, then its utterances have meaning in exactly the way mine do.

That the robot looks and smells different from a human, that its "brain" is a structure of silicon pico-chips, is in the end irrelevant to whether or not it believes things, wants things, understands what it hears—in general, whether its states have intentionality. As Douglas Hofstadter has pointed out (in conversation), if simply looking different and having different bodily parts were decisive in determining intentionality, then one could envision much the same argument used persistently by male humans to conclude that females do not have states with original, nonderived, *real* intentionality. They have merely "femintentionality." Or, obviously, the roles could be reversed, and women could claim that men do not have original nonderived, *real* intentionality. They have merely "mascintentionality."

Finally, as noted in discussing Popper's argument, the discovery that we humans were actually the product of extraterrestrial intelligence should make no difference to whether we (really) have beliefs, desires, and thought and whether our utterances (really) mean something. The complex inferential-computational relations between representational items in a system are whatever they are, regardless of where the system ultimately came from. But if the antireductionist argument were correct, then such a discovery concerning our origins should make us conclude that we do not have *real* intentionality after all. Rather, it should make us "conclude," since of course we could not really conclude anything.

Whether a robot has intentional states *at all* will depend, inter alia, on how complex its internal informational network of states is, on its sensory detectors, and on its motor effectors, but it is important to stress two points here. First, there is no criterion for exactly specifying when the complexity is enough and when it is not, or for saying just how the system of representational states must hook up to the world. If the internal informational network is as complex as that enjoyed by an adult human, it is enough, but if it is as simple as that of a sea squirt or a thermostat, it is not enough. The extremes are clear enough, then, but in the middle ground we are less sure. At this stage of our understanding, determining whether something has intentional states is mostly a matter of guessing how like us it is—the greater the resemblance, the more likely we will say that it has intentional states. This is not because we know what it is for a system to represent, but because we don't know, so we proceed with the founding assumption that we are paradigmatic representers. The problem is that in the absence of a robust *theory* of information processing there can be no precise criterion for exactly how complex an internal network must be and how it must hook up to the world in order to count as bestowing genuine meaningfulness.[11]

Accordingly, the imprecision here is at least in part a function of theoretical immaturity. There are theoretically embedded definitions that specify exactly when something is a protein or an amino acid, because chemical theory is a well-developed theory. Until there is a more developed empirical theory about the nature of representing in organisms, greater precision will have to wait. The fact is, we simply do not know very much about how organisms represent, and what sort of business representing is, or even whether our concept of having a representational system delimits a natural kind. And even when we do know more, imprecision may be our lot, as it is in the case of "species." To force precision by grinding out premature definitions enlightens nobody. Nor, I suspect, will repeated analysis of the folk psychological category of meaning avail us much. (See especially Dennett 1986.)

8.5   Concluding Remarks

The common theme uniting the objections to intertheoretic reduction considered in this chapter has been that mental states are not physical states, either because they are the states of a nonphysical substance or because they are emergent nonphysical states of the brain in the sense that they cannot be explained in terms of neuronal states and processes. None of these objections seems to me compelling. Dualists, however, are not the only ones to raise objections. Surprisingly perhaps, some physicalists have generated antireductionist arguments of their own from within a broadly physicalist framework. Though there is the obvious major disagreement on the question of dualism, nonetheless, these newer arguments share with the older arguments a devotion to the idea that it is because mental states have meaning and because mental states enjoy logical relations to one another that the reductive program is forever thwarted. Their brand of dualism is a dualism of theory, not a dualism of substance. But "antireductionism" is rather more fashionable than "dualism," and hence the implicit dualism of theory and the entailed dualism of properties is played down. The antireductionist arguments are perhaps more subtle than Popper's variety, but their root motivation derives from a common conviction about the irreducibility of intentionality. I shall try to bring these arguments into focus in chapter 9.

Selected Readings

Biro, J. I., and R. W. Shahan, eds. (1982). *Mind, brain, and function*. Norman, Okla.: University of Oklahoma Press.

Churchland, Paul M. (1984). *Matter and consciousness: A contemporary introduction to the philosophy of mind*. Cambridge, Mass.: MIT Press.

Churchland, Paul M. (1985). Reduction, qualia, and the direct introspection of brain states. *Journal of Philosophy* 82:8–28.

Dennett, Daniel C. (1978). *Brainstorms: Philosophical essays on mind and psychology*. Montgomery, Vt.: Bradford Books. (Reprinted (1984) Cambridge, Mass.: MIT Press.)

Flanagan, Owen J., Jr. (1984). *The science of the mind*. Cambridge, Mass.: MIT Press.

Jackson, Frank (1982). Epiphenomenal qualia. *Philosophical Quarterly* 32:127–136.

Nagel, Thomas (1974). What is it like to be a bat? *Philosophical Review* 83:435–450.

Popper, Karl R. (1977). Part I of *The self and its brain*. Berlin: Springer-International.

Stich, Stephen P. (1983). *From folk psychology to cognitive science: The case against belief*. Cambridge, Mass.: MIT Press.

Chapter 9
Functionalist Psychology

Further information should allow us to replace the single concept of mind and mental activity by others more fully descriptive of the modes of action of brain processes.
J. Z. Young, 1978

9.1 Introduction

We come now to the most sophisticated arguments against the reductionist program. These arguments have a foot in both folk psychology and scientific psychology and typically involve both an *analysis* of folk psychological categories and an *empirical theory* about the general nature of information and information processing in the mind-brain. The dominant theme has three movements: (1) there are categories of folk psychology that are fundamentally correct for characterizing mental states; (2) these categories delimit *intentional* states and *logical* processes, and they will figure essentially in both the research and the evolving theories of a science of the mind; (3) these categories, essential to the psychological level of description, will not reduce to categories at the neurobiological level of description.

The implication for a scientific psychology, or at least some non-trivial domain of a scientific psychology, is that no reduction to neurobiology can be expected. The implication for research in the relevant domain of scientific psychology is that neurobiology is largely irrelevant to discovering an adequate theory of information processing at the psychological level.

In most variations on this antireductionist theme the computer metaphor is prominent, for a number of reasons. One is that a fairly clear sense can be given to the notion of *levels* of description in the case of computers. The machine can be considered to have three basic levels of description: the semantic level, the syntactic level, and the level of the mechanism. At the semantic level the machine can be described as (for example) having certain goals, computing a square root, sacrificing a rook, or inferring a conclusion from the premises. At the syntactic level the nature of its code, its symbolic system, its access principles, and so forth, are described. The mechanism level concerns the nature of the machine's architecture and hence its physical constraints and capacities. A theory of cognitive information processing is, on this view, a theory of the dynamics of the semantic level as governed by the logical rules and control principles at the syntactic level. By contrast, neurobiology is assumed to address neither of these levels but rather to be focused on the architecture—that is, on the level of the mechanism. This hypothesis concerning the levels in the mind-brain has strongly colored the perception of what research strategies will be productive and whether neuroscience is relevant to psychological research.

A further reason for the prominence of the computer metaphor is that the notions of symbol manipulation and computation are quite well defined within computer science, and the central empirical hypothesis is that cognition is a species of computation. The underlying basis for this hypothesis is the idea that reasoning is the model for cognitive information processing *generally*. This means that cognition is largely symbol manipulation and that the important relations in cognitive information processing are thus the logical relations between the symbols. Now modern logic has provided immense resources for understanding reasoning in terms of logical systems: deductive logic, inductive logic, modal logic, decision-theoretic logic, and so on. Accordingly, it is argued, we can study cognitive processes by programming a computer to honor the relevant logical relations, and thus we can explore what the sequence of symbol manipulations must be in order to get a complex output such as problem solving, pattern recognition, or answering a question. The antireductionist arguments wish to make much of a fundamental contrast between the cognitively relevant *logical* operations on symbols and the cognitively irrelevant *causal* relations among physical states of the implementing mechanism. (See especially Pylyshyn 1984.)

Simplifying somewhat, on this view the mind is essentially a serial machine governed by rules of logic that operate on sentence-like representations. This research outlook has generated enormous appeal, partly because it has held promise that the powerful systematic resources of logic and computer science could jointly solve puzzles about the nature of the internal processes intervening between input and output. It has thus drawn into a cooperative venture logicians, philosophers of mind, researchers in artificial intelligence, and cognitive psychologists.

In this chapter I will try to show where I think the antireductionist's arguments fail and why the isolationist research ideology is to be avoided. More than that, this chapter will be the occasion for staging a general assault on the theory that identifies cognition with reasoning and that models representations generally on sentences. I do not doubt that some internal processes are instances of reasoning, but I do emphatically doubt both that cognition in general is anything like reasoning and that sentence-like symbols are in general the mode of representation. In place of the isolationist research ideology I shall recommend a co-evolutionary approach wherein neurobiology as well as psychology and computer modeling have a central role. In place of the venerable sentence-logic paradigm I shall in chapter 10 sketch the outlines of new theoretical frameworks in which representations and computations are conceived in a markedly different manner.

9.2 Antireductionism in Functionalist Theories of the Mind

Functional Types and Structural Implementations
The core idea of functionalism is the thesis that mental states are defined in terms of their abstract causal roles within the wider information-processing system. A given mental state is characterized in terms of its abstract causal relations to environmental input, to other internal states, and to output. Being in pain, on this account, is a state characterized by its causal relations to behavior such as wincing and crying out, by its causal relations to external input such as the skin being burned, by its causal relations to other internal states such as the desire to make the pain go away, beliefs about the source of the pain and about what will bring relief, and so forth. The characterization of having the goal of, say, finding a mate will follow a similar pattern: the goal state will be connected to a complex range of beliefs and desires, will prompt a diverse range of plans and actions, and will be connected in rich and complicated ways to perceptual states (Putnam 1967, Fodor 1975, Lycan 1981b).[1]

In general, functional kinds are specified by reference to their roles or relational profiles, not by reference to the material structure in which they are instantiated. What makes a certain part of an engine a valve lifter is that, given a specified input, it has a certain output, namely the lifting of the valves, and it might be instantiated in various physical devices, such as a rotating camshaft or a hydraulic device. More humbly, "mousetrap" is a functional kind, being implementable in all manner of physically different devices: spring traps, assorted cage traps, a sack of grain falling when a trip line is wriggled, or perhaps even a cat or a specially bred killer rat. There is nothing in the specification "mousetrap" that says it must have a tin spring or a wooden housing. Being a mousetrap or a valve lifter is therefore a functional kind, not a physical kind, though mousetraps and valve lifters are implemented in physical stuff and every implementation or "token" is a physical device.

According to functionalism, then, mental states and processes are functional kinds. Functionalists have typically sided with physicalism by claiming that our mental states are implemented in neural stuff, not, as the dualist would have it, in spiritual stuff. At one level of description we can talk about the causal and logical relations among perceptions, beliefs, desires, and behavior, and at the structural level we can talk about spiking frequencies of neurons, patterns of excitations, and so forth. It is because neurons are orchestrated as they are that the system has the functional organization it does, and thus the physical substratum subserves the functional superstratum. In our case the functional organization that is our psychology is realized in our neural "gubbins." In similar fashion, it is because on-off switches in a computer are orchestrated as they are that it adds, finds square roots, and so forth. The computer's program is realized in its electronic "gubbins." The functionalist theory is thus as roundly physicalist as it can be, yet despite their adherence to physicalist principles, functionalists have typically rejected reductionism and ignored neuroscience. Why?

Plainly, it is not because functionalists suppose that mental states have no material realization. Rather, it is because they envision that types of mental states could have *too many* distinct material realizations for a reductive mold to fit. As functionalists see it, for a reductive strategy to succeed, a type of mental state must be identical to a type of physical state, but, they argue, the identities are not forthcoming. The reason is that one and the same cognitive organization might be realized or embodied in various ways in various stuffs, which entails that there cannot be one-to-one relations between functional types and structural types. A cognitive organization is like the computational organization of a computer executing a program: computational processes are logical, or at least semantically coherent, and they operate on symbols as a function of the symbol's meaning, not as a function of its physical etiology in the machine, and the same program can be run on different machines (Putnam 1967, Pylyshyn 1984). There is nothing in the specification of a cognitive organization, the functionalist will remind us, that says that pain must be subserved by substance P in a given set of neurons or that a goal-to-find-a-mate state must be linked to testosterone. This oversimplifies, of course, but the main point is clear enough.

In a general way one can imagine that on another planet there might have evolved creatures who, though very different from us in physical structure, might have a cognitive organization much like our own. Suppose, for example, they were silicon-based instead of carbon-based as we are. For these animals, having a goal will be functionally like our having a goal, but such a state will not be identical to having neurons n–m responding thus and so, though to be sure the goal state will be embodied in their physical structure. Or suppose that in time we figure out how to manufacture a robot that has the same functional organization as a human: it has goals, beliefs, and pains, and it solves problems, sees, and moves about. Its information-processing innards are not neurons but microchips, and its cognitive organization cannot therefore be identical to a particular neuronal organization, since *neural* stuff it has not got. Instead, its cognitive economy will be instantiated in electronic stuff. As we shall see, the plausibility of these thought-experiments depends on a crucial and highly suspect assumption—namely, that we know at what level the biology does not matter.

Fictional examples are not really needed to make the point anyhow, since there are certain to be neural (structural) differences between functionally identical states in distinct species. An echidna and a yak may both be in pain or have the goal of finding a mate and hence be in the same functional state, though the neural events and processes subserving their states may differ considerably. The same is probably true of more closely related species such as chimpanzees and gorillas. Moreover, it is continued, there may be nontrivial differences in structural detail between two *humans* in a functionally identical state: the neural events that subserve my adding 29 and 45 may not be the same as those in the brain of a calculating prodigy or a mathematician or a child or a street vendor. Indeed, on different occasions different neuronal events may realize *my* adding 29 and 45, depending on what else my brain is doing and heaven knows what other matters. We know quite well that two computers can be in the same type of functional state and yet have very different structural states. For example, two computers can be executing the same program written in BASIC, though their hardware and even their assembly language may be quite different (Fodor 1975).

Identity of functional-state types with structural-state types, argues the functionalist, is therefore hopelessly unrealistic, and since reduction requires such identities, *tant pis* for reduction. Physicalist principles are in no way sundered, however, for all that physicalism requires is that any given *instance* of a functional-state type (a token of that type) be realized in physical stuff, and this the functionalist heartily agrees to and insists upon. He therefore describes himself as espousing *token-token* identity of mental states with physical states, but denying *type-type* identity and therewith reductionism (Putnam 1967, Dennett 1978b).

This foray against the reductionist program is known as the argument from *multiple instantiability* or *multiple realizability*. Functional states are multiply instantiable, and the range of physical implementations will be so diverse that we cannot expect it to form a natural kind. Apart from its implications for the theory that mental states are identical with brain states, the argument has been deployed to methodological purpose in the following way.

If mental states and processes are functional kinds, then to understand how cognitively adept organisms solve problems, think, reason, and comport themselves intelligently, what we need to understand is their functional organization. Research on neurons is not going to reveal the nature of the functional organization, but only something about the embodiment of the functional organization— and just one sort of instantiation at that. Neuroscience, it has been argued, is focused on the engineering details rather than on the functional scheme, and to this extent it is removed from the level of description that is appropriate to answering questions concerning learning, intelligence, problem solving, memory, and so forth. Knowledge of the structural minutiae is important for repairs, of course, and to this extent neuroscience has obvious medical significance, but structural theory will not enlighten functional hypotheses and functional models. To put it crudely, it will not tell us how the mind works. Cognitive psychology, in contrast, is focused at the appropriate level of description, and in cooperation with research in artificial intelligence it constitutes the best strategy for devising a theory of our functional cognitive economy. Thus the crux of the argument.

As Pylyshyn (1980) sees it, the research labor can be divided along these lines: the cognitive scientists will figure out the functional/ cognitive theory, and the neuroscientists can untangle the underlying physical devices that instantiate the cognitive "program." On an extreme version of this view, nothing much of the details of neuronal business need be known by the cognitive scientist—or the philosopher, either—since the way the functional organization is instantiated in the brain is a quite separate and *independent* matter from the way our cognitive economy is organized. Pylyshyn comes close to this in his claim that computational questions can be addressed exclusively at a privileged (functional) level of algorithms and symbolic manipulation (1980:111). He says, ". . . in studying computation it is possible, and in certain respects essential, to factor apart the nature of the symbolic process from the properties of the physical device in which it is realized" (p. 115).

Neuroscience, on this picture, is irrelevant to the computational questions of cognitive science. What it is relevant to are implementation issues, such as whether a particular computational model of cognitive business is in fact implemented in the neural structure. Computational (functional) psychology is thus conceived as an *autonomous* science, with its proprietary vocabulary and its own domain of questions, the answers to which, as Pylyshyn remarks, ". . . can be given without regard to the material or hardware properties of the device on which these processes are executed" (p. 115). It may even be suggested that the less known about the actual pumps and pulleys of the embodiment of mental life, the better, for the less there is to clutter up one's functionally oriented research.

Whether anyone really holds the extreme version of the research ideology is doubtful, but certainly milder versions have won considerable sympathy, and sometimes cognitive science programs permit or encourage neglect of neuroscience, where the autonomy of psychology is the rationale. How influential the view is I cannot estimate, but some philosophers are still wont to excuse those colleagues who take neuroscience seriously as having not quite managed to master the distinction between functional and structural descriptions. The methodological point should be taken seriously because functionalism is now the dominant theory of the mind espoused by philosophers as well as by many cognitive scientists. Even so, there are significant differences among functionalists on a number of issues, including the relevance of theories of brain function to theories of psychological function. Dissent from the methodological point is not without voice in cognitive psychology (for example, McClelland and Rumelhart 1981, Posner, Pea, and Volpe 1982), philosophy (for example, Enç 1983, Hooker 1981, Paul M. Churchland 1981), and computer science (for example, Anderson and Hinton 1981). My lot is thrown in with the dissenters, because I think both the antireductionist argument and the research ideology it funds are theoretically unjustified and pragmatically unwise to boot. In what follows I shall try to show why.

9.3   In Defense of Reductionism

There are two principal sources of error in the antireductionist views outlined above. The first concerns the background assumptions about the nature of intertheoretic reduction; the second concerns the conception of levels—how many there are, their nature, their discovery, and their interconnections. These sources of error will be considered in sequence.

Intertheoretic Reduction and Functionalism

Functionalists appear to assume that intertheoretic reduction cannot come off unless the properties in the reduced theory have a *unique* realization in physical stuff. This assumption is crucial in the case against reduction, and it is what floats the methodological claim for the autonomy of cognitive psychology.[2] Is the assumption justified?

One way to test the claim is to see whether it conflicts with or comports with the paradigm cases of reduction in the history of science. "Temperature" is a predicate of thermodynamics, and as thermodynamics and molecular theory co-evolved, the temperature of gases was found to reduce to the mean kinetic energy of the constituent molecules. That is, a corrected version of the classical ideal gas law was derived from statistical mechanics together with certain assumptions. Several features of this case are immediately relevant to the issue at hand. Notice that what was reduced was not temperature tout court, but temperature of a gas. The temperature of a gas *is* mean kinetic energy of the constituent molecules, but the temperature of a solid is something else again; the temperature of a plasma cannot be a matter of kinetic energy of the molecules, because plasmas are high-energy states consisting not of molecules but of dissociated atoms; the temperature of empty space as embodied in its transient electromagnetic radiation is different yet again. (Paul M. Churchland 1984 and Enç 1983 also make this point.) And perhaps there are states as yet undiscovered for which temperature is specified in none of these ways. The initial reduction in thermodynamics was relative to a certain domain of phenomena, to wit, gases, but it was a bona fide reduction for all that. Nor is this domain-relativity used as grounds for saying that thermodynamics is an autonomous science, independent and separate from physics. Quite the contrary, the co-evolution of corpuscular physics and thermodynamics was of the first importance to both physics and thermodynamics.

Yet if we heed the functionalist assumption at issue, we ought to withhold the stamp of reduction on grounds that temperature must be a functional property that is multiply realized in distinct physical structures. Now, however, this looks like a merely verbal recommendation about what to call reductions in cases where the predicates in the reducing theory are relativized to certain domains (cf. Cummins 1983). As such, it implies nothing about the derivation of one theory from another or about the autonomy of the sciences. No grand methodological strictures about what is and is not relevant to the "functional" theory will be in order. As a merely verbal recommendation it is not especially objectionable, but it has no obvious utility either.

Dialectically, it does the functionalist no good to deny reduction in thermodynamics, for then he loses the basis for saying that psychology is on an entirely different footing from the rest of science (Enç 1983). After all, if psychology is no worse off than thermodynamics, then reductionists can be cheerful indeed. At any rate, the requirements for the reduction of psychology should not be made stiffer than those for intertheoretic reduction elsewhere in science. (See also Richardson 1979, Paul M. Churchland 1984.)

The main point of the example drawn from thermodynamics is that reductions may be reductions *relative to a domain of phenomena*. Though this is called "multiple instantiability" and is draped in black by the functionalist, it is seen as part of normal business in the rest of science. By analogy with the thermodynamics example, if human brains and electronic brains both enjoy a certain type of cognitive organization, we may get two distinct, domain-relative reductions. Or we may, in the fullness of time and after much co-evolution in theories, have one reductive account of, say, goals or pain in vertebrates, a different account for invertebrates, and so forth. In and of itself, the mere fact that there are differences in hardware has no implications whatever for whether the psychology of humans will eventually be explained in neuroscientific terms, whether the construction of psychological theories can benefit from neuroscientific information, and whether psychology is an autonomous and independent science. That reductions are domain-relative does not mean they are phony reductions or reductions manqué, and it certainly does not mean that psychology can justify methodological isolation from neuroscience.

Enç (1983) draws a further point out of the thermodynamics case. Two volumes of a gas might have the same temperature, but the distributions of velocities of their constituent molecules will be quite different even while their mean value is the same. To be consistent, functionalists should again deny reductive success to statistical mechanics since, as they would put it, *temperature of a gas* is differently realized in the two cases. If, on the other hand, they want to concede reduction here but withhold its possibility from psychology, they need to do more than merely predict hardware differences between species or between individuals.

If it turns out that we are lucky enough to get a reduction (domain-relative) of *human* psychology to neuroscience, what does this do to the thesis that mental kinds are functional kinds? Nothing, for that thesis is independent of the antireductionist argument, and it stands on its own feet after the argument from multiple instantiability falls. The thesis that mental states are identified in terms of their abstract causal roles in the wider information-processing system is the core conception that makes functionalism functionalism, and it is entirely neutral on the question of reducibility. Functionalists can be true blue functionalists without naysaying reduction. Functionalism as it lives and breathes, however, is another matter, and frequently functionalists have wished to argue for a package: the functional characterization of mental states, the nonreducibility of psychology, and the autonomy (in some degree) of psychology from the more basic sciences. As a result, the term "functionalism" is typically if inappropriately associated with the whole package.

The point of this section has been a very general one: intertheoretic reductions are not conditional on a one-to-one mapping of predicates of the higher-level theory onto predicates of the reducing theory. Antireductionists may wish to concede the general point but to continue by arguing that the details of the case at hand rule out reduction. In so arguing, they will point to radical differences between the neuronal level of explanation and the functional-computational level, and they will point out that the multiplicity of instantiations of psychological predicates can be so profuse, diverse, and arbitrary that the case cannot be likened to the thermodynamics–statistical mechanics example. In a word, they claim that the case of psychology is special.

Levels of Organization in the Mind-Brain
There is a good deal that is uncontroversial in the antireductionist's appreciation that there must *be* a set of levels of organization. A theory of cellular and synaptic changes occurring during learning will be more fine-grained than a theory of how an interactive network learns, which will be more fine-grained than a theory of what anatomical structures subserve learning, which will be more fine-grained than a theory that postulates a coding mechanism, retrieval mechanisms, and so forth. What is controversial is the assumption that the trilevel model suitable to Von Neumann computers is also suitable to organic brains. That there should be some division of labor is also beyond dispute; no one since Bacon could take all knowledge as his province. Indeed, no one since Helmholtz could take even all of

neuroscience as his province. What is regrettable, however, is the divisive research ideology based on the trilevel model.

As we have seen, the hypothesis based on the computer analogy is that the mind-brain has three levels of organization: the semantic, the syntactic, and the mechanistic—the level of *content*, the level of the *algorithm*, and the level of *structural implementation*. The principal problem with the computer metaphor is that on the basis of the complexity we already know to be found in the brain, it is evident that there are *many* levels of organization between the topmost level and the level of intracellular dynamics. (See also Lycan 1981a.) And even if there were just three, neurobiological theory (see chapter 10) challenges that way of specifying their organizational description. How many levels there are, and how they should be described, is not something to be decided in advance of empirical theory. Pretheoretically, we have only rough and ready—and eminently revisable—hunches about what constitutes a level of organization.

As a first approximation, we can distinguish the following levels of organization: the membrane, the cell, the synapse, the cell assembly, the circuit, the behavior. And within each level further substrata can be distinguished. If, however, neurons are organized into modules, each perhaps playing a role in several distinct information-processing modules, and if modules themselves are members of higher-order "metamodules," again with membership being a diverse and distributed affair, or if some cell assemblies or modules have a transient membership or a transient existence, we may then find a description of levels that is orthogonal to the first.

Another preliminary and related way to demarcate a level is to characterize it in terms of the research methods used. Certainly this is a very rough way of defining levels of organization, but it may be useful until the research reveals enough for us to see what the levels really are. For example, in research on learning and memory one can discern many different methods that, compared to one another, are more or less fine-grained. The cellular approach taken by Kandel and his colleagues (Hawkins and Kandel 1984) showing modification in presynaptic neurotransmitter release in habituation is in some sense at a lower level than studies by Lynch and his colleagues (Lee et al. 1980) showing modification of synapse numbers and synaptic morphology correlated with plasticity in behavior, which in turn is at a (slightly) lower level than the studies by Greenough and his colleagues (Greenough, Juraska, and Volkmar 1979) on the effect of maze training on dendritic branching. We then ascend to the multicellular studies in the hippocampus done by Berger, Latham, and Thompson (1980), and from there up (a bit) to the cell assembly studies in the olfactory bulb by Freeman (1979), which uses an 8×8 electrode array and evoked response potential averaging techniques. Upward again to the studies of Nottebohm (1981) on the seasonal changes in the "songster" nuclei of the canary brain or to the animal models of human amnesia studied by Zola-Morgan and Squire (1984). At yet a different level are the studies by Jernigan (1984) and Volpe et al. (1983) of correlations between neural tissue atrophy and memory performance using neural imaging techniques (CBF, PET). Finally there are neurological studies of human amnesia (Weiskrantz 1978, Squire and Cohen 1984), ethological studies of such things as how bees remember flowers (Gould 1985), and psychological studies of memory capacities and skills of college undergraduates (Norman 1973, Tulving 1983). This is obviously a very fast Cook's ascent at just one point through the research strata, but a more leisurely tour will reinforce the impressions.

It is simply not rewarding to sort out this research in terms of the trilevel computer analogy, nor is there any useful purpose to be served by trying to force a fit. Moreover, at each of the research levels one can distinguish among questions concerning the nature of the capacity, questions concerning the processes subserving the capacity, and the matter of the physical implementation. The point is, even at the level of *cellular* research, one can view the cell as being the functional unit with a certain input-output profile, as having a specifiable dynamics, and as having a structural implementation in certain proteins and other subcellular structures.

What this means is that one cannot foist on the brain a monolithic distinction between function and structure, and then appoint psychologists to attend to function and neuroscientists to attend to structure. Relative to a lower research level a neuroscientist's research can be considered functional, and relative to a higher level it can be considered structural. Thus, Thompson's work on multicellular response profiles in the hippocampus is perhaps structural relative to Squire's work on the recognition capacities of amnesic humans but functional relative to Lynch's work on plasticity of synaptic morphology. The structure-function distinction, though not without utility, is a *relative*, not an absolute, distinction, and even then it is insufficiently precise to support any sweeping research ideology.

In addition, we simply do not know at what level of organization one can assume that the physical implementation can vary but the capacities will remain the same. In brief, it may be that if we had a complete cognitive neurobiology we would find that to build a computer with the same capacities as the human brain, we had to use as structural elements things that behaved very like neurons. That is, the artificial units would have to have both action potentials and graded potentials, and a full repertoire of synaptic modifiability, dendritic growth, and so forth, though unlike neurons they might not need to have, say, mitochondria or ribosomes. But, for all we know now, to mimic nervous plasticity efficiently, we might have to mimic very closely even certain subcellular structures.

There is a further assumption, usually unstated, that lends credence to the ideology of autonomy and should be debunked. This assumption is that neuroscience, because it tries to understand the physical device—the brain itself—will not produce *theories* of functional organization. Now we have already seen that the functional-structural distinction will not support the simplistic idea that psychology does functional analysis and neuroscience does structural analysis, and that there are bound to be many levels of organization between the level of the single cell and the level at which most cognitive psychologists work. It is important as well to emphasize that when neuroscientists do address such questions as how neurons manage to store information, or how cell assemblies do pattern recognition, or how they manage to effect sensorimotor control, they are addressing questions concerning neurodynamics—concerning information and how the brain processes it. In doing so, they are up to their ears in theorizing, and even more shocking, in theorizing about representations and computations. If the representations postulated are not sentence-like, and if the transformations postulated do not resemble reasoning, this does not mean the theory is not functional theory, or not real theory, or not relevant to theories at a higher level. Some examples of such theorizing—which is as unequivocally "functional" as anything in cognitive psychology—will be presented in chapter 10. The existence of bona fide *neurofunctional* theorizing is perhaps the most resounding refutation of the second assumption.

My general conclusion, therefore, is that it is supremely naive to assume that we know what level is functional and what is structural, and that neurons can be ignored as we get on with the functional specification of the mind-brain.[3] This explains my earlier warning (section 9.2) about the multiple instantiation thought-experiments that are endlessly invoked by antireductionists. Nevertheless, antireductionists will argue for the autonomy of cognitive psychology not merely on the basis of the trilevel hypothesis but also on the grounds that the categories and generalizations appropriate to the cognitive levels are special. For reasons to be examined, these categories are believed to have an invulnerable theoretical integrity and to be irreducible to physical categories. In section 9.5 I shall outline and criticize the arguments on behalf of this thesis, but first, to prepare the ground, I shall present a co-evolutionary research ideology to compete with the ideology of autonomy of cognitive psychology.

9.4   The Co-evolutionary Research Ideology

The Division of Research Labor
According to the functionalist research ideology, the task of cognitive psychology is to determine what "programs" the mind-brain runs in virtue of which it has certain cognitive capacities, and the job of neuroscience is to find out whether the brain really implements the hypothesized programs. Moreover, this ideology recommends that cognitive psychology is to be *autonomous* with respect to neuroscience, in the sense that neurobiological data are irrelevant to figuring out the cognitive "program" the mind-brain runs.

Five general reasons speak against the autonomy ideology and in favor of embracing an ideology of co-evolutionary development:

1. Our mental states and processes *are* states and processes of our brains (chapter 8).
2. The human nervous system evolved from simpler nervous systems.
3. Brains are by far the classiest information processors available for study. In matters of adaptability, plasticity, appropriateness of response, motor control, and so forth, no program has ever been devised that comes close to doing what brains do—not even to what lowly rat brains do. If we can figure out how brains do it, we might figure out how to get a computer to mimic how brains do it.
4. If neuroscientists are working on problems such as the nature of memory and learning, studying cellular changes, synaptic changes, the effects of circumscribed lesions, and so forth, it is perverse for a cognitive scientist trying to understand memory and learning to ignore systematically what the neuroscientists have discovered.
5. Categories at any level specifying the fundamental *kinds* may need to be revised, and the revisionary rationales may come from research at any level.

Philosophers are sometimes fond of arguing that certain things are possible *in principle,* and in this context it may be argued that it is in principle possible for psychology to hew out a functionalist cognitive theory without interleaving itself with neuroscience. I don't know whether this is true, and I have no sense of how to assess the claim.

My guess is that it shares a flaw with many other philosophical thought-experiments: too much thought and not enough experiment. What I think is clear is that the history of science reveals that co-evolution of theories has typically been mutually enriching. In practice at least, psychology as a discipline has nothing to gain from adopting an isolationist methodology. In what follows I shall explain the competing research ideology, namely the co-evolution of research, drawing on examples outside the fields at issue. Then, using the case of research on memory and learning, I shall indicate why psychology should prefer the co-evolutionary ideology.

The Benefits of Co-evolutionary Development
The case of thermodynamics and statistical mechanics displays especially well the mutual benefits of concordant development. Our understanding of the nature of temperature, equilibrium, and entropy was expanded and readjusted as discoveries were made at *both* the macro and the micro levels. Hooker's swift synopsis of the co-evolution of the two gives the flavor:

> First, the mathematical development of statistical mechanics has been heavily influenced precisely by the attempt to construct a basis for the corresponding thermodynamical properties and laws. For example, it was the discrepancies between the Boltzmann entropy and thermodynamical entropy that led to the development of the Gibbs entropies, and the attempt to match mean statistical quantities to thermodynamical equilibrium values which led to the development of ergodic theory. Conversely, however, thermodynamics is itself undergoing a process of enrichment through the injection "back" into it of statistical mechanical constructs, e.g. the various entropies can be injected "back" into thermodynamics, the differences among them forming a basis for the solution of the Gibbs paradox. More generally, work is now afoot to transform thermodynamics into a generally statistical theory, while retaining its traditional conceptual apparatus, and there is some hope that this may eventually allow its proper extension to non-equilibrium processes as well . . .
> (1981:49)

The value of co-evolution can also be seen in the development of physics and chemistry, of astronomy and dynamics, of the theory of infectious disease and microbiology, of classical genetics and molecular genetics, and more recently of nonequilibrium thermodynamics and biology, and of immunology and genetic engineering. In these instances discoveries at one level often provoke further experiments and further corrections at the other level, which in turn provoke questions, corrections, and ideas for new explorations.

It may be objected that the example of classical genetics and molecular genetics is in fact a bad example of what I wish to show, because it conflicts with the idea that co-evolution will lead to reduction. The trouble, it will be said, is that molecular genetics has not succeeded in reducing "gene" to a structural basis, and there is well-reasoned skepticism that it never will do so. (See especially Hull 1974.) This case is worth a closer look because of the analogies between it and the case of psychology and neurobiology.

Reduction and Co-evolution
In classical genetics genes are the units of hereditary transmission, mutation, and recombination. Their role in the theory is to explain why there is a given output (phenotypic traits) given a certain input (fertilization), and they are specified essentially in terms of their causal properties. Looked at in this way, a gene is a set of functional properties. The problem for molecular genetics was to find what structural mechanism in the organism could be identified as the gene for a particular phenotypic trait. The early expectations were that it would be some identifiable segment of a chromosome, and later, some identifiable strip of DNA. It became evident that matters were exceedingly complex and that many mechanisms and many biochemical conditions contributed to the expression of a trait. Not that the complexity by itself was thought to frustrate reduction, but what did seem discouraging was the discovery that differences in the structure of the DNA did not always result in differences in the phenotype, owing to compensating biochemical circumstances; and conversely that the same DNA base could yield distinct phenotypic traits, again owing to divergent matters in the biochemical surround. In short, instead of the coveted one-to-one relation between genes as functionally specified and genes as structurally specified, there is a *many-to-many* relation between the genes of classical genetics and the genetic material of molecular genetics. And perhaps, it has been suggested, it may be so bad as to be a many-to-(indefinitely)many relation. As Philip Kitcher puts it, "There is no molecular biology of the gene. There is only molecular biology of the genetic material" (1982:357).

Importantly, those who have rejected reduction in genetics as a hopeless cause have not wished to claim that molecular genetics cannot explain the input-output phenomena described by transmission genetics, or that transmission genetics is an autonomous science, or that molecular genetics is irrelevant to transmission genetics. On the contrary, they typically agree with reductionists in arguing exactly the reverse. The heart of the disagreement, then, concerns the significance of one-to-one mappings between the functional units of the molar theory and the structural units of the molecular theory. This issue is of central importance to those who see the reductionist program in neuroscience blocked by the possibility that psychological categories will not map one to one onto neurobiological categories. Now from the reductionist viewpoint, this possibility does not look like an obstacle to reduction so much as it predicts a fragmentation and reconfiguration of the psychological categories. Indeed, there are already signs of a fragmentation of the folk psychological category of memory. (See section 4.1.) To show why the reductionist's course is reasonable, I shall explore the issue more fully.

When a property of a system is postulated on the basis of the input-output profile of the system, the natural expectation is that there is a (unitary) mechanism for accomplishing the effect, and the reasonable research strategy is to try to find that unitary mechanism. However reasonable the expectation and the research, it is a frustrating truth that functions postulated at the input-output level do not always map onto unitary structures. This is especially likely to be so when the system is complex—that is, when there is a long and complicated route between input and output. The following simple but compelling example from Dewan 1976, described by Hooker, makes this sort of situation clear.

> Consider a set of electrical generators G, each of which produces alternating current electrical power at 60Hz but with fluctuations in frequency of 10% around some average value. Taken singly, the frequency variability of the generators is 10%. Taken joined together in a suitable network, their collective frequency variability is only a fraction of that figure because, statistically, generators momentarily fluctuating behind the average output in phase are compensated for by the remaining generators, and conversely, generators momentarily ahead in phase have their energy absorbed by the remainder. The entire system functions, from an input/output point of view, as a single generator with a greatly increased frequency reliability, or, as control engineers express it, with a single, more powerful, "virtual governor". The property "has a virtual governor of reliability f" is a property of the system as a whole, but of none of its components. Does this render it irreducible? Yes, and no. For, once the mechanism of the system's operation is understood, it is seen that this property's being a property of this system is entailed by the conjunc-

tion of laws for the individual generators plus specification of system structure. Its being so is not, however, entailed by the laws of the component generators alone. In this sense, the property *is* irreducibly a property of the whole system—the system *structure* obtaining is essential to *its* obtaining. But from an ontological point of view, there is nothing to the system over and above its components and the physical relations between them (however physically realized). This latter point is driven home by enquiring *"what thing* is the virtual governor?" (a real governor, one on each component generator, is an actual physical device), *"where* is the virtual governor?" and so on. The answers must be that, in the sense of the questions, there is no thing which is the virtual governor, so "it" cannot be localized more closely than the system as a whole. (This is why engineers refer to it as a virtual governor.) (Hooker 1981:509)

Genes, it appears, are more like the virtual governor in the example than like a distinct component such as a generator. One way to describe the situation in genetics, therefore, is to say that there really are no genes, *in the sense specified* by such questions as "What thing in the DNA is a gene?" or "Where are the genes?" The assumption that there is a single structural unit is an assumption that has to be dropped. Instead, there is a complex set of conditions and mechanisms, some of which are themselves functionally specified at some level down from the top, and DNA segments figure prominently but not exclusively in that set.

The many-to-many tangle will resolve into a one-to-one pattern so long as the micro half of the relation is permitted to include things beyond the DNA configuration, things like the biochemical milieu. (Unless of course, the system's macro properties are indeterministic with respect to its biochemical properties, but neither party to the debate makes this implausible claim.) Moreover, given the levels of organization to be found in organisms, part of the story may involve specification of middle-range input-output functions that are in turn explained by lower-level mechanisms. As to the macro half of the relation, it is evident that input-output characterizations of the system as a whole and of subsystems at various levels within modify and are modified by molecular as well as high-level discoveries. For example, the specification of what is a phenotypic trait is not theory-neutral either and has itself undergone modifications to reflect deeper understanding in both classical and molecular genetics. (For example, Benzer's modification 1957; see discussions in Philip Kitcher 1982, Hull 1974.)

Very roughly, reduction will still have been accomplished if the input-output effects described by a suitably evolved macrogenetic theory can be explained by molecular goings-on. Following Hooker here, the crux of what is required is that the laws (in general, the true sentences) of the evolved transmission genetics have an "image" in the theorems of the reducing theory. A bit more specifically, this requires that (1) initial macrolevel inputs are identified with initial states of mechanisms, (2) final macrolevel outputs are identified with final states of mechanisms, and (3) for every macrolevel input-to-output function there is a class of mechanisms nomically relating the relevant input and output states (1981:516).[4]

If such a reduction were to emerge, notice that we could describe it as occupying a place on the revisionary end of the spectrum if we think of Mendel's theory (his laws and his specification of "factor" (= gene) and "dominance") as the theory that is reduced/replaced. Alternatively, given the co-evolution of transmission genetics and molecular genetics, future historians of science might prefer to say that what was reduced was the *evolved* macrotheory T*, that it was essentially retained by the evolved microtheory M*, and that the reduction was smooth, macrolevel properties having been identified with microlevel complex conditions. The first reading seems rather perverse because it does not acknowledge the historical fact of co-evolution of the theories preceding reduction. However, on the second reading the important addendum is that one effect of the co-evolution of transmission and molecular genetics will have been to revise rather radically the causal mainstay of Mendelian genetics as the macro- and microtheories approached reductive integration.

If anything, genetics is an especially good case rather than a problematic one to consider as we view the prospects for co-evolution and reduction of psychology and neuroscience.[5] Three major themes resonate through Hooker's analysis of the genetics case, all of which are here applicable: (1) input-output functional properties are not always subserved by unitary mechanisms, but are the outcome of the orchestration of diverse mechanisms, no one of which can be suitably identified as the realization of the macrolevel property, (2) this tends to be the case the more levels of organization there are in the system and the more complex the route between input and output, and (3) because of these and other factors, the characterization of input-output functions and input-output laws will be revised to mesh more closely with lower-level discoveries.

Co-evolution of Research on Memory and Learning
A predictable outcome of the co-evolution of psychology and neuroscience is that some types of mental state, specified by folk psychology in terms of their presumed causal properties, will turn out to be "virtual governors." It is of enormous philosophical interest that this is already happening in the case of two interconnected categories whose role is quite central in folk psychology, namely memory and learning. "Memory," as a category characterized within folk psychology, is at least as bad as a virtual governor.

As indicated earlier (section 4.1), "learning" does not define a single kind of business; among the various kinds can already be distinguished habituation, sensitization, imprinting, one-trial learning, classical conditioning, instrumental conditioning, and place-learning. Suppose these to be "basic" kinds of plasticity, the list must then be expanded to include so-called higher learning, and here too the general catchall category appears ready to fragment into a number of distinct classes with distinct underlying neuronal systems. Perceptual-motor skills may differ along certain dimensions from "purely" cognitive skills, and the mechanisms subserving language learning appear to be different from those subserving facial recognition or cognitive mapping. And some of the research raises deep problems for the commonsense conception of "control" in human mental life, and for the role of consciousness. The theoretical future of a unified folk psychology category, "memory," or "learning," looks bleak because the domain of input-output phenomena is itself undergoing redescription and reclassification. And the interconnected set of categories "consciousness," "awareness," and "attention" are themselves evolving and may in time be transformed rather radically.

Moreover, the research on memory and learning illustrates very well the mutual benefits of co-evolution at all levels of research. Having shed the confining Skinnerian dogma that knowledge of the internal mechanisms would contribute nothing to understanding behavioral plasticity, and taking advantage of recent electronic and micro technology, the memory and learning field has in the last twenty-odd years become a classical exhibit of productive research on a nervous system capacity at many levels at once. Research influences go up and down and all over the map. Though I cannot give anything like a review of the enormous relevant literature, I want to provide a few samples to illustrate the interdisciplinary nature of the research program.

At the cellular and molecular level Kandel and his colleagues (1976, Hawkins and Kandel 1984) have discovered much concerning the neurobiological basis for habituation, sensitization, and classical conditioning in the invertebrate *Aplysia Californica* (figure 2.26). (See also section 2.3.) These discoveries are truly remarkable both because they represent a landmark in the attempt to understand the neurobiological basis of plasticity and because they show that memory and learning can, despite the skepticism, be addressed neurobiologically. Quinn and his colleagues (Quinn and Greenspan 1984) have found a complementary account to explain why certain mutant populations of *Drosophila* are learning disabled, and thus a connection has been made between specific genes and the production of an enzyme known to have a causal role in learning. The neurobiological basis of imprinting in the chick is slowly coming into focus (Horn 1983), as are the neural circuitry underlying classical conditioning in the mammalian brain (McCormick 1984) and the neural circuitry underlying song learning in the canary (Nottebohm 1981).

The discovery that bilateral surgical removal of the medial temporal lobe, amygdala, and hippocampus in humans resulted in profound amnesia for events occurring after surgery (Scoville and Milner 1957; see the discussion below) led to intensive study of the role of those structures in animal models. Some of this work has involved complex testing of residual capacities after making circumscribed lesions at various sites, and some has involved recording from specified areas in the hippocampus.

In one of the latter experimental attempts Berger, Thompson, and their associates found that after training there was a sort of cellular representation of the behavioral response in the hippocampus, and this "representation" developed during the training phase of classical conditioning (Berger and Thompson 1978, Berger, Latham, and Thompson 1980). In the performance of the learned response, it occurred prior to the onset of the behavioral response. Interestingly, however, lesioning of the hippocampus does not prevent classical conditioning, though lesioning of the interpositus nuclei of the cerebellum does. Anatomical studies reporting pathways and connections have formed the basis for hypotheses to explain the effects, and these hypotheses were important to those studying humans and those studying animal models. Zipser (1985) has developed a theoretical model to explain hippocampal learning during classical conditioning that draws on some principles found to apply in *Aplysia*. Vertebrate nervous systems are much more complicated than those of invertebrates, but the *Aplysia* research has provided a framework of hypotheses that structures research on the cellular basis of habituation, sensitization, and classical conditioning in the vertebrate brain.

The amnesic syndromes found in Korsakoff's patients, whose intellectual degeneration is correlated with many years of alcohol abuse, and in Alzheimer's patients, patients who have undergone electroconvulsive therapy, and patients with tumors or with other lesions have been intensively studied and compared both at the performance level and in terms of the underlying pathology. Important differences have emerged, and the data have suggested to some neuropsychologists that there are at least two distinct physiological systems subserving higher long-term learning and memory.

One line of evidence in favor of the hypothesis depends on showing that the two capacities are dissociable, and the most striking example of such dissociation is displayed by Milner's patient, H.M. At age 27 H.M. underwent surgery as a means of last resort to control his intractable epilepsy. The surgery involved bilateral resectioning of the medial temporal lobe and hippocampal structures (figures 3.3 and 3.5) (Scoville and Milner 1957). In tests following the surgery an unexpected side effect was discovered: H.M. has profound anterograde amnesia and can recall virtually nothing of any events that have happened since the surgery. As Scoville and Milner have observed, he appears to forget everything as soon as it happens. He cannot remember what he had for lunch or whether he had lunch, he cannot recall having met the hospital staff he sees many times a day or how to get to the bathroom. Nor can he recall being told that his favorite uncle has died, and each time he inquires about his uncle and is told of his death, his grief is renewed. His IQ was slightly above average preoperatively and is still so postoperatively. H.M. has quite good retrograde memory, especially for events a year or so before surgery, and he easily recalls events from his early life. Eventually H.M. came to understand that something was very wrong in his life, and he commented,

> Right now, I'm wondering. Have I done or said anything amiss? You see, at this moment everything looks clear to me, but what happened just before? That's what worries me. It's like waking from a dream; I just don't remember. (Milner 1966:115)

Despite his severe anterograde memory deficit, it has been found that H.M. does have a retained capacity for learning certain kinds of things. For example, Milner (1966) showed that he could learn a mirror tracing task, and Corkin (1968) showed that he could learn rotary pursuit and manual tracking. Although these achievements might be considered merely noncognitive, sensorimotor skills, it is remarkable that H.M. has also mastered, at a normal rate, the Tower of Hanoi puzzle (figure 4.1). That is, when presented with the puzzle, H.M. can solve it in the optimal number of steps, and he can proceed to the end if started anywhere in the middle (Cohen and Corkin 1981). This is a nontrivial intellectual feat.

More puzzling still, on each occasion when he is asked to attempt the puzzle, he does not recall having learned how to do it, and he does not even recall having encountered it before. That is, he has no conscious recognition of the puzzle that he can verbally report. When, having solved the puzzle in the optimal number of steps, H.M. is asked to explain his expertise, he shrugs it off with a confabulatory explanation, such as that he is good at puzzles, this one is easy, and so forth. He has acquired an impressive cognitive-cum-motor skill, yet so far as he is able to *tell* us, the puzzle is always a complete novelty. Control is therefore also problematic here because H.M. can initiate and successfully complete an extended, intellectually demanding task, even though he has no awareness that he has the knowledge or that he is executing his knowledge on the task at hand. If H.M. has no awareness of his skill, how, one wonders, does the nervous system execute the long sequence of steps necessary for the puzzle's solution? The point is, in some sense H.M. is not aware of what he is doing, yet what he is doing is cognitive, complex, and, should we say, intentional. To put it crudely, it is as though some part of H.M.'s nervous system knows what it is doing and has the relevant complex intentions, but H.M. does not. What does H.M. think he is doing? Thus the problem of control. (See also Warrington and Weiskrantz 1982.)

It is this unpredicted dissociation of capacities that has moved some neuropsychologists to postulate two memory systems, each with its own physiological basis. In attempting to key onto the criterial features of the lost and the retained capacities of H.M., Squire and Cohen (1984) propose that the distinction be made as follows: "descriptive memory" is the capacity to verbally report recollections, and "procedural memory" is the capacity to exhibit a learned skill. Although this way of framing the distinction is useful in some measure, it is acknowledged by Squire and Cohen to be a preliminary and imprecise taxonomy, and much remains to be discovered about the range and nature of each capacity, assuming there are indeed two.

Studies of animal models tend to confirm the fractionation of memory components (Weiskrantz 1978, Mishkin and Petri 1984, Zola-Morgan 1984), but interpretive questions remain concerning which anatomical structures explain the observed deficits and the degree to which animal models illuminate the human cases. Anatomical studies are certainly important in determining whether there are distinct anatomical structures subserving dissociable memory systems and in suggesting further ways to test amnesic patients in order to determine just which capacities are retained and which are lost. It could be that PET and cerebral blood flow scans will help resolve some of the issues currently in dispute. (For a cautionary discussion concerning the Squire version of the two-systems hypothesis, see Weiskrantz (forthcoming).)

At the same time, of course, psychologists have collected immense amounts of data concerning learning and remembering in the intact human. Learning curves, forgetting curves, distinctions between unaided recall, cued recall, and recognition, and the role of attention, for example, have been enormously useful and have been employed at other levels of investigation. Some psychologists have framed a "two-systems" hypothesis but have drawn the boundaries quite differently from the neuropsychologists. Tulving (1972, 1983) distinguishes episodic from semantic memory (neither of which encompasses cognitive skills), and Kinsbourne and Wood (1975) have used this distinction in their research on amnesia. Others (Norman and Rumelhart 1970) have distinguished between memory for item and memory for context, and this rather different taxonomy has also been used in interpreting data on amnesics (Huppert and Piercy 1976).

The assorted more-than-one-system hypotheses have provoked widespread testing of intact humans and have occasioned new studies on skills (Kolers 1975, Rumelhart and Norman 1982), the role of consciousness in the various kinds of memory (Posner 1984, Poulos and Wilkinson 1984), and so forth, in order to try to discover the nature of the two capacities, if such there really be, and whether there is theoretical justification for postulating yet other capacities. What is striking about the research on memory and learning is its interdisciplinary character. Researchers working at one level are always on the lookout for, and are often successful in finding, results elsewhere that can help them in devising useful experiments or in reconfiguring the memory-learning taxonomy.

One hope concerning the research in memory and learning is that the explanation of the biological basis of relatively simple plasticity such as habituation in *Aplysia* can be used as a scaffolding for addressing the neurobiology of other kinds of learning and for figuring out the neurobiology both of habituation and (eventually) of other kinds of plasticity in humans. The current classification of kinds of learning may well be reconfigured even further in unpredictable ways as the research at all levels continues. There is a sense in which, so far as higher learning is concerned, we cannot be at all sure yet what the explananda are. For example, we do not have a principled way to characterize either the capacity that is preserved in H.M. or the capacity that is lost.

One response to those who advocate the autonomy of psychology is therefore this: it would be simply boneheaded for a cognitive psychologist working on learning and memory to refuse to care about animal models, pathway research, clinical cases, imprinting in chicks, song learning in canaries, and habituation in *Aplysia*. We simply don't know remotely enough yet to know what is not relevant. And learning and memory are not some recherché capacities of tangential connection to intelligent behavior; they are as central to cognitive psychology as anything could be.

Co-evolution, Reduction, and Cognitive Neurobiology
Although some functionalists have also made the point that input-output operations will be realized in no unitary mechanisms at intermediate or lower levels, there has been little inclination to envisage either that such circumstances might provoke thoroughgoing reconceptualization of the input-output operations or that neuroscience might inform us about the nature and organization of the intermediate levels (see, for example, Cummins 1983). There is a tendency to assume that the capacities at the cognitive level are well defined and hence that the route of research influence will be from higher levels to lower levels. As we see in the case of memory and learning, however, the categorial definition is far from optimal, and remembering stands to go the way of impetus.

A misleading but popular metaphor for the co-evolution of psychology and neuroscience pictures the two tunneling through a mountain, working from opposite ends. It is misleading because co-evolution typically is far more interactive than that, and involves one theory's being susceptible to correction and reconceptualization at the behest of the cohort theory. Neuroscience and psychology need each other. Crudely, neuroscience needs psychology because it needs to know what the system does; that is, it needs high-level specifications of the input-output properties of the system. Psychology needs neuroscience for the same reason: it needs to know what the system does. That is, it needs to know whether lower-level specifications bear out the initial input-output theory, where and how to revise input-output theory, and how to characterize processes at levels below the top. Psychology cannot know what the system does simply on the basis of input-output hypotheses, for, as it now seems clear, such hypotheses may postulate what turn out to be "virtual governors"; worse, they may postulate input-output operations that are completely misconceived. Worse again, they may depend on a mis-conception, deeply entrenched in folk psychology, of the phenome-non to be explained. As neuroscience and psychology co-evolve, both will need *folk* psychology less and less. A metaphor that is perhaps more apt likens the co-evolutionary progress to two rock climbers making their way up a wide chimney by bracing their feet against the wall, each braced against the back of the other.

What the mind-brain is doing—even as described at the level of input-output functions of the system—is not an observational matter, to be read off simply by looking at the behaving organism. Rather, it is a deeply theoretical matter. Some initial theory is essential to get the whole enterprise going, and broadly speaking, folk psychology is that initial theory. We have already gone beyond folk psychology, and as neuroscience and psychology co-evolve, the likelihood is that the initial theory will by inches be revised, lock, stock, and barrel. (For more specific arguments demonstrating weakness in folk psy-chology, see section 9.5.)

The co-evolutionary development of neuroscience and psychology means that establishing points of reductive contact is more or less inevitable. As long as psychology is willing to test and revise its theory and hypoth-eses when they conflict with confirmed neurofunctional and neuro-structural hypotheses, and as long as the revisions are made with a view to achieving concord with the lower-level theory, then the capacities and processes described by psychological theory will finally find explanations in terms of neuroscientific theory. (The same is true, of course, for the revisions and reconstructions in neurosci-ence.) If certain capacities specified in folk psychology turn out to be "virtual governors" so far as neuroscience can determine, then a coevolutionary strategy will elicit revisionary descriptions of the capacities, based on what seems pretty certain at the neurofunctional level. The capacities, newly described, will be explained by the neurofunctional theory that prompted them. Obviously, this is an oversimplification of what is a horrendously complex business, but I am after the general features at this point. The heart of the matter is that if there is theoretical give and take, then the two sciences will knit themselves into one another.

How thoroughgoing a reduction will ultimately be achieved re-mains, of course, to be seen, and a rich reductive integration could be frustrated by a variety of factors. First are the practical difficulties, such as disruption to research—by plagues, wars, and so forth. Sec-ond, the problem of understanding how the mind-brain works may be beyond our finite capacities. The brain, in the event, *may* be more complicated than it is smart, in which case reductive consummation of neuroscience and psychology may forever elude us. One does not *believe* this, but it is a possibility to be admitted. Third, and not unrelated, we may simply lack the mathematics adequate to the task. The sobering example here is the reduction of chemical properties to quantum mechanical properties, where the general outlines are clear enough but in all save the simplest of cases actual reduction is thwarted by want of the necessary mathematics. The chemical properties are not, however, seen to be *emergent* in some metaphysical sense, and new mathematical breakthroughs may resolve the problems. (See the earlier discussion in section 7.3.)

Fourth, it may be in the nature of things that psychology is not reducible to neuroscience. Consider by way of analogy that though the theory of optics and the theory of particle mechanics co-evolved, the first never did and never will reduce to the second, since light turned out to be electromagnetic radiation and the theory of optics was instead reduced to the theory of electromagnetic radiation. Thus, optics and mechanics went their separate ways. An empirical possibility that cannot be ruled out a priori is that mental states have certain properties not explicable in terms of neurofunctional organization or neurostructural dynamics.

There are, however, disanalogies between the case of light and the case of mental states and processes, the most salient of which is this: the expectation that mechanics would reduce optics was nurtured by the belief that the fundamental properties of matter were mechanical and was dashed by the discovery that electrical properties are also fundamental. For the case of psychology to be exactly like that, it would have to turn out that mentality is somehow a *fundamental property of matter*, and for that there is not the smallest shred of evidence. But perhaps in some other quirky and unforeseen way, psychology will resist reduction. Just perhaps, for science is full of surprises. To concede that it is empirically possible that psychology, however richly co-evolved with neuroscience, might be of such a nature as never to reduce, is just to concede a very bare possibility. It means only that there is no contradiction in supposing psychology is irreducible. It is not to envision a *positive reason* why it will not reduce, and it is not to concede the wisdom of an isolationist methodology for psychology.

To argue the merits of co-evolution of theories is not to advocate anything at all specific by way of research methods, and I do not mean to imply that every researcher needs to know what every other researcher is up to. No one *could* do that even if he wanted to. On a strong version of the autonomy thesis, psychology goes its own way, and in so doing, it is essentially isolated both in matters of discovery and in matters of disconfirmation from neuroscience. On the co-evolutionary picture of science, psychology and neuroscience should each be vulnerable to disconfirmation and revision at any level by the discoveries of the other. And when inquiries converge on a subject matter, as for example they do on learning, memory, attention, and perception, each should be open to discoveries of the other. The isolation of psychology from the disconfirmatory reach of neuroscience would be a mistake, because in general it is such susceptibility that keeps a science honest. Short-run isolation of a science while it works up a head of steam is one thing, but isolation in the long run, isolation *in principle*, is quite another.

The unity of science is advocated as a working hypothesis not for the sake of puritanical neatness or ideological hegemony or old positivistic tub-thumping, but because theoretical coherence is the "principal criterion of belief-worthiness for epistemic units of all sizes from sentences on up" (Paul M. Churchland 1980). Once a theory is exempt from having to cohere with the rest of science, its confirmation ledger is suspect and its credibility plummets. To excuse a theory as hors de combat is to do it no favors (Oppenheim and Putnam 1958, Feyerabend 1963a, 1963b). (For the contrary view, see Fodor 1974 and 1975.)

A mainstay assumption of the autonomy thesis concerns the *integrity* of the sentential-logical model of representations and computations and its absolute irreducibility. Thus, it may be conceded that lines may be redrawn in demarcating learning and memory capacities, but nevertheless it will be insisted that the fundamental theoretical framework characterizing representations and computations is sound, to be neither revised by nor reduced to neuroscience. In section 9.5 I shall present the case for this view, and in section 9.6 I shall argue against it, showing that there are compelling reasons for seeing even the sentential paradigm as problematic and thus for unequivocally preferring the co-evolutionary ideology.

9.5 Representations and Reduction

In dismissing the reductive program, functionalists rely not only on the distinction between function and structure but also on a distinction between *logical/meaning* relations and *causal* relations. Psychological states, as we have seen it claimed many times, stand to one another in logical and meaningful relationships. Psychological states are representational, and changes of state are explainable in terms of rules followed for the manipulation of representations. This connection between cognitive processes, on the one hand, and symbol manipulation and rule following on the other, explains the mutual admiration of orthodox artificial intelligence research and cognitive psychology.

Beliefs, desires, goals, hopes, thoughts, intentions, expectations, and so forth, are mental states referred to in the explanation of behavior, and what is alleged to make them indispensable for psychology but unfathomable by neuroscience is that they form a *semantically coherent* system, as opposed to a *causally interconnected* system. In the terminology used earlier (chapter 8), they have *content*; they are *intentional*. They are *about* things, they can be true or false of the world, and they stand to one another in logical relationships such as entailment and contradiction. The objection to a reductionist program runs as follows: psychological explanations of human behavior rely essentially on the ascription of representational states to the person and they exploit the rule-governed relationships between the contents of the states. Because mental states are identified in terms of their logical and semantical relations, and because transitions between mental states are determined by the logical relations between representations, mental states are special. *Logical relations cannot be reduced to causal relations*; consequently, psychological theory is autonomous and the prospect of reduction is patently hopeless.[6]

We have already seen Popper's development of this common intuition concerning the specialness of logical relations, and the criticism of it (section 8.4). This version offers additional considerations, however, and it avoids some of the weaknesses of Popper's arguments. What makes this version different is that it does not deny that mental states are in causal interaction, but only that what matters for psychological explanation and for the development of a scientific cognitive psychology are the logical relations and semantic representations. In defense of this idea it claims that the categories of psychological theory will cross-classify those of neurobiology, in the sense that the former will at best map onto an *indefinite* number of *arbitrarily* related neurobiological categories. In this sense, the generalizations of psychology are emergent with respect to neurobiological theory.

Logical Relations and Biological Relations
In more detail, the arguments proceed in the following vein. Consider, for example, that in explaining why Smith shot his horse, it may be said: Smith believed his horse had broken its leg and believed that whenever a horse has a broken leg, the only thing to do is destroy it. Sense is made of Smith's action in terms of his beliefs and the logical relations obtaining between them. More specifically, Smith's decision to destroy the horse follows logically from the con-

tent of two of his beliefs: "Whenever a horse breaks a leg, the only thing to do is destroy it" and "This horse broke its leg." The causal relations, whatever they may be, between the physiological realizations of the representational states are not what matters to the explanation. Rather, what matters are the logical (i.e., formal) relations between the *contents* of his beliefs, desires, intentions, and so on. Mental states do stand in causal relations to other mental states, but, as Fodor says, "mental representations have their causal roles in virtue of their formal properties" (1981:26). We have access to the causal relationships between mental states only via access to their representational relationships. Thus the crux of the antireductionist argument from rules and representations.

The point is grounded in the machine analogy. Consider an electronic symbol-manipulating device, such as a pocket calculator. The explanation of why it printed out 27 will proceed by citing the input (9, ×, 3) and the arithmetic rule for multiplication. What is needed to explain the behavior is an understanding of the calculator's representations and the rules for manipulating the representations. Not only do the electronic events underlying the changes of state differ from machine to machine; they will not yield an explanation of the phenomenon in question in any event (Fodor 1975). Descriptions of such events can be useful, but not for explaining why the calculator printed out 27. Pylyshyn says, "We explain why the machine does something by referring to certain interpretations of its symbols in some intended domain. This is, of course, precisely what we do in describing how (and why) people do what they do" (1980:113). The real obstacle to reduction, it is claimed, is the intentionality of mental states; that is, the fact that they have content. For explanations at the intentional level are of a radically different nature from those at levels that do not advert to representations and content. The latter explanations have a good and useful place, but they cannot do justice to the representational dimension of psychological life.

But why, precisely, not? The heart of the rationale is this: the categories of psychological theory will radically cross-classify the categories of neurophysiological theory, and consequently neurophysiological generalizations will miss entirely important relations describable only at the level where representations are referred to. That is, at best the psychological categories will map onto an indefinite jumble of neurobiological categories, and it *will* be a jumble, in the sense that the neurobiological categories in question will not form a natural kind. Neurophysiological explanations, therefore, will not explain the same things that a psychology of representations will explain (Pylyshyn 1980, Fodor 1981). In Fodor's words, ". . .we are driven to functionalism (hence to the autonomy of psychology) by the suspicion that there are empirical generalizations about mental states that can't be formulated in the vocabulary of neurological or physical theories. . ." (1981:25). The best way to understand this claim is through an example Pylyshyn presents.

Suppose someone comes to believe that there is a fire in her building and so dials the fire department on her telephone. Now coming to believe there is a fire in the building is coming to have a certain kind of representation, and whoever believes there is a fire in her building has the same representation. And if in consequence she dials the fire department, we understand the whys and wherefores of her behavior in the same way. However, underlying the commonality of representation may be a dismaying diversity of physiological states. Someone can come to believe the building is on fire in a variety of ways: she might smell smoke, see smoke, see flames, feel a hot wall, hear someone call "Fire," hear a smoke detector, and on and—indefinitely—on. Each of these distinct ways of coming to have the representation "There is a fire in the building" will have a distinct physiological causal story, at least for the obvious reason that different sensory receptors are involved. In this sense, the categories of psychology cross-classify or are orthogonal to the categories of neuroscience.

Because the neurophysiological realizations are distinct, the neurophysiological generalizations will not capture what is similar in each of these instances—to wit, that the person believed there was a fire in the building. The neurophysiological explanations of why the person dialed the number 911 will be *different* in each case, whereas the psychological explanation will do justice to the abstract— semantically coherent—similarity prevailing in each case and will explain the behavior by reference to the commonly held belief. In sum, certain generalizations, vital for the explanation of behavior, will be missed by neuroscience but will be captured by psychological theory (Pylyshyn 1980, Fodor 1981). Neuroscience, therefore, cannot explain phenomena characterized by our psychological theory. Thus the irreducibility and autonomy of cognitive psychology.[7]

Two preliminary remarks: (1) These arguments against reduction in no way depend on ascribing a nonphysical status to representations. In contrast to Popper's arguments from intentionality (section 8.4), this view asserts that every instance of a mental state has a physical realization. (2) The psychological states for which these arguments are most plausible are the sentential attitudes (beliefs, desires, thoughts, and so forth). The arguments are decidedly less plausible in regard to memory, many kinds of learning, sensory states, consciousness, attention, pattern recognition, facial recognition, the emotions, habits, cognitive skills, and so on. The reason is that in the latter cases there is no theory (not even palpable folk theory) of how to characterize the relevant semantical/logical representations, *if* such there be, or how they relate to one another. By contrast, in the case of the sentential attitudes the theory is straightforward: content is specified by a sentence, and the relations between sentences are defined by logic (see below). Given the limited application of the argument, it may be assumed that it is meant to defend not the autonomy of psychology in general but the autonomy of sentential attitude psychology in particular.

On the other hand, Pylyshyn (1980, 1984) argues unequivocally that cognitive psychology as a whole should be modeled on sentential attitude psychology. This suggests that the scope of the argument is intended to be very wide indeed. Thus, to be as liberal as possible I shall take it to defend the autonomy of cognitive psychology, assuming that sentential attitude theory occupies a central position therein. This is inevitably an unsatisfactory carving of the territory, since many psychologists who consider themselves in the cognitive swim but who work on learning or attention, for example, will not wish to have their discipline hived off from neuroscience. Certainly it will distress those researchers who describe their work as *cognitive neuroscience* (for example, Patricia Goldman-Rakic, Michael Gazzaniga). Nevertheless, granting a certain vagueness about how much of cognitive science is at stake, let us proceed.

Autonomy and Irreducibility Assessed
What the arguments from intentionality show is not that cognitive psychology should be autonomous, or that cognitive psychology is irreducible to neuroscience, but only that cognitive psychology is respectable. Taken as arguments for the view that cognitive psychology is worth pursuing and is a necessary, indispensable part of the enterprise of coming to understand how the mind-brain works, I think they are fair enough, and I have no quarrel. What are contentious are the much larger claims of irreducibility and autonomy, and these go beyond what the premises can support. That the arguments have overextended their reach is evidently not obvious, to say the least, since many philosophers have been convinced of the autonomy of psychology after taking to heart these very arguments. Indeed, autonomy's opposite, interdependence, is within philosophy a minority opinion.

The brunt of my reply attacks the central idea that logical relations between states cannot be explained in terms of causal relations between neurobiological states. I think this opinion is fundamentally a myth, unsupported by any cogent arguments. Where the idea does get support is (1) from the venerable tradition in philosophy according to which the logical-meaningful dimension of mental business cannot be explained naturalistically and (2) from unjustified assumptions about limitations of neuroscience. It assumes either that there can be no theory in neuroscience, or that neuroscience is forever limited to specifying interactions at the level of the single cell, or that neuroscience is too hard to ever tell us much. It therefore fails to recognize that theorizing about information processing in cell assemblies, groups of such assemblies, and so on up, is as much a part of neuroscience as recording from a single cell. An essential part of my reply will therefore be the demonstration, in chapter 10, of what theorizing in neuroscience looks like and, more importantly, of what neurobiological theorizing about *representations and computations* looks like.

First, a general point: the argument from intentionality is in fact a special case of the argument from multiple instantiability (section 9.3), and the observations and remarks made earlier regarding what the multiple instantiability argument does and does not prove are all relevant here. And as we have seen in the preceding section, the arguments for the enriching effect of the co-evolution of theories greatly weaken the ideology of autonomy and irreducibility.

The naturalist's additional point in reply is this: if there really is a commonality of psychological state in the heads of all who come to believe there is a fire in the building, then there is every reason to expect that *at some appropriate level* of neurophysiological organization, this commonality corresponds to a common neurobiological configuration. After all, the heads all house human brains, and human brains have a common evolutionary history. They are not the product of entirely different designs in Silicon Valley and at Mitsubishi. It should be possible, therefore, to explain neurobiologically what is going on, unless the psychological level is indeterministic with respect to the relevant neurophysical level. For that there is no evidence, nor do the antireductionists wish to embrace such an unlikely view.

Envisage a neurobiological theory, of some appropriate level of organization, that addresses the question of representations and computations in the brain, but where the representations are not sentence-like and the computations are not inferences but are, say, mathematical—just the sort to be executed by suitably configured neuronal arrays. Why should not such a theory explain the logical and meaningful relations between states at the psychological level? How, a priori, do philosophers know that it cannot? What can be their special source of knowledge? I suspect that the philosophical tradition of veneration for inference and the sentential attitude has generated a kind of fetishism with respect to logic as the model for inner processes. A reverent attachment to this aspect of folk psychology, together with ignorance about neuroscience, has made the naturalistic program seem pathetically hopeless.

So long as neuroscience can address the functional questions concerning how information is stored and processed by neuronal ensembles, it is addressing levels of organization above that of the single cell. At the appropriate *neurofunctional* level, therefore, psychological states of a given type may be found to have a common neurofunctional property. That is, assuming the reality of a commonality at the topmost psychological level of organization, it could turn out that whenever someone comes to have a belief that the building is on fire, a certain neuronal *assembly* somewhere in the hierarchy of organization has a particular and identifiable configuration. On the other hand, it may be that the state of having the belief that the building is on fire is analogous to a "virtual governor," and the neural conditions ramify across diverse neuronal assemblies. In that event readjustment of macrolevel theory and macrolevel description may be elicited, and in a science fiction parallel to the case of genetics it may eventually be said that there is no neurophysiology of individual beliefs; there is only a neurophysiology of information fermenphorylation (to take a made-up name). On either scenario, and this is the important point, there will be an explanation of macrolevel effects in terms of microlevel machinations, of macrolevel categories in terms of microlevel business. Insofar as there are such explanations, reductive integration will have been achieved.

Moreover, there is already evidence that the folk psychological categories of belief and desire are bound to fragment at the hands of science and hence that, like the virtual governor and like learning and memory, they will have no unitary explanation at lower levels. One important reason here derives from the original work of Stephen Stich (1983), and the difficulty centers on the nature of the way we ascribe beliefs (desires, etc.) within the folk psychological framework—that is, the bases on which we say what it is someone believes. More exactly, the difficulty is that belief ascription is context-relative, and depending on interests, aims, and sundry other considerations, different criteria are variously used to specify the content of a given mental state. Even worse, sometimes different criteria will give conflicting answers to the question of what someone believes. So the first problem is that folk psychology as it stands does not have a *single,* unified, well-defined notion of content, but rather a set of vague notions flying in loose formation. This may be all very well for a folk theory going about its humdrum business, but if there is no such thing as *the* content of someone's propositional attitudes, then the project of finding a place for the propositional attitudes in cognitive psychology, let alone neurobiology, is severely hampered.

The second problem is that some of the criteria routinely invoked within folk psychology for specifying content rely on features that are *irrelevant to the causal role* of the mental state in interaction with other mental states, stimuli, and behavior. Noteworthy culprits here are semantic features—namely, truth, reference, and meaning. Now such criteria will give completely irrelevant content specifications if what we seek are psychological generalizations that articulate the causal role in cognition of beliefs and desires. The brain, as Dennett (1981) has put it, is a syntactic engine, not a semantic engine. That is, roughly, the brain goes from state to state as a function of the causal properties of the antecedent states, not as a function of what the states are "about" or whether they represent something true about the world. So far as the question of reduction is concerned, this means that at best, considerable correction and reconfiguration of the folk psychological concepts of belief and desire are required. It may be possible, however, that a syntactic analogue of the sentential attitudes will be able to do duty in a scientific psychology and will fit in comfortably with a cognitive neurobiology in the geometric style (sections 10.3–10.6). Even so, of course, these newly characterized states and the relations between them can be expected to have a neurobiological reduction, for the reasons just discussed.

Semantical issues are notoriously difficult, and this is not the place to do anything but take the lid off the jar and let a few odors escape. Suffice it to say that Stich's breakthrough on the question of semantics bears importantly on the possibility of smoothly reducing folk psychology to neurobiology, as well as on how representational states are to be understood in cognitive science. If Stich is right, and I think he is, then it is already clear that the propositional attitudes, qua folk psychological categories, are coming apart. Therefore, when antireductionists parade these categories in all their folk psychological regalia as irreducible, the irony is that it is their lack of empirical integrity that prevents their reduction.

Revisionary Reductions and Folk Psychology
If the reduction is smooth, relatively little revision of the top-level theory may be required; if it is bumpy, conceptual revision may be greater. Notwithstanding reduction and revision, belief talk, like gene talk, could continue to have a useful role—and not just after

hours but also in research (cf. also Newtonian mechanics and the special theory of relativity). It may be this prospect that encourages the antireductionist to plead the case for autonomy. The point does nothing to that end, however. It is a practical observation about conceptual usefulness, and all it really supports is the less controversial notion that research needs to be conducted at many levels, one of which describes mental states. That is perfectly consistent with reductionist goals, and though sound enough, it is a far cry from autonomy.

Raising the matter of revisions emphasizes once more that the psychological categories valued by the antireductionist are categories of a *theory*, and in the main the theory that embeds these categories is folk psychology. It is an empirical question how good a theory of mind-brain function folk psychology is, and how much reconceptualization is required. Notice in particular that if the categories of folk psychology radically cross-classify those of neuroscience, and if, in addition, no explanation of folk psychology by neuroscience can be achieved, it may be because folk psychology is radically misconceived. Ironically for its champions, folk psychology may be irreducible with respect to neuroscience—irreducible because dead wrong.

The price of claiming autonomy for an immature theory is that one shields it from the very revisionary forces essential to its reaching maturity. The price of claiming autonomy for a theory when it has a powerful replacement is that one protects it from disconfirmation and closes oneself off from the explanatory and experimental opportunities made available by the competing theory. As an example of the first situation, consider that for thermodynamics in its early days to have been granted autonomous status from mechanics would have denied it the benefits of co-evolution. As for the second, if physicists in the seventeenth century had taken Aristotelian physics as autonomous with respect to Newtonian physics, it would have been viciously stultifying for physicists determined to be Aristotelian. It is *respectability* that should be claimed for cognitive psychology, not autonomy or irreducibility.

The computer metaphor should be handled with extreme caution. As we have seen, the theory of levels borrowed from computer science defines prematurely and inappropriately the levels of organization in the brain. There are additional reasons for caution. In the case of pocket calculators we know what generalizations describe their behavior, what categories apply, and what rules they follow. We build them precisely so that they will operate according to arithmetic rules and so that they can represent numbers. Their symbol-manipulating capacities are understood because we have built them in, and the generalizations that are true of them are so by virtue of their manufacture. By contrast, human brains were not literally built to instantiate the generalizations of folk psychology, and what generalizations do truly describe our inner processes is a matter for empirical research. In the case of evolved organisms, ourselves and others, we must find out what generalizations are true and what categories apply. As a matter of discovery, there may be much to be learned about how we manipulate symbols and what symbols we manipulate by studying how symbol manipulation evolved and how (and whether) it is accomplished in simpler nervous systems. (See chapter 10 for further discussion of the respects in which the computer metaphor misleads us.)

Folk psychology, like other folk theories before it, may be misconceived in many dimensions, and under pressure from discoveries at diverse levels it can be expected to evolve. Even the characterization of what needs to be explained may be revised. The domain of phenomena that allegedly cannot be explained by neuroscience but only by intentional psychology is a domain specified by intentional psychology. Change that, and the domain description changes too. It is spectacularly evident that newer theories do not always espouse the explananda of the older theories. (See chapter 7.) Neuroscience may fail to explain phenomena characterized in folk psychology for the same reason Newtonian physics fails to explain what turns the crystal spheres and modern biology fails to explain how the vital spirits are concocted. The complaint that neuroscience cannot in principle do justice to the generalizations of psychology errs in two directions: it is overconfident about the integrity of folk psychology and it underestimates the value of co-evolution of theories.

Are Sentential Attitudes Important to Theorizing in Psychology?
Sentential attitudes and *logical* inference occupy center stage in the disagreement between those who defend autonomy and those who defend co-evolution and interdependence. But are the sentential attitudes really so very important in folk psychology or in cognitive psychology? Would thoroughgoing revision of their theory be so very revolutionary?

The answer to both questions is a resounding yes. Beliefs, desires, thoughts, intentions, and the like, are invariably assumed to mediate between input and output and to have a crucial role in the causation of behavior. Moreover, to echo an earlier remark, it is only in the case of the sentential attitudes that we have something approaching a systematic theory both of the nature of the representations and of the rules that govern the transitions between representations. Most of the generalizations routinely used in the explanation of human behavior advert to sentential attitudes and their interplay. One of the beauties of sentential attitudes as a theoretical postulate is that they can also be given a role in nonconscious processes and hence can be invoked to describe cognitive business a long way down. Additionally, we can exploit deductive logic and such inductive logic and decision theory as are available to extend our theory of the rules followed by internal states. Dismantle sentential attitude theory, and we no longer have any idea how to explain behavior—we no longer have any idea of what is going on inside. Fodor (1975) grittily describes the situation: it's the only theory we've got.

The theoretical blessings of sentential attitude psychology are undeniably rich, and it is entirely reasonable to try to develop a scientific psychology by extending and pruning the sentential attitude base. Consequently, the suggestion that substantial revisions to this base resulting from co-evolution are likely will fall on ungrateful ears. It is of course no defense of the truth of a theory that it's the only theory we've got. (Compare some fictional Aristotelian, circa 1400: "It's the only theory we've got.") What the lack of alternatives implies is that one has no choice but to *use* the available theory, and this is consistent with its falsity and with trying to construct a better competing theory. In view of the continual harping on the theme of revision, the advocates of theory interdependence must finally square up to this question: is the prospect of revision to sentential attitude psychology serious or frivolous? That is, does it rest on substantial grounds, or is it just a pie-in-the-sky possibility?

We have already seen in Stich's research compelling reason to suppose that the folk psychological categories of belief, desire, and so forth, will require substantial revision. In addition, there are substantial reasons for predicting that at best inference and sentence-like representations will have a small role in the theory of information processing, and for predicting quite radical revisions in folk psychology. These matters will be discussed in the next section.

9.6   Information Processing and the Sentential Paradigm

The Sentential Manifesto

An information-processing theory is *sentential* if it adheres to the following tenets (Patricia S. Churchland 1980b):

> 1. Like beliefs and desires, the cognitively relevant internal states are states that have content, where the content is identified via a sentence. The identification is presumed to be possible by virtue

of an isomorphism holding between the states of the person (his brain) and the relevant sentences of a set.

2. The theoretically important relations between cognitive states are characterized by means of the resources of logic. These obtain in virtue of the aforementioned isomorphism. (Various theories of logic will be variously favored by cognitive scientists.)

3. The transitions between states are a function of the logical relations holding between the sentences identifying the states, which in the most straightforward case will consist of inference, abductive and deductive. Again, by virtue of the isomorphism.

4. The evaluation of the cognitive virtue (rationality) of a system is a function of the extent to which it succeeds in doing what the favored theory of state transition (i.e., theory of logic) says it ideally should do.

Any sentential theory needs a theory of how it is that internal states have content, since it is plainly ad hoc to suppose it a lucky accident that the relevant isomorphisms systematically obtain. Fodor's theory (1975, 1981) is that sentential attitudes (alias propositional attitudes) are relational states, where one of the relata is a sentence in the organism's *language of thought.* Thus, if Smith has the thought that gulls' eggs are delicious, then he stands in a certain relation to a sentence in his language of thought, namely the sentence whose English translation is "Gulls' eggs are delicious." Broadly speaking, the information processing is manipulation of representations, and representations are symbols of the language of thought. Thinking is, to put it crudely, sentence-crunching, and the machine analogy underwrites the intended sense of symbol manipulation.

Within cognitive science there is considerable loose talk about cognitive representations, where the question of the nature and status of representations is left conveniently vague. Fodor's theory makes explicit what is an implicit commitment in sentential/representational hypotheses generally. There are, it should be emphasized, many cognitive psychologists who do not adhere to the sentential theory and who investigate cognitive capacities while awaiting the development of a nonsentential theory of representations.

The foregoing is just a thumbnail sketch of the main features of a sentential theory of information processing, but the finer points and the in-house disputes can for now be set aside.

Cognition and Sentence-Crunching
How plausible are the framework assumptions of the sentential paradigm? The theme of the ensuing section is that as an approach to

cognitive activity in general, they have serious flaws. Language is a social art, and linguistic behavior serves a communicative function. We may stand to enhance our cognitive repertoire as a result of acquiring linguistic skill, inasmuch as such a skill structures and enables certain cognitive capacities. On the other hand, there is something deeply mystifying in the idea that all of our cognitive activity, including cognitively dependent perception, pattern recognition, and the cognitive activity of infants, is language-like, in the sense that it consists of sentence manipulation.

If we think of linguistic behavior as something that evolved because it provided for a quantum jump in the information available to organisms by allowing for complex exchange between individuals, then the enthusiasm for cognition as sentence-crunching seems insensitive to evolutionary considerations. Sentence-crunching is certain to have been a cognitive latecomer in the evolutionary scheme of things, and it must have knit itself into the preexisting nonsentential cognitive organization, or, perhaps one should say, it must have evolved out of preadaptive nonsentential structures. To be sentence-crunching "all the way down" implies either that cognition must have been sentence-crunching "all the way back," which is implausible, or that sentence-crunchers have no cognitive heritage from earlier species, which is also implausible given the evolution of the brain.

The objections in the literature to the sentential paradigm condense around several prominent problems, which I shall consider briefly in turn.

The Infralinguistic Catastrophe
It is a problem for the sentential paradigm that intelligent behavior is displayed by organisms who have no overt linguistic capacity. Consider the case of a nonverbal deaf-mute who was committed to an asylum for the insane as a result of misdiagnosis (and some malice). He made his escape after what must have been elaborate planning, deception, and arranging, and the escape must be considered intelligent by any standard. The behavior of chimpanzees in getting what they want or where they want is also as obviously intelligent as much behavior of the overtly verbal human (Menzel 1974). The orangutans who make umbrellas of jungle leaves have an intelligent solution to a comfort problem. The octopi who unscrew mason jars to get the food inside, the macaques who wash their sandy potatoes in the sea, and the rooks who drop stones on would-be invaders all display a solution that is in some degree intelligent (Griffin 1984). Nonverbal human infants learn the language of their peers, a cognitive feat of monumental proportions.

Short of conceding that there is substantial nonsentential representation, two solutions are possible. (1) One can argue that behavior in the infralinguistic organism is not really a cognitive product. Language learning by the toddler, on this view, is not in fact cognitive in the intended sense. (2) One can argue that since the behavior in question is cognitive, then the infraverbal organisms have a language of thought in which they reason, solve problems, etc. (Fodor 1975).

The first alternative in effect defines a cognitive process as a sentence-crunching process. Accordingly, it becomes true *by definition* that cognition is essentially sentence-crunching, but this leaves it entirely open whether much of the information processing subserving intelligence is cognitive in this special sense.

The second alternative suffers from diminished credibility. It is a strain to see the justification for supposing that orangutans, infant humans, and all the rest have a language of thought, Mentalese, in which they frame hypotheses, test them against the evidence, draw deductive inferences, and so forth. Mentalese, as Fodor (1975) depicts it, is a full-fledged language, with a syntax, a semantics, and a finite vocabulary—as indeed it must be if it is to be the wherewithal for sentence-crunching. An additional difficulty that Fodor himself draws out concerns how the infant uses Mentalese to learn the language of his peers. If the infant learns English by hypothesizing what chunks of English can be correlated with concepts in Mentalese, then he can only acquire English concepts for which there are Mentalese correlates. This means that there is no such thing as real concept learning, in the sense that wholly new concepts are added to the conceptual repertoire.

This consequence is sufficiently unacceptable to be a reductio of the Mentalese hypothesis. For it entails that the ostensibly new concepts evolving in the course of scientific innovation—concepts such as atom, force field, quark, electrical charge, and gene—are lying ready-made in the language of thought, even of a prehistoric hunter-gatherer. It is difficult to take such an idea seriously, even supposing there is something like a language of thought in linguistically accomplished humans. The concepts of modern science are defined in terms of the theories that embed them, not in terms of a set of "primitive conceptual atoms," whatever those might be. To suppose they are ready-made in Mentalese is to suppose the embedding theory is somehow (miraculously) ready-made in Mentalese. This cannot be right. (For a fuller discussion, see Patricia S. Churchland 1980b.) If it is not, then however learning of a first language is accomplished, it is not by sentence-crunching in the language of thought. Something entirely different is going on.

The Problem of Tacit Knowledge
Under the lens of philosophical analysis, the concept of belief as it lives in folk psychology shows serious theoretical defects, and if the theory cannot be modified to correct the problems, then radical revision of the theory may have to be considered. The philosophical analysis can be understood as a testing of the internal coherence of the theory, and some of the results are very puzzling. Tacit beliefs are a case in point. (See especially Dennett 1975, 1984a, Lycan (forthcoming).)

Some of the things Smith believes are things he is dwelling on right now, as for example when he says silently to himself, "My fern needs water." Other things are allegedly not part of his current silent monologue, but were part of past monologues, such as what he said to himself as he drove to work, namely, "Flin Flon is on the migration route of polar bears." What else does Smith believe? Well, suppose we determine the range of what he believes by querying him. We ask, "Is Medicine Hat on the migration route of polar bears?" and when he says no, we can add the negation of our question to the list of what he believes. Why not ask him the same question about Tallahassee, Dallas, and so forth? Why not ask him whether polar bears are made of sand, of salt, of spaghetti, . . . ? Again, with additions to the belief-list. Why not ask him, for every number *n* greater than 7, whether he believes that polar bears are less than *n* meters tall? Since he will answer yes each time, his answers to these questions can also be added. The trouble is, things are getting out of hand, and the modest Smith is now credited with an infinite number of beliefs.

Philosophers have tried to augment and exploit the resources of folk theory to save it from the extravagance of infinite belief stores. Call "tacit" any belief that one really has but has not explicitly entertained. The problem then is how to specify conditions under which someone does really have "P" as a tacit belief, where the conditions are not so broad as to entail that we all have an infinity of beliefs. The problem seems manageable enough at first blush, but it turns out to be stubbornly resistant to solution.

The austere solution is simply to cut out tacit beliefs altogether. The price of that solution is that the consequences of one's beliefs—even the dead obvious consequences—are no longer things one believes. Smith believes that all men are mortal, and he believes that Trudeau is a man, but, busy with other things, he has never troubled to explicitly draw the conclusion: Trudeau is mortal. But it is an obvious consequence of his beliefs, he would assent in a flash if asked, and it can be shown to have a causal role in his behavior if we set up the right circumstances. (Suppose Smith is a prairie socialist who attends the opposition's rally and hears an Ottawa Liberal say, "Trudeau will live forever." Smith, ever forthright and voluble, unhesitatingly shouts out, "Trudeau is mortal.") Given these considerations, it seems reasonable to say that Smith all along believed that Trudeau is mortal, notwithstanding the implicit status of the belief. The austere solution looks unacceptable.

The trick is to find a principled way of dividing, among the sentences Smith will assent to, those that are really tacit beliefs, with real causal effects, and those that are not. If an extrapolator-deducer mechanism is postulated, this explains how Smith (really) has the belief that Trudeau is mortal (it gets deduced from other beliefs in the store), but it also brings additional problems. Are *all* the consequences of all of Smith's beliefs things he believes? Alas, no, since no one will assent to every such consequence, and some, such as theorems of mathematics, will not even be recognized, let alone assented to. Nor will it do to take all the *obvious* consequences of Smith's beliefs as what he tacitly believes, because what is obvious depends on who the person is, and there is no independent measure. What was obvious to Gödel is not obvious to me (Field 1977). Moreover, all of us—irrationally, one might say—can fail on occasion to see the "obvious" consequences of our beliefs (Nisbett and Ross 1980). On the other side of the coin, even some of the far-flung consequences Smith does assent to are not plausible candidates as tacit beliefs if they were assented to on the spot, so to speak, rather than having been cranked out by the extrapolator-deducer working behind the scenes (see especially Lycan (forthcoming)).

Moreover, when we look closely at how the extrapolator-deducer mechanism might be expected to operate, there are intractable problems. How does it "know" what beliefs in the store are relevant to deducing an answer to a particular question? Does it have its own store of beliefs about what is relevant to what questions? Is there a higher-order extrapolator-deducer mechanism to handle that? And what of *its* beliefs? (See Dennett 1975.) In many examples it is not evident either what could be the input to the extrapolator-deducer or what the chain of reasoning might have been. For example, I suppose it must be said that I believe that the computer on which I now enter this word will not blow up in the next ten seconds. But that is not a belief that until this moment figures in my speech, silent or overt, so it must be deducible from my other beliefs. Like what? That computers never blow up? (I don't know if I believe that.) That North Star computers never blow up? That computers only blow up if . . . if what? I really don't have the faintest idea. (See also Dreyfus 1979, 1981.)

With the failure of internal solutions to the problem of tacit beliefs, it must be suspected that there is a framework mistake somewhere, perhaps infecting the statement of the problem itself. Thus, the supposition that the knowledge store is a sentence (belief) store comes to be regarded as untenable. Abandoning that supposition, we can try instead the idea that tacit knowledge is not (mainly not) a corpus of tacit beliefs. It may be that on some occasions sentences are stored, as for example when the exact words of Macbeth's death speech are burned into memory, but verbatim storage may be the exception rather than the rule.

What is stored is generally something else, something that may be verbally encoded on demand, but need not be verbally encoded to be cognitively engaged. Accordingly, even those sentences that have been explicitly assented to or that figured in silent speech are generally not stored as sentences. If such information is nonconsciously used in the course of solving a problem, or if it serves as a background assumption, there is no reason to assume it must first acquire a sentential encoding. Sometimes the background assumptions that affect behavior and problem solving can be verbalized only with immense effort or perhaps not at all. Think, for example, of social knowledge, or of a farmer's "bovine knowledge," or of a woodsman's "bush knowledge."[8] The scope of sentential representation and sentential manipulation now looks more limited than the sentential paradigm assumes. Other sorts of representational structures will need to be postulated; hence the interest in nonsentential representations such as prototypes (Rosch 1973), images (Kosslyn 1975), and frames (Minsky 1975). (See also chapter 10.)

The Problem of Knowledge Access

An organism's knowledge store is a waste of resources unless it can be used, and that means that the right bits must be available at the right times. For motile creatures, survival and reproductive success depend upon being able to use the stored information for fleeing, fighting, feeding, and reproducing. It does a bull moose no good to know what a female moose looks like if that information remains untapped during rutting season. Notice too that the point holds whether the information is innate or acquired. So much, I think, is obvious. What is not obvious is how an information-processing system knows which of the many things in its store is relevant to the problem at hand. If everything in the store is accessed, then the system will be swamped and unable to make a speedy decision (starving to death while it continues to canvass information), but if relevant information is unavailable, the organism's environment will make it pay. As noted earlier, something akin to this question troubled Peirce profoundly, and the form it took for him was how humans happen to light upon relevant hypotheses to explain an event.

At first encounter the problem of relevant access might seem merely a philosopher's curiosity, but it turns out to be much more. This becomes most clearly visible in the context of artificial intelligence (AI), where the problem is to program a robot that can interact with the world using a knowledge store. Consider the following example, adapted from Dennett 1984a. The robot's task is to survive, and it is told that the spare battery it needs is in a room where a time bomb is set to explode soon. Suppose that the battery is on a wagon, and, having entered the room, the robot pulls the wagon out of the room. The bomb explodes and destroys both the battery and the robot, because the bomb, it turns out, was also on the wagon. Apparently the robot knew that but failed to see an obvious consequence of its behavior, so its program must be improved to allow for that.

Having modified the program, we try again. This time the robot goes into the room and, after pulling out the wagon, begins to crank out the consequences of its behavior, and the consequences of the consequences, including such things as "Some heat will be generated by the action of the wheels on the floor" and "Pulling out the wagon will not change the color of the walls," and the bomb explodes while it is still cranking.

The defect, it seems, is that the robot needs to distinguish between relevant and irrelevant consequences, and what it needs is a mechanism for lighting on the relevant ones. Our parents would say to us, "Use your common sense: the color of the walls does not matter, but the bomb's still being on the wagon does." But how do we translate our parents' advice into an instruction the robot can follow? Should it have the following instruction in its store: if you are trying to get your battery away from a bomb, make sure they are not both on the same wagon, and all else is irrelevant? This is both too specific and too general. Many other things could indeed be relevant, such as: if there is water nearby, don't put the battery in that; if there is apple juice nearby, don't put the battery in that; don't put the bomb in a fire; don't let yourself be near the bomb; if the bomb can be switched off, do that; and so on and drearily on. Moreover, it seems too specific if it is to mimic human knowledge, since we do not have explicit instructions for what to do when finding bombs and babies on wagons, yet we would typically behave successfully.

Suppose, on the other hand, we give the robot the more general instruction, "If you find a hazard situated close to your battery, separate them by a good distance." More will still be needed, however—

namely, a list of what to count as hazards, and how close "close" is, and how far a "good" distance is. Part of the trouble is that the last measure varies as a function of the hazard, and even what counts as a hazard depends on what else is around. A meter is far enough from a sharp knife, "in the cottage" is far enough from a bear, two feet is far enough from a smoldering camp fire but not far enough from a roaring one.

It is now deeply puzzling how the robot might be instructed so as not to be a fool, a problem that in AI research is called the *frame problem* (McCarthy and Hayes 1969).[9] How do humans manage not to be fools? What does our "common sense" or "intelligence" consist in? The more we try to solve the robot's problem of sensible behavior, the more it becomes clear that *our* behavior is not guided by explicit sentential instructions in our store of knowledge (Dennett 1984a). Specifying the knowledge store in sentences is a losing strategy. We have knowledge, all right, but it does not consist in sets of sentences. We know about moving babies away from hazards without having detailed lists of what counts as a hazard and how far to move the baby. Our "relevant-access mechanism" is imperfect, since we are tripped up from time to time, and tort law is full of instances of such imperfection. The right things do not always occur to us at the right times. Nevertheless, we manage on the whole to survive, reproduce, and do a whole lot more.

Somehow, nervous systems have solved the problem of knowledge access. Once that solution is understood, we may be amazed at how different it is from what we imagined, and we may find that we had even naively misconceived the problem itself. It is of course no mere trifle that can be isolated as we get on with understanding the rest of cognition. It is the problem of explaining how an organism can behave intelligently, and it is therefore at the very heart of questions concerning learning, memory, attention, problem-solving, and whatever else of a smart sort the mind-brain does.

Even relatively simple nervous systems have solved the problem of knowledge access, insofar as past experiences modify their behavior. The evolution of increasingly complex nervous systems must involve increasingly complex solutions to the problem of knowledge use. One strategy for coming to understand what is going on is to study learning, memory, and knowledge use in simpler systems and to see how Nature in fact solved the problem. The answers found at that level may well be illuminating for more complex nervous systems. Ethologists learning ever more about the nature of animal behavior, such as imprinting and song learning, and neuroscientists finding mechanisms that subserve that behavior (Kandel 1976, Horn 1983, Nottebohm 1981) can thus put a squeeze on the questions.

The co-evolution of ethology and neuroscience is already well underway, and the two have coalesced at some points in what goes by the name of *neuroethology*. (See for example Horn 1983, Nottebohm 1981, Hoyle 1984.) The complaint that the simpler nervous systems do not display intelligence is premature: we will not know what intelligence is until we have a solution to the problem of knowledge use. In any event, if there are grades of intelligence, understanding the lower grades may be essential to understanding the higher grades.[10] (See also chapter 10.)

The problems of tacit knowledge and knowledge access are not unrelated, and together with the infralinguistic problem they make an impressive case for assessing the sentential paradigm as unsound. The sententialist is of course right about this much: if cognition is not *in general* the manipulation of sentences, then we don't know what is going on. The antecedent of this conditional seems to me inescapable, and since my extrapolator-deducer is in good order, I conclude that indeed we do not know what is going on. Not, however, that I see that as cause for despair; it is what we would expect for a science in *statu nascendi*. Compare the lament of the vitalist in the nineteenth century: if there is no such thing as vital spirit, then we do not have any idea what makes living things alive and different from nonliving things. Biochemistry eventually changed all that.

Eliminative Materialism
Once folk psychology is held at arm's length and evaluated for theoretical strength in the way that any theory is evaluated, the more folkishly inept, soft, and narrow it seems to be. The crucial first step is to see that it *is* a theory, notwithstanding its observational application to oneself and others, and notwithstanding its overpowering obviousness and familiarity. Insofar as it is a theory, it is an empirical, not an a priori, question how good a theory in fact it is, and its "obviousness" will not protect it from revision or replacement if it is flawed.

Like other folk theories, folk psychology is not without virtue, and within certain circumscribed domains it has considerable predictive success. It has at least been good enough to survive until now. On the other hand, it would be astonishing if folk psychology, alone among folk theories, was essentially correct. The mind-brain is exceedingly complex, and it seems unlikely that primitive folk would have lit upon the correct theoretical framework to explain its nature where they failed with motion, fire, heat, the weather, life, disease, the sky, the stars, and so forth. Even if folk psychology is in some degree "built in," as perhaps folk physics may be, such innateness does not guarantee its truth, its adequacy, or its immunity from revision.

These are general considerations, but as the foregoing section shows, there are in addition detailed reasons for supposing that folk psychology is misconceived in a number of dimensions. The sentential paradigm seems increasingly problematic, and interest in alternatives is on the rise. In such an environment, new theories, looking at first damp and frail, will hatch and struggle to fly. (See chapter 10.)

By "eliminative materialism" I mean the view that holds

1. that folk psychology is a theory;
2. that it is a theory whose inadequacies entail that it must eventually be substantially revised or replaced outright (hence "eliminative"); and
3. that what will ultimately replace folk psychology will be the conceptual framework of a matured neuroscience (hence "materialism").

(For philosophers who defend this view, see Feyerabend 1963b, 1963c, Rorty 1970, Paul M. Churchland 1981, Stich 1983. For neuroscientists whose views are very close to this, see Young 1978 and Crick 1979.)

As eliminative materialism sees it, the sentential attitudes do not play a preeminent role in our cognitive economy. At best they have a limited and rather superficial role. There is some sentence-crunching, almost certainly, but it is not constitutive of cognitive activity. As Hooker reminds us, "Language will surely be seen as a surface abstraction of much richer, more generalized processes in the cortex, a convenient condensation fed to the tongue and hand for social purposes" (1975:217). Sentences are linguistic entities, and language is principally a device for communication.

In order to get a perspective on how parochial it may be to assume that communicative structures are the model for cognitive structures, recall that humpbacked whales communicate by means of "melodies." Imagine that whales have a theory of "melodic attitudes," in virtue of which they explain and predict one another's behavior, where having a certain melodic attitude is understood on the model of overt melody-making. The content of the attitudes is specified by a particular melody, and a whale has a certain melodic attitude just in case he stands in a certain relation to a melody in his "score of internal-music." In the whales' scheme of things, internal cognitive processing is conceived to be essentially melody-crunching, and problem solving is melody-chaining, or "fugueing." Now some of their cognition may really consist in melody-crunching, but that is likely to be at best a small part of the story. Most of it will be understood in the same way our cognition is understood, in terms neither of sentence-crunching nor of melody-crunching. (For another fanciful example, imagine creatures who communicate by producing mosaics of colored patches on their foreheads. They might have a theory of "mosaic attitudes," where cognition is viewed as essentially a matter of mosaic-crunching. The recipe is obvious.)

But if folk psychology is a much-muddled theory, it is by no means clear how it should be revised, nor what the replacing theory would look like. Certainly there is no question of discarding folk psychology until there is a suitable theory to take over the explanatory burden. Even a misconceived theory is better than no theory at all. In any event, folk psychology and its upgraded successors will be crucial elements in the co-evolutionary scenario described earlier.

The prospect of transforming folk psychology as we know and love it has prompted objections, some of which I have already covered, but others of which I must consider separately here. One popular objection is that eliminative materialism is self-refuting. In order to state his position, the argument goes, the eliminativist must believe what he says, but what he says is "There really are no such states as beliefs." However, if there are no beliefs, then the eliminativist cannot believe what he says. Or if he believes what he says, then there really are beliefs. The eliminativist can expect to be taken seriously only if his claim cannot, and he therefore refutes himself.

What the eliminativist is fumbling to say is that folk psychology is seriously inadequate as a theory. Now within the confines of that very theoretical framework we are bound to describe the eliminativist as believing there are no beliefs; however, this is not because folk psychology *is bound to be true*, but only because we are confined within the framework the eliminativist wishes to criticize and no alternative framework is available. If the eliminativist is correct in his criticisms, and if the old framework is revised and replaced, then by using the new vocabulary the eliminativist's criticisms could be restated with greater sophistication and with no danger of pragmatic contradiction. (For example, the new eliminativist might declare, "I gronkify beliefs," where gronkification is a neuropsychological state defined within the mature new theory.) It would be foolish to suppose folk psychology must be true because at this stage of science to criticize it implies using it. All this shows is that folk psychology is the only theory available *now*.

By way of analogy, consider a biologist in the early nineteenth century who wishes to criticize vitalist theory as misconceived. He suggests that there is no such thing as vital spirit and that other accounts must be found to distinguish living things from nonliving things. Consider the following fanciful defense of vitalism:

> The anti-vitalist says that there is no such thing as vital spirit. This claim is self-refuting; the speaker can be expected to be taken seriously only if his claim cannot. For if the claim is true, then the speaker does not have vital spirit and must be *dead*. His claim is meaningful only if it is false. (Patricia S. Churchland 1981d)

The vitalist makes exactly the same mistake here as is made in the foray against the eliminativist. He misidentifies the *unique availability* of a theory with the *truth* of the theory. I suspect that any grand-scale criticism of a deeply entrenched, broadly encompassing theory will seem to have a self-refuting flavor so long as no replacement theory is available. The reason is this: the available theory specifies not only what counts as an explanation but also the explananda themselves. That is, the phenomena that need explaining are specified in the vocabulary of the available theory (for example, the turning of the crystal spheres, the possession by demons, the transfer of caloric, the nature of consciousness). To tender sweeping criticisms of the entire old theory while still *within its framework* will therefore typically sound odd. But odd or not, such criticism nonetheless serves an essential role in steering a theory into readiness for revision.

Finally, it may be objected that the sentential paradigm will survive, whatever the theoretical revolutions and however thorough our understanding of the brain, because it is useful and natural and forms the nexus of our moral conceptions concerning responsibility, praise, and blame. By way of reply, it should first be mentioned that the issue now concerns a *prediction* about what will in fact be the social outcome of a theoretical revolution, and my inclination is to back off from making predictions about such matters.

Nevertheless, it may be useful to consider that objections cut from the same cloth were made on behalf of the geocentric theory of the universe and the creationist theory of man's origins. These theories were defended on grounds that they were useful and natural and were crucial elements in Christian doctrine. If the geocentric theory was wrong, if the creationist story was wrong, then crucial sections of the Bible could not be literally true and man's conception of himself and his place in the universe would be changed.

The new physics and the new biology each did, in some degree, undermine the power of the Christian church and naturalize man's understanding of himself and the universe. But perhaps that was not a bad thing. At a minimum it is worth considering whether transformations in our moral conceptions to adhere more closely to the discovered facts of brain function might be no bad thing as well. Whether this is so will be a complex matter about which I feel ignorant, but it is certainly not a closed matter. It is at least conceivable that our moral and legal institutions will be seen by future generations to be as backward, superstitious, and primitive as we now see the Christian church's doctrine of past centuries concerning the moral significance of disease and the moral propriety of anesthesia, immunization, and contraception (White 1896).

9.7 Conclusions

The goal of this chapter has been to defuse the antireductionist arguments of the functionalists. Mental states may be functional states, but this does not imply that the specification of their functional profile based in folk psychology is correct, either in general or in detail.[11] Nor does it imply that psychology cannot be reduced to neuroscience. The claims for the autonomy of psychology are therefore misbegotten. Psychology stands to profit from a co-evolutionary development with ethology and neuroscience, partly because there are common areas of research, and partly because the sentential paradigm appears to have fundamental shortcomings. New theories about the nature of information processing and about the nature of information-bearing structures are badly needed. In the next chapter I wish to discuss some attempts to ascend beyond the level of the single cell—attempts to theorize about representations and computations in *systems* of neurons.

Selected Readings

Churchland, Paul M. (1981). Eliminative materialism and the propositional attitudes. *Journal of Philosophy* 78:67–90.

Churchland, Paul M. (1984). *Matter and consciousness: A contemporary introduction to the philosophy of mind.* Cambridge, Mass.: MIT Press.

Dennett, Daniel C. (1975). Brain writing and mind reading. In *Language, mind and knowledge,* ed. K. Gunderson. (Minnesota Studies in the Philosophy of Science 7.) Minneapolis: University of Minnesota Press. (Reprinted in D. C. Dennett (1978). *Brainstorms.* Cambridge, Mass.: MIT Press.)

Dennett, Daniel C. (1984). Cognitive wheels: The frame problem of artificial intelligence. In *Minds, machines, and evolution,* ed. C. Hookway, 129–151. Cambridge: Cambridge University Press.

Fodor, Jerry A. (1981). *Representations*. Cambridge, Mass.: MIT Press.

Fodor, Jerry A. (1985). Fodor's guide to mental representation: The intelligent auntie's vade-mecum. *Mind* 94:76–100.

Lycan, William G. (1981). Form, function and feel. *Journal of Philosophy* 78:24–50.

Pylyshyn, Zenon (1984). *Computation and cognition*. Cambridge, Mass.: MIT Press.

Stich, Stephen P. (1983). *From folk psychology to cognitive science: The case against belief.* Cambridge, Mass.: MIT Press.

PART III

A Neurophilosophical Perspective

Chapter 10
Theories of Brain Function

What we require now are approaches that can unite basic neurobiology and behavioral sciences into a single operational framework.
Dominick Purpura, 1975

10.1 Introduction

An enormous amount is known about the structure of nervous systems. What is not understood is how nervous systems function so that the animal sees or intercepts its prey, remembers where it cached nuts, and so forth. We are beginning to understand the behavior of an individual neuron—its membrane properties, the spiking properties of its axon, the synaptic phenomenology, its patterns of connectivity, the transport of intracellular materials, its metabolism, and even something of its embryological migration and development. To be sure, many unanswered questions remain, and major breakthroughs are yet to be made, but the neuron is not a smooth-walled mystery. Neuroscientists have considerable confidence at least about what sort of research would lead to answers to outstanding questions, and they have a general picture of what, more or less, the answers will look like. On the other hand, the state of theory of how *ensembles* of neurons result in an owl's being able to intercept a zigzagging mouse, for example, or how any creature visually recognizes a given object, is markedly different. Here there is no widely accepted theoretical framework, nor even a well-defined conception of what a theory to explain such things as sensorimotor control or perception or memory should look like.

Theorizing about brain functions is often considered slightly disreputable and anyhow a waste of time—perhaps even "philosophical." A neuroscientist randomly plucked out of the crowd at the Society for Neuroscience meetings and asked about the role of theories in the discipline will likely answer with one or all of the following: (1) "The time for theories has not yet arrived, since not enough is known about the structural detail," (2) "What is available by way of theory is too abstract, is untestable, and is anyhow irrelevant to experimental neuroscience," (3) "You cannot get a grant for that sort of monkey-business." (For a sophisticated version of (1), see Selverston 1980.)

One cannot escape having some sympathy with these sentiments. If one is going to do research, one must attract grants and get results. And at least if one is doing experiments, the techniques, the methods, and the procedures are often clear enough. One can lesion, implant electrodes, perfuse neurotransmitters, and so forth. If theorizing is the task, however, the techniques and methods are dis-couragingly amorphous. There is no reliable routine or well-honed method—just the rather empty exhortation to "have good ideas." There is, moreover, a substantial risk in spending time and effort in understanding a theory well enough to figure out ways to test it, and then spending yet more time and effort in conducting the experi-ments. If the theory turns out to be a flop, and in the absence of a mature paradigm it well may, then the investment may be a career disaster. So the decision to adopt a policy that says "Leave theorizing to the theorizers" is by no means irrational.

On the other hand, the value of theory is that it motivates and organizes experimental research, and good theory opens doors to important experimental results. By shunning theory, one runs the risk that the data-gathering may be random and the data gathered, trivial. This is not an idle worry in the current state of neuroscience, for as a number of scientists have pointed out, many grant proposals are not motivated by a genuine hypothesis at all. It sometimes hap-pens that a piece of research is undertaken not in virtue of a larger program for which the results are important, but because the re-searcher has mastered a certain technique, and there are always more measurements he can make. The technique comes to structure and govern the research program rather than the other way around. The justification offered for such research is the "maybe-mightbe" two-step: "If . . . then maybe . . . , and then my results might be important."

The consequence of research thus motivated is a huge stockpile of data whose relevance is God knows what. The idea that all results are important or will some time be found to be important is an example of the *inductivist fallacy*. According to the inductivist strategy, one first gathers all the data, and only then can one set about theorizing. Progress in science is seldom made that way, but is made instead by approaching Nature with specific questions in mind, where the ques-tions are spawned in the context of a hypothesis (Popper 1935, 1963). Consider, for example, how Crick and Watson figured out the molecular structure of DNA. Not, evidently, by first gathering all data and then letting them fall into place, but rather by trying a hypothesis, finding it in ruins, then dreaming up another hypothesis and testing it, and so on and inventively on, until a fit was found. Many of the data gathered in a random data-gathering venture will be useless. It is therefore troubling that a fast sampling of researchers at the poster sessions of the Society for Neuroscience meetings will yield at least several unblushing instances of the "maybe-mightbe" two-step.

In a general sense the best experiments are those whose results shake loose important information, but to design such an experiment one must know what are the right questions to ask. The more coherent and rich the available theoretical framework, the greater the potential for putting to Nature the right questions. Once a theoretical framework matures, the symbiosis between the theory and the experiments causes both to flourish, and the better the theory, the better the questions put to experimental test. Physics and genetics are renowned illustrations of the fruitful symbiosis of theory and experiment.

Moreover, it is an illusion to suppose that experimental research *can* be completely innocent of theoretical assumptions. So long as there is a reason for doing one experiment rather than another, there must be some governing hypothesis or other in virtue of which the experimental question is thought to be a good question, and some conception of why the experiment is worth the very considerable trouble. There must, that is, be some sense of how the results are significant for the larger picture of how the brain works (Kuhn 1962). This conglomeration of background assumptions, intuitions, and assorted preconceptions, however loose and vague, is the theoretical backdrop against which an experimenter's research makes sense to him. What is wanted, therefore, is not *no* theory but rather *good* theory—testable, coherent, richly ramified theory. The dearth of fleshed-out, testable theory is therefore something to be rectified, not patiently endured. (This point has by no means gone unnoticed in the neurosciences. See, for example, the commentaries on Selverston 1980, especially Calabrese 1980, Hoyle 1980, and Lent 1980.)

A third and rather obvious point is also relevant. Theories will not of their own accord waft up out of the data. If we are to explain how ensembles of neurons succeed in, say, coordinating movement, then we need a functional story that will explain how the structure works. The structural details are, to be sure, crucially important, but even when they are known, there remains the problem of accounting for *how the ensemble works*. And the function of the ensemble cannot be just read off the data concerning the participating neurons since, among other things, the interactions between components are non-linear. Whatever it is that ensembles do, it will not *look* like what components do, nor will it be a summation of what components do. (See also Bullock 1980, Davis 1980.)

How to characterize the mathematical relationships between the response profiles of the input and output ensembles is not something that in effect falls out of an array of data, though it may well be inspired by it. Theories are interpretations of the data; they are not merely generalizations over data points. Additionally, and this cuts against the idea that a complete collection of the data must be in place before theorizing is useful, whether some aspect of neuronal or ensemble business is a "relevant structural detail" may in fact be recognized only under the auspices of a theory that purports to explain ensemble function. For example, unless you think that DNA is hereditary material, you will not think the organization of nucleotides is relevant to determining the phenotype.

Although there is an undercurrent of reticence regarding theory in neuroscience, nonetheless there is a growing recognition of the need for theorizing. If neuroscience is to have a shot at explaining—really explaining—how the brain works, then it cannot be theory-shy. It must construct theories. It must have more than anatomy and pharmacology, more than physiology of individual neurons. It must have more than patterns of connectivity between neurons. What we need are small-scale models of subsystems and, above all, grand-scale theories of whole brain function.

The cardinal background principle for the theorist is that there are no homunculi. There is no little person in the brain who "sees" an inner television screen, "hears" an inner voice, "reads" the topographic maps, weighs reasons, decides actions, and so forth. There are just neurons and their connections. When a person sees, it is because neurons, individually blind and individually stupid neurons, are collectively orchestrated in the appropriate manner. So much seems obvious, and even a brief immersion in the neurosciences should proof one against the seductiveness of homuncular hypotheses. Surprisingly, however, homunculi, or at least the odor of homunculi, drift into one's thinking about brain function with embarrassing frequency.

Part of the explanation for the enduring presence of homuncular preconceptions is that folk psychology still provides the basic theoretical framework within which we think about complex behavior. Unless warned off, it insinuates itself into our thinking about brain function as well. In a relaxed mood, we still understand perceiving, thinking, control, and so forth, on the model of a self—a clever self—that does the perceiving and thinking and controlling. It takes effort to remember that the cleverness of a brain is explained not by the cleverness of a *self* but by the functioning of the neuronal machine that is the brain. (See also Crick 1979.)

Crudely, what we have to do is explain the cleverness not in terms of an equally clever homunculus, and so on in infinite regress, but in terms of suitably orchestrated throngs of stupid things (Dennett 1978a, 1978b). In one's own case, of course, it seems quite shocking that one's cleverness should be the outcome of well-orchestrated stupidity. The sobering reminder here is that so far as neuronal organization is concerned, there appears to be no rationale for giving a system conscious access to all—or even very many—of the brain's states and processes.

10.2 In Search of Theory

What is available by way of theory? Are there theories that have real explanatory power, are testable, and begin to make sense of how the molar effects result from the known neuronal structure? Less demandingly, are there theoretical approaches that look as though they will lead to fully fledged theories?

The fast answer is that a lot of very creative and intelligent work is going on in a number of places, but it is uneven, and it is difficult to determine how seminal most of it is. I began scouting the theoretical landscape with neither a clear conception of what I was looking for nor much confidence that I should recognize it if I found it. Most generally, I was trying to see if anywhere there was a kind of "Galilean combination": the right sort of simplification, unification, and above all, *mathematization*—not necessarily a fully developed theory, but something whose explanatory beginnings promised the possibility of real theoretical growth.

In coming to grips with the problems of getting a theory of brain function, I had to learn a number of general lessons. First, there are things that are advertised as theories but are really metaphors in search of a genuine theoretical articulation. One well-known example is the suggestion first floated by Van Heerden (1963) that the brain's information storage is holographic. (See also Pribram 1969.) Now the brain is *like* a hologram inasmuch as information appears to be distributed over collections of neurons. However, beyond that, the holographic idea did not really manage to explain storage and retrieval phenomena. Although significant effort went into developing the analogy (see, for example, Longuet-Higgins 1968), it did not flower into a credible account of the processes in virtue of which data are stored, retrieved, forgotten, and so forth. Nor does the mathematics of the hologram appear to unlock the door to the mathematics of neural ensembles. The metaphor did, nonetheless, inspire research in parallel modeling of brain function. (See section 10.5.)

The dominant metaphor of our time likens the brain to a computer, though this dominance is perhaps owed less to tight-fitting similarities than to the computer's status as *the* Technological Marvel of our time. Only in a *very* abstract sense is the brain like a computer: in both the brain and the electronic machine the output is a function of the input and the internal processing of the input. But this is clearly a highly abstract similarity, drawing merely on the presumption of systematicity between input and output. Finding the *relevant* points of similarity such that knowing some fact about computers will teach us some principles of brain function is very difficult, and how helpful the computer metaphor really is remains an open question. Certainly there are profound dissimilarities between brains and standard serial electronic computers (see section 10.9), and it is arguable that for many brain functions the computer metaphor has been positively misleading. (See discussions by Von Neumann 1958 and Rosenblatt 1962.) Most pernicious perhaps is the suggestion that the nervous system is just the hardware and that what we really need to understand is its "cognitive software." The hardware-software distinction as applied to the brain is dualism in yet another disguise. In any case, which differences and similarities are trivial and which are significant cannot be determined independently of knowing something about how both brains and computers work. Metaphors can certainly catalyze theorizing, but theories they are not.

Second, flowcharts describing projection paths in vertebrate nervous systems are sometimes characterized as theories. Insofar as they are theories, they are typically theories of anatomical connections, sometimes with a highly schematic complement of physiological connections. Although they may suggest a rough description of what happens at each stage, they do not really explain the processes such that from a given kind of input, a given kind of output results. For example, the circuit diagram for the cerebellum is sometimes taught as though it were a theory of how the cerebellum coordinates movement, but in reality it is no such thing. (This example will be more fully discussed in the next section.) Circuit diagrams often represent a huge experimental investment, and they are absolutely essential in coming to understand the brain's functional properties, but theories of brain function they are not.

Third, sometimes a list of ingredients important for getting a theory is offered as the theory itself, but evidently such a list is not per se a theory of what processes intervene between input and output. A list may include items such as that the brain is in some sense self-organizing, that it is a massively parallel system, and that functions are not discretely localizable but in some sense distributed. But a list of this sort does not add up to a *theory*, though the items are relevant considerations to be stirred into the pot. Like the prohibition against homunculi, they might be construed as constraints that any serious theory will ultimately have to honor. Or in more old-fashioned language, they might be called "prolegomena for future theorizing." (See also below.)

Fourth, as Crick has said, it is important to know what problems to try to solve first, and what problems to leave aside as solvable later. Because one is ever on the brink of being thrown into a panic by the complexity of the nervous system, it is necessary at some point to put it all at arm's length and ask: What answers would make a whole lot of other cards fall? What are the fundamental things a nervous system must do? This of course will be a guess, but an educated guess, not a blind one. The hope of any theorist is that if the basic principles governing how nervous systems operate are discovered, then other operations can be understood as evolution's articulation and refinement of these basic principles. Simplifications, idealizations, and approximations, therefore, are unavoidable as part of the first stage of getting a theory off the ground, and the trick is to find the simplification that is the Rosetta stone, so to speak, for the rest. In physics, chemistry, genetics, and geology, simplifying models have permitted a clarity of analysis that lays the foundation for coping with the tumultuous complexity that exists. Accordingly, Ramón y Cajal's warning against ". . . the invincible attraction of theories which simplify and unify seductively" should not be taken too much to heart. If a theory is on the right track, then the initial simplifications will grow into more comprehensive articulations; otherwise, it will shrivel and die.

The guiding question in the search for theory is this: What sort of organization in neuron-like structures *could* produce the output in question, given the input? Different choices will be made concerning which output and input to focus on. For example, one might select motor control, visual perception, stereopsis, memory, or learning about spatial relations as the place to go in. What is appealing about visual perception is that we know a great deal about the psychology of perception and about the physiology of the retina, the lateral geniculate nuclei, and the visually responsive areas of the cortex. What we do not understand, among other things, is how to characterize the output at various anatomical stages. On the other hand, what is appealing about motor control is the inverse. We know what the output is—namely, motor behavior—and we know quite a lot about the structural layout of the cerebellum, the motor cortex, and other motor-relevant parts of the brain. But we do not understand how to give a functional characterization of the input to motor structures. Different theorizers, accordingly, will have different hunches about the best place to dig in.

In the most general terms, we are looking for a description of the processes intervening between the input and the output. Constraining the theory-construction will be facts at all levels of organization. Thus, if we are theorizing about how a visual representation is constructed from light patterns falling on the retina, we must bear in mind fine-grained facts (such as that the only light-sensitive elements are rods and cones), larger-grained neural facts (such as that there are numerous topographic maps on the cortex), and psychological facts (such as that color perception remains constant under varying conditions of illumination). In addition, there are facts about visual deficits under specified neurological insult. For example, monkeys with bilateral lesions to the inferior temporal cortex are selectively impaired in visual recognition tests, whereas monkeys with lesions to the posterior parietal cortex are selectively impaired in landmark discrimination (Mishkin, Ungerleider, and Macko 1983).

There are also real-time constraints. In other words, the time it actually takes the nervous system to accomplish something, together with the facts of conduction velocities and synaptic transmission times, will put an upper limit on what to hypothesize as the number of steps intervening between input and output. For example, if it takes about 500 msec for a person to respond in a visual recognition test, then there must be no more than about 100 synaptic steps between the input and the output. Accordingly, a hypothesis that envisages a serial processing unit for visual recognition with 300 or 1,000 steps cannot be right. This observation is usually followed by the inference that the brain, unlike the standard electronic computing device, is a massively parallel machine (Feldman and Ballard 1982, Brown 1984). The point is, 100 steps in a serial processing program is far too few to do anything very fancy. Certainly it is not remotely enough to do the sorts of superlatively complex things our brains routinely do. Considerations of real-time constraints have, accordingly, militated against the idea that the brain's mode of operation can be modeled by a sequential program.

In the remaining sections I shall offer a small sample of some of the kinds of theoretical ventures currently undertaken. Opinions diverge widely concerning what has promise and where the gold is. Generally speaking, theoretical approaches originating with neuroscientists are decried by those in the computer science business as "computationally naive"; on the other side of the coin, neurobiologists usually deplore the "neurobiological naivete" of those whose theories originate in computer science laboratories. So long as there is no theoretical approach known to do for neuroscience what Newton did for physics, we are all naive. Inevitably, there is a tendency to see one's own simplifications as "allowable provisionally" and someone else's as a fatal flaw. To one convinced of the gold in his own bailiwick, other theoretical diggings may seem crackpot. Additionally, if a theory has quite grand ambitions, it stands to be derided as "pie-in-the-sky"; if, on the other hand, a theory is narrow in scope and highly specific, it risks being labeled "uninteresting."

My approach here will be to present three quite different theoretical examples with a view to showing what virtues they have and why they are interesting. Each in its way is highly incomplete; *of course* each makes simplifications and waves its hands in many important places. Nevertheless, by looking at these approaches sympathetically, while remaining sensitive to their limitations, we may be able to see whether the central motivating ideas are powerful and useful and, most importantly, whether they are experimentally provocative. My strategy can be defended quite simply: if one adopts a sympathetic stance, one has a chance of learning something, but if one adopts a carping stance, one learns little and eventually sinks into despair.

Regardless of whether any of the three examples has succeeded in making a Grand Theoretical Breakthrough, each illustrates some important aspect of the problem of theory in neuroscience: for example, what a nonsentential account of representations might look like, how a massively parallel system might succeed in sensorimotor control, pattern recognition, or learning, how one might ascend beyond the level of the single cell to address the nature of cell assemblies, how co-evolutionary exchange between high-level and lower-level hypotheses can be productive. They all try to invent and perfect new concepts suitable to nervous system function, and they all have their sights set on explaining macro phenomena in terms of micro phenomena. Being selective means that I necessarily leave out much important work, but given the limitations of space, that is something I can only regret, not rectify.

Two of the examples originate from within an essentially neurobiological framework. The first focuses on the fundamental problem of sensorimotor control and offers a general framework for understanding the computational architecture of nervous systems. The authors of this approach are Andras Pellionisz and Rodolfo Llinás, and owing to the very broad scope and the general systematicity their theory seeks to encompass, I shall discuss it at considerable length. The second, originating with Francis Crick examines the neurobiological basis for certain attentional mechanisms specified by psychological hypotheses. This is more narrowly focused and can be discussed quite succinctly. The third approach, discussion of which I sandwich between these two, is a new development within the wider field of artificial intelligence research and goes by the name of *connectionism* or the modeling of *parallel distributed processing* (PDP). Connectionist researchers are trying to figure out the computational operations used in nervous systems, and the strategy has been to use computer models of parallel distributed systems to try to generate the appropriate macro phenomena from neuron-like elements in a network-like arrangement. In contrast to the other two, this approach is essentially based in computer science, but unlike standard artificial intelligence research, it is informed and constrained by neurobiology.

10.3   Tensor Network Theory

Because there are general philosophical lessons to be drawn concerning the possibility of a new "neurocognitive" paradigm and concerning the co-evolution of functional and structural hypotheses, it will be useful to place the opening discussion of tensor network theory within the context of its inception—of what led to the first fumblings and how the general idea of phase spaces and coordinate transformations slowly took shape.

The place to start, then, is where the theory started: the cerebellum. With only some exaggeration it can be said that almost everything one would want to know about the micro-organization of the cerebellum is known. For neuroanatomists the cerebellum has been something of a dream of experimental approachability, because it has a limited number of neuron types (five, plus two incoming fibers), each one morphologically distinctive and each one positioned and connected in a characteristic and highly regimented manner (figure 2.4). The output of the cerebellar cortex is the exclusive job of just one type of cell, the Purkinje cell (of which more anon), and the input is supplied by just two, very different cell systems, the mossy fibers and the climbing fibers. This investigable organization has made it possible to determine the electrophysiological properties of each distinct class of neuron and to study in detail the nature of the Purkinje output relative to the mossy fiber–climbing fiber input. The neuronal population in the cerebellum is huge—something on the order of 10^{10} neurons— and there is at least another order of magnitude in synaptic connections. Nonetheless, basic structural knowledge of the cerebellum has made it possible to construct a schematic wiring diagram that illustrates the pathways and connectivity patterns of the participating cells (figure 10.1). The first point, then, is that a great deal is understood at the level of micro-organization.

Exactly *what* the cerebellum contributes to nervous system function is not well understood, however. What is known is that it has an important role in coordinating movement, as well as in moving the whole body. It is what permits one to smoothly touch one's nose, catch an outfield fly, or land a snowball on a passing car. The complexity underlying any of these feats puts high demands on a nervous system. For example, in catching a fly ball, a baseball player must estimate the trajectory of the ball and keep his eyes on it while running to where it is expected to fall. So he has to run, visually track, maintain balance, reach to intercept, and finally catch the ball.

Subjects with cerebellar lesions show a decomposition of movement, almost as though the various parts of each movement had to be thought out one by one. Undershooting and overshooting the target and moving the limb in the wrong direction are also typical dysmetric signs in cerebellar subjects. Cerebellar patients also have difficulties in checking a fast movement, such as a swing of the arm. There are commonly problems in gait, showing themselves especially in unsteadiness and large stride. Depending on the area of lesion, there may also be motor impairment of speech (dysarthria). Playing baseball is out of the question.

It is known that the cerebellum is not essential for movement because subjects with a nonfunctioning cerebellum can still make voluntary movements. But evidently it is essential for well-controlled, well-timed, well-spaced movement. Plasticity in the nervous system does permit some compensation in the event of cerebellar lesions occurring early in development. Children whose cerebellar hemispheres are damaged early in life may nonetheless develop quite good motor control, so long as the more medial structures in the cerebellum (the flocculonodular lobe and the vermis) are undamaged. But if these structures are also damaged and the entire cerebellum is nonfunctional, the child remains ataxic (that is, suffers deficits in motor coordination) and dysmetric.

The evolution in complexity and size of the cerebellum in humans is at least as striking as that of the cerebrum. Correcting for body size, humans have a larger cerebellum than, for example, chimpanzees, whose cerebellum in turn is larger than that of horses or dogs. As one

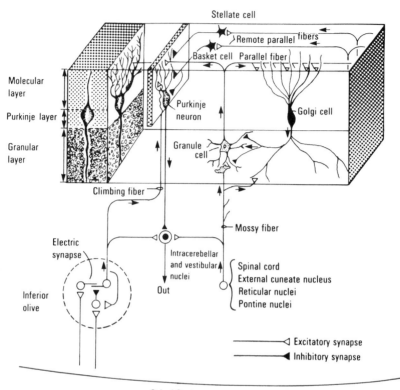

Stellate cell

Molecular layer

Purkinje layer

Granular layer

Purkinje neuron

Golgi cell

Granule cell

Remote parallel fibers

Basket cell Parallel fiber

Climbing fiber

Mossy fiber

Electric synapse

Intracerebellar and vestibular nuclei

Out

Spinal cord
External cuneate nucleus
Reticular nuclei
Pontine nuclei

Inferior olive

◁ Excitatory synapse
◀ Inhibitory synapse

Spinal Cord

Figure 10.1
Circuit diagram for the cerebellar cortex. Purkinje cells are excited directly by climbing fibers and indirectly (via parallel fibers from the granule cells) by the mossy fibers. Stellate and basket cells, which are excited by parallel fibers, act as inhibitory interneurons. The Golgi cells act on the granule cells with feedback inhibition (when excited by parallel fibers) and feedforward inhibition (when excited by climbing and mossy fiber collaterals). The output of the Purkinje cell is inhibitory upon the cells of the intracerebellar and vestibular nuclei. (Modified from Ghez and Fahn (1981). Ch. 30 of *Principles of Neural Science,* ed. E. R. Kandel and J. H. Schwartz, pp. 334–346. Copyright 1981 © by Elsevier Science Publishing Co., Inc.)

might predict, therefore, human versatility in motor control is remarkable. To mention only a tiny sample, we can swim, pole-vault, climb trees, use knives, speak languages, whistle, draw, skate, and play musical instruments. For each of these accomplishments the nervous coordination of muscles is a stunningly complex affair.

What is the input on which the cerebellum can work its miracles? It includes massive inputs from the cerebral cortex—the motor strip and nearly everywhere else—as well as from other brain regions subserving motor function. The cerebellum also receives afferent inputs from all types of sensory receptors. Some of the cortical inputs are thought to be grossly specified motor commands for which the cerebellum provides the finely tuned, detailed commands. (This will be elaborated below.) In the absence of the cerebellum the motor commands of the cerebral cortex are conveyed down the spinal cord without the coordinative tuning of the cerebellum.

Now if we know so much, in a general fashion, about what the cerebellum does, and if we know so much about the fine-grained structural facts, we ought to be able to figure out *how* the cerebellum does what it does. We ought, that is, to be able to explain how the activity of the collections of cells produces coordinated movement. For anyone who hoped that the theory would simply tumble out once so many details were available, the cerebellum seemed strangely frustrating. Because what remained mysterious was the functional story—intermediate between the gross functional description and the wiring diagram—that would explain exactly what role the cerebellum plays in the administration of motor control. The epistemological situation provoked diverse researchers into trying to find a fruitful theoretical orientation (for example, Braitenberg and Onesto 1961, Marr 1969, Ito 1970).

The line that Pellionisz and Llinás pursued depended on their determination to take as the starting point the parallel nature of information processing in the brain, and in the cerebellum in particular. If the cerebellum has a parallel architecture, in the sense that many channels are simultaneously processing information, then, they argued, it is a fair assumption that the computational processes are suited to that architecture. To understand what the computational processes might be, they followed the idea that they needed to know about the *patterns* of activity within large *arrays* of neurons.

A "wiring diagram" of cerebellar neurons is useful in describing in a highly schematic way the connections between input and output. Typically, however, the diagram displays one or two schematic neurons and their connections, whereas in fact these are embedded in an array of thousands of cells. That is, the massively parallel nature of the network is, for graphic convenience, suppressed. Such suppression will not matter if the schematic neuron is a faithful representative of every neuron in its array—if, that is, the system is essentially redundant. On the other hand, if the global connectivity pattern within the array is itself crucial to how the array processes information, then we pay for the convenience of the suppression, inasmuch as we mask exactly the detail we need in order to understand the system.

Now in fact neurons in an array do appear to differ in number of synaptic connections with a given incoming neuron (convergence), number of neurons to which they project (divergence), synaptic morphology, and so forth. For example, and this example will be important in the tensor network theory, sets of Purkinje cells positioned at different sites along a beam of incoming parallel fibers have different outputs, and the differences are systematic (Pellionisz, Llinás, and Perkel 1977). At least in this case the schematic neuron is not a faithful representative of all neurons in its array, and the differences, argued Pellionisz and Llinás, are not trivial but essential to the nature of the array's output. As they saw it, to understand those differences is to get close to understanding the functional story implemented in the parallel architecture.

Given this starting point, the task was to find out more about the patterns of activities between neuronal arrays. Because of the technological difficulties involved in simultaneous intracellular recording from multiple adjacent cells, Pellionisz and Llinás began instead by modeling a segment of a frog cerebellum in a computer in order to force more pattern into the open (Pellionisz, Llinás, and Perkel 1977). By drawing on the available knowledge of cell connectivity and morphology, they programmed a computer to "grow" huge numbers of cells (8,285 Purkinje cells, 1.68 million granule cells, 16,820 mossy fibers), with the appropriate connectivity network, thereby creating a fictive cerebellum in the computer to simulate the real thing. They could then activate specific input cell populations and investigate the patterns of activity in large populations of receiving cells.

The model is, of course, just a model, limited by whatever anatomical and physiological data are built into it. Therefore, no grand and incontestable conclusions about how the cerebellum works should be drawn directly from it. Nevertheless, the model is a valuable heuristic device because it enables us to see something not visible through single-cell recordings—namely, *patterns of activity* in huge (fictive) neuronal ensembles. It enables the theoretical imagination to transcend the limits of the schematic wiring diagram and single-cell recordings and to begin to come to terms with the parallel nature of the system. So even if no computational *conclusions* can be drawn, *testable computational hypotheses* may germinate.

Once convinced that the connectivity of arrays of neurons is crucial to explaining how a given input yields a given output, the investigator must find a way to characterize the relation between input arrays and output arrays. In mulling over the patterns the computer simulation yielded and the problems the cerebellum had to be solving as its contribution to sensorimotor control, Pellionisz and Llinás began to think that what the network of cerebellar cells did to its input could be characterized by means of a tensor—a generalized mathematical function for transforming a vector into another vector, no matter what the frames of reference involved. The basic mathematical insight was that if the input is construed as a vector in one coordinate system, and if the output is construed as a vector in a different coordinate system, then a tensor is what effects the mapping or transformation from one vector to the other. Which tensor matrix governs the transformation for a given pair of input-output ensembles is an empirical matter determined by the requirements of the reference frames in question. And that matrix is implemented in the connectivity relations obtaining between input arrays and output arrays.

Let us consider this step by step. Vectors are represented geometrically as directed line segments in a specified coordinate system (frame of reference). The various components of the vector are given in terms of their values as specified in relation to the relevant coordinate axes (figure 10.2). If each neuron in a network of input neurons specifies an axis of a coordinate system, then the input of an individual neuron—its spiking frequency—defines a point on the axis, and the input of the whole array of neurons can then be very neatly given as a vector in that space. Similarly, the output of an array can be specified as a vector in the space defined by the set of output neurons. (For an introduction to the basic concepts, see Jordan 1986).

Given the data on input vectors and output vectors supplied in the model, Pellionisz observed that from a mathematical standpoint, the connectivity relations between input and output neurons serve as a matrix, such that any input vector is transformed into an output vector. That is, the nature of the regularity in the patterns of activity of the neuronal arrays represented in the model invited the hypothesis that the arrays are doing *matrix multiplication*. In particular, the systematic differences in response profiles of sets of Purkinje cells situated at different locations on the same beam of parallel input fibers could be explained as the outcome of matrix multiplication (figure 10.2).

So far the vector-matrix mathematics seems like a marvelously convenient way to order a lot of messy, fine-grained detail, but suppose that the cerebellum's susceptibility to a vector-matrix analysis reflects a deeper functional reality. With this thought in mind, Pellionisz began to pursue a further hunch: suppose that ensemble activity can be described as mapping vectors onto vectors not as a matter of mere mathematical convenience but because ensembles really represent coordinate systems, and a fundamental *functional* problem for a nervous system consists in making translations from one coordinate sys-

V = (3, 2)

$$M = \begin{bmatrix} 6 & 4 & 3 \\ -2 & -5 & 1 \end{bmatrix}$$

$$\begin{aligned} V' = M \cdot V = (3 \cdot 6) + (2 \cdot -2) &= 14 \\ (3 \cdot 4) + (2 \cdot -5) &= 2 \\ (3 \cdot 3) + (2 \cdot 1) &= 11 \end{aligned}$$

V' = (14, 2, 11)

Figure 10.2
Consider a simple case of a 2 × 3 matrix—that is, two rows and three columns, as illustrated. Let the vector be (3,2). To find the dot product, multiply the first component of the vector by the matrix number in row one, column one; multiply the second component by the matrix number in row two, column one. Add the two products to yield the first component of the resultant vector. Repeat for columns two and three to find the second and third components.

tem to another. What coordinate systems? Well, those defined by the representational job of a given ensemble.

To begin with, there will be the coordinate system specified by visual or olfactory or vestibular input arrays and the very different coordinate system specified by motor output arrays. Suppose, indeed, that the fundamental computational problem of sensorimotor control *is* the geometrical problem of going from one coordinate system (e.g., visual) to another, very different coordinate system (e.g., motor). Then arrays of neurons are interpretable as executing vector-to-vector transformations because that is what they really *are* doing— the computational problems a nervous system has to solve are fundamentally geometrical problems. The idea seemed to have plausibility not only for the cerebellum but for wider domains as well.[1]

A tensor is a *generalized* mathematical function for transforming vectors into other vectors, irrespective of the differences in metric and dimension of the coordinate systems. If the basic functional problem of sensorimotor control is getting from one very different coordinate system to another, then tensorial transformations are just what the nervous system should be doing. Accordingly, the hypothesis is that the connectivity relations between a given input ensemble and its output ensemble are the physical embodiment of a tensor.

The geometric characterization of the problem of sensorimotor control, and of neurofunctional capacities generally, is neither immediately compelling nor, for that matter, immediately comprehensible. What is required is something on the order of a major conceptual shift. The phenomenological scenario here seems to be confusion and incomprehension in the first phase, followed, as understanding flowers, by a gathering sense of obviousness adhering to the general principles. The detailed hypotheses are, evidently, a further matter. My own understanding here began to find its feet as Paul M. Churchland and I constructed a cartoon story of a highly simplified creature who faces a sensorimotor control problem of the utmost simplicity.[2] In what follows I shall use the cartoon story in trying to outline the Pellionisz-Llinás picture of the brain's geometrical problems and its geometrical solutions. With that in hand, we shall return to nervous systems and to the cerebellum in particular. First, however, a brief philosophical aside.

For purists of the top-down persuasion, the cardinal article of faith is that first you figure out *what* the mind-brain does, and secondarily you find out how it might implement the functions described. Granted, in a certain sense, any theorizing about mind-brain function has a veneer of top-downishness, else it would not be theorizing but data-gathering. If the dominant connotation of "top-down" is that of the purists, however, then to the degree that the theorizing is highly constrained and richly informed by implementation-level data, it is decidedly confounding to label the enterprise as "top-down."

In the case of tensor network theory the insights concerning the functional nature of sensorimotor control grew out of reflections on the significance of vector-matrix descriptions at the level of cell assemblies, which were themselves enabled by computer simulations dependent on a massive data bank of *structural* detail. In short, the high-level functional hypothesis was suggested by the low-level functional hypothesis, which in turn was a consequence of adopting a strategy based on essentially structural considerations. This is exactly the reverse of the order of discovery advised by the top-down purist. Poetic distortion aside, it is tempting to see the conceptual genesis of the tensor network theory as an instance of figuring out *how* something works before figuring out *what* it is doing.

I do not wish to make excessively much of this point, and it by no means entails anything terribly grand, such as that there is no distinction between functional capacities and their structural implementation. Nevertheless, I do see it as enfeebling the methodological advice of the top-down purists, as well as bolstering the stock of the co-evolutionary approach to cognitive neurobiology.

10.4   Cartoon Story of What a Tensor Does in Sensorimotor Control

The cartoon world is inhabited by a very simple crab-like critter, Roger. He is equipped with a pair of eye-like devices for detecting the position of an apple in external space, where each eye can rotate in a socket so as to get the apple in register with its "sweet spot" (fovea, as it were). The eyes can rotate ninety degrees either to the right or to the left of their straight ahead position. Roger also has an arm-like device, a two-jointed limb that consists of a forearm and an upper arm, the latter projecting from midway in the center structure. The arm is used to make contact with the apple (figure 10.3). Although conceptually Roger is a three-dimensional critter, his existence as a computer-generated display means he is limited to activity in just two dimensions, as though he never pays any attention to height. His world, to make things simple, is really just a 2-D, flatlander world. Figure 10.3 (part b) shows this world viewed from above.

The apple has a position in external space, what we shall call 2-D external Euclidean space. The position of the apple in this external space can be given by drawing a pair of coordinate axes and specifying the position in terms of the coordinates. Its position can also be represented in *visual phase space*—that is, its position in *the natural coordinate system of Roger's sensory equipment*. How do we characterize Roger's visual phase space? Since each eye can rotate, the position of each eye can be specified by the angle it subtends as it turns away

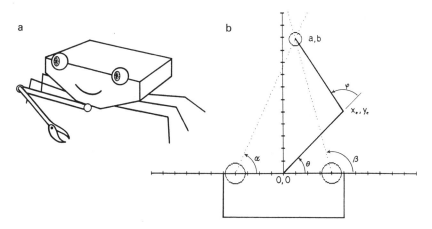

Figure 10.3
The problem of sensorimotor coordination. (a) and (b) depict a crab-like robot with rotatable eyes and an extendable arm. As the eyes triangulate a target by assuming angles (α, β), the arm joints must assume angles (θ, φ) such that the tip of the forearm makes contact with the target. (Adapted from Paul M. Churchland (forthcoming).)

from the straight ahead position (see figure 10.3). It is most convenient to characterize the straight ahead position as 90; hence, all eye positions can be specified as the angle subtended by the horizontal axis and the "fovea line." For example, suppose that the apple is at (1.2, 10.8) in external space. Then to foveate it, the eyes must rotate: the left, such that the angle subtended by the horizontal and the "fovea line" is 65 degrees; the right, such that the relevant angle is 105 degrees. In Roger's visual phase space, therefore, the position of the apple is given by the ordered pair of position angles for each eye, namely (65, 105).

Roger's visual space is a *phase space* in which the position of the apple is represented by the two eye-rotation angles, alpha and beta, that jointly triangulate it. Any coordinate system specifies a phase space, and here "position in phase space" simply refers to the global condition of the physical system being represented. Phase spaces may differ as a function of the number of coordinate axes (2, 3, 50, 10,000, etc.) and the angles of their axes (at right angles to each other, or nonorthogonal). A hyperspace is a phase space with more than three dimensions. A phase space may be Euclidean, but it need not be. It could, for example, be Riemannian, in which case the interior angles of a triangle inscribed in that space need not sum to 180 degrees. (A caution: the term "phase space" is commonly used in classical mechanics to denote a specific coordinate space of six dimensions, three for position and three for momentum. But as I use the term here, it has the entirely general meaning of "coordinate space" or "state space." See also Suppe 1977.)

Note that for any position of the apple in external space, there is a corresponding position of the apple in Roger's visual phase space. Accordingly, we can say that Roger's visual vector, such as (65, 105), *represents* the position of the apple in the world, since there is a systematic relation between where the apple is in the world, as described in external coordinates, and "where" in visual phase space it is, as specified by a pair of eye-angle coordinates (figure 10.4a).

Just as Roger has a 2-D visual space in which the position of the object is represented, so he has a 2-D motor space in which its arm position can be represented. But, and this is crucial, these two phase spaces are very different. How do we characterize Roger's motor phase space? Again, by specifying the axes appropriate to his motor equipment. This time, the position of his limb in phase space is given by the two angles by which it deviates from a standard position. Thus, let the zero position of the upper arm be flush with the horizontal axis. Then a position of 45 on the upper-arm axis will represent an upper-arm position of 45 degrees off the horizontal (figure 10.3). Cor-

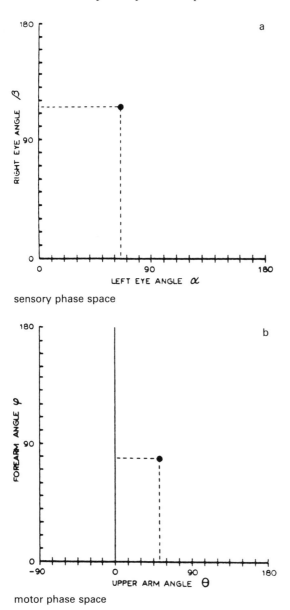

sensory phase space

motor phase space

Figure 10.4
The respective configurations of the crab's sensory and motor systems can each be
represented by an appropriate point in a corresponding phase space: (a), (b). The crab
needs a function from points in sensory phase space to points in motor phase space.
(Adapted from Paul M. Churchland (forthcoming).)

relatively, let the zero position of the forearm be its position when extended straight out from the upper arm, wherever the upper arm happens to be positioned. Accordingly, a position of 78.5 on the forearm axis represents the forearm as rotated 78.5 degrees counterclockwise from the line extending out from the upper arm, whatever the position of the upper arm. Notice, therefore, that we can give the overall position of Roger's arm in motor phase in terms of the two angles as (45, 78.5). Moreover, we can specify the position of the apple by specifying that arm position where the tip of the forearm just touches the apple. The sensory phase space and the motor phase space are represented in Roger's "brain" and reflect the unique nature of the sensory apparatus and the motor apparatus, respectively (figure 10.4).

Now for the action (figure 10.5). The eyes, having detected the apple, announce its position: "Apple at (55, 85)." Notice that if the arm were to take as its command, "Go to (55, 85)," then it would

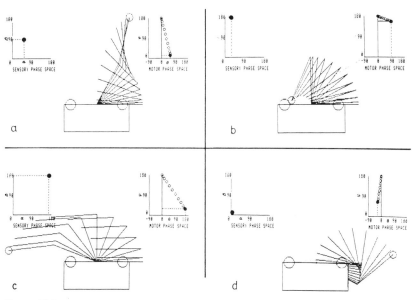

Figure 10.5
The successfully coordinated crab. In this computer simulation the sensory phase space position is entered as input, and the motor phase space position is computed as output. The arm configuration is then directed along a straight line in motor phase space, from its folded rest position (0, 180), toward its target position. See upper right inset in each example. That position places the arm in physical contact with the target object in real space. (Adapted from Paul M. Churchland (forthcoming).)

execute that command by putting the upper arm at 55 and the forearm at 85. This would be disastrous, because it would put the arm nowhere near the apple. In other words, *the position of the apple in visual space is not the position of the apple in motor space.* From figure 10.5 (part a) it is evident that if the apple is at (55, 85) in visual space, it is at (62, 15) in motor space. What Roger needs, therefore, is something to tell him what coordinates in motor space correspond to a given set of coordinates in visual space. If Roger's arm is to go where the apple is, he needs to know its "apple-touching" position, and figure 10.5 shows the path in motor phase space his hand should follow from its starting position folded up against his chest. That is, he needs something that will tell his limbs where to go in motor space on the basis of where the apple is in visual space. He needs a mathematical function that will specify where in motor space to go, given the location of the target in visual space—in other words, something to effect a *transformation of coordinates.* Figure 10.5 shows three other movements the arm makes (b, c, d), depending on where the target is placed. In general, the mathematical function will compute the target's position in motor space on the basis of its detected position in sensory space.

Let us consider the desired mathematical function in pictorial terms. Figure 10.6 (part a) displays Roger's sensory or eye-position phase space, and the visible grid lines represent that portion of the phase space such that Roger's eyes converge on a point within reach of Roger's modest arm. Figure 10.6 (part b) displays Roger's motor phase space, but with a grid of curving lines superimposed on it. Their significance is as follows. For each point in sensory phase space, there is a uniquely corresponding point in motor phase space, a point that specifies Roger's arm as touching the triangulated target. If we now consider an entire *grid* of points in sensory phase space, there will of course be a corresponding "grid" of positions specified in motor phase space. That is what we see in figure 10.6. But as projected onto motor phase space, that "grid" is *deformed* relative to the original sensory grid. (The triangle and rectangle are added to help the reader locate the original positions within the deformed grid.) Accordingly, we may think of the coordinate-transforming function at issue as a transformation that deforms sensory phase space in order to put all the points in it into proper register with the desired points in motor phase space. "Proper register" here just means that Roger's arm systematically reaches out to wherever his eyes triangulate.

Exactly what transformation is required is clearly very sensitive to the details of Roger's sensory and motor equipment. If his eyes were

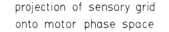

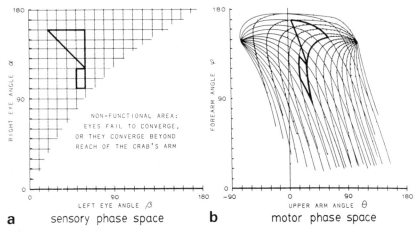

Figure 10.6
The coordinate transformation, graphically represented. The grid in (a) represents the set of points in sensory phase space that correspond to a triangulated object within reach of the crab's arm. For each such point in (a), its corresponding position in motor phase space is entered in (b). The entire set of corresponding points in (b) displays the global transformation of phase-space coordinates effected by the crab's coordinating function. The heavily scored triangle and rectangle illustrate corresponding positions in each space. (Adapted from Paul M. Churchland (forthcoming).)

farther apart, or if his arm segments were of different lengths, a somewhat different transformation would be in order.

The critical point, therefore, is that we need a way of going from points or vectors in sensory space to points or vectors in motor space. Clearly there must be a systematic relationship between the "sensory position" and the "motor position" of the apple, or else poor Roger would never manage to grasp what he senses. A mapping from vectors in one space to vectors in another space can be usefully represented as a general transformation of the coordinates of the one space into the coordinates of the other. For spaces in general (including non-Cartesian spaces) the coordinate transformer is called a *tensor*. In real animals, Pellionisz and Llinás argue, the intrinsic geometry of nervous subsystems need not be limited to phase spaces with orthogonal (Cartesian) axes, and thus the relevance of tensors. But the point of our cartoon story is merely to illustrate the principle of coordinate transformation, and so we shall pass by the complexities of the fully general case.

In this cartoon story the position of the apple in real space is the *invariant*, which the visual system and the motor system both represent, each in its different way, while the coordinate transformer tells the effector system what it must do to make contact with the invariant. In geometrical terms, the coordinate transformation tells us how we have to *deform* one phase space to get at the object in the other phase space. Tensors are a means whereby the nervous system can represent the very same thing many times over, despite the differences in coordinate systems in which the thing is represented. In sum, then, *representations are positions in phase spaces, and computations are coordinate transformations between phase spaces.*

Bear in mind, however, that even equipped with a coordinate transformer to translate sensory locations into the correct motor locations, Roger is radically simplified—so much so that he would not stand a chance in the real, cutthroat, biological world. Even the humblest nervous systems are more complex and more sophisticated than Roger's. To begin with, his is a 2-D world, and ours is a 4-D space-time world. As soon as we consider the sensorimotor control problems that must be solved by the brains of real creatures, making their living in a 4-D space-time world, the necessity of elaborating on the simple coordinate transformer of the cartoon story is plain. Moreover, Roger never moves his whole body, and he never has the problem of maintaining posture and balance. All he does is visually locate the apple and then touch it. He does not flee or hide from any predator, he does not mate, he does not build a nest or dig a hole, he does not even chew up and swallow the apple he touches. Consider also that although Roger has merely two phase spaces—one afferent and one efferent—this is an unrealistic arrangement for a real nervous system, which could be expected to have some number of intervening phase spaces as well. Nevertheless, the crux of the Pellionisz-Llinás approach is this: the sensorimotor problems faced by more realistic creatures can be understood as reducing at bottom to the same general type of problem that Roger faces—namely, the problem of making coordinate transformations between different phase spaces. And the solution found for Roger's cartoon world illustrates the general nature of the solution evolved by organic brains in the real world.

Roger is simplified in a further dimension. He has neither muscles nor neurons to make muscles contract. When he moves an arm, that is really just the computer painting lines across the CRT screen. When a real crab moves a claw, it does so by virtue of the precise orchestration of muscle contraction by neurons. Let us wallow a bit in the sensorimotor predicament of a real crab foraging for food. Supposing it spots an edible chunk of fish, it must move toward it, grasp it with its claw, and get it into its mouth. It has to contend with six legs;

moreover, each leg has three joints, each joint is served by at least two muscles, and each muscle consists of many muscle cells and is innervated by a large number of neurons. If the object to be intercepted is itself moving, the control problem becomes very complex. But it is approachable by using the same basic mathematical idea used in solving Roger's problem.

If we can think of the crab's arm as specifying a phase space, then the set of muscles concerned may also be thought of as specifying a phase space, where the positions of each muscle are represented on a proprietary axis of that space, and where a vector in that space is determined by the degree of contraction of the component muscles. A phase space of yet higher dimensions is specified by the motor neurons innervating the muscles, where each neuron is given a dimension and its firing frequency will be represented as a point along that axis. Notice that we can expect there to be systematic relationships between positions in the skeletal phase space, positions in the muscle phase space, and positions in the neuronal phase space. The central idea is quite simple: the limbs move the way they do because the muscles contract the way they do, where that pattern of effects is in turn caused by a pattern of neuronal activation of the muscle units.

Animals' motor systems had to evolve systematic relationships among the phase spaces of motor neurons, muscle cells, and limbs if they were going to use neurons to control the movement of muscles and thereby control the movement of limbs. Any animal whose motor system lacks such relationships will not be able to move properly, and its survival time will be brief. From the perspective of tensor network theory, to look for the functional relations between connected cell assemblies is to investigate the properties of the relevant phase spaces—that is, to determine their geometries, and to determine the transformations that will take us *from* the representation of some external invariant in a given space *to* its representation in a different phase space. Knowing the geometry of the limb phase space, therefore, will guide us in approaching the motor neuron phase space.

Similar points apply of course to matters on the afferent end. Roger does not detect the presence of the target by virtue of photosensitive neurons. Biological organisms with real eyes do. Nevertheless, the basic principle of representation as position in phase space and computation as coordinate transformation can be invoked. That is, in real organisms retinal neurons will specify a phase space, vestibular neurons will specify a phase space, and so forth. If the afferent system is to play a role in the organism's feeding, fleeing, and so forth, then afferent phase spaces will have to be coordinated with efferent phase spaces. Sensory phase spaces are bound to be different from motor phase spaces, since, to put it schematically, the first must be an "as-the-world-presents-itself" representation, whereas the second must be an "as-my-body-should-be" representation. If nervous systems are to represent an invariant, as they must do if animals are to intercept prey, then tensors appear to be an efficient way in which the sensory representations can be transformed into output representations in motor phase spaces. And we can envision the evolution of fancier sensorimotor control aided by the development of phase spaces intervening between afferent and efferent. If a tensor equation is valid in one frame of reference, it is valid in all, regardless of how deformed one space is relative to another or whether the spaces differ in dimensions. On this view, the specific connectivity of distinct neuronal arrays has evolved to effect these general tensorial transformations under the specific conditions of a given species of organism.

In living organisms, then, it is arrays of neurons that must represent positions in phase spaces such as visual space or motor space, and it is a neuronal network that must make coordinate transformations. To see how a neuronal network can be suited to the implementation of coordinate transformations, let us start with a simple schematic vector-to-vector transformation. Consider an input system of four dimensions whose inputs a, b, c, d are transformed into output values x, y, z, of a three-dimensional system. The input can also be regarded as a point in the 4-D phase space, or as a vector whose base is at the origin of the relevant phase space and whose tip is specified by the four components of the input. Similarly, the output can be regarded as a point in 3-D phase space, or as a vector whose tip is determined by the output values.

Suppose the input vector is transformed into the output vector by matrix multiplication. This mathematical operation can be realized rather simply by the schematic neural array in figure 10.7. The array consists of three main structures: the parallel input fibers, the dendritic tree of the receiving cells, and the axons carrying the output of these cells x, y, and z. The parallel fibers carry excitatory input in the form of action potentials, and the values a, b, c, d are determined by the momentary spiking frequency of each of the four fibers. Every parallel fiber makes synaptic contact with each of the three dendritic trees. The output frequency of spike emissions for each neuron is determined by (1) the frequency of input stimulations it receives from all incoming signals and (2) the nature of the synaptic connectivity of each input junction, where this includes such factors as distance from the axon hillock, size of receptor site, and so forth. The latter values are represented by the numbers in the matrix in figure 10.7. The neural connectivity, therefore, models the matrix. The signals are

Parallel fibre
input

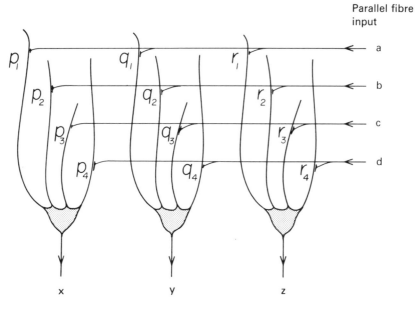

Purkinje cell output

Figure 10.7
Coordinate transformation by matrix multiplication, neurally implemented. The input
vector $\langle a, b, c, d \rangle$ is physically represented by four spiking frequencies, each of which is
above (positive number) or below (negative number) the baseline spiking frequency of
the input pathway. Each input element synapses onto all of the output cells, and the
weight of each synaptic connection implements the corresponding coefficient of the
abstract matrix. Each cell "sums" its incoming stimulations and emits spikes down its
output axon with a frequency proportionate to its summed input. Thus results the
output vector $\langle x, y, z \rangle$. (Adapted from Paul M. Churchland (forthcoming).)

"summed" at each axon hillock and a spike train is emitted. Thus, the
output vector has as its components x, y, and z, the three output
frequencies. Vectors (input) are thus transformed into vectors (output) via matrix multiplication.

Although the model neuron array is highly schematic, it is fairly
easy to imagine how to embellish it. For example, the dimensionality
of the phase spaces can be increased by adding neurons, redundancy
can be accommodated if needed by "twinning" neuron configurations, the matrix can be made plastic by allowing for modifiability of synaptic junctions or for the addition of receptor sites.
Moreover, something resembling this neuronal array does exist in the
cerebellar cortex. Indeed, it was precisely by pondering the regimented organization of parallel fibers and Purkinje cells in the cere-

bellar cortex that Pellionisz and Llinás came to the view that their basic principle of operation was vector-to-vector transformation. (See again figure 10.2.) The set of incoming parallel fibers specifies a vector, the connectivity interface of parallel fibers and Purkinje dendrites models a matrix, and the axons of the Purkinje cells specify the suitably transformed output vector (figure 10.8).

There are in the cerebellum other matters to be factored in, such as the role of incoming climbing fibers (one to each Purkinje cell with multiple synaptic contacts) and the function of neurons in the cerebellar nucleus. But Pellionisz and Llinás consider that these can be accommodated within the basic framework of phase space representation and vector-to-vector transformation (Pellionisz and Llinás 1982). If the cerebellum is executing tensorial transformations, the next question is this: what is the character of those phase spaces such that a vector from one is transformed into a vector of the other? The answer to that depends on the empirical facts about what the motor cortex and the cerebellum are really up to, but at least a rough answer, based on clinical, physiological, and anatomical data, is already discernible.

Crudely, the plot line is this: the input from the cerebral cortex specifies in a *general* way what bit of behavior is called for. For example, suppose the incoming "intention" to my cerebellum is "Touch *that* (apple) with my right hand." The incoming "intention" vector specifies this position in a sensorimotor coordinate system (touch *that* seen/heard object), but it does not specify a curve in the motor space that says exactly how the goal position is to be achieved such that the target is intercepted. It is the job of the cerebellum to transform that intention vector into an execution vector that will orchestrate the motor neurons in order to produce a precisely and smoothly coordinated sequence of muscular contractions. It will have to coordinate all the muscles relevant to the behavior, based on an updated representation of the body's current configuration. No matter what my body's starting position—arms hanging straight down, arms over the head, arms behind the back, fingers in ipsilateral ears, fingers in contralateral ears, fingers between the toes—I can still touch my nose, and touch it in one smooth, graceful, fast movement. Nor is feedback necessary, except at the tail end of the movement as the finger closes in on the target, and then, notice, the finger decelerates. Often a movement is too fast to exploit feedback, as for example in the case of the finger movements of an accomplished violinist, or in catching an egg after it slips from one's hand. In such cases the conduction velocities of neurons are too slow to permit feedback data to be used to inform the next motor command, and the movement

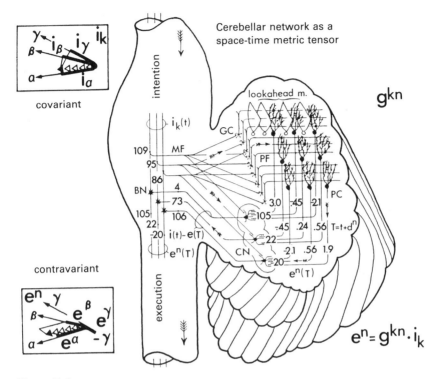

Figure 10.8
Schematic diagram of the cerebellum acting as a space-time metric tensor of the motor hyperspace. The diagram represents the cerebellar input as a covariant vector, and the cerebellar network transforms it into a contravariant output vector. Abbreviations: MF, mossy fibers; GC, granule cells; PF, parallel fibers; PC, Purkinje cells; CN, cerebellar nuclei; BN, brain stem nuclei. The $i_k(t)$ motor intention components refer to time-point t; the $e^n(T)$ motor execution components refer to time-point T, where $T = t + d^n$. The matrix elements in the array between Purkinje cells and cerebellar nuclei show the coefficients by which the mossy fiber information must be multiplied to yield the components of the execution vector expressed in summed firing frequencies of Purkinje axons arriving at cerebellar nuclei. $e^n = (105, 22, -20)^T$. The Purkinje cell arrangement along a parallel fiber beam represents a "temporal lookahead module," implying that some supernumerary Purkinje cells take first- or second-order time derivatives of the input. (From Pellionisz 1984.)

must be composed as a unified sequence without waiting for feedback. The coordinate transformation idea explains how this can be done.

Further evidence for the composition of motor sequences in the absence of feedback is available from both animal and clinical studies. Deafferentation of a body part means that all afferent neurons from that body part are rendered unable to transmit their input to the CNS.

This includes not only skin afferents but also muscle and joint afferents. In experiments on monkeys it has been found that the animal can make good use of deafferented limbs to reach, grasp, climb, and walk; moreover, it can learn new movements (Taub 1976). In a rare case of deafferentation in a human, caused by a peripheral sensory neuropathy in which the motor neurons were spared, the patient remained able to perform many motor skills. For example, without visual feedback he could easily touch his nose, touch each finger sequentially with the thumb, and draw (on command) circles, squares, and figure eights. Evidently in these instances he was executing the sequence of movements without benefit of any feedback at all. Remarkably, this patient was even able to drive a car with a gear shift, though when he bought a new car he could not learn to drive it and had to resort to driving the old car (Marsden, Rothwell, and Day 1984). Given the touchy and idiosyncratic nature of clutches, this is not surprising.

Now the general principle proposed for cerebellar motor coordination is that the incoming "intention" vector is transformed, via a tensor, into an execution vector that specifies the detailed sequencing of muscle cell activity. Failure of the cerebellum to function means that the "intention" vector rather than the "execution" vector is the motor command directly transmitted down the spinal cord, and the result is inadequate muscular coordination and inappropriate timing. The finger overshoots or undershoots, and the movement lacks grace and smoothness, not unlike Roger's fumble if his visual space coordinates are directly used to specify his arm position in intercepting the target. Of course, the cerebellum may be doing other things as well, and it is also likely that there is not one massive connectivity matrix for motor coordination, but rather sets and even hierarchies of matrices. Nevertheless, the hypothesis invites us to see tensorial transformation as a fundamental principle of operation.

In sum, the tensor network hypothesis says that a neuronal network implements its general function as a connectivity matrix to transform input vectors into output vectors. There are, accordingly, two important strands in the hypothesis: the first accommodates the fact that the coordinate systems of neuronal ensembles will specify different frames of reference but must be systematically related, and the second accommodates the parallel nature of neuronal networks, by proposing that individual neurons in the array contribute the components to the vectors, while the structure of the connectivity between neuronal arrays determines the tensorial matrix. It is by trying to do justice to the parallel nature of nervous systems that one comes to fathom how they could use tensorial transformations to achieve sensorimotor control.

The idea that the tensor network approach really provides a theoretical framework within which questions about brain function can be addressed and answered is still very new, and not surprisingly the assessment within neuroscience varies. Some neuroscientists are suspicious that it comes from the "in-a-single-bound-Jack-was-free" school of thought. Some are uncertain about what it all comes to experimentally and whether this is really what a large-scale theoretical approach should look like. Others are enthusiastic because they have begun to envision how they can apply it in their own experimental research and because it literally gives them interpretive hypotheses for their data.

Naturally, it is possible that the tensor network theory is, after all, merely a dead-ender, despite the conviction of Pellionisz and Llinás that it is the real McCoy, or at least a robust and fertile ancestor of a real McCoy. In beginning to determine this, what essentially matters is whether the tensor network theory makes a difference in explaining and predicting experimental results. Quite simply, to be taken seriously it must engage the data: it must unify results, it must give coherent explanations, it must be testable, and it must open experimental doors.

We have already seen a crude analysis of its explanatory capacity with respect to the motor coordination function of the cerebellum, but in order to get a better look at the explanatory potential of the Pellionisz-Llinás approach, it will be useful to focus more closely on other domains where it appears to yield results. Let us therefore leave Roger in his simple, timeless, flatlander world and return to the neuronosphere.

10.5 Tensor Network Theory and the Vestibulo-Ocular Reflex

Gaze control is a rather complex affair involving many elements, including image-slip on the retina, contraction of the neck muscles, contraction of the muscles controlling eyeball movement, and motion of fluid in the vestibular apparatus of the inner ear. The vestibulo-ocular reflex (hereafter, the VOR) contributes one dimension to gaze control, and although in reality it is not isolated from other aspects, to begin by treating it as isolated is a useful idealization.

The VOR is the neuronal arrangement whereby a creature can continue to look at an object even though the head moves in any of its possible directions (all directions, if the creature is an owl). Rotation of the eyes is produced to compensate precisely for the movement of the head. As the head rotates to the right, the eyes track the object by rotating to the left. Here is a simple way to show yourself how clever the VOR is. First, stretch a hand in front of your eyes and, while holding your head steady, wave the hand back and forth quite quickly. Visually track the hand, and try to keep a steady, clear visual image. What you will get instead is a smeary image. For the contrast, keep the hand steady, and move your head back and forth at a good clip. Now the image of the hand is not smeary, as before, but clear and quite steady. That effect is owed to the VOR.

How does the VOR work? First we need to know what neuronal structures are involved. Principal elements are as follows: First, there are the semicircular canals of the vestibular apparatus in the ear, three canals on each side, one in each of the three planes. Although commonly thought to be precisely at right angles to each other, the canals in some species deviate considerably from the presumed ideal. Second, each eyeball has six extraocular muscles (muscles attached to the eyeball exterior) for rotating the eyeball in its socket. Basically, the VOR system circuit is at least a three-stage affair connecting vestibular receptors, via three stages of neuronal links, to the eyeball muscles. These stages consist of (1) the neurons responding to input signals from vestibular receptor cells, which synapse on (2) neurons in the vestibular nuclei (called secondary vestibular neurons), which synapse on (3) oculomotor neurons that innervate the muscles (figure 3.9). Notice that although only one neuron is sketched in to depict each stage, in reality of course there is a large array of neurons at each stage.

The problem for the system to solve is how much each muscle unit should contract in order that the eyeball move to compensate for the movement of the head. If we conceive the problem in terms of the tensor approach, it takes this form: Assume the system wants to keep a particular object in view while the head turns. Then the system needs to convert a new "head position" vector into a new "muscle-position" vector. The input space will have three dimensions, one for each canal, and the relevant point along the axis for each canal is determined by the angle from the "initial" position (figure 10.9). As the head deviates from the initial position, we can describe its movement as a sequence of points in this vestibular phase space. For that sequence of points, we must find the "compensating" sequence of points in the muscle phase space. If the vestibular coordinates are directly used for specifying where the muscles should go, then the eyeball will end up in the wrong place, much as Roger's arm ends up in the wrong place if visual coordinates are not transformed into the coordinates of his motor space. For simplicity, the diagram assumes

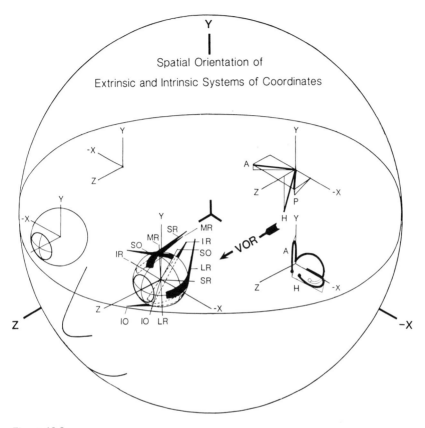

Figure 10.9
The vestibular semicircular canals (A, anterior; P, posterior; H, horizontal) can be characterized by their rotational axes. For the motor system, the rotational axes of the eye correspond to the pull of extraocular muscles (LR, lateral rectus; MR, medial rectus; SR, superior rectus; IR, inferior rectus; SO, superior oblique; IO, inferior oblique). The rotational axes of the vestibular semicircular canals and the extraocular muscles constitute two built-in frames of reference for the CNS to measure a head movement and to execute a compensatory gaze-shift. (From Pellionisz (1985). In *Adaptive Mechanisms in Gaze Control*, ed. A. Berthoz and G. Melvill Jones. Copyright © 1985 by Elsevier Science Publishing Co., Inc.)

that the head is moving purely horizontally, so that the input maximally registers yaw, as opposed to pitch and roll.

There are six extraocular muscles, so the muscle phase space is six-dimensional, and the muscle vector will have as its components the points on the axes for each muscle. Where any muscle is on its axis will be a function of its degree of contraction from a standard position, say when the eyeball is positioned directly ahead. Experimental data are available expressing the relation between muscle contraction

PHYSICAL GEOMETRY :   ROTATIONAL AXES

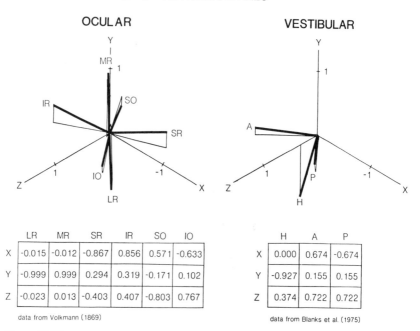

OCULAR

VESTIBULAR

	LR	MR	SR	IR	SO	IO
X	-0.015	-0.012	-0.867	0.856	0.571	-0.633
Y	-0.999	0.999	0.294	0.319	-0.171	0.102
Z	-0.023	0.013	-0.403	0.407	-0.803	0.767

data from Volkmann (1869)

	H	A	P
X	0.000	0.674	-0.674
Y	-0.927	0.155	0.155
Z	0.374	0.722	0.722

data from Blanks et al. (1975)

Figure 10.10
The sensory and motor systems of coordinates of the VOR, intrinsic to CNS function, as defined by the vestibular matrix and eye muscle matrix. The directions in three-dimensional XYZ space of the unit rotational axes, belonging to individual eye muscle contractions, are shown on the left; that is, this illustration shows how the eyeball moves in 3-space relative to the activity of a given muscle. The excitatory activation-axes of the combined semicircular canals of the two vestibuli are shown on the right. These two frames of reference therefore delimit the phase spaces within which the nervous system must function such that gaze control is achieved. To facilitate visual perception of the three-dimensional directions of the axes, their orthogonal projection to the XYZ plane is also indicated. The numerical values are based on anatomical data. (From Pellionisz (1985). In *Adaptive Mechanisms in Gaze Control*, ed. A. Berthoz and G. Melvill Jones. Copyright © 1985 by Elsevier Science Publishing Co., Inc.)

and eyeball rotation (Volkmann 1869) and describing the excitatory sensitivity-axes for each vestibular canal (Blanks et al. 1975). Given these data, it is therefore possible to describe the vestibular phase space and the oculomotor phase space for a given head rotation. This is the basis for the quantitative description in figure 10.10.

According to the tensor network theory, there ought to be a tensorial transformation of the vestibular vector into the oculomotor vector. The Pellionisz-Llinás hypothesis is that a tensorial transformation takes place at each of the three synaptic levels, the last of which transforms a premotor vector into a motor vector that tells the muscles what the position in muscle phase space should be—in other words, how much each muscle should contract (figure 10.11). Since we can figure out what the positions of the eyeball should be given the position of the head, we can determine the tensorial transformations needed. Then we can work backward and figure out what the participating neurons at each stage should be doing. This in turn can be tested by seeing whether the neurons really do behave as the hypothesis says they should. As more is discovered about the neuronal basis, the basic hypothesis may be corrected and elaborated, and thus theory and experimental research co-evolve.

To give an example of a testable hypothesis emerging out of the theoretical considerations: Pellionisz reasoned that the vestibular apparatus should have a preferred position, called the eigenposition, in which the output vector is different merely in magnitude from the input vector, and thus the tensorial transformation is maximally simple. Mathematically it can be shown that there is indeed a set of such positions, though it differs from species to species. In humans the head's "best" position ought to be tilted slightly upward at a pitch of 21 degrees; in rabbits, at 24 degrees. This in fact appears to be so.

The tensor network strategy then exploits this idea: there should be a systematic relation between the vestibular phase space and the neurons that, by their pattern of firing frequencies, represent the position of the head. That is, there should be a systematic relation between the phase space of the vestibular canals and the phase space of the vestibular *neurons*, and similarly for the eyeball muscles and the oculomotor neurons. If we can generate hypotheses about the phase spaces of the sensory and motor systems, this allows us to generate fine-grained hypotheses about the neuronal implementation and to test the hypotheses against the facts of neuronal responses. This is the framework for experimental investigation.

A further test of the hypothesis is how well it fares in computer simulation. The answer is that the Pellionisz computer model (1985) of gaze control involving the VOR and neck muscle coordination is certainly impressive. It uses a realistic basis for specifying components of vestibular vectors and oculomotor vectors. One virtue of a computer model is that it permits us to test the theory by asking the model whether the neuronal array *could* be executing tensorial transformations on its input, given the experimentally constrained configuration of neurons and their electrophysiological properties in the model. If the answer in a highly constrained computer model is no, then the answer forthcoming from the brain itself is not likely to be yes. The answer from the Pellionisz-Llinás computer model

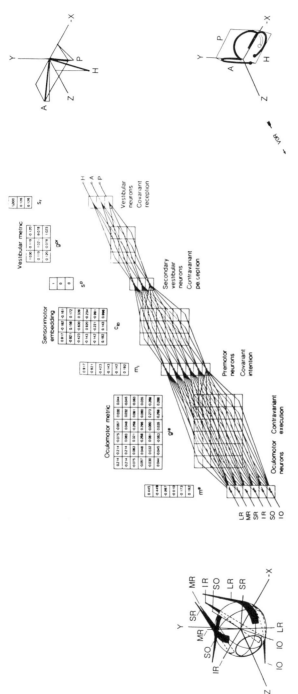

Figure 10.11
Tensorial solution for the VOR sensorimotor transformation and its quantitative (matrix and network) implementation. For each of the three synaptic junctions, there is an appropriate transformation. The result is the conversion of a three-dimensional covariant vector s_r (upper right) into a six-dimensional contravariant extraocular vector m^e (lower left). In this example the vestibular input vector corresponds to the case of maximal horizontal stimulation, and the numerical values represent deviation in base firing rate. The illustrated scheme can be used for calculation of any eye-muscle activation emerging from a given vestibular input. The lenslike character of the sequence of transformations is especially evident in this illustration. (From Pellionisz (1985). In *Adaptive Mechanisms in Gaze Control*, ed. A Berthoz and G. Melvill Jones. Copyright © 1985 by Elsevier Science Publishing Co., Inc.)

appears to be that the VOR neuronal array could indeed be transforming covariant vectors into contravariant vectors—that the connectivity and electrophysiology could support such a function.

As indicated at the outset, matters are much more complicated than the three-stage characterization of the VOR implies. No circuit is as isolated from other fields of neuronal activity as the schematic description of a reflex would permit us to suppose. As Sherrington observed (1906), "a simple reflex is probably a purely abstract conception, because all parts of the nervous system are connected together and no part of it is probably ever capable of reaction without affecting and being affected by various other parts. . . ."

First of all, there are connections to the vestibular nuclei from the cerebellum, which figure in the saccadic movement of the eyes. Moreover, since not all objects are tracked, there must be factors in virtue of which the tracking response is differentially engaged, according to interest, motivation, and such. The neck muscles are a crucial part of the story since the head moves, and there is feedback from them. And from behavioral output, we know there must be connections to visual perception. Additionally, the VOR is in some measure plastic, since it can adjust to reversing prisms on the eye (Gonshor and Jones 1976).

These complexities can be addressed within the framework of tensor network theory, and with the basic schema in place it is possible to envision how to begin to factor in additional features. In this spirit, Pellionisz has sketched a schematic frog nervous system that gives a rough picture of how tensor network theory means to encompass representation and computation from the initial sensory input to the final motor output (figures 10.12, 10.13). For example, in this sketch reception vectors from the visual and auditory receptors are integrated in the superior colliculus by a tensorial transformation. The idea is that different modalities can be understood as different axes in a phase space. A position in the multimodal phase space will be determined by the components of the various axes, and what is perceived is hence a unified, objective target, as opposed to the-object-as-seen or the-object-as-heard.

Further elements in the sketch envision the sensory cortex determining whether the target should be snapped at, the vestibulocerebellum determining how posture would need to be corrected in that event, the motor cortex relaying a vector specifying what configuration the body should go into relative to the target, and the cerebellum transforming that vector into a vector that specifies in detail how the body (hindlimbs, neck, forelimbs) should achieve that configuration, given its starting position, in order to converge on the

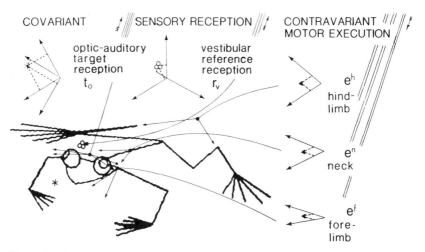

Figure 10.12
Symbolic depiction of natural frames of reference in which multisensory-multimotor transformations are implemented in neuronal networks of the frog CNS, perhaps in the tectum. In this example the CNS integrates information from several sensory modalities and transforms the coordinated sensory output of the colliculus into different optional motor responses. The coordination problem is complex, because in snapping at a fly, the frog must use coordinated input from vision, audition, and the vestibular system, and snapping may involve a "whole body saccade" to a target, using hindlimb muscles, and stabilization of the head by neck and forelimb muscles. (From Pellionisz 1983b.)

target. At each stage the model conforms to the basic principles of tensor network theory: representations are positions in phase spaces, and computation is coordinate transformation via tensors. This model is obviously highly schematic, and it is a long way both to a computer simulation of such a frog and to physiological understanding. So no one should be under the misapprehension that the schematic model has all the nitty-gritty details nailed down. (The question of plasticity and network modifiability will be deferred until section 10.7.)

Having emphasized the visionary nature of the schema, I must also say that I see it as no bad thing at this stage. In the case of a large-scale theory, there must be some demonstration of how experimental data can fit, but at the same time the general framework must be big and bold and ambitious enough to generate projects and programs. That is what is essential for the "Galilean combination." The work on the VOR addresses the first consideration, and the amphibian nervous system schema addresses the second. Both are necessary. One can of course always dun any theory coming and going—by criticizing its visionary projections as insufficiently snug with the experimental

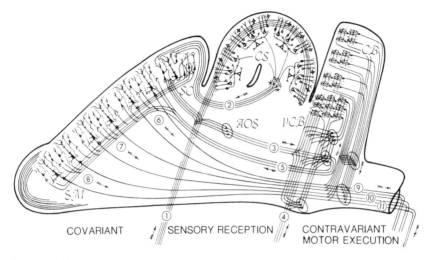

Figure 10.13
Highly schematic characterization of the CNS neuronal networks of amphibia to depict the hypothesized implementation of coordinate transformations as described in figure 10.12. Abbreviations: CS superior colliculus (a.k.a. optic tectum); VCB, vestibulocerebellum; AOS, accessory optic system; SC, sensory cortex; SM, sensorimotor cortex. (From Pellionisz 1983b.)

nitty-gritty, and by criticizing the experimentally close work as insufficiently wide in what it explains.

10.6 Phase Space Sandwiches

A further demonstration of the fertility of the tensor network concerns coordinate transformations between phase spaces with *two* dimensions. Paul M. Churchland (forthcoming) has suggested that when the relevant phase spaces are two-dimensional, the neurons can pattern themselves so as to constitute a literal, physical map of the relevant space. If two adjacent neuronal grids are metrically deformed so as to be in the appropriate register with each other, then they can make the required coordinate transformations directly by means of vertical connections that join corresponding points in the two spatially contiguous grids. Moreover, such grids, justified by the economy of engineering, will have a topographical organization displaying neighborhood relations of the represented space. It thus has the added virtue that it comports with, and perhaps provides one explanatory basis for, some instances of the topographical organization of large areas of gray matter in nervous systems and the vertical cross-laminar connections that frequent gray matter.

The hypothesis is best understood as a special case of the more general theoretical approach advocated by Pellionisz and Llinás. In more detail the idea is this:

> If we suppose that our crab [Roger; section 10.4] contains internal representations of both its sensory phase space and its motor phase space, then the following arrangement will effect the desired transformation. Let its sensory phase space be represented by a physical grid of signal-carrying fibres, a grid that is metrically deformed in real space in just the way displayed in figure [10.14]. Let its motor phase space be represented by a second grid of fibres, in undeformed orthogonal array. Place the first grid over the second, and let them be connected by a large number of short vertical fibres, extending downwards from each vertex in the sensory grid to the nearest vertex in the underlying motor grid, as in figure [10.14].
>
> The system functions as follows. Depending on where each eye is positioned, a signal is sent down a particular fibre in the appropriate bundle, a fibre which extends into the sensory grid from the appropriate radial point. Joint eye position is thus reliably registered by a joint stimulation at a unique coordinate intersection.
>
> In the lower grid, a stimulation at any coordinate intersection is conveyed outwards along the relevant pair of motor fibres, each of which induces its target limb joint to assume the appropriate angle. We need now suppose only that the vertical connections between the upper and lower grids all function as "and-gates" or "threshold switches", so that a stimulatory signal is sent down a vertical connection to the motor grid exactly if and exactly where the relevant sensory intersection point is simultaneously stimulated by both of its intersecting fibres. Such a system will "compute" the desired coordinate transformations to a degree of accuracy limited only by the grain of the two grids, and by the density of their vertical connections. Because the upper map is *metrically deformed* in the manner described, the points in sensory space are brought into appropriate register with the points in motor space. As the eyes fixate, so fixates the arm: it reaches out to precisely the point triangulated by the crab's eyes. (Paul M. Churchland (forthcoming))

For reasons reflecting the overtly geometrical nature of the idea, Churchland has called this the *phase-space sandwich* hypothesis. By spatially organizing themselves into maps, and by layering so that the maps are in suitable register, neurons might, with utmost simplicity,

COORDINATE TRANSFORMATION BY
CONTIGUOUS TOPOGRAPHIC MAPS

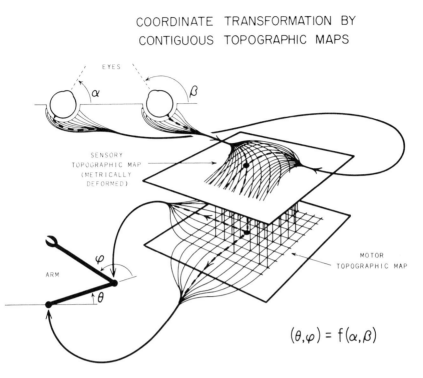

$$(\theta, \varphi) = f(\alpha, \beta)$$

Figure 10.14
The coordinate transformation, physically implemented. Joint eye position is registered
in the upper map by a simultaneous stimulation at a unique intersection. Acting as
and-gates, the vertical connections convey a signal down to the motor map from
exactly that position. From there, activity is conducted out both of the intersecting
motor fibers, with the result that each arm joint assumes an angle appropriate to the
fiber containing the signal. (Adapted from Paul M. Churchland (forthcoming).)

execute any 2-D to 2-D transformation whatsoever. Within these limits,
the principle could be applicable quite generally, whatever the nature
of the phase space transformations, and whether the features represented are internal or external.

   Although in the cartoon case the sensory space and the motor space
are directly connected in a single phase space sandwich, in real brains
one would expect a number of phase spaces to intervene between the
initial sensory space and the final motor space, and one would expect
distinct phase spaces for each sensory modality. Some intervening
phase spaces can be predicted to be quite abstract in what they represent. As sketched, the basic idea is quite simple, but if it is implemented in nervous tissues, naturally there would be complicating
factors (Paul M. Churchland (forthcoming)).

Evidence that some parts of the nervous system may in fact conform in some measure to the phase space sandwich configuration can be found in studies on the superior colliculus (also known as the optic tectum, especially in lower animals). High on the midbrain are two pairs of lumps, the uppermost pair being the superior colliculus (see section 3.2). Known to be important in foveating a target, the superior colliculus has a laminar architecture, in which the topmost lamina receives input from the retina and is organized to map the retina topographically. The bottom layer sends motor output to the extraocular muscles and is topographically mapped so that stimulation of a visual cell will cause the eyes to move so as to foveate that part of the visual field represented by the stimulated cell in the overlying visual layer. It looks as though the retinotopic map and the extraocular-muscle map are pretty much in register, with the result that vertical connections (direct or stepwise) from the retinotopic map can excite the motor neurons to move the eyeball so that it foveates on that part of the visual field wherein the target was first detected (figure 10.15). This sketch is an oversimplification, of course. For one thing, in mammals the superior colliculus is a tightly integrated part of a larger complex system that includes inputs from the visual cortex and the frontal eye fields. Nevertheless, the suggestion is that the phase space sandwich may constitute the fundamental organizing plan in the superior colliculus, overlying which may be an encrustation of modifications, cobble-ups, and jury-rigged inventions. The idea is useful, therefore, to the extent that it reveals some simple computational pattern at the core of the immense complexity.

In the superior colliculus are a number of intervening layers, one of which contains an auditory map that permits the animal to foveate what it hears. In some animals one layer is a "whisker" map, which enables the organism to foveate what its whiskers sense. As one would expect, the neck muscles are also represented, so that in some cases foveation is accomplished by moving both the head and the eyeball. The principle of laminating suitably deformed topographical maps and making vertical connections between them means that phase space transformations can be executed very simply and very quickly. And the problem of neurogenesis looks more tractable the simpler the computational principle.

Once this geometric technique of performing transformations is understood, it will be observed that the maps representing phase spaces on which transformations are to be made need not be literally stacked one on top of the other. Maps can exploit the phase space sandwich principle even though they are spatially distant from each other, so long as the set of fibers connecting them preserves the

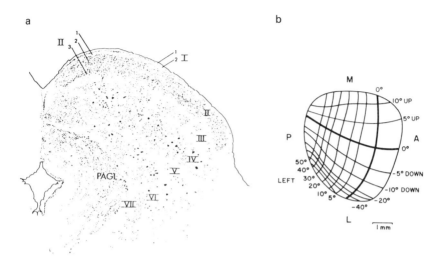

Figure 10.15
(a) Projection drawing of Nissl-stained cross section of cat superior colliculus illustrating laminar organization. Dots correspond to cell bodies of collicular neurons. (From Kanaseki and Sprague 1974.) (b) Retinotopic map: a metrically deformed topographic map of the visual hemifield, in rectangular coordinates, on the superficial layer of the right colliculus of the cat. Abbreviations: M, medial; L, lateral; P, posterior. (Adapted from Schiller 1984.)

relevant topographical relations. Additionally, it must be stressed that even if we know that a cortical area is topographically organized, it is a further and more difficult question what *phase space* is there represented. The more complex the nervous system, the more abstract will be the phase space representations deep in the neuroaxis. Such abstract maps are what Konishi (forthcoming) calls "centrally synthesized maps." Notice also that it would be simple enough to add a lamina representing real space (figures 10.16, 10.17) that could be used in calculating the trajectory of a moving object.

The discovery that nervous systems abound in topographical maps and relation-preserving interconnections (chapter 3) has long seemed an organizational key that ought to help solve the functional mysteries. The phase space sandwich hypothesis is one possible way of finding a fit between some anatomical facts and a computational theory.[3] It should be emphasized that the hypothesis suggests only *one* way in which sensorimotor computations might be executed, and other computational principles such as matrix multiplication, winner-take-all strategies, and error-correcting strategies (see section 10.9) may also have a place. Nervous systems likely use assorted tricks and devices, and the phase space sandwich may be but one among many.

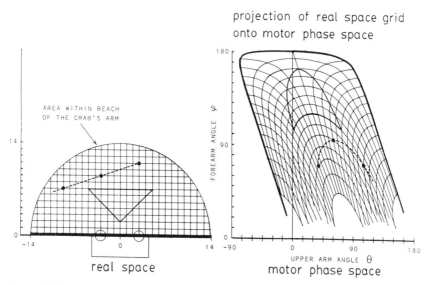

Figure 10.16
The transformation of real-space coordinates into motor phase space. The semicircular grid in (a) represents the set of points in *real* space within reach of the crab's arm. The deformed grid in (b) displays the corresponding points in motor phase space. The large triangle is for orientation, and the three rectilinear points represent an object moving at uniform velocity in front of the crab. (Adapted from Paul M. Churchland (forthcoming).)

10.7   *Tensor Network Theory: Further Questions*

Many questions about brain function remain to be addressed in discussing the tensor network theory. Perhaps the most prominent question concerns learning, and whether the tensor network approach can accommodate some kinds of plasticity. Pellionisz and Llinás (1985b) have indicated that they think it can. They suggest that in a broad sense learning is the process whereby geometries of ensembles are modified in order that they come, by increments, to more closely approximate a homeomorphic relationship. Feedback, on this analysis, enables one geometry to be modified so as to give a more faithful representation. The modification in geometry will be the result of modification along various dimensions of the participating neurons. As Pellionisz schematically puts it:

> . . . metric tensors, embodied in neuronal networks, may interact through invariants or through common vectorial expressions in such a manner that they organize, generate, and modify one another. (1983a:206)

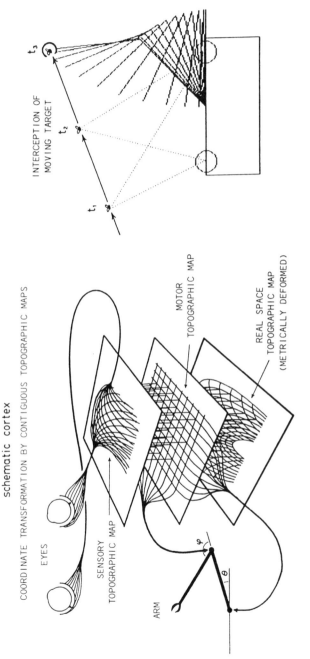

Figure 10.17
A metrically deformed topographic map of real space is here added to the robot crab's "cortex" as a bottom layer, to which vertical connections extend from the upper layers. This layer provides the crab with an internal representation of the position of objects in real space. Given two sequential points in real space, a lookahead feature built into the third layer can project a colinear third point. A signal from this point in the lower map, conducted back up to the motor map, will position the arm to catch a moving object on the fly. (Adapted from Paul M. Churchland (forthcoming).)

Thus, he envisages a hierarchy of nested geometries that interact with one another and with the external geometry.

This very general outline of an approach to plasticity and learning is given some substance in a recent paper by Pellionisz and Llinás (1985b), in which they address the specific problem of "tuning" the cerebellum so that it effects the correct transformation from the "motor intention vector," which issues from the higher motor centers, to the "motor execution vector," which finally directs the muscles. Pellionisz and Llinás show how the covariant proprioception vector, which provides a form of feedback concerning actual motor performance, can be iteratively fed back into the transforming cerebellar matrix in such a fashion that, after a number of iterations, the matrix relaxes into a state in which the relevant eigenvectors are identical. In this state the matrix effects the *correct* coordinate transformation. The authors further suggest that the climbing fibers of the cerebellum—which had no role in their initial theory of cerebellar function—constitute the special pathway by which such reverberative feedback modifies the transformational properties of the cerebellar network. Such a "relaxation" process constitutes a possible point of contact with the "relaxation" algorithms advanced by the "connectionists" in AI, whose work will be discussed in section 10.9.

This approach comports with the general hypothesis that learning new motor skills essentially begins with the modification and assembling of preexisting motor programs. On this view, the developing brain will grow certain motor programs in the normal course of maturation, whether or not there is feedback. The modification and novel sequencing of available skills to make new skills are the basic ingredients of motor "learning." This is not to say that new skills are nothing other than constructs of old skill-atoms, since genuine novelty does appear—skating is not just sliding one foot in front of the other, for example. But it does suggest that the learning of new skills draws on available skills and exploits error correction in order to produce a novel motor program. Thus, for example, in learning to pole-vault we begin by assembling a set of already existing skills—running, grasping, pushing the body, and so forth—and error-correct until a new smooth sequence is produced. It is in error correction that feedback becomes crucial.

Whether detailed explanations of learning within the tensor network theory will be forthcoming and whether they can exploit what is already known at the molar level about feedback and feedforward mechanisms remains to be seen. It may be that the tensor network approach can consort fruitfully with other approaches to neuronal learning already feathering out, such as the parallel models of associative memory and feature recognition (Rumelhart and Zipser 1985, Willshaw 1981, Kohonen, Oja, and Lehtiö 1981). Since the parallel modeling strategies for learning and recognition also use a vector-matrix approach, some of this research may be immediately useful in addressing the problem of learning motor skills in terms of phase space modification. (For more on this, see section 10.9.)

From what is already apparent, it can be concluded that a variety of types of process are indifferently lumped together in the vernacular as "learning." As things look now, some of these processes may be understandable in the way Pellionisz and Llinás envisage, whereas others may be understandable only by invoking quite different principles, perhaps as an overlay on a geometrical analysis, perhaps in terms of principles altogether independent of it. A vector-matrix theory may, for example, give a good account of motor learning and certain kinds of recognition but not of some types of cognitive learning in humans.

Then again, perhaps such processes as concept acquisition, which have so far resisted an analysis in terms of symbol manipulation, will be made comprehensible in terms of modifications to the geometry of highly abstract phase spaces. Additionally, it seems to me quite possible that some capacities hitherto considered strictly cognitive may be discovered to share fundamental elements with paradigmatic motor skills. One is certainly nudged in that direction by data on profoundly amnesic patients who can learn not only new motor skills but also how to solve highly complicated—and ostensibly cognitive—puzzles (such as the Tower of Hanoi puzzle). (See the discussion in chapters 4 and 9.)

In addition to learning, some provision will need to be made for other factors crucial to behavioral output such as hunger, thirst, arousal, sexual interest, attention, and so forth. I see no evidence that such features positively *cannot* be encompassed within a phase space framework, though on the other hand I have no idea whatever of how to do it.

So far the emphasis has been on the programmatic virtues of the tensor network theory, but naturally the question of testing detailed hypotheses is ever at hand. Novel ways to test the theory will undoubtedly be found by experimental neuroscientists who know intimately their particular subfield. Computer modeling will be a means of first resort, but if we are to know whether arrays of neurons fit the tensor network hypothesis, ways must also be found for getting exacting detail on the response profile of a large battery of input neurons, parallel fibers, Purkinje cells, and so forth.

At the moment, the neuron-by-neuron test is not available, because the test requires *simultaneous* recording of multiple, adjacent cells and that in turn requires a major technological breakthrough. A number of laboratories are trying to solve this problem, and Llinás's laboratory at New York University has developed some techniques for recording from 24 adjacent cells simultaneously (Bower and Llinás 1983). Although this is a striking achievement, much larger numbers may need to be accommodated.

What gives a theory the right "feel" in its early stages is whether or not it is capable of making sense of the phenomena, whether it shows itself capable of fitting in with established theory elsewhere in science (biology, genetics, physics, chemistry), whether it can unify and explain, and perhaps, whether it is simple and elegant. There are, alas, no formal procedures for telling whether a theory is on the right track, let alone whether it is elegant, and perhaps the best indicator here is whether a theory captures the imagination of other scientists who, in making it their own, get it to reveal satisfying answers to important questions and solutions to long-standing mysteries. I think this has begun to happen in this case (Peterson et al. 1985, Gielen and Van Zuylen (1986), locomotion studies under way in Larry Jordan's laboratory); but for more, we shall have to wait and see.

So much tentativeness is characteristic, in any event, for a theory in its first stages, and any nascent theory can be swamped by a deluge of "what-about's." But the tensor network theory does have what I earlier characterized as the Galilean combination of simplicity, unifying principles, and mathematization. Which is not to say that it is *right*, but only that it is *a Theory*—a large-scale, ambitious, fertile theory—a phenomenon unusual enough in neuroscience to make it worth a long look.[4]

10.8   What Has Motor Control Got to Do with Mental States?

It will perhaps seem odd that nothing has yet been said to make contact with the processes that are typically in the forefront of philosophers' discussions. Why should philosophers care about a theory whose general shape is dictated by problems of sensorimotor control?

This is a fair question, and its answer depends on thinking about the human mind-brain as something that evolved from simpler nervous systems. If we think of motor control as a fundamental function for nervous systems, then increasing sophistication in nervous systems is, in this broad sense, understandable as an increasingly sensitive means of controlling behavior on the basis of sensory information. As organisms compete for scarce resources, efficiency of motor control is at a premium, and nervous systems with more sophisticated motor control will have a selective advantage over those whose motor control is less efficient. For example, motor systems that enable a creature to build a nest, swing through the trees, use warning calls, or learn to make dipping sticks are all refinements that amount to improved motor control.

To follow evolution's footsteps in discovering how basic principles of motor control are refined and upgraded to yield more complex systems is a productive strategy. Additionally, it may be a shift in focus that allows us a breakthrough in the attempt to understand the higher functions. As Pellionisz and Llinás see it, if they have the general principles right—even roughly right—then it is a start, and a start in the right place. If we can see how the complexity in behavior that we call cognition evolved from solutions to basic problems in sensorimotor control, this can provide the framework for determining the nature and dynamics of cognition.

There is an assumption, popular among philosophers, that the brain processes that make for cognition are one sort of thing and that the brain processes that contribute to motor control belong to an entirely different category. Accordingly, the assumption may be used to justify a disregard of research on motor control by those doing research on cognition. But if we look at matters from an evolutionary and neurobiological point of view, the assumption is not only naive, it in fact trammels the theoretical imagination. It is like trying to do physics on the assumption that one set of laws and principles applies to the sublunary sphere, and a quite different set to the superlunary sphere.[5]

Higher functions are surely not discontinuous with lower functions; they are not a sphere unto themselves. Needless to say, this does *not* mean that psychological investigations of perception, memory, and the like, are therefore inappropriate. At the risk of being repetitive, I would note again that the co-evolutionary strategy discussed in chapter 9 envisages research proceeding at all levels, with a rich interanimation between levels. But it does mean that if we want to understand the fundamental principles of cognition, we may need to understand the emergence in evolution of those paradigmatically cognitive processes, and hence we may need to understand their origins in sensorimotor control. It does mean, therefore, that a principled disregard of sensorimotor control by philosophers may deprive them of just the perspective needed to understand the fundamental principles underlying intelligent behavior.

More than that, the tensor network theory provides an answer to those advocates of a sentential theory of representation and cognition who say that their theory is the only game in town (Fodor 1975, 1981).

The only theory of representations and representing we've got, runs the lesson, is sentential. Critics of the sentential paradigm have often been challenged to present an alternative theory of representing, where the implicit rider is that if the critic cannot say even what a competing theory would look like, then he ought to keep mum. The discussion of the tensor network theory so far has emphasized the *computational* power of the theory in addressing the computational questions of how the brain solves sensorimotor problems. But it is important to see that it also shows great promise in the way it addresses the questions concerning how the brain *represents.*

The tensor network theory opens a door, through which we can begin to envisage a radically different paradigm in which *representations,* even at fairly abstract levels of organization, are interpreted as *points in phase spaces,* and where tensorial transformations effect transitions between phase spaces. Although some cognitive activity probably is understandable as the manipulation of sentential representations according to logical rules, many cognitive processes likely are not. Indeed, the processes underlying sentential representation are surely themselves nonsentential in nature. What is needed is a way to conceive of what nonsentential representing might be, and the tensor network theory provides that much, even if, in the end, it turns out not to be right.

Unbuttoning a bit, let us indulge in some unrestrained speculation concerning how some cognitive representing might be understood within the tensor network hypothesis. Consider the problem of recognizing faces, or the problem of how we can recognize a phonemic string as the sort that *could* be an English word, even though it is not. Both feats of recognition are accomplished routinely and effortlessly, yet both stubbornly resist a sentential analysis. Since a new approach is called for, envisage instead the possibility that facial recognition involves a feature phase space with as many dimensions as there are recognitionally relevant features. The neurons keyed to respond to individual features are the axes of the coordinate space, and the activity levels of the neurons jointly specify a point in phase space.

Suppose, to make it simple, that one neuron is sensitive to size of eyes, another to shape of eyes, another to distance between eyes, another to nose length, another to mouth width, and so on. There may be several hundred dimensions to this facial phase space, and a given face will therefore occupy a specific point in the phase space. More likely, the system wants less precision, and two presentations of the same face may have only approximately the same point in phase space. The response patterns of the input neurons will determine where in the phase space the face is, and hence a face is represented when a given response pattern obtains. Notice that this view precisely does *not* say there is a "grandmother neuron," but says rather that there is a *response pattern* of a whole set of neurons that, within limits, covaries with the presentation of Grandmother.

A phase space of course has a metric, easily visible in the figures of the sensory and motor grids, and a phase space representation embodies the metrical relations between distinct possible positions within it. A given point in a phase space will be closer to certain points than to others, and by definite amounts. If the phase space is devoted to facial recognition, then closely resembling faces will occupy adjacent regions, and very different faces will be correspondingly further apart. This is why we can recognize someone even after an absence of five years, why the bank teller reminds us of Aunt Bessie, and why there are perceived family resemblances. Undoubtedly certain features are more salient than others, and the geometry of the phase space will be warped to reflect this. Eyes, for example, appear to be more important than freckles; thus, I can easily recognize a photo of Einstein whether or not it has been doctored with freckles, but change the eyes and the recognition problem is more difficult. Presumably this is the sort of thing cartoonists exploit. It is also remarkable that we can recognize degraded presentations of faces, and this too looks as though it can easily be explained on the phase space model. A subset of features may be enough to define a uniquely populated volume in facial phase space—no one else might have just the bony facial contours of Lincoln, or the caterpillar mustache on the squat facial contour characteristic of Hitler. This suggests too how small lesions can easily be compensated for, and hence why loss of a small section of the phase space will not show up as an isolated inability to recognize a particular person at a particular age (e.g., Churchill at the end of the war).

Suppose that a specific volume of the phase space is occupied by a prototype face, or more specifically by, say, a prototype female face. Conceivably, the prototypes are in some degree hard-wired in (Rosch 1973, Rosch and Lloyd 1978). Part of what goes into facial recognition might be distance in the phase space from the prototype, and learning the variant on the basic prototype for a specific culture will be a matter of modifying the relevant volume of the phase space to accord with peer practice. Orientation of faces seems to be important in their recognition; hence, a photo of Einstein will be instantly recognizable if presented right side up but recognizable only with considerable effort if presented upside down (Rock 1983). This could be explained on grounds that the prototype of the human face has eyes in the upper quadrants, mouth in the lower.

A suitably amended story might be told for recognition of phonemic strings as could-be words. Suppose a given set of neurons is sensitive to distinctive phonemic features and forms a coordinate system of as many axes as there are features. A given phonemic string is then represented as a point in phase space. In the linguistically accomplished, a certain scattered volume of the phase space will be carved out as high density, thus forming a subspace of prototypically English phoneme strings (words).[6]

Color perception is another area where the phase space model of representation naturally suggests itself. It is remarkable that we see an object as having a constant color even when viewed under a wide variety of illumination conditions. Land's results (1977) indicate that color perception is a function not of radiant energy impinging on the photoreceptors but of computed "lightness" values of objects at three wavelengths.

The photoreceptors responsible for color vision are the cones, and a cone may have one of three types of visual pigment, with differing sensitivity to specific light wavelengths. The "long-wave cones" are maximally sensitive to light at wavelengths of 450 nanometers, the "middle-wave cones" are sensitive over a large range but peak at about 535 nanometers, and the "short-wave cones," whose area of sensitivity largely overlaps with that of the middle-range cones and partly overlaps with that of the long-wave cones, have a sensitivity peak at 565 nanometers.

The computational problem for the visual system is how to get reflectance efficiency (lightness) values out of values for light flux on the receptors.[7] The representation problem is how a given triplet of reflectance values yields the representation of a unique color. It appears that this problem can be given a simple geometric solution.

Once the system has obtained reflectance efficiency values at each of the three wavelengths, perception of a given color is determined by the relations among the three reflectance efficiency values. But what is remarkable is that, as Land points out, any specific color can be represented as a point in a three-dimensional "color space" (1977:120). The three coordinate axes of the color space are the lightness or reflectance efficiency values at each of the three wavelengths. Any color we can see has a location in the color space, and to each triplet of reflectance efficiencies computed by the visual system there corresponds a specific color. The space has a metric, and hence shades of yellow are closer to each other than to shades of blue, the very dark colors are found in one corner of the lowest level, the very lightest colors are found in the opposite corner of the highest level, and so forth.

The possibility that presents itself is that the phase space of per-ceived color has as its physical substrate a neuronal phase space, whose axes are three streams of neurons carrying information about reflectance efficiency values at the three wavelengths. The *representa-tion problem* for color perception, therefore, can be addressed thus: colors are represented as points in a three-dimensional neuronal phase space.

Moved by the hypothesis concerning color perception, one might go on to speculate that the perception of tastes and odors and the neural substrate of these perceptions can perhaps also be addressed within the same general framework. Consider: the human gustatory system appears to have just four distinct types of receptors for taste—sweet, salt, sour, and bitter—and yet we perceive an astounding number of distinct flavors. The receptors do not themselves have axons, but they convey information across a synapse to the next stage of neurons, whose response is substantially a function of the receptor type to which it is specifically linked, though its response is also affected to a subtle degree by activity in other receptor types. Now if we think of each postreceptor neuron type as constituting one axis in a four-dimensional phase space, then the activity of neurons on each axis specifies a position in the 4-D phase space. Different positions in taste phase space will be determined by the varying activity of the relevant neurons.

For example, suppose the salt receptor and the sweet receptor are excited, but the bitter and sour receptors are not. The activity in the relevant postreceptor neurons will specify a particular position in the neuronal taste phase space, and it will be a different position from that determined by excitation of, say, just the bitter receptors or the bitter and sour and sweet receptors. Degree of excitation also allows for further resolution within the taste phase space. Accordingly, the taste of Jonathan apples will be a position in phase space, different from the position occupied by the taste of absinthe, and even in minor degree from the position occupied by the subtly different flavor of McIntosh apples. The flavor of orange will be closer in the phase space to the flavor of grapefruit than to the flavor of mustard. A similar conceptual approach may be appropriate for odors, if, as it seems, the human olfactory system relies for its perception of a vast range of distinct odors on a finite number (perhaps just five) of recep-tor types.

The notion of quality spaces is by no means new, but I think it worth dwelling in this context on the possibility of making a connection between the phase spaces defined at the neuronal level and quality spaces defined at the cognitive level. The basic thesis of prototype theory (Rosch 1973, Rosch and Mervis 1975) is that many concepts should be understood not on the model of lists of necessary and sufficient conditions for application but rather as stored prototypes or "focal examples." On this view, recognition and perception involve similarity matching with the prototype. The behavioral data show that subjects conform to a metric in classifying objects as (for example) birds or vegetables or colors. For instance, robins are more readily classifiable as birds than are chickens, carrots are more readily classifiable as vegetables than radishes, and radishes, in turn, more than parsley. Using prototype theory, the interpretation of the data is that robins are more centrally located than chickens in the (bird) phase space, and carrots are more centrally located than radishes (which are in turn more centrally located than parsley) in the (vegetable) phase space.

The possibility being explored is that we can understand the physical substrate for cognitive quality spaces in terms of phase spaces defined by neurons at some suitable level of organization, and this in turn may plough back insights concerning the nature of cognitive quality spaces. At the very least, it is striking that a *nonpropositional* cognitive theory should dovetail so suggestively with a geometrical theory of neuronal representation and computation.

This is all the more striking because research in AI in the *parallel modeling* school (see section 10.9) has had considerable success in modeling visual recognition (Hinton and Sejnowski 1983a), word recognition (McClelland and Rumelhart 1981), and memory (Willshaw 1981) using a vector-matrix approach. The computing basis for these models is binary state neuron-like elements arranged in parallel, with synapse-like connections whose weights are altered as the network "learns." Unlike conventional cognitive simulation programs in serial machines where representations are equated with *symbols,* in these models representations are *patterns of activity* distributed across a set of units. Transformations are achieved by matrix multiplication followed by thresholding or some similar nonlinear operation.

Finally, it may be that the geometric approach will not so much compete with the propositional-logical conception of cognition as explain and absorb it. It is known that the resources of phase space analysis are sufficiently powerful to model the structures and relations of logic and language. That is, logicians have shown (Van Fraassen 1970, 1972, Van Fraassen and Hooker 1976) that linguistic structure and the logical relations between them can be handled simply and elegantly within a geometric framework. Propositions, for example, are modeled as subspaces of a *logical* phase space, and inferences can be modeled as vector-to-vector transformations. Hooker has suggested (in correspondence) that it is therefore possible to envision a unified cognitive neurobiology in which logic and the propositional attitudes, characterized in terms of phase spaces, vectors, and matrices, fit in quite naturally with a wider geometric theory of representations and computation. In that event, the psychology of sentential attitudes and reasoning might reduce rather smoothly to neurobiology.

Whether such a reduction can be achieved is obviously an empirical question, but Hooker's idea is that the general framework permits us to begin to reconceive the structures and relations of logic and language and to exploit the geometric conception in developing models of the relations between subcognitive domains and the propositional attitudes. Thus, on this vision of things, the propositional paradigm would be reinterpreted geometrically.

Even granting the power and elegance of the geometrical characterization of logic and logical structures, however, one should probably not be very sanguine about the *smoothness* of any prospective reduction of folk psychology. One important reason here derives from the work of Stephen Stich (1983), which, as we saw in section 9.5, shows that the folk psychological categories of belief, desire, and so forth, have internal deficiencies which entail that they must be reconfigured if they are to be used by a scientific psychology. Stich's view is that at best, reconfigured *analogues* of these categories will be used by a scientific psychology. If any sentence-like representations are to be reduced in the manner envisioned by Hooker, therefore, it will be these reconfigured analogues of folk psychological categories.

Some of this section is philosophical, in the sense that it flies some theoretical balloons. I readily admit that a great deal of tough empirical slogging needs to be done to take it from the realm of the possible to the realm of the actual. But a major goal has been to respond to those who assumed that nothing in a theory of sensorimotor control can be relevant to philosophical questions concerning mental states and cognitive processes. My summary answer is that as a result of considering a theory of the basic principles of sensorimotor control, we can begin to see the shape of a new and powerful paradigm for understanding computational processes executed by the mind-brain and for understanding how the mind-brain represents at a variety of organizational levels. The multidimensional phase space appears to be a very powerful means for representation-in-general, and clearly it is no longer acceptable to say that the sentential theory of representing is the only game in town. But this section is also philosophical in the (perhaps different) sense that it tries to limn the general shape of a unified theory of the mind-brain.

In this chapter I have tried to achieve a balance between being sympathetic enough to give the tensor network theory a fair hearing and being distant enough to spot egregious weaknesses. Almost certainly others will see in this work flaws, as well as virtues, to which I have been blind. The overarching aim throughout has been not so much to defend a particular theory as to try to convey a sense both of why it matters so tremendously to have *a* theory and of what a general theory of neuronal ensembles might look like. One important aspect of the tensor network theory that was insufficiently developed is its conceptual affinity with those computer-simulation approaches to vision, learning, and so forth, that begin with a biologically faithful basis of neuron-like elements. This is the work in parallel modeling, which is interesting not only for how it might cross-fertilize with the tensor network approach but also for its insightful simulations of nervous system functions. I shall therefore continue in the next section with a succinct discussion of parallel modeling.

10.9   Parallel Models of Neuronal Computation

Within the AI community there is a growing dissatisfaction concerning the adequacy of sequential models to simulate the cognitive processes of creatures with brains. Although sequential models can be extremely powerful, they have been disappointing in the simulation of fundamental cognitive processes such as pattern recognition and knowledge storage and retrieval. As Rumelhart[8] has observed, for those things we humans find quite difficult, such as chess and theorem-proving, conventional AI approaches have been quite successful, but for those things we find easy, such as perceptual recognition and speech comprehension, the success of the conventional approaches has been negligible. One line of reasoning is that the conventional simulations will never be very good, however many bells and whistles are added, because they depend on assumptions that are at odds with the biology of nervous systems, and a nervous system is still the most impressive example we have of an information-processing device.

For an example of the *dissimilarity* between computers and nervous systems, consider that in conventional computers memory is likened unto a library, with each piece of data located in its own special space in the memory bank, data that can be retrieved only by a central processor that knows the address in the memory bank for each datum. Human memory appears to be organized along entirely different lines. For one thing, from a partial or a degraded stimulus human memory can "reconstruct" the rest, and there are associative relationships among stored pieces of information based on considerations of *content* rather than on considerations of *location*.

The effects of brain lesions on memory functions also suggest that the principles of information storage in nervous systems are unlike those used by computers. If each datum were stored in a precise location, then destruction of tissue should produce highly specific losses in memory. For example, if my memory for facts about Churchill or for the tune of "Greensleeves" is stored in a precise location, then by abolishing the neurons at that location, we should be able to abolish my ability to sing "Greensleeves" or to recollect who was the British prime minister during World War II, while leaving intact my recollection of who was British prime minister during the Crimean War and my memory for "Mud, Mud, glorious Mud." It appears doubtful that lesions produce data losses of that degree of specificity. Rather, they result in a general degrading of memories. There is more specificity in nervous tissue than Lashley thought, but it now appears doubtful that individual neurons are so specific that they are tuned to respond to a single item and nothing else. Thus, connectionist models tend to devise and use *distributed* principles, which means that elements may be selective to a range of stimuli and there are no "grandmother cells" (Anderson and Mozer 1981).

The learning of cognitive skills and the significance of rehearsal are decidedly troublesome for the computer memory metaphor, as are the dynamics of memory consolidation and the pattern of developing amnesia in Korsakoff's patients such that the older the memories, the more likely they are to be preserved. Information storage, it appears, is in some ill-defined sense a function of connectivity among sets of neurons. This implies that there is something fundamentally wrong in understanding the brain's memory on the model of individual symbols stored at unique addresses in a data bank (Anderson and Hinton 1981). Consequently, these differences have made the metaphor that identifies the brain with a computer seem more than a trifle thin. And they have implied that a good deal of simulation research conducted under the justificatory shelter of the metaphor has been misdirected.

A further source of misgivings about the computer metaphor concerns real-time constraints. Although the signal velocities in nervous systems are quite slow in comparison to those in computers, brains are nonetheless far, far faster than electronic devices in the execution of their complex tasks. For example, human brains are incomparably faster than any computer in word-nonword recognition tasks. As McClelland says,

If current estimates of the number of synapses in the brain are anywhere near correct, it would take even the fastest of today's computers something between several years and several centuries to simulate the processing that can take place within the human brain in one second. (unpublished:22)

Feldman and Ballard express the modeling constraints implied by temporal limitations as the "hundred-step rule." As they explain,

The critical resource that is most obvious is time. Neurons whose basic computational speed is a few milliseconds must be made to account for complex behaviors which are carried out in a few hundred milliseconds (Posner 1978). This means that *entire complex behaviors are carried out in less than a hundred time steps.* Current AI and simulations programs require millions of steps. (1982:206)

The known parallel architecture of the brain and the suspected distributed nature of information storage has suggested to some researchers that greater success in understanding cognitive functions might be achieved by a radical departure from the sequential stereotype. The idea has been to try to understand how interconnected neuron-like elements, simultaneously processing information, might accomplish such tasks as pattern recognition and learning. As Anderson and Hinton have assessed the situation with respect to memory,

If we abandon the idea that the basic method of retrieving items is via their addresses, we can use parallel computation in systems of interconnected elements to achieve content-addressable memory. (1981:10)

The principal articles of faith for conventional simulation research are that processing is sequential and that what makes a process a *cognitive* process is that it manipulates symbols (Pylyshyn 1984). The parallel modeling strategy (also called "connectionism") divests itself of both articles. As noted earlier, whereas in a conventional model a representation is a symbol, in the parallel models it is a pattern of activity distributed across a network. In the words of Anderson and Hinton,

The basic notion in all these models is the idea of a *state vector,* that is, that the currently active representations within the system are coded as patterns of activity simultaneously present on the set of elements that comprise the system. (1981:17)

The notion of a state vector will already be familiar in view of the earlier discussion concerning phase space representation in motor control.

In a clear statement of connectionist principles—a sort of connectionist manifesto—Feldman and Ballard characterize the new approach:

> The fundamental premise of connectionism is that individual neurons *do not transmit large amounts of symbolic information.* Instead, they compute by being *appropriately connected* to large numbers of similar units. This is in sharp contrast to the conventional computer model of intelligence prevalent in computer science and cognitive psychology. (1982:208)

Expressing essentially the same point, Von der Malsburg and Willshaw say of connectionist models,

> In computer terminology, *the programme resides in the structure of the local interactions;* the result of the computation being the globally ordered state, which is arrived at by a parallel computation, and which is resistant to small alterations. (1981:83; my emphasis)

The connectionists have abandoned the exclusively top-down approach characteristic of much research in AI and are looking for principles to explain how elements in networks interact to produce global results. The two types of approach need not be at loggerheads on all counts, however, for it may be that serial simulations could be appropriate for some types of cognitive activity or for certain levels of cognitive organization, even if not for all. Moreover, the problems, strategies, and lessons, learned in the course of developing serial programs to simulate cognitive processes, are there for the parallel modelers to exploit should they prove useful. Let us now take a closer look at what the parallel modelers are trying to do. The centerpiece problem for organizing the discussion is the problem of how we see.

Global Effects and Local Interactions
In order for an organism to see, its nervous system must be affected by the world external to it. The fundamental fact constraining any hypothesis about how a brain can have visual perception is that the input to the visual system is the two-dimensional array of light falling on the retina. Out of that stimulus array, the brain must concoct an interpretation of what in the external world corresponds to the received pattern of light. And of course, there is no one inside to see the array and identify it as the sort of pattern made by, say, a bird or a pineapple. There are just networks of neurons that interact with each other and that, as a result of the interconnections, yield the global effect that is an interpretation of the 2-D array. Since it cannot be

magic, there must be mechanisms. Hence, the problem is to figure out by what principles the brain visually recognizes objects.

Though it has evolved close connections to neurobiology, the parallel modeling strategy is still sometimes referred to as "top-down" (see, for example, Marr and Poggio 1976). This is largely because of Marr's influence, for in his articulation of the strategy one first had to figure out a computational schema that would solve a problem (say, for visual recognition) and only then could one usefully address the question of whether and how the brain implemented that schema. Not even Marr adhered strictly to the doctrine, however, and some of the most successful parallel models are avowedly inspired and constrained by neurobiology. (See, for example, Hinton and Sejnowski 1983a, 1983b, and 1986.)

Sometimes even the neurobiologically inspired and constrained models may be characterized as "top-down," however, and this is presumably because the motivating question is something like this: "How *could* neuron-like elements in a network N interact to produce global effect E?" Presumably this question contrasts with a different sort of question: "Do the neurons in network N produce global effect E by conforming to algorithm A?" On the basis of that contrast, one might call the first question "top-down" and the second "bottom-up." Although the contrast is clear enough, the labels strike me as misleading. I prefer to mark the contrast between these two types of questions not as "top-down versus bottom-up" but as follows: the first is a *theory-devising* question, and the second a *theory-testing* question.

Typically, what determines whether "top-down" is applicable to a strategy is whether or not the strategy cares how the brain performs the processing under study. To call the first question "top-down" is to deprive that label of whatever significance it has, because the "how could" questions of the connectionists are constrained by considerations of neuronal architecture and physiology in a way that classical top-down computer models (for example, Schank and Abelson 1977) simply are not. However, this is an issue about what words to use, and perhaps the "top-down–bottom-up" contrast is not very useful anyhow at this point. It might be best simply to see parallel models as *theories* concerning brain processes intervening between input and output, or theories of how macro effects are produced by microstructure.

There are many variations on the parallel model theme. For example, there are linear models (Kohonen, Oja, and Lehtio 1981) and nonlinear models (Hinton 1981) of simple associative memory. Addressing mechanisms are replaced in some parallel models by hardware connections (Fahlman 1981) and in others by patterns of activity where data are stored by modification of "synaptic" weights (Hinton 1981). In some the computation used is matrix multiplication (Kohonen, Oja, and Lehtio 1981), and in others it is a relaxation algorithm (Marr and Poggio 1976, Hummel and Zucker 1980). The unifying element is the contrast to conventional computers in architecture (parallel versus serial), in the method for data storage, and in the nature of representation.

In order to convey a sense of what makes the approach interesting, I shall illustrate with an example of one such model, drawing on the recent work on visual recognition done by Hinton and Sejnowski (1983a, 1986); Ballard, Hinton, and Sejnowski (1983). The rationale for choosing vision modeling for illustration is that it seems to me substantially richer as well as closer to the neurobiology than the work in memory and learning. Perhaps, after all, this might be expected, since the neural substrate of vision is far better understood than the neural substrate of memory. Although impressive in their own right, the memory models are, as Sejnowski (1981) comments, "uncomfortably abstract," and his observation on Kohonen's memory model, for example, seems apt: ". . . , [it] resembles memory in the way that a toy glider resembles a bird. It does fly, in a rigid sort of way, but it lacks dynamics and grace" (p. 203). The work on higher functions is nevertheless important, at least because it illustrates how such problems as learning, memory, and knowledge chunking can be addressed, and to some nontrivial degree solved, within a new paradigm. (See especially the theory of reading devised by McClelland and Rumelhart (1981) and theory of learning developed by Rumelhart and Zipser (1985).)

In the Hinton-Sejnowski system for visual recognition, the network consists of two sets of binary units: detectors for receiving input from the external world, and units connected to detectors and to other nondetecting units. The task of the system is to interpret the image array on the detectors. When a unit is in its "true" state (true = 1, false = 0), this can be understood as a sort of vote for the hypothesis it represents. Final hypotheses are determined by fit with the image and by fit with other hypotheses, so that the winning hypothesis emerges after extended voting competitions with others. This type of procedure for searching for the best hypothesis is called *cooperative search*.

Whereas in some models the search procedure assigns numbers to units as representing the probability that the unit's hypothesis is true, the Hinton-Sejnowski model is a bit different. If a given hypothesis has a probability of .8, then the unit that represents that hypothesis

has a .8 probability of being in the "true" state. In this sense, therefore, the model is stochastic, a feature that enables it to avoid certain
problems (see below). Note also that the relation between two units is
a matter of "synaptic" weighting and that such weighting implements constraints between hypotheses. It will be evident that if the
synaptic weights can be changed, then the relations between hypotheses thereby change, and the system is capable of learning. That is,
one hypothesis can acquire a higher probability given a particular
image by virtue of modifying the probabilities for the relevant unit's
being in the "true" state in those conditions.

Relaxation: Searching for the Best Hypothesis
The general idea of *relaxation* is that a network converges on a global
result on the basis of local interactions, where units have access to the
responses of their neighbors and adjust their own responses according to how their neighbors are responding. By iterative modification
of responses on the part of units according to certain simple rules, the
network as a whole eventually "relaxes" into a stable, optimal state. If
the connections are symmetric, and if the updating is asynchronous,
then a system allowed to run will relax into a stable configuration.
This resulting state is, in effect, the system's answer to the question
posed by the stimulus. Within this general conception of cooperative
search, therefore, the problem is to find an assignment of the weights
to connections between units such that a system of interacting units
can relax into an optimal answer.

Once the detectors are activated by a stimulus, a range of connected units are activated, which means that a certain range of hypotheses are "in the game," as it were. Some units activate certain
units and inhibit other units. The system thus moves away from some
of the less probable hypotheses toward more probable hypotheses as
a result of the "voting" interactions. Incompatible hypotheses will
compete until the more probable wins. Less probable hypotheses will
be in the "true" state with decreasing frequency and hence will have
decreasing influence on connected units. The general character of the
probability relationships between hypotheses is Bayesian.

Figure 10.18 shows a very simple constraint network for cooperative search, where the hypothesis for the network to find is the one
that best fits the input and therefore specifies the orientation of the
object. Each unit is a hypothesis concerning a vertex of the Necker
cube; incompatible hypotheses are negatively connected, and consil-
ient hypotheses are positively connected. In this system weights are
assigned such that two negative inputs balance three positive inputs.
Each unit has three neighbors connected positively and two competi-

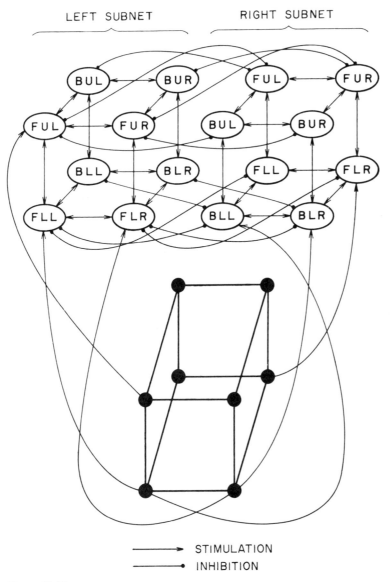

LEFT SUBNET   RIGHT SUBNET

⟶ STIMULATION
⟶• INHIBITION

Figure 10.18
A simple network representing some of the constraints involved in perceiving the
Necker cube. Abbreviations: B, back; F, front; L, left; R, right; U, upper; L, lower. Each
unit in the network represents a hypothesis concerning a vertex in a line drawing of a
Necker cube. The network consists of two interconnected subnetworks—one corre-
sponding to each of the two possible interpretations. (From Rumelhart et al. (1986). In
Parallel Distributed Processing: Explorations in the Microstructure of Cognition. Vol. 2: *Applications*, ed. J. L. McClelland and D. E. Rumelhart. Cambridge, Mass.: MIT Press.)

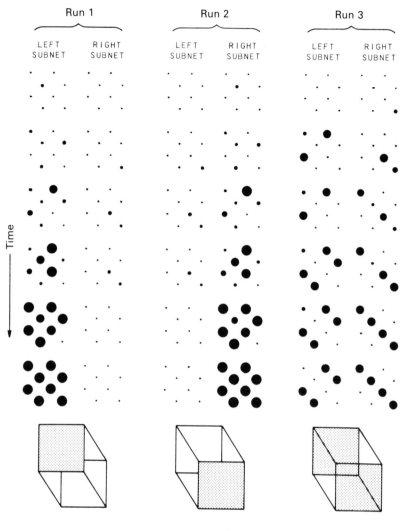

Interpretations

Figure 10.19
Three different runs of a simulation based on the network shown in Figure 10.18. The size of the circles indicates the activation value of each unit. The units are arranged in the shape of the subnetwork, with each circle shown in its position corresponding to the vertex of the cube from which it is receiving input. The states are shown after every sixth update. (Modified from Rumelhart et al. (1986). In *Parallel Distributed Processing: Explorations in the Microstructure of Cognition*. Vol. 2: *Applications*, ed. J. L. McClelland and D. E. Rumelhart. Cambridge, Mass.: MIT Press.)

tors connected negatively, and each unit receives one positive input from the stimulus. To see how the system will run, suppose all units are off, and then give one unit a positive value (input). Eventually, the system will settle into a state where all units in one subnetwork are activated and all units in another subnetwork are turned off. This can be understood as the system's having relaxed into an interpretation of the line drawing either as a right-facing Necker cube or as a left-facing Necker cube. Figure 10.19 shows three different states the network might relax into, depending on what unit is first activated. This cartoon network is not an example of how a visual system is thought to solve the object orientation problem. Rather, it is included to illustrate as simply as possible some fundamental principles of networks for cooperative search.

If units in a network are interpreted as hypotheses, then the connections between the units can be interpreted as *constraints* among the hypotheses. The input to the system can also be thought of as a constraint; hence, when the system is stimulated by an input, the locally optimal state to which it relaxes is a state that satisfies as many constraints as possible. Kirkpatrick, Gelatt, and Vecchi (1983) have pointed out that there is a provocative connection between cooperative search and thermodynamics, inasmuch as the network and its behavior also have a model in energy distribution. The central idea is that we can understand how the network finds a good combination of hypotheses on the model of a physical system settling into a minimal energy state.

More specifically, Kirkpatrick and his colleagues have suggested that we take as the appropriate metaphor the annealing of metals. Given the proper cooling schedule, the heated metal will appropriately anneal into the desired crystalline structure. In this case we know that as the metal cools, highly improbable states are eventually replaced by more probable states as energy is distributed and the system comes to find (relaxes into) the global energy minimum. The idea is that in cooperative search, the system simulates annealing, in the sense that parts find local energy minima and the system gradually finds the most probable answer—the global energy minimum.

Part of the value of the thermodynamic analogy, aside from its intrinsic suggestiveness, is that it makes available to the modeler the range of laws, concepts, and equations in thermodynamics that he can then use to explore and create new features and principles in parallel networks. In other words, it imports a whole dimension of *systematicity* for free,[9] as it were, and this systematicity provides an exploratory framework. More than that makes the analogy appealing, however. The analogy suggests the possibility of finding a concept that does for brain theory what the concept of energy did for physics.

Hinton and Sejnowski (1983a) exploit the analogy as follows: Let any given state of the system have an associated "energy," and let higher energy states be the degree to which the constraints are violated, and lower energy states be the degree to which constraints are satisfied.[10] Search can then be understood in thermodynamic terms as the system's finding energy minima as it cools. Having high temperature is therefore analogous to having a great deal of noise in the system, and cooling is analogous to the emergence of the winning hypothesis (the signal). As Hinton and Sejnowski say, ". . . so in minimizing its energy, it is maximizing the extent to which it satisfies constraints" (1983a:449). Assuming that the connections between search units are symmetrical and that they are updated asynchronously, then it is a fact about the system that it will settle into a local energy minimum.

Using the thermodynamic analogy, Hinton and Sejnowski express the rule for minimizing the energy contributed by a unit in a deterministic system as follows: *Adopt the true state if your total input from the other units and from outside the system exceeds your threshold.* (See figure 10.20 for an example of what this model can do.) This looks both simple and elegant as a mechanism for a network to produce a best-fit combination of hypotheses from a set of hypotheses activated by an image array. It also permits certain assumptions about the physical world to be built into the interactions between units. For example, it is probable that two adjacent points on a surface have the same reflectance, though they may not. Such information can be built into the synaptic weights of a set of units. (Concerning the kinds of assumptions about the physical world that might be built into nervous systems, see Gibson 1968, Ullman 1979.)

The settling into local minima will occur whether the system is stochastic or not, but a flaw in the deterministic version of cooperative search is that a unit's change in energy levels must always be down, never up. The consequence is that sometimes the system gets stuck at some *local* minimum and hence never reaches the *global* minimum. Or, in the "hypothesis and constraint" language, a combination of hypotheses can be favored too early in the game by a segment of units, and there is no way to let an *overall* better combination of hypotheses, outvoted in the early rounds, have another go.

The thermodynamic analogy suggests the probabilistic strategy. Different cooling schedules produce different molecular organizations in the annealing process, some of which yield a crystalline structure with global energy minimum and some of which do not. To

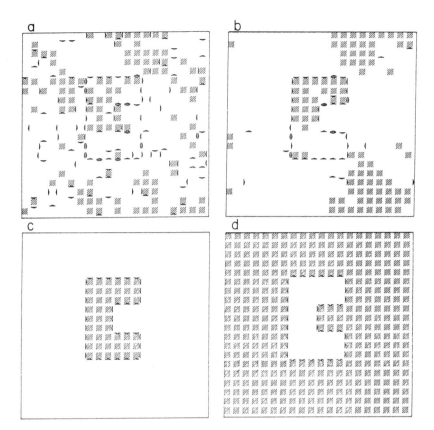

Figure 10.20
This diagram shows three successive stages in simulated annealing as the network solves the problem of separating figure from ground. (Hatchmark squares ⬚ are figure units, ◄ are edge units.) Physical constraints, such as that edges tend to be continuous and that figures are internally connected, are built into the algorithm. (a) shows the network at "high temperature," where the figure and edge units make a structureless pattern. In (b) the network has "cooled" to "medium temperature," and more structure appears as figure units support edge units whose orientation is consistent with them. (c) At "low temperature" local inconsistencies are resolved, the entire network "crystallizes" to the correct solution, and the block letter "C" appears as figure against a bare background. In (d) the center of attention shifts to the outside and causes a figure-ground reversal. (Courtesy T. Sejnowski. Based on Sejnowski and Hinton (forthcoming).)

achieve an annealing with the *global* energy minimum, a very gradual schedule is wanted. In informational terms this is analogous to adding noise to the system, and thus it becomes possible to see how to improve upon the cooling schedule where the system gets stuck at local minima. Fluctuations (noise) allow the system to break out of superficial minima, so that, after a while, the lower a minimum is, the more likely it is that the system will be there (Ackley, Hinton, and Sejnowski 1985).

The advantage of the stochastic version, therefore, is that states can occasionally jump to higher-level energy states—that is, relatively improbable hypotheses can occasionally come up for reconsideration. To achieve this effect, Hinton and Sejnowski use a modification of an algorithm concerning average energy distributions devised by Metropolis et al. (1953). The effect of the addition is that *noise* is added to the decision rule. Occasionally, therefore, a unit will adopt a hypothesis that is less consistent with the hypothesis gaining strength in its neighborhood, and the locally improbable hypothesis could eventually win global status depending on how it comports with hypotheses in other neighborhoods. On this view of matters, noise in the system turns out not to be an incidental and ignorable property of the system, but to be important to its efficient functioning. If this is right, then the probabilistic nature of neuronal responsiveness has an important function. As Hinton and Sejnowski (1983b) say,

> We suggest that fluctuations may be deliberately added to neural signals to avoid locking the network into unwanted local optima and to provide the linear conditions needed for efficient learning. The issue of noise in the nervous system deserves renewed experimental investigation and further theoretical analysis. (p. 5)

The hypothesis concerning noise is interesting for another, philosophical, reason. As Mark Wilson has remarked (personal communication), if one took the view that psychology should be autonomous with respect to neuroscience and that the details of the neuronal machine were irrelevant to understanding cognitive functions, then noise in networks would be exactly the sort of thing one would miss. And yet it may be exactly the sort of thing that needs to be considered in order to get an adequate explanation of cognitive processes.

Do Real Neuronal Systems Work This Way?
Relaxing into an optimal hypothesis may be *a* way to do pattern recognition and so forth, but is it the *brain's* way? As a first consideration, recall that because the machine that implements the program has a parallel architecture, and because the units are neuron-like,

with connectivity grossly patterned to simulate neuronal connections, the Hinton-Sejnowski model is to a surprising degree biologically constrained. Therefore, it is not merely *a* way, an any-old-way,
to do pattern recognition. More specifically, it is a way for a set of
simple units, organized in parallel, with rich cross-talk potential and
interaction constraints such as "synaptic weights," to do pattern
recognition.

For the model to provide a theory of certain brain functions such as
pattern recognition, it will need to account both for fine-grained anatomical and physiological data and for higher-level psychological
data. As in the case of the tensor network theory, we shall need to
evaluate how well it explains and unifies the data, how it can be
tested, and whether it is rich enough to suggest new experimental
tests. To be fair, we must bear in mind that the parallel modeling
strategies are of very recent vintage and that what we see thus far is
really just a beginning. What we have is not so much a theory of how
the visual system functions, or even how one aspect of it functions,
but rather an approach that may lead to a theory of the phenomena.

There are anatomical and physiological facts about the visual system that at some suitable stage need to be embraced within the
model, assuming it is adequate enough to be worth extending—for
example, the center-surround organization of the retina, the X, Y,
and W ganglion-cell pathways with their distinct properties, the retinotopic maps in distinct areas of the cortex, and the characteristic
columnar architecture and connectivity patterns. Some researchers
have taken steps in this direction. For example, Zucker and Hummel
(1983) claim that their relaxation model is faithful to and accounts for
both the processing in the X-pathway and the center-surround organization of retinal cells.

Certain psychological features of vision seem to be difficult to account for within computer vision models. For example, subjective
contours are a puzzle because there is nothing on the 2-D image array
that corresponds to the subjective edge and contrast in color perceived. It may be that these features are not the outcome of low-level
vision modules, as David Marr has claimed, but essentially involve
the contribution of higher centers, as for example, Irvin Rock (1983)
claims. Marr (1982) hoped that he could elicit subjective contours in
his computer model as part of the normal process of edge filling-in,
but Rock points out that many cases of subjective contours cannot be
handled that way and need a figure-ground distinction. Such a distinction may need higher-level "hypotheses" to solve the problem for
the lower-level module. The recent finding by von der Heydt,
Peterhans, and Baumgartner (1984) showing that there are cells in

area 18 that can be driven by subjective contours indicates, nonetheless, that ostensibly high-level business can be investigated neurobiologically, and this may encourage the connectionists. Many other features also suggest "intelligence in perception" to Rock, such as size constancy and orientation constancy.

Although Marr's particular computer vision model does seem vulnerable to these objections, the Hinton-Sejnowski model may have the flexibility to accommodate the intervention of high-level hypotheses in visual perception. One can envisage stages of relaxation in the visual system, such that a hypothesis submitted by one level could be rejected at a higher level, with instructions sent below to rework the data and, subject to certain constraints, to come up with a better hypothesis. In other words, the relaxation process could sweep up a wider and wider range of "hypotheses," and the stochastic nature of the processes will permit *initially* improbable combinations of hypotheses to win out. This conception is compatible, of course, with the view that vision is often subject to descending control.

In a recent paper, however, Sejnowski and Hinton (forthcoming) propose a cartoon story to indicate how a network can solve figure-ground problems by relaxing to a best-fit hypothesis. The model was designed so that missing line segments could be filled in, and a shift in an attentional "spotlight" permits the network to relax into a new hypothesis specifying what is figure and what is ground. (On the attentional spotlight, see Crick 1984 and section 10.10.) The success of this model in handling the faces/vase case of figure-ground ambiguity indicates that at least some figure-ground solutions are well within the capacity of cooperative search.

A further question concerning the neurobiological fidelity of the model arises in connection with the basic units. Recall that these are simple binary units, whereas real neurons are not simple on-off units. A neuron has a spontaneous firing rate that can be increased by depolarization and decreased by hyperpolarization. Its firing frequency can be affected by a large assortment of factors apart from the current changes caused by input neurons (chapter 2). Extracellular circumstances, the recent history of the neuron's behavior, and the intrinsic properties of particular neurons will bear upon its spiking profile. The graded potentials induced at postsynaptic regions also have a complex profile not captured by the simplifications of the computer model (Freeman 1975). The question, therefore, is whether the simple units of the model can be translated into the more complex neuronal units that actually exist.

The optimistic answer is that networks of binary units engaged in cooperative search are rather like the cartoon story of Roger, in the sense that they simplify, idealize, and approximate. But if the basic principles of organization are right, then they can be fancied up to make the cartoon story more closely resemble the real story. Additionally, Hinton has pointed out (personal communication) that if one regards the output of a neuron over a very short time period, such as a few milliseconds, it really is a stochastic binary device. That the firing rate over the longer time period is fundamental seems unlikely on the assumption that neuronal ensembles do avail themselves of something like cooperative search, since there would be insufficient time for voting and revoting.

Additionally, it is not clear that the model is fast enough. Relaxation techniques do have great appeal, but cross-talk, voting, and revoting take time. To repeat an earlier point: if a recognition response occurs 500 msec after the stimulus, there is time for only about twenty synaptic relays; if it has a 1,000 msec latency, there is time for only about forty synaptic relays. Moreover, the response latency includes the time taken to mobilize and execute the motor response, not just the time taken to reach a consensual decision on categorization of the input. Still, as Hinton has remarked (personal communication), there is time for about twenty iterations (individual spikes) in 100 msec, so perhaps time constraints are not a problem. I do not say that these models *are* too slow, but only that speed is a major concern.

Finally, we may want to pose to connectionist models of pattern recognition, memory, or learning the following question: How are the proposed solutions meant to fit into the wider story of the brain's solutions to the fundamental problem of sensorimotor coordination? Put crudely, brains are not in the business of pattern recognition for its own sake, and the nature of pattern recognition, as accomplished by brains, must be understood in the context of its role in how brains achieve motor control. Evolution being what it is, pattern recognition is there to subserve motor coordination. And what goes for pattern recognition in this regard goes also for learning and memory. Since pattern recognition is not the *end* of the sensorimotor coordination story, but only a means to a motor control end, we need to ask connectionists with vision models, *What happens next?* How are the results of a relaxation algorithm to figure in the theory of how the organism moves? Are the results such that they can be used in motor control?

By raising these questions I do not mean to imply either that connectionists are unaware of them or that they will be unable to answer them. Rather, the implication is that if we ignore motor control as the context within which we try to understand pattern recognition, we run the risk of generating biologically irrelevant solutions. The computer, of course, does not have to feed itself, build a nest, mate, or hide; hence, it can afford idly to deploy pattern recognition, platonically unconcerned with matters motoric. The brain, making its living in a rough world, red in tooth and claw, cannot afford such purely contemplative luxury. The point, therefore, is that insofar as evolution solved the problems of sensory processing and motor control simultaneously, we may find it profitable—nay, *essential*—in shaping our theories, to mimic evolution and aim for simultaneous solutions as well. (See also Llinás (forthcoming) and Foss 1986.)

10.10   *The Neurobiology of an Attentional Operation*

The final example of a theoretical development to be discussed here has as its major target the neurobiological mechanisms that subserve visual attention, and its author is Francis Crick (1984).

The background problem for this theoretical venture must be understood first. A fundamental puzzle concerning visual perception arises from the fact that cells in different areas of the cortex appear to be specialized to respond to distinct dimensions of the physical stimulus. Cells in some areas are maximally responsive to movement, others to lines in specific orientations, others to conspecific faces, others to colors, others to stereoptic disparity, and so forth (chapter 3). In other words, perceptual features seem arranged by topic and dispersed hither and thither around the visual cortex. Our perceptions, by contrast, show no such disunity. One sees a unified composite, such as a running black dog or a falling yellow ball. We seem driven to the inference that there must be neuronal means for conjoining distinct properties—yellow color and roundness—such that what is seen is a yellow ball.

There is an additional important element in this puzzle. Although we appear to be able to perceive an indefinite number of distinct combinations, there cannot be hard-wired in distinct cells corresponding to every one of these combinations because there is insufficient neuronal hardware for that. Therefore, Crick suggests, in order to express the particular conjunction of properties in the stimulus, there must be temporary associations of cells, where each represents a property from a distinct dimension. The association is to be temporary so that a set of cells can on one occasion participate in the "yellow ball" combination, on another occasion a "yellow box" combination, and so forth.

To a first approximation, then, we can expect the visual system to generate perceptual combinations by temporarily associating in some manner sets of appropriate cells, where the association has downstream effects on the animal's behavior. Not all conjunctions need to be so formed. Some, of especial biological significance, may be hardwired in genetically, and others, subserving the perception of words, for example, may be permanent cell assemblies resulting from "overlearning." Even granting large numbers of such permanently associated cell groups, it is evident that many associations expressing perceived conjunctions will have to be temporary.

Given the background problem, what we should like to know is how the nervous system accomplishes the association, and knowing the answer would add an important piece to the puzzle of how we see. Certain data from psychophysics appear to offer clues about the kind of process underlying perceived conjunctions. Anne Treisman and her colleagues (1980, 1982) have found that illusory conjunctions of properties are perceived when a scene is flashed very briefly or when distracting elements are present in the scene.

For example, when flashed a picture of a woman in a red hat and a black dress, roughly half the subjects report seeing the opposite conjunction: a woman in a black hat and a red dress. Or again, presented briefly with a green H and a red T, roughly half the subjects report a red H and a green T. Treisman has also found that a subject searching a presented card for a single feature—say just the H-shape (color does not count)—takes roughly about the same amount of time regardless of the number of items, whereas when he is searching for a color-shape conjunction—say, a green H—his search time is a linear function of the number of items in the array. Speaking loosely, the feature seems to "pop out," whereas finding the conjunction requires attentive scanning of about 50–70 msec per item. (See also Julesz 1980.)

The psychological data suggest that "pop out" is a preattentive result but that conjunction perception is the result of attentive scanning of items. Treisman has conjectured that there is a kind of attentive "searchlight," moving from one item to the next, until the sought item has been found. The searchlight is not the only attentional mechanism exploited by the nervous system. Also in evidence, for example, is an attentional effect when one's eyes saccade to a movement in peripheral vision or when one's head moves to foveate the area from which a loud sound emanates or where one expects to see a bright light. (For a review of the neurobiological investigation of these phenomena, see Rizzolatti 1983.)

Assuming there is an attentional searchlight in the specified sense, Crick has raised the question of how the nervous system might effect a searchlight operation. Notice that this does not imply that we understand very well the psychological function and need merely to find its structural realization. Rather, by considering the nature of the neurobiological processes, we can raise new questions about the nature of the attentional processes. As we shall see, this is a good, if embryonic, example of the co-evolution of neurobiological and psychological hypotheses.

The central ideas of Crick's hypothesis for the attentional searchlight derive from reflecting on what the searchlight hypothesis requires of nervous tissue and from considering what likely piece of architecture has properties suited to satisfying those requirements. It is thus directly informed and inspired by neurobiological data concerning patterns of connectivity, response properties of cells, and time constants for physiological events.

Crick has suggested that the reticular complex of the thalamus is a candidate for controling the searchlight, principally because (1) it is on the route of highly specific reciprocal connections between the dorsal thalamus and the cortical visual areas and is therefore strategically located to "sample" activity and determine "where the action is," and (2) its neurons have extensive inhibitory collaterals projecting to thalamic neurons that may permit it to select a narrow thalamic region where there is the greatest activity (figure 10.21)

Many neurons in the thalamus itself have a remarkable response profile, discovered by Llinás and Jahnsen (1982). If, following a brief hyperpolarization, they are depolarized, they respond with a short burst of activity, and then return to the resting state and do not burst

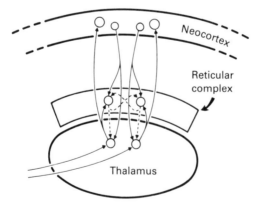

Figure 10.21
The main connections of the reticular complex, highly diagrammatic and not drawn to scale. Solid lines represent excitatory axons. Dashed lines show inhibitory (GABAergic) axons. Arrows represent synapses. (From Crick 1984.)

again for another 80–150 msec. One possibility, therefore, is that neurons of the reticular complex respond to incoming activity by giving the thalamic neurons a hyperpolarizing shot, but when these neurons are subsequently depolarized by the visual stimulus, they go into rapid firing mode. If the wiring is right, neighboring thalamic cells of the relevant sort will go into bursting mode once those adjacent have ceased, and so on in sequence.

Why this is interesting will soon become apparent. Crick suggests that the chief principle guiding the formation of temporary associations of cells—cell assemblies—is fine-time coincidence of high levels of activity in neurons. To a first approximation, simultaneously occurring high activity is necessary for cells to form the association that expresses property conjunctions. Using some ideas of Christoph von der Malsburg (1981), Crick adds the hypothesis that the physical basis for the association is temporary alterations in the synapses by which the two cell sets are connected. He calls synapes that alter in the requisite fashion "Malsburg synapses." Whether Malsburg synapses actually exist and how, over a short time course, synaptic modification might come to be are not known, so these are some of the questions yet to be resolved.

On Crick's hypothesis, the sequential bursting activity of thalamic cells is the operation of the searchlight, and the effect of the bursting response is to enable the formation of temporary cell assemblies by virtue of fine-time coincidence in firing. To summarize, Crick's hypothesis incorporates four basic elements (1984:4588):

(1) The searchlight is controlled by the reticular complex of the thalamus.
(2) The expression of the searchlight is the production of rapid firing in a subset of active thalamic neurons.
(3) The conjunctions produced by the searchlight are mediated by Malsburg synapses, especially by rapid bursts acting on them.
(4) Conjunctions are expressed by cell assemblies, especially of assemblies of cells in different cortical regions.

In brief, therefore, when presented with a stimulus consisting of a green H and a red T, the subject sees it so if there is sufficient time for the thalamic searchlight to select coactivated neuronal groups and for neurons in these groups to undergo temporary synaptic modification to enhance their activity and so express a perceptual conjunction. Consequently, illusory conjunctions are essentially noise, occurring in perception when there is insufficient time for the thalamic searchlight to do its work and hence for the relevant cell assemblies to form.

Crick is quick to point out that the theory is of course imprecise in many places and that many empirical questions have yet to be answered. As examples, he mentions that it is not known how the thalamic neurons might enable the formation of cell assemblies, or in just what cortical areas neurons might be involved in expressing perceptual conjunctions. Whether the relations between neurons in the reticular complex and neurons in the thalamus are in fact those specified in the hypothesis is also not known. If the thalamus effects the searchlight operation, then there should be at least two searchlights (one for each hemithalamus), and perhaps in addition to vision there are searchlights for other modalities. (Consider Deutsch 1984 and illusory conjunctions in audition.) Psychological tests may bear upon this question. Further questions concern the role of the superior colliculus in visual attentive processes and the downstream effect of temporary cell associations. (See Moran and Desimone 1985 for a study of the effects of selective attention on single cells in the extrastriate cortex.)

Evidently Crick's hypothesis provokes both neurobiological and psychological questions, and thus the initial statement of the hypothesis may be just the beginning of a fruitful co-evolutionary exchange. Certainly one does not expect anything approaching completeness at this stage, but the signs are that the hypothesis may be rich enough in experimental potential and sound enough in the definition of the large-scale problem that some coevolutionary good will come of it. Of course both the psychological searchlight hypothesis and Crick's neurobiological account may be quite wrong, but both are eminently investigable. What is already visible is that neurophysiologists as well as psychologists working on attention and visual perception are very much in the game of testing the predictions of the hypothesis, suggesting revisions, and so forth.

10.11 Concluding Remarks

The plan for this chapter has been to provide only a sample of the *type of thing* that I take to be a theory in neuroscience of how macro phenomena are produced by neuronal phenomena. The choice of examples is self-conscious and necessarily reflects my idiosyncratic hunches and biases about what directions seem especially promising. Other researchers, with a different set of hunches and biases, may find themselves tugged in rather different directions. To present a thorough survey of theoretical approaches, though desirable, is not something I could reasonably undertake. For one thing, one has to toy and tinker with a theory for a long while before getting a feel for its capabilities and its limitations. Furthermore, a survey, properly done, would itself comprise an impossibly large volume.[11]

Selected Readings

Ballard, D. H. (1986). Cortical connections and parallel processing: Structure and function. *Behavioral and Brain Sciences* 9/1.

Braitenberg, Valentino (1984). *Vehicles*. Cambridge, Mass.: MIT Press.

Churchland, Paul M. (forthcoming). Cognitive neurobiology: A computational hypothesis for laminar-cortex. *Biology and Philosophy* 1:25–51.

Crick, F. H. C. (1979). Thinking about the brain. *Scientific American* 241:219–232.

Feldman, J. A., and D. H. Ballard (1982). Connectionist models and their properties. *Cognitive Science* 6:205–254.

Hinton, Geoffrey E., and James A. Anderson, eds. (1981). *Parallel models of associative memory*. Hillsdale, N.J.: Erlbaum.

Llinás, Rodolfo R. (forthcoming). "Mindness" as a functional state of the brain. In *Mind matters*, ed. C. Blakemore and S. Greenfield. Oxford: Basil Blackwell.

McClelland, James L., and David E. Rumelhart (1986). *Parallel distributed processing: Explorations in the microstructure of cognition*. Vol. 2: *Applications*. Cambridge, Mass.: MIT Press.

Pellionisz, Andras (1984). Coordination: A vector-matrix description of transformations of overcomplete CNS coordinates and a tensorial solution using the Moore-Penrose generalized inverse. *Journal of Theoretical Biology* 110:353–375.

Pellionisz, Andras, and Rodolfo R. Llinás (1985). Tensor network theory of the metaorganization of functional geometries in the central nervous system. *Neuroscience* 16:245–273.

Rumelhart, David E., and James L. McClelland (1986). *Parallel distributed processing: Explorations in the microstructure of cognition*. Vol. 1: *Foundations*. Cambridge, Mass.: MIT Press.

Chapter 11
Closing Remarks

So my hope is that the application of scientific language to describe ourselves may lead to an improvement in powers of communication and cooperation, perhaps even to a revolution in their effectiveness.
J. Z. Young, 1978

At this stage in their history the brain and behavioral sciences are monumentally exciting, for we appear to have embarked upon a period when an encompassing scientific understanding of the mind-brain will, in some nontrivial measure, be ours. Theories—of the large-scale, governing-paradigm, unifying-framework kind—are beginning to emerge, and they will evolve and come to structure both the research enterprise and, undoubtedly, our very way of thinking about ourselves. And it would be amazing if the new theories and the new discoveries did not contain surprises of such magnitude as to constitute a revolution in understanding. In its power to overturn the "eternal verities" of folk knowledge, this revolution will be at least the equal of the Copernican and Darwinian revolutions. It is already evident that some deeply central folk psychological concepts, such as memory, learning, and consciousness, are either fragmenting or will be replaced by more adequate categories.

Those who suppose that science and humanism must be at loggerheads will greet this forecast of the future with no enthusiasm. They may tend to see the revision of folk theory and the rise of neurobiological-psychological theory as the irreparable loss of our humanity. But one can see it another way. It may be a loss, not of something necessary for our humanity, but of something merely familiar and well-worn. It may be the loss of something that, though second nature, blinkers our understanding and tethers our insight.

The gain, accordingly, may be a profound increase in the understanding of ourselves, which, in the deepest sense, will contribute to, not diminish, our humanity. The loss, moreover, may include certain folk presumptions and myths that, from the point of view of fairness and decency, we come to see as inhumane. And among the desirable losses may also be numbered certain widespread and horrible diseases of the mind-brain.

Divesting ourselves of such things as these is clearly in the spirit of both humanism and science. In any case, it is a mistake to see science as standing in opposition to humanism; rather, it is the political and entrepreneurial *abuses* of scientific knowledge that have displayed a catastrophic disregard for humanistic principles. And we shall certainly have to guard against similar abuses of neuroscientific knowledge.

A primary objective of this book has been to show that neuroscience matters to philosophy. I have advanced three general lines of argument in support of this view: (1) mental processes are brain processes, (2) the theoretical framework resulting from a co-evolution of neuroscience and psychology is bound to be superior to folk psychology, and (3) it is most unlikely that we can devise an adequate theory of the mind-brain without knowing in great detail about the structure and organization of nervous systems.

The correlative theme is that philosophy matters to neuroscience. My strategy here has been to sound that theme less by explicit argument than by implicit demonstration. The central point, nevertheless, is that neuroscience needs philosophy because ongoing research must have a synoptic vision within which the immediate research goals make sense. Such a synoptic vision, transcending disciplinary boundaries but informed by the relevant disciplines, testing the integrity of the governing paradigm and investigating alternatives, is philosophy. At least, it is one very traditional way of doing philosophy. But this sort of philosophy is not an a priori discipline pontificating grandly to the rest of science; it is in the swim with the rest of science and hence stands to be corrected as empirical discovery proceeds.

Moreover, discoveries in neuroscience will undoubtedly change out of all recognition a host of orthodoxies beloved in philosophy. Barring a miracle (or a calcified stubbornness), it will in particular transfigure epistemology, as we discover what it really means for brains to learn, to theorize, to know, and to represent. Neuroscience may even teach us a substantial thing or two about how science and mathematics are themselves possible for our species.

So it is that the brain investigates the brain, theorizing about what brains do when they theorize, finding out what brains do when they find out, and being changed forever by the knowledge.

Notes

Chapter 1

1. The word "neuron" is Greek in origin, and the Greeks used it to mean "nerve" (large, visible cable), though they sometimes also used it to mean "tendon," which makes for confused reading.
2. James Bogen has reminded me of the delicate and difficult aspects of Golgi staining, appreciation of which makes the reticularist's position seem more understandable than it otherwise might.

Chapter 2

1. "Process" seems at first a rather odd word for structures, applying as it commonly does to a train of events. But it is the standard word and I shall use it hereafter in its neurobiological sense.
2. For instance, if you carefully remove the soft white piece of spinal cord in the cleft of the vertebral bone of a lamb chop and cut through it cleanly, you will see the central gray (approximately in a butterfly shape) surrounded by white matter.
3. Receptors for the benzodiazepines (e.g., Valium and Librium) have been found in the brain (discussed in Braestrup and Nielsen 1980), as well as a peptide that naturally occurs in the brain, acts at the benzodiazepine receptor, and increases anxiety (Ferraro, Guidotti, Conti-Tronconi, and Costa 1984).
4. This is true of mammals, where males have an X and a Y chromosome and females have two X chromosomes. However, in birds the females are heterogametic (XY) and the males are homogametic (XX), and in some reptiles the sex of offspring is determined not genetically but by environmental factors such as temperature of the incubating sand. If you are a snapping turtle, you will be female if your mother laid the egg you are in on sand whose temperature is at the extreme low of 20 degrees Celsius or the extreme high of about 30 degrees Celsius; you will be male if the temperature is somewhere in between (Harvey and Slatkin 1982).
5. The hyperstriatum ventrale, pars caudale (HVc), and the robust nucleus of the archistriatum (RA).

Chapter 3

1. Each neuron has a favored sound frequency—called its "characteristic" or "best" frequency—at which it maximally responds even when the sound is very faint. Typically it will respond to a range of slightly higher and slightly lower tones if the decibels are increased.

2. There are other types of interneuron as well, though their physiology is less well understood. For a short discussion of interneurons and their functions, and of the columnar aggregates as input-output modules, see Jones 1981.
3. What should exist, but does not, is a complete compendium of all anatomical data, at all levels of grain. It would need to be done on computer, with weekly updates, standardized terminology, bibliographical references, and access by computer network. Then if one needed to know all the connections, say, in and out of lamina 4 of area MT, available information could be quickly retrieved. Ideally, a computer graphics accompaniment would give visual representation to the data. As it is, the data are spread all over innumerable journals and books, and even anatomists are not familiar with all the anatomical information there is.

Chapter 4

1. Neuropsychologists (Squire and Cohen 1984) have suggested that the phenomena invite a distinction between *declarative* and *procedural* memory, where what is declarative is in some sense accessible to conscious awareness and what is procedural is not. There are some animal models using monkeys (Zola-Morgan 1984) that confirm the dissociability of the two capacities, but since the monkeys do not literally "report" anything, this basis for the distinction is acknowledged to be still a provisional labeling of the assortment of things amnesics respectively can and cannot remember. To this extent, it is essentially a behavioral labeling, rather than a theoretically embedded categorization. (See also section 9.4.)
2. A *lesion* is any damage to nervous tissue that impairs normal functioning of the neurons. For example, a lesion could be caused by surgery, disease, a tumor, vascular abnormalities, drugs, pressure, or a blow to the head.
3. The problem is with what Kolb and Whishaw (1980) call "the n = 1 studies."
4. Spencer argued thus:

> If there is some organization, it must consist in that same "physiological division of labour" in which all organization consists; and there is no division of labour, physiological or other, of which we have any example, or can form any conception, but what involves the concentration of special kinds of activity in special places (1855:611).

5. Grünbaum changed his name to Leyton in 1915.

Chapter 5

1. What seems phenomenologically unappealing about the Crick-Mitchison theory is that it doesn't appear to account for regularities in dream content. For example, in adolescence (at least) many dreams are of a sexual nature, and from adolescence onward people also report countless variations on the "test" dream. Freud's theory, unappealing on other grounds, does have some strengths on this issue. In support of the Crick-Mitchison hypothesis, however, is the finding by Hopfield, Feinstein, and Palmer (1983) that connectionist models quickly suffer from overload unless there is a "forgetting" procedure.
2. There is some controversy concerning one specific tracer technique developed by Sokoloff and his colleagues. The Sokoloff technique uses 2-deoxy-glucose, an analogue of glucose, and the questions pertain to the basic biochemical and metabolic assumptions of the technique. (See Fox 1984 and a response by Raichle and Ter-

Pogossian 1984.) The controversy is not yet settled, but in any event it attaches only to the 2-deoxy-glucose tracer, and this is not the only tracer technique usable in PET scanning.

3. There were in fact several very small patches in the left visual field that were considered spared, on the basis of conventional clinical assessment.

4. G. H. Hardy (1940) recalls,

> I remember once going to see him when he was lying ill at Putney. I had ridden in taxicab number 1729 and remarked that the number seemed to me rather a dull one, and that I hoped it was not an unfavorable omen. "No," he replied, "it is a very interesting number; it is the smallest number expressible as the sum of two cubes in two different ways."

5. The ventricles are cavities in the brain filled with cerebrospinal fluid (figure 3.6). Sometimes the canals connecting the cavities are blocked and the cerebrospinal fluid cannot drain out but continues to collect and press against the ventricle walls. (See section 3.2.)

Chapter 6

1. I realize that this caveat may not do me much good. In trying to keep the discussion simple, I will inevitably slight many a nicety and outrage some historian or other. Philosophers are notoriously sensitive, perhaps even testy, about the history of their subject, and for some, every nuance and every shade must be honored. My choice was simple: either run the risk of offending those historians who find any simplification a brutal oversimplification, or omit altogether the history relevant to the wider project. The choice was obvious. As usual, selected readings will be provided at the chapter end.

2. Mill was the exception to this empiricist principle, since he thought even mathematical principles were, when you got to the heart of the matter, empirical.

3. There are, or course, many versions of idealism. The common theme is the view that the fundamental reality is mind, not matter. Furthermore, idealism typically is antinaturalist in the sense that it is opposed to the view that the operations of the mind can be understood in terms of causes and effects. Nineteenth-century idealists also adopted the view, owed to Kant, that experience is not merely "given" but involves some sort of organization, categorization, and interpretation. This conception of the mind as actively contributing to experiences rather than passively recording it figured in the idealists' opposition to naive realism, which says that our perceptions closely resemble the external objects perceived. Hegel was the dominant figure in the idealism of the later part of the nineteenth century. A noted British idealist of the 1920s was J. M. E. McTaggart, who wrote in rather mystical fashion of the unreality of space, time, and matter. It was this thesis that scientifically attuned philosophers found particularly offensive and worthy of ridicule.

4. Though ardor for this sort of argument has visibly cooled, it is by no means dead. For a recent example, see Anthony Kenny, Master of Balliol College, Oxford, scold Richard Gregory for having fallen into fallacious ways of talking about the visual system (Kenny 1984).

Chapter 7

1. See Dennett's illuminating discussion of an imaginary psychological example, "fatigues," in the introduction to his 1978b book.
2. For further discussion of reduction, see especially Hooker 1981, Wimsatt 1976a, 1976b, Philip Kitcher 1982.
3. For more discussion, see Chihara and Fodor 1965, Dennett 1978b, Paul M. Churchland 1979 and 1984, and Stich 1983.
4. Nonverbal animals would be ascribed beliefs and desires by analogy.
5. It is uncontentious so long as one is not a dualist, and this matter will be taken up in chapter 8.
6. By "suitably liberal" I mean only that we do not limit cognitive activity to linguistically mediated activity. (See also chapters 9 and 10.) It is obviously uncontentious if knowing that one is aware involves linguistically anchored predicates such as "awareness" or "consciousness."

Chapter 8

1. I explore these and other examples in considerable detail in the aforementioned paper (1983).
2. One argument for substance dualism (see Eccles 1977) derives from certain neurophysiological results obtained by Benjamin Libet et al. (1979). The argument is particularly interesting because it is perhaps the only argument based solely on objective empirical data. According to Eccles and Libet, the data show that a mental event *precedes in time* the brain states causally responsible for it. In their judgment this can best be explained in terms of the nonphysical mind antedating the experience in time. As Eccles and Libet see it, if the mental event and the physical counterpart are not cotemporaneous, they cannot be identical.

   After analyzing Libet's papers, I came to the conclusion that the interpretation of the data was unwarranted and that other simpler and more straightforward interpretations were readily available. In brief, I could not find any grounds for concluding that mental states are distinct from brain states. The experimental setup and the interpretation of the data are too complex to present here, and for an account of the disagreement between Libet and me on this question I refer the reader to Patricia S. Churchland 1981a, 1981b, and Libet 1981.
3. Others who have explored this view, either critically or sympathetically, include Robinson (1982), Campbell (1983), Margolis (1978), Dennett (1978b, forthcoming), Shoemaker (1981).
4. Here is a simple way of summing up the difficulties by drawing on distinctions used in philosophical logic. Either the contexts of the premises are transparent or they are opaque. If they are transparent, then the second premise is justified only by begging the question. If they are opaque, then the properties are not extensional, Leibniz's law does not apply, and the arguments are fallacious. Either way, the arguments fail. I suspect that part of the appeal of arguments (A) and (B) lies in their being readable either as transparent or as opaque. Just as one pins down the error on one reading, the other reading, like a Necker cube, flips into focus and seems to be the intended reading. And so it proceeds, flipping back and forth between the criticisms.
5. For a similar version, see also H. Robinson 1982.
6. For a thought-experiment that indicates how it is conceivable that our heroine

might use her utopian neuroscience to introspect the state of her mind-brain, see Paul M. Churchland 1985.

7. For a different view on these questions, see Stich and Nisbett 1980.

8. I owe this argument to Paul M. Churchland.

9. This argument bears a superficial similarity to Searle's (1980) argument, but it is importantly different. As I understand it, Searle's argument contains a crucial qualification in premise (2), namely that no computer model that mimics mind-brain capacities only at their highest level of organization can be adequate, though one that mimicked "all the causal powers of the brain" would be. Searle is a physicalist, and his argument is directed not against reductionism but against what he calls the "formal models" in artificial intelligence and cognitive psychology. It is not altogether clear what is embraced and what is excluded by "formal," but if "purely formal" is roughly equivalent to "sentential," then there is some agreement between us since I am critical of the sentential paradigm. (See chapter 9.) If it is not equivalent or roughly so, then perhaps some of my objections will ruffle Searle's argument as well.

10. For a more fully developed account, see Paul M. Churchland 1979, Stich 1983. For a different account, see Dretske 1981.

11. Nor is it clear that we need to care very much if what we want is a science of the mind-brain, since the assignment of content to internal states may not figure in the generalizations that describe information processing in cognitive organisms. For arguments in support of this view, see Stich 1983.

Chapter 9

1. So far as I can determine, Sperry's (1976, 1980) conception of mental states aligns itself more with functionalism than with anything else, though his arguments against reductionism seem confused to me. To the extent that I can understand them, they seem to have a family resemblance to those considered in this and the subsequent section.

2. Or perhaps some subdomain of cognitive psychology. Exactly what categories and generalizations are at issue here is not very clear, but the intent, at least of Pylyshyn and Fodor, is to include the whole of cognitive psychology.

3. Perhaps these are the sorts of considerations that lay behind Searle's (1980) criticism of functionalism.

4. This is just a partial specification of what is needed; for Hooker's complete account, see Hooker 1981, part III. The rest is not unimportant, but I think it need not be set out here.

5. For a discussion of the opposite view, see Patricia Kitcher 1980, 1982.

6. Something like this argument may also be what moves Sperry (1976, 1980).

7. There are other variations on this theme to the effect that meanings are irreducible to physical states, but I take the presented version to be the most coherent and most persuasive. Davidson (1970) most particularly has proposed antireductionist arguments, and though his work has been widely discussed in the philosophical literature, I find Dennett 1978b, Fodor 1975, 1981, and Pylyshyn 1984 clearer and deeper. For a Davidsonian attack on the position I defend, see Horgan and Woodward 1985. For yet other arguments defending antireductionism, see Margolis 1978, C. Taylor 1971, Vendler 1984.

8. This idea has been intensively explored by Dreyfus (1979, 1981).

9. As I understand it, the frame problem refers to a rather more circumscribed prob-

lem within AI, and hence I felt bound to select "knowledge access" as the name for this more general problem. For my purposes the differences are not important. The research on the problem in AI has been crucial in bringing the problem itself into clear focus.

10. Since Menzel (1983) is surely right when he says that no animals are simple, I should clarify that by "simpler system" I here mean any organism lower on the phylogenetic scale than *Homo sapiens*. Thus, the term obviously includes a lot of profoundly complex brains. Rhesus monkey brains are scarcely less complex than ours, but they are more researchable. The nervous system of *Aplysia Californica* is considerably less complex than that of a monkey, but even so it is a wonder of complexity.

11. I omit here certain interesting problems with the functionalist theory of mental states. These problems center on giving a functional analysis of qualia and consciousness. For discussions of these issues, see Block 1978, Churchland and Churchland 1981, Shoemaker 1981, Lycan 1981a, Paul M. Churchland 1985, and Dennett (forthcoming).

Chapter 10

1. Pellionisz and Llinás are by no means alone nor the first in taking representations to be vectors in coordinate spaces and computations to be vector-to-vector transformations. For an early application, see Pitts and McCulloch 1947. The vector-matrix approach was also used by Rosenblatt 1962 in the perceptron work. For recent examples, see Kohonen et al. 1977, Anderson and Mozer 1981, Ballard 1986. The novel aspect to the Pellionisz-Llinás approach is their generalization of the abstract formalism from vector to tensor analysis and their conception of representation.

2. Lest I be misunderstood on the matter, I should emphasize that the computer display of the cartoon organism is in no way intended to be a contribution to computer science. It was merely an (auto)didactic device that made the problem simple enough so that we could begin to understand the fundamental principles Pellionisz and Llinás were talking about. Obviously, far more sophisticated robotic devices have been created in AI labs. However, if the Pellionisz-Llinás approach is basically right, then it may be that it holds implications for robotics.

3. As Michael Arbib has pointed out to me, there are similarities between the phase space sandwich model and the model of distributed motor control in the superior colliculus devised by Pitts and McCulloch in 1947. (See also Arbib 1981.) In the Churchland model what plays the central role are the notions of phase spaces and the coordinate transformation of positions in one phase space to positions in a different phase space. Hence, the relative *deformation* of topographically mapped surfaces is critical in effecting the appropriate transformation. But certainly Pitts and McCulloch did make the parallel and distributed nature of nervous systems and the topographic mapping of collicular layers the key elements in their seminal model.

4. For a discussion critical of the tensor network theory, see Arbib and Amari 1985. See Pellionisz and Llinás (1985b) for their reply.

5. On this theme, see also Piaget 1971.

6. This example was suggested to me by Ray Jackendoff.

7. McCollum, Pellionisz, and Llinás (1983) have proposed a tensorial hypothesis to show how the visual system can solve the computational problem. A difficulty with this germinal hypothesis is that it presents the computation as handled en-

tirely at the retinal level, whereas recent data from Land et al. (1983) indicate that in mammals the cortex is required for color constancy. Nevertheless, whether the computation is executed by the retina or whether it is done higher up, it remains significant that the computational problem can be solved rather simply using the tensor network approach.

8. In conversation. See also McClelland, Rumelhart, and Hinton 1986.

9. This way of expressing the value of a systematicity imported from another theory is borrowed from Jerry Fodor.

10. "The global energy of the system is defined as:

$$E = -\tfrac{1}{2} \sum_{i \neq j} \sum w_{ij}\, s_i s_j - \sum_i \eta_i s_i,$$

where n_i is the external input to the ith unit, w_{ij} is the strength of the connection (synaptic weight) from the jth to the ith unit, s_i is a boolean truth value (0 or 1) and 0_i is a threshold." (Hinton and Sejnowski 1983a:449).

11. Other theorists whose work ideally should have been discussed include Michael Arbib (1981, 1982), Valentino Braitenberg (1984), Gerald Edelman (1978), Walter Freeman (1975), Günter Palm (1982), and Christoph von der Malsburg (1973, 1981).

Bibliography

Ackley, David H., Geoffrey E. Hinton, and Terrence J. Sejnowski (1985). A learning algorithm for Boltzmann machines. *Cognitive Science* 9:147–169.

Adams, R. D., and M. Victor (1981). *Principles of neurology*. 2nd ed. New York: McGraw-Hill.

Akil, Huda, S. J. Watson, E. Young, M. E. Lewis, H. Khachaturian, and J. M. Walker (1984). Endogenous opioids: Biology and function. *Annual Review of Neuroscience* 7:223–255.

Allen, Max (1983). Models of hemispheric specialization. *Psychological Bulletin* 93:73–104.

Allman, John (1977). Evolution of the visual system in early primates. *Progress in Psychobiology and Physiological Psychology* 7:1–53.

Allman, John (1982). Reconstructing the evolution of the brain in primates through the use of comparative neurophysiological and neuroanatomical data. In *Primate brain evolution*, ed. E. Armstrong and D. Falk, 13–28. New York: Plenum.

Allman, John, and Jon Kaas (1971). Representation of the visual field in striate and adjoining cortex of the owl monkey (*Aotus trivirgatus*). *Brain Research* 35:89–106.

Altman, Joseph (1972). Postnatal development of the cerebellar cortex in the rat. *Journal of Comparative Neurology* 145:353–397.

Anderson, James A., and Geoffrey E. Hinton (1981). Models of information processing in the brain. In G. E. Hinton and J. A. Anderson, eds. (1981), 9–48.

Anderson, James A., and Michael C. Mozer (1981). Categorization and selective neurons. In G. E. Hinton and J. A. Anderson, eds. (1981), 213–236.

Angevine, J. B., Jr., and C. W. Cotman (1981). *Principles of neuroanatomy*. New York: Oxford University Press.

Arbib, Michael (1981). Perceptual structures and distributed motor control. In *Handbook of physiology: The nervous system II*, ed. V. B. Brooks, 1449–1480. Bethesda, Md.: American Physiological Society.

Arbib, Michael (1982). Modelling neural mechanisms of visuomotor coordination in Frog and Toad. In *Competition and cooperation in neural nets*, ed. S. Amari and M. Arbib, 342–370. Berlin: Springer-Verlag.

Arbib, Michael, and Shun-Ichi Amari (1985). Sensorimotor transformations in the brain (with a critique of the tensor theory of cerebellum). *Journal of Theoretical Biology* 112:123–155.

Asanuma, H. (1975). Recent developments in the study of the columnar arrangement of neurons within the motor cortex. *Physiological Review* 55/2:143–156.

Asanuma, H., and I. Rosen (1972). Topographical organization of cortical efferent zones projecting to distal forelimb muscles in monkey. *Experimental Brain Research* 14:243–256.

Aserinsky, E., and N. Kleitman (1953). Regularly occurring periods of eye motility, and concomitant phenomena during sleep. *Science* 118:273–274.

Atkinson, R. C., and R. M. Shiffrin (1968). Human memory: A proposed system and its control processes. In *The psychology of learning and motivation*, vol. 2, ed. K. W. Spence and J. T. Spence. New York: Academic Press.

Auburtin, S. A. E. (1861). Reprise de la discussion sur la forme et le volume du cerveau. *Bulletin du société d'anthropologie de Paris* 2:209–220. (Excerpted and translated in E. Clarke and C. D. O'Malley (1968), 492–494.)

Ayer, A. J., ed. (1959). *Logical positivism*. New York: Free Press.

Ballard, D. H. (1986). Cortical connections and parallel processing: Structure and function. *Behavioral and Brain Sciences* 9/1.

Ballard, D. H., Geoffrey E. Hinton, and Terrence J. Sejnowski (1983). Parallel visual computation. *Nature* 306/5938:21–26.

Bantle, J. A., and W. E. Hahn (1976). Complexity and characterization of polyadenylated RNA in the mouse brain. *Cell* 8:139–150.

Barker, C. F., and R. E. Billingham (1977). Immunologically privileged sites. *Advances in Immunology* 23:1–54.

Barlow, Horace B. (1972). Single units and sensations: A neuron doctrine for perceptual physiology? *Perception* 1:371–394.

Barr, Murray L. (1974). *The human nervous system: An anatomical viewpoint.* 2nd ed. New York: Harper and Row.

Bartholow, R. (1874). Experimental investigation into the functions of the human brain. *American Journal of Medical Sciences* 67:305–313.

Bell, Charles (1823). Second paper on the nerves of the orbit. *Philosophical Transactions of the Royal Society* 113:289–307.

Bellugi, Ursula, Howard Poizner, and Edward S. Klima (forthcoming). *What the hands reveal about the brain.* Cambridge, Mass.: MIT Press.

Benzer, Seymour (1957). The elementary units of heredity. In *The chemical basis of heredity*, ed. W. McElroy and B. Glass, 70–93. Baltimore: The Johns Hopkins University Press.

Berger, T. W., R. I. Latham, and R. F. Thompson (1980). Hippocampal unit-behavior correlations during classical conditioning. *Brain Research* 193:483–485.

Berger, T. W., and R. F. Thompson (1978). Identification of pyramidal cells as the critical elements in hippocampal neuronal plasticity during learning. *National Academy of Sciences of the United States of America. Proceedings. Biological Sciences* 75:1572–1576.

Berkeley, George. *The Works of George Berkeley.* (1948–1957). 9 vols. Ed. A. A. Luce and T. E. Jessop. London: Nelson.

Berker, Ennis A. (1985). Principles of brain function in neuropsychological development of hydrocephalics. Doctoral dissertation, University of Michigan, Ann Arbor.

Berlin, Charles I. (1977). Hemisphere asymmetry in auditory tasks. In S. Harnad et al., eds. (1977), 303–323.

Berlucchi, Giovanni, and James M. Sprague (1981). The cerebral cortex in visual learning and memory, and in interhemispheric transfer in the cat. In F. O. Schmitt, F. G. Worden, G. Adelman, and S. G. Dennis, eds. (1981), 415–440.

Bianchi, Leonardo (1895). The functions of the frontal lobes. (Translated from the original ms by A. de Watteville.) *Brain* 18:497–522. (Excerpted and translated in Clarke and O'Malley (1968), 544–545.)

Biro, J. I., and R. W. Shahan, eds. (1982). *Mind, brain, and function.* Norman, Okla.: University of Oklahoma Press.

Bisiach, Edoardo, Erminio Capitani, Claudio Luzzatti, and Daniela Perani (1981). Brain and conscious representation of outside reality. *Neuropsychologia* 19:543–551.

Bisiach, E., and C. Luzzatti (1978). Unilateral neglect of representational space. *Cortex* 14:129–133.

Bisiach, E., D. Perani, C. Papagno, and A. Berti (unpublished). Unawareness of disease following lesions of the right hemisphere: Anosognosia for hemiplegia and anosognosia for hemianopia.

Bjorklund, Anders, and Ulf Stenevi (1977). Reformation of severed hippocampal cholinergic pathway in the adult rat by transplanted septal neurons. *Cell Tissue Research* 185:289–302.

Bjorklund, Anders, and Ulf Stenevi (1984). Intracerebral neural implants: Neuronal replacement and reconstruction of damaged circuitries. *Annual Review of Neuroscience* 7, 279–308.

Blakemore, Colin (1977). *Mechanics of the mind.* Cambridge: Cambridge University Press.

Blakemore, Colin, and Susan Greenfield, eds. (in press). *Mind matters.* Oxford: Basil Blackwell.

Blanks, R. H. I., I. S. Curthoys, and C. H. Markham (1975). Planar relationships of the semicircular canals in man. *Acta Otolaryngolica* 80:185–196.

Block, Ned (1978). Troubles with functionalism. In *Perception and cognition. Issues in the foundation of psychology*, 261–325. (Minnesota Studies in the Philosophy of Science 9.) Minneapolis: University of Minnesota Press. (Reprinted in N. Block, ed. (1981). *Readings in the philosophy of psychology*, 268–305. Cambridge, Mass.: Harvard University Press.)

Bloom, F. E. (1980). Neuropharmacology and the adaptive regulation of receptor sensitivity: An overview. *Neurosciences Research Program Bulletin* 18/3:429–435.

Bodian, R. (1967). Neurons, circuits, and neuroglia. In *The neurosciences: A study program*, ed. G. C. Quarton, T. Melnechuck, and F. O. Schmitt, 6–24. New York: Rockefeller University Press.

Bogen J. E., E. D. Fisher, and P. J. Vogel (1965). Cerebral commissurotomy: A second case report. *Journal of the American Medical Association* 194:1328–1329.

Bonin, G. von, ed. (1960). *Some papers on the cerebral cortex.* Springfield, Ill.: Charles C. Thomas.

Boolos, George S., and Richard C. Jeffrey (1974). *Computability and logic.* Cambridge: Cambridge University Press.

Bower, J., and R. Llinás (1983). Simultaneous sampling of the responses of multiple, closely adjacent, Purkinje cells responding to climbing fiber activation. *Society for Neuroscience Abstracts* 9:607.

Bradshaw, J. L., and N. C. Nettleton (1981). The nature of hemispheric specialization. *Behavioral and Brain Sciences* 4/1:51–63.

Braestrup, Claus, and Mogens Nielsen (1980). Multiple benzodiazepine receptors. *Trends in Neurosciences* 3:301–303.

Braitenberg, Valentino (1984). *Vehicles.* Cambridge, Mass.: MIT Press.

Braitenberg, V., and N. Onesto (1961). The cerebellar cortex as a timing organ. Discussion of an hypothesis. *Proceedings of the 1st Annual Conference on Medical Cybernetics*, 1–19. Naples: Giannini.

Brazier, Mary A. B. (1982). The problem of neuromuscular action: Two 17th century Dutchmen. In *Historical aspects of the neurosciences*, ed. F. C. Rose and W. F. Bynum, 13–22. New York: Raven.

Brazier, Mary A. B. (1984). *A history of neurophysiology in the 17th and 18th centuries.* New York: Raven.

Broadbent, D. E. (1970). Stimulus set and response set. Two kinds of selective attention. In *Attention: Contemporary theory and analysis*, ed. D. Mostofsky, 51–60. New York: Appleton-Century-Crofts.

Broca, Pierre-Paul (1861). Remarques sur le siège de la faculté du langage articulé; suivies d'une observation d'aphémie (perte de la parole). *Bulletin de la société anatomique de Paris* 36:330–357. (Translated as "Remarks on the seat of the faculty of articulate language, followed by an observation of aphemia" in G. von Bonin, ed. (1960), 49–72.)

Broca, Pierre-Paul (1863). Localisation des fonctions cérébrales: Siège du langage articulé. *Bulletin de la Société d'anthropologie. Paris* 4:200–202.

Brodmann, Korbinian (1909). *Vergleichende Lokalisationlehre der Grosshirnrinde in ihren Prinzipien dargestellt auf Grund des Zellenbaues*. Leipzig: J. A. Barth.

Brookshire, R. H., and L. E. Nicholas (1984). Comprehension of directly and indirectly stated main ideas and details in discourse by brain-damaged and non-brain-damaged listeners. *Brain and Language* 21:21–36.

Brown, C. M. (1984). Computer vision and natural constraints. *Science* 224:1299–1305.

Bryden, M. P. (1982). *Laterality: Functional asymmetry in the intact brain*. New York: Academic Press.

Buchsbaum, M. S., J. Cappelletti, R. Ball, et al. (1984). Positron emission tomographic measurement in schizophrenia and affective disorders. *Annals of Neurology (Supplement)* 15:S157–S165.

Buchsbaum, M. S., and R. J. Haier (1978). Biological homogeneity, symptom heterogeneity, and the diagnosis of schizophrenia. *Schizophrenia Bulletin* 4:473–475.

Buchsbaum, M. S., D. H. Ingvar, R. Kessler, et al. (1982). Cerebral glucography with positron tomography. *Archives of General Psychiatry* 39:251–259.

Bullock, T. H. (1980). Reassessment of neural connectivity and its specification. In *Information processing in the nervous system*, ed. H. M. Pinsker and W. D. Willis, Jr., 199–220. New York: Raven.

Bullock, T. H. (1984). Comparative neuroscience holds promise for quiet revolutions. *Science* 225:473–478.

Bullock, T. H., and G. A. Horridge (1965). *Structure and function in the nervous systems of invertebrates*. San Francisco: W. H. Freeman.

Bullock, T. H., R. Orkand, and A. Grinnell (1977). *Introduction to nervous systems*. San Francisco: W. H. Freeman.

Bunge, Richard P. (1968). Glial cells and the central myelin sheath. *Physiological Review* 48:197–251.

Burklund, C. W., and Aaron Smith (1977). Language and the cerebral hemispheres. *Neurology* 27:627–633.

Butterfield, Herbert (1968). *The origins of modern science 1300–1800*. Toronto: Clarke, Irwin and Co.

Calabrese, Ronald L. (1980). Invertebrate central pattern generators: Modeling and complexity. (Commentary on Selverston 1980.) *Behavioral and Brain Sciences* 4/3:542–543.

Campbell, Keith (1983). Abstract particulars and the philosophy of mind. *Australasian Journal of Philosophy* 61:129–141.

Campion, J., R. Latto, and Y. M. Smith (1983). Is blindsight an effect of scattered light, spared cortex, and near-threshold vision? *Behavioral and Brain Sciences* 6:423–486.

Carew, T. J., E. T. Walters, and E. R. Kandel (1981). Classical conditioning in a simple withdrawal reflex in *Aplysia Californica*. *Journal of Neuroscience* 1:1426–1437.

Carnap, Rudolf (1928). *Der logische Aufbau der Welt*. Berlin: Weltkreis-Verlag. (Translated by R. A. George (1967). *The logical structure of the world*. London: Routledge and Kegan Paul.)

Carnap, Rudolf (1932). Überwindung der Metaphysik durch logische Analyse der Sprache. *Erkenntnis* 2:219–241. (Translated by A. Pap as The elimination of metaphysics through logical analysis of language. Reprinted in A. J. Ayer, ed. (1959). *Logical positivism*, 60–81. New York: Free Press.)

Carnap, Rudolf (1950). Empiricism, semantics and ontology. *Revue internationale de philosophie* 4:20–40. (Reprinted (1956) in *Meaning and necessity*, 2nd ed., 205–221. Chicago: Chicago University Press.)

Chihara, C. S., and Jerry Fodor (1965). Operationalism and ordinary language: A critique of Wittgenstein. *American Philosophical Quarterly* 2:281–295.

Chomsky, Noam (1965). *Aspects of the theory of syntax*. Cambridge, Mass.: MIT Press.

Christensen, B., H. Krausz, R. Perez-Polo, and W. D. Willis, Jr. (1980). Communication among neurons and neuroscientists. In *Information processing in the nervous system*, ed. H. M. Pinsker and W. D. Willis, Jr., 339–359. New York: Raven.

Church, Alonzo (1936). An unsolvable problem of elementary number theory. *American Journal of Mathematics* 58:345–363.

Churchland, Patricia Smith (1980a). A perspective on mind-brain research. *Journal of Philosophy* 77/4:185–207.

Churchland, Patricia Smith (1980b). Language, thought, and information processing. *Nous* 14:147–170.

Churchland, Patricia Smith (1981a). On the alleged backwards referral of experiences and its relevance to the mind-body problem. *Philosophy of Science* 48:165–181.

Churchland, Patricia Smith (1981b). The timing of sensations: Reply to Libet. *Philosophy of Science* 48:492–497.

Churchland, Patricia Smith (1981c). How many angels. . . . ? (Commentary on Puccetti 1981.) *Behavioral and Brain Sciences* 4/1:103–104.

Churchland, Patricia Smith (1981d). Is determinism self-refuting? *Mind* 90:99–101.

Churchland, Patricia Smith (1982). Mind-brain reduction: New light from the philosophy of science. *Neuroscience* 7/5:1041–1047.

Churchland, Patricia Smith (1983). Consciousness: The transmutation of a concept. *Pacific Philosophical Quarterly* 64:80–95.

Churchland, Paul M. (1970). The logical character of action explanations. *Philosophical Review* 79:214–236.

Churchland, Paul M. (1975). Two grades of evidential bias. *Philosophy of Science* 42:250–259.

Churchland, Paul M. (1979). *Scientific realism and the plasticity of mind*. Cambridge: Cambridge University Press.

Churchland, Paul M. (1980). Critical notice: Joseph Margolis: *Persons and minds: The prospects of nonreductive materialism*. *Dialogue* 19:461–469.

Churchland, Paul M. (1981). Eliminative materialism and the propositional attitudes. *Journal of Philosophy* 78/2:67–90.

Churchland, Paul M. (1984). *Matter and consciousness: A contemporary introduction to the philosophy of mind*. Cambridge, Mass.: MIT Press.

Churchland, Paul M. (1985). Reduction, qualia, and the direct introspection of brain states. *Journal of Philosophy* 82:8–28.

Churchland, Paul M. (forthcoming). Cognitive neurobiology: A computational hypothesis for laminar cortex. *Biology and Philosophy* 1:25–51.

Churchland, Paul M., and Patricia Smith Churchland (1981). Functionalism, qualia, and intentionality. *Philosophical Topics* 12:121–145. (Reprinted in J. I. Biro and R. W. Shahan, eds. (1982), 121–145.)

Clarke, Edwin, and C. D. O'Malley (1968). *The human brain and spinal cord: A historical study illustrated by writings from antiquity to the twentieth century*. Berkeley and Los Angeles: University of California Press.

Clement, John (1982). Students' preconceptions in introductory mechanics. *American Journal of Physics* 50:66–71.

Clemes, S., and W. Dement (1967). The effect of REM sleep deprivation on psychological functioning. *Journal of Nervous and Mental Disorders* 144:485–491.

Cohen, N. J., and S. Corkin (1981). The amnesic patient. H. M.: Learning and retention of cognitive skill. *Society for Neuroscience Abstracts* 7:517–518.

Constantine-Paton, Martha (1981). Induced ocular-dominance zones in tectal cortex. In F. O. Schmitt, F. G. Worden, G. Adelman, and S. G. Dennis, eds. (1981), 47–67.

Constantine-Paton, Martha, and Margaret I. Law (1982). The development of maps and stripes in the brain. *Scientific American* 247/6:62–70.

Cooper, J. R., F. E. Bloom, and R. H. Roth (1982). *The biochemical basis of neuropharmacology*. 2nd ed. New York: Oxford University Press.

Corkin, Suzanne (1968). Acquisition of motor skill after bilateral medial temporal-lobe excision. *Neuropsychologia* 6:255–265.

Cornsweet, Tom N. (1970). *Visual perception*. New York: Academic Press.

Cowan, W. Maxwell (1978). Aspects of neural development. In *International review of physiology*. Vol. 17: *Neurophysiology III*, ed. R. Porter, 149–191. Baltimore: University Park Press.

Cowan, W. Maxwell (1979). The development of the brain. *Scientific American* 241/3:112–133.

Cowan, W. Maxwell (1981). Keynote to *The organization of the cerebral cortex*. In F. O. Schmitt, F. G. Worden, G. Adelman, and S. G. Dennis, eds. (1981), xi–xxi.

Cowey, A. (1981). Why are there so many visual areas? In F. O. Schmitt, F. G. Worden, G. Adelman, and S. G. Dennis, eds. (1981), 395–413.

Coyle, J. T., D. L. Price, and M. R. DeLong (1983). Alzheimer's disease: A disorder of cortical cholinergic innervation. *Science* 219:1184–1190.

Craik, F. I. M. (1984). Age differences in remembering. In L. R. Squire and N. Butters, eds. (1984), 3–12.

Craik, F. I. M., and R. S. Lockhart (1972). Levels of processing: A framework for memory research. *Journal of Verbal Learning and Verbal Behavior* 11:671–684.

Crick, F. H. C. (1979). Thinking about the brain. *Scientific American* 241:219–232.

Crick, F. H. C. (1984). Function of the thalamic reticular complex: The searchlight hypothesis. *National Academy of Sciences of the United States of America. Proceedings. Biological Sciences* 81:4586–4590.

Crick, F. H. C., and Graeme Mitchison (1983). The function of dream sleep. *Nature* 304/5922:111–114.

Critchley, Macdonald (1962). Speech and speech-loss in relation to the duality of the brain. In *Interhemispheric relations and cerebral dominance*, ed. V. B. Mountcastle, 208–213. Baltimore: The Johns Hopkins University Press.

Critchley, MacDonald (1979). *The divine banquet of the brain*. New York: Raven.

Crow, T. J., A. J. Cross, Eve C. Johnstone, and F. Owen (1982). Two syndromes in schizophrenia and their pathogenesis. In F. A. Henn and H. A. Nasrallah, eds. (1982), 196–234.

Crowe, Raymond R. (1982). Recent genetic research in schizophrenia. In F. A. Henn and H. A. Nasrallah, eds. (1982), 40–60.

Cummins, Robert (1983). *The nature of psychological explanation*. Cambridge, Mass.: MIT Press.

Cupples, Brian (1977). Three types of explanation. *Philosophy of Science* 44:387–408.

Davidson, Donald (1970). Mental events. In *Experience and theory*, ed. L. Foster and J. W. Swanson, 79–101. Amherst, Mass.: University of Massachusetts Press.

Davis, J. M., and D. L. Garver (1978). Neuroleptics: Clinical use in psychiatry. In *Handbook of psychopharmacology*, vol. 10, ed. L. L. Iverson, S. D. Iverson, and S. H. Snyder, 129–164. New York: Plenum.

Davis, William J. (1980). Neurophilosophical reflections on central nervous pattern generators. *Behavioral and Brain Sciences* 3:543–544.

Dawkins, Richard, and John Krebs (1978). Animal signals: Information or manipulation? In *Behavioral ecology: An evolutionary approach*, ed. J. R. Krebs and N. B. Davies, 282–309. Oxford: Basil Blackwell.

Deiters, Otto F. K. (1865). *Untersuchungen über Gehirn und Rückenmark des Menschen und der Säugethiere*. (Posthumous.) Braunschweig: Vieweg. (Excerpted and translated in E. Clarke and C. D. O'Malley (1968), 67–70.)

Déjerine, J. (1892). Contribution à l'étude anatomoclinique et clinique des différentes variétés de cécité verbale. *Comptes rendus des séances de la Société de Biologie et de ses filiales* 4:61–90.

De Lacoste-Utamsing, C., and R. L. Holloway (1982). Sexual dimorphism in the human corpus callosum. *Science* 216:1431–1432.

Dennett, Daniel C. (1975). Brain writing and mind reading. In *Language, mind and knowledge*, ed. K. Gunderson. (Minnesota Studies in the Philosophy of Science 7.) Minneapolis: University of Minnesota Press. (Reprinted in D. C. Dennett (1978b).)

Dennett, Daniel C. (1978a). Artificial intelligence as philosophy and as psychology. In *Philosophical perspective on artificial intelligence*, ed. M. Ringle. New York: Humanities Press and Harvester Press.

Dennett, Daniel C. (1978b). *Brainstorms: Philosophical essays on mind and psychology*. Montgomery, Vt.: Bradford Books. (Reprinted (1984). Cambridge, Mass.: MIT Press.)

Dennett, Daniel C. (1979). On the absence of phenomenology. In *Body, mind, and method: Essays in honor of Virgil Aldrich*, ed. D. Gustafson and B. Tapscott, 93–113. Dordrecht, Holland: D. Reidel.

Dennett, Daniel C. (1980). The milk of human intentionality. (Commentary on Searle 1980.) *Behavioral and Brain Sciences* 3:428–430.

Dennett, Daniel C. (1981). Three kinds of intentional psychology. In *Reduction, time, and reality*, ed. R. Healey, 37–61. Cambridge: Cambridge University Press.

Dennett, Daniel C. (1982). Notes on prosthetic imagination. *New Boston Review*, June:3–7. (Reprinted, with revision, as "The imagination extenders" in *Psychology Today*, December 1982:32–39.)

Dennett, Daniel C. (1983). Intentional systems in cognitive ethology: The "Panglossian Paradigm" defended. *Behavioral and Brain Sciences* 6:343–390.

Dennett, Daniel C. (1984a). Cognitive wheels: The frame problem of artificial intelligence. In *Minds, machines, and evolution*, ed. C. Hookway, 129–151. Cambridge: Cambridge University Press.

Dennett, Daniel C. (1984b). *Elbow room: The varieties of free will worth wanting*. Cambridge, Mass.: MIT Press.

Dennett, Daniel C. (1986). Can machines think? In *How we know*, ed. M. Shafto, 1–26. San Francisco: Harper and Row.

Dennett, Daniel C. (forthcoming). Quining qualia. In *The Intentional Stance*. Cambridge, Mass.: MIT Press.

Descartes, René (1644). *The principles of philosophy*. English translation in E. S. Haldane and G. R. T. Ross (1911). *The philosophical works of Descartes*. 2 vols. Reprinted (1968). Cambridge: Cambridge University Press.

Descartes, René (1649). *Les Passions de l'âme*. English translation in E. S. Haldane and G. R. T. Ross (1911). *The philosophical works of Descartes*. 2 vols. Reprinted (1968). Cambridge: Cambridge University Press.

Descartes, René (1664). *Traité de l'homme*. Paris: Angot. French text with English translation in Thomas Steele Hall (1972). *Treatise on man*. Cambridge, Mass.: Harvard University Press.

Desimone, R., T. D. Albright, C. G. Gross, and C. Bruce (1984). Stimulus-selective properties of inferior temporal neurons in the macaque. *Journal of Neuroscience* 4:2051–2062.

Desmedt, J. E., ed. (1979). *Cognitive components in cerebral event-related potentials and selective attention*. Basel: Karger.

Desmedt, John E., Julien Debecker, and Donald Robertson (1979). Serial perceptual processing and the neural basis of changes in event-related potentials components and slow potential shifts. In J. E. Desmedt, ed. (1979), 53–79.

Deutsch, Diana (1984). Memory for nonverbal information: A link between behavioral and physiological studies. In L. R. Squire and N. Butters, eds. (1984), 45–54.

DeVoogd, T. J., and F. Nottebohm (1981). Sex differences in dendritic morphology of a song control nucleus in the canary: A quantitative Golgi study. *Journal of Comparative Neurology* 196:309–316.

Dewan, E. M. (1976). Consciousness as an emergent causal agent in the context of control system theory. In *Consciousness and the brain*, ed. G. Globus, G. Maxwell and I. Savodnik, 181–198. New York: Plenum.

Dijkgraaf, S. (1967). Biological significance of lateral line organs. In *Lateral line detectors*, ed. P. Cahn, 83–95. Bloomington: University of Indiana Press.

Dismukes, R. K. (1980). What is a modulator? *Neurosciences Research Program Bulletin* 183:390–394.

Donchin, E. (1975). Brain electrical correlates of pattern recognition. In *International symposium on signal analysis and pattern recognition in biomedical engineering*, ed. G. F. Inbar, 199–218. New York: Wiley.

Donchin, E., G. McCarthy, M. Kutas, and W. Ritter (1983). Event-related potentials in the study of consciousness. In *Consciousness and self-regulation*, vol. 3, ed. G. E. Schwartz and D. Shapiro, 81–121. New York: Plenum.

Dray, William (1963). The historical explanation of action reconsidered. In *Philosophy and history*, ed. S. Hook, 105–135. New York: New York University Press.

Dretske, Fred I. (1981). *Knowledge and the flow of information*. Cambridge, Mass.: MIT Press.

Dreyfus, Hubert L. (1979). *What computers can't do*. 2nd ed. New York: Harper and Row.

Dreyfus, Hubert L. (1981). From micro-worlds to knowledge representation: AI at an impasse. In *Mind design*, ed. J. Haugeland, 161–204. Cambridge, Mass.: MIT Press.

Du Bois-Reymond, Emil (1849). *Untersuchungen über thierische Elektricität*. Vol. 2. Berlin: Reimer. (Excerpted and translated in E. Clark and C. D. O'Malley (1968), 197.)

Duhem, Pierre (1914). *La théorie physique: Son object, sa structure*. Paris: Rivière et Cie. (Translated (1953) by Philip Weiner as *The aim and structure of physical theory*. Princeton, N.J.: Princeton University Press. Reprinted (1962). New York: Atheneum.)

Duncan-Johnson, C. C., and E. Donchin (1977). On quantifying surprise: The variation of event-related potentials with subjective probability. *Psychophysiology* 14:456–467.

Eccles, John C. (1977). Part II of *The self and its brain* (Popper and Eccles 1977), 225–406.

Eccles, John C., M. Ito, and J. Szentágothai (1967). *The cerebellum as a neuronal machine*. New York: Springer-Verlag.

Eccles, John C., and Daniel N. Robinson (1984). *The wonder of being human*. New York: Free Press.

Edelman, Gerald M. (1978). Group selection and phasic reentrant signalling: A theory of higher brain function. In *The mindful brain*, G. M. Edelman and V. B. Mountcastle, 51–100. Cambridge, Mass.: MIT Press.

Edelman, Robert (1984). The clinicians's guide to the theory and practice of NMR scanning. *Discussions in Neurosciences* 1/1:9–48.

Ehrhardt, A. A., and S. W. Baker (1974). Fetal androgens, human CNS differentiation, and behavior sex differences. In *Sex differences in behavior*, eds. R. C. Friedman, R. M. Richart, and R. L. van de Wiele, 33–51. New York: Wiley.

Einstein, Albert (1949). Autobiographical notes. In *Albert Einstein: Philosopher-Scientist*, ed. P. Schilpp, 3–95. Evanston, Ill.: The Library of Living Philosophers.

Enç, Berent (1983). In defense of the identity theory. *Journal of Philosophy* 80:279–298.

Fahlman, Scott (1979). *NETL: A system for representing and using real-world knowledge.* Cambridge, Mass.: MIT Press.

Fahlman, Scott (1981). Representing implicit knowledge. In G. E. Hinton and J. A. Anderson, eds. (1981), 145–159.

Feder, H. H. (1984). Hormones and sexual behavior. *Annual Review of Psychology* 35:165–200.

Feindel, W., R. S. J. Frackowiak, D. Gadian, P. L. Magistretti, and M. R. Zalutsky, eds. (1985). Brain metabolism and imaging. *Discussions in Neurosciences* 2/2 (special issue).

Feldman, J. A. (1985). Connectionist models and their applications: Introduction. *Cognitive Science* 9:1–2 (special issue).

Feldman, J. A., and D. H. Ballard (1982). Connectionist models and their properties. *Cognitive Science* 6:205–254.

Feldman, Robert S., and Linda F. Quenzer (1984). *Fundamentals of neuropsychopharmacology.* Sunderland, Mass.: Sinauer.

Ferraro, P., A. Guidotti, B. Conti-Tronconi, and E. Costa (1984). A brain octadecaneuropeptide generated by tryptic digestion of DBI (Diazepam Binding Inhibitor) functions as a proconflict ligand of benzodiazepine recognition sites. *Neuropharmacology* 23:1359.

Ferrier, David (1876). *The functions of the brain.* London: Smith, Elder.

Ferrier, David (1890). *The Croonian lectures on cerebral localisation.* London: Smith, Elder.

Feyerabend, Paul K. (1962). Explanation, reduction, and empiricism. In *Minnesota studies in the philosophy of science*, vol. 3, ed. H. Feigl and G. Maxwell, 28–97. Minneapolis: University of Minnesota Press. (Reprinted in P. K. Feyerabend (1981). *Philosophical papers*, vol. 1, 44–96. Cambridge: Cambridge University Press.)

Feyerabend, Paul K. (1963a). How to be a good empiricist: A plea for tolerance in matters epistemological. In *Philosophy of science, the Delaware seminar*, vol. 2, ed. B. Baumrin, 3–39. New York: Interscience. (Reprinted in H. Morick, ed. (1972), 164–193.)

Feyerabend, Paul K. (1963b). Materialism and the mind-body problem. *The Review of Metaphysics* 17:49–66. (Reprinted in C. V. Borst, ed. (1970). *The mind/brain identity theory*, 142–156. London: Macmillan.)

Feyerabend, Paul K. (1963c). Mental events and the brain. *Journal of Philosophy* 60:295–296.

Feyerabend, Paul K. (1981). *Philosophical papers.* Vols. 1 and 2. Cambridge: Cambridge University Press.

Field, Hartry (1977). Logic, meaning, and conceptual role. *Journal of Philosophy* 74:379–408.

Field, Hartry (1978). Mental representation. *Erkenntnis* 13:9–61. (Reprinted in N. Block, ed. (1981). *Readings in the philosophy of psychology*, vol. 2, 78–114. Cambridge, Mass.: Harvard University Press.)

Fine, Michael, Donald A. Keefer, and George R. Leichnetz (1982). Testosterone uptake in the brainstem of a sound-producing fish. *Science* 215/4537:1265–1267.

Flanagan, Owen J., Jr. (1984). *The science of the mind.* Cambridge, Mass.: MIT Press.

Flourens, Pierre (1824). Recherches expérimentales sur les propriétés et les fonctions du système nerveux dans les animaux vertébrés. (Translated as "Investigation of the properties and the functions of the various parts which compose the cerebral mass" in G. von Bonin, ed. (1960), 3–21.)

Fodor, Jerry A. (1974). Special sciences. *Synthese* 28:77–115. (Reprinted in J. A. Fodor (1981).)

Fodor, Jerry A. (1975). *The language of thought.* New York: Crowell. (Paperback edition (1979). Cambridge, Mass.: Harvard University Press.)

Fodor, Jerry A. (1981). *Representations.* Cambridge, Mass.: MIT Press.

Fodor, Jerry A. (1985). Fodor's guide to mental representation: The intelligent auntie's vade-mecum. *Mind* 94:76–100.

Forel, August-Henri (1887). Einige hirnanatomische Betrachtungen und Ergebnisse. *Arch. Psychiat. NervKrankh.* 18:162–198. (Excerpted and translated in E. Clarke and C. D. O'Malley (1968), 105–109.)

Foss, Jeffrey (1986). Abstract solutions vs. neurobiologically plausible problems. (Commentary on Ballard 1986.) *Behavioral and Brain Sciences* 9.

Foulkes, D. (1966). *The psychology of sleep.* New York: Scribner's.

Fox, Jeffrey L. (1984). PET scan controversy aired. *Science* 224:143–144.

Freed, W. J. (1983). Functional brain tissue transplantation: Reversal of lesion-induced rotation by intraventricular substantia nigra and adrenal medulla grafts, with a note on intracranial retinal grafts. *Biological Psychiatry* 18/11:1205–1267.

Freeman, Walter (1975). *Mass action in the nervous system.* New York: Academic Press.

Freeman, Walter (1979). Nonlinear dynamics of paleocortex manifested in the olfactory EEG. *Biological Cybernetics* 3:21–37.

Frege, Gottlob (1952). *Translations from the philosophical writings of Gottlob Frege,* trans. and ed. P. Geach and M. Black. Oxford: Basil Blackwell.

Fritsch, G., and E. Hitzig (1870). Über die elektrische Erregvarkeit des Grosshirns. *Archiv für Anatomie, Physiologie und Wissenschaftliche Medizin.* (Translated as "On the electrical excitability of the cerebrum" in G. von Bonin, ed. (1960), 73–96.)

Furshpan, E. J., and D. D. Potter (1959). Transmission at the giant motor synapses of the crayfish. *Journal of Physiology* 145:298–325.

Gainotti, Guido, Carlo Caltagirone, and Gabriele Miceli (1983). Selective impairment of semantic-lexical discrimination in right-brain-damaged patients. In E. Perecman, ed. (1983), 149–167.

Galaburda, Albert M., and Marek-Marsel Mesulam (1983). Neuroanatomical aspects of cerebral localization. In A. Kertesz, ed. (1983b), 21–61.

Galambos, Robert, and Steven A. Hillyard, eds. (1981). *Electrophysiological approaches to human cognitive processing.* (Based on a work session of the Neurosciences Research Program, 1981.) *Neurosciences Research Program Bulletin* 20:141–265.

Galen. *Galen on anatomical procedures. Translation of the surviving books with introduction and notes.* (1956). C. Singer. London: Oxford University Press.

Gall, Franz Josef (1812). *Anatomie et physiologie du système nerveux en général, et du cerveau en particulier.* Vol. 1. Paris: Schoell. (Excerpted and translated in E. Clarke and C. D. O'Malley (1968), 476–480.)

Gardner, Howard, Hiram H. Brownell, Wendy Wapner, and Diane Michelow (1983). Missing the point: The role of the right hemisphere in the processing of complex linguistic material. In E. Perecman, ed. (1983), 169–191.

Gazzaniga, Michael S. (1970). *The bisected brain.* New York: Appleton-Century-Crofts.

Gazzaniga, Michael S. (1975). Brain mechanisms and behavior. In *Handbook of psychobiology*, ed. M. S. Gazzaniga and C. Blakemore, 565–590. New York: Academic Press.

Gazzaniga, Michael S. (1983). Right hemisphere language following brain bisection: A twenty year perspective. *American Psychologist* 38/5:525–537.

Gazzaniga, Michael S. (1984a). Advances in cognitive neurosciences: The problem of information storage in the human brain. In G. Lynch, J. L. McGaugh, and N. M. Weinberger, eds. (1984), 78–88.

Gazzaniga, Michael S., ed. (1984b). *Handbook of cognitive neuroscience*. New York: Plenum.

Gazzaniga, Michael S. (1985). *The social brain: Discovering the networks of the mind*. New York: Basic Books.

Gazzaniga, Michael S., Joseph E. Bogen, and Roger W. Sperry (1962). Some functional effects of sectioning the cerebral commissures in man. *National Academy of Sciences of the United States of America. Proceedings. Biological Sciences* 48:1765–1769.

Gazzaniga, Michael S., and Joseph E. LeDoux (1978). *The integrated mind*. New York: Plenum.

Gazzaniga, Michael S., and Charlotte S. Smylie (1984). What does language do for a right hemisphere? In M. S. Gazzaniga, ed. (1984b), 199–209.

Gazzaniga, Michael S., and R. W. Sperry (1967). Language after section of the cerebral commissures. *Brain* 90:131–148.

Geschwind, Norman (1965). Disconnexion syndromes in animals and man. *Brain* 88:237–294, 585–644.

Ghez, Claude, and Stanley Fahn (1981). The cerebellum. In E. R. Kandel and J. H. Schwartz, eds. (1981), 334–346.

Gibson, J. J. (1968). What gives rise to the perception of motion? *Psychological Review* 75:335–346.

Gielen, C. C. A. M., and E. J. van Zuylen (1986). Coordination of arm muscles during flexion and supination. *Neuroscience*.

Glees, P., and J. Cole (1950). Recovery of skilled motor functions after small repeated lesions of motor cortex in macaque. *Journal of Neurophysiology* 13:137–148.

Gleitman, Henry (1981). *Psychology*. New York: Norton.

Goldman, P. S., H. T. Crawford, L. P. Stokes, et al. (1974). Sex-dependent behavioral effects of cerebral cortical lesions in the developing rhesus monkey. *Science* 186:540–542.

Goldman-Rakic, P. S. (1981). Development and plasticity of primate frontal association cortex. In F. O. Schmitt, F. G. Worden, G. Adelman, and S. G. Dennis, eds. (1981), 69–97.

Goldman-Rakic, P. S. (1984). Modular organization of the prefrontal cortex. *Trends in Neurosciences* 7/11:419–424.

Golgi, Camillo (1883). Recherches sur l'histologie des centres nerveux. *Archs. ital. Biol.*, 3:285–317. (Excerpted and translated in E. Clarke and C. D. O'Malley (1968), 92–96.)

Golgi, Camillo (1908). La doctrine du neurone. In *Les Prix Nobel en 1906*. Stockholm: P. A. Norstedt & Söner. (Excerpted and translated in E. Clarke and C. D. O'Malley (1968), 96.)

Goltz, F. L. (1892). Der Hund ohne Grosshirn. Siebente Abhandlung über die Verrichtungen des Grosshirns. *Pflügers Arch.* 51:570–614. (Excerpted and translated in E. Clarke and C. D. O'Malley (1968), 560–565.)

Gonshor, A., and G. Melvill Jones (1976). Extreme vestibulo-ocular adaptation induced by prolonged optical reversal of vision. *Journal of Physiology* 256:381–414.

Gordon, Harold W. (1980). Right hemisphere comprehension of verbs in patients with complete forebrain commissurotomy: Use of the dichotic method and manual performance. *Brain and Language* 11:76–86.

Gorski, R. A. (1979a). Nature of hormone action in the brain. In *Ontogeny and reproductive hormone action*, ed. T. H. Hamilton and W. A. Sadler, 371–392. New York: Raven.

Gorski, R. A. (1979b). Long-term hormonal modulation of neuronal structure and function. In F. O. Schmitt and F. G. Worden, eds. (1979), 969–982.

Gorski, R. A., J. H. Gordon, J. E. Shyrne, and A. M. Southam (1978). Evidence for a morphological sex difference within the medial preoptic area of the rat brain. *Brain Research* 148:333–346.

Gould, James L. (1985). How bees remember flower shapes. *Science* 227:1492–1494.

Goy, Robert W., and Bruce S. McEwen (1977). *Sexual differential of the brain.* (Based on a work session of the Neurosciences Research Program.) Cambridge, Mass.: MIT Press.

Goy, Robert, W., John E. Wolb, and Stephen G. Eisele (1977). Experimental female hermaphroditism in rhesus monkeys: Anatomical and physiological characteristics. In *Handbook of sexology*, ed. J. Money and H. Muspah, 139–156. Amsterdam: Elsevier/Excerpta Medica.

Greenough, W. T., J. M. Juraska, and F. R. Volkmar (1979). Maze training effects on dendritic branching in occipital cortex of adult rats. *Behavioral and Neural Biology* 26:287–297.

Griffin, Donald R. (1984). *Animal thinking.* Cambridge, Mass.: Harvard University Press.

Gross, C. G., C. E. Rocha-Miranda, and D. B. Bender (1972). Visual properties of neurons in inferotemporal cortex of the macaque. *Journal of Neurophysiology* 35:96–111.

Grossberg, Stephen (1982). *Studies of mind and brain.* Dordrecht, Holland: D. Reidel.

Grünbaum, A. S. F. (see Leyton, A. S. F.)

Hannover, Adolph (1840). Die Chromsäure, ein vorzügliches Mittel bei den mikroskopischen Untersuchungen. *Archiv für Anatomie, Physiologie und wissenschaftliche Medizin*, 549–558. (Excerpted and translated in E. Clarke and C. D. O'Malley (1968), 60–61.)

Hansen, J. C., and S. A. Hillyard (1983). Selective attention to multidimensional auditory stimuli. *Journal of Experimental Psychology: Human Perception and Performance* 9:1–19.

Hanson, N. R. (1967). Observation and interpretation. In *Philosophy of science today*, ed. S. Morgenbesser, 89–99. New York: Basic Books.

Hardy, G. H. (1940). *Ramanujan.* London: Cambridge University Press.

Harlow, J. M. (1868). Recovery from the passage of an iron bar through the head. *Massachusetts Medical Society Publications* 2:327–347.

Harnad, Stevan, R. W. Doty, L. Goldstein, J. Jaynes, and G. Krauthamer, eds. (1977) *Lateralization in the nervous system.* New York: Academic Press.

Harrington, Anne (1985). Nineteenth-century ideas on hemisphere differences and "duality of mind." *Behavioral and Brain Sciences* 8/4:617–659.

Harvey, Paul H., and Montgomery Slatkin (1982). Some like it hot: Temperature-determined sex. *Nature* 296:807–808.

Hawkins, Robert D., and Eric R. Kandel (1984). Steps toward a cell-biological alphabet for elementary forms of learning. In G. Lynch, J. L. McGaugh, and N. M. Weinberger, eds. (1984), 385–404.

Hebb, D. O. (1939). Intelligence in man after large removals of cerebral tissue: Report of four left frontal lobe cases. *Journal of General Psychology* 21:73–87.

Hebb, D. O., and W. Penfield (1940). Human behavior after extensive bilateral removals from the frontal lobes. *Archives of Neurology and Psychiatry* 44:421–438.

Hecaen, Henri, and Martin L. Albert, eds. (1978). *Human neuropsychology.* New York: Wiley.

Heilman, Kenneth M. (1979). Neglect and related disorders. In K. M. Heilman and E. Valenstein, eds. (1979), 268–307.

Heilman, Kenneth M., Gregory Howell, Edward Valenstein, and Leslie Rothi (1980). Mirror-reading and writing in association with right-left spatial disorientation. *Journal of Neurology, Neurosurgery, and Psychiatry* 43:774–780.

Heilman, Kenneth M., and Edward Valenstein, eds. (1979). *Clinical neuropsychology.* New York: Oxford University Press.

Heilman, Kenneth M., Robert R. Watson, Edward Valenstein, and Antonio R. Damasio (1983). Localization of lesions in neglect. In Andrew Kertesz, ed. (1983b), 471–492.

Heimer, Lennart (1983). *The human brain and spinal cord: Functional neuroanatomy and dissection guide.* New York: Springer-Verlag.

Heimer, Lennart, and Martine J. Robards, eds. (1981). *Neuroanatomical tract-tracing methods.* New York: Plenum.

Held, Hans (1897). Beiträge zur Structur der Nervenzellen und ihrer Fortsätze. Zweite Abhandlung. *Arch. Anat. Physiol. (Anat. Abt.),* 204–294. (Excerpted and translated in E. Clarke and C. D. O'Malley (1968), 119–120.)

Helmholtz, Hermann L. F. von (1850). Vorläufiger Bericht über die Fortpflanzungsgeschwindigkeit der Nervenreizung. *Archiv für Anatomie, Physiologie und wissenschaftliche Medizin,* 71–73. (Translated in W. Dennis (1948). *Readings in psychology,* 197–198. New York: Appleton-Century-Crofts.)

Hempel, Carl (1945). A definition of "degree of confirmation." *Philosophy of Science* 12:98–115.

Hempel, Carl (1965). *Aspects of scientific explanation.* New York: Free Press.

Henn, Fritz, A., and Henry A. Nasrallah, eds. (1982). *Schizophrenia as a brain disease.* New York: Oxford University Press.

Heritage, Aileen S., and Walter Stumpf (1980). Brain catecholamine neurons are target sites for sex hormones. *Science* 207/4437:1377–1379.

Hesse, Mary (1970). Is there an independent observation language? In *The nature and function of scientific theories,* ed. R. Colodny, 36–77. Pittsburgh: University of Pittsburgh Press.

Heuser, J. E., and T. S. Reese (1979). Synaptic vesicle exocytosis captured by quick-freezing. In F. O. Schmitt and F. G. Worden, eds. (1979), 573–600.

Hillyard, S. A., G. V. Simpson, D. L. Woods, S. van Voorhis, and T. Munte (1984). Event-related brain potentials and selective attention to different modalities. In *Neural integration at basic and cortical levels: IBRO conference,* ed. F. Reinoso, 395–414. New York: Raven.

Hillyard, S. A., and M. Kutas (1983). Electrophysiology of cognitive processing. *Annual review of psychology* 34:33–61.

Hinton, Geoffrey E. (1981). Implementing semantic networks in parallel hardware. In G. E. Hinton and J. A. Anderson, eds. (1981), 161–187.

Hinton, Geoffrey E., and James A. Anderson, eds. (1981). *Parallel models of associative memory.* Hillsdale, N.J.: Erlbaum.

Hinton, Geoffrey E., And Terrence J. Sejnowski (1983a). Optimal perceptual inference. *Proceedings of the IEEE Conference on computer vision and pattern recognition* (Washington, D.C., June 1983), 448–453. Silver Spring, Md.: IEEE Computer Society Press.

Hinton, Geoffrey E., and Terrence J. Sejnowski (1983b). Analyzing cooperative computation. In *Proceedings of the 5th annual conference of the Cognitive Science Society, Rochester, N.Y.*

Hinton, Geoffrey E., and Terrence J. Sejnowski (1986). Learning and relearning in Boltzmann machines. In D. E. Rumelhart and J. L. McClelland, eds. (1986).

Hirano, Asao, and Herbert M. Dembitzer (1967). A structural analysis of the myelin sheath in the central nervous system. *Journal of Cell Biology* 34:555–567.

His, Wilhelm (1888). Über die embryonale Entwickelung der Nervenbahnen. *Anat. Anz.* 3:499–505. (Excerpted and translated in E. Clarke and C. D. O'Malley (1968), 103–104.)

Hitzig, G., and G. T. Fritsch (1870) Über die elektrische Erregbarkeit des Grosshirns. *Archiv für anatomie, Physiologie und wissenschaftliche Medizin*, 300–332. (Translated as "On the electrical excitability of the cerebrum" in G. von Bonin, ed. (1960), 73–96.)

Hodgkin, A. L., and A. F. Huxley (1952). A quantitative description of membrane current and its application to conduction and excitation in nerve. *Journal of Physiology* 117:500–544. (Reprinted in C. D. Barnes and C. Kircher, eds. (1968). *Readings in neurophysiology*, 205–249. New York: Wiley.)

Holtzman, Jeffrey D., and Michael S. Gazzaniga (1982). Dual task interactions due exclusively to limits in processing resources. *Science* 218:1325–1327.

Hooker, C. A. (1975). Systematic philosophy and meta-philosophy of science: Empiricism, Popperianism, and realism. *Synthese* 32:177–231.

Hooker, C. A. (1981). Towards a general theory of reduction. Part I: Historical and scientific setting. Part II: Identity in reduction. Part III: Cross-categorial reduction. *Dialogue* 20:38–59, 201–236, 496–529.

Hopfield, J. J., D. I. Feinstein, and R. G. Palmer (1983). "Unlearning" has a stabilizing effect in collective memories. *Nature* 304:158–159.

Horgan, Terrence, and James Woodward (1985). Folk psychology is here to stay. *Philosophical Review* 44:197–226.

Horn, G. (1983). Information storage in the brain: A study of imprinting in the domestic chick. In *Advances in vertebrate neuroethology: Proceedings of a NATO Advanced Study Institute*, ed. J.-P. Ewart, R. Capranica, and D. J. Ingle, 511–541. New York: Plenum.

Hoyle, Graham (1980). Expectation and achievement in analysis of motor program generation: Commentary on Selverston. *Behavioral and Brain Sciences* 3:552–553.

Hoyle, Graham (1984). The scope of neuroethology. *Behavioral and Brain Sciences* 7:367–412.

Hrdy, Sarah Blaffer (1981). *The woman that never evolved.* Cambridge, Mass.: Harvard University Press.

Hubel, D. H., and T. N. Wiesel (1965). Receptive fields and functional architecture in two non-striate visual areas (18 and 19) of the cat. *Journal of Neurophysiology* 28:229–289.

Hubel, D. H., and T. N. Wiesel (1968). Receptive fields and functional architecture of monkey striate cortex. *Journal of Physiology* 195:215–243.

Hubel, D. H., and T. N. Wiesel (1972). Laminar and columnar distribution of geniculocortical fibres in the macaque monkey. *Journal of Comparative Neurology* 146:421–450.

Hubel, D. H., and T. N. Wiesel (1977). Functional architecture of macaque visual cortex. *Proceedings of the Royal Society of London. Series B* 198:1–59.

Hubel, D. H., T. N. Wiesel, and S. LeVay (1977). Plasticity of ocular dominance columns in monkey striate cortex. *Philosophical Transactions of the Royal Society of London* 278/961:377–409.

Hughes, John, T. W. Smith, H. W. Kosterlitz, et al. (1975). Identification of two related pentapeptides from the brain with potent opiate agonist activity. *Nature* 258:577–579.

Hull, David (1974). *Philosophy of biological science.* Englewood Cliffs, N.J.: Prentice-Hall.

Hume, David (1739). *A treatise of human nature.* Modern edition by L. A. Selby-Bigge (1888). Oxford: Clarendon Press.

Hume, David (1748). *Enquiry concerning human understanding.* Modern edition by L. A. Selby-Bigge (1894). *Hume's enquiries.* Oxford: Clarendon Press.

Hummel, R. A., and S. W. Zucker (1980). On the foundation of relaxation labelling processes. *Technical Report 80–7.* Montreal: Computer Vision and Graphics Laboratory, McGill University.

Huppert, F. A., and M. Piercy (1976). Recognition memory in amnesia patients: Effect of temporal context and familiarity of material. *Cortex* 12:3–20.

Ingvar, D. H. (1982). Mental illness and regional brain metabolism. *Trends in Neurosciences* 5/6:199–203.

Ito, M. (1970). Neurophysiological aspects of the cerebellar motor control system. *International Journal of Neurology* 7:162–176.

Iverson, Leslie L. (1979). The chemistry of the brain. *Scientific American* 241/3:134–149.

Iverson, Leslie L., and Martin M. Rosser (1984). Human learning and memory dysfunction: Neurochemical changes in senile dementia. In G.Lynch, J. L. McGaugh, and N. M. Weinberger, eds. (1984), 363–367.

Jackson, Frank (1982). Epiphenomenal qualia. *Philosophical Quarterly* 32:127–136.

Jackson, J. Hughlings (1864). Loss of speech with hemiplegia on the left side, valvular disease, epileptiform convulsions affect the side paralyzed. *Medical Times Gazette* 2:166. (Reprinted in James Taylor, ed. (1932). *Selected writings of John Hughlings Jackson.* 2 vols. London: Staples Press.)

Jackson, J. Hughlings (1875). *Clinical and physiological researches on the nervous system.* (Contains a reprinting of "On the anatomical and physiological localisation of movement in the brain," first published in *Lancet* 1873,i:84–85.) London: Churchill.

Jackson, J. Hughlings (1881). Remarks on dissolution of the nervous system as exemplified by certain post-epileptic conditions. *Medical Press and Circular* 1:329. (Reprinted in James Taylor, ed. (1932). *Selected writings of John Hughlings Jackson.* 2 vols. London: Staples Press.)

James, William. *Pragmatism: A new name for some old ways of thinking.* New York: Longmans, Green. (Reprinted in Frederick Burkhardt and Fredson Bowers, eds. (1975). *Pragmatism and the meaning of truth.* Cambridge, Mass.: Harvard University Press.)

Jernigan, Terry L. (1984). The study of human memory with neuro-imaging techniques. In L. R. Squire and N. Butters, eds. (1984), 258–265.

Jolly, Alison (1972). *The evolution of primate behavior.* New York: Macmillan.

Jones, E. G. (1981). Anatomy of cerebral cortex: Columnar input-output organization. In F. O. Schmitt, F. G. Worden, G. Adelman, and S. G. Dennis, eds. (1981), 199–235.

Jordan, M. I. (1986). An introduction to linear systems. In J. L. McClelland and D. E. Rumelhart, eds. (1986).

Jouvet, M. (1967). Neurophysiology of the states of sleep. *Physiological Review* 47:117–177.

Julesz, Bela (1980). Spatial nonlinearities in the instantaneous perception of textures with identical power spectra. *Philosophical Transactions of the Royal Society of London. Series B* 290:83–94.

Junge, Douglas (1981). *Nerve and muscle excitation.* 2nd ed. Sunderland, Mass.: Sinauer.

Kaas, J. H., R. J. Nelson, M. Sur, and M. M. Merzenich (1979). Multiple representations of the body within the primary somatosensory cortex of primates. *Science* 204:521–523.

Kass, J. H., R. J. Neslon, M. Sur, and M. M. Merzenich (1981). Organization of somatosensory cortex in primates. In F. O. Schmitt, F. G. Worden, G. Adelman, and S. G. Dennis, eds. (1981), 237–261.

Kanaseki, T., and J. M. Sprague (1974). Anatomical organization of pretectal nuclei and tectal laminae in the cat. *Journal of Comparative Neurology* 158:319–337.

Kandel, Eric R. (1976). *Cellular basis of behavior: An introduction to behavioral neurobiology.* San Fransisco: W. H. Freeman.

Kandel, Eric R. (1979). Small systems of neurons. *Scientific American* 241/3:66–76.

Kandel, Eric R. (1981a). Synaptic transmission I: Postsynaptic factors controlling ionic permeability. In E. R. Kandel and J. H. Schwartz, eds. (1981), 63–80.

Kandel, Eric R. (1981b). Synaptic transmission II: Presynaptic factors controlling transmitter release. In E. R. Kandel and J. H. Schwartz, eds. (1981), 81–90.

Kandel, Eric R. (1981c). Somatic sensory system III: Central representation of touch. In E. R. Kandel and J. H. Schwartz, eds. (1981), 184–198.

Kandel, Eric R., and James H. Schwartz, eds. (1981). *Principles of neural science.* New York, Amsterdam, Oxford: Elsevier/North-Holland.

Kant, Immanuel (1781). *Kritik der reinen Vernunft.* 2nd ed. (1787). Translated and edited by N. Kemp Smith (1929). *Immanuel Kant's critique of pure reason.* Reprinted (1964). London: Macmillan.

Kelley, Darcy B. (1980). Auditory and vocal nuclei in the frog brain concentrate sex hormones. *Science* 207/4430:553–555.

Kelly, Dennis D. (1981). Physiology of sleep and dreaming. In E. R. Kandel and J. H. Schwartz, eds. (1981), 472–485.

Kelly, James P. (1981a). Visual system II: Anatomy of the central visual pathways. In E. R. Kandel and J. H. Schwartz, eds. (1981), 226–235.

Kelly, James P. (1981b). Vestibular system. In E. R. Kandel and J. H. Schwartz, eds. (1981), 406–418.

Kemeny, J. G., and O. Oppenheim (1956). On reduction. *Philosophical Studies* 7:6–17.

Kenny, Anthony (1984). *The legacy of Wittgenstein.* Oxford: Basil Blackwell.

Kertesz, Andrew (1983a). Issues in localization. In A. Kertesz, ed. (1983b), 1–20.

Kertesz, Andrew, ed. (1983b). *Localization in neuropsychology.* New York: Academic Press.

Kety, S. S. (1978). The biological roots of mental illness: Their ramifications through cerebral metabolism, synaptic activity, genetics, and the environment. *Harvey Lecture* 71:1–22.

Kety, S. S., D. Rosenthal, P. H. Wender, F. Schulsinger, and B. Jacobsen (1975). Mental illness in the biological and adoptive families of adopted individuals who have become schizophrenic: A preliminary report based on psychiatric interviews. In *Genetic research in psychiatry*, ed. R. R. Fieve, D. Rosenthal, and H. Brill, 147–165. Baltimore: The Johns Hopkins University Press.

Kimura, D. (1967). Functional asymmetry of the brain in dichotic listening. *Cortex* 3:163–178.

Kinsbourne, Marcel (1971). The minor cerebral hemisphere as a source of aphasic speech. *Archives of Neurology* 25:302–306.

Kinsbourne, Marcel (1974). Lateral interactions in the brain. In *Hemisphere disconnection and cerebral function*, ed. M. Kinsbourne and W. L. Smith, 239–259. Springfield, Ill.: Charles C. Thomas.

Kinsbourne, Marcel (1977). Hemi-neglect and hemispheric rivalry. In *Hemi-inattention and hemispheric specialization. Advances in neurology,* ed. E. A. Weinstein and R. P. Friedland, 41–49. New York: Raven.

Kinsbourne, Marcel (1980). Brain-based limitations on mind. In *Body and mind: Past, present and future,* ed. R. Rieber, 155–175. New York: Academic Press.

Kinsbourne, Marcel (1982). Hemisphere specialization and the growth of human understanding. *American Psychologist* 37:411–420.

Kinsbourne, Marcel, and Elizabeth Warrington (1963a). The localizing significance of limited simultaneous visual form perception. *Brain* 86:697–705.

Kinsbourne, Marcel, and Elizabeth Warrington (1963b). Jargon aphasia. *Neuropsychologia* 1:27–37.

Kinsbourne, Marcel, and Elizabeth Warrington (1964). Observations on color agnosia. *Journal of Neurology, Neurosurgery, and Psychiatry* 27:296–299.

Kinsbourne, Marcel, and F. Wood (1975). Short-term memory processes and the amnesic syndrome. In *Short-term memory,* ed. D. Deutsch and J. A. Deutsch, 257–291. New York: Academic Press.

Kirkpatrick, S., C. D. Gelatt, and M. P. Vecchi (1983). Optimization by simulated annealing. *Science* 220:671–680.

Kitcher, Patricia (1980). How to reduce a functional psychology? *Philosophy of Science* 47:134–140.

Kitcher, Patricia (1982). Discussion: Genes, reduction, and functional psychology. *Philosophy of Science* 49:633–636.

Kitcher, Philip (1982). Genes. *British Journal for the Philosophy of Science* 33:337–359.

Kitcher, Philip (1984). 1953 and all that: A tale of two sciences. *Philosophical Review* 93:335–373.

Klima, Edward, and Ursula Bellugi (1979). *The signs of language.* Cambridge, Mass.: Harvard University Press.

Koenigsberger, L. (1906). *Hermann von Helmholtz.* English translation by F. A. Welby (1965). New York: Dover.

Koester, J. (1981). Resting membrane potential. In E. R. Kandel and J. H. Schwartz, eds. (1981), 27–35.

Kohonen, Teuvo, Pekka Lehtio, P. Rovamo, J. Hyvarinen, K. Bry, and L. Vainio (1977). A principle of neural associative memory. *Neuroscience* 2:1065–1076.

Kohonen, Teuvo, Erkki Oja, and Pekka Lehtiö (1981). Storage and processing of information in distributed associative memory systems. In G. E. Hinton and J. A. Anderson, eds. (1981), 105–143.

Kolata, Gina (1979a). Report: New drugs and the brain. *Science* 205/4408:774–776.

Kolata, Gina (1979b). Report: Sex hormones and brain development. *Science* 205/4410:985–987.

Kolata, Gina (1982). Report: Grafts correct brain damage. *Science* 217/4557:342–344.

Kolb, Bryan, and Ian Q. Whishaw (1980). *Fundamentals of human neuropsychology.* San Francisco: W. H. Freeman.

Kolb, Bryan, and Ian Q. Whishaw. (1984). Decortication abolishes place but not cue learning in rats. *Behavioral Brain Research* 11/2:123–134.

Kolers, Paul (1975). Specificity of operation in sentence recognition. *Cognitive Psychology* 7:289–306.

Konishi, Masakazu (forthcoming). Centrally synthesized maps of sensory space. *Trends in Neurosciences.*

Konishi, Masakazu, and Mark E. Gurney (1982). Sex differentiation of brain and behavior. *Trends in Neurosciences* 5/1:20–23.

Kosslyn, Stephen M. (1975). Information representation in visual images. *Cognitive Psychology* 7:341–370.

Krebs, J. R., and N. B. Davies, eds. (1978). *Behavioral ecology: An evolutionary approach.* Sunderland, Mass.: Sinauer.

Kuffler, S. W., J. G. Nicholls, and A. R. Martin (1984). *From neuron to brain: A cellular approach to the function of the nervous system.* 2nd ed. Sunderland, Mass.: Sinauer.

Kuhn, Thomas S. (1962). *The structure of scientific revolutions.* 2nd ed. (1970). Chicago: University of Chicago Press.

Kühne, Willy (1862). *Über die peripherischen Endorgane der motorischen Nerven.* Leipzig: Engelmann. (Excerpted and translated in E. Clarke and C. D. O'Malley (1968), 75–77.)

Kummer, Hans (1968). *Social organization of Hamadryas baboons.* Chicago: University of Chicago Press.

Kupfer, D. J., and F. G. Foster (1972). Interval between onset of sleep and rapid eye movement sleep as an indicator of depression. *Lancet* 2:684–686.

Kupfer, D. J., and F. G. Foster (1975). The sleep of psychotic patients: Does it all look alike? In *The biology of the major psychoses: A comparative analysis,* ed. D. X. Freedman, 143–164. New York: Raven.

Kutas, M., and S. A. Hillyard (1980). Reading senseless sentences: Brain potentials reflect semantic incongruity. *Science* 207:203–205.

Kutas, M., and S. A. Hillyard (1984). Event-related potentials in cognitive science. In M. Gazzaniga, ed. (1984b), 387–409.

Kutas, M., G. McCarthy, and E. Donchin (1977). Augmenting mental chronometry: The P300 as a measure of stimulus evaluation time. *Science* 197:792–795.

La Mettrie, Julien Offray de (1748). *L'Homme machine.* (Published anonymously.) Leyden: Luzac. (Translation into English by E. Luzac and G. Smith (1750), London, and G. C. Bussey (1912), Chicago.)

Land, Edwin (1977). The retinex theory of color vision. *Scientific American* 237:108–128.

Land, Edwin H., David H. Hubel, Margaret S. Livingstone, S. Hollis Perry, and Michael M. Burns (1983). Colour-generating interactions across the corpus callosum. *Nature* 303:616–618.

Larsen, T. Andreo, and Donald B. Calne (1982). Recent advances in the study of Parkinson's disease. (Review.) *Trends in Neurosciences* 5/1:10–12.

Lashley, Karl S. (1933). Integrative functions of the cerebral cortex. *Physiological Review* 13:1–42.

Lashley, Karl S. (1937). Functional determinants of cerebral localization. *Archives of Neurology and Psychiatry* 38:371–387.

Lassen, N. A., D. H. Ingvar, and E. Skinhoj (1978). Brain function and blood flow. *Scientific American* 239:62–71.

Lee, K. S., F. Schottler, M. Oliver, and G. Lynch (1980). Brief bursts of high-frequency stimulation produce two types of structural change in rat hippocampus. *Journal of Neurophysiology* 44:247–258.

Lent, Charles M. (1980). On neuronal nihilism: Commentary on Selverston. *Behavioral and Brain Sciences* 3:555–556.

Levy, J. (1982). Mental processes in the nonverbal hemisphere. In *Animal mind-human mind,* ed. D. R. Griffin, 57–73. Berlin: Springer-Verlag.

Levy, J., and M. L. Reid (1976). Variations in writing posture and cerebral organization. *Science* 194:337.

Levy-Agresti, J., and R. W. Sperry (1968). Differential perceptual capacities in major and minor hemispheres. *National Academy of Sciences of the United States of America. Proceedings. Biological Sciences* 6:1151.

Levy, J., C. Trevarthen, and R. W. Sperry (1972). Perception of bilateral chimeric figures following hemisphere disconnection. *Brain* 95:61–78.

Lewis, David (1983). Postscript to "Mad pain and Martian pain." In *Philosophical papers,* vol. I, 122–130. New York: Oxford University Press.

Leyton (Grünbaum), A. S. F., and C. S. Sherrington (1917). Observations on the excitable cortex of the chimpanzee, orangutan, and gorilla. *Quarterly Journal of Experimental Physiology* 11:135–222. (Reprinted in G. von Bonin, ed. (1960). 283–396.)

Libet, Benjamin (1981). The experimental evidence for subjective referral of a sensory experience backwards in time: Reply to P. S. Churchland. *Philosophy of Science* 48:182–197.

Libet, Benjamin, E. W. Wright, Jr., B. Feinstein, and D. K. Pearl (1979). Subjective referral of the timing for a conscious sensory experience: A functional role for the somatosensory specific projection system in man. *Brain* 102:191–222.

Lindsay, Peter H., and Donald A. Norman (1977). *Human information processing.* 2nd ed. New York: Academic Press.

Llinás, Rodolfo R. (1975). The cortex of the cerebellum. *Scientific American* 232/1:56–71.

Llinás, Rodolfo R. (1979). The role of calcium in neuronal function. In F. O. Schmitt and F. G. Worden, eds. (1979), 555–571.

Llinás, Rodolfo R. (1981). Electrophysiology of the cerebellar networks. In *Handbook of physiology.* Vol. 2: *The nervous system, Part II,* ed. V. B. Brooks, 831–876. Bethesda, Md.: American Physiological Society.

Llinás, Rodolfo R. (1982). Calcium in synaptic transmission. *Scientific American* 247:56–65.

Llinás, Rodolfo R. (1984a). Comparative electrobiology of mammalian central neurons. In *Brain slices,* ed. R. Dingledine, 7–42. New York: Plenum.

Llinás, Rodolfo R. (1984b). The squid giant synapse. In *Current topics in membranes and transport.* Vol. 22: *The squid axon,* ed. A. Kleinzeller and P. F. Baker, 519–546. New York: Academic Press.

Llinás, Rodolfo R. (1984c). Rebound excitation as the physiological basis for tremor: A biophysical study of the oscillatory properties of mammalian central neurones *in vitro.* In *Movement disorders: Tremor,* ed. L. J. Findley and R. Capildeo, 165–182. London: Macmillan.

Llinás, Rodolfo R.(1984d). Possible role of tremor in the organization of the nervous system. In *Movement disorders: Tremor,* ed. L. J. Findley and R. Capildeo, 475–477. London: Macmillan.

Llinás, Rodolfo R. (forthcoming). "Mindness" as a functional state of the brain. In *Mind matters,* ed. C. Blakemore and S. Greenfield. Oxford: Basil Blackwell.

Llinás, Rodolfo R., R. Baker, and C. Sotelo (1974). Electronic coupling between neurons in the cat inferior olive. *Journal of Neurophysiology* 37:560–571.

Llinás, Rodolfo R., and R. Hess (1976). Tetrodotoxin-resistant dendritic spikes in avian Purkinje cell. *National Academy of Sciences of the United States of America. Proceedings. Biological Sciences.* 73:2520–2523.

Llinás, Rodolfo R., and D. E. Hillman (1969). Physiological and morphological organization of the cerebellar circuits in various vertebrates. In *Neurobiology of cerebellar evolution and development,* ed. R. Llinás, 43–73. Chicago: American Medical Association.

Llinás, Rodolfo R., and H. Jahnsen (1982). Electrophysiology of mammalian thalamic neurons *in vitro. Nature* 297:406–408.

Llinás, Rodolfo R., and M. Sugimori (1979). Calcium conductances in Purkinje cell dendrites: Their role in development and integration. In *Progress in Brain Research.* Vol. 51: *Development and chemical specificity of neurons,* ed. M. Cuenod, G. W. Kreutzberg, and F. E. Bloom, 323–334. Amsterdam: Elsevier.

Llinás, Rodolfo R., and M. Sugimori (1980). Electrophysiological properties of in vitro

Purkinje cell somata in mammalian cerebellar slices. *Journal of Physiology London* 305:171–195.

Longuet-Higgins, H. C. (1968). The non-local storage of temporal information. *Proceedings of the Royal Society of London. Series B* 171:327–334.

Lycan, William G. (1981a). Form, function and feel. *Journal of Philosophy* 78:24–50.

Lycan, William G. (1981b). Toward a homuncular theory of believing. *Cognition and Brain Theory* 4:139–159.

Lycan, William G. (forthcoming). Tacit belief. In *Belief*, ed. R. J. Bogdan. Oxford: Oxford University Press.

Lynch, Gary, James L. McGaugh, and Norman M. Weinberger, eds. (1984). *Neurobiology of learning and memory*. New York: Guilford.

McCarthy, J., and P. Hayes (1969). Some philosophical problems from the standpoint of Artificial Intelligence. In *Machine intelligence*, vol. 4, ed. B. Meltzer and D. Michie, 463–502. New York: Harper and Row.

McClelland, James L. (unpublished). Models of perception and memory based on principles of neural organization. Carnegie-Mellon University, Pittsburgh, Pa.

McClelland, James L., and David E. Rumelhart (1981). An interactive activation model of the effect of context in letter perception. Part I: An account of basic findings. *Psychological Review* 88:375–407.

McClelland, James L., and David E. Rumelhart (1986). *Parallel distributed processing: Explorations in the microstructure of cognition*. Vol. 2: *Applications*. Cambridge, Mass.: MIT Press.

McClelland, James L., David E. Rumelhart, and Geoffrey E. Hinton (1986). The appeal of parallel distributed processing. In D. E. Rumelhart and J. L. McClelland, eds. (1986). Cambridge, Mass.: MIT Press.

McCloskey, Michael (1983). Intuitive physics. *Scientific American* 248/4:122–130.

McCloskey, Michael, Alfonso Caramazza, and Annamaria Basili (forthcoming). Dissociations of number system processes. In *Mathematical disabilities: A cognitive neurophysiological perspective*, ed. G. Eeloshe and X. Seron. Hillsdale, N.J.: Erlbaum.

McCloskey, Michael, Alfonso Caramazza, and Bert Green (1980). Curvilinear motion in the absence of external forces: Naive beliefs about the motion of objects. *Science* 210/4474:1139–1141.

McCollum, G., A. Pellionisz, and R. Llinás (1983). Tensorial approach to color vision. *Journal of Theoretical Neurobiology* 2:23–28.

McCormick, David (1984). Cerebellum: Essential involvement in a simple learned response. Doctoral dissertation, Stanford University.

McDowell, Fletcher (1979). Cerebrovascular diseases: Section fourteen. In *Textbook of medicine*, ed. Paul B. Beeson, Walsh McDermott, and James B. Wyngaarden, 777–801. Philadelphia: Saunders.

McEwen, Bruce S. (1976). Interaction between hormones and nervous tissues. *Scientific American* 235/1:48–58.

McEwen, Bruce S., Carl J. Denef, John L. Gerlach, and Linda Plapinger (1974). Chemical studies of the brain as a steroid target tissue. In F. O. Schmitt and F. G. Worden, eds. (1974), 599–620.

McGinn, Colin (1982). *The character of mind*. Oxford: Oxford University Press.

MacKay, D. M. (1978). Selves and brain. *Neuroscience* 3:599–606.

McKeever, Walter F. (1979). Handwriting posture in left handers. *Neuropsychobiology* 17:429–444.

McKeever, Walter F. (1981). On laterality research and dichotomania. (Commentary on Bradshaw and Nettleton 1981.) *Behavioral and Brain Sciences* 4/1:73–74.

MacVicar, B., and F. E. Dudek (1980). Dye-coupling between CA3 pyramidal cells in slices of rat hippocampus. *Brain research* 196:494–497.

Magendie, F. J. (1822a). Expériences sur les fonctions des racines des nerfs rachidiens. *J. Physiol. Exp. Path., Paris* 2:276–279. (Excerpted and translated in E. Clarke and C. D. O'Malley (1968), 300.)

Magendie, F. J. (1822b). Expériences sur les fonctions des racines des nerfs qui naissent de la moelle épinière. *J. Physiol. Exp. Path., Paris* 2:366–371. (Excerpted and translated in E. Clarke and C. D. O'Malley (1968), 301–302.)

Magistretti, Pierre J., John H. Morrison, and Floyd E. Bloom, eds. (1984). *Nervous System Development and Repair. Discussions in Neurosciences* 1/2 (special issue).

Makowski, Lee, D. L. D. Caspar, W. C. Phillips, and D. A. Goodenough (1977). Gap junction structures. II: Analysis of X-ray diffraction data. *Journal of Cell Biology* 74:629–645.

Margolis, Joseph (1978). *Persons and minds: The prospects of nonreductive materialism.* Dordrecht, Holland: D. Reidel.

Marr, David (1969). A theory of cerebellar cortex. *Journal of Physiology* 202:437–470.

Marr, David (1982). *Vision.* San Francisco: W. H. Freeman.

Marr, David, and T. Poggio (1976). Cooperative computation of stereo disparity. *Science* 194:283–287.

Marsden, C. D., J. C. Rothwell, and B. L. Day (1984). The use of peripheral feedback in the control of movement. *Trends in Neurosciences* 7:253–257.

Marshall, John C. (1981). Hemispheric specialization: What, how, and why. (Commentary on Bradshaw and Nettleton 1981.) *Behavioral and Brain Sciences* 4/1:72–73.

Marx, Jean L. (1982). Transplants as guides to brain development. *Science* 217/4557:340–341.

Mateer, Catherine A. (1983). Localization of language and visuospatial functions by electrical stimulation. In A. Kertesz, ed. (1983b), 153–183.

Matsui, Takayoshi, and Asao Hirano (1978). *An atlas of the human brain for computerized tomography.* Tokyo/New York: Igaku-Shoin.

Mayer, D. J. (1975). Pain inhibition by electrical stimulation: Comparison to morphine. *Neurosciences Research Program Bulletin* 13:94–100.

Mazziotta, J. C. (1985). PET scanning: Principles and applications. *Discussions in Neurosciences* 2:9–47.

Mazziotta, J. C., M. E. Phelps, R. E. Carson, and D. E. Kuhl (1982). Tomographic mapping of human cerebral metabolism: Auditory stimulation. *Neurology* 32:921–937.

Mendelson, Wallace B., J. Christian Gillin, and Richard Jed Wyatt (1977). *Human sleep and its disorders.* New York: Plenum.

Menzel, E. W. (1974). A group of young chimpanzees in a one-acre field. In *Behavior of nonhuman primates,* vol. 5, ed. A. M. Schrier and F. Stollnitz, 83–153. New York: Academic Press.

Menzel, E. W. (1983). Parlez-vous baboon, Bwana Sherlock? (Commentary on Dennett 1983.) *Behavioral and Brain Sciences* 3:371–372.

Merzenich, M. M., and J. F. Brugge (1973). Representation of the cochlear partition on the superior temporal plane of the macaque monkey. *Brain Research* 50:275–296.

Merzenich, M. M., and J. H. Kaas (1980). Principles of organization of sensory-perceptual systems in mammals. *Progress in Psychobiology and Physiological Psychology* 9:1–42.

Metropolis, N., A. Rosenbluth, M. Rosenbluth, A. Teller, and E. Teller (1953). Equation of state calculations for fast computing machines. *Journal of Chemical Physics* 6:1087.

Miczek, Klaus A., M. L. Thompson, and L. Shuster (1982). Opioid-like analgesia in defeated mice. *Science* 215/4539:1520–1522.

Milner, Brenda (1966). Amnesia following operation on the temporal lobes. In *Amnesia*, ed. C. W. M. Whitty and O. Zangwill, 109–133. London: Butterworth.

Milner, B., S. Corkin, and H.-L. Teuber (1968). Further analysis of the hippocampal amnesic syndrome: 14-year follow-up study of H. M. *Neuropsychologia* 6:215–234.

Milner, B., and M. Petrides (1984). Behavioral effects of frontal-lobe lesions in man. *Trends in Neurosciences* 7/11:403–407.

Milner, B., and T. Rasmussen (1966). Evidence for bilateral speech representation in some non-right handers. *Transactions of the American Neurobiological Association* 91:306–308.

Minsky, Marvin (1975). Frame-system theory. In *Theoretical issues in natural language processing*, ed. R. Schank and B. Nash-Webber, 118–130. (Reprinted in P. Johnson-Laird and P. Wason, eds. (1977). *Thinking: Readings in cognitive science*, 355–376. Cambridge: Cambridge University Press.

Mishkin, Mortimer, and Herbert L. Petri (1984). Memories and habits: Some implications for the analysis of learning and memory. In L. R. Squire and N. Butters, eds. (1984), 287–296.

Mishkin, Mortimer, Leslie G. Ungerleider, and Kathleen A. Macko (1983). Object vision and spatial vision: Two cortical pathways. *Trends in Neurosciences* 6:414–417.

Mohr, J. P. (1973). Rapid ameliorization of motor aphasia. *Archives of Neurology* 28:77–82.

Mooney, R. D., B. G. Klein, M. F. Jacquin, and R. W. Rhoades (1984). Dendrites of deep layer, somatosensory superior collicular neurons extend into superficial laminae. In *Abstracts: Society for Neuroscience. 14th Annual Meeting* 10:158.

Moran, Jeffrey, and Robert Desimone (1985). Selective attention gates visual processing in the extrastriate cortex. *Science* 229:782–784.

Morgan, M. J. (1981). Hemisphere specialization and spatiotemporal interactions. (Commentary on Bradshaw and Nettleton 1981.) *Behavioral and Brain Sciences* 4:74–75.

Morick, Harold, ed. (1972). *Challenges to empiricism.* Belmont, Calif.: Wadsworth.

Morrell, Joan I., and Donald W. Pfaff (1981). Autoradiographic technique for steroid hormone localization: Application to the vertebrate brain. In *Neuroendocrinology of reproduction*, ed. Norman T. Adler, 519–531. New York: Plenum.

Mountcastle, Vernon (1957). Modality and topographic properties of single neurons of cat's somatic sensory cortex. *Journal of Neurophysiology* 20:408–434.

Mountcastle, Vernon (1979). An organizing principle for cerebral function: The unit module and the distributed system. In F. O. Schmitt and F. G. Worden, eds. (1979), 21–42. (Reprinted in G. M. Edelman and V. B. Mountcastle (1978). *The mindful brain*, 7–50. Cambridge, Mass.: MIT Press.)

Müller, Johannes (1835). *Handbuch der Physiologie des Menschen für Vorlesungen.* Vol. 1, bk. 3, sec. 4. Coblenz. (Excerpted in E. Clarke and C. D. O'Malley (1968), 205–206.)

Myers, P. S. (1978). Analysis of right-hemisphere communicating deficits: Implications for speech pathology. In *Clinical aphasiology: Conference proceedings*, ed. R. H. Brookshire. Minneapolis: BRK.

Myers, P. S., and C. W. Linebaugh (1981). Comprehension of idiomatic expressions by right-hemisphere damaged adults. In *Clinical aphasiology: Conference proceedings*, ed. R. H. Brookshire, 254–261. Minneapolis: BRK.

Myers, R. E., and R. W. Sperry (1958). Interhemispheric communication through the corpus callosum: Mnemonic carry-over between the hemispheres. *Archives of Neurology and Psychiatry* 80:298–303.

Naeser, A. M., M. Alexander, N. Helm-Estabrooks, et al. (1982). Aphasia with predominantly subcortical lesion sites. *Archives of Neurology* 39:2–14.

Nagel, Ernest (1961). *The structure of science.* New York: Harcourt, Brace, and World.

Nagel, Thomas (1974). What is it like to be a bat? *Philosophical Review* 83:435–450.

Neher, E., and C. F. Stevens (1979). Voltage-driven conformational changes in intrinsic membrane proteins. In F. O. Schmitt and F. G. Worden, eds. (1979), 623–629.

Neisser, Ulric (1966). *Cognitive psychology.* New York: Appleton-Century-Crofts.

Neuburger, Max (1897). *Die historische Entwicklung der experimentellen Gehirn- und Rückenmarksphysiologie vor Flourens.* Stuttgart: Ferdinand Enke Verlag. (English translation by Edwin Clarke (1981). *The historical development of experimental brain and spinal cord physiology before Flourens.* Baltimore: The Johns Hopkins University Press.)

Neurath, Otto (1932). Protokollsätze. *Erkenntnis* 3:204–214. (Translated by G. Schlick and reprinted as "Protocol sentences" in A. J. Ayer, ed. (1959). *Logical positivism.* New York: Macmillan.)

Nicholls, J. G., and D. A. Baylor (1968). Specific modalities and receptive fields of sensory neurons in the CNS of the leech. *Journal of Neurophysiology* 31:740–756.

Nicoll, Roger A. (1982). Neurotransmitters can say more than just "yes" or "no." *Trends in Neurosciences* 5:369–374.

Nisbett, Richard, and Lee Ross (1980). *Human inference: Strategies and shortcomings of social judgment.* Englewood Cliffs, N.J.: Prentice-Hall.

Norman, D. A. (1969). *Memory and attention: An introduction to human information processing.* New York: Wiley.

Norman, D. A. (1973). Memory, knowledge, and the answering of questions. In *The Loyola symposium on cognitive psychology,* ed. R. Solso, 135–165. Washington, D.C.: Winston.

Norman, D. A., and D. E. Rumelhart (1970). A system for perception and memory. In *Models of human memory,* ed. D. A. Norman. New York: Academic Press.

Northcutt, R. Glenn (1977). Nervous system (vertebrate). In *McGraw-Hill encyclopedia of science and technology,* vol. 9, 90–96. New York: McGraw-Hill.

Nottebohm, F. (1981). Laterality, seasons and space governing the learning of a motor skill. *Trends in Neurosciences* 4/5:104–106.

Ojemann, George A. (1983). Brain organization for language from the perspective of electrical stimulation mapping. *Behavioral and Brain Sciences* 6/2:189–230.

O'Keefe, J., and L. Nadel (1978). *The hippocampus as a cognitive map.* Oxford: Clarendon Press.

Olton, D., J. T. Becker, and G. E. Handelmann (1979). Hippocampus, space, and memory. *Behavioral and Brain Sciences* 2:313–365.

Oppenheim, P., and H. Putnam (1958). Unity of science as a working hypothesis. In *Minnesota studies in the philosophy of science,* vol. 2, ed. H. Feigl et al., 3–36. Minneapolis: University of Minnesota Press.

Palm, Günther (1982). *Neural assemblies: An alternative approach to artificial intelligence.* Berlin: Springer-Verlag.

Patterson, Paul H., and Dale Purves, eds. (1982). *Readings in developmental neurobiology.* Cold Spring Harbor, N.Y.: Cold Spring Harbor Laboratory.

Paupardin-Tritsch, D., and H. M. Gerschenfeld (1975). 2-hydroxytryptamine as a synaptic transmitter of excitation and inhibition. In *Golgi centennial symposium proceedings,* ed. M. Santini, 487–501. New York: Raven.

Peirce, Charles Sanders (1931–1935). *The collected papers of Charles Sanders Peirce,* vols. 1–6, ed. C. Hartshorne and P. Weiss. Cambridge, Mass.: Harvard University Press.

Pellionisz, Andras (1983a). Brain theory: Connecting neurobiology to robotics. Tensor analysis: Coordinates to describe, understand and engineer functional geometries of intelligent organisms. *Journal of Theoretical Neurobiology* 2:185–211.

Pellionisz, Andras (1983b). Sensorimotor transformations of natural coordinates via neuronal networks: conceptual and formal unification of cerebellar and tectal models. In *Proceedings of workshop on visuomotor coordination in frog and toad*. (Organized by R. Lara and M. Arbib.) Computer and Information Science: University of Massachusetts Technical Report 83–19.

Pellionisz, Andras (1984). Coordination: A vector-matrix description of transformations of overcomplete CNS coordinates and a tensorial solution using the Moore-Penrose generalized inverse. *Journal of Theoretical Biology* 110:353–375.

Pellionisz, Andras (1985). Tensorial aspects of the multidimensional approach to the vestibulo-oculomotor reflex and gaze. In *Adaptive mechanisms in gaze control*, ed. A. Berthoz and G. Melvill Jones, 231–296. Amsterdam: Elsevier.

Pellionisz, A., and R. Llinás (1979). Brain modeling by tensor network theory and computer simulation. The cerebellum: Distributed processor for predictive coordination. *Neuroscience* 4:323–348.

Pellionisz, A., and R. Llinás (1982). Space-time representation in the brain. The cerebellum as a predictive space-time metric tensor. *Neuroscience* 7:2249–2970.

Pellionisz, A., and R. Llinás (1985a). Cerebellar function and the adaptive feature of the central nervous system. In *Adaptive mechanisms in gaze control*, ed. A. Berthoz and G. Melvill Jones, 223–232. Amsterdam: Elsevier.

Pellionisz, A., and R. Llinás (1985b). Tensor network theory of the metaorganization of functional geometries in the central nervous system. *Neuroscience* 16:245–273.

Pellionisz, A., R. Llinás, and D. H. Perkel (1977). A computer model of the cerebellar cortex of the frog. *Neuroscience* 2:19–36.

Penfield, Wilder, and Herbert Jasper (1954). *Epilepsy and the functional anatomy of the human brain*. Boston: Little, Brown and Co.

Penfield, Wilder, and Lamar Roberts (1959). *Speech and brain mechanism*. Princeton, N.J.: Princeton University Press.

Perecman, Ellen, ed. (1983). *Cognitive processing in the right hemisphere*. New York: Academic Press.

Perenin, M. T., and M. Jeannerod (1978). Visual function within the hemianopic field following early cerebral hemidecortication in man. I. Spatial localisation. *Neuropsychologia* 16:1–13.

Perenin, M. T., J. Ruel, and H. Hecaen (1980). Residual visual capacities in a case of cortical blindness. *Cortex* 16:605–612.

Perry, Elaine K., and Robert H. Perry (1982). The cholinergic system in Alzheimer's disease. *Trends in Neurosciences* 5:261–262.

Peterson, B., J. Baker, C. Wickland, and A. Pellionisz (1985). Relation between pulling directions of neck muscles and their activation by the vestibulocollic reflex: Tests of a tensorial model. *Society for Neuroscience Abstracts* 11:83.

Pfaff, Donald W. (1980). *Estrogens and brain function*. New York: Springer-Verlag.

Pfaff, Donald, W., and Bruce S. McEwen (1983). Actions of estrogens and progestins on nerve cells. *Science* 219:808–814.

Pflug, B., and R. Tolle (1971). Therapy of endogenous depression by sleep deprivation: Practical and theoretical consequences. *Nervenarzt* 42:117–124.

Phelps, Michael E., David E. Kuhl, and John C. Mazziotta (1981). Metabolic mapping of the brain's response to visual stimulation: Studies in humans. *Science* 211:1445–1448.

Phelps, Michael E., and John C. Mazziotta (1985). Positron emission tomography: Human brain function and biochemistry. *Science* 228:799–809.

Piaget, Jean (1971). *Insights and illusions of philosophy.* Translation by Wolfe Mays. New York: World Publishing Co.

Picton, T. W., and S. A. Hillyard, H. I. Krausz, and R. Galambos (1974). Human auditory evoked potentials. I. Evaluation of components. *Electroencephalography and Clinical Neurophysiology* 36:179–190.

Pitts, W. H., and W. S. McCulloch (1947). How we know universals: The perception of auditory and visual forms. *Bulletin of Mathematical Biophysics* 9:127–147.

Plato. *Plato: The collected dialogues.* (1961). Ed. Edith Hamilton and Huntington Cairns. New York: Bollingen Foundation.

Popper, Karl R. (1935). *Logik der Forschung.* Vienna: Springer-Verlag. Translated (1959) as *The logic of scientific discovery.* London: Hutchinson. (Reprinted (1965). New York: Harper Torchbooks.)

Popper, Karl R. (1963). *Conjectures and refutations: The growth of scientific knowledge.* New York: Basic Books (2nd ed. (1965). New York: Harper and Row.).

Popper, Karl R. (1972). *Objective knowledge.* Oxford: Clarendon Press.

Popper, Karl R. (1977). Part I of *The self and its brain* (Popper and Eccles 1977), 3–223.

Popper, Karl R., and John C. Eccles (1977). *The self and its brain* (Parts I and II). Berlin: Springer-International.

Poritsky, Raphael (1969). Two and three dimensional ultrastructure of boutons and glial cells in the motoneuronal surface of the cat spinal cord. *Journal of Comparative Neurology* 135:423–452.

Posner, Michael I. (1978). *Chronometric explorations of the mind.* Hillsdale, N.J.: Erlbaum.

Posner, Michael I. (1984). Selective attention and the storage of information. In G. Lynch, J. L. McGaugh, and N. M. Weinberger, eds. (1984), 89–101.

Posner, Michael I., Roy Pea, and Bruce Volpe (1982). Cognitive-neuroscience: Developments toward a science of synthesis. In *Perspectives on mental representation,* ed. J. Mehler, E. Walker, and M. Garrett, 69–85. Hillsdale, N.J.: Erlbaum.

Poulos, Constantine X., and D. Adrian Wilkinson (1984). A process theory of remembering: Its application to Korsakoff amnesia and a critique of context and episodic-semantic theories. In L. R. Squire and N. Butters, eds. (1984), 67–82.

Pribram, Karl (1969). The neurophysiology of remembering. *Scientific American* 220:73–86.

Puccetti, Roland (1981). The case for mental duality: Evidence from split-brain data and other considerations. *Behavioral and Brain Sciences* 4/1:93–99.

Purkyně, J. E. (1837). *Bericht über die Versammlung deutscher Naturforscher und Ärzte in Prag im September, 1837.* This report of the paper presented by Purkyně has been reprinted in his *Opera selecta.* (Excerpted and translated by E. Clarke and C. D. O'Malley (1968), 53–56.)

Purpura, Dominick P. (1975). Introduction and perspectives. In *Golgi centennial symposium: Perspectives in neurobiology,* ed. M. Santini, xiii–xvii. New York: Raven.

Putnam, Hilary (1967). The nature of mental states. In *Art, mind and religion,* ed. W. H. Capitan and D. D. Merrill, 37–48. Pittsburgh: University of Pittsburgh Press. (Original title was "Psychological predicates.") (Reprinted in D. M. Rosenthal, ed. (1971), 150–161.)

Pylyshyn, Zenon (1980). Computation and cognition: Issues in the foundation of cognitive science. *Behavioral and Brain Sciences* 3/1:111–134.

Pylyshyn, Zenon (1984). *Computation and cognition.* Cambridge, Mass.: MIT Press.

Quine, W. V. O. (1953). Two dogmas of empiricism. In *From a logical point of view.* Cambridge, Mass.: Harvard University Press.

Quine, W. V. O. (1960). *Word and object.* Cambridge, Mass.: MIT Press.

Quine, W. V. O. (1969). Epistemology naturalized. In *Ontological relativity and other essays*, 69–90. New York: Columbia University Press.

Quinn, William G., and Ralph J. Greenspan (1984). Learning and courtship in *Drosophila:* Two stories with mutants. *Annual Review of Neuroscience* 7:67–93.

Raichle, Marcus E., and Michel M. Ter-Pogossian (1984). Letter in reply to Fox: PET scan controversy. *Science* 224:934.

Raisman, G., and P. M. Field (1973). Sexual dimorphism in the neuropil of the preoptic area of the rat and its dependence on neonatal androgen. *Brain Research* 54:1–29.

Rakic, Pasko (1975). Cell migration and neuronal ectopias in the brain. *Birth Defects: Original Article Series* 11:95–129.

Rakic, Pasko (1981). Developmental events leading to laminar and areal organization of the neocortex. In F. O. Schmitt, F. G. Worden, G. Adelman, and S. G. Dennis, eds. (1981), 7–28.

Ramón y Cajal, Santiago (1888). Estructura del cerebelo. *Gac. méd. Catalana* 11:449–457. (Excerpted and translated in E. Clarke and C. D. O'Malley (1968), 111–113.)

Ramón y Cajal, Santiago (1908). Structure et connexions des neurones. *Les Prix Nobel en 1906*, 1–25. Stockholm: P. A. Norstedt & Söner. (Excerpted and translated in E. Clarke and C. D. O'Malley (1968), 128–129.)

Ranson, Stephen W., and Sam L. Clark (1959). *The anatomy of the nervous system.* Philadelphia: Saunders.

Rasmussen, T., and B. Milner (1977). The role of early left-brain injury in determining lateralization of cerebral speech functions. *Annals of the New York Academy of Science* 299:355–369.

Rehfeld, Jens F. (1980). Cholecystokinin. *Trends in Neurosciences* 3/3:65–67.

Reichardt, Werner E. (1981). Introduction to *Theoretical approaches in neurobiology*, ed. W. E. Reichardt and T. Poggio, 1–4. Cambridge, Mass.: MIT Press.

Remak, Robert (1838). *Observationes anatomicae et microscopicae de systematis nervosi structura.* Berlin: Reimer. (Excerpted and translated in E. Clarke and C. D. O'Malley (1968), 51–52.)

Rescher, Nicholas (1970). *Scientific explanation.* New York: Free Press.

Richards, Whitman (1973). Visual processing in scotomata. *Experimental Brain Research* 17:333–347.

Richards, Whitman (1983). Is hindsight better than blindsight? (Commentary on Campion, Latto, and Smith 1983.) *Behavioral and Brain Sciences* 6:461.

Richardson, Robert (1979). Functionalism and reductionism. *Philosophy of Science* 46:533–558.

Rizzolatti, Giacomo (1983). Mechanisms of selective attention in animals. In *Advances in vertebrate neuroethology*, ed. J.-P. Ewart, R. R. Capranica, and D. J. Ingle, 261–297. New York: Plenum.

Robinson, D. A. (1972). Eye movements evoked by collicular stimulation in the alert monkey. *Vision Research* 12:1795–1808.

Robinson, Howard (1982). *Matter and sense: A critique of contemporary materialism.* Cambridge: Cambridge University Press.

Rock, Irvin (1983). *The logic of perception.* Cambridge, Mass.: MIT Press.

Roffwarg, H. P., J. N. Muzio, and W. C. Dement (1966). Ontogenetic development of the human sleep-dream cycle. *Science* 152:604–619.

Rorty, Richard (1965). Mind-body identity, privacy, and categories. *Review of Metaphysics* 19:24–54. (Reprinted in D. M. Rosenthal, ed. (1971), 174–199.)

Rorty, Richard (1970). In defense of eliminative materialism. *Review of Metaphysics* 24:112–121. (Reprinted in D. M. Rosenthal, ed. (1971), 223–231.)

Rosch, E. (1973). On the internal structure of perceptual and semantic categories. In

Cognitive development and the acquisition of language, ed. T. Moore, 111–144. New York: Academic Press.

Rosch, E., and B. B. Lloyd, eds. (1978). *Cognition and categorization*. Hillsdale, N.J.: Erlbaum.

Rosch, E., and C. Mervis (1975). Family resemblances: Studies in the internal structure of categories. *Cognitive Psychology* 7:573–605.

Rose, Clifford F., and W. F. Bynum (1982). *Historical aspects of the neurosciences*. New York: Raven.

Rosenberg, Jay (1974). *Linguistic Representation*. Dordrecht, Holland: D. Reidel.

Rosenberg, Roger N. (1980). Genetic variation and neurological disease. *Trends in Neurosciences* 3/6:144–148.

Rosenblatt, Frank (1962). *Principles of neurodynamics*. Washington, D.C.: Spartan Books.

Rosenthal, D. M., ed. (1971). *Materialism and the mind-body problem*. Englewood-Cliffs, N.J.: Prentice-Hall.

Rubens, Alan B., and D. Frank Benson (1971). Associative visual agnosia. *Archives of neurology* 24:305–316.

Rumelhart, David E., and Donald A. Norman (1982). Simulating a skilled typist: A study of skilled cognitive-motor performance. *Cognitive Science* 6:1–36.

Rumelhart, David E., and James L. McClelland (1986). *Parallel distributed processing: Explorations in the microstructure of cognition*. Vol. 1: *Foundations*. Cambridge, Mass.: MIT Press.

Rumelhart, D. E., P. Smolensky, J. L. McClelland, and G. E. Hinton (1986). Schemata and sequential thought processes in PDP models. In J. L. McClelland and D. E. Rumelhart, eds. (1986).

Rumelhart, David E., and David Zipser (1985). Feature discovery by competitive learning. *Cognitive Science* 9:75–112.

Russell, Bertrand (1914). On the nature of acquaintance. In *Logic and knowledge* (1956), ed. R. Marsh, 127–174. London: Allen and Unwin.

Russell, Bertrand (1924). Logical atomism. In *Logic and knowledge* (1956), ed. R. Marsh, 321–343. London: Allen and Unwin.

Russell, Bertrand, and A. N. Whitehead (1910–1913). *Principia mathematica*. 3 vols. Cambridge: Cambridge University Press.

Sacks, Oliver (1985). The twins. *New York Review of Books* 32:16–20.

Salmon, Wesley (1971). *Statistical explanation and statistical relevance*. Pittsburgh: University of Pittsburgh Press.

Saunders, J. B. de C. M., and C. D. O'Malley (1950). *The illustrations from the works of Andreas Vesalius*. Cleveland: The World Publishing Co.

Schank, Roger, and Robert Abelson (1977). *Scripts, plans, goals and understanding*. Hillsdale, N.J.: Erlbaum.

Schiller, P. H. (1984). The superior colliculus and visual function. In *Handbook of physiology. Section I: The nervous system*, ed. I. Darian-Smith, vol. 3, 457–504. Bethesda, Md.: American Physiological Society.

Schiller, P., and M. Stryker (1972). Single-unit recording and stimulation in superior colliculus of the alert rhesus monkey. *Journal of Neurophysiology* 35:915–924.

Schlick, Moritz (1936). Meaning and verification. *Philosophical Review* 46:339–369.

Schmitt, F. O., and F. G. Worden, eds. (1974). *The neurosciences: Third study program*. Cambridge, Mass.: MIT Press.

Schmitt, F. O., and F. G. Worden, eds. (1979). *The neurosciences: Fourth study program*. Cambridge, Mass.: MIT Press.

Schmitt, F. O., F. G. Worden, G. Adelman, and S. G. Dennis, eds. (1981). *The organization of the cerebral cortex*. Cambridge, Mass.: MIT Press.

Schwartz, James H. (1981). Chemical basis of synaptic transmission. In E. R. Kandel and J. H. Schwartz, eds. (1981), 106–120.

Scoville, W. B., and B. Milner (1957). Loss of recent memory after bilateral hippocampal lesions. *Journal of Neurology, Neurosurgery, and Psychiatry* 20:11–21.

Searle, John R. (1980). Minds, brains, and programs. *Behavioral and Brain Sciences* 3/ 3:417–457.

Searle, John R. (1983). *Intentionality: An essay in the philosophy of mind.* Cambridge: Cambridge University Press.

Sejnowski, Terrence J. (1981). Skeleton filters in the brain. In G. E. Hinton and J. A. Anderson, eds. (1981), 189–212.

Sejnowski, Terrence J., and Geoffrey E. Hinton (forthcoming). Separating figure from ground with a Boltzmann machine. In *Vision, brain, and cooperative computation,* ed. M. Arbib and A. R. Hanson. Cambridge, Mass.: MIT Press.

Sellars, Wilfrid (1963). *Science, perception and reality.* London: Routledge and Kegan Paul.

Selverston, Allen I. (1980). Are central pattern generators understandable? *Behavioral and Brain Sciences* 4/3:535–571.

Shepherd, Gordon M. (1983). *Neurobiology.* New York: Oxford University Press.

Sherman, Murray S., and Peter D. Spear (1982). Organization of visual pathways in normal and visually deprived cats. *Physiological Reviews* 62/2:738–855.

Sherrington, C. S. (1906). *The integrative action of the nervous system.* New Haven, Conn.: Yale University Press.

Shoemaker, Sydney (1981). Functionalism, qualia, and intentionality. *Philosophical topics* 12:93–118. (Reprinted in J. I. Biro and R. W. Shahan, eds. (1982). *Mind, brain, and function,* 93–118. Norman, Okla.: University of Oklahoma Press.)

Sigworth, Frederick J., and Erwin Neher (1980). Single Na+ channel currents observed in cultured rat muscle cells. *Nature* 287:447–449.

Smith, Aaron (1966). Speech and other functions after left (dominant) hemispherectomy. *Journal of Neurology, Neurosurgery, and Psychiatry* 29:467–471.

Smith, Aaron (1972). Dominant and nondominant hemispherectomy. In *Drugs, development, and cerebral function,* ed. W. L. Smith, 37–68. Springfield, Ill.: Charles C. Thomas.

Smith, Aaron (1984). Early and long-term recovery from brain damage in children and adults: Evolution of concepts of localization, plasticity and recovery. In *Early brain damage, Vol. 1,* ed. C. R. Almli and S. Finger, 229–324. New York: Academic Press.

Snyder, Solomon H. (1976). The dopamine hypothesis of schizophrenia: Focus on the dopamine receptor. *Journal of American Psychiatry* 133:197–202.

Snyder, Solomon H. (1980). Brain peptides as neurotransmitters. *Science* 209/4460:976–983.

Sokoloff, Louis (1981). The relationship between function and energy metabolism: Its use in the localization of functional activity in the nervous system. *Neurosciences Research Program Bulletin* 19:159–210.

Sokoloff, Louis (1984). *Metabolic probes of central nervous system activity in experimental animals.* Sunderland, Mass.: Sinauer.

Sousa-Pinta, A. (1973). The structure of the first auditory cortex (AI) in the cat. Light microscopic observations on its organization. *Archives Italiennes de biologie* 111:112–137.

Spencer, Herbert (1855). *The principles of psychology.* London: Longman, Brown, Green & Longman.

Sperry, R. W. (1963). Chemoaffinity in the orderly growth of nerve fiber patterns and connections. *National Academy of Sciences of the United States of America. Proceedings. Biological Sciences* 50:703–710.

Sperry, R. W. (1974). Lateral specialization in the surgically separated hemispheres. In F. O. Schmitt and F. G. Worden, eds. (1974), 5–19.

Sperry, R. W. (1976). Mental phenomena as causal determinants in brain function. In *Consciousness and the brain*, ed. G. Globus, G. Maxwell, and I. Savodnik, 163–177. New York: Plenum.

Sperry, R. W. (1980). Mind-brain interaction: Mentalism, yes; dualism, no. *Neuroscience* 5:195–206.

Sperry, R. W. (1982). Some effects of disconnecting the cerebral hemispheres. *Science* 217/4566:1223–1226.

Sperry, R. W., and Michael Gazzaniga (1967). Language following surgical disconnection of the hemispheres. In *Brain mechanisms underlying speech and language*, ed. C. Millikan and F. Darley, 108–115. New York: Grune & Stratton.

Spitzer, Nicholas C., ed. (1982). *Neuronal development*. New York: Plenum.

Spokes, E. G. S. (1981). The neurochemistry of Huntington's chorea. *Trends in Neurosciences* 4/5:115–118.

Sprague, J. M., J. Levy, A. DiBerardino, and G. Berlucchi (1977). Visual cortical areas mediating form discrimination in the cat. *Journal of Comparative Neurology* 172:441–448.

Springer, Sally P. (1977). Tachistoscopic and dichotic-listening investigations of laterality in normal human subjects. In S. Harnad et al., eds. (1977), 325–336.

Springer, Sally P., and Georg Deutsch (1981). *Left brain, right brain*. San Francisco: W. H. Freeman.

Squire, Larry R., and Nelson Butters, eds. (1984). *Neuropsychology of memory*. New York: Guilford.

Squire, Larry R., and Neal J. Cohen (1984). Human memory and amnesia. In G. Lynch, J. L. McGaugh, and N. M. Weinberger, eds. (1984), 3–64.

Stent, Gunther S., and William B. Kristan, Jr. (1981). Neural circuits generating rhythmic movements. In *Neurobiology of the leech*, ed. K. J. Muller, J. G. Nicholls, and G. S. Stent, 113–146. Spring Harbor, N.Y.: Cold Spring Harbor Laboratory.

Stich, Stephen P. (1978). Beliefs and subdoxastic states. *Philosophy of Science* 45:499–518.

Stich, Stephen P. (1983). *From folk psychology to cognitive science: The case against belief.* Cambridge, Mass.: MIT Press.

Stich, Stephen P., and Richard E. Nisbett (1980). Justification and the psychology of human reasoning. *Philosophy of Science* 47:188–202.

Stone, Jonathan (1983). *Parallel processing in the visual system*. New York: Plenum.

Stone, Jonathan, and Bogdan Dreher (1982). Parallel processing of information in the visual pathways. *Trends in Neurosciences* 5/12:441–446.

Suga, N. (1977). Amplitude spectrum representation in the Doppler-shifted CF processing area of the auditory cortex of the mustache bat. *Science* 196:64–67.

Suppe, Frederick (1977). The search for philosophic understanding of scientific theories. In *The structure of scientific theories*, ed. F. Suppe, 3–232. Urbana, Ill.: University of Illinois Press.

Sur, M., M. Merzenich, and J. H. Kaas (1980). Magnification, receptive field area and "hypercolumn" size in areas 3b and 1 of somatosensory cortex in owl monkeys. *Journal of Neurophysiology* 44:295–311.

Sutton, S., P. Teuting, J. Zubin, and E. R. John (1967). Information delivery and the sensory evoked potential. *Science* 155:1436–1439.

Swammderdam, Jan (1737 and 1738). *Biblia naturae*. Published posthumously by H.

Boerhaave. Amsterdam: Severinus. Translated into English by T. Flloyd (1758). London.

Swets, J. A., W. P. Tanner, and T. G. Birdsall (1964). Decision process in perception. In *Signal detection and recognition by human observers*, ed. J. A. Swets, 3–57. New York: Wiley.

Szabo, T. (1974). Anatomy of the specialized lateral line organs of electroreception. In *Handbook of sensory physiology*, vol. III/3, ed. A. Fessard. New York: Springer-Verlag.

Szentágothai, J. (1975). The "module concept" in cerebral cortex architecture. *Brain Research* 95:475–496.

Szentágothai, J. (1979). Local neuron circuits of the neocortex. In F. O. Schmitt and F. G. Worden, eds. (1979), 399–415.

Tarski, Alfred (1944). The semantic conception of truth and the foundations of semantics. *Journal of Philosophy and Phenomenological Research* 4:341–375.

Taub, Edward (1976). Movement in nonhuman primates deprived of sensory feedback. *Exercise Sport Science Review* 4:335–374.

Taylor, Charles (1971). Interpretation and the sciences of man. *Review of Metaphysics* 25:1–32, 35–45. (Reprinted in Charles Taylor (1985). *Philosophy and the human sciences: Philosophical papers*, vol. 2. Cambridge: Cambridge University Press.)

Taylor, P. A., and T. W. Stone (1981). Neurotransmodulatory control of cerebral cortical neuron activity. In F. O. Schmitt, F. G. Worden, G. Adelman, and S. G. Dennis, eds. (1981), 347–357.

Ter-Pogossian, Michel M., Marcus E. Raichle, and Burton E. Sobel (1980). Positron-emission tomography. *Scientific American* 243:171–181.

Thompson, R. F. (1967). *Foundations of physiological psychology*. New York: Harper and Row.

Thompson, Richard F. (1975). *Introduction to physiological psychology*. New York: Harper and Row.

Toran-Allerand, Dominique C. (1978). Gonadal hormones and brain development: Cellular aspects of sexual differentiation. *American Zoologist* 18:553–565.

Tranel, Daniel, and Antonio R. Damasio (1985). Knowledge without awareness: An autonomic index of facial recognition by prosopagnosics. *Science* 228:1453–1454.

Treisman, A. M. (1969). Strategies and models of selective attention. *Psychological Review* 76:282–299.

Treisman, A. M., and G. A. Gelade (1980). A feature integration theory of attention. *Cognitive Psychology* 12:97–136.

Treisman, A. M., and H. Schmidt (1982). Illusory conjunctions in the perceptions of objects. *Cognitive Psychology* 14:107–141.

Trevarthen, C. (1970). Experimental evidence for a brain stem contribution to visual perception in man. *Brain, Behaviour and Evolution* 3:338–352.

Truman, James W. (1984). Cell death in invertebrate nervous systems. *Annual Review of Physiology* 7, 171–188.

Tulving, Endel (1972). Episodic and semantic memory. In *Organization of memory*, ed. E. Tulving and W. Donaldson. New York: Academic Press.

Tulving, Endel (1983). *Elements of episodic memory*. Oxford: Clarendon Press. (Precis with commentaries and replies in *Behavioral and Brain Sciences* (1984), 7:223–268.)

Turing, A. M. (1937a). On computable numbers, with an application to the Entscheidungsproblem. *Proceedings of the London Mathematical Society* 42:230–265.

Turing, A. M. (1937b). Computability and lambda-definability. *Journal of Symbolic Logic* 2:153–163.

Ullman, Shimon (1979). *Interpretation of visual motion*. Cambridge, Mass.: MIT Press.

Uttal, William R. (1973). *The psychobiology of sensory coding*. New York: Harper and Row.
Valenstein, Elliot S. (1973). *Brain control*. New York: Wiley.
Van Essen, David C., and John H. R. Maunsell (1983). Hierarchical organization and functional streams in the visual cortex. *Trends in Neurosciences* 6:370–375.
Van Fraassen, Bas C. (1970). On the extension of Beth's semantics of physical theories. *Philosophy of Science* 37:325–338.
Van Fraassen, Bas C. (1972). A formal approach to the philosophy of science. In *Paradigms and paradoxes*, ed. R. Colodny, 303–366. Pittsburgh: University of Pittsburgh Press.
Van Fraassen, Bas C. (1980). *The scientific image*. Oxford: Clarendon Press.
Van Fraassen, Bas C., and C. A. Hooker (1976). A semantic analysis of Niels Bohr's philosophy of quantum theory. In *Foundations of probability theory, statistical inference and statistical theories of science*, vol. 3, ed. W. L. Harper and C. A. Hooker, 221–241. Dordrecht, Holland: Reidel.
Van Heerden, P. J. (1963). Theory of optical information in solids. *Applied optics* 2:393–400.
Van Wagenen, W., and R. Herren (1940). Surgical division of commissural pathways in the corpus callosum. *Archives of Neurology and Psychiatry* 44:740–759.
Vendler, Zeno (1984). *The matter of minds*. Oxford: Clarendon Press.
Vesalius, Andreas (1543). The *Epitome* of the *De Humani Corporis*. Brussels. Reproduced in J. B. de C. M. Saunders and C. D. O'Malley (1950).
Vignolo, Luigi A. (1983). Modality specific disorders of written language. In A. Kertesz, ed. (1983b), 357–369.
Virchow, Rudolf (1856). *Gesammelte Abhandlungen zur wissenschaftlichen Medizin*. Frankfurt: Meidinger. (Excerpted and translated in E. Clarke and C. D. O'Malley (1968), 86–87.
Vogel, G. W., S. Thurmond, P. Gibbons, et al. (1975). REM sleep reduction effects on depression syndromes. *Archives of General Psychiatry* 32:765–777.
Volkmann, A. W. (1869). Zur Mechanik der Augenmuskeln. *Ber. sachs. Gesamte. Akad. Wiss.* 21:28–69.
Volpe, B. T., P. Herscovitch, M. E. Raichle, M. S. Gazzaniga, and W. Hirst (1983). Cerebral blood flow and metabolism in human amnesia. *Journal of Cerebral Blood Flow and Metabolism* 3:5.
Volpe, Bruce T., John J. Sidtis, and Michael S. Gazzaniga (1981). Can left-handed writing posture predict cerebral language laterality? *Archives of Neurology* 38:637–638.
Von Békésy, G. (1960). *Experiments in hearing*. New York: McGraw-Hill.
Von der Heydt, R., E. Peterhans, and G. Baumgartner (1984). Illusory contours and cortical neuron responses. *Science* 224:1260–1262.
Von der Malsburg, Christoph (1973). Self-organizing of orientation sensitive cells in the striate cortex. *Kybernetik* 14:85–100.
Von der Malsburg, Christoph (1981). Internal report 81–2. Göttingen, F. R. G.: Department of Neurobiology, Max-Planck-Institute for Biophysical Chemistry.
Von der Malsburg, Christoph, and David Willshaw (1981). Cooperativity and brain organization. *Trends in Neurosciences* 4:80–83.
Von Neumann, John (1958). *The computer and the brain*. New Haven, Conn.: Yale University Press.
Waber, D. (1976). Sex differences in cognition: A function of maturation rate? *Science* 192:572–573.
Wada, J. (1949). A new method for the determination of the side of cerebral speech

dominance. A preliminary report on the intracarotid injection of sodium amytal in man. *Medical Biology* 14:221–222.

Wada, J., and T. Rasmussen (1960). Intracarotid injection of sodium amytal for the lateralization of cerebral speech dominance. Experimental and clinical observations. *Journal of Neurosurgery* 17:266–282.

Waldeyer-Hartz, H. W. G. von (1891). Über einige neuere Forschungen im Gebiete der Anatomie des Centralnervensystems. *Dt. med. Wschr.* 17:1213–1218, 1244–1246, 1267–1269, 1287–1289, 1331–1332, 1352–1356. (Excerpted and translated in E. Clarke and C. D. O'Malley (1968), 114–117.)

Warrington, Elizabeth K. (1979). Neurophysiological evidence for multiple memory systems. In *Brain and Mind*, Ciba Foundation Symposium (new series). 69:153–185. Amsterdam: Elsevier, Excerpta-Medica, North-Holland.

Warrington, Elizabeth K., and L. Weiskrantz (1982). Amnesia: A disconnection syndrome? *Neuropsychology* 20:233–248.

Weinstein, Edwin A., and Robert L. Kahn (1955). *Denial of illness.* Springfield, Ill.: Charles C. Thomas and Oxford: Basil Blackwell.

Weisblat, D. A., and W. B. Kristan, Jr. (1985). The development of serotonin-containing neurons in the leech. In *Model neural networks and behavior*, ed. A. I. Selverston, 175–190. New York: Plenum.

Weiskrantz, L. (1978). A comparison of hippocampal pathology in man and other animals. In *Functions of the septo-hippocampal system.* Ciba Foundation Symposium (new series) 58:373–406. Amsterdam: Elsevier, Excerpta-Medica, North-Holland.

Weiskrantz, L. (forthcoming). On issues and theories of the human amnesic syndrome. In *Memory Systems of the Brain: Animal and Human Cognitive Processes*, ed. N. M. Weinberger, J. L. McGaugh, and G. Lynch, 380–415. New York: Guilford.

Weiskrantz, L., and A. Cowey (1967). A comparison of the effects of striate cortex and retinal lesions on visual acuity in the monkey. *Science* 155:104–106.

Weiskrantz, L., E. K. Warrington, M. D. Sanders, and J. Marshall (1974). Visual capacity in the hemianopic field following a restricted occipital ablation. *Brain* 97:709–728.

Wender, P. H., D. Rosenthal, and S. S. Kety (1974). Crossfostering. *Archives of General Psychiatry* 30:121–128.

Wernicke, C. (1874). Der aphasische Symptomenkomplex. Breslau: Cohn & Weigert.

White, Andrew Dickson (1896). *A history of the warfare of science with theology.* Vol. 2. Reprinted (1978). Gloucester, Mass.: Peter Smith.

Whitehouse, Peter J., Donald L. Price, Robert G. Strubble, et al. (1982). Alzheimer's disease and senile dementia: Loss of neurons in the basal forebrain. *Science* 215/4537:1237–1239.

Willshaw, David (1981). Holography, associative memory, and inductive generalization. In G. E. Hinton and J. A. Anderson, eds. (1981), 83–104.

Wilson, D. H., A. G. Reeves, M. S. Gazzaniga, and C. Culver (1977). Cerebral commissurotomy for the control of intractable seizures. *Neurology* 27:708–715.

Wimsatt, W. (1976a). Reductive explanation: A functional account. In *PSA 1974* (Proceedings of the Philosophy of Science Association), ed. R. S. Cohen, C. A. Hooker, A. C. Michalos, and J. W. van Evra, 671–710. Dordrecht, Holland: D. Reidel.

Wimsatt, W. (1976b). Reduction, levels of organization, and the mind-body problem. In *Consciousness and the brain*, ed. G. Globus, G. Maxwell, and I. Savodnik, 199–267. New York: Plenum.

Witelson, S. F. (1976). Sex and the single hemisphere: Specialization of the right hemisphere for spatial processing. *Science* 193:425–427.

Wittgenstein, Ludwig (1922). *Tractatus logico-philosophicus.* Modern edition with translation by D. F. Pears and B. F. McGuiness (1961). London: Routledge and Kegan Paul.

Wood, C. C. (1978). Variations on a theme by Lashley: Lesion experiments on the neural model of Anderson, Silverstein, Ritz and Jones. *Psychological Review* 85:582–591.

Wood, C. C. (unpublished). Brain macropotentials, brain mechanisms, and cognitive processes: A critique. Colloquium presentation for the Society for Philosophy and Psychology, Chicago 1981.

Wood, C. C., and Truett Allison (1981). Interpretation of evoked potentials: A neurophysiological perspective. *Canadian Journal of Psychology* 35:113–135.

Young, J. Z. (1978). *Programs of the brain*. Oxford: Oxford University Press.

Zaidel, Eran (1975). A technique for presenting lateralized visual input with prolonged exposure. *Vision Research* 15:283–289.

Zaidel, Eran (1978). Auditory language comprehension in the right hemisphere following cerebral commissurotomy and hemispherectomy: A comparison with child language and aphasia. In *Language acquisition and language breakdown: Parallels and divergences*, ed. A. Caramazza and E. Zurif, 229–275. Baltimore: The Johns Hopkins University Press.

Zangwill, O. L. (1975). Excision of Broca's area without persistent aphasia. In *Cerebral localization*, ed. K. J. Zulch, O. Creutzfeld, and G. C. Galbraith, 258–263. Heidelberg and New York: Springer-Verlag.

Zipser, David (1985). A theoretical model of hippocampal learning during classical conditioning. *Behavioral Neuroscience*.

Zola-Morgan, S. (1984). Toward an animal model of human amnesia: Some critical issues. In L. R. Squire and N. Butters, eds. (1984), 316–329.

Zola-Morgan, S., and L. R. Squire (1984). Preserved learning in monkeys with medial temporal lesions: Sparing of motor and cognitive skills. *Journal of neuroscience* 4:1072–1085.

Zollinger, R. (1935). Removal of left cerebral hemisphere. *Archives of Neurology and Psychiatry* 34:1055–1064.

Zucker, Steven W., and Robert A. Hummel (1983). Receptive fields and the reconstruction of visual information. *Technical report no. 83–17*. Montreal: Computer Vision and Robotics Laboratory, Department of Electrical Engineering, McGill University.

Index

cytoarchitectural map of, 102, *105*
divisions of, 100, *101* (*see also specific structures*)
functional architecture of, 137, 415, 460
sexual bipotentiality of, 89
Brain disorders, as neurochemical diseases, 85–86
Brain grafts. *See* Neural implants
Brentano, Franz, 336
Bridge principles, 258, 280, 281, 282
Broca, Paul, **159–160**, 161
Broca's aphasia, 160, 189, 229
Broca's area, 159–160, *160*, 189, 201, 202, 259–260
Brodmann, Korbinian, 102
Brodmann's areas, 102, *105*, 117, 201–202, 224. *See also* Motor cortex; Primary visual cortex
Brookshire, R. H., 188
Bullock, T. H., 209
Burklund, C. W., 188

Calcium ions (Ca⁺⁺), 48, 51, 52, 62, 64–66
and plasticity, 67, 70, 72
Calculating oddities, **232–234**
California Institute of Technology, 121, 176
California series, 176, 183–186, 187
"Caloric," 280
Canary, 94
Cantor, Georg, 182
Carmine stain, 27
Carnap, Rudolf, 253
Cartesian argument, **308–310**. *See also* Descartes, René
Cat, 176
Category error, 273
Cations, 48, 49
Causal relations, 246–247, 304, 376, 380
Cell assemblies. *See* Neuronal ensembles
Cell membrane, **48–50**
excitability of, 57
potential difference across, *51*
Cells. *See* Neurons
Cellular "alphabet," 72
Center-surround organization, 100
Central nervous system (CNS), 38, *101*
and electrical synapses, 62
and gonadal hormones, 88
and tensor network theory, *441*

Cerebellar cortex, *414*
Cerebellum, 100, *103*, 296
and cerebral cortex, 414
evolution of, 413–414
function of, 104
inputs to, 412, 414–415
lesions of, 413
micro-organization of, **412–413**
neuronal network of, *431*
Cerebral blood flow (rCBF) studies, 217–**218**, *220*
Cerebral cortex, 102, *103*, 414
Cerebral hemispheres, *37*, **100–102**
Cerebrospinal fluid (CSF), 106
C-fibers, 41
Characteristic frequency, 125, 483n3.1
"Chemical affinity," and neurogenesis, 140, 141
Chemical synapses, 62, 65
Chick, 140, 369
Chimeric stimuli, 177–178, *179*
Chimpanzee, *168*
Chloride ions (Cl⁻), 48, 52
Chlorpromazine, 82, 83
Cholecystokinin, 78
Cholinergic neurons, 78
Christensen, B., 100
Churchland, Paul M., 269, 327, 331, 419, 441, 442 (quoted)
Circuits, neuronal, **69–76**, *414*, 415
for cerebellar cortex, *414*
and learning, 369
as level of organization, 359
as theory, 408
Classical conditioning, 71–72
Classical empiricism, **244–247**
Classical mechanics, **286–288**, 289–291, 302
Climbing fibers, in cerebellum, 412, 430, 448
"Clinical neurology," as term, 153, 154
Cocaine, 82
Cochlea, 125, *126*
Cochlear nuclei, 125
Cochleotopic maps, **125–127**, *128*, 444
Co-evolution
and attentional hypotheses, 476
benefits of, **363–364**
and cognitive psychology, 354–356
and folk psychology, 482
of macro- and microtheory, 6, 8

Academic Press Series in Communications, Networking, and Multimedia

EDITOR-IN-CHIEF

Jerry D. Gibson
Southern Methodist University

This series has been established to bring together a variety of publications that represent the latest in cutting-edge research, theory, and applications of modern communication systems. All traditional and modern aspects of communications as well as all methods of computer communications are to be included. The series will include professional handbooks, books on communication methods and standards, and research books for engineers and managers in the world-wide communications industry.